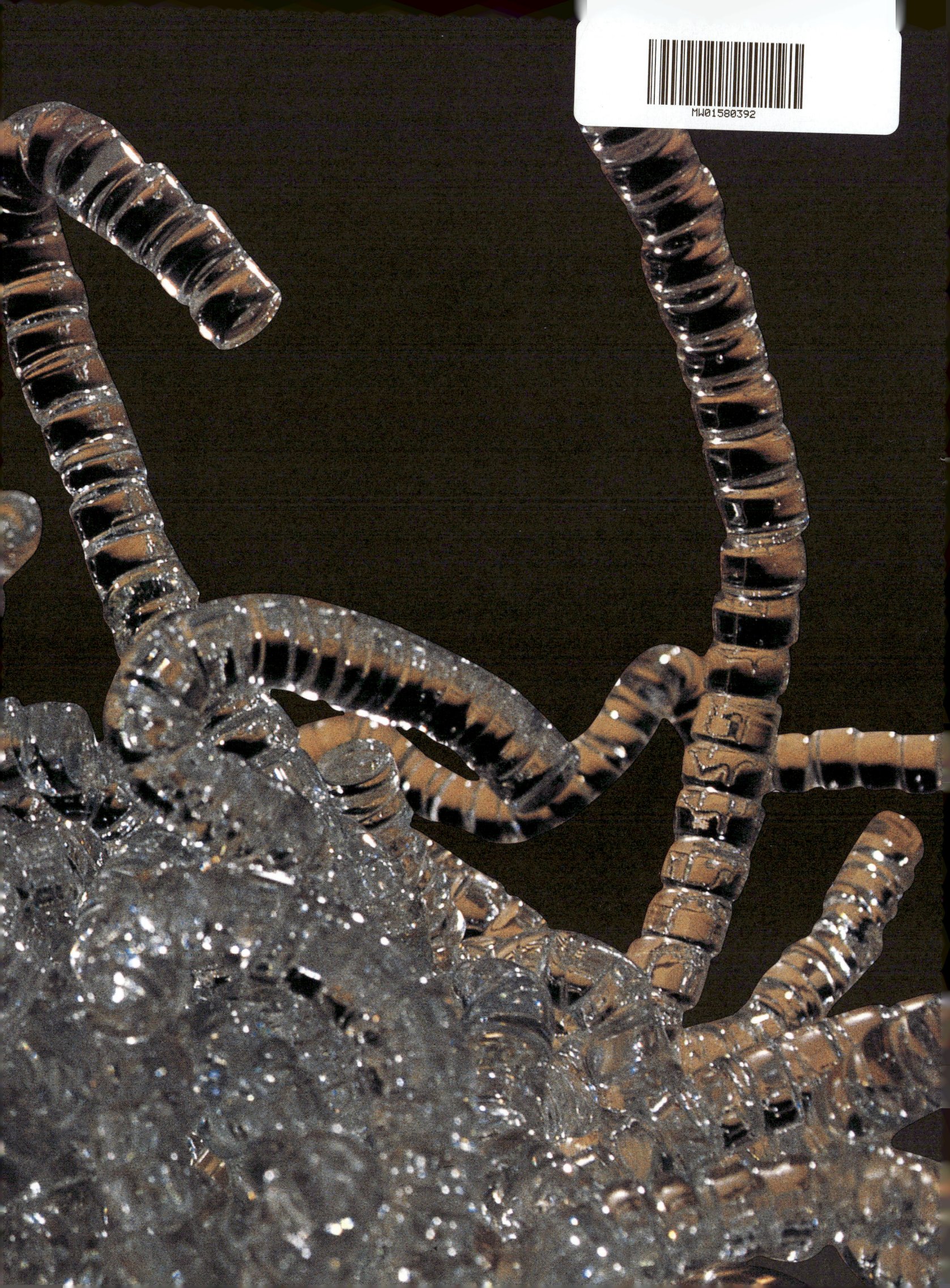

WOMEN WORKING IN GLASS

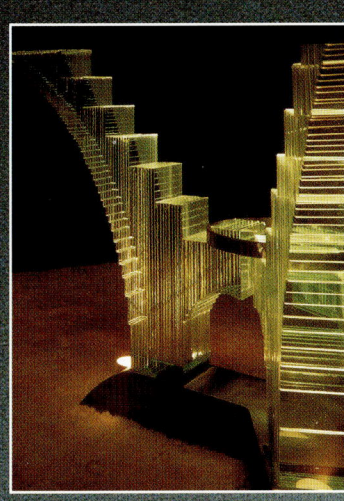

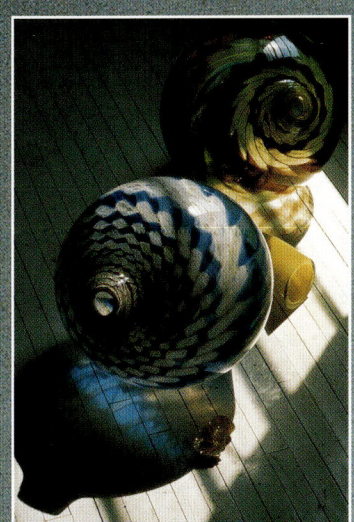

LUCARTHA KOHLER

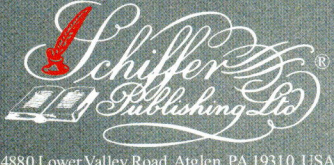

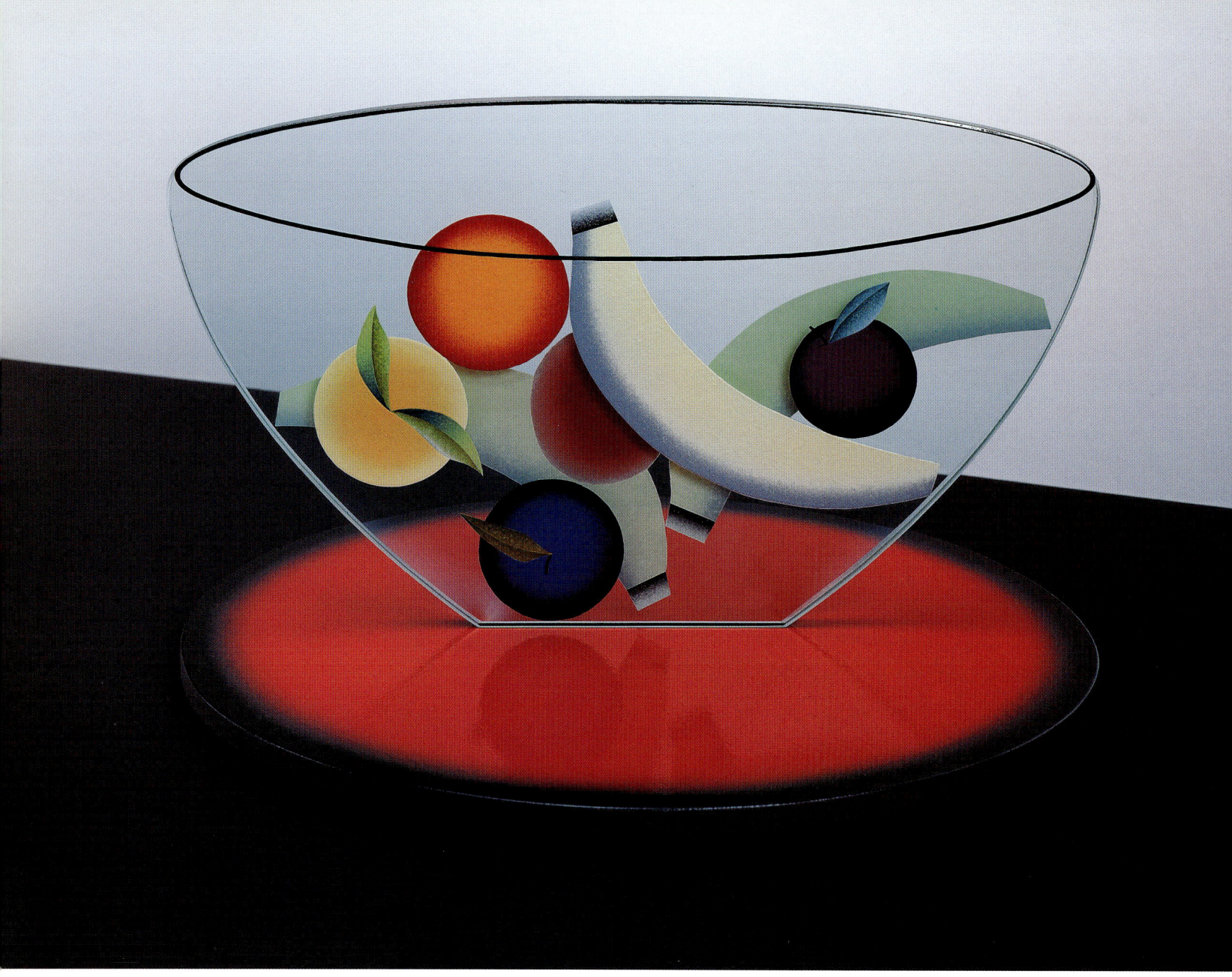

Library of Congress Cataloging-in-Publication Data

Kohler, Lucartha.
Women working in glass / by Lucartha Kohler.
p. cm.
ISBN 0-7643-1807-1 (Hardcover)
1. Glass art. 2. Women glass artist--United States.
I. Title.
NK5112.K65 2003
748'082'0973--dc21
2003006883

Copyright © 2003 by Lucartha Kohler

All rights reserved. No part of this work may be reproduced or used in any form or by any means—graphic, electronic, or mechanical, including photocopying or information storage and retrieval systems—without written permission from the publisher.

The scanning, uploading and distribution of this book or any part thereof via the Internet or via any other means without the permission of the publisher is illegal and punishable by law. Please purchase only authorized editions and do not participate in or encourage the electronic piracy of copyrighted materials.

"Schiffer," "Schiffer Publishing Ltd. & Design," and the "Design of pen and ink well" are registered trademarks of Schiffer Publishing Ltd.

Designed by Bonnie M. Hensley
Cover design by Bruce Waters
Type set in Lydian BT/Lydian BT

ISBN: 0-7643-1807-1
Printed in China

Published by Schiffer Publishing Ltd.
4880 Lower Valley Road
Atglen, PA 19310
Phone: (610) 593-1777; Fax: (610) 593-2002
E-mail: Info@schifferbooks.com
Please visit our web site catalog at
www.schifferbooks.com
We are always looking for people to write books on new and related subjects. If you have an idea for a book please contact us at the above address.

This book may be purchased from the publisher.
Include $3.95 for shipping.
Please try your bookstore first.
You may write for a free catalog.

In Europe, Schiffer books are distributed by
Bushwood Books
6 Marksbury Ave.
Kew Gardens
Surrey TW9 4JF England
Phone: 44 (0)20-8392-8585
Fax: 44 (0)20-8392-9876
E-mail: Bushwd@aol.com
Free postage in the UK. Europe: air mail at cost

Contents

Acknowledgments 4	Susie Krasnican 92	Sabrina Knowles/Jenny Pohlman 149
Preface 5	Elizabeth Ryland Mears 95	Maria Lugossy 151
Introduction 6	Nancy Mee 97	Linda MacNeil 153
In the beginning: Herstory 8	Kathleen Mulcahy 99	Jackie Pancari 155
	Flo Perkins 101	Sally Prash 157
The Sixties 28	Judith Schaechter 103	Amy Roberts 159
The Artists 35	Kathleen Sheard 105	Linda Ross 161
Paula Bartron 36	Molly Stone 107	Ginny Ruffner 163
Asa Brandt 38	Debbie Tarsitano 109	Lisabeth Sterling 165
Jane Bruce 40	Yaffa Todd 111	Raquel Stolarski-Assael 167
Pat Esch 42	Ulrica Valien 113	Cappy Thompson 169
Audrey Handler 44		Pamina Traylor 172
Harriet Hyams 46	**The Eighties** 115	Dana Zamecnikova 174
Joan Reep 48	**The Artists** 121	
Pauline Solven 50	Tina Betz 122	**The Nineties** 176
Sylvia Vigiletti 52	Jody Bone 124	**The Artists** 189
Mary White 54	Anna Boothe 125	Robin Cass 190
	Ruth Brockman 127	Dorothy Hafner 192
The Seventies 56	Carol Cohen 129	Beth Hylen 194
The Artists 75	B. Jane Cowie 131	Karen Lomonte 196
Cristine Barney 76	KeKe Cribbs 133	Beth Lipman 198
Bonnie Biggs 78	Laura Donefer 135	Kristina Logan 200
Sonja Blomdahl 80	Susan Edgerley 137	Amy J. Schwartz 202
Rene Culler 82	Irene Frolic 139	Celeste Starita 204
Diana Hobson 84	Robin Grebe 141	
Joey Kirkpatrick/Flora C. Mace 86	Shari Hopper 143	**Glossary of Glass Terms** 206
Margie Jervis and Susie Krasnican .. 89	Dinah Hulet 145	**Endnotes** 207
Margie Jervis 90	Judy Jensen 147	**Selected Bibliography** 208

Acknowledgments

I want to thank Robin Rice for editing my chapter texts, and for helping me to understand communicating through the written word. I hope, in exchange, I have helped her to understand the history and making of glass. Beth Hylan of the Rakow Library of the Corning Museum of Glass who helped and encouraged me to write the book in the first place. For Beth again and Gail Bardham, for their endless hours of research, saving some of these women from obscurity. Audrey Handler and Sylvia Vigiletti, for providing me with valuable insights and archival material. Elizabeth Byrd Jackson from The Glass Art Society staff and Gay Taylor from the Museum of American Glass. Eugene Bolt from the University of the Arts for his Photoshop help, Ken Andersen from the USPS for yeoman duty through "rain, sleet, hail, and …" In addition, special thanks to all of the artists who provided me with their material for the artist pages and text of the book.

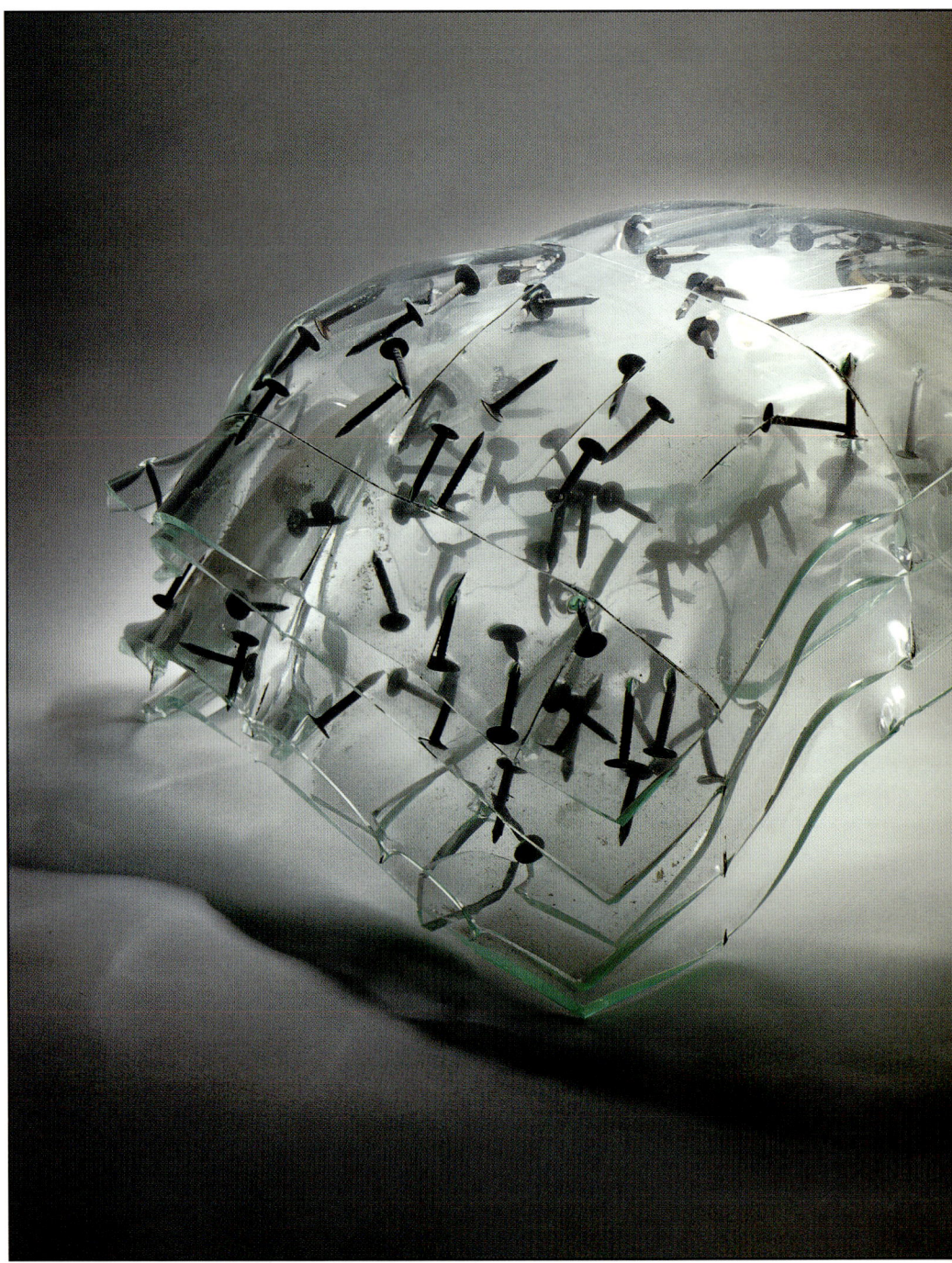

Preface

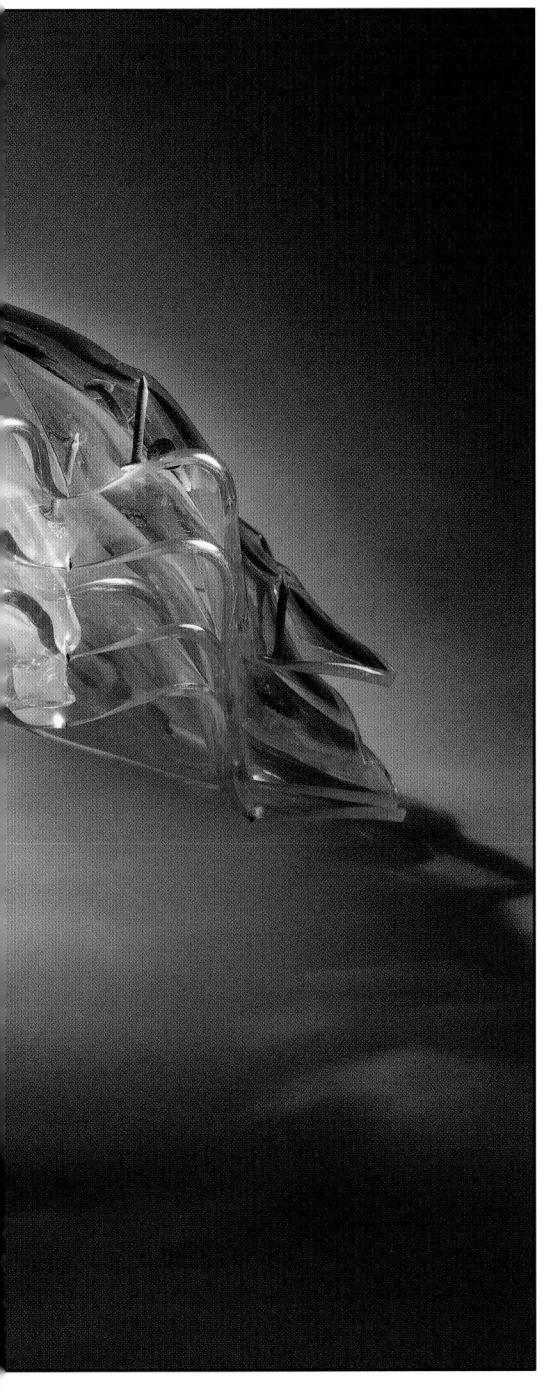

Today we recall that once woman was dubbed the "weaker vessel." Nevertheless, though she might have been considered flawed as a vessel of knowledge or virtue, no one has ever questioned her unique power as a reproductive biological vessel. It is a curious fact that man has often enviously restricted the right of vessel-making to himself. The history of glass is, of course, much concerned with vessels — fragile ones at that. However, in Lucartha Kohler's engaging account of women as makers of glass, from the earliest times up to the contemporary period, we find evidence of significant contributions to the medium. Although women's participation in this art form has sometimes been undervalued, actively discouraged, and, seemingly, willfully forgotten, throughout history they have consistently returned to this primordial yet infinitely subtle medium.

When Lucartha asked me to edit this volume, I felt well prepared by my acquaintance with the work of a number of today's women glass artists. Many, including Lucartha, herself, have been Resident Fellows at the Creative Center for Glass in America, where I, too, had fellowships as an art writer. I *was* prepared to approach the history of women in glass with a technical vocabulary, but I found that I was not aware of many earlier women who have too often been neglected by art and craft historians. When they are discussed, these artists are sometimes marginalized as isolated, even eccentric examples. Lucartha's research brings a sense of continuity to centuries of contributions by women significant to the field.

An equally praiseworthy aspect of Lucartha's accomplishment is the richness and range of illustrations she has selected. From the functional to lush surrealism to minimal light-saturated geometries, the achievements of women in glass are a visual delight. It is an honor to be associated with this project.

Robin Rice
2 March 2003

Introduction

When I was very young I had a vision of myself as an artist. Growing up I painted on everything, including the floors and walls of our house. My parents were very supportive and encouraged my creativity; I came to believe I could become a successful artist. Even while attending a women's art college, I found no serious obstacles in my way. I truly believed that, if I made good art, I would become successful as an artist. It was only after I left the women's art school environment and chose to focus on training to make sculpture that I began to encounter gender blocks. My generation of women, who entered college in the fifties and sixties, had to work much harder to be taken seriously when competing with men on their turf. Fine arts fields like sculpture, specifically metal casting and fabrication, were especially difficult to find support, although most craft mediums welcomed women. Many modern crafts traditions grew from the work women historically did, like making pottery, weaving, embroidery, and china painting. Since glass is such a young art medium, and more closely aligned to its fire-born macho/factory history, it adopted the same attitude about women as did sculpture. An example of how this attitude about women sculptors has persisted throughout recent history was found in a review about Louise Nevelson's work appearing in *Cue Magazine*, October 4, 1941.

> We learned the artist is a woman, in time to check our enthusiasm. Had it been otherwise we might have hailed these sculptural expressions as by surely a great figure among moderns.[1]

There have been courageous female pioneers in all of the arts, as well as women who chose professional careers when it was a difficult choice. My own mother was appointed as a court recorder to the Orphans Court of Pennsylvania; a job traditionally filled by men. The history of strong, intelligent and independent women working in all fields including the arts and especially with glass as a material has been far more extensive than I first imagined when I set out to research the subject. Part of the adventure of writing this book has been the unexpected paths I have been led down. One such example is finding a book through research, on a library bookshelf written twenty-five years ago by a classmate from the women's college I attended. In her book, *Women and Creativity*, Joelynn Snyder-Ott writes…

> Researching women artists is a difficult, but rewarding task, and one begins to feel like an archaeologist, crying out in delight on finding a small reference to a woman artist buried or wedged in between long articles and color representations of a male artist's work. As Simone de Beauvoir states in *Force of Circumstance*, upon finding information, one must then try to pierce through the mythological, prejudicial and sexist documentation in which most women artists have been recorded, destroying the myth of femininity which usually veils women's accomplishments.[2]

Now, in the twenty-first century, the attitude toward women as artists has changed considerably. Young women today find it difficult to imagine that there really was a problem. In the past women seeking to make their mark in the art world had a difficult task. Many women felt that they were not taken seriously and their work was of inferior quality. These attitudes contributed to how a woman artist saw herself in relation to her male peers. It is obvious that good art has no sex, however, the prevailing attitude as late as the 1980s was that art by women and women's art just was not good art.

Perhaps there is a feminine aesthetic or perhaps, because the material is so seductive and attracts the feminine side of all of us, there appears to be an inherent dichotomy within the material and the process. Even the way hot glass is formed with caressing touches and gentle breathing to encourage the molten glass into a form is feminine. Yet, the handling of heavy material at the end of a blow-pipe and the intense heat of the furnace make glassblowing a macho male chore. The end result of a blown form is often referred to by adjectives such as lush and sensuous. Other forming techniques such as kiln work have a definite tie to women's work. Many of the activities of slumping, fusing, and casting simulate work in the kitchen. Painting on glass and stained glass assembly were early crafts where women excelled. Engraving and cutting, even sandblasting, go back several hundred years as work women were permitted to do in factories. Women have proved over and over again that their approach to making work with glass has made them determined to overcome the physical demands, limitations, and challenges placed on them by society.

There is little doubt that women played an important role in the early history of glass making and more recently glass art, just as they have in the history of art. I have approached the task of writing this book as though I were rescuing these women from obscurity. When women are treated as equals, their work can be judged on its own merit. Until recently young women had limited access to women's work in glass and have had few female teachers, mentors, role models, and heroines. That is changing; women today can and do believe they can be successful.

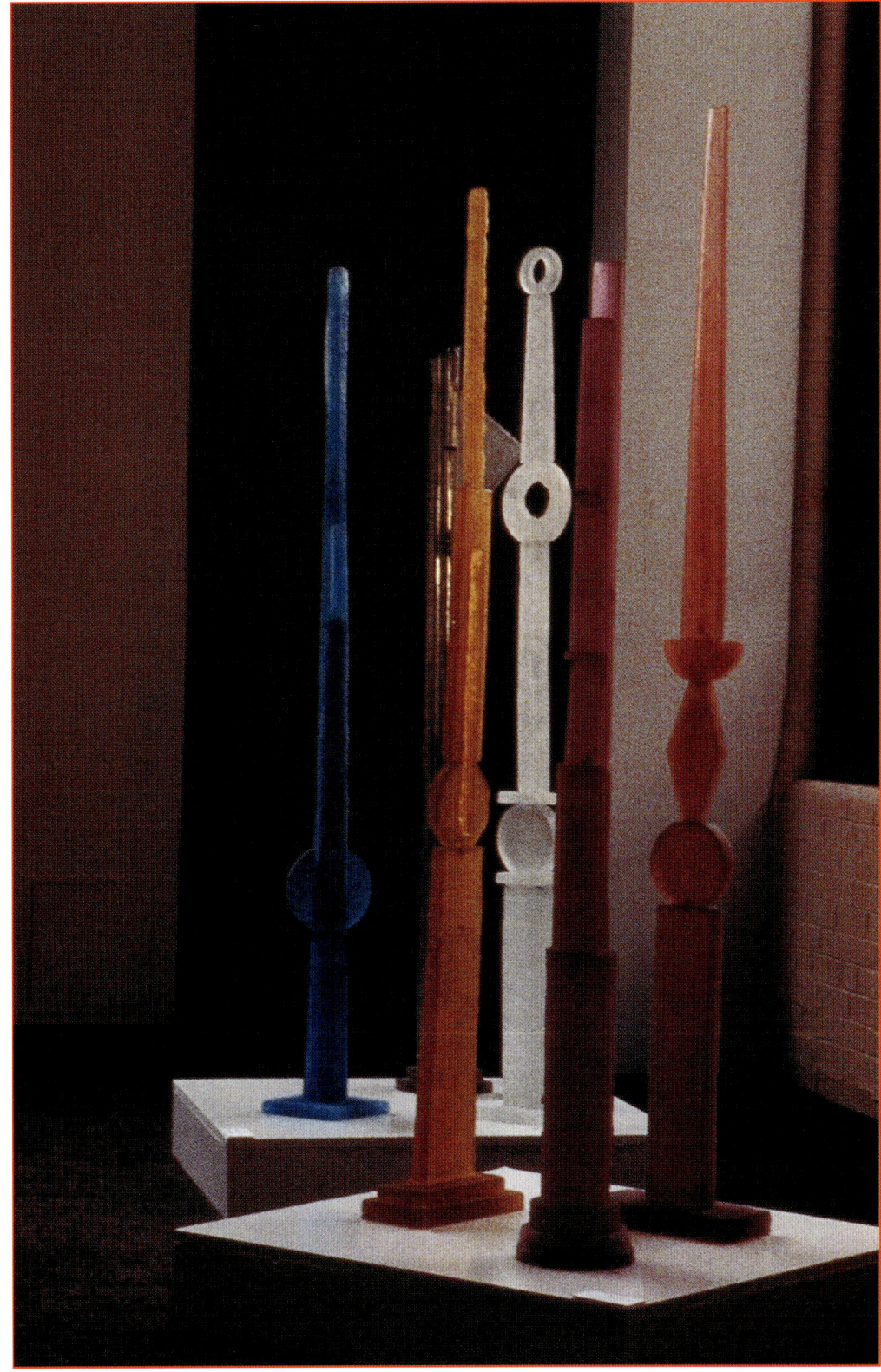

In the Beginning: Herstory

Since ancient times the aura surrounding glass objects and their manufacture has been mysterious and secretive. We really don't know which gender of our early ancestors actually did make glass. Recorded history assumes that it was men; however, no one until recently took the time to investigate other possibilities. In prehistoric cultures, the division of labor was very different from ours. During the Paleolithic period (35,000 to 10,000 years ago), woman made most of the clothing, hunting, and cooking gear as well as spiritual objects. She gathered food and supplies and generally managed domestic life [the cave] while the men were out hunting. Evidence to suggest that women had the power and potential to control their environment is found in research as early as the nineteenth century. Both Johann Bachofen, a German classical scholar, and Lewis Henry Morgan, an American anthropologist, present convincing evidence of matriarchal societies.[1] The use of figurines in sympathetic magic to aid fertility is well documented. A woman wishing to become pregnant would make a model of herself pregnant and carry it around with her, hoping the spirits would honor her intentions and present her with a child. This creative act was quite possibly the origins of woman as artist. The next 10,000 years saw many changes in cultural patterns. In Neolithic villages men stayed home more often than they did in Paleolithic cultures to help with the chores but women still did most of the making. Very early in the course of human evolution women developed the skills needed to run a family of five (or a multinational corporation). At the same time they had enormous amounts of creativity. Somewhere around 5,000 years ago, when glass was first made, women were still considered equal, if not superior to men. That was the era of the Great Mother Goddess in many cultures. Later, during the third millennium BC, a power shift in gender politics occurred and "female deities" had to take a back seat to "male deities." That was the time when writing and record keeping were invented, along with many of the sciences, poetry, and music.

The myths of diverse cultures from this period tell of a descent into the underworld by a powerful female deity. As the story is told, she is transformed into a subordinate spirit and then re-emerges. The same tale occurs in classic Greek myths two millennia later. Other stories tell of the battle for dominance between Zeus and the goddess Hera on Mount Olympus. This redefinition of gender roles among the gods reflected sweeping changes in most aspects of life back then and showed up in almost all cultures. According to modern psychology, the shift was from intuitive/creative (feminine) centered thinking to rational/logical (masculine) centered thinking. Somehow, over time, rational thinking came to be associated with power and strength. Of course in ancient times a woman's physical strength was unquestioned. Women typically carried their babies and small children with them wherever they went and, in the case of nomadic tribes, transported an entire family's possessions. Granted, women back then needed to have several weeks of maternity leave from heavy chores, but between babies and other tasks, there was still plenty of time to make a goblet for the tribal chief's dinner. There have been many women in heroic situations rising above ordinary expectations, cultural mores, and established patterns of behavior. During the

Celtic Iron Age in Britain, women were sometimes warriors. The most famous was Boudica from East Anglia who led the British revolt against the Romans in 60 AD.[2] Considering countless such examples of women who were bold innovators in many fields of endeavor, why couldn't we expect that our venerable foremothers experimented with the new material, glass? I think there probably were many women glassmakers, but since men have written most history, women were either inadvertently overlooked or deliberately ignored.

Early pottery remains do not carry a signature, yet it's known that Indian women from the Americas and many other cultures have made pottery for hundreds, perhaps even thousands, of years.[3] Were potters unique? Did women everywhere make pottery? In Ancient Egypt, during the time of the pyramid builders, women had many rights and privileges. They could own property, run a business, perhaps even be a sculptor. How many male gender-specific arts and crafts forms were there? How many women created anonymous works of art? Virginia Woolf's remark when speaking of women writers, "anonymous was a woman" must surely apply to the visual arts as well as to literature.

Courageous women archeologists today are indeed finding evidence to support the idea that women were involved as artisans in ancient times. In her paper "Neikais—A Woman Glassblower of the First Century A.D.?" E. Marianne Stern cites evidence of at least three women glassmakers from the Roman Empire. Little is known about early glassmaking, so there are few references to individual glassblowers. One way of identification is by a mold blown signature. A name was carved into the wooden mold and when glass was blown into the mold the signature became part of the design on the vessel. It is assumed by many modern experts that the name was that of the artisan who made the vessel. The most renowned name in Roman times was Ennion. Over thirty glass vessels with his signature have been found in the countries around the Mediterranean. The names of 130 Roman glassblowers are known. Two of the names are definitely female, Sentia Secunda and Ennia Fortuna. A third name, Nekais, is probably a woman's name.[4]

The fall of the Roman Empire was followed by a long period of religious expansion and territorial wars. The limited power accorded women in Greek and Roman society was further undermined in the late

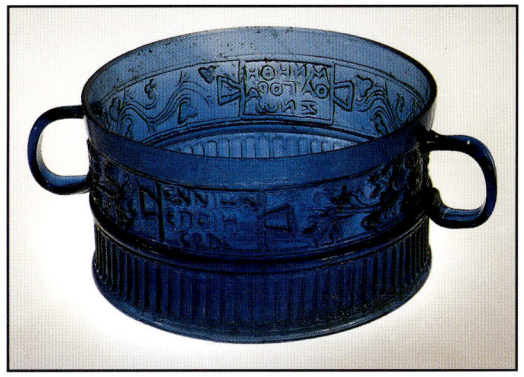

Neikais, Beaker signed by Neikais, probably mid-first century A.D. Roman Empire. *Photograph courtesy of the Corning Museum of Glass.*

Roman Empire by the rise of Christianity and was lost until the last half of the twentieth century. The religious views of the early Christian church were strongly patriarchal. As late as the third and fourth century AD, many women in the Roman Empire worshiped the Goddess Isis as a powerful Earth Mother. In an attempt to gain converts to Christianity, the church leaders had to give them a goddess, so, they adopted Isis from Pagan religions and adapted her to fit the new Christianity. Unfortunately in the process the once robust and strong Earth Mother lost her power. Depictions of women as frail and less powerful than their ancient foremothers stem from the early Christian era.

Religion aside, the making of glass continued and spread to most corners of the

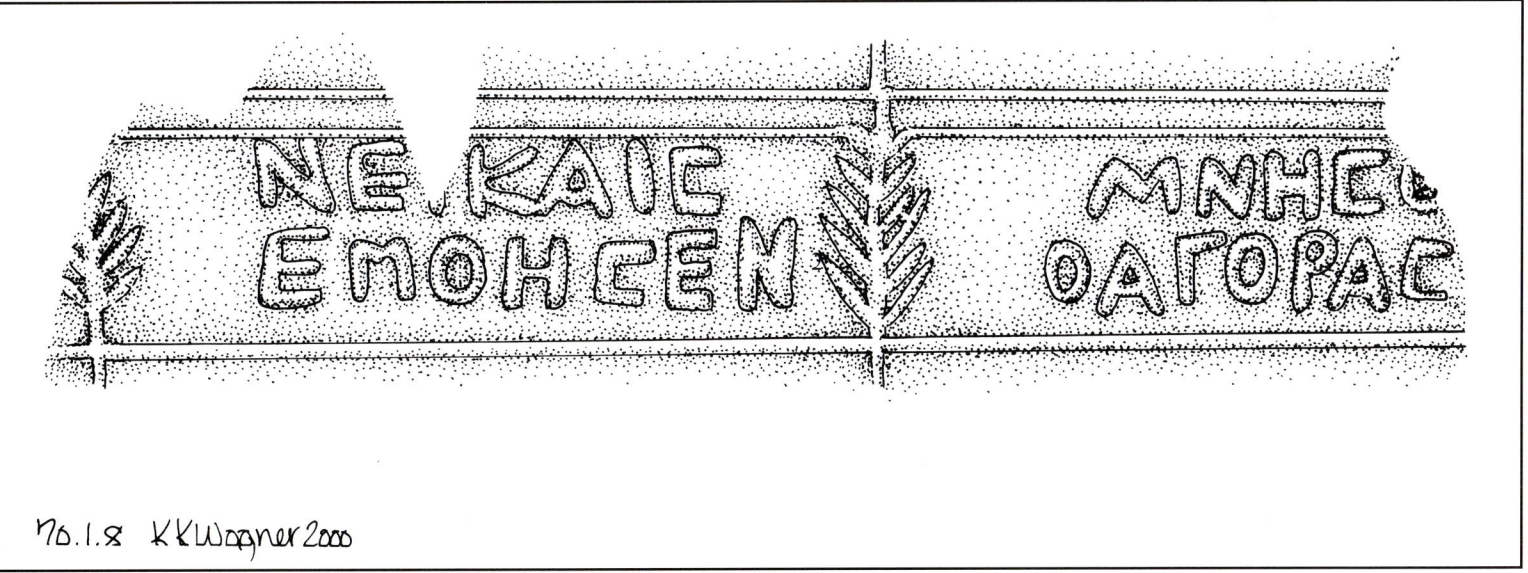

Neikais, drawing for beaker, drawn by Kim Kelly Wagner. *Courtesy The Corning Museum of Glass.*

known world. Glass became a material for the manufacture of a utilitarian product for window glazing, for drinking vessels, for transporting oils and wines, for body adornment, and for illumination. In the Middle Ages a woman had almost no rights. Prior to marriage she belonged to her father and after marriage to her husband. Unmarried women of good family often joined a nunnery; there they were well educated and could spend time devoted to painting and sculpture for religious purpose as well as avoid male domination. Also during the Middle Ages crafts were organized into Guilds. These Guilds were intended to protect their workers' skills and were based on male heredity. Skills were treated as property and were passed down from man to man. This led to the apprentice/master system that dominated craft and art production well beyond the Industrial Revolution, which began in 1760 in England. In medieval glassmaking, women were usually restricted to auxiliary jobs such as sorting cullet for remelting and washing and cleaning the glass. In rare instances they were permitted on the blowing floor.

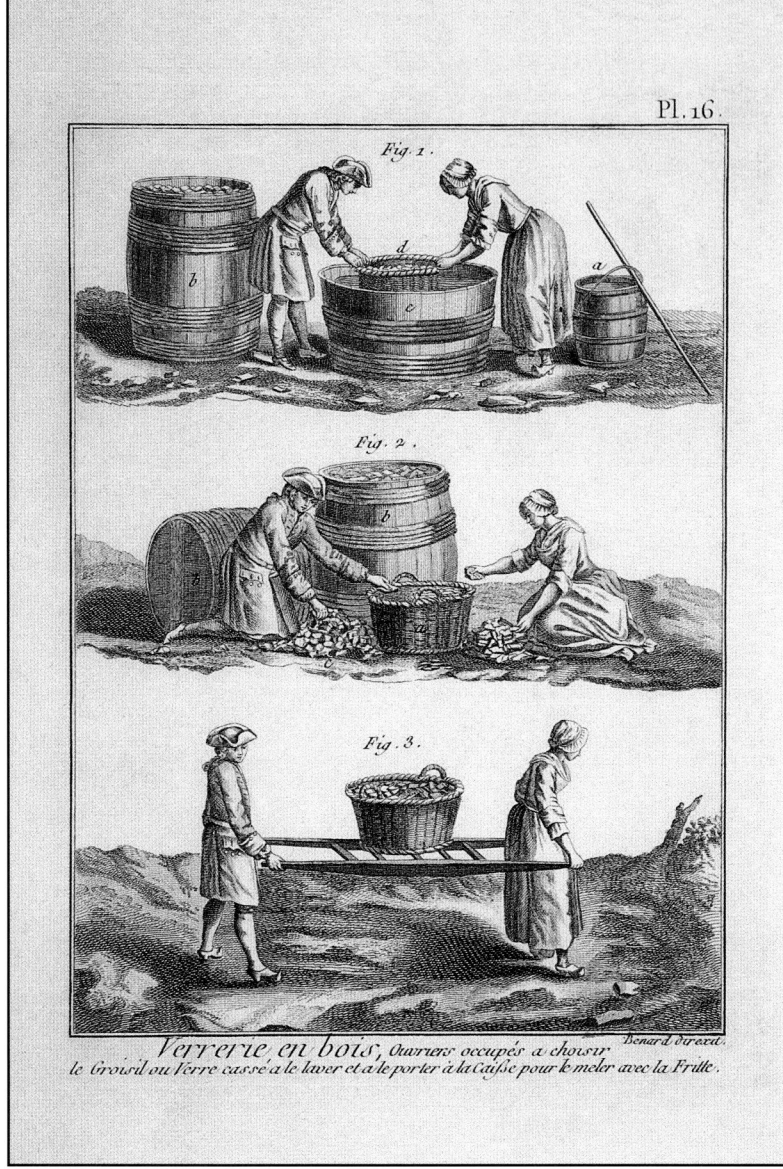

Diderot Drawing, washing and cleaning cullet, "Verrerie en bois, Ouvriers occupes a chosisir le Groisil ou Verre cassè a le laver et a le porter à la Caisse pour le meler avec la fritte" from Diderot Denis and others. Encyclopedia, eighteenth century. *Courtesy The Rakow Research Library.*

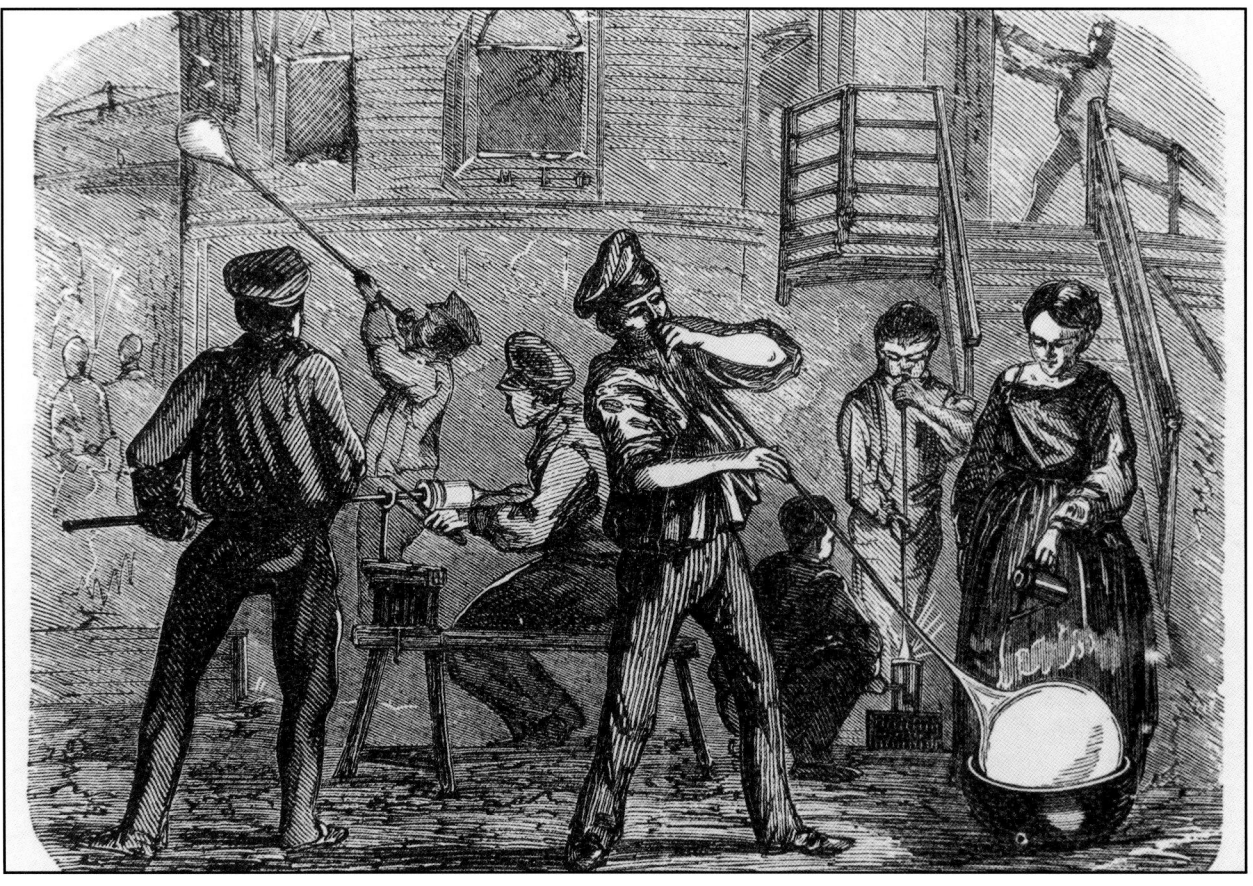

Goblet Makers, from One Hundred Years Progress of the United States, 1872. Print courtesy of The Museum of American Glass, Wheaton Village.

In modern times the island of Murano in Venice has come to be known as an important glass center. Glass only arrived on the island in the eleventh century when the glass houses in Venice posed a fire threat to the city. By the thirteenth century, glass bead making was one of the first organized crafts to have an impact on female labor. Many shops employed women who worked at home as both bead makers and bead stringers. Generally guilds did not give women rights of membership, although they were allowed to work if they were wives or daughters of a master in the trade. In many jobs women and boys were preferred for delicate handwork because of their manual dexterity. By the fifteenth century glass beads were such a popular export that shops and factories employed street women as stringers just to have enough of a labor force. Since there is little documentation of the gender division of labor in the making of glass in Venice, research can only rely on isolated stories. One such tale attributes the invention of chevron beads in the fifteenth century to Maria Barovier, daughter of Angelo, the most famous Renaissance glass blower. A chevron bead was made by layering many colors of glass one over the other to form a large bead. Once the bead cooled the layers were ground away revealing a complex pattern. Among the treasures Christopher Columbus brought to the new world were Venetian chevron beads. By the eighteenth century women were both lamp-bead artisans and bead stringers, but given the illegal nature of women's employment, it was difficult to know how many there were and if their work was limited to bead making. The tradition of employing women as bead makers continued well into the nineteenth century. In his novel *The Ashbern Papers. Louisa Pallant. The Modern Warning*, which is set in Venice during the 1880s, Henry James describes one of these artisans.

> This was a young lady with powdered face, a yellow cotton gown and *much leisure*, who used often to come to see him. She practiced, *at her convenience*, the art of a stringer of beads (these ornaments are made in Venice, in profusion; she had her pocket full of them and I used to find them on the floor of my apartment) (James 1888: 93)[5]

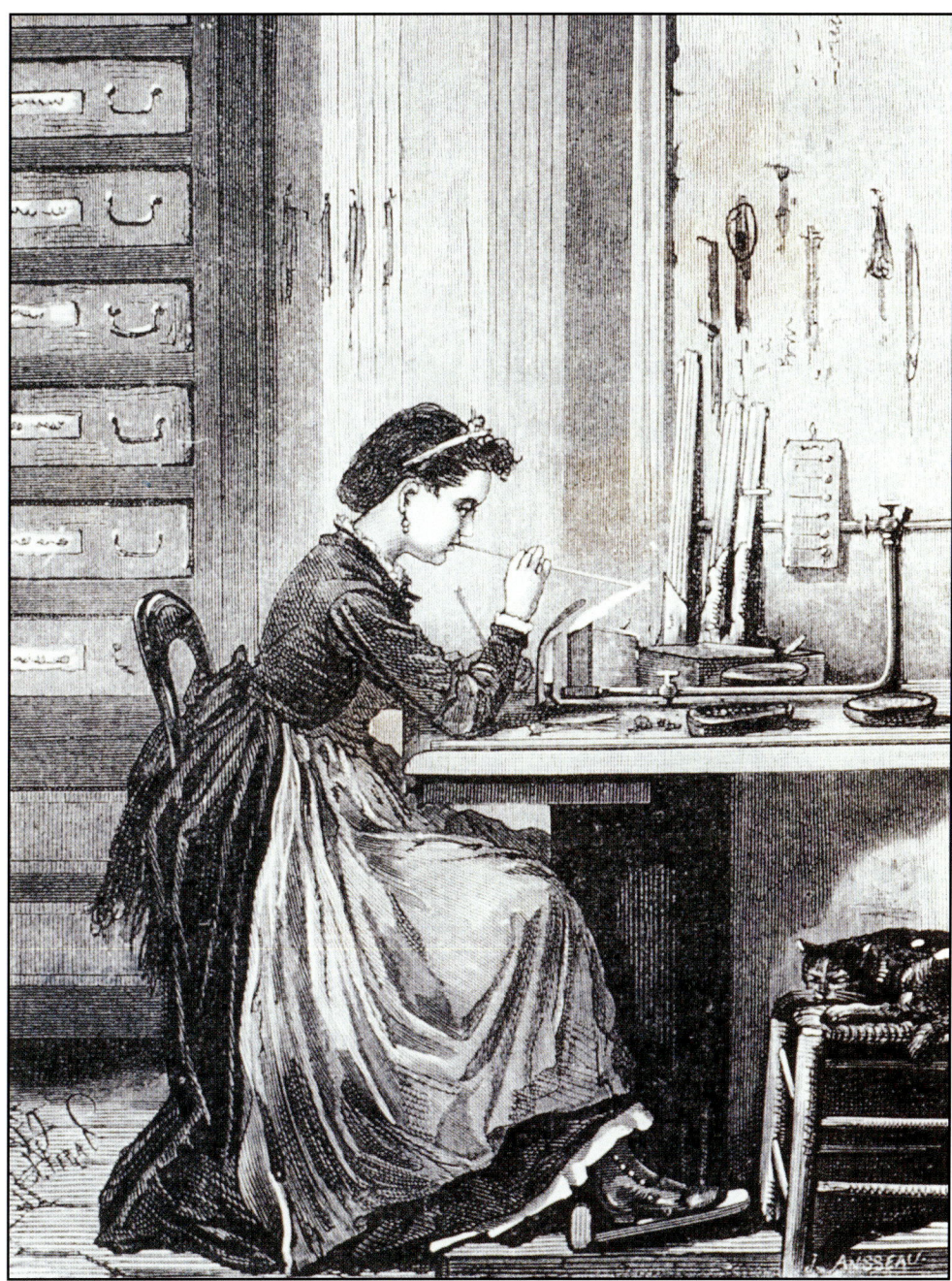

Beadmaking Parisian Worker making a false pearl. *Courtesy The Rakow Research Library, Chambon Collection.*

Glass painting was an art practiced by women for hundreds of years. Here are a few names from the British Society of Master Glass Painters: in the early fourteenth century, Margaret de Sez from Paris; in the fifteenth century, Katheryn de Ringle from Belgium; and in the eighteenth century, Mlle de Montigny, also from Paris and Barbara von Esch from Switzerland. The tradition continued in England and by the nineteenth century many women's names are listed in the Society records. These women not only did tracing and painting, but in some cases designed and executed panels for windows.[6]

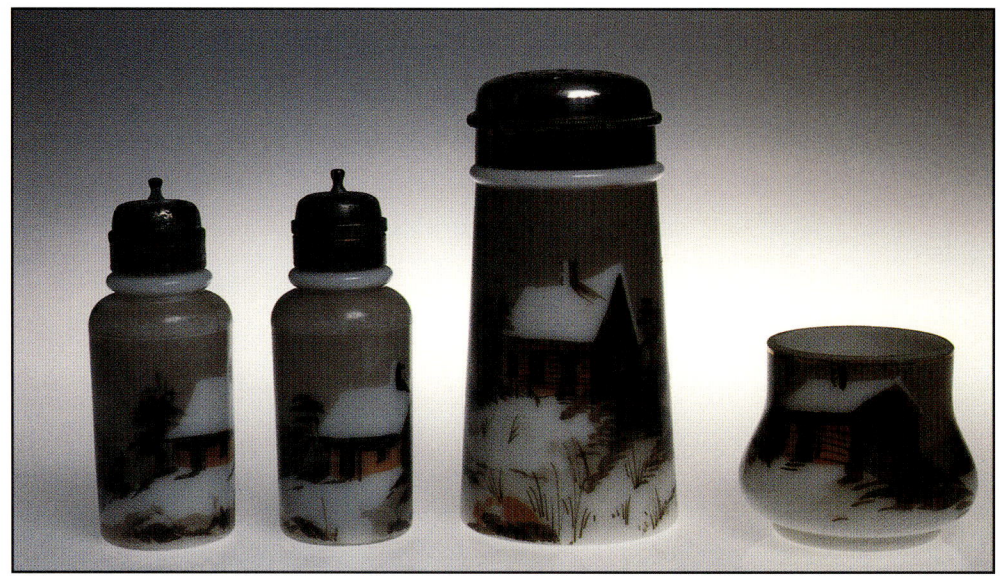

Salt Shakers, Muffineer, and Toothpick Holder painted by Mary Gregory ca. 1880-1884. Photo Courtesy of the Sandwich Glass Museum.

The tradition of glass painting continued in the American industry which produced tableware and lighting. Women were employed to paint designs on lamps and vases. The most famous name from the nineteenth century was Mary Gregory.[7] Although Ms. Gregory did not personally paint the beautiful images of children for which she became famous, she and her sister did work for the Boston and Sandwich Glass Company prior to 1865 and painted landscapes and winter scenes on lamps and vases and tableware.

During the late nineteenth century in America Louis Comfort Tiffany, son of the famous jeweler, made a decision to focus his attentions on the decorative arts instead of fine arts and opened Tiffany Studios. In the mid-1880s, he attempted to replace his older male employees with young males at lower salaries. The older men rebelled and went on strike; Tiffany let them go and hired young women from art schools to work at even cheaper wages. After hiring women for economic interests, he discovered they were better equipped to carry out his designs than the male employees were. By 1894, Tiffany employed about fifty women in various aspects of glass art production. Most of his female artists did not gain recognition, even for their most successful designs. Mrs. Clara Driscoll Mae Wolcott's *Dragonfly Lampshade* was a rare exception. The now famous *Wisteria Lampshade* design was obtained from Mrs. Curtis Freschel, a client of Tiffany's, who commissioned him to make some furnishings for her home. Tiffany acquired the design, made it, and was inspired to do a line of floral lamps.[8]

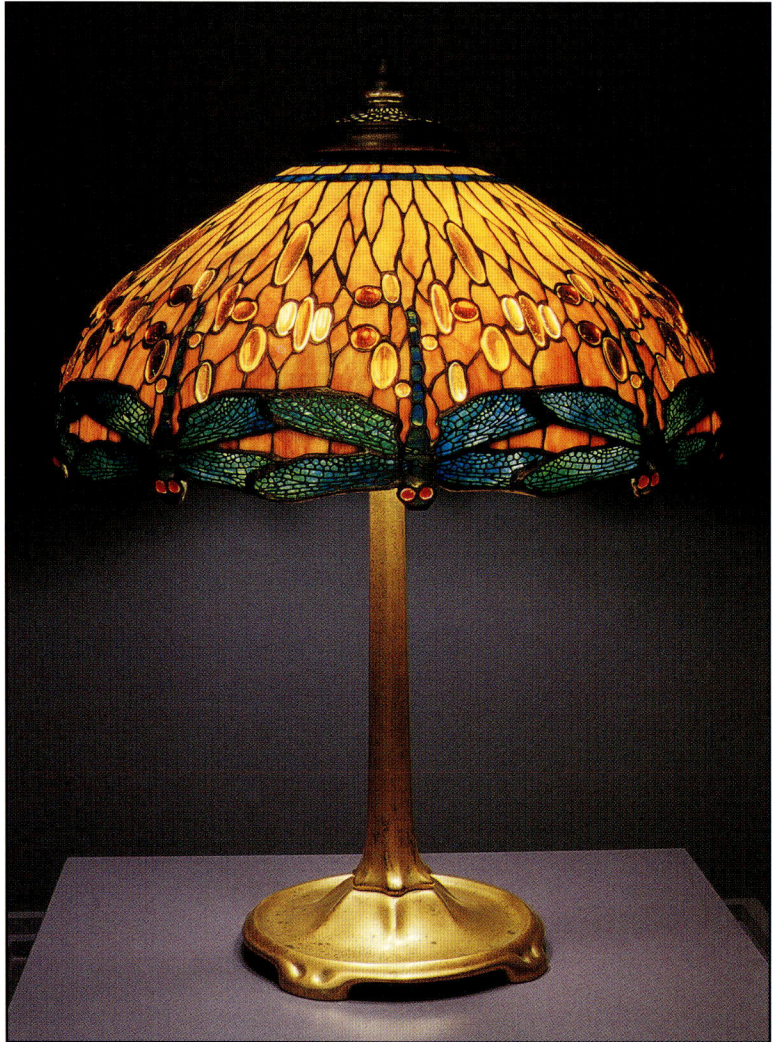

Dragonfly Lampshade,
Tiffany Studios.
Courtesy of the
Neustadt Museum of
Tiffany Art, New York.

Opposite page:
Wisteria Lampshade,
Tiffany Studios.
Courtesy of the
Neustadt Museum of
Tiffany Art, New York.

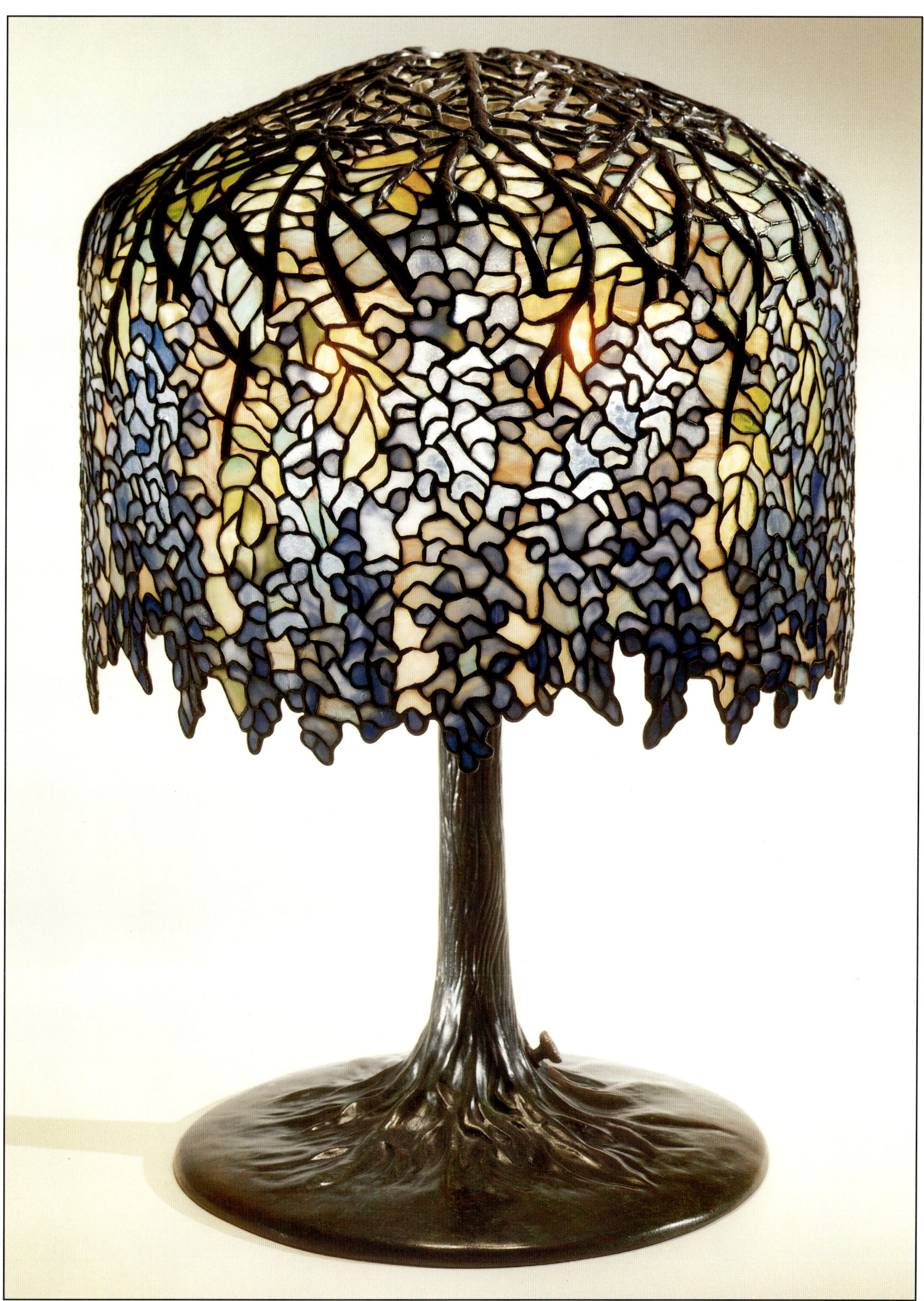

14   In the beginning: Herstory

According to some critics, Tiffany's landscapes were considered to be his best products. Some of these landscapes were designed by Agnes Northrop, who joined the studio in 1884; but she was never credited for her work. Tiffany's opinion of female artisans was corroborated by a U.S. Bureau of Labor report in 1902. It says that

> some manufacturers do not want female designers, on account of a prejudice against women taking up the work of men. But where they are once employed they are preferred, because they are naturally of a more artistic temperament. They display more taste, are always reliable, and can do fully as good work as men. It is the opinion that the competition and employment of women in the field of design ... has tended to improve the work of men.[9]

There were many other jobs that women did in glass factories. An illustration from the early nineteenth century shows "Bottles coming out of the furnace at Verriers de Jumet, Belgium," another illustration shows them sandblasting bottles. In yet another factory in Belgium women are carrying glass cylinders, splitting cylinders, and flattening them.

Top to bottom:
"Grinding Room," T.C. Wheaton Glass Co. ca. 1900. *Photo courtesy of The Museum of American Glass, Wheaton Village.*

Bottle factory: Postcard showing bottles coming out of the furnace, at Verriers de Jumet, Jumet, Belgium, about 1910. *Courtesy of the Rakow Research Library, Chambon Collection.*

Postcard showing the splitting of glass cylinders at Verrierie H. Lambert about 1900, Belgium, Ed Neis. *Courtesy of the Rakow Research Library, Chambon Collection.*

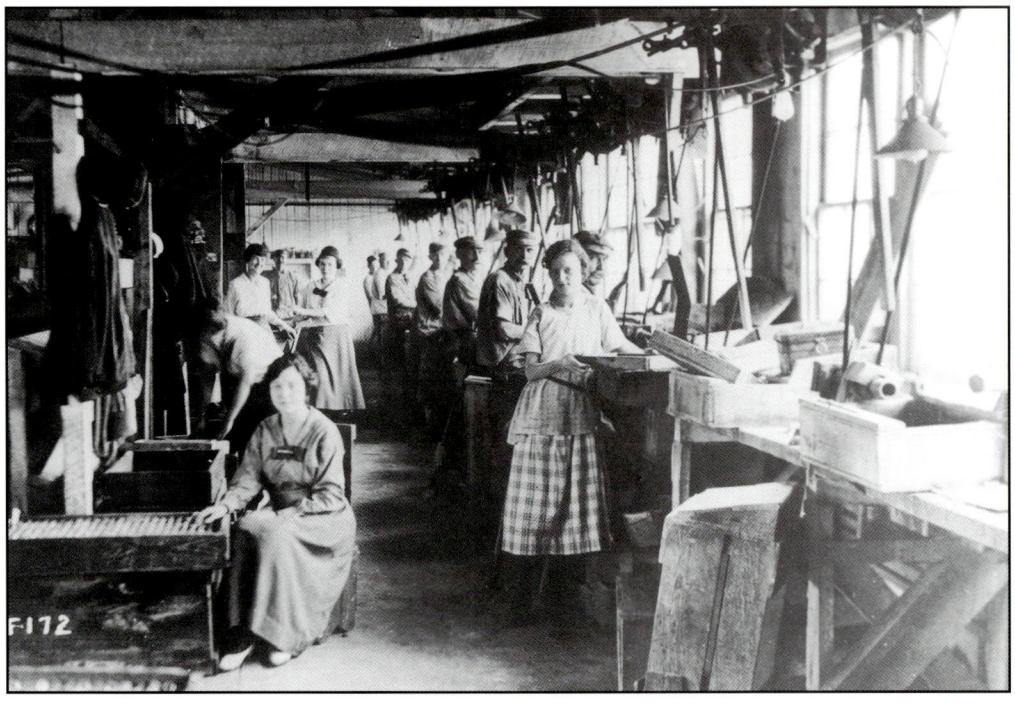

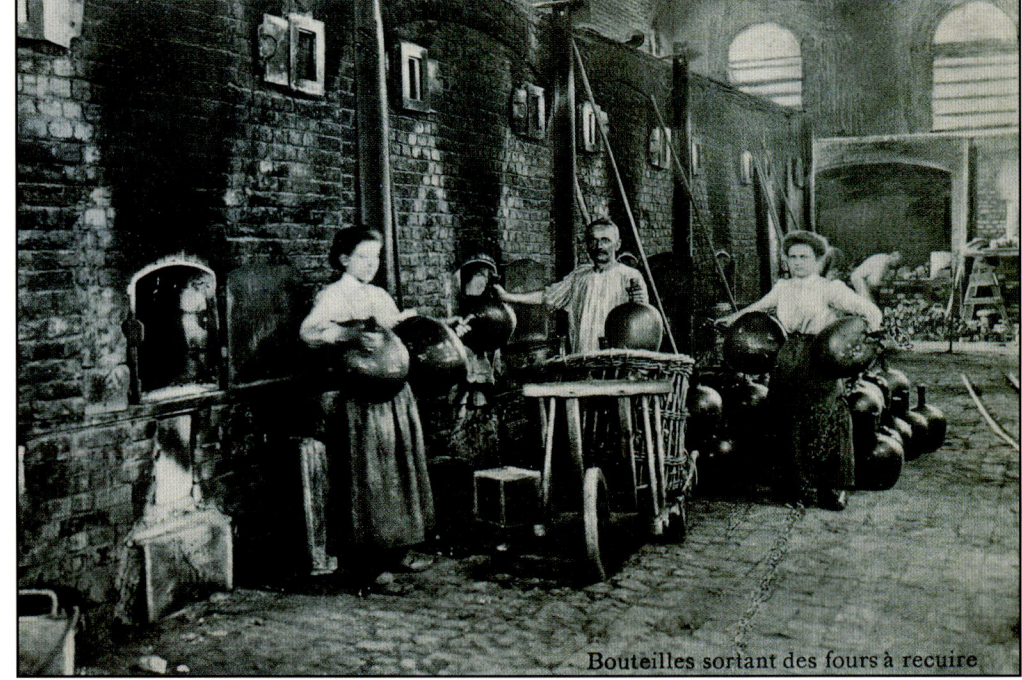

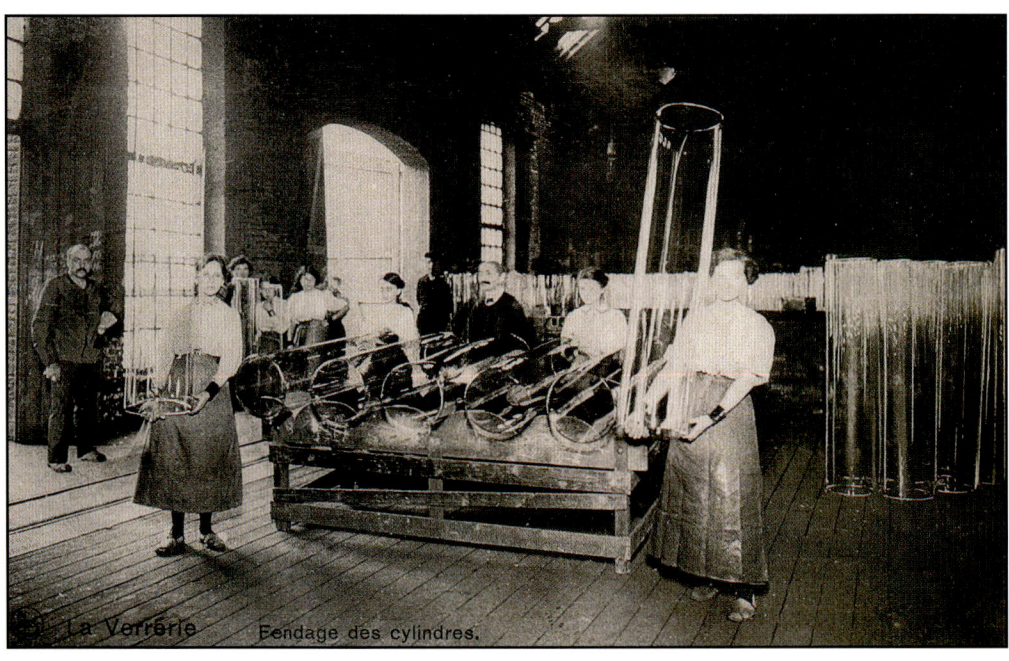

In the beginning: Herstory 15

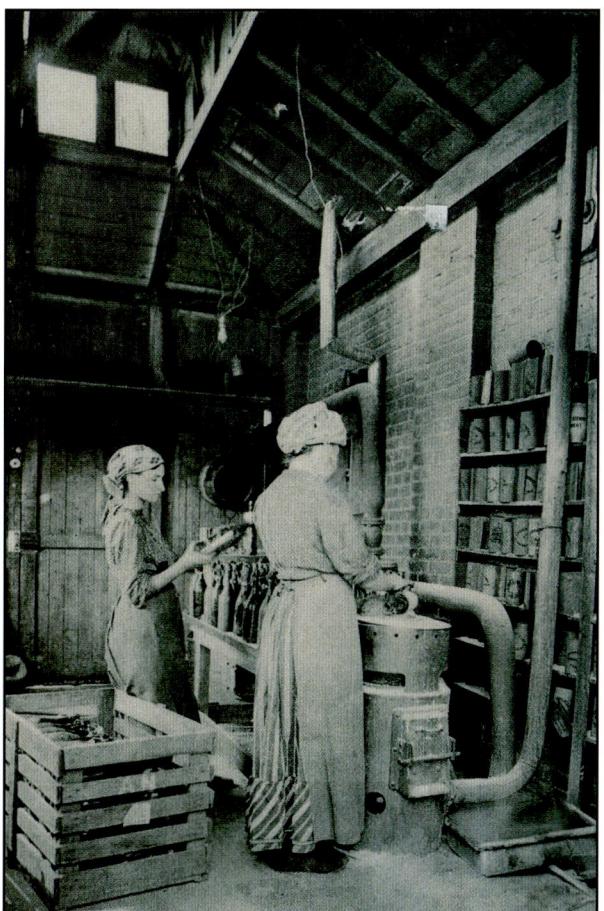

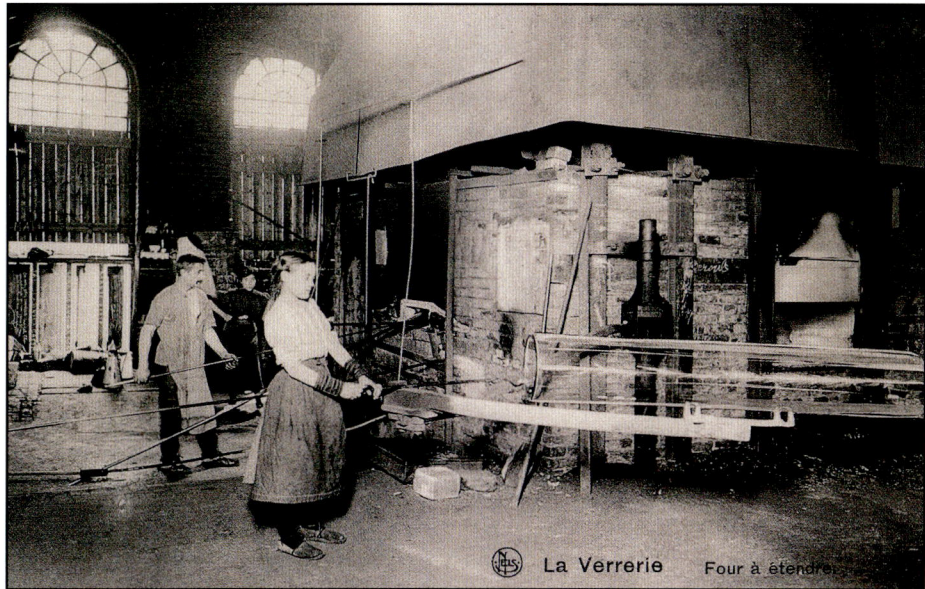

Sandblasting: Postcard showing women sandblasting bottles, at Verriers de Jumet, Jumet, Belgium, about 1910. *Courtesy of the Rakow Research Library, Chambon Collection.*

Postcard showing furnace for flattening glass cylinders at Verrierie H. Lambert about 1900, Belgium, Ed Neis. *Courtesy of the Rakow Research Library, Chambon Collection.*

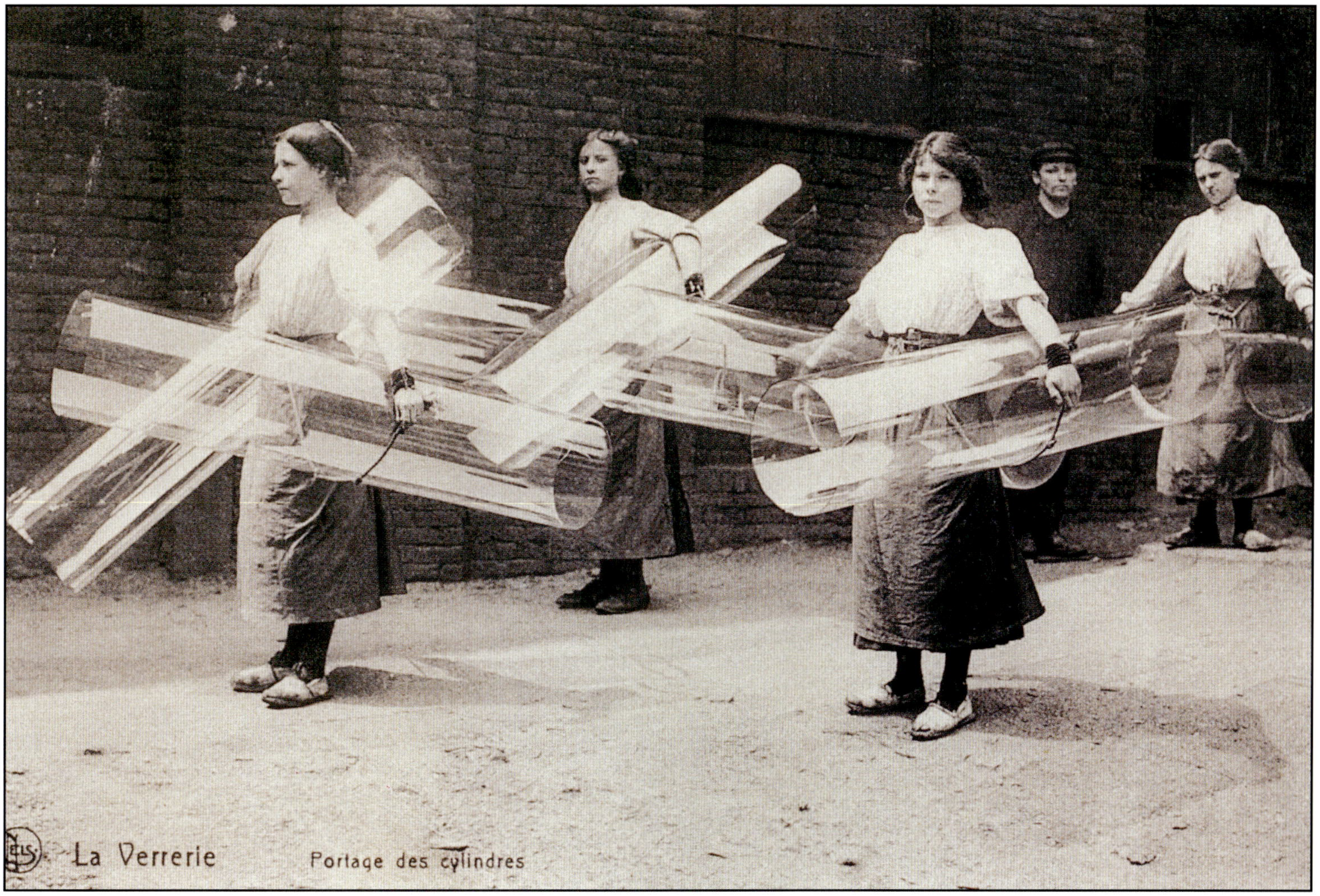

Postcard showing women carrying glass cylinders at Verrierie H. Lambert about 1900, Belgium, Ed Neis. *Courtesy of the Rakow Research Library, Chambon Collection.*

The Industrial Revolution saw many changes in labor laws as trade unions eventually replaced the medieval guilds. Factories were replacing small shops and machines were replacing jobs. The prevailing attitude in the unions was that factories were not a place for women and glass blowing was certainly not a woman's task. In England and America women gained entry into the glass factories as strike breakers. According to a report citing examples from the United States Bureau of Labor, in 1889 there was a strike in a Pennsylvania plant because the firm wanted to employ girls for engraving glass. When ordered to teach them, the men went on strike; the girls were hired. In 1890, men in another Pennsylvania plant making tableware and shades went on strike and their places were filled with women.

According to a spoof review, "Women in Glass, a tardy book notice," written by Paul Hollister in 1975 about an old book he came across, The Employment's of Women: A Cyclopaedia of Woman's Work, written by Virginia Penny in 1877, this useful volume gives statistical information for the years 1859-1861 showing that women were underpaid and undervalued compared to male workers. Ms Penny indicates types of employment and the wages paid for specific jobs. The lowest wages were for sorting, packing, and affixing labels. The average pay for this type of work was $3.00 per week. At this time Penny says, in England and Europe women could be found cutting, grinding, etching, and engraving glass. Enameling, staining, and painting glass are also tasks often done by women. Penny mentions a woman in England who filled large orders for church and cathedral windows in America and Europe, while in France some stained glass was made in a Carmelite Convent. The nuns supplied windows for churches all over Europe - even some in America. Mostly the nuns supervised the making of the windows, but a few of them were occupied in painting the glass.

The book also lists some industrial statistics for several months in Paris, for the year 1848.

Glassblowers	76 men	6 women
Painters and gilders	108 men	8 women
Cutters, Engravers, Polishers	327 men	8 women
Makers of glass beads	13 men	90 women[10]

After 1850 there was a large increase in women as well as children working in factories in the US according to the US Bureau of Labor.[11] This increase in part reflects a growth in the number of factories making glass between 1870 and 1880. Some women gained entry to the factories as strike breakers, especially in the cutting shops. Sand blasting was invented during that decade; however, there is little evidence of women using the process until later. The discovery of natural gas stimulated the building of even more factories between 1880 and 1890. In order to keep wages low, women were employed to do jobs usually carried out by men. Some parts of the workload were adjusted and new methods were devised so that women could be employed. The census indicated the average age of female glass workers was sixteen to twenty old years with a small percent of women forty-five and older.

Women continued to do lamp working into the twentieth century. Bead making continued, mostly in Europe, with factories in Venice and Bavaria [former Czechoslovakia]. Even today most beads and Christmas ornaments are handmade. Specialized scientific apparatus was becoming more important as research in science and medicine was rapidly expanding. The invention of the electric light bulb provided employment opportunities for female glass workers in America.

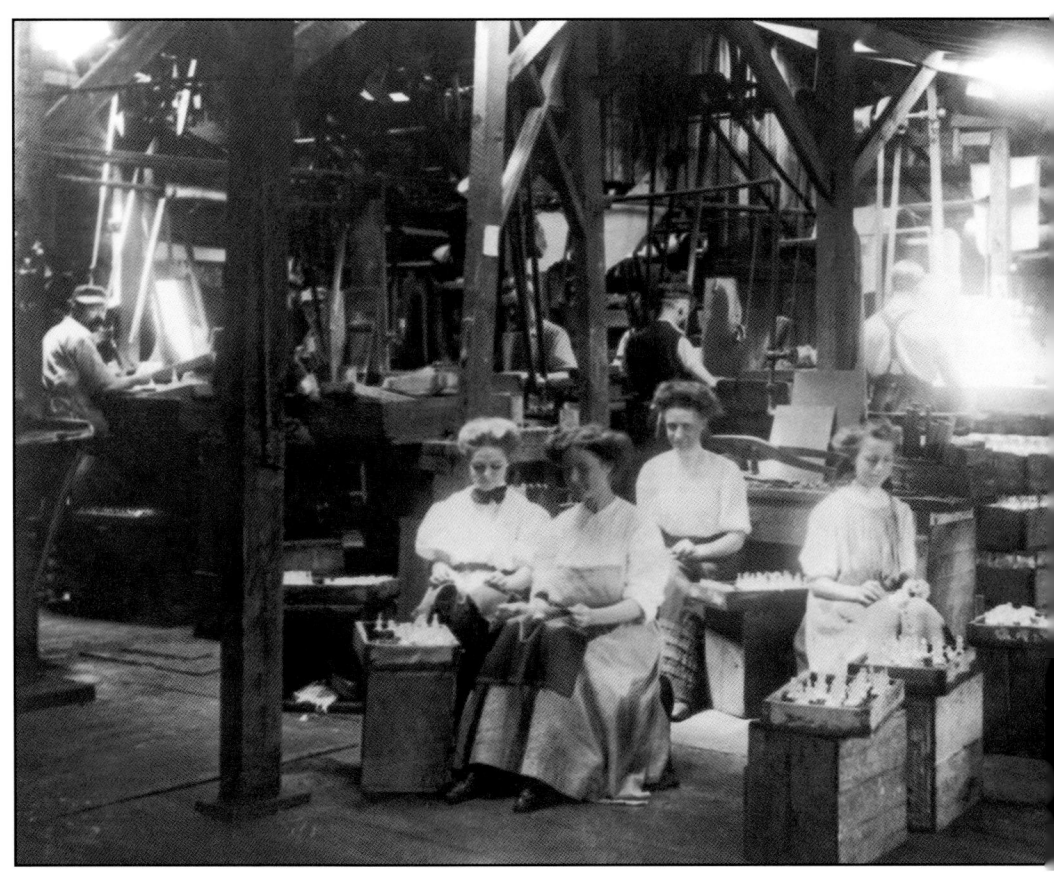

"Women and Children in Factories," T.C. Wheaton Glass Company, ca 1890. Photo courtesy of The Museum of American Glass, Wheaton Village.

In the beginning: Herstory

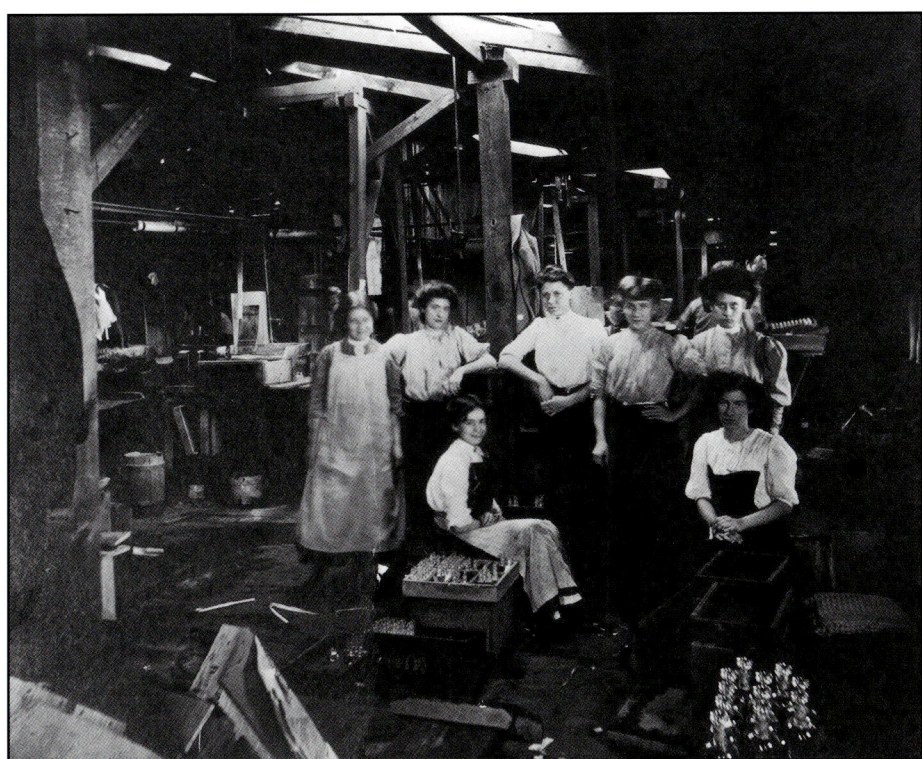

"Women and Children in Factories," T.C. Wheaton Glass Company, ca 1890. *Photo courtesy of The Museum of American Glass, Wheaton Village.*

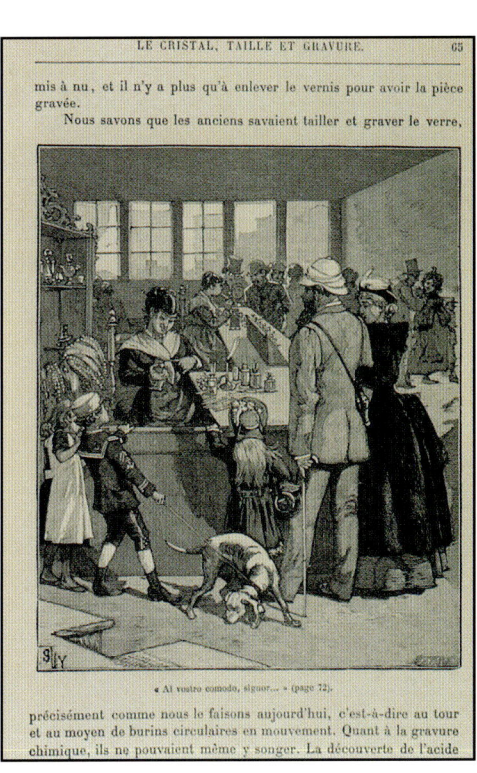

Lamp workers, late nineteenth century. From Bitard. Les Arts et metiers illus. Paris: 1890-1900, p.65. *Courtesy The Rakow Research Library.*

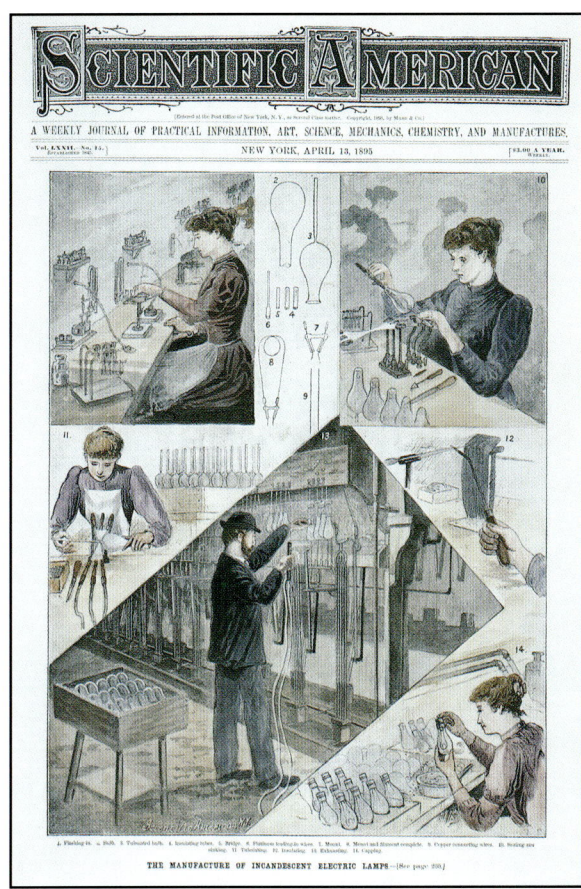

"The Manufacture of Incandescent Electric Lamps," *Scientific American*, April 13, 1895. *Courtesy Rakow Archives, Corning Museum of Glass.*

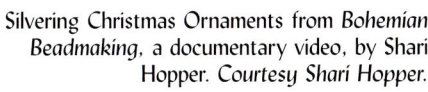

Silvering Christmas Ornaments from *Bohemian Beadmaking*, a documentary video, by Shari Hopper. *Courtesy Shari Hopper.*

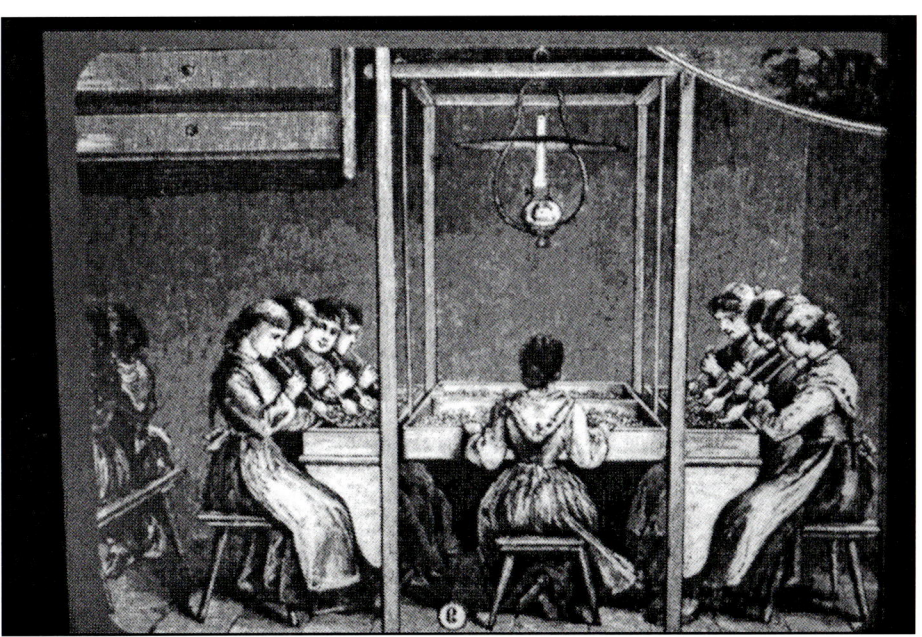

Art education was difficult if not impossible for women in the nineteenth century, except for those who could afford to take private classes. Wives or daughters of men in the fine arts or trades were sometimes allowed private instruction in order to lend a helping hand in the studio. Trade apprenticeships excluded women for fear of taking men's jobs, especially in metalwork and glassblowing. Crafts that did not compete with men for employment were deemed suitable for women. By the 1890s a movement to educate women in feminine crafts began in Britain. Schools in Birmingham and Glasgow began teaching classes in jewelry and metalwork in addition to embroidery, lace making, and painting. An art movement known as "Art Nouveau," emerging in Britain and Europe from 1888 to 1920, owed much to the contributions of women artists. A significant influence was the Glasgow School of Art where a number of talented female students became important figures in the avant-garde design of the period. Young artists including Margaret Macdonald and her sister Frances, Ann Macbeth, Jessie Newberry, and Jessie M. King formed The Glasgow Society of Lady Artists Club, the first residential art club for women.[11] Margaret Macdonald later married Charles Rennie Macintosh. Though she continued to work, she chose to remain in his shadow. Nevertheless, she contributed original designs, probably including designs for stained glass panels, to his architectural interiors and exercised a considerable influence on his work. Margaret Macdonald and her sister are said to have designed the famous *Glasgow rose*, often executed in glass, which came to symbolize the entire Glasgow art movement.

In America, by the mid-nineteenth century, women were becoming increasingly dependant on their own financial resources and art-related occupations were acceptable as suitably lady-like. Mrs. Sarah Worthington King Peter of Philadelphia founded The Philadelphia School for Design for Women in 1844, now the Moore College of Art and Design. In 1871 Walter Smith, a headmaster from Leeds School of Art in Yorkshire, England, came to America to become Director of Drawing for the Boston Schools and Massachusetts State Director of Art Education. Walter Smith's attitude toward art education for women was progressive for his time.

> My own fear has been, and now is, that hitherto women have been treated as pets and playthings, to be indulged and delighted in, but not to be held responsible for anything; have been educated with the view that all should become merely the ornaments of society and not its essentials, and the important half of its structure; that, finally, men have come to regard women with a patronizing feeling, in which there is an infinite amount of good nature in some cases, but no justice in any case…we educate women superficially, and then smugly say they have no minds; we withhold reasoning processes from them, and then say they cannot argue, but jump to conclusions; we train and grind up our boys in athletic sports, in Euclid and conic sections, and the differential calculus, and our girls in Berlin wool work, in waltz playing, and the Paris fashions, and then proclaim that men can reason, women only perceive, men can create, women only appreciate…half of the troubles we find in the world arise from, and are a just judgment upon, our presumption in making distinctions between them, in fostering the self-conceit of the one, and sacrificing the independence of the other. Let the same education from the first to the last, physical and mental, be furnished for both sexes.[12]

Idealism at the turn of the century influencing both the gender issue and the art-verses-craft issue was short lived and did not return again until the 1980s.

The widespread influence of the Art Nouveau and later Art Deco movements in Europe involved another famous family of artists. René Lalique, a French jeweler turned glassmaker, was responsible for introducing both hand and machine pressed glass primarily used for perfume bottles by France's best perfume houses. His daughter Suzanne became a painter and decorator and sometimes turned her talents toward designs for glassware and perfume bottles sold under the labels of big stores rather than perfumeries. Lalique's granddaughter, Marie-Claude Lalique, until recently directed the firm Cristal Lalique and was its exclusive designer since 1977.

From the beginning of the twentieth century, women in Europe were often trained in the design arts. Tyra Lundgren, born in 1897 in Stockholm, was trained as a designer in ceramics and glass in Sweden then worked in Italy for Paulo Scarpa, head designer for Vennini, an Italian Glass company in the 1930s.

In response to the collapse of the stock market in 1929 and the great depression of the 1930s, artists formed an Unemployed Artists Association to press for government relief. Many of those artists were women. The federal government responded through various programs, collectively called the New Deal. The new federal art programs were required to follow an equal opportunity policy. "Perhaps for the first time in world history women were hired without discrimination, in proportions that bore some relation to their numbers in population."[14]

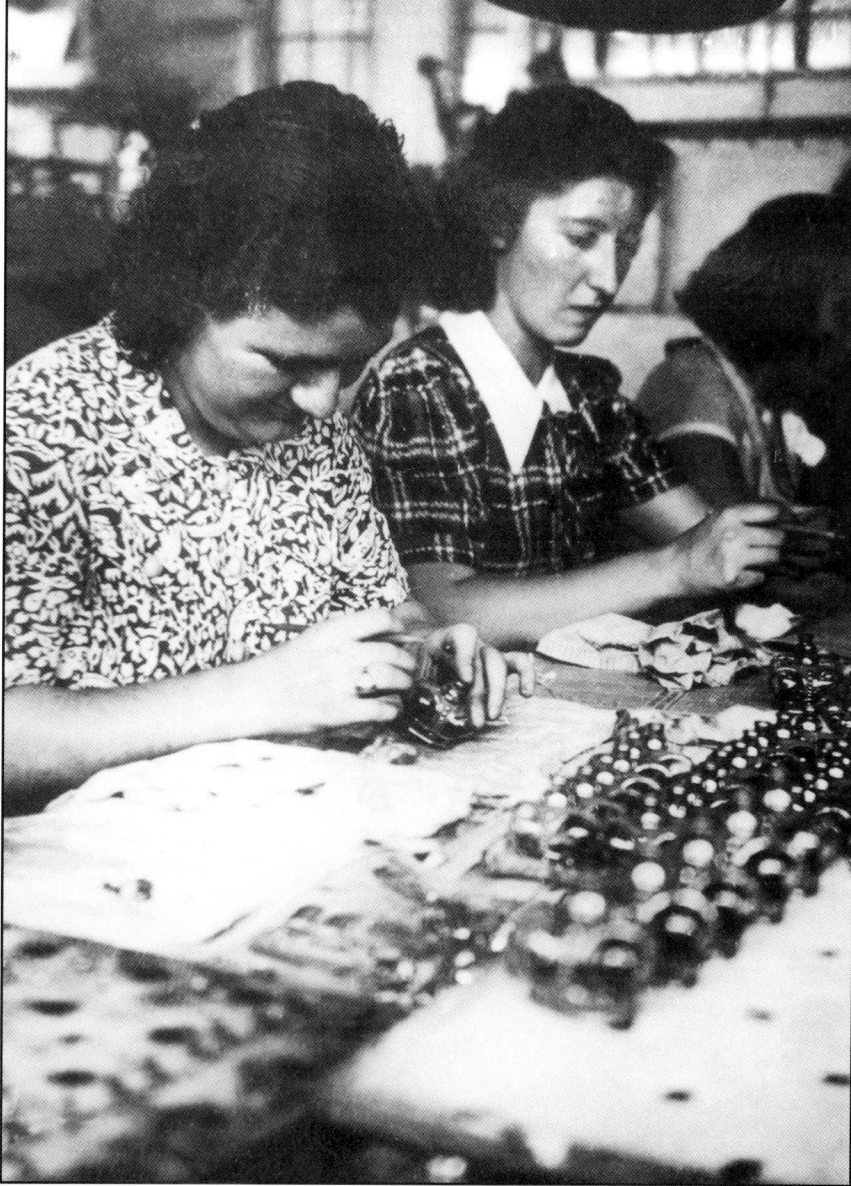

"Gold painting perfume bottles," ca. 1925, T.C. Wheaton Glass Co. *Photo courtesy of The Museum of American Glass, Wheaton Village.*

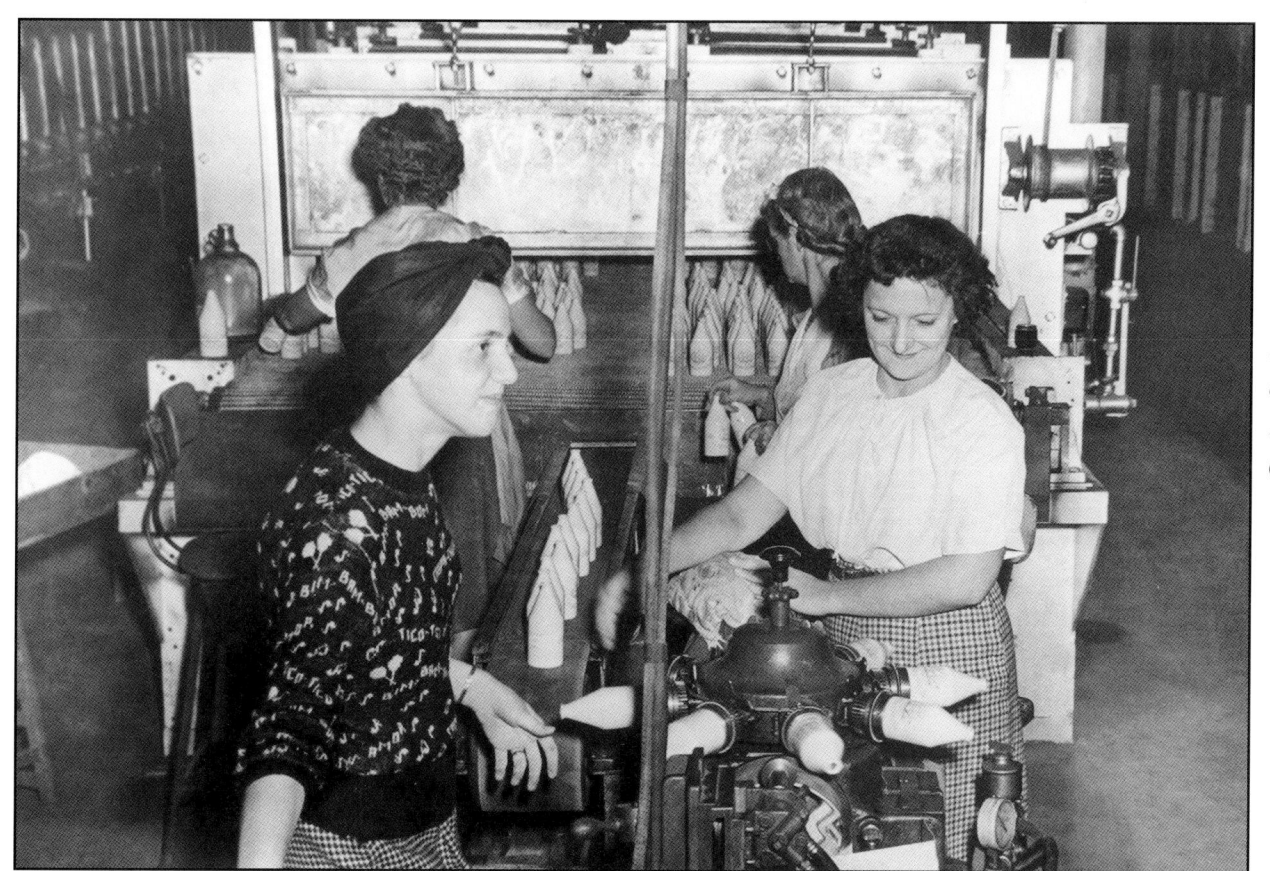

"Schulton automatic bottle decorating machine," ca. 1942. *Photo courtesy of The Museum of American Glass, Wheaton Village.*

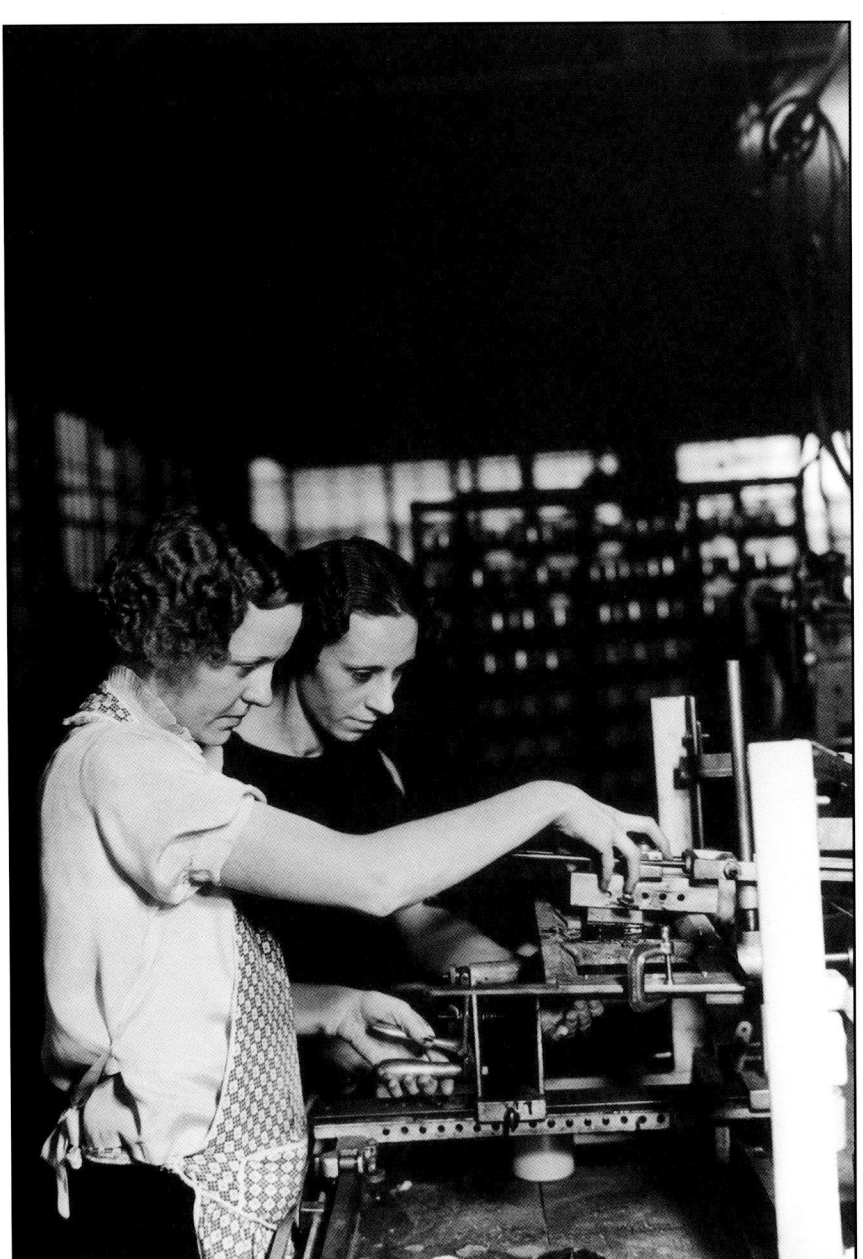

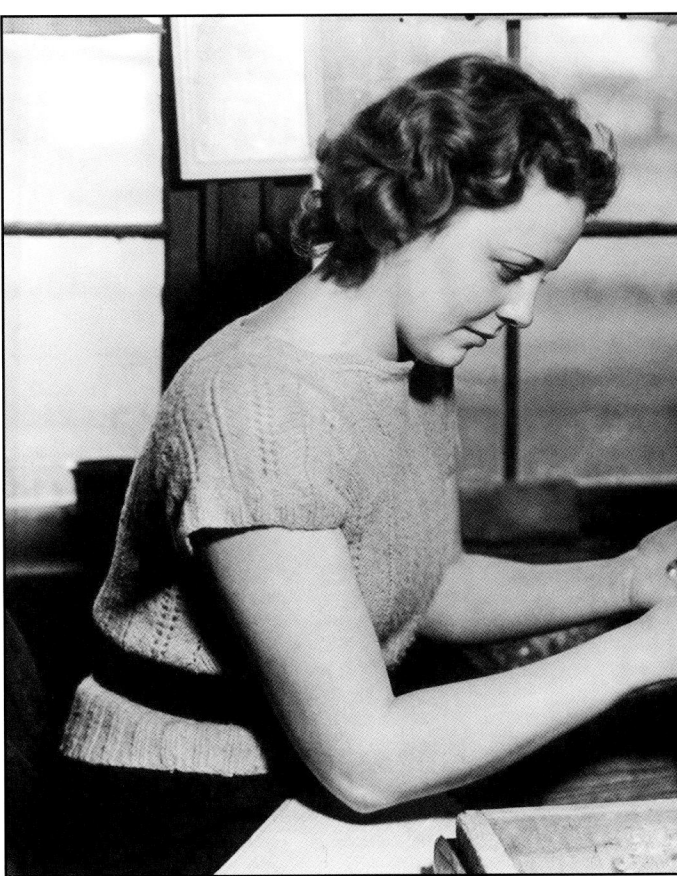

"Silkscreen hand decorating" photo, WPA project, Lewis Hine. Photo courtesy of The Museum of American Glass, Wheaton Village.

"Grinding" photo, WPA project, Lewis Hine. Photo courtesy of The Museum of American Glass, Wheaton Village.

"Tying stoppers" photo, WPA project, Lewis Hine. Photo courtesy of The Museum of American Glass, Wheaton Village.

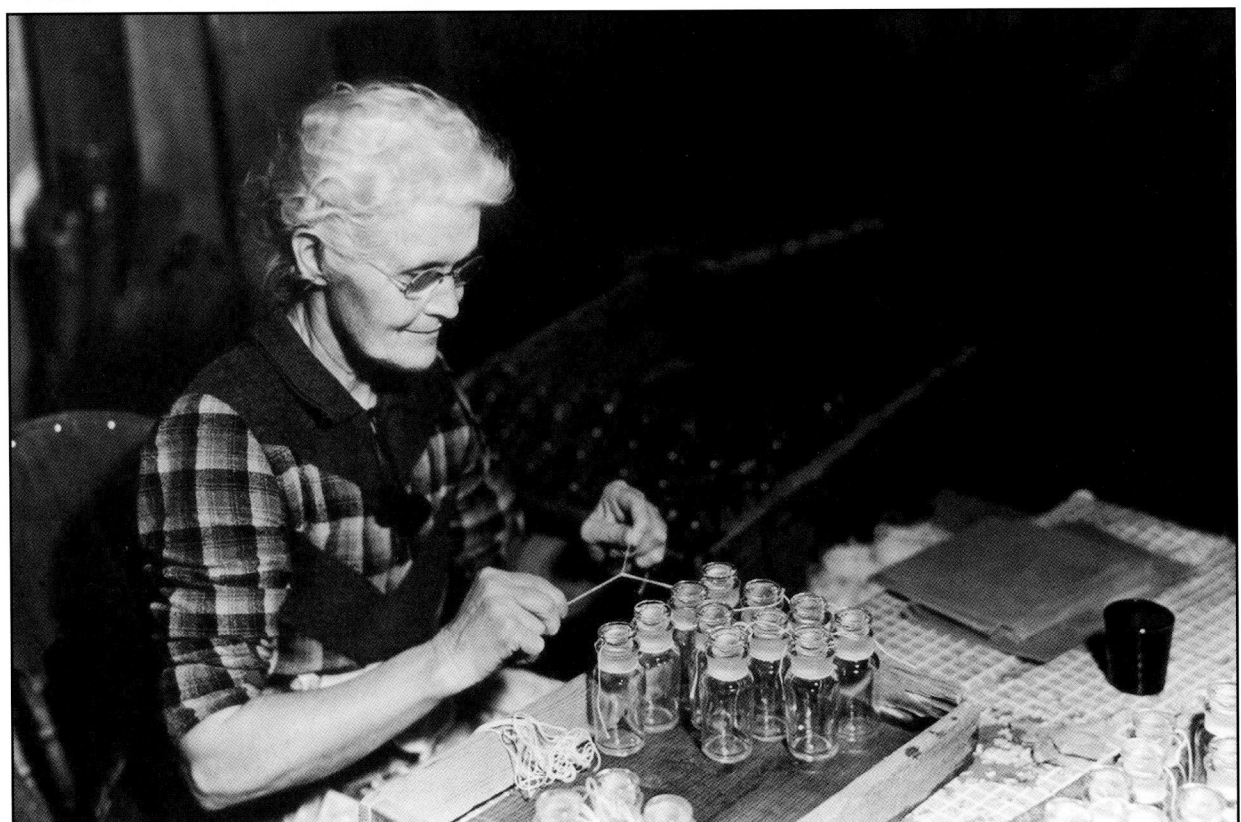

In the beginning: Herstory

During World War II, many American women responded to the government's encouragement to join the war effort by entering the war production job market. These women were trained as skilled laborers doing traditionally "men's work." The *Rosie the Riveter* poster from 1943 depicts a worker with an attitude. Unfortunately, the sense of power women achieved with that effort soon ceased to exist; after the war, women were encouraged to return to their homes or resume their pink-collar jobs.

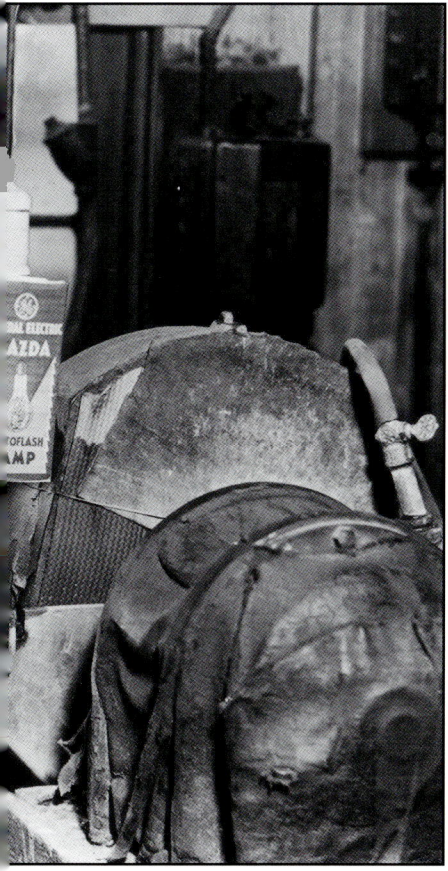

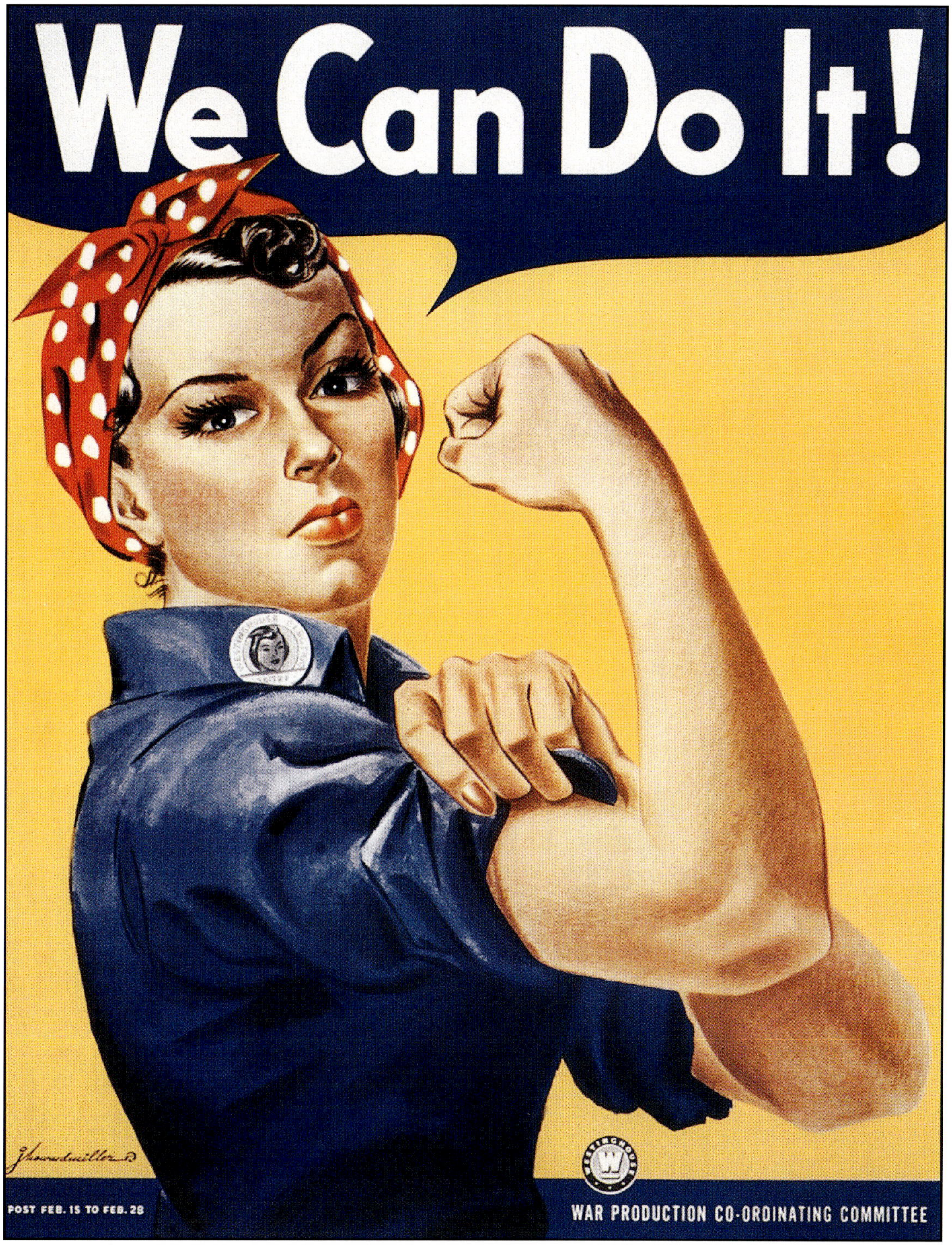

"We Can Do It" Poster created by J. Howard Miller and produced by Westinghouse for the War Production. *Courtesy of US National Archives.*

In the beginning: Herstory

The prevailing attitude prior to Word War II - that women belonged in the home - returned with a vengeance.

> As Betty Friedan has pointed out, when the G.I.'s returned after World War II, the era of the flight to the suburbs and the Baby Boom began, and women were informed once more that true happiness for them lay in the kitchen and the bedroom rather than in factories or professions.[13]

With a few exceptions, in the 1950s, most high school age young women wanted to get married and raise a family. The idea that a woman could have a successful career as an artist was discouraged. Those that did enter college did so for the most part to find a "suitable" husband, to acquire, as the joke went, not a BA after her name but an "MRS" before it. There were many more women artists working and many more art schools educating women than in past decades. One would think that the time was right for women to achieve success but the opposite proved to be true. When Peggy Guggenheim championed the new American artists, including women in her New York gallery, the success of the new American art, referred to as the New York School in both Europe and America caused male artists concern. They formed an unofficial and exclusive old boy's club in which women were not welcome; however, a number of female artists from that period did become successful. Overall, artists and the art world were rather unfriendly to women, but crafts embraced them. Many women students enrolled in colleges in the 1940s and '50s majored in art education in order to be able to teach in primary or secondary schools. Acceptable art courses at that time included drawing, painting, and craft mediums such as jewelry, ceramics, weaving.

Frances Higgins was born in 1912 in Haddock, Georgia, and received a BS in Art from Georgia State College for Women. Higgins was quoted in *Glass Focus Magazine*.[14]

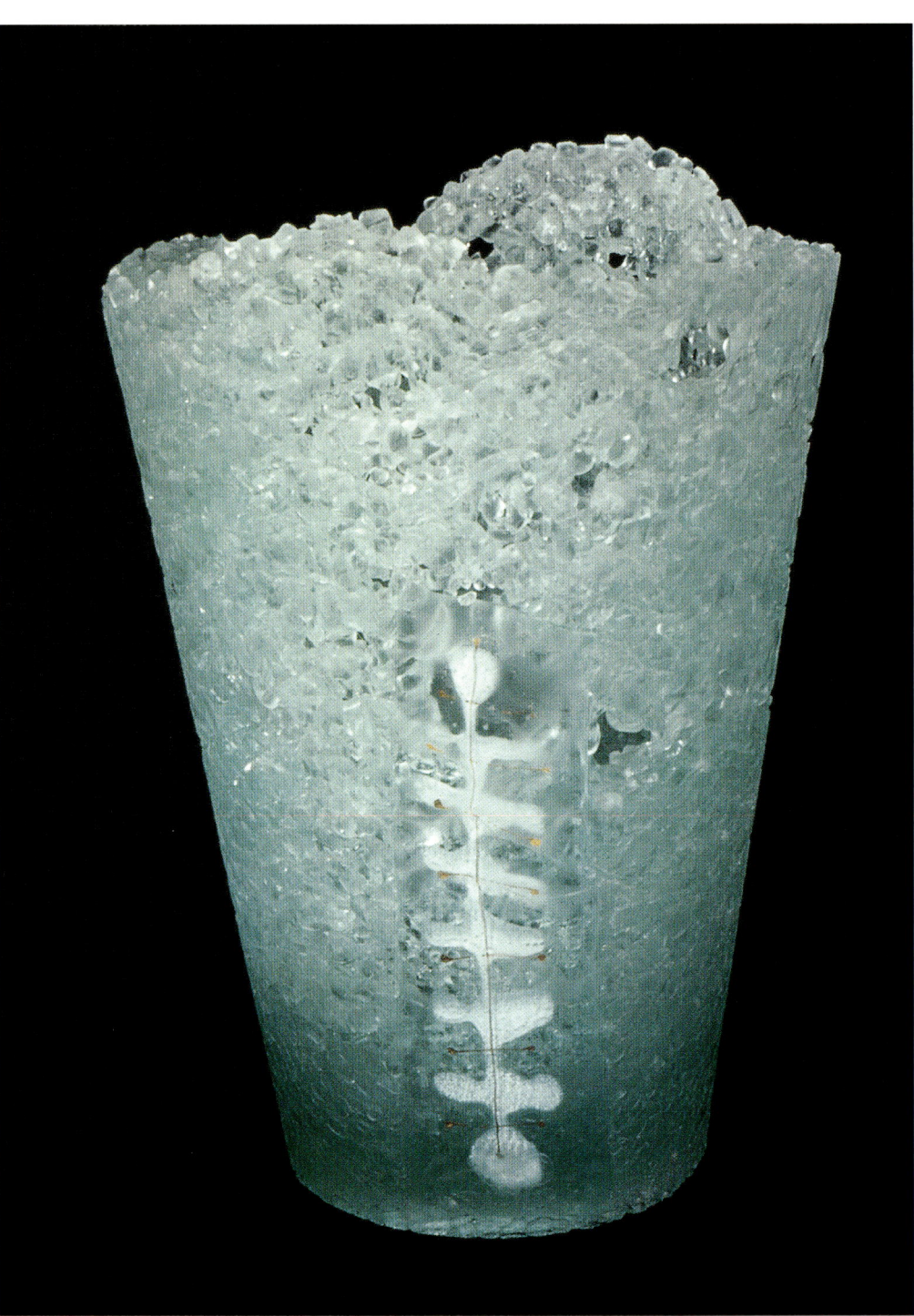

Francis Higgens, Vessel, about 1955, 23.5 cm x 16.6. cm d, crushed glass fused in a mold, enameled. *Photograph courtesy of The Corning Museum of Glass.*

In the beginning: Herstory   23

> "I majored in art in college. I got a B.S. degree so I could teach because that was about all a woman could do in Georgia." After her degree she went on to Ohio State where she taught pottery and other general craft courses. She first became interested in glass around 1942 when she saw a demonstration at a Ceramic Society meeting of glass medallions being made from a mold. She thought, "If they can do that, I can make a plate."

She did… In 1948 Frances Higgins moved to Chicago to get her Masters degree at the Institute of Design. That is where she met her future husband Michael. Soon after they married, they settled in Chicago. Most of the work from their long and productive career in glass was a combined effort of both talents.

Another pioneer from that same period was Edris Eckhardt, born 1910 in Cleveland, Ohio. She attended the Cleveland Institute of Art, specializing in sculpture and ceramics. She began her teaching career at the Cleveland Institute of Art and moved on to teach in other universities where she earned national recognition in ceramics. Her earliest glass experiments began in 1953 when she rediscovered the methods used by the Romans in the manufacture of gold glass. This event, along with the discovery of how to duplicate the reds and blues found in European stained glass windows, earned her a Guggenheim Fellowship and a Tiffany Fellowship, both in 1959. From an unpublished paper titled "Finding A Future In The Past," written by Edris Eckhardt in October 1961,[15] Eckhardt describes her experience of the art world in the early fifties:

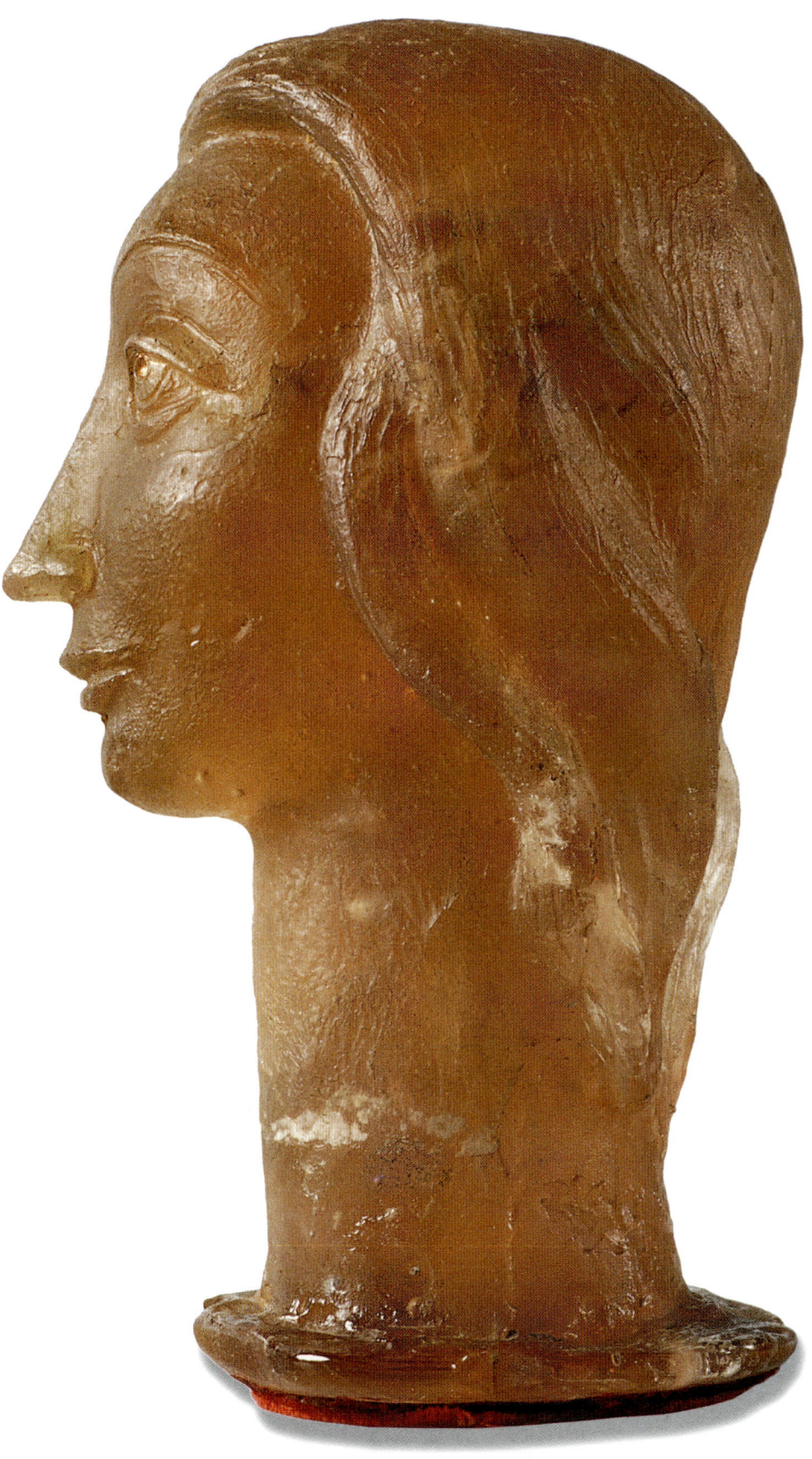

Edris Eckhardt, *Summer Day*, 1967, sculpture cast in amber colored glass, 9 inches high. *Chrysler Museum of Art, Norfolk, VA, Museum Purchase and Gift of Mr. And Mrs. Arthur Diamondstien.*

> I realized how cults, fashions and brain washing prevailed in the art field. One could lead or follow, there was very little middle road.
>
> Every artist must occasionally take stock of himself, his time, his relation to it. He must constantly change, enlarge, diversify or be left stranded on an island of his own making while the stream of life flows by.
>
> In such a frame of mind I visit the Metropolitan Museum of Art in 1953. I quite accidentally saw a case of Byzantine gold glass that held my attention with potent hypnotic force. It occurred to me that here was an art long dormant. That glass making as a one-man operation or art belonged to the past. I recalled that some of the most exciting glass came from periods when glass was hand-made by the artist. I felt this field was wide open—no standards, no rules, no fashions, no cults.

She converted her ceramic kiln for glass working. In the electric ceramic kiln she melted her own batch, laminated and fused commercial glass, and eventually began lost wax casting, sometimes with crushed glass. If she wanted a glossy finish, she poured molten glass directly into the preheated mold while it was in the kiln.

After many years of glass working, Eckhardt still remained enthused and excited, constantly experimenting, and then, sharing. She predicted in 1950 that glass would be a very important development in the arts in the near future.

In the Bohemian Black Forest, glass making has been around since antiquity. A unique and distinct style of glassware developed there and many glass making families' histories go back centuries. So it is with Jaroslava Brychtova. She came from a family of artists; her mother was involved with textiles and founded a textile-weaving workshop, her father was trained as a sculptor, but turned to glassmaking and co-founded the school for glassmaking at Zelenzy Brod. Brychtova was born in 1924, and showed early signs of exceptional talent. At sixteen she began to collaborate with her father to make small pate de verre sculpture for jewelry. In 1945 she entered the School for Applied Arts in Prague. She married Milos Zahradnik in 1947 and had three children, all the while working on architectural designs in glass. In 1956 Brychtova began a creative collaboration with Stanislav Libensky which lasted until his death in 2002. They eventually divorced their respective spouses and in 1963 they married.[16] Their collaborative work has inspired many artists, both men and women, and will probably find a place in history alongside Michelangelo.

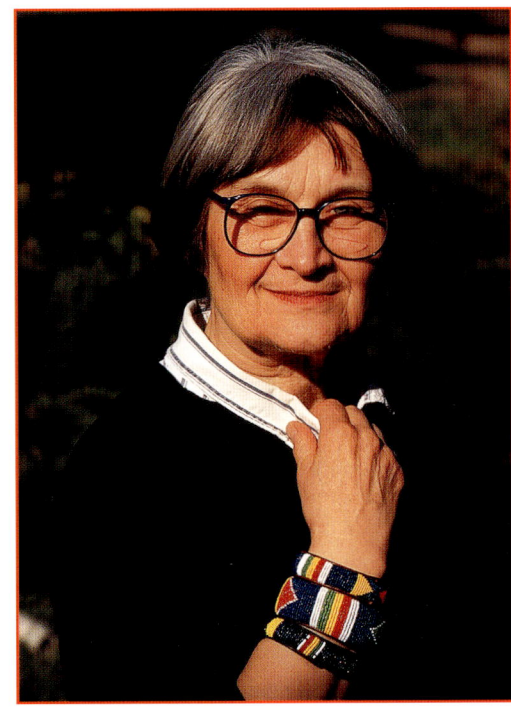

Jaraslava Brychtova photograph. *Photograph courtesy of Russell Johnson.*

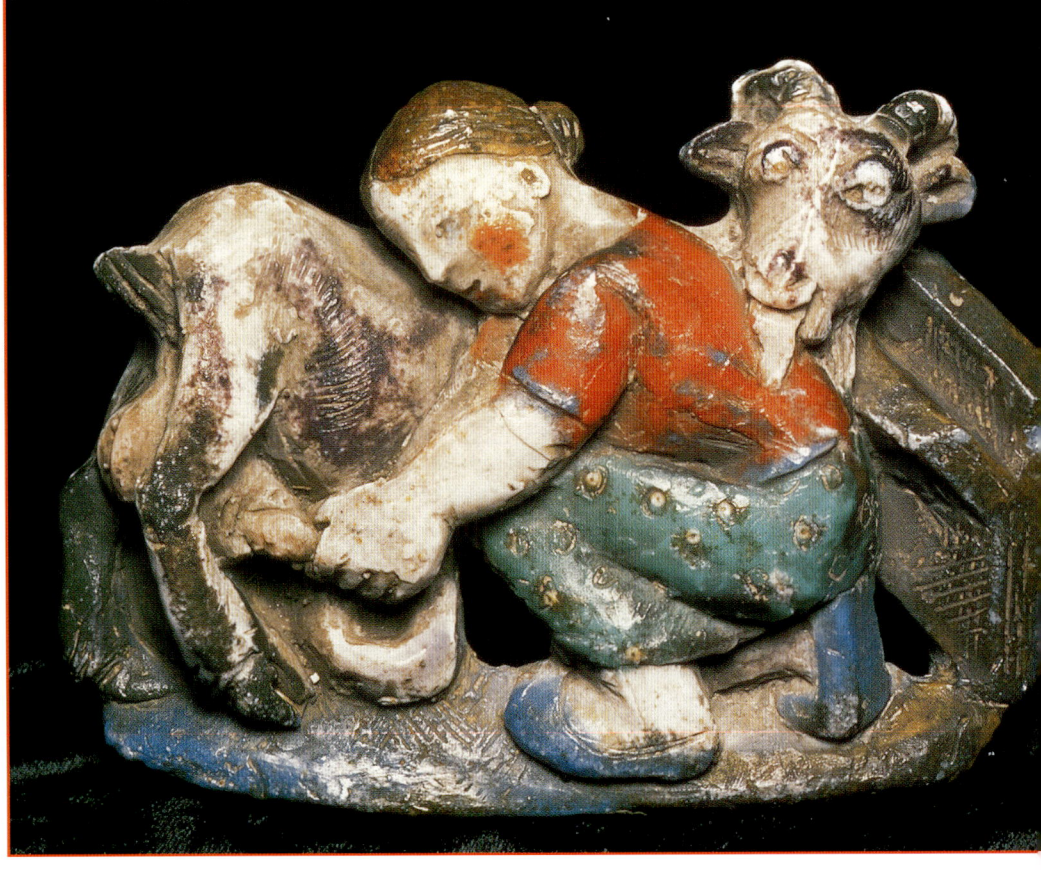

Milking, 1947, 12 cm h x 18 cm w, photo: Miroslav Vojtechovsky. *Photo courtesy of the artist.*

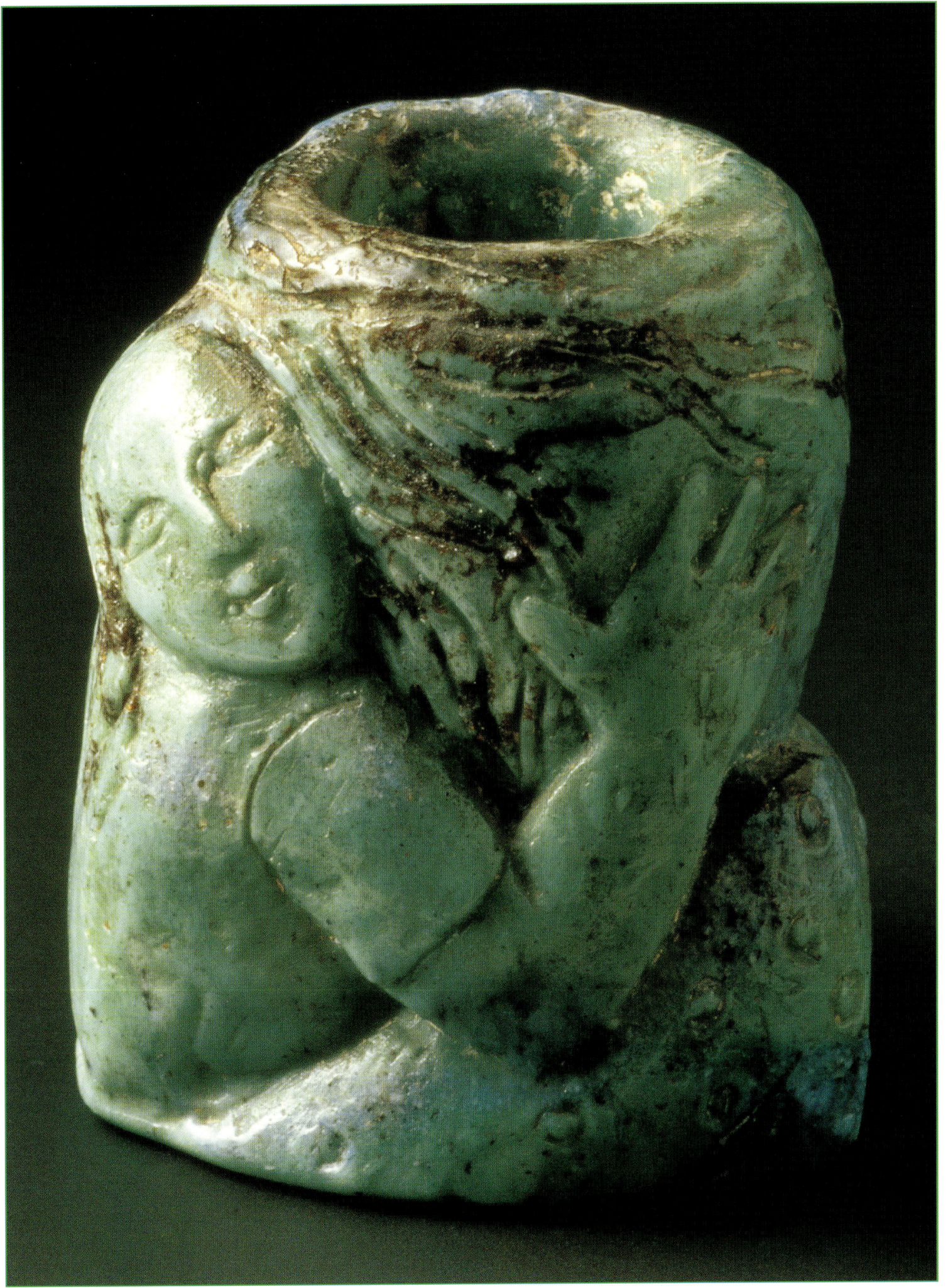

Woman with Vessel, 1947, 13 cm h, photo: Miroslav Vojtechovsky. *Photo courtesy of the artist.*

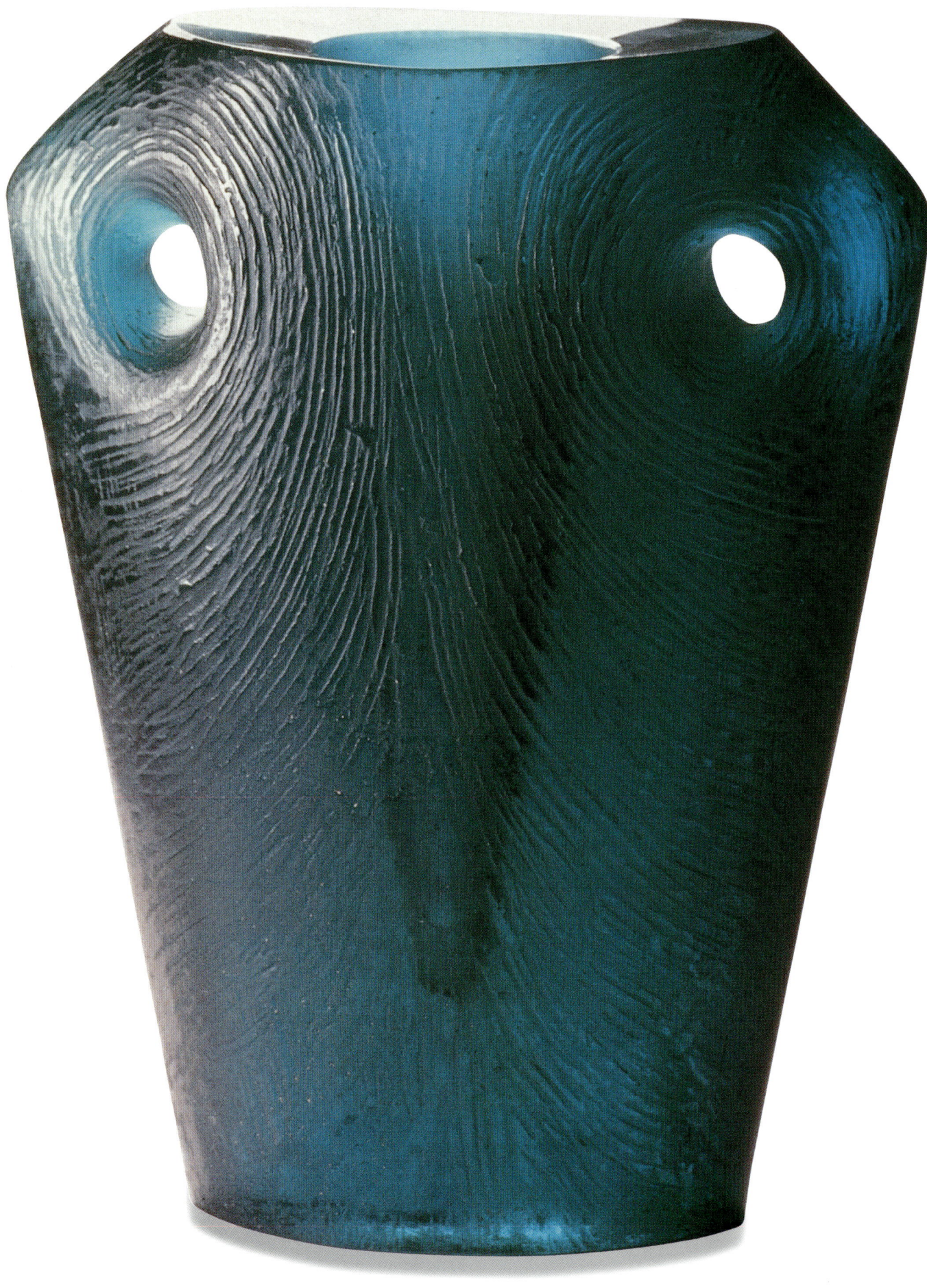

Vase with Inner Structure, 1953, 20.4 cm h x 13.3 cm w,
photo: Frank J. Borkowski. Photo courtesy of the artist.

In the beginning: Herstory 27

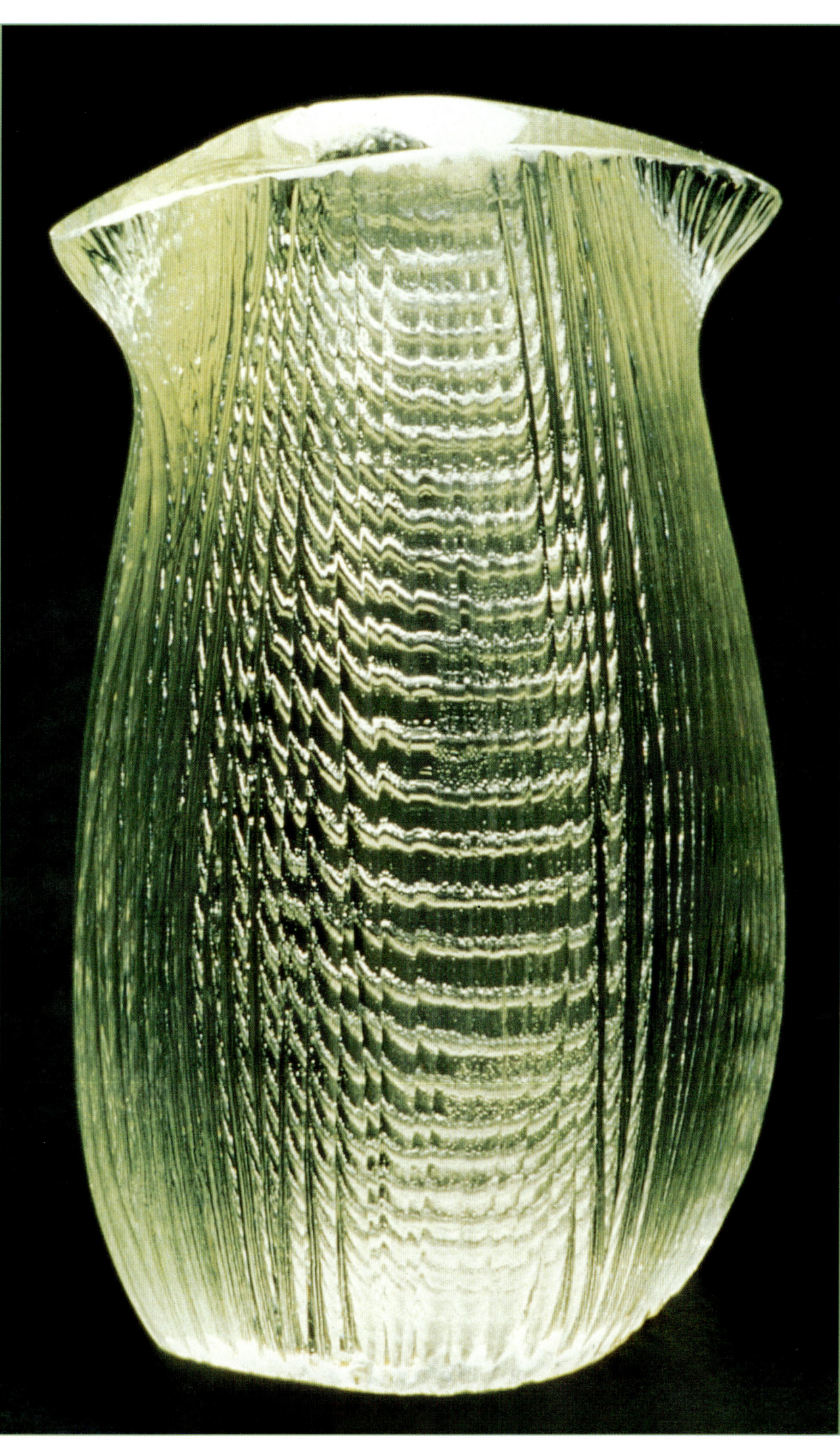

Vase with Inner Structure,
1953, 23.5 cm h x 17.5
cm w, photo: Gabriel
Urbanek (green-blue).
*Photo courtesy of the
artist.*

The Sixties

The 1960s saw more radical change, protest, and political upheaval than any other decade in recent history. Civil rights and women's rights, human rights and religious rights all played a part in shaping the last half of the twentieth century. A president and two powerful political leaders were assassinated. Domestic dissent caused by the Viet Nam war led to protests, draft card burnings, and a mass exodus of able-bodied draft age men to Canada and other safe havens. We put the first man in space and a man on the moon. The introduction of the "pill" in 1960 transformed attitudes about sex for both men and women. The gender revolution begun in 1848 reached a milestone in 1920 when women finally won the right to vote, but another forty years brought even more substantive changes. The "Women's Lib" movement fueled by Betty Friedan's book *The Feminine Mystique* ushered in an era of feminism leading to the founding of the National Organization for Women.

The arrival in America of the Beatles changed popular music forever. Hippies, the decade's flower children, with their "Peace not war mantra," invaded a small upstate New York town with a music festival/concert that has never been duplicated, though occasionally imitated. Experimentation with communal living, Eastern philosophies, and mind-altering drugs challenged everyone's complacent acceptance of the status quo.

Despite these revolutionary events, men continued to dominate the art world. Very few galleries would even show work done by women, an ironic state of affairs considering that many galleries were owned or operated by women. American art for the first time became valuable as a collectable commodity. This was also a time of rapidly changing trends and the making of super stars in the art world. "Dealers and collectors waited eagerly for each new avant-garde movement to be identified and labeled by critics and curators, so they could buy early when the prices were low and resell as the values skyrocketed."[1]

The emotional, painterly Abstract Expressionism of the previous decade gave way to a cool minimal and hard edge art. Pop Art, and Art and Technology, a marriage of art made from the materials and technology found in industrial fabrication factories were the stars of the decade. Chryssa was an early woman pioneer in the Art and Technology movement with her welded steel and neon constructions, originally made with real commercial signs and assembled in a factory. Eventually she set up her own shop and hired glassblowers and foundries to fabricate her work. The experimental Fluxus group believed ... "that art should be lived—should generate a new way of thinking and seeing rather than produce commodities to be bought and sold."[2] The group staged happenings, events, and performances, and attracted many avant-garde artists in New York. It had several important women followers. Yoko Ono was one of the earliest members.[3] In her 1964 *Morning Piece*, she labeled broken shards of heavy glass with specific future mornings and times such as "August 12 2002, early in the morning." She kept a detailed list of these future mornings, and faithfully recorded which were sold and which mornings were still available. Another 1964 Ono work employing glass was titled *pointedness*, according to Erica Adams' review of *Yes Yoko Ono*, a current traveling retrospective exhibition of Yoko Ono's work published in *This Side Up*.[4] Adams quotes Ono, " '*Pointedness*' was inspired, Ono says, by moonlight flooding a Zen garden "as if it was daylight, now became a pointedness in my heart. It seemed as if we were a million miles away from the moon-

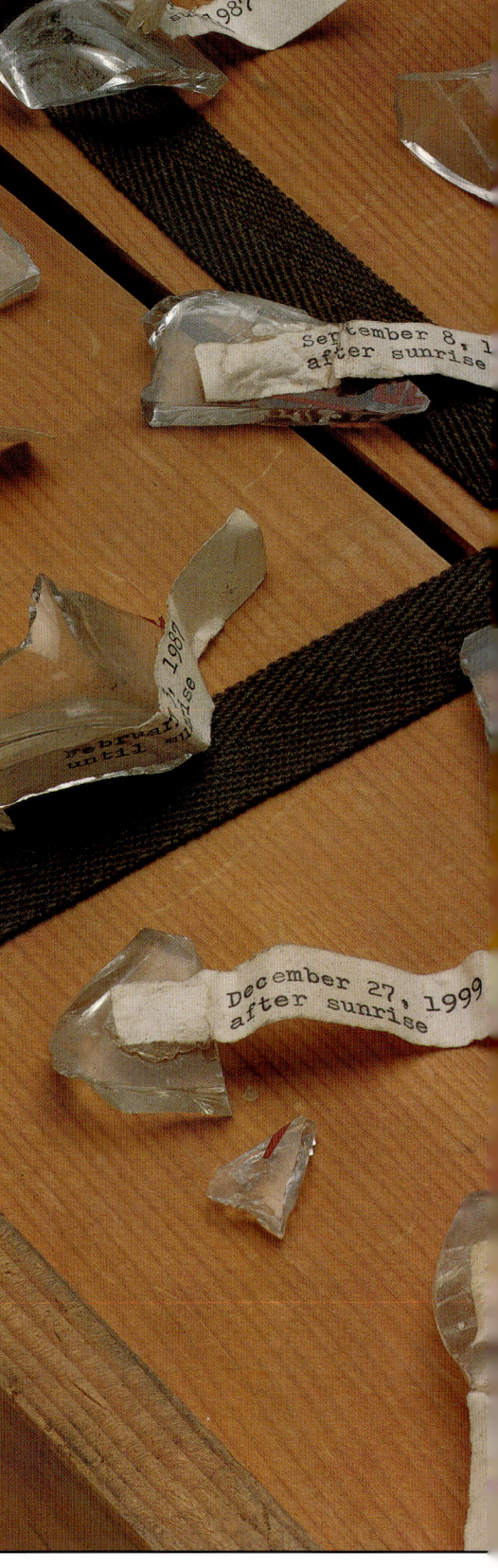

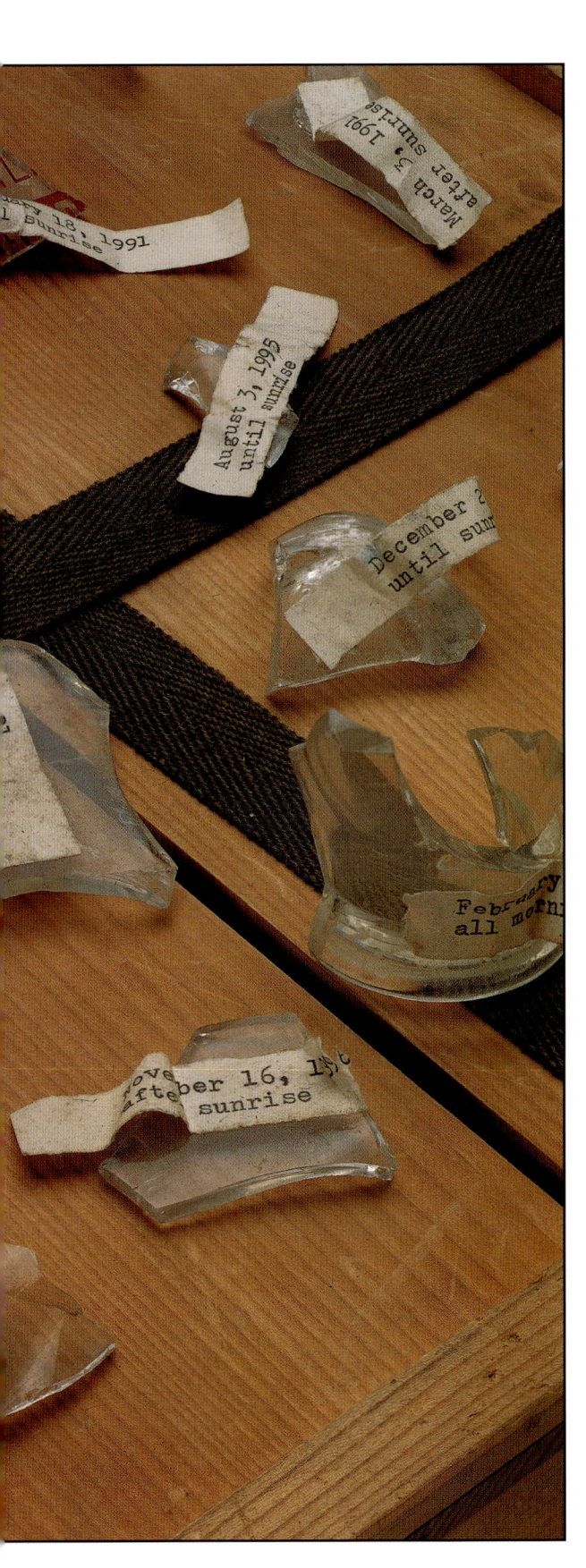

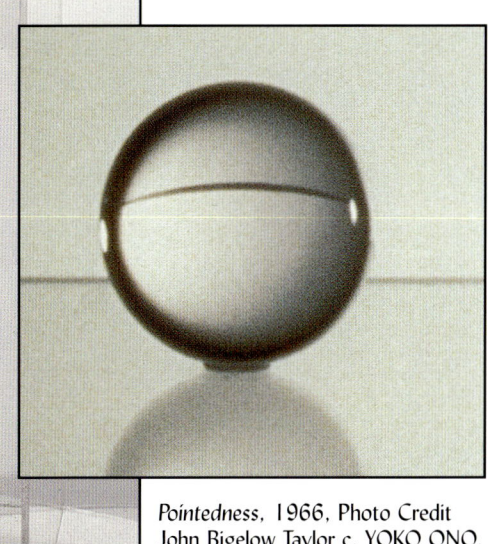

Left:
Mornings For Sale (detail), 1964, Photo Credit John Bigelow Taylor c. YOKO ONO. Courtesy of Lenono Photo Archive.

Right:
Pointedness, 1966, Text inscribed on pedestal reads: POINTEDNESS YOKO ONO 1966
THIS SPHERE WILL BE A SHARP POINT WHEN IT GETS TO THE FAR CORNERS OF THE ROOM IN YOUR MIND
First exhibited at: *Unfinished Paintings and Objects*
Indica Gallery, London, 1966.
Photo Credit John Bigelow Taylor c. YOKO ONO. Courtesy of Lenono Photo Archive.

Pointedness, 1966, Photo Credit John Bigelow Taylor c. YOKO ONO. Courtesy of Lenono Photo Archive.

light." Glass and bronze versions each express two different political eras. Both are inscribed with her instructions: **"This sphere will be a sharp point when it gets to the far corners of the room in your mind."** The sixties crystal sphere is receptive, fluid, reflective, floating on the then new utopian material Plexiglas. Glass is suspended motion slowed into a believable solidity.

"*Glass Keys to Open the Skies*" brings two of Yoko Ono's important themes together. For her, the sky represents timelessness, constancy, and unlimited space, while the key serves as a metaphor for knowledge. The glass keys are fragile and can only be used for a conceptual or magical opening.[5]

The Craft as Art movement also began in the sixties. Not only was the art world chauvinistically male at that time, it was also elitist, segregating "high art" from "low art"

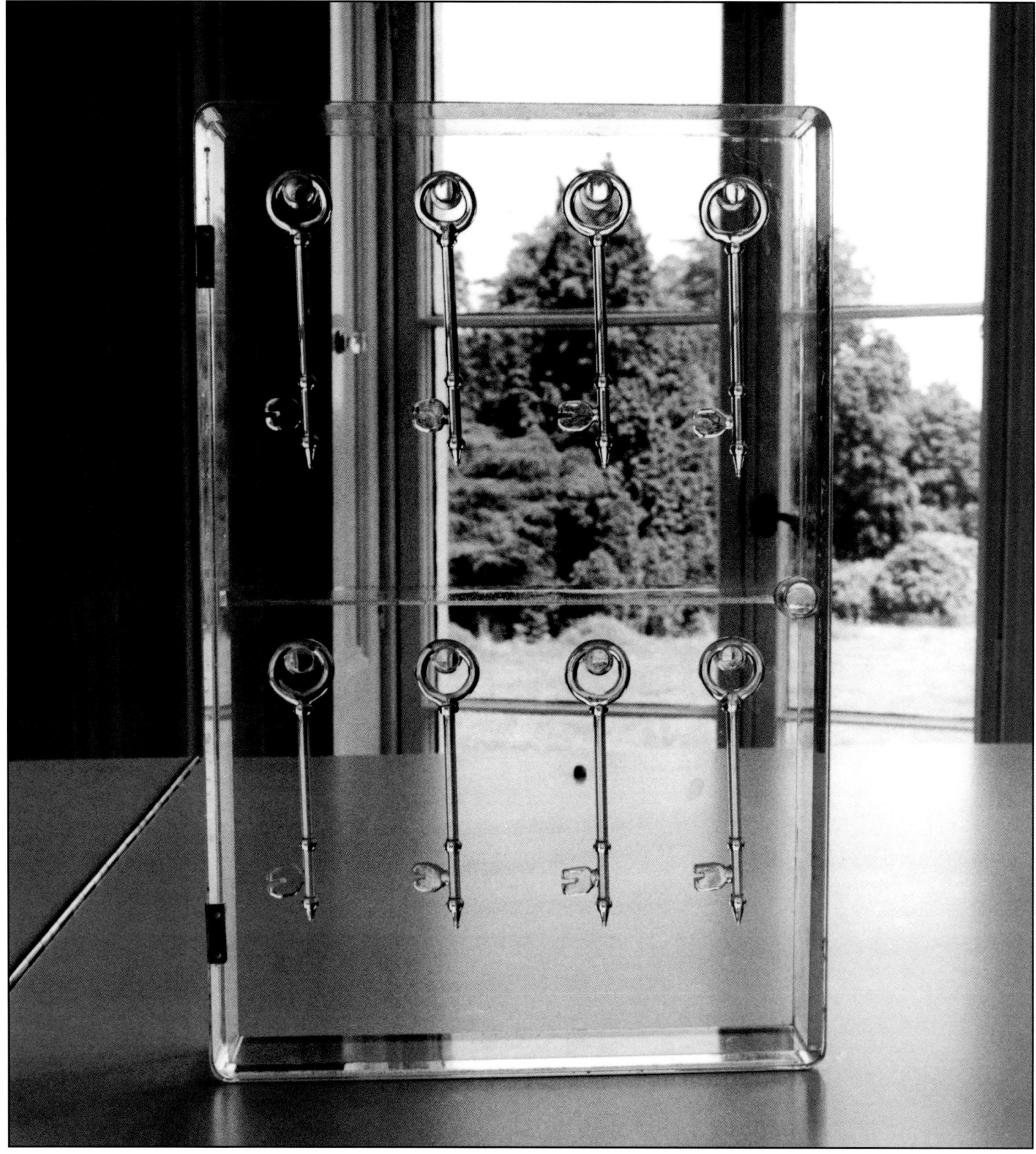

Glass Keys, 1966, 7.5" h x 10" w x 1.5" d, keys 1.5". Glass keys in Plexiglas box, Photographed at Ascot, England, Photo: Peter Fordham c. 1970 YOKO ONO.

(crafts). Lenore Tawney, a weaver, chose a medium that has historically been used primarily by women and created architectural scale panels she called "woven works" emulating grid-like paintings. Soon after, other artists associated with the crafts and decorative arts followed.

Following the trend, a man named Harvey Littleton had a vision. He, like Edris Ekhardt, had the idea that glass, an ancient discovery which modern industry had adapted to make products for the consumer marketplace, could become a medium for fine art. Harvey Littleton grew up in Corning, New York, where he spent summers working for The Corning Glassworks, where his father worked as a physicist. He majored in ceramics in college and later taught summer workshops in ceramics at the Toledo Art Museum and the University of Wisconsin. During the summer of 1959 at the American Craft Council meeting held at Lake George, Littleton presented his idea to try to build a small furnace to blow glass creatively. If successful, glass blowing could be taught as part of a university curriculum. In the summer of 1962 the Craft Council gave him a grant; The Toledo Art Museum gave him some space. Dominick Labino, a research technician from Johns-Manville who was already interested in blowing glass, helped set up the equipment.[6]

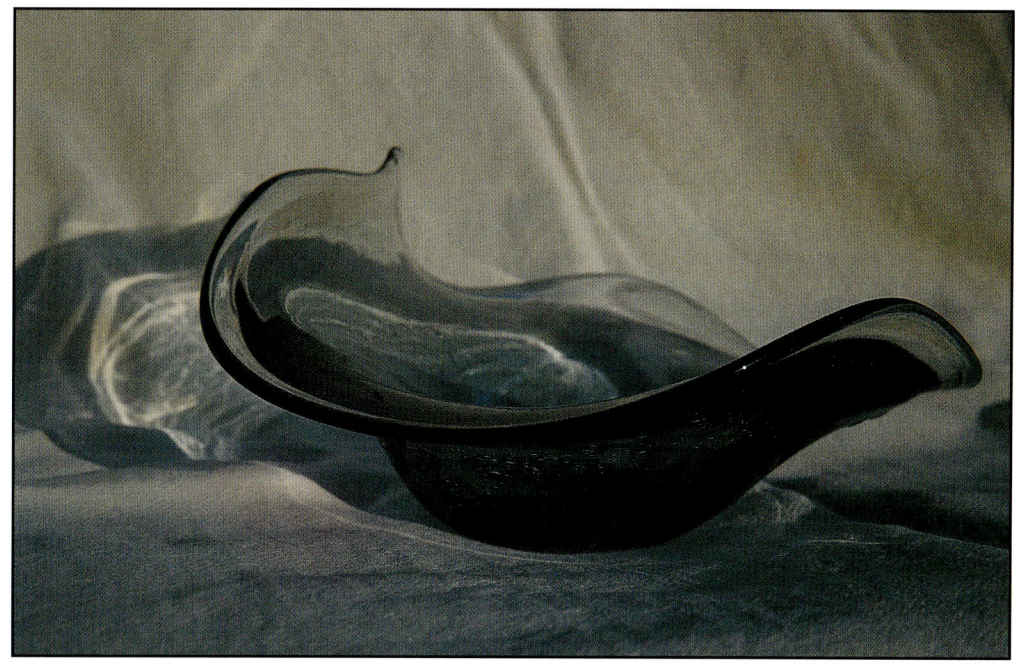

Pat Esch, 1964, bowl, blown glass. *Photo courtesy of the artist.*

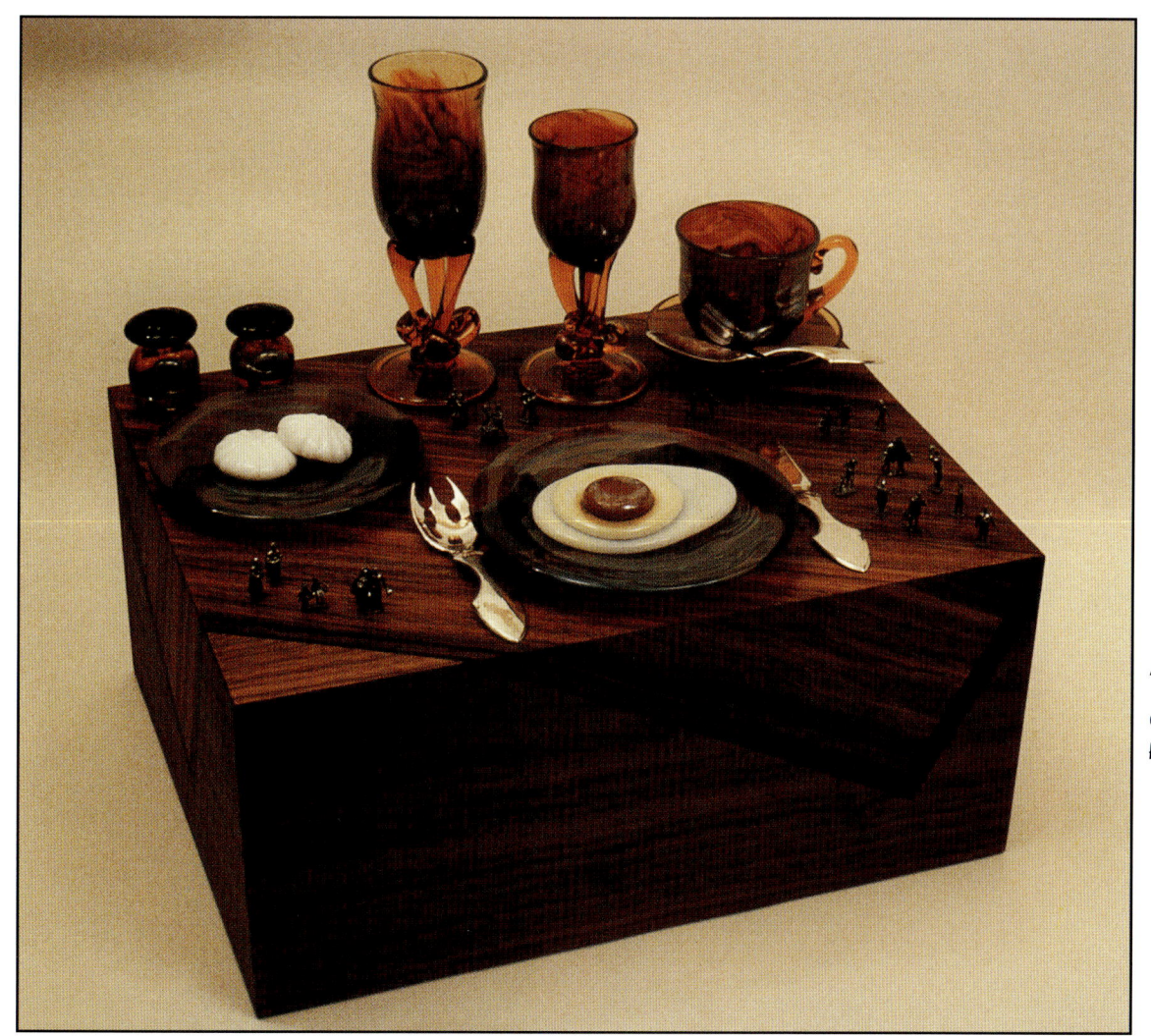

Audrey Handler, *Wedding Breakfast*, c. 1970s, 14.75" x 12.50" x 16.25". *Collection Corning Museum of Glass, photo courtesy of the artist.*

The following year, 1963, the first class in creative glass blowing was offered for credit in an American college. Littleton offered the class to his graduate ceramic students at The University of Wisconsin, Madison, and has had a glass blowing course ever since. Among the first group of students were a number of women; Pat Esch, Joan Falconer Byrd, Monona Rossol, and Audrey Handler. Audrey Handler is still working in glass today. Joan Falconer Byrd remained working in ceramics, but wrote extensively about the studio movement and glass in North Carolina. Monona Rossol became an advocate for health and safety issues and has authored a number of books, including The Artist's Complete Health and Safety Guide and is founder and president of ACTS, Arts, Crafts, and Theater Safety.

One of Harvey's early students, Sam Herman, went to Britain in 1966 on a Fulbright to study with Helen Monroe Turner, a respected cutter and engraver at the Edinburgh College of Art. He stayed in England and became a research fellow at the Royal College of Art from 1967 to 1968 where he was responsible for developing the hot glass program for students to blow their own forms. Prior to 1969 a technician executed the students' designs. Pauline Solven and Asa Brandt from Sweden were the first women students to blow their own work. Herman's presence had an impact on the studio movement throughout Britain. With the aid of Graham Hughes, chairman of the Crafts Center of Great Britain and Susannah Robbins, its director, he set up The Glasshouse on Neal St. in Covent Garden; a workshop where recent graduates from The Royal College of Art could make and sell work.[7] Another of Harvey Littleton's early students, American Audrey Handler, spent a year in 1968 at The Royal College of Art as a research fellow.

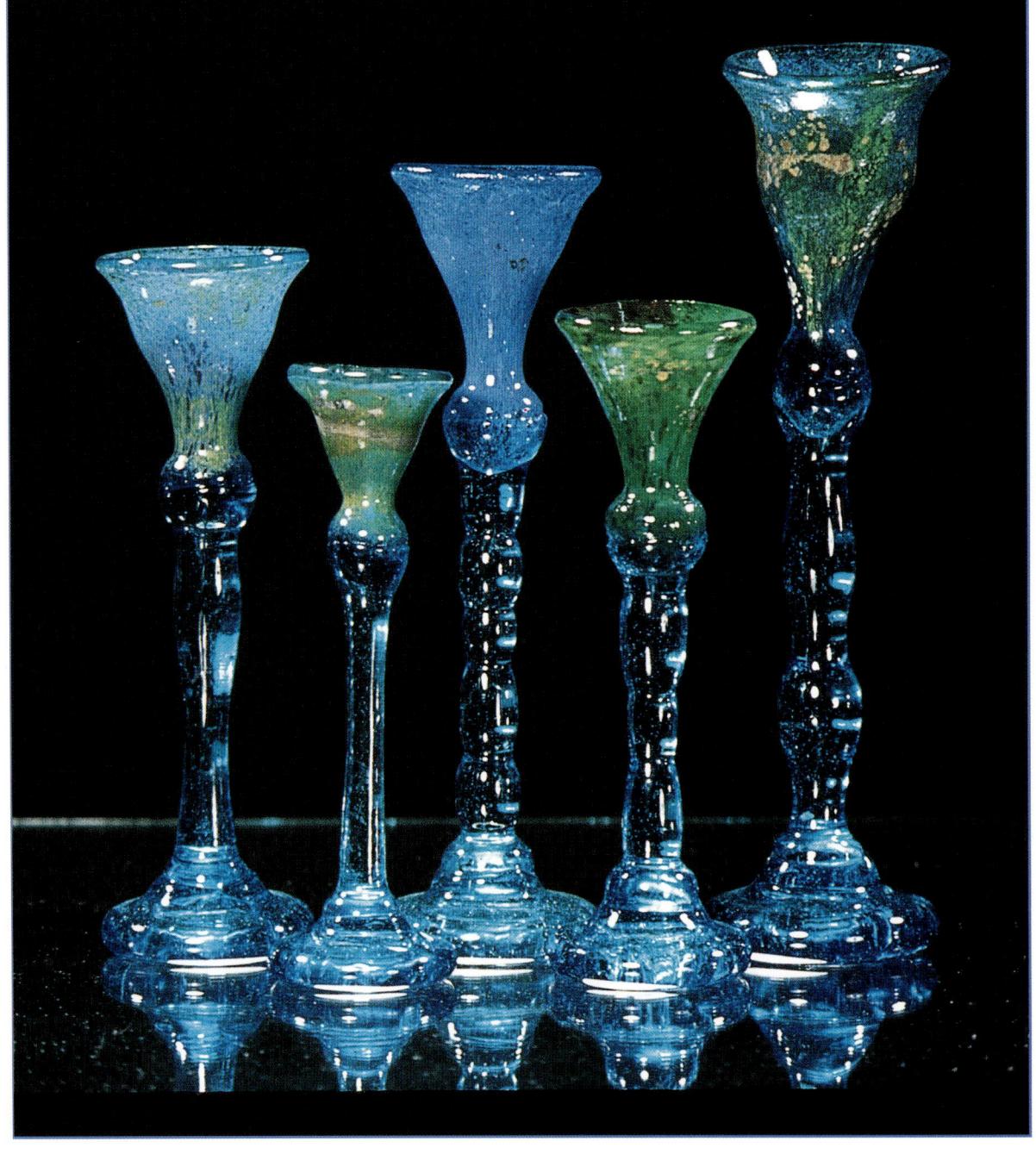

Asa Brandt, "glass," 1968.
Photo courtesy of the artist.

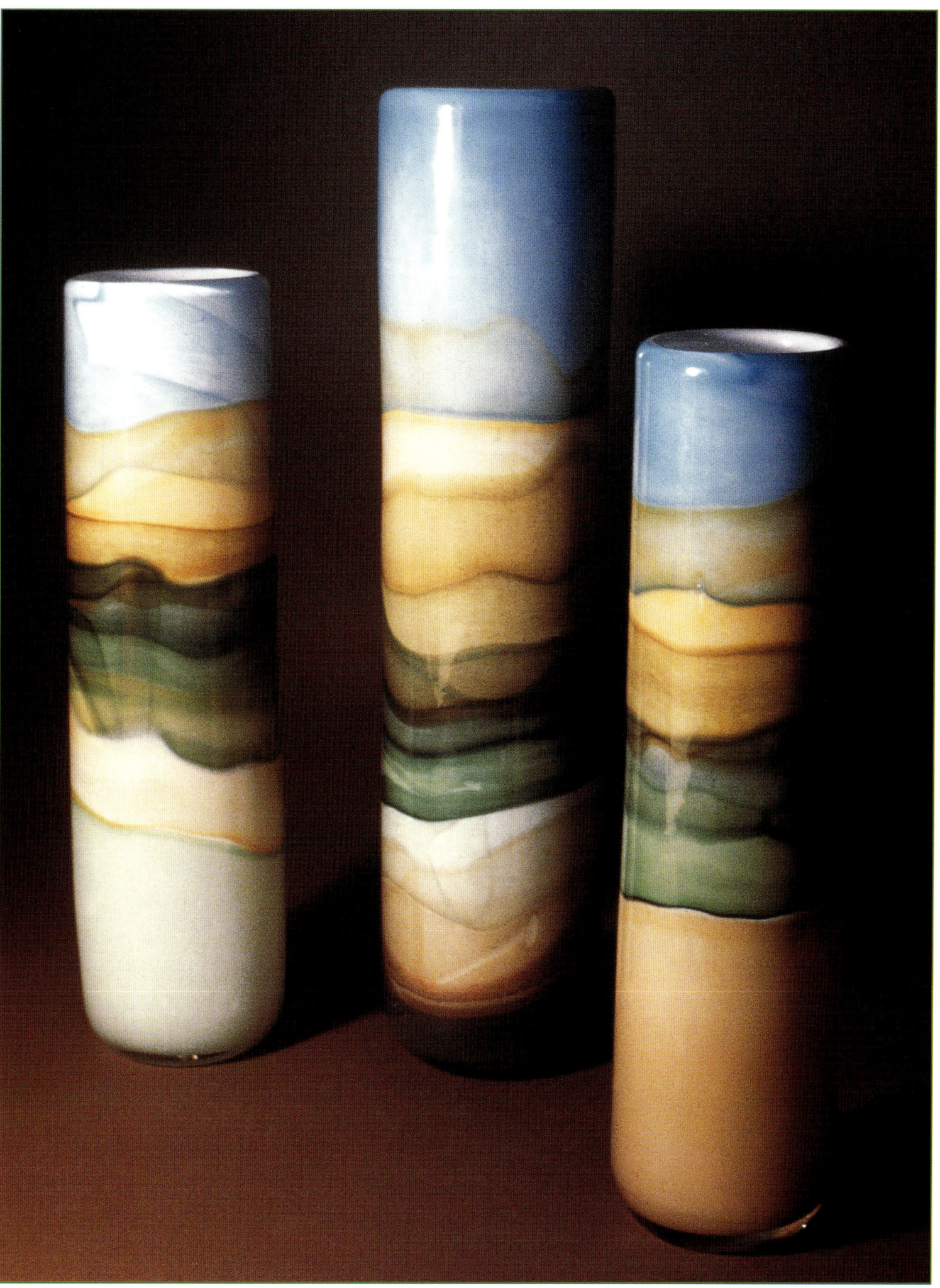

Pauline Solven, *Fragmented Landscape*, 1980. Photo courtesy of the artist.

In the United States, The Toledo Museum of Art began organizing glass exhibitions beginning in 1966. The first "Toledo Glass National" featured the work of seven women. There were several other Glass Nationals sponsored by The Toledo Museum of Art as well as Corning Museum of Glass. Audrey Handler said she felt for a long time that she was one of a few token women in many of the early exhibitions.

Since that time glass artists have taken two different paths. Some chose to make art from glass while others chose to make consumer products. In some cases the two paths intertwine. The latter is more closely related to the long history of glass. In addition, the cost of melting glass in a studio furnace prevents many artists from full time art making with glass. Women seem to be drawn to one-of-a-kind art making, rather than concentrating on a line of production pieces. Perhaps that is the feminine difference. Rosmarie Lierke, a glass artist from Germany, addresses this question in an article written for *Neus Glas* in 1983.

"Women working with hot glass; Is this actually a topic for discussion? Are there differences?" ... "I don't know, but, I do know that women have a special relationship to this material that was inaccessible to them for hundreds of years. Women on the way to emancipation work with a substance that is attempting to free itself from the functional servitude which often overshadows its true material character in order to emerge as an independent artistic medium. Hot glass is feminine."[8]

The artists who began working with glass during the sixties all had an enormous amount of courage, both men and women. The material is seductive and scary, heavy and hot, difficult to form, expensive, and above all highly addictive, yet the list of artists grows ever longer. The numbers of women were few in the early days; some stayed with it and some went on to other careers. Sylvia Vigiletti, active for many years in her own studio and a foundation pillar for the Glass Art Society, has recently turned her attention to photography. Mary White, an early student at California College of Arts and Crafts, has been actively showing her work since then, teaching and providing an example as a role model for young glass artists. I will allow the ones that I could find speak for themselves.

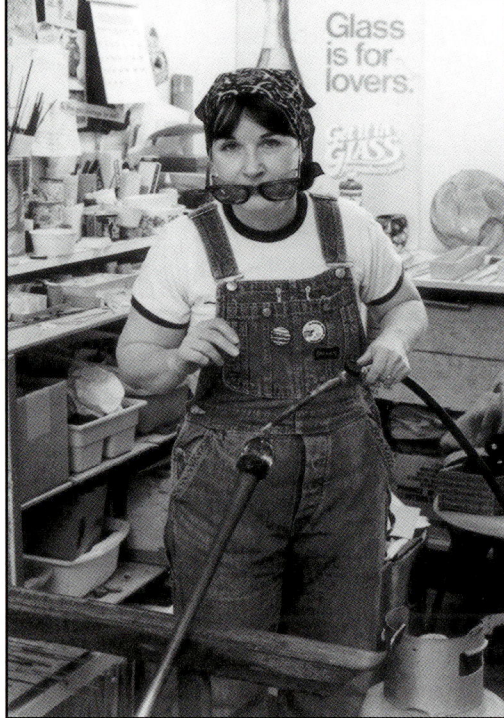

Sylvia Vigiletti, studio photograph. *Photo courtesy of the artist.*

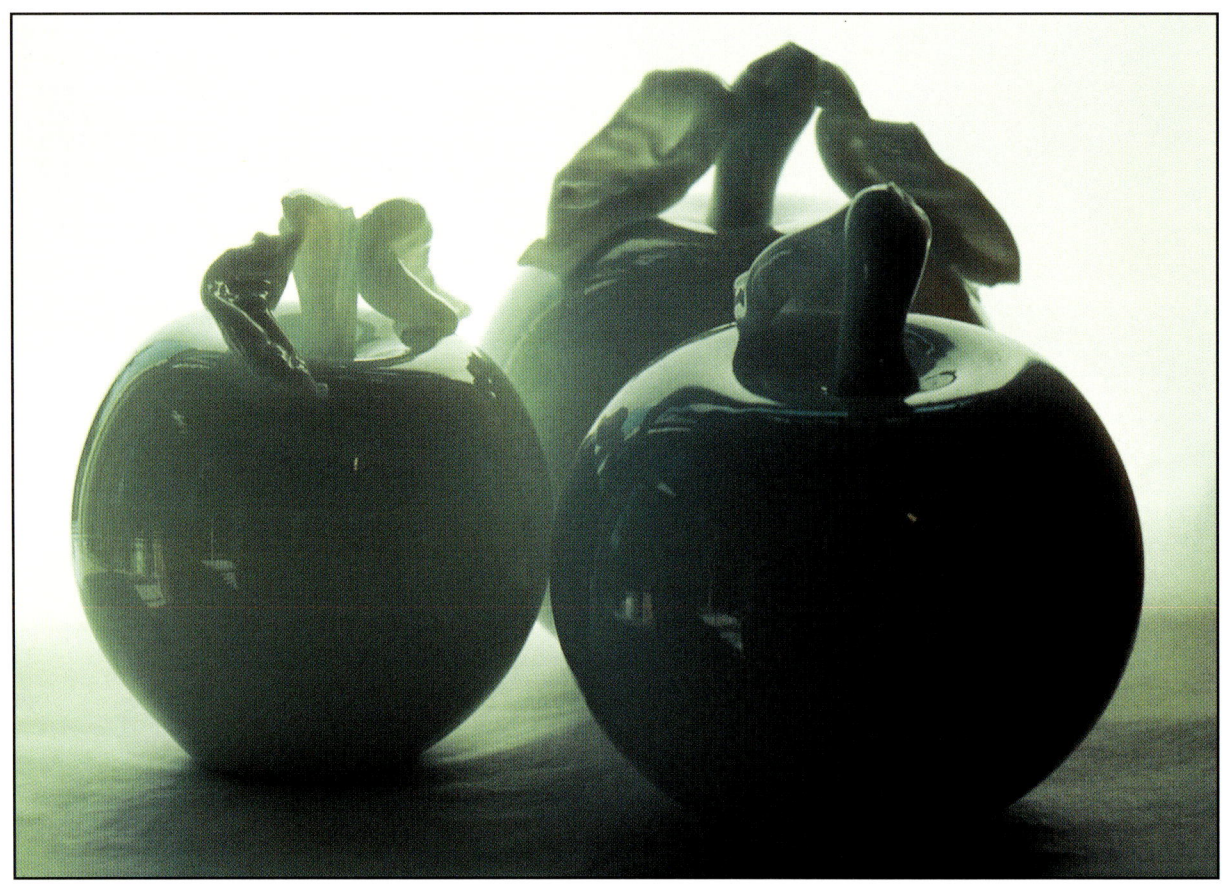

Mary White, *Apples de Maria Blanca*, 1974, blown glass, 5" x 8". *Photo courtesy of the artist.*

The Artists

Paula Bartron

The forms are simple and conjure up associations with primitive things, vessel forms, and even material, earth, clay, and iron. I want them to contain an atmosphere of pureness, tranquility, and balance – a timeless intensity and quiet presence. There is also a continual juxtaposition of opposite qualities such as light and heavy, an inner glow of hidden transparence emanating only when the work is hit with side light. Important also are the relationships of four sided forms: squares, rectangles, inner and outer, open and closed.

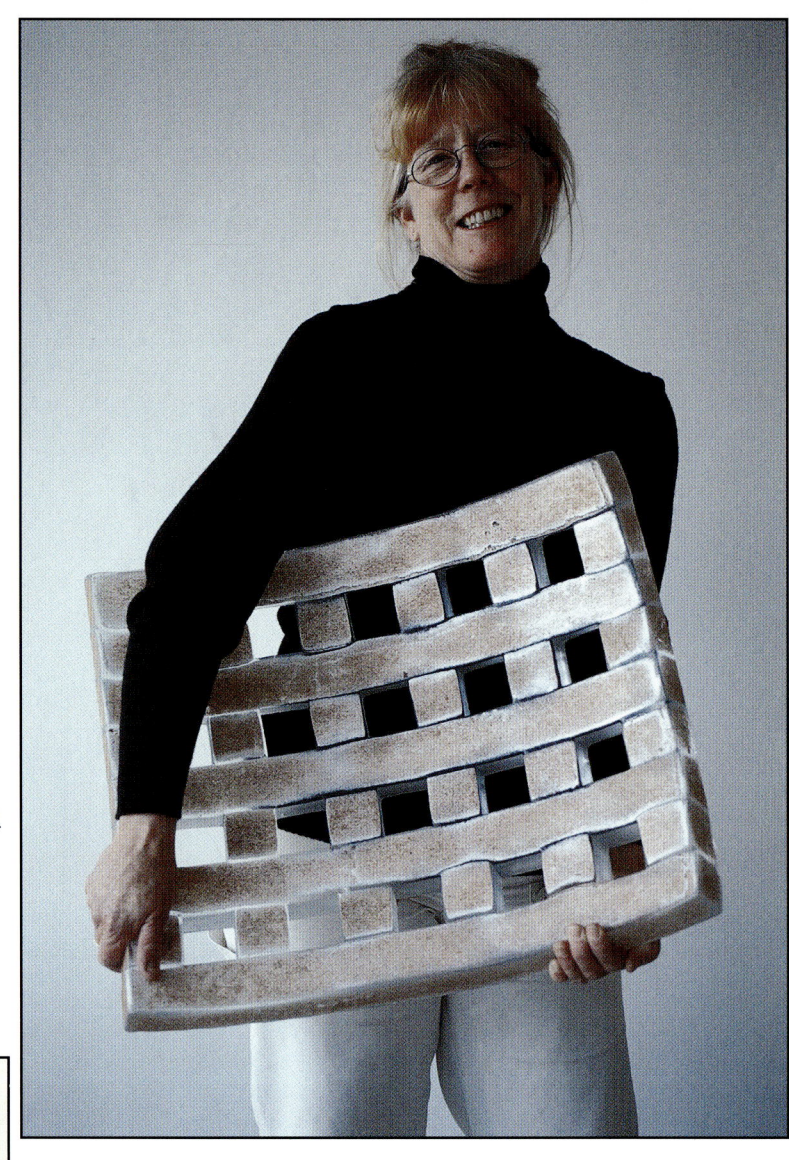

Paula Bartron. *Photo by Simon Whitfield.*

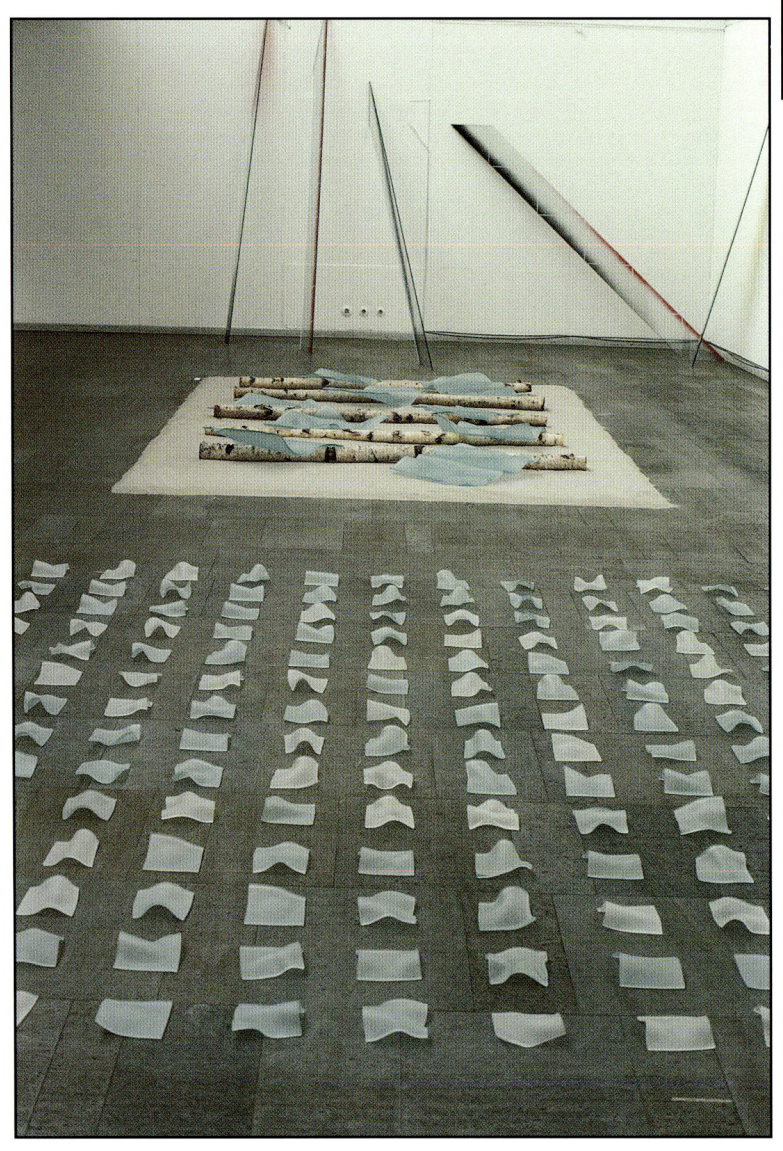

Hav, 1983, 3.5 meters x 4.5 meters installation, Lunds Kontsthall, Sweden. *Photo courtesy the artist.*

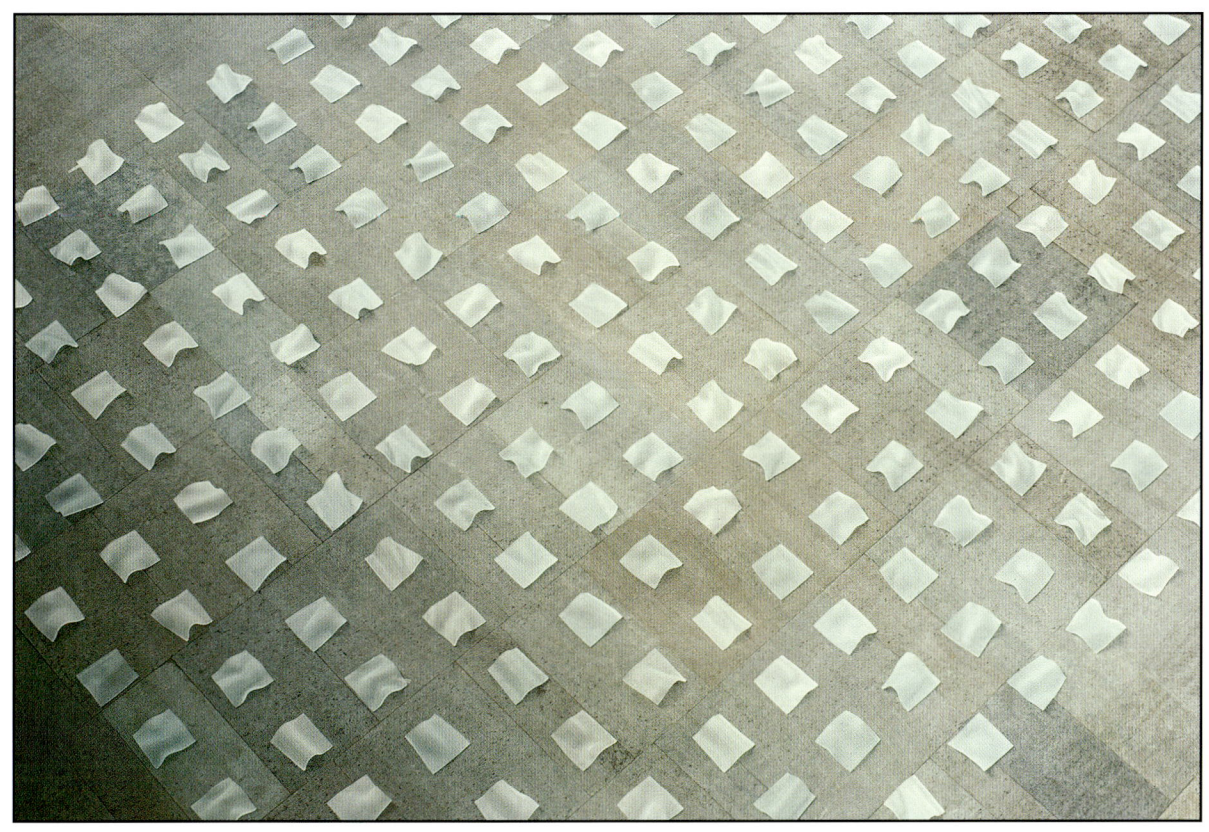

Hav, 1983, 3.5 meters x 4.5 meters installation, Lunds Kontsthall, Sweden, detail. *Photo courtesy the artist.*

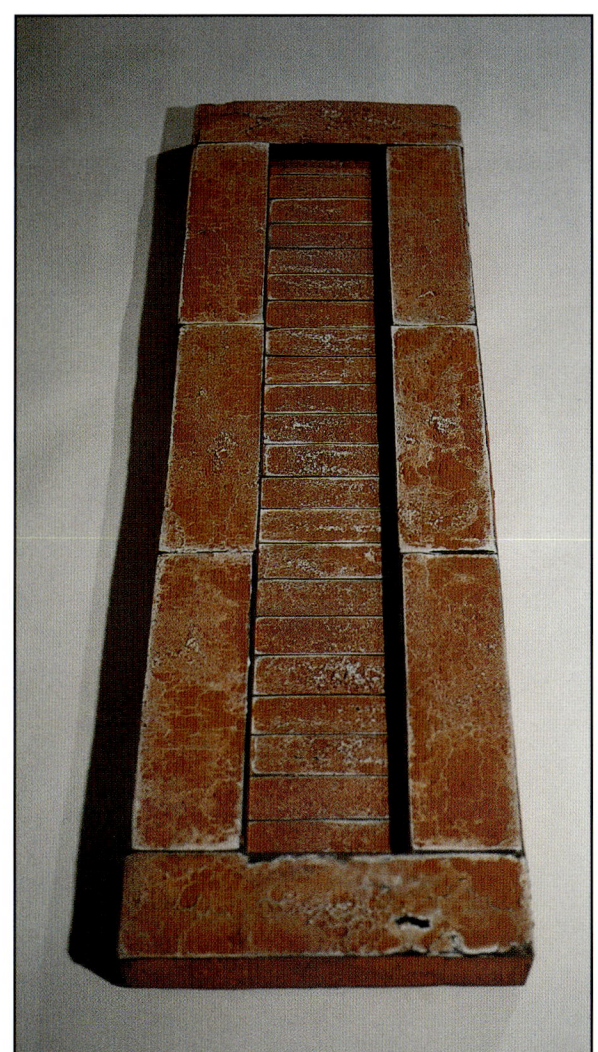

White Basin, 1997, 40.5 cm x 51 cm, sandcast, sawed, fused glass. *Photo courtesy the artist.*

White Basin, 1998, 127 cm x 35 cm x 7 cm, sandcast glass. *Photo courtesy the artist.*

Asa Brandt

Asa Brandt does not care for the formal tradition of Swedish glass; she plays and lets her imagination wander with the glass mass and hopes that the joy she feels herself with the glass will be transferred to others.

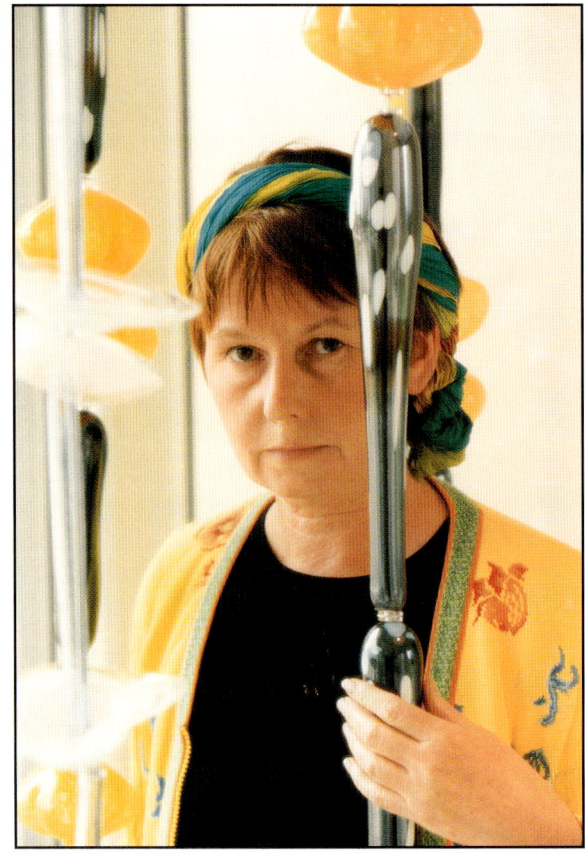

Asa Brandt.

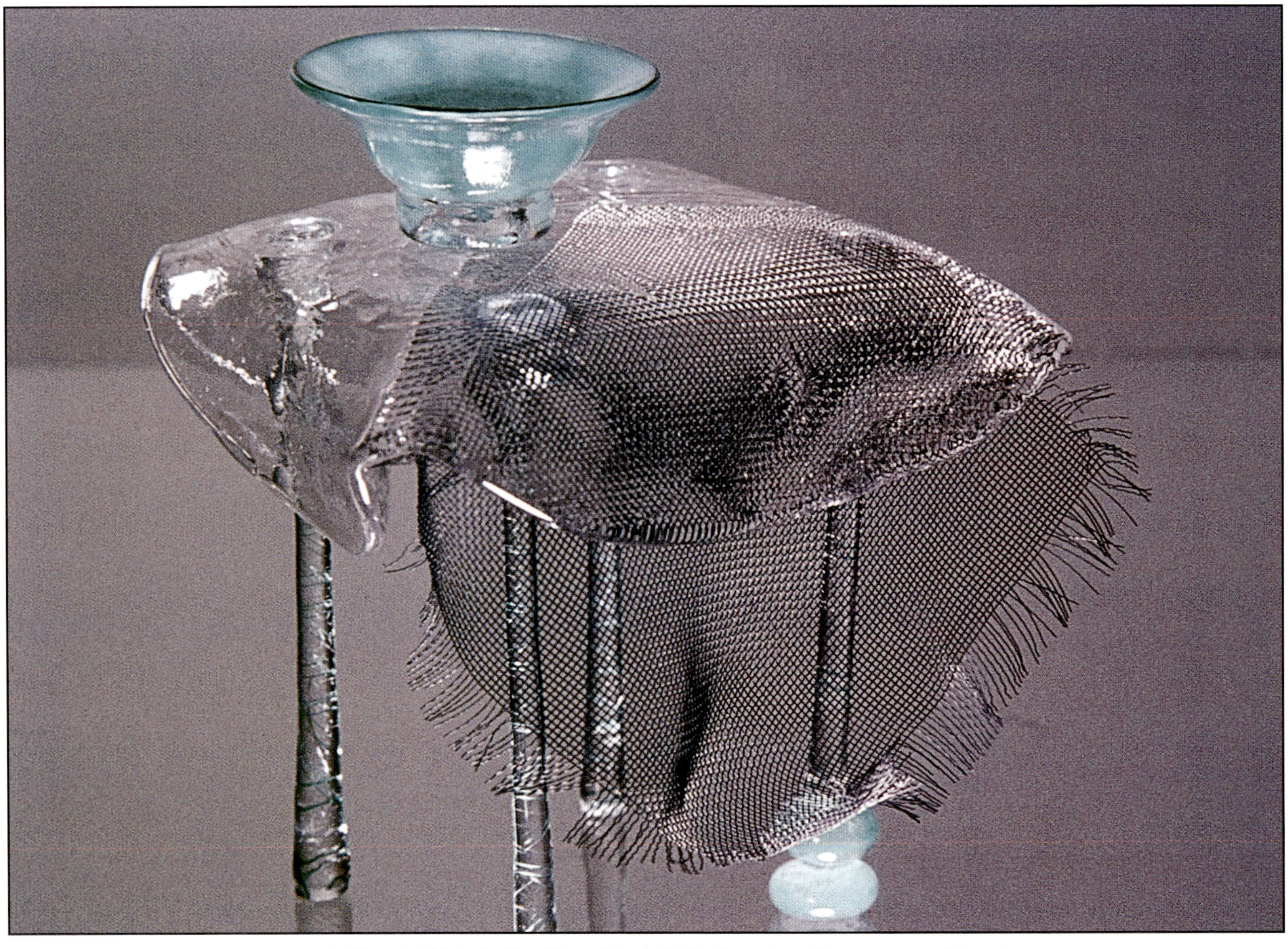

Miniature Table with Tablecloth of Iron Net and Bowl, 1972, blown glass. Photo courtesy of the artist.

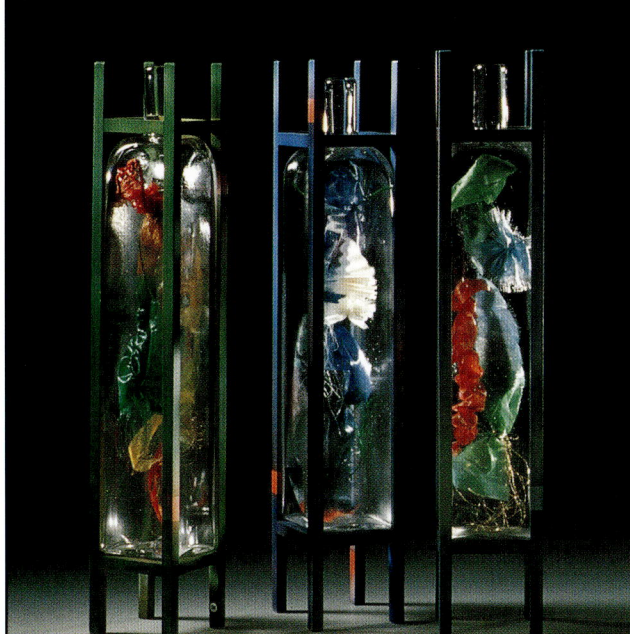

Blown Bottles with Painted Textile Hanging Inside, 1989. Photo courtesy of the artist.

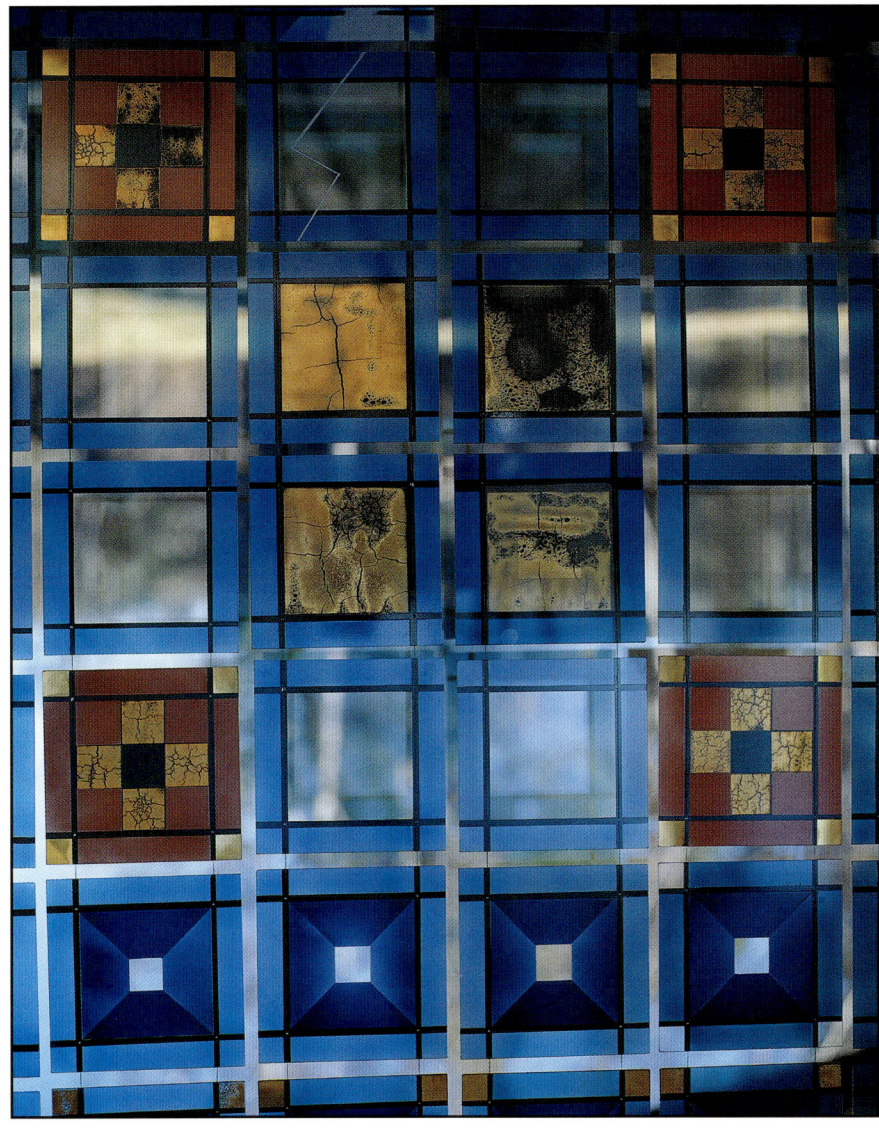

I Am Thinking of Tutanchamon, 2000, painted plane glass, 160 cm x 120 cm x 0.2 cm. Photo courtesy of the artist.

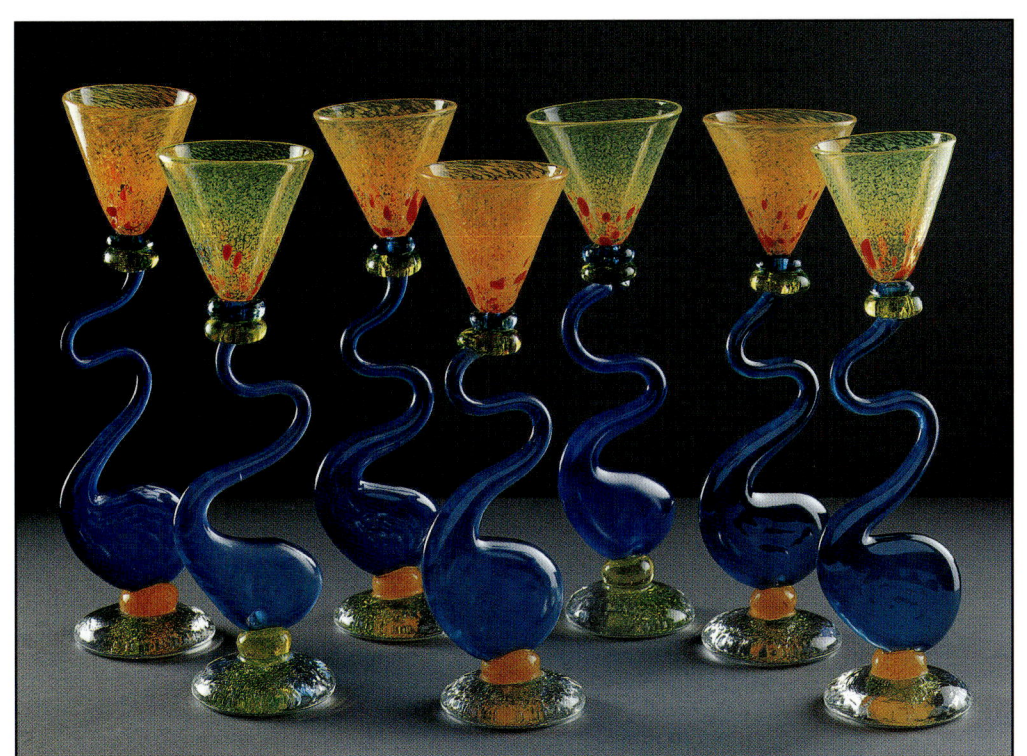

Goblets, 1998, blown glass, photo credit, Anders Qwarnstrom. Photo courtesy of the artist.

Jane Bruce

The focus of my current practice is the "space between." The space between "craft" and "Art" – "function" and "Non-function." The space between "Form" and "viewer," from hand-pedestal to one where the work confronts the viewer in space as an equal.

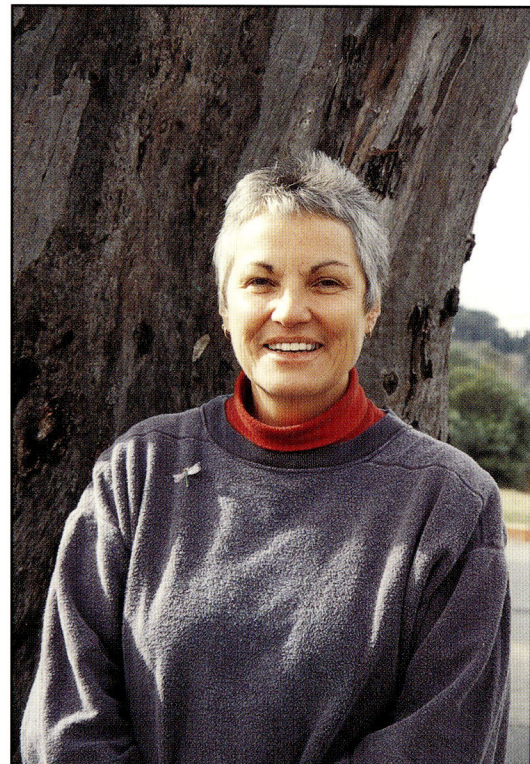

Jane Bruce.

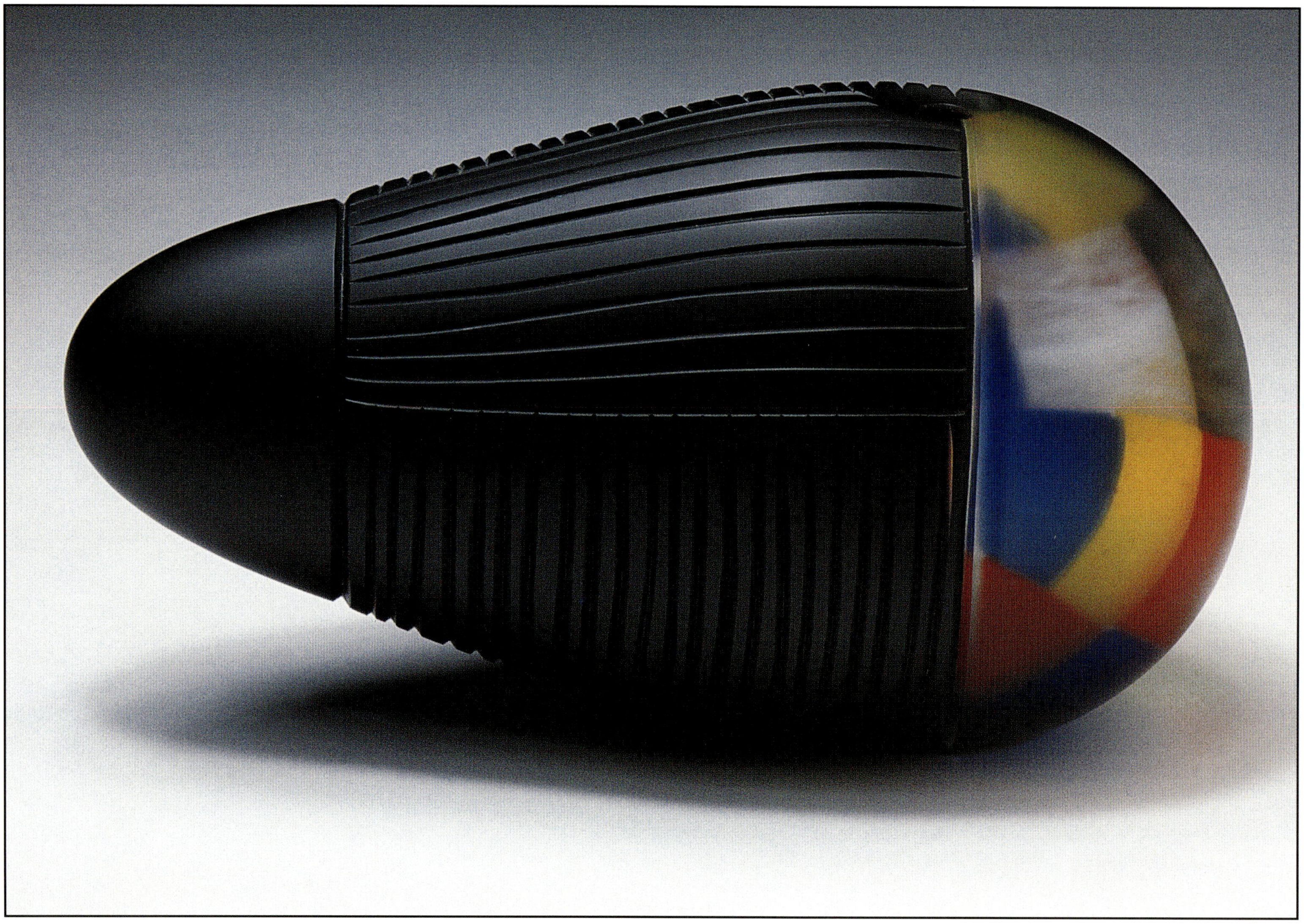

Bullseye Object, 1996, 6.5" x 6.5" x 11", kiln formed Bullseye glass, wheel cut, hand finished. *Photo courtesy of the artist.*

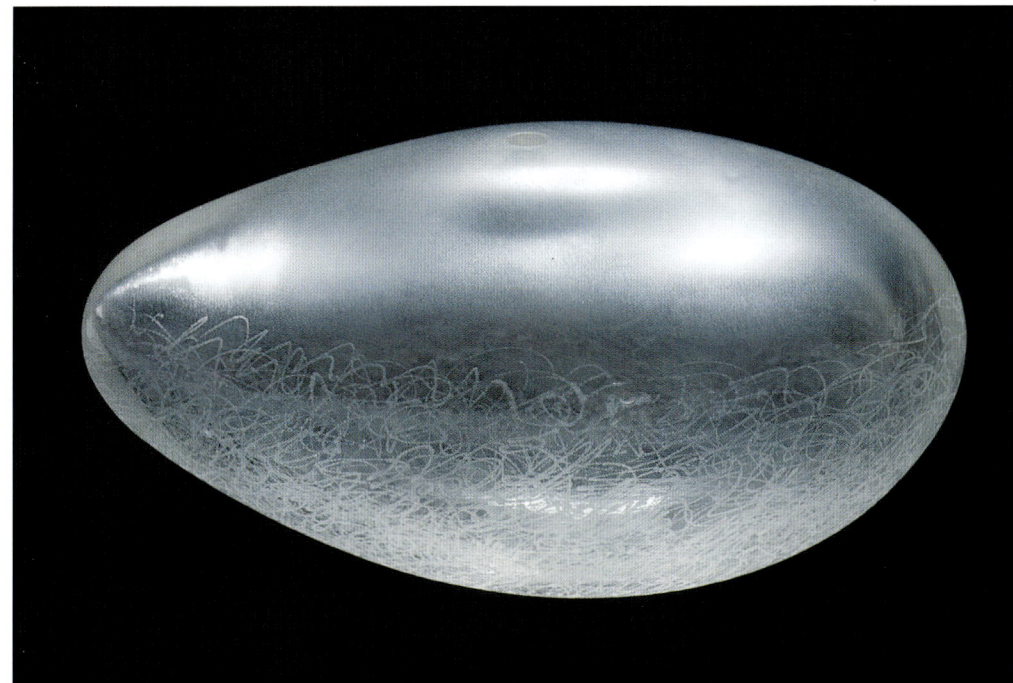

Clear Engrave, Object #5, 1998, 4.5" x 4" x 10", blown, engraved, hand finished. Photo courtesy of the artist.

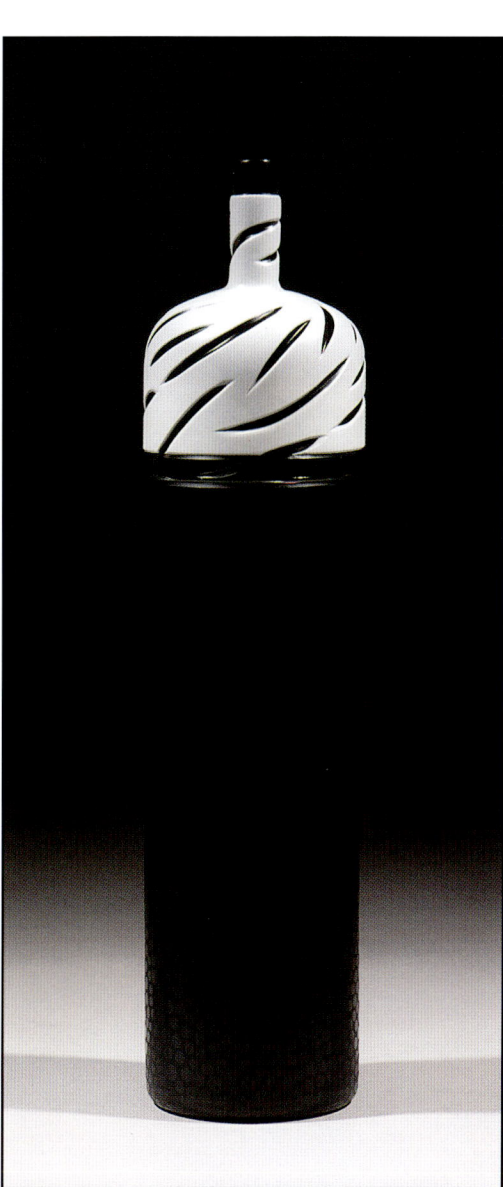

White/Purple/Black Lidded Vessel (series IV), 2002, 22.5" x 5" d, blown glass, wheel cut, sandblasted, hand-finished. Photo courtesy of the artist.

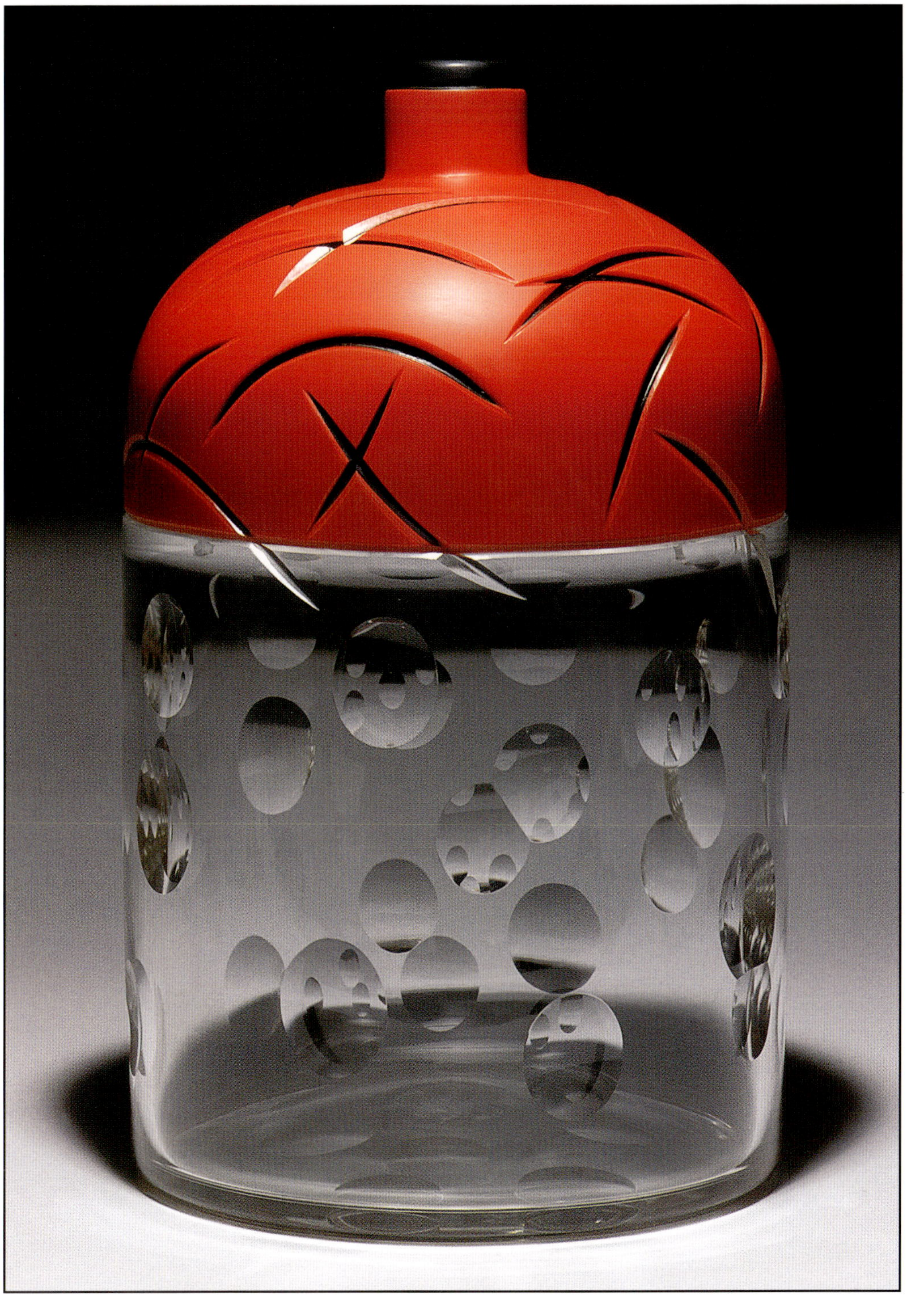

Red/Purple/Clear Lidded Vessel (series III), 2000, 15.75" x 9.5". Photo courtesy of the artist.

Pat Esch

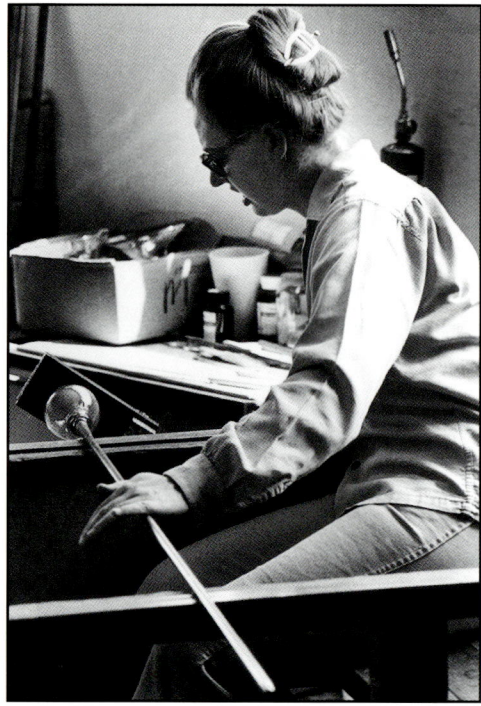

Pat Esch.

I set up a studio in Denver, Colorado, in 1965 and started blowing glass for a living in an old house in the downtown area. I later moved to the suburbs and was a studio glass-blower until 1974 when I sold my equipment and returned to Madison, Wisconsin, where I have been a pastry chef. Most recently I am making furniture as a hobby.

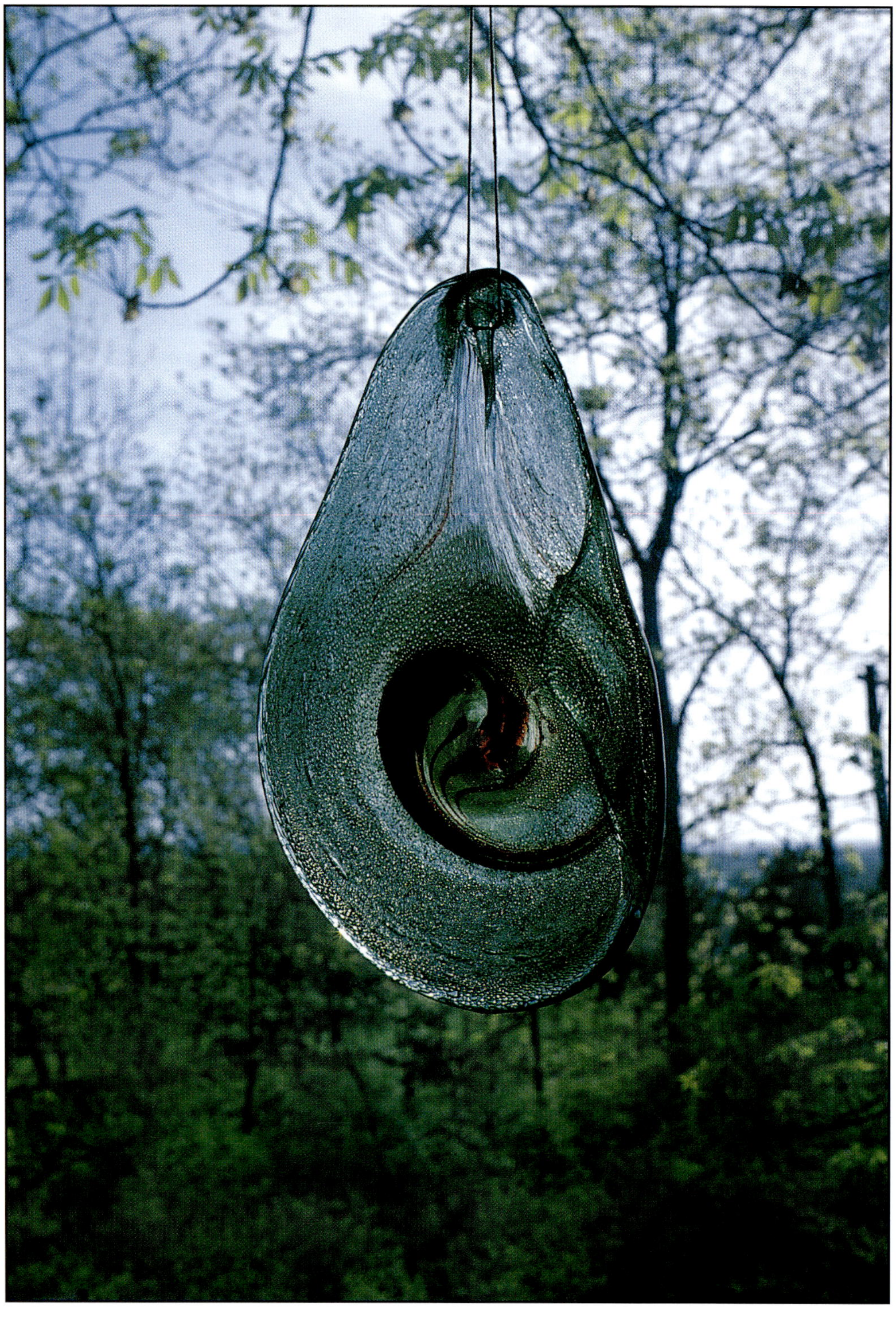

Window Hanging, 1965, 10" h.
Photo courtesy of the artist.

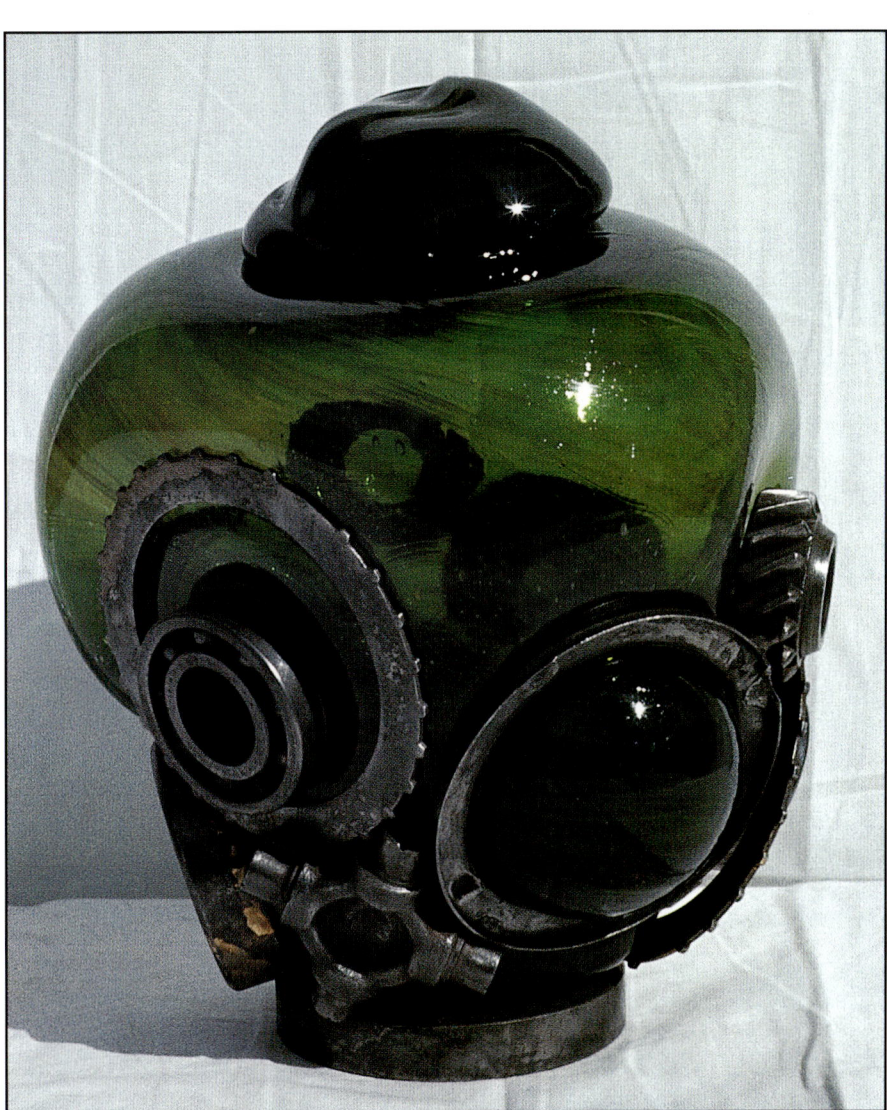

*Glass and Metal #2, 1971, 8" x 6" d.
Photo courtesy of the artist.*

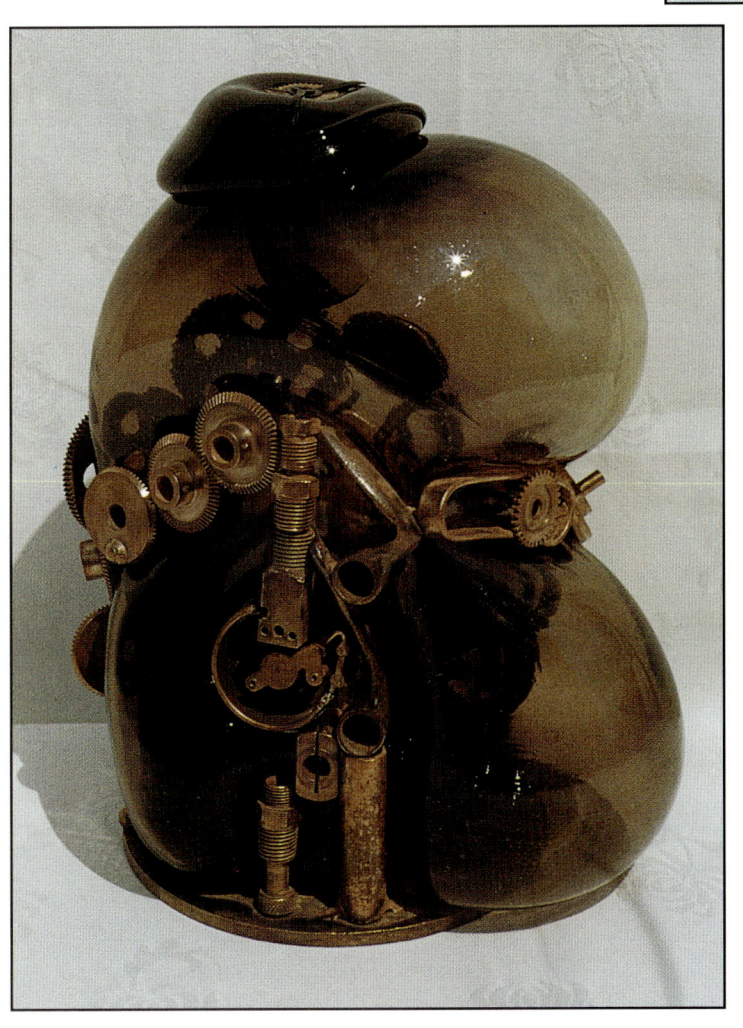

*Glass and Metal #3, 1972, 8" x 6" d.
Photo courtesy of the artist.*

Audrey Handler

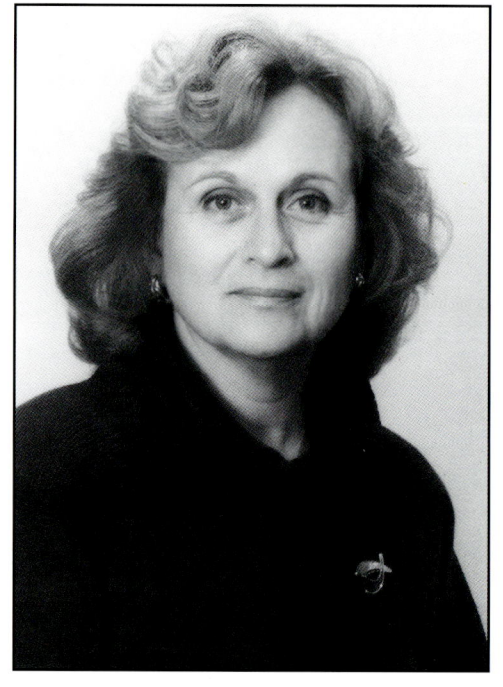

Audrey Handler.

I have always been interested in glass. I remember the small perfume bottles that I collected and treasured as a small child.

My ideas and concepts come from my own life experiences. There were always bowls of fruit on my mother's table waiting for some guest to just drop in. The apple, which symbolizes life and, for me, home and love has become a central theme in my work.

In the beginning the struggle to control the glass was so overwhelming that I concentrated on making controlled shapes like vases and bowls with a landscape motif. But as more colors became available and the glass better, I began to use symbolism in my work. I love to tell a story and so I began to create my sculptures, not only in glass, but also in wood and gold and silver to help illustrate an idea.

The larger table setting sculptures are personal statements and comments on life. They usually concern women and their social situations. The cup represents entrapment, the apple home, and the pear life. These sculptures are small worlds or landscape portraits with life-sized objects and sometimes tiny silver or gold people. They create a surrealistic time and place. *The Wedding Breakfast* in the Corning Museum Collection is ironically a breakfast for one. My recent work consists of bowls of realistic fruit. I also make bowls of vegetables and larger than life-sized apple forms that I call "*Pomes*."

I have been working in glass since 1965 and the love and obsession I have for this medium is still fresh. I love the way the glass colors look when they are hot, when it is transparent, translucent or opaque. Soft, but yet hard, this incredible medium, transformed by heat, expresses diversity and beauty. It continually transfixes me with awe.

I work alone in my studio, which is an old Wisconsin cheese factory that I have renovated several times since I first opened the studio in 1970. It is out in the country and is an ideal situation with lots of room for my creative energies. This year I have completely rebuilt the glass working equipment and now my studio, equipment, and I are truly in the twenty-first century.

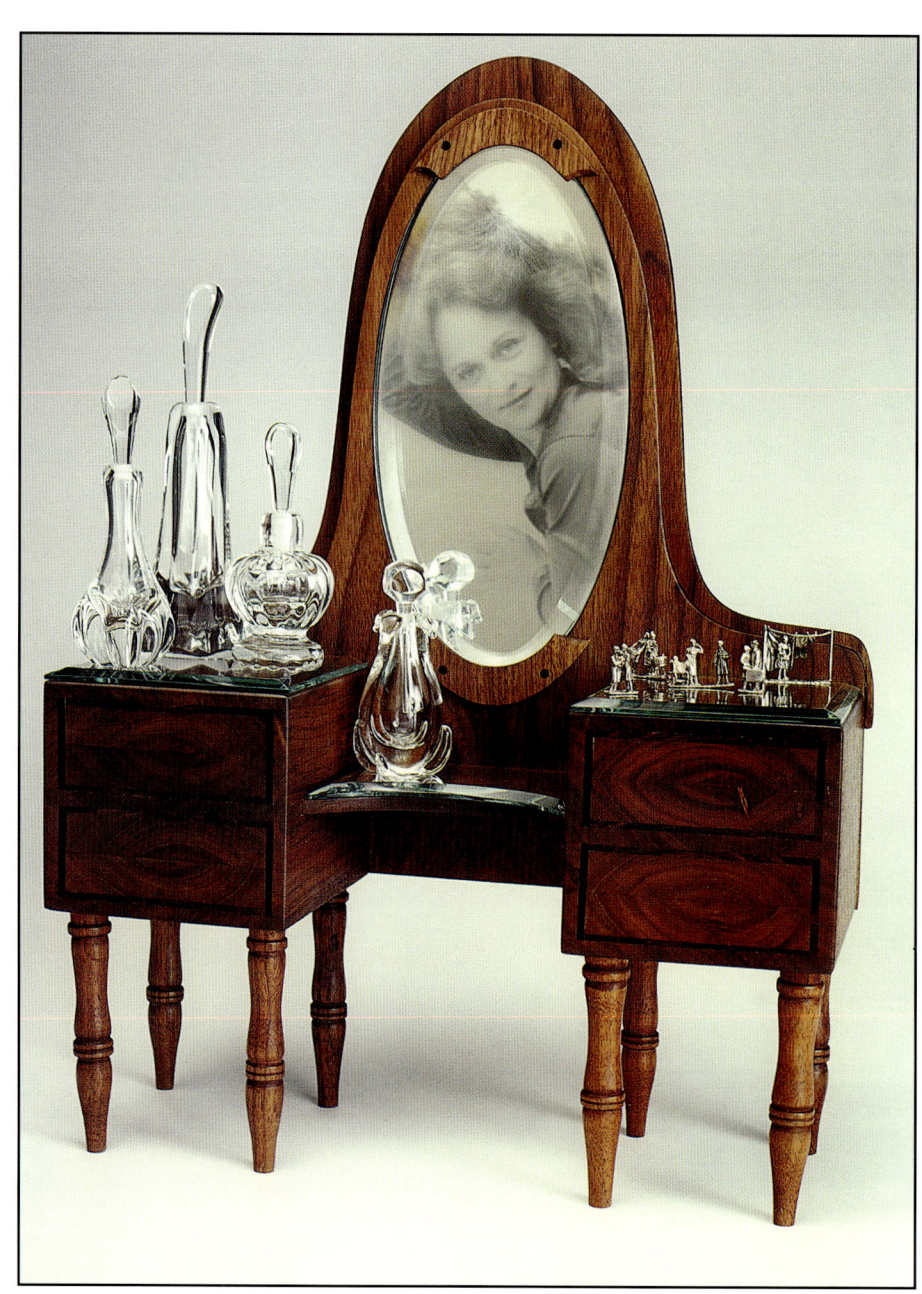

Vanity, 1983, 14" x 13" x 5", blown glass, walnut and rosewood, sterling silver, photo emulsion. *Photo courtesy of the artist.*

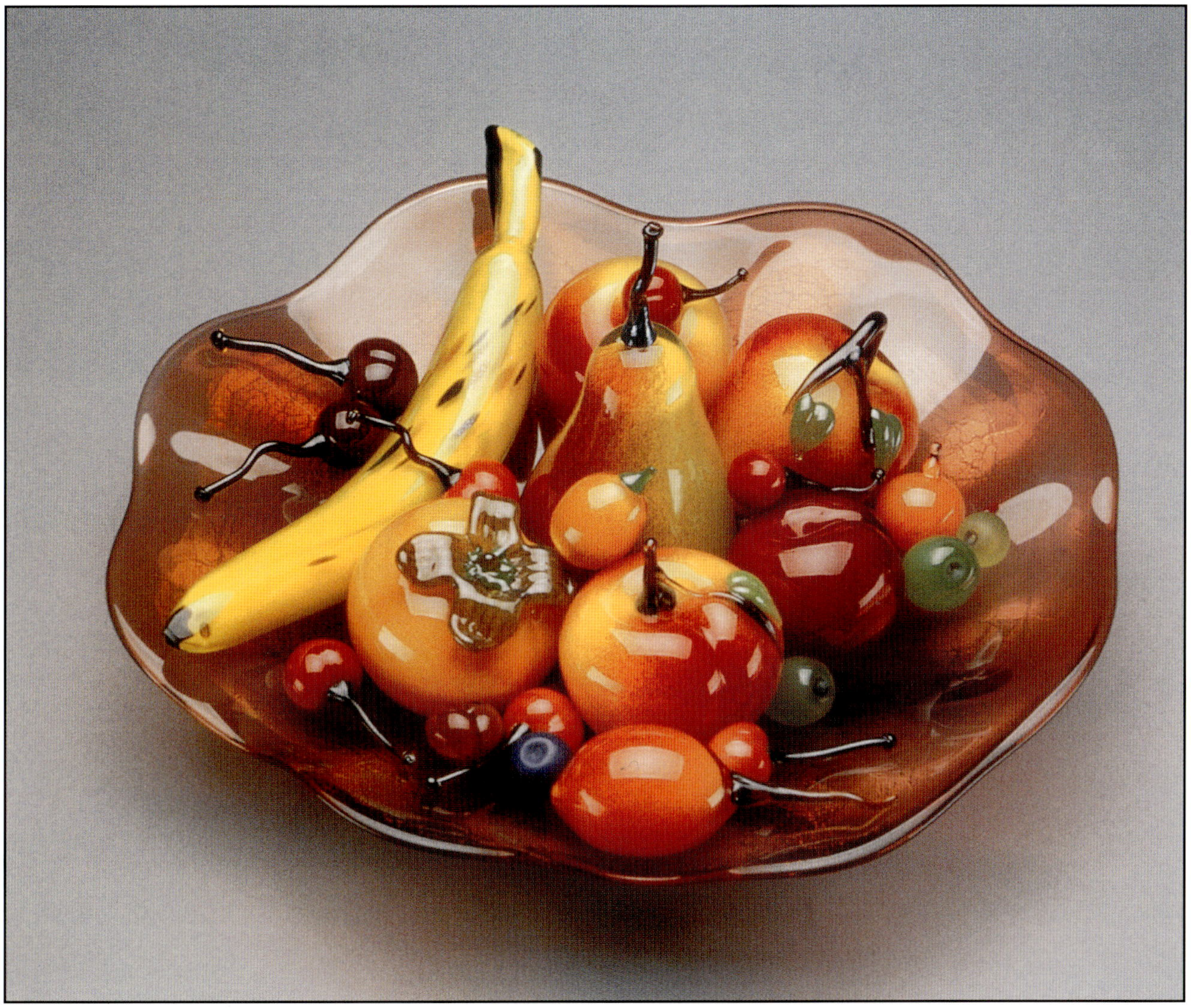

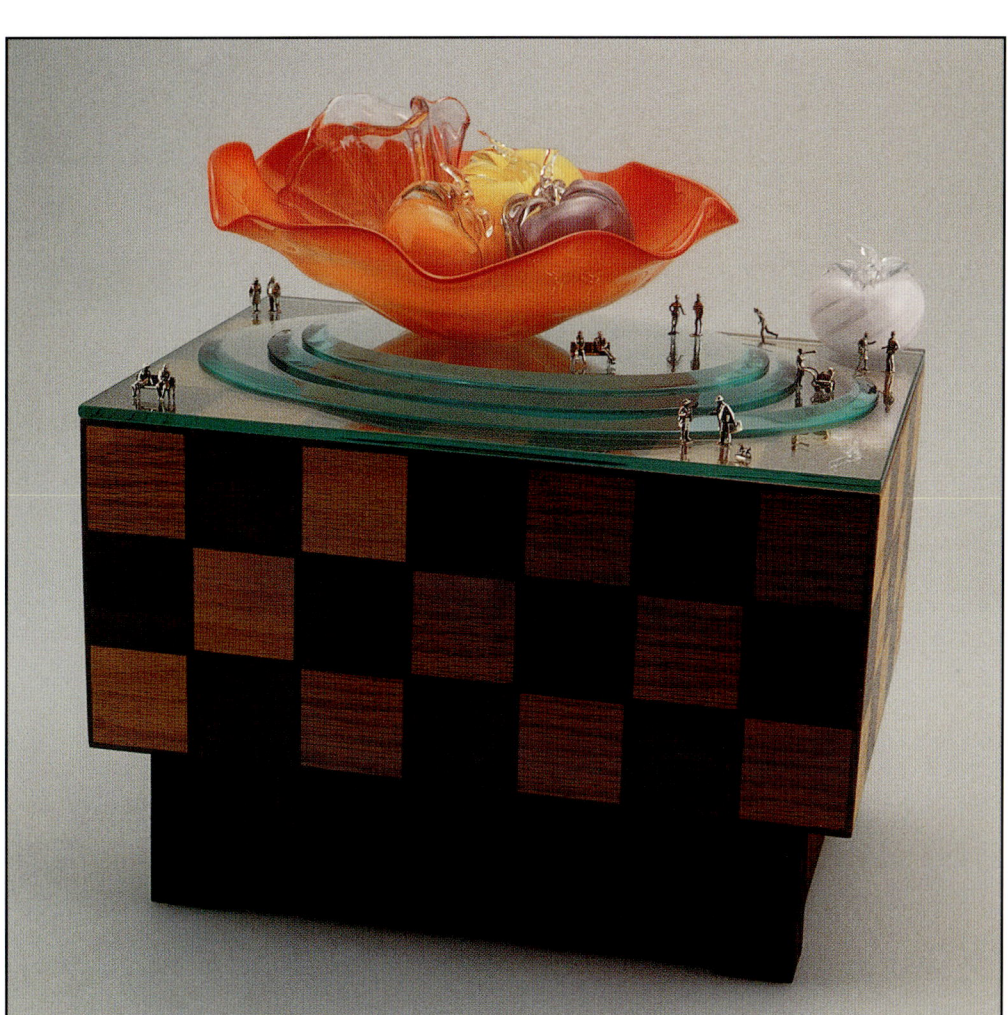

Bowl of Fruit, 1997, 7" h x 12" w x 7" d, blown glass. Photo courtesy of the artist.

Moments in a Park, 1988, 10" x 14" x 14", blown glass. Photo courtesy of the artist.

Harriet Hyams

Stone, wood, and welded steel were the starting point of my career. When I discovered glass in the mid-sixties, I knew I'd come home: to a journey that would lead me to discoveries and adventures of all kinds.

Glass has taught me about myself and the world in the most unexpected ways. I try to make sense of the chaos and arrange and rearrange shapes and colors while exploring light to make windows that are beautiful and mysterious. I love to do this.

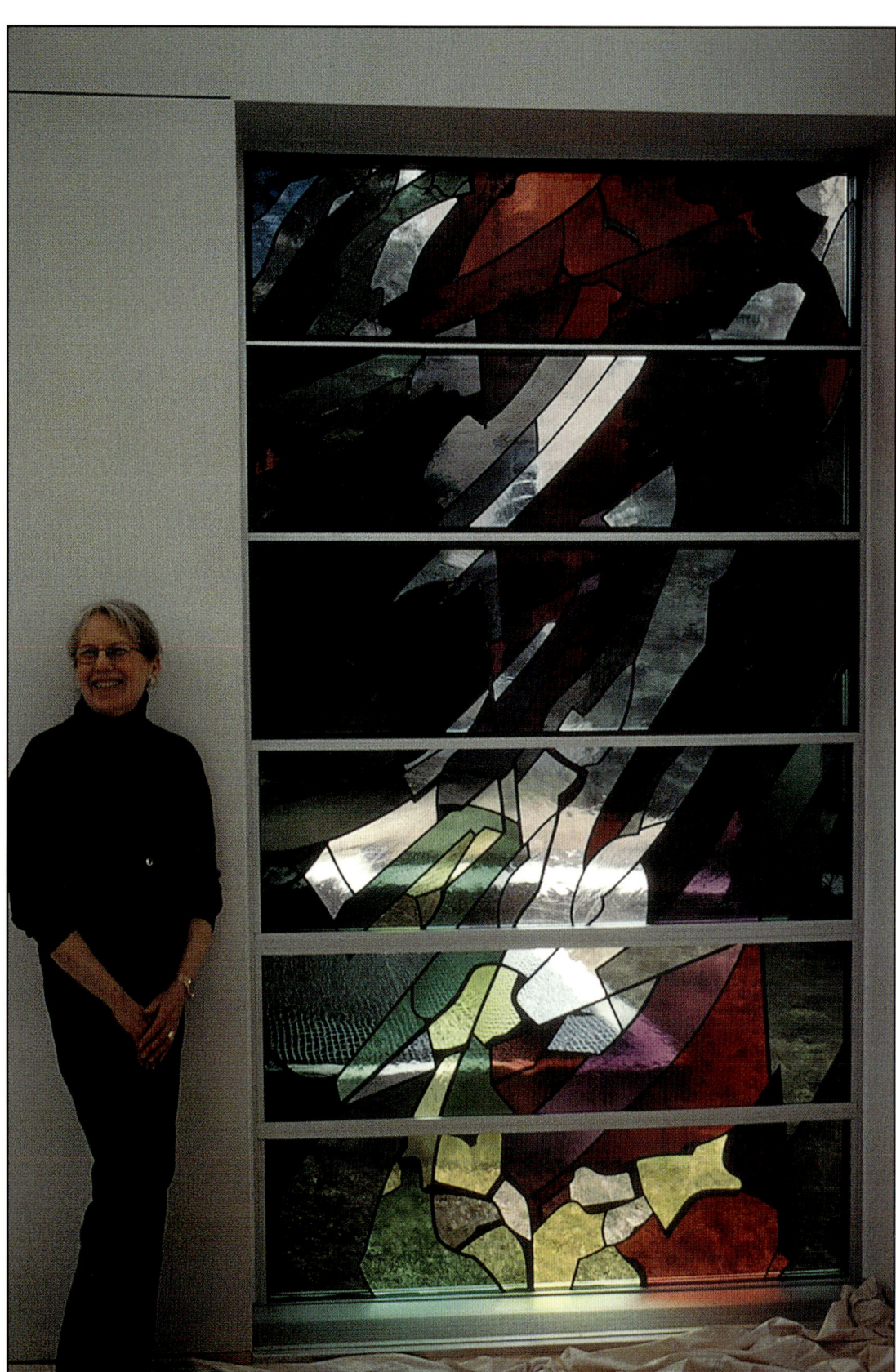

Harriet Hyams, Photo: Charles Shimel.
Photography courtesy of the artist.

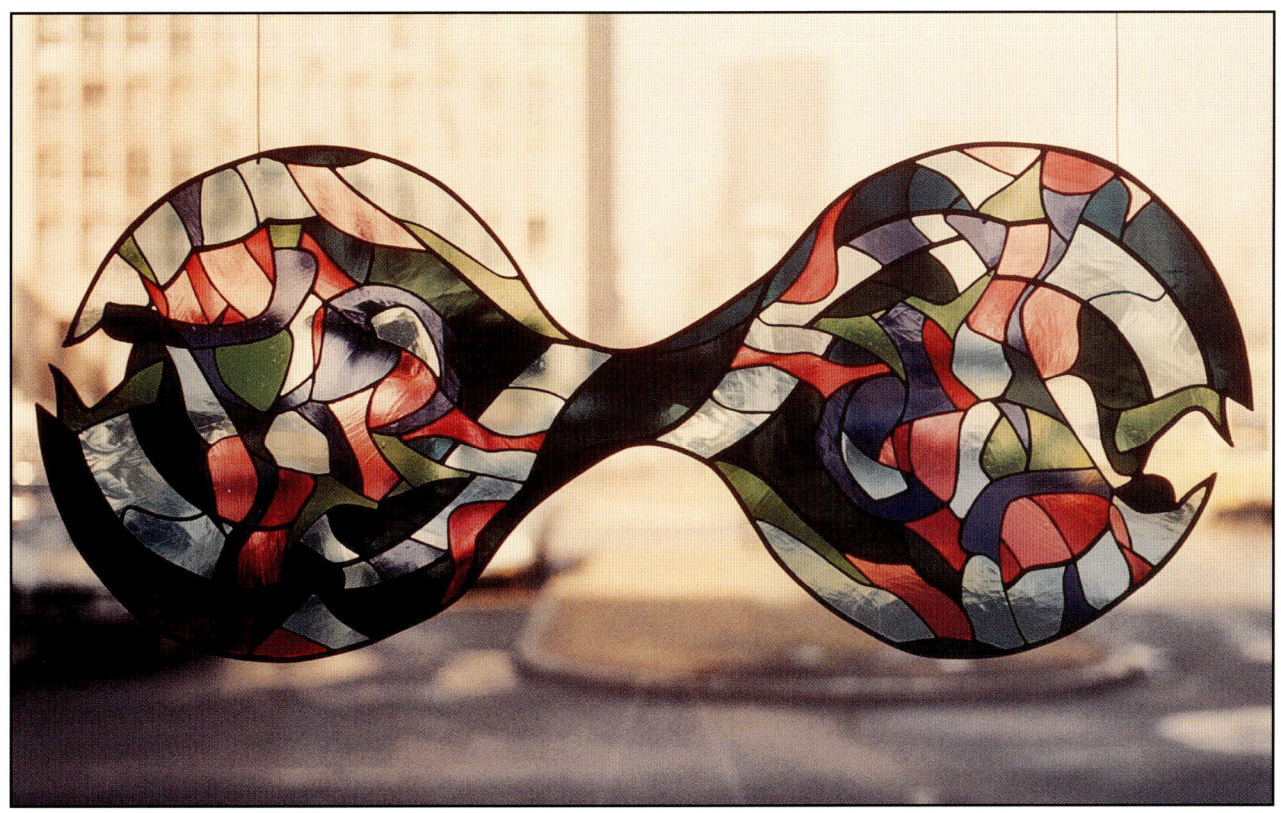

Perception, 18" x 44", stained glass sculpture. Photograph courtesy of the artist.

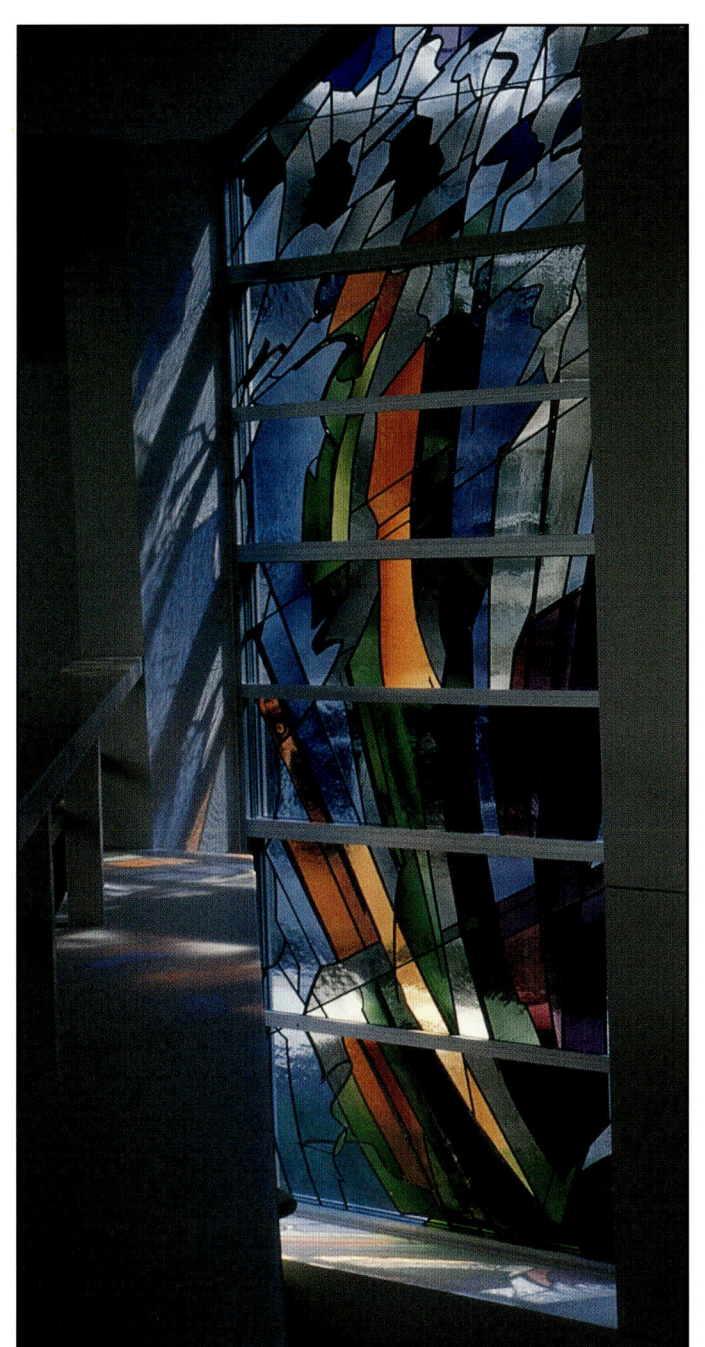

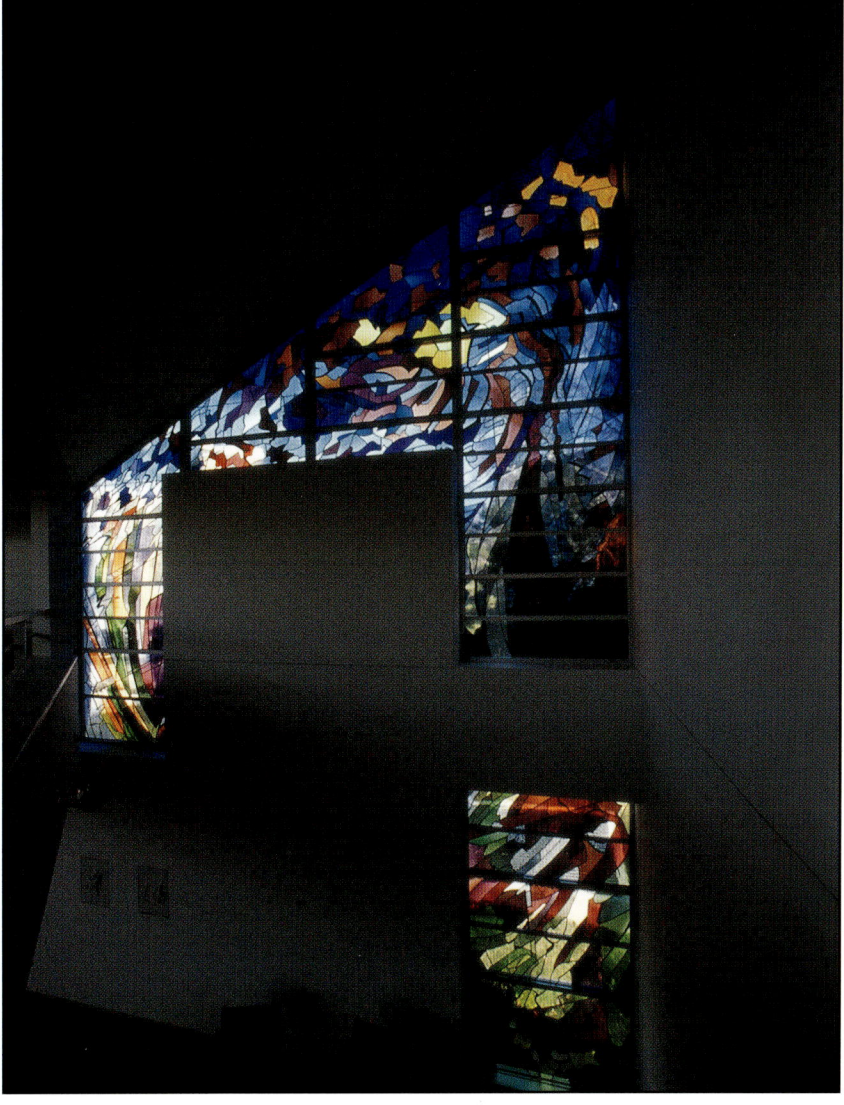

Eucharist Window, 2001, 29' x 20', Dominican Chapel, Our Lady of the Rosary, Sparkill, New York. Photo: Charles Shimel. *Photograph courtesy of the artist.*

Detail of *Eucharist Window*, 2001, 29' x 20', Dominican Chapel, Our Lady of the Rosary, Sparkill, New York. Photo: Charles Shimel. *Photograph courtesy of the artist.*

Joan Reep

In 1969, I started glassblowing at Patricia Esch's studio in Arvada, Colorado. With a background in painting and sculpture, my only intention was to add blown glass to my sculptures. I became completely enchanted with the material and the entire glassblowing process. Soon I was doing not only glass sculpture, but blowing functional pieces as well. Prior to that time, I was incorporating factory made slab glass into my bronzes.

Glass has been my passion for over thirty years. While following my bliss I have traveled the world and met so many wonderful people.

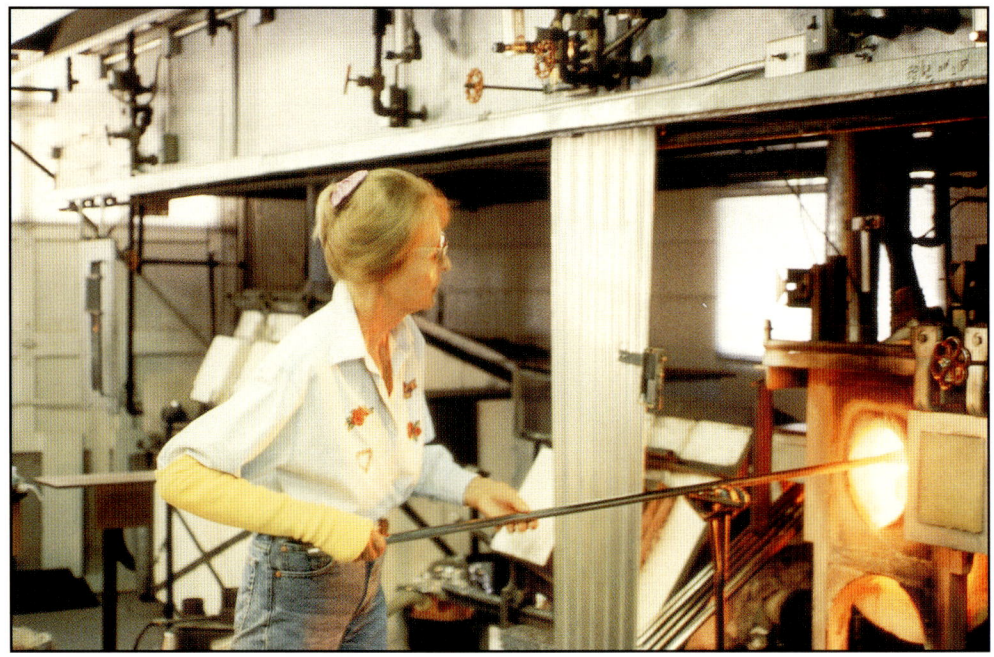

Joan Reep.

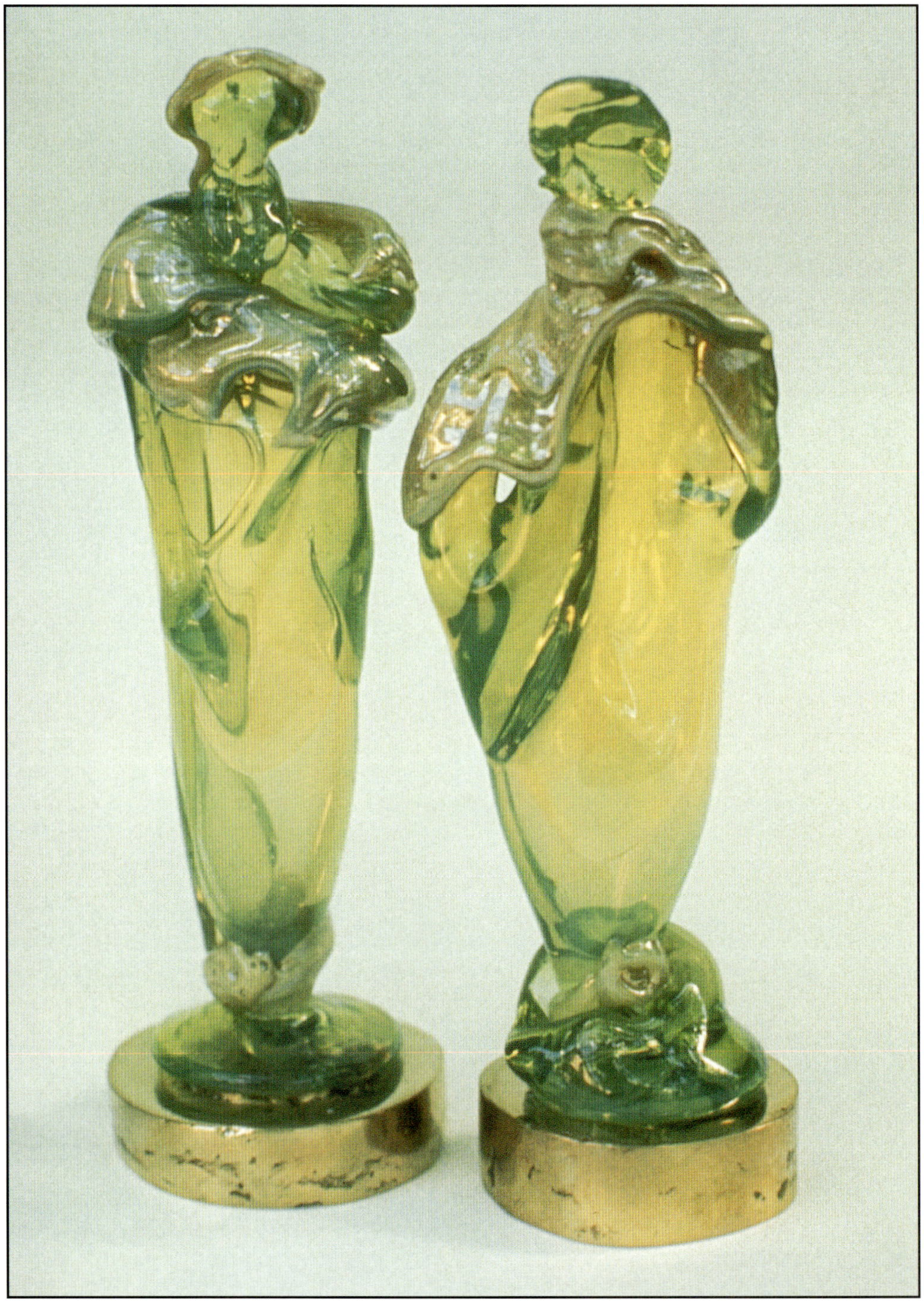

Haute Couture, c. 1971, blown and hand-formed silver with bronze fabricated base, 9" h. *Photo credit the artist.*

The Sixties - The Artist   49

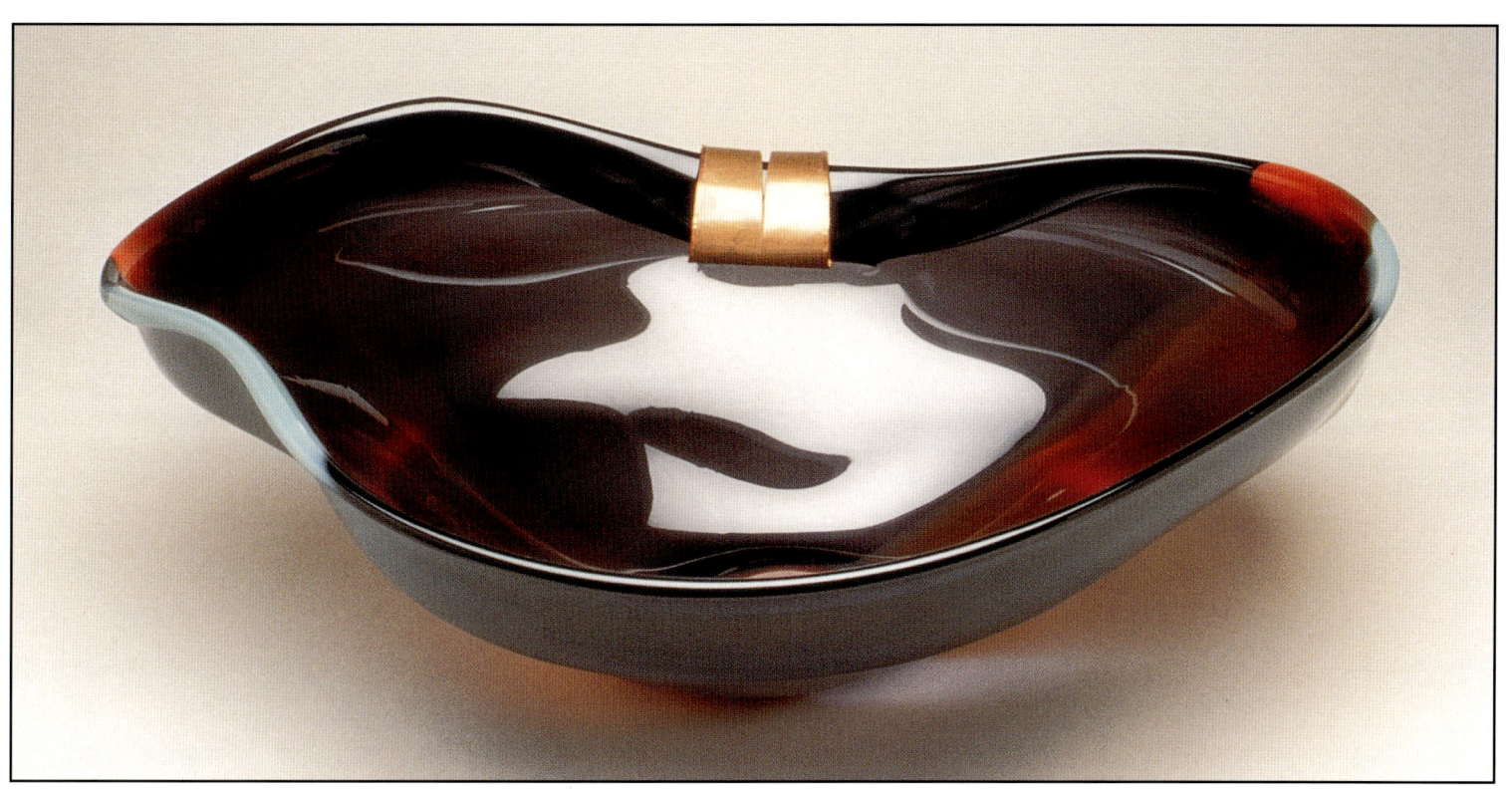

Blown glass vessel with copper, 1999, 16" d x 5" h. Photo credit the artist.

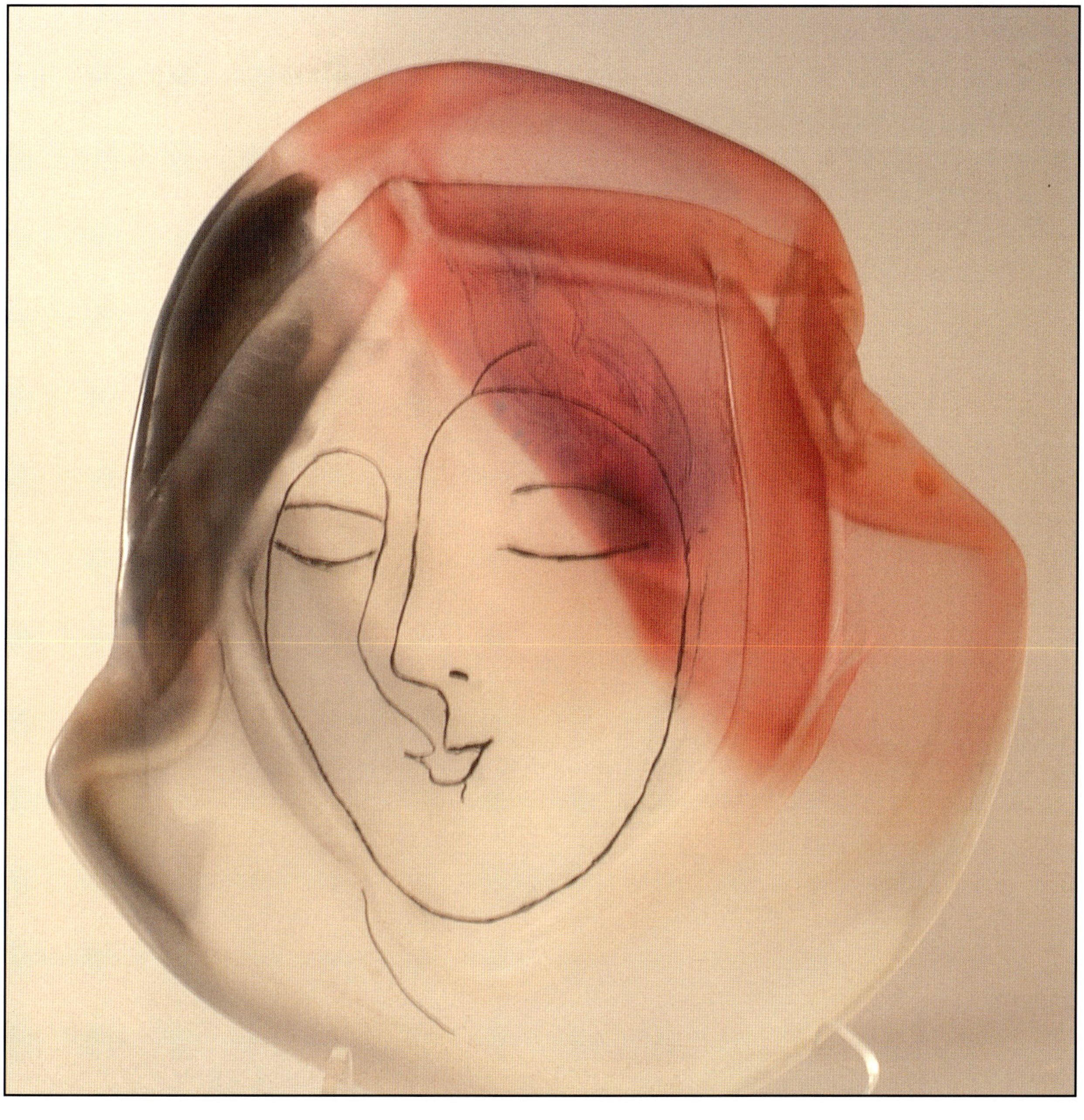

Dreaming of Picasso, 2002, slumped blown glass with drawing, 16.75" x 17.5". Photo credit the artist.

Pauline Solven

I take a painterly approach to my glass, and while my sources of inspiration lie in fine art, architecture, and nature, the work is usually abstract. Organization of colour is a principal concern, and I often express in the pieces a feeling for an observed situation or experienced moment in time.

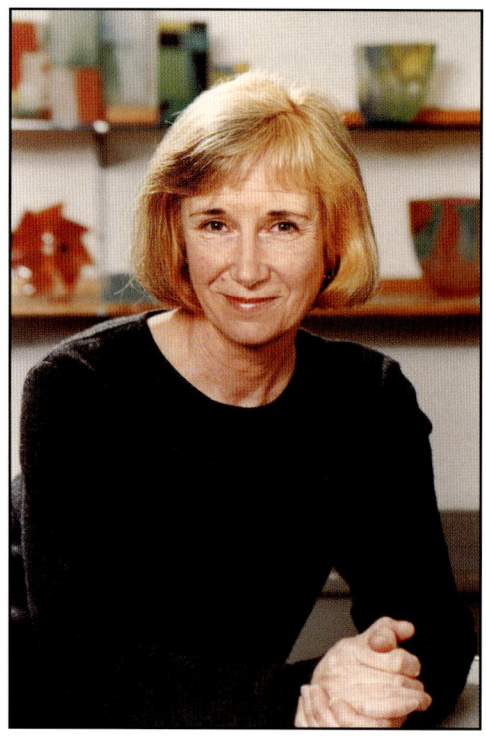

Pauline Solven.

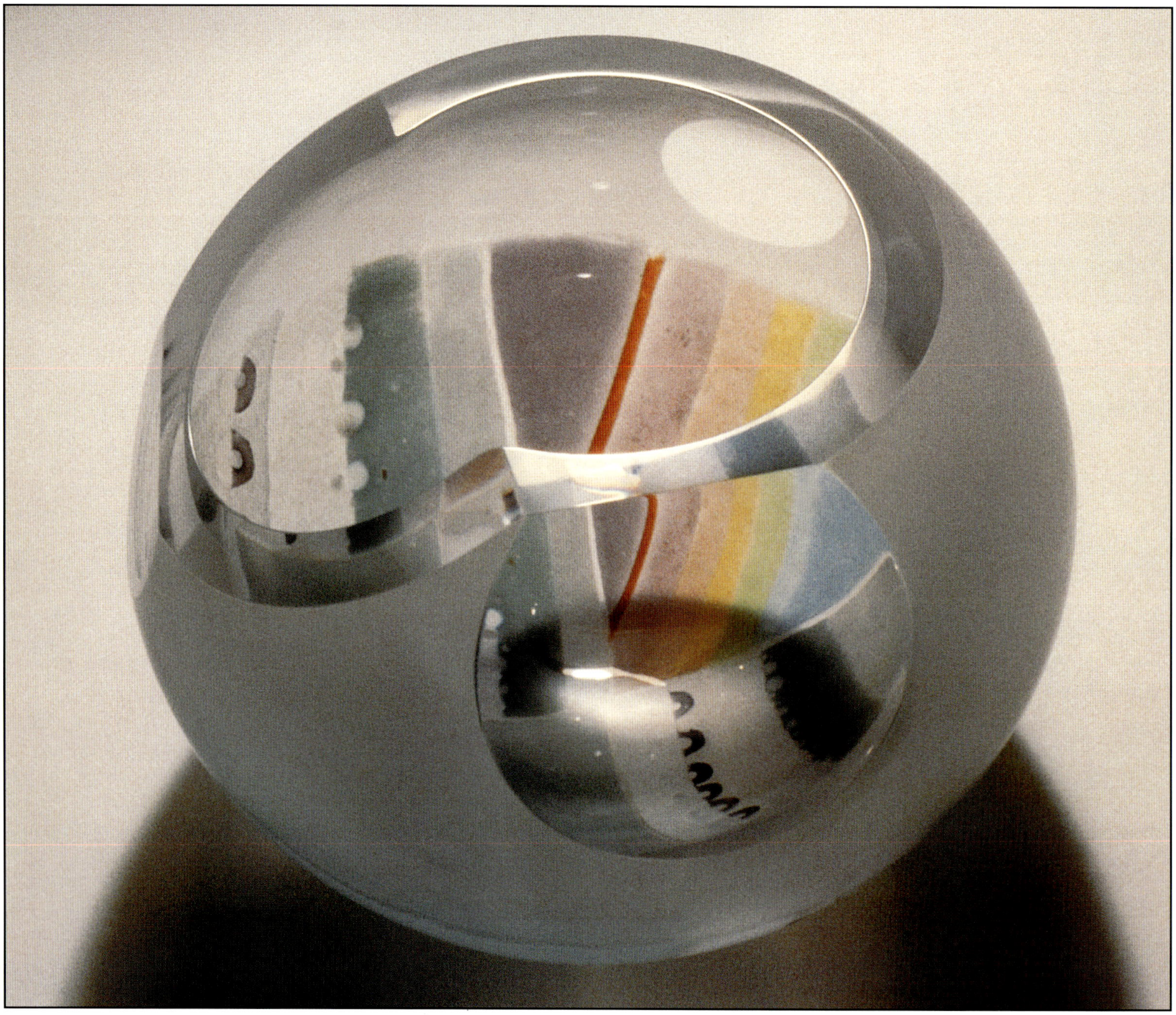

Sail D'azure, 1983. Photo courtesy of the artist.

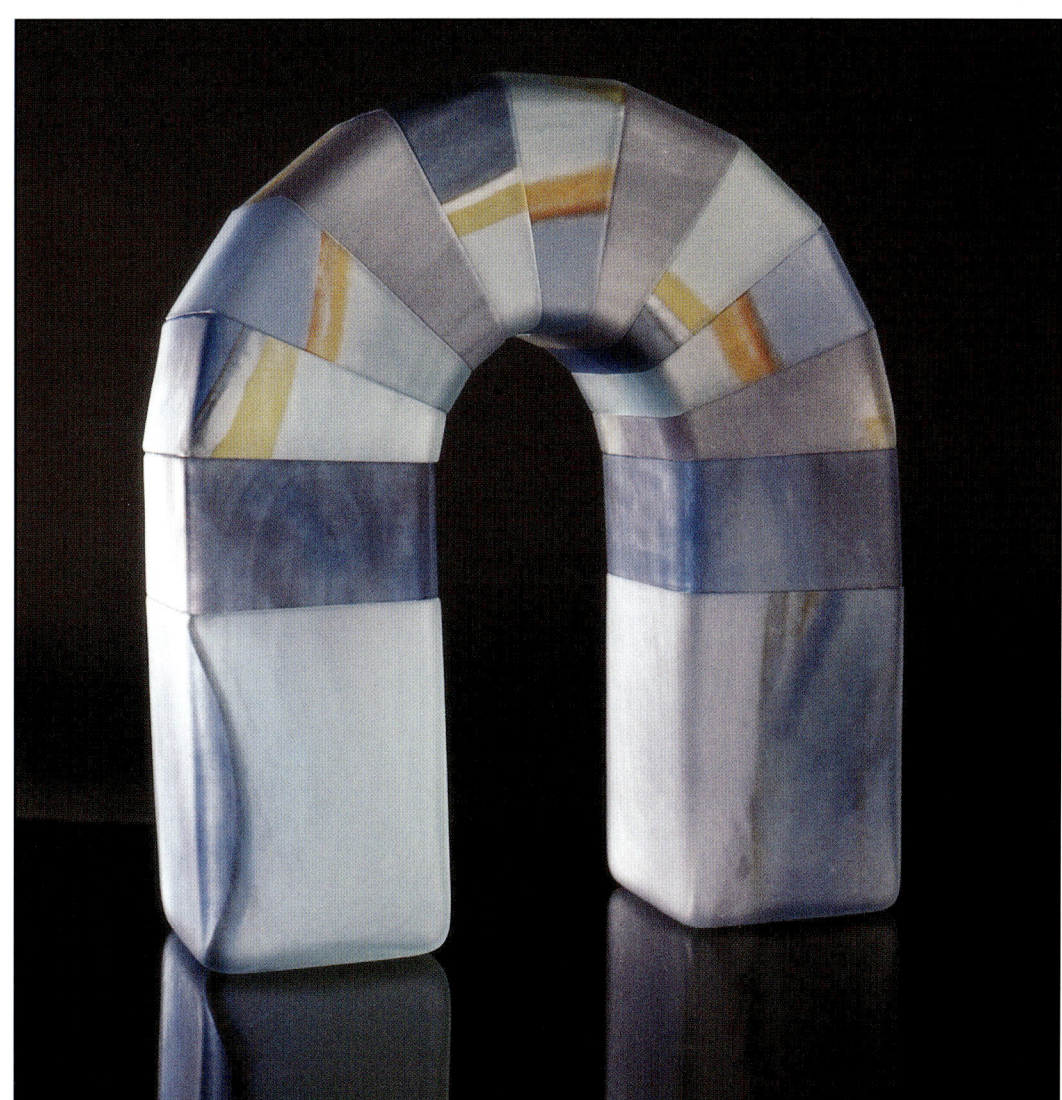

*Emerging Sun I, 1999.
Photo courtesy of the artist.*

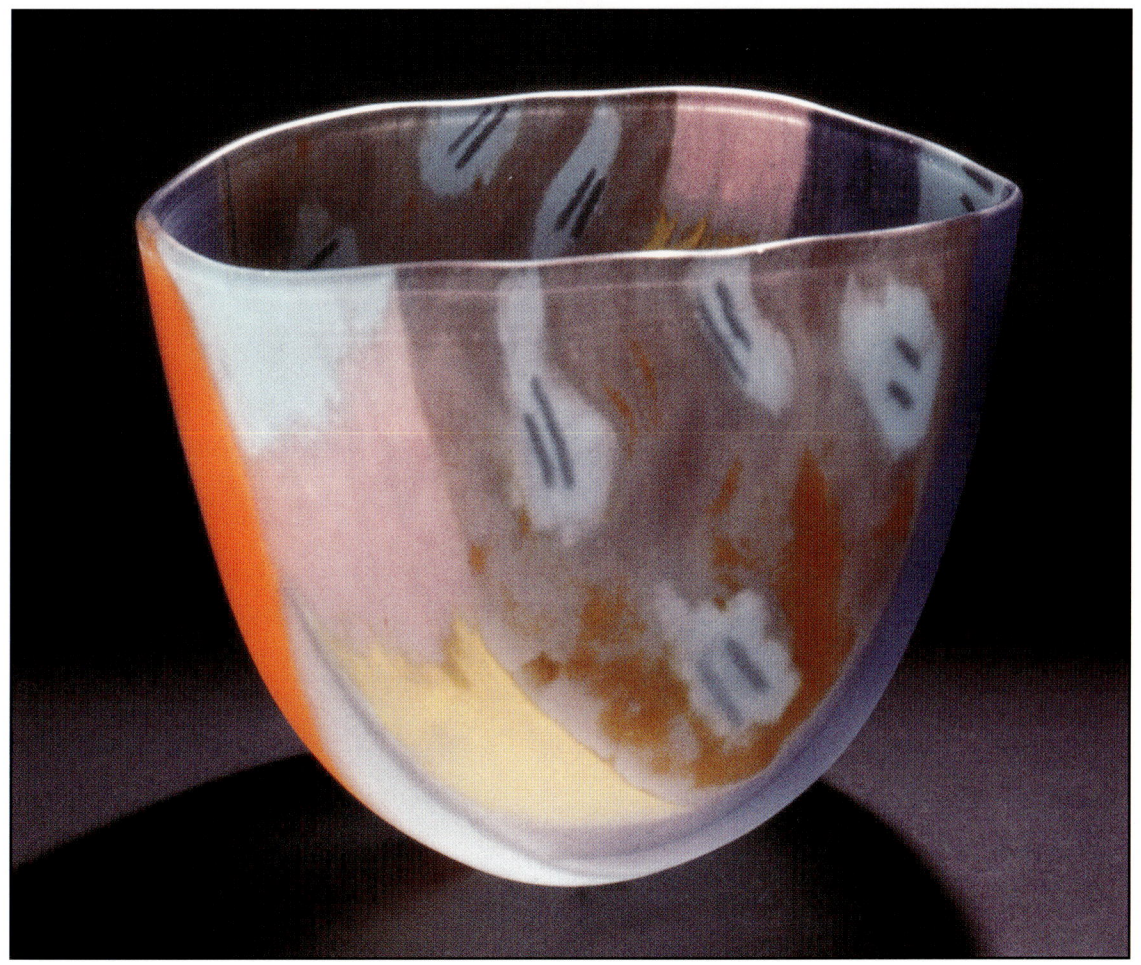

*Paintwork VII, 2002. Photo
courtesy of the artist.*

Sylvia Vigiletti

My favorite and most recognized work done in glass has been the small veiled forms, especially the *"Tension Series."* These are very intimate pieces that need to be viewed at close range. The way the bubble touches or invades the layers...the depth of colors...the tension felt as the layers are distorted...all are important elements that describe a particular time in my life.

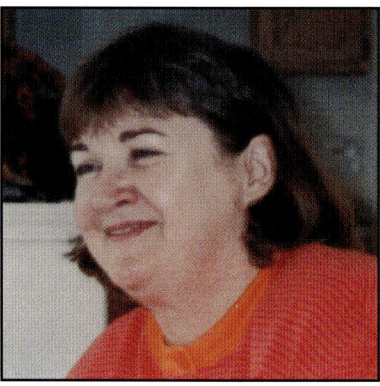

Sylvia Vigiletti. Photo credit: Ken Vigiletti.

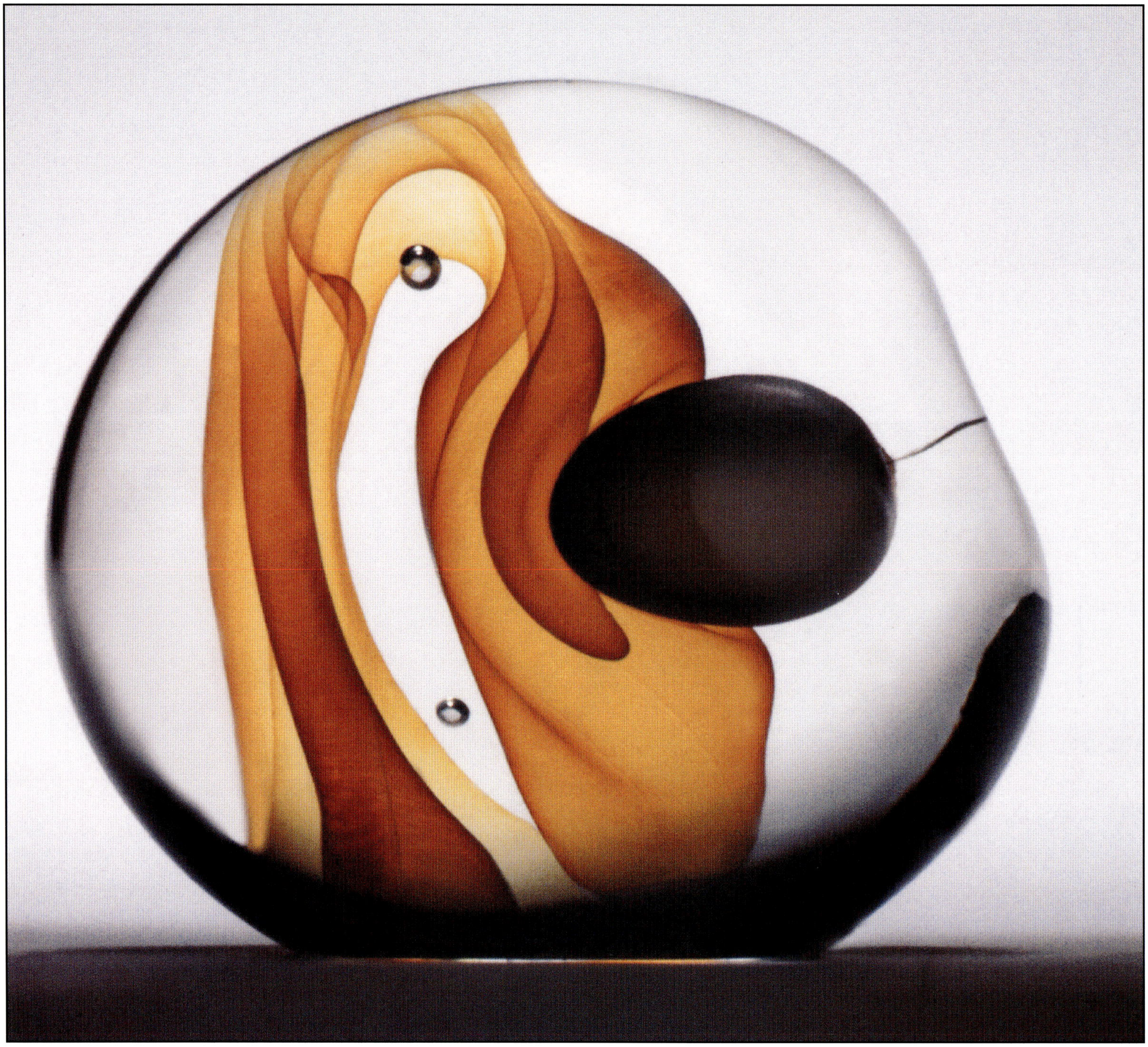

Black Pearl Tension Series, 1983, 4" x 4.5" x 1.75", photo: Robert Vigiletti. *Courtesy the artist.*

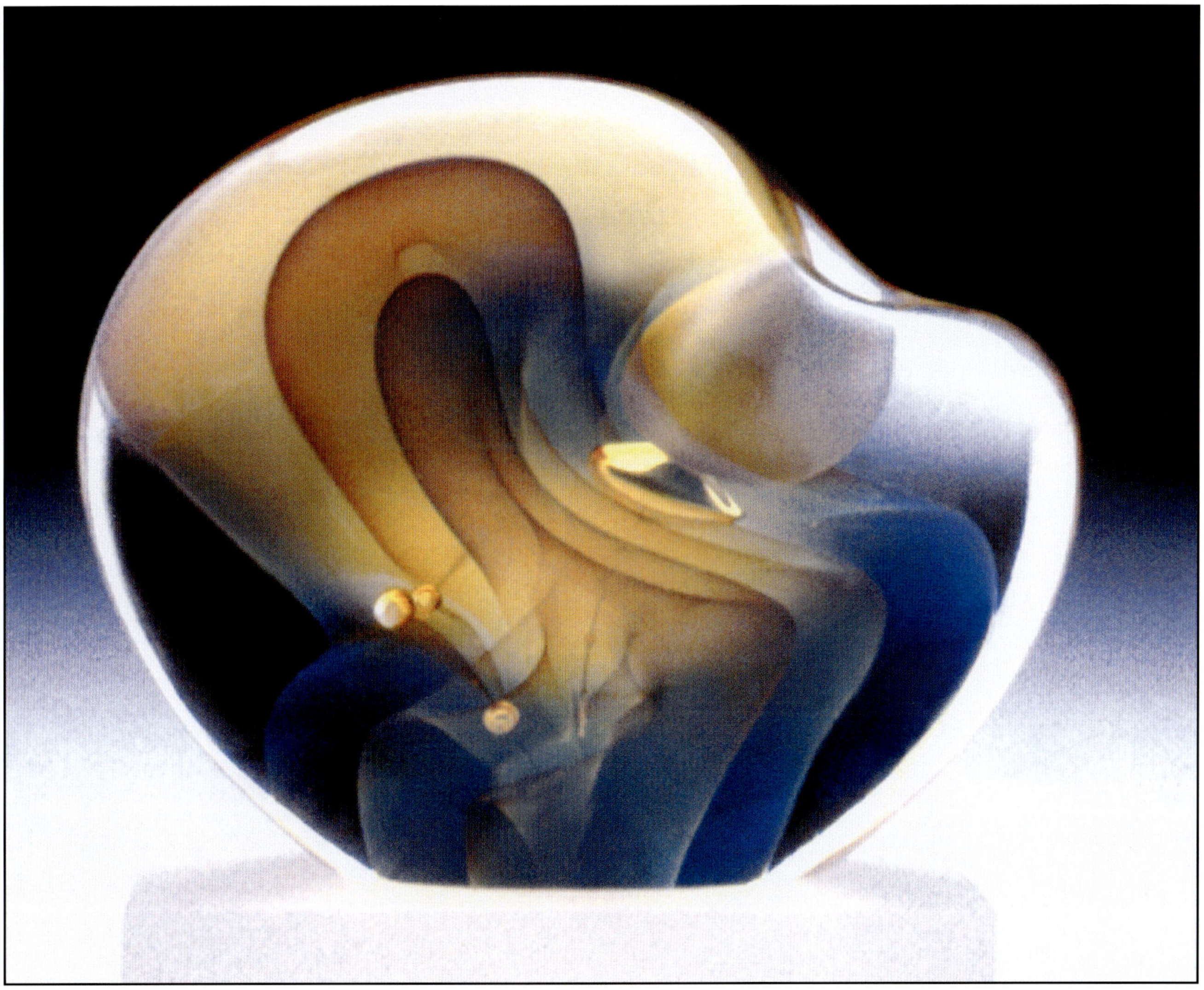

The Sixties - The Artist   53

Veiled Form Tension Series, 1981, photo: Robert Vigiletti. *Courtesy the artist.*

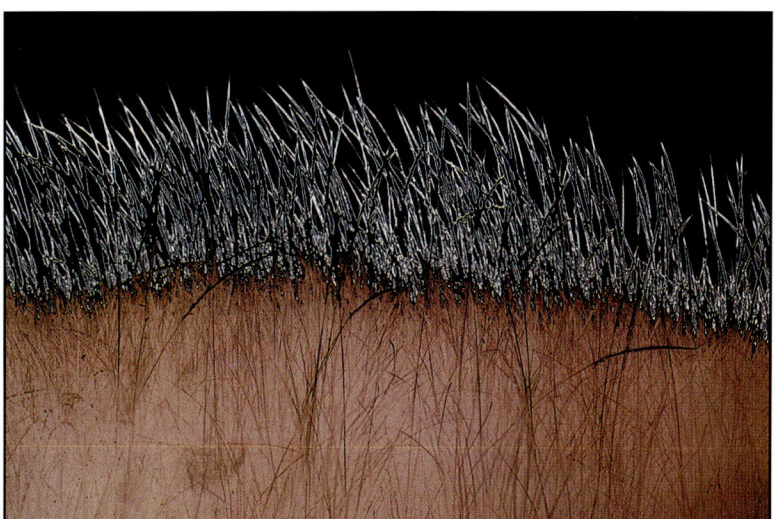

Midnight Grasses, 2001, 16" x 19", photograph. *Photo courtesy of the artist.*

During the last few years Sylvia has concentrated her creative energies on photography.

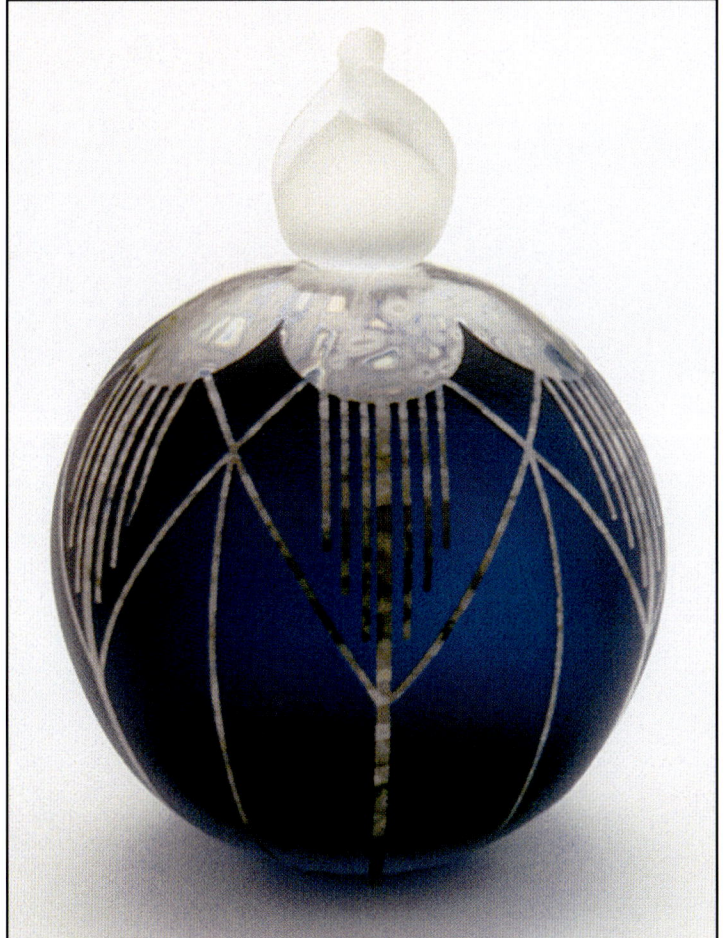

Deco Series Perfume Bottle, c. 1986, photo: Robert Vigiletti. *Courtesy the artist.*

Mary White

Dwelling on dwellings, healing, and other states of mind

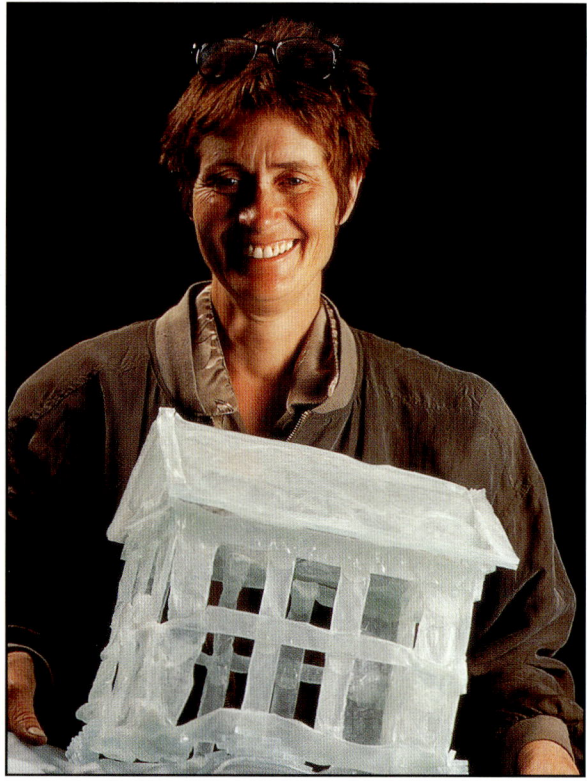

Mary White photo – *Portrait of the Artist* with *Living on the Wave*, 1999. Photo courtesy of the artist.

My work is an exploration of spirit and the soul. I want to evoke the wonder and surprise of natural and spiritual phenomenon.

I have moved several times, from Philadelphia mainline to Chicago south side to an Iowa farm to Oxford, England, to a Colorado ranch to an Indiana campus to Michoacan, Mexico, and finally, to the Bay area of California, where I have lived for many years. "Home" is a spirit as much as a place. My work is an expression of the transitory, yet substantial quality of the inner dwelling: a place of healing and substance.

As a child hiking in the Colorado Rocky Mountains, the old worn abandoned miner's cabins in the high meadows, near rushing glacial streams and rivers, offered us warmth, protection, and shelter from mountain storms. They were one-room shelters, built of rough boards and scrap wood, with no furniture. Mountain flowers like Indian Paint Brush often grew in profusion near the door. Sparse, but dry and safe from the lightning and sudden torrential storms. The image of a simple cabin, near the ancient mining shafts, close by a rushing creek, surrounded by chaotic colors of mountain flowers often comes to mind when I visualize shelter. The cabin foundations became metaphors in my houses for the strong and sudden forces, some joyful, some heart breaking, that life brings daily.

In 1994, when I finally decided I wanted to have a "house," I found and bought an old dilapidated 1893 Victorian surrounded by warehouses in West Berkeley, the industrial area of the city. My partner and I raised the house ten feet up and built our wood and glass shops below. For three years, as we did all of the construction necessary to close up the stripped bared house, we camped out with no kitchen or furniture, fixing one room at a time as the house swayed in the winds on the pilings. It was like living in a boat, close to the elements. I started making the glass houses during the time I started working on my own house, visualizing "home," thinking of the foundations as the story of the house, as the bearer of the spirit.

I like to use reused materials: discarded window glass, construction lumber, and metal to make the pieces. It seems important to recreate beauty out of objects considered unusable. Most of the house forms I make have inner lights. Eventually I will figure out how to make them solar powered lights so that they are self-sustainable systems.

I look for the inner light of the spirit of the home just as I look for the inner light of all other living beings.

Reverse glass paintings in the seventeenth century were often votive offerings, painted to place on walls near the church alter, evoking the healing of a relative or friend. I have followed the same tradition, documenting my internal hopes and dreams in the small panels that are then grouped together to evoke healing spirits who might bring the qualities of reconciliation and peaceful and creative interchange into our midst.

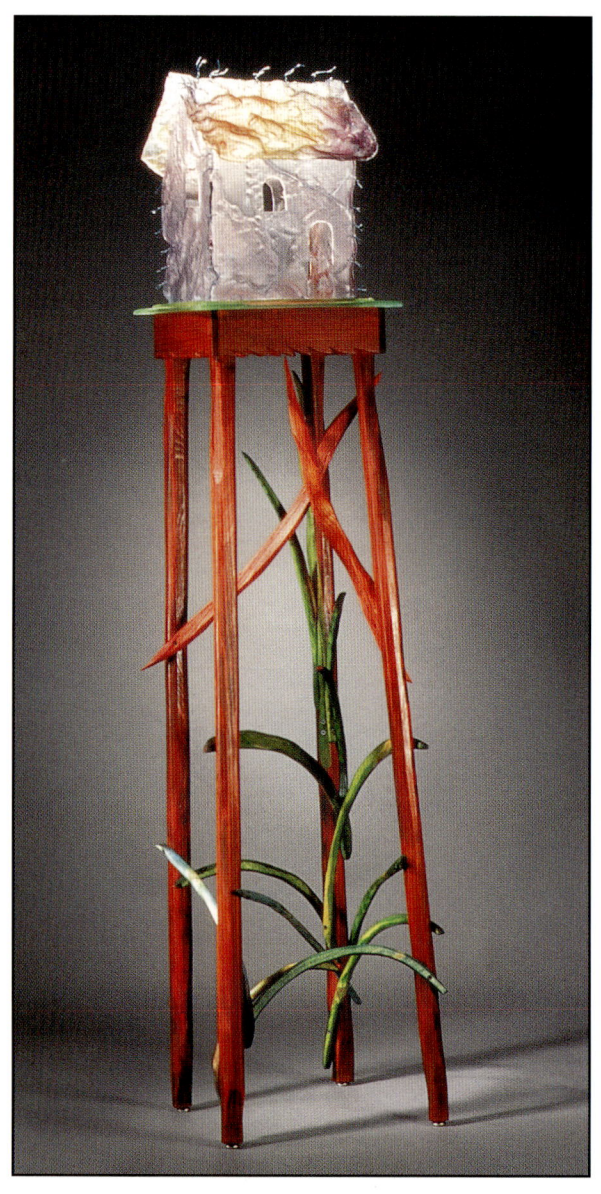

Dwelling on Sunrise, 2002, 72" x 14" x 13", fused plate glass, wood, paint, photo credit: Richard Sargent. Photo courtesy of the artist.

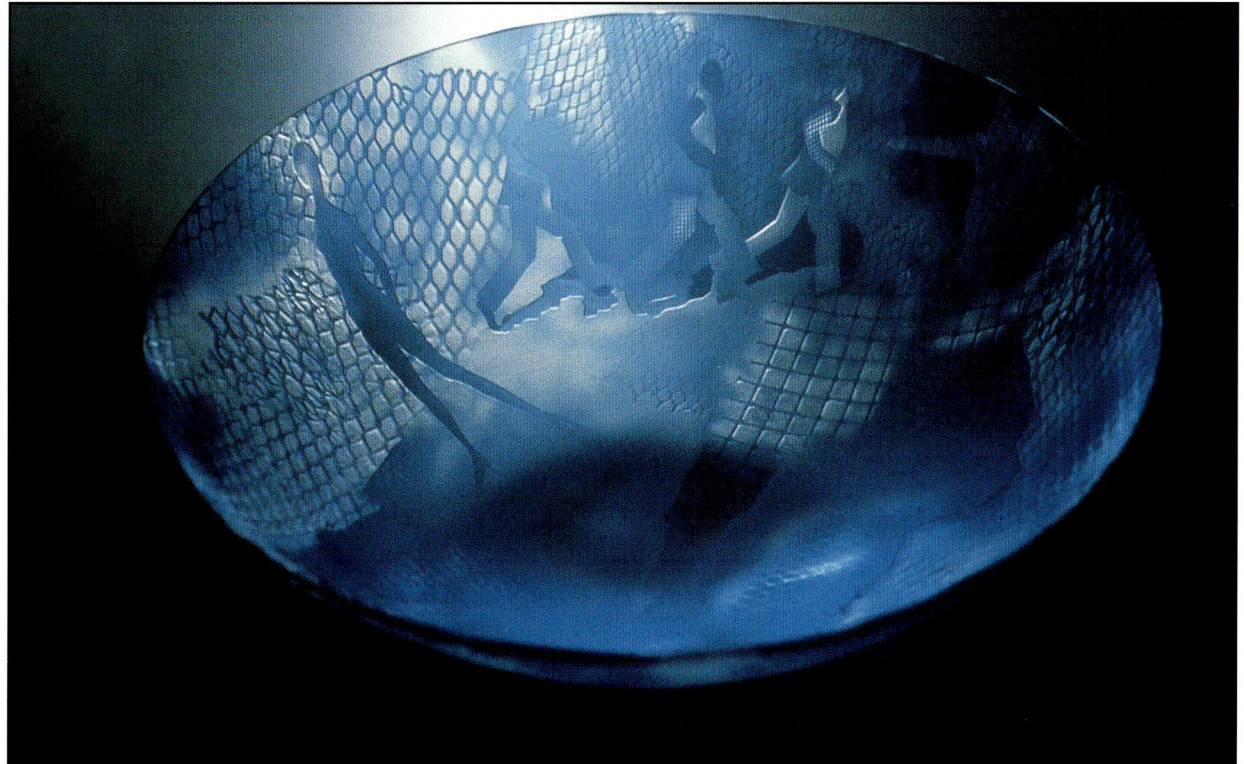

Waiting for Godot, 1980, carved slumped glass. Photo courtesy of the artist.

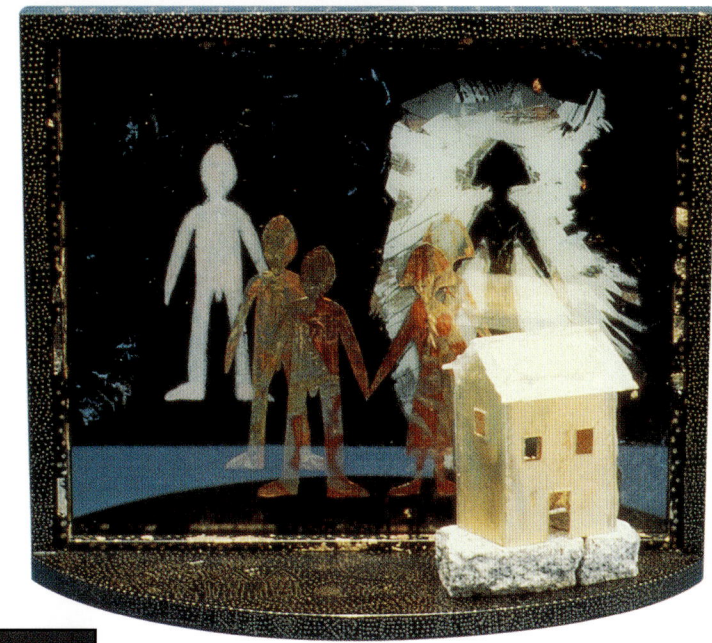

Opposites Attract, 1989, 11" x 13", painting, wood, glass. Photo courtesy of the artist.

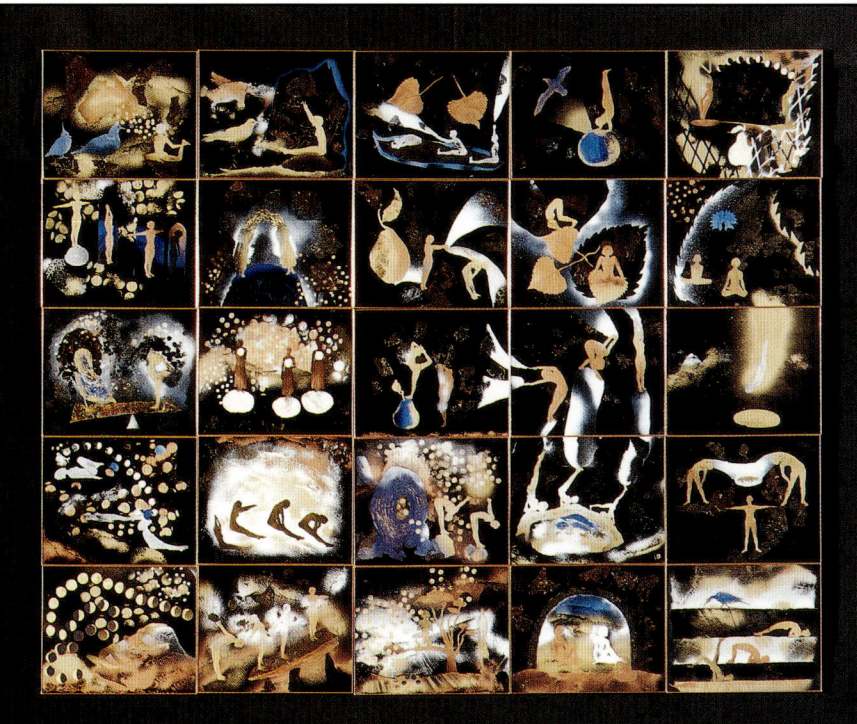

The Healing Wall, 2001, 9" x 11" reverse painting on glass, 55" x 45", photo credit: Richard Sargent. *Photo courtesy of the artist.*

The Seventies

The decade of the seventies arrived a midst military tension and turmoil. In 1970 Richard Nixon escalated the war in Vietnam, causing outrage on college campuses. At Kent Sate University in Ohio the Ohio National Guard was called to quell a riot: four students were killed: two men and two women.

It was a time of expansion in education, especially in the Crafts. Many colleges and universities were adding craft disciplines to their curriculums, including new glass departments.

Spurred along by the new feminist consciousness women began to demand recognition for themselves. Galleries, museums, and critics would not pay attention to women artists so, aware of their situation, they began to organize and protest. A group of New York artist's led by critic Lucy Lippard formed a committee that demanded equality at the prestigious Whitney Museum annual exhibitions. "Forced into guerilla tactics, the protestors left eggs and tampax all over the shiny Whitney Museum floors and staged a sit-down in the middle of the opening of the 1970 Whitney Annual."[1]

A 1972 survey of commercial art galleries revealed that only eighteen percent of them carried the work of women. As a result, women's co-op galleries, such as AIR and Soho 20 in New York, and others across the country were founded to exhibit work these dealers refused to show.

Simultaneously, the place of craft in the art world was undergoing a metamorphosis. Many women artists were incorporating craft techniques in their art, sometimes as a deliberate reference to the traditional occupations of women, and many craft artists were gaining recognition for their work. A number of art movements in the '70s can be directly attributed to women. Some, such as the Pattern and Decoration movement helped to break down the barriers between art and craft. Judy Chicago incorporated ceramics, china painting, and embroidery in her project *The Dinner Party*, which was a tribute to powerful women throughout history: Ruth Duckworth, Mary Frank, Toshiko Takaezu, and Lucy Rei in ceramics, Suzanne Benton in metals, and Lenore Tawny in fibers, all worked to raise the level of craft arts to that of fine art. In 1972 the Women's Caucus for Art was formed and began to campaign for equal exhibition opportunities for women.

A ground breaking article in the January 1971 issue of *ARTnews*, written by Dr. Linda Nochlin, a professor of Art History at Vassar College and an important activist in the woman's art movement, paved the way for younger women to gain the respect and recognition they deserve. Her article titled "Why Have There Been No Great Women Artists?" looks at past attitudes that shaped how women artists have been treated by society. Her article draws attention to how the lack of proper art education, the male dominated art world, and a woman's own self identity played a part in the formation of these attitudes. As an example, Dr. Nochlin cites a remark made as late as the 1970s:

Again, lest we feel that we have made a great deal of progress in this area in the past 100 years, I might bring up the remark of a bright young doctor who when the conversation turned to his wife and her friends "dabbling" in the arts snorted, "well, at least it keeps them out of trouble!"[2]

This belittling viewpoint was still held in the seventies by many male artists and dealers, as well as by fathers, brothers, and husbands of women seeking a career in the arts. Many women as well bought into the idea that having a career in the arts was difficult and required sacrifice. The barriers women faced in the art world were often sufficient to prevent them from pursuing professional careers in the arts.

Nochlin concludes,

> What is important is that women face up to the reality of their history and of their present situation. Disadvantage may indeed be an excuse; it is not, however, an intellectual position. Rather, using their situation as underdogs and outsiders as a vantage point, women can reveal institutional and intellectual weaknesses in general, and, at the same time that they destroy false consciousness, take part in the creation of institutions in which clear thought and true greatness' are challenges open to anyone-man or woman- courageous enough to take the necessary risk, the leap into the unknown.[3]

The year 1971 was an important year for the studio glass movement. Pilchuck, the famous glass school just north of Seattle, Washington, was born. Glass artist, Dale Chilhuly, usually receives credit for establishing the school. Chilhuly, a native of Tacoma, Washington, had the vision to build a summer camp on the West Coast for glass blowing similar to the one at Haystack on Deer Island in Maine. Chilhuly, along with Ruth Tamura, then chairman of the glass department at California College of Art and Craft, were awarded a $2,000 grant from the Union of Independent Colleges of Art for an experimental summer program in glass. Jack Lenore Larson, a friend and mentor to Dale, suggested he approach Seattle Art patrons Ann and John Hauberg for help. They offered some land on their ranch fifty miles north of Seattle.

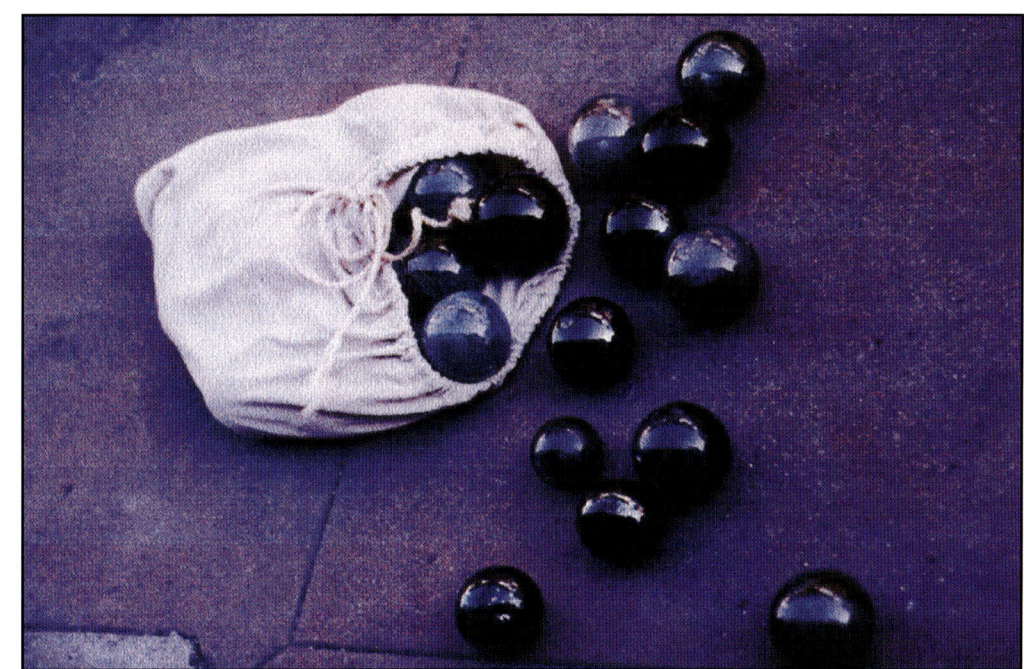

Ruth Tamura, *Bag of Marbles,* 1969, marbles were 6" diameter. A live marble game with three dressed players happened. The gallery floor was covered with sand ... the marbles were scattered around the sand – and the game began. *Photograph courtesy of California College of Arts and Crafts, photo archives.*

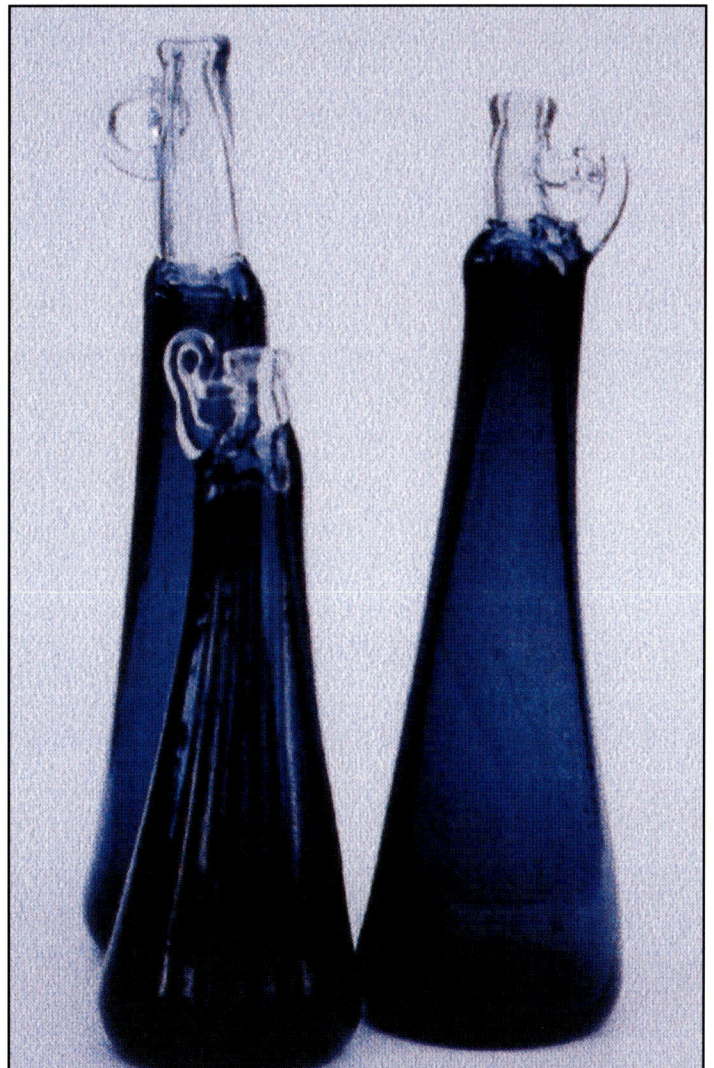

Ruth Tamura, *Vases,* 1969, assorted sizes. *Photograph courtesy of California College of Arts and Crafts, photo archives.*

58 The Seventies

Most of that summer of 1971 was spent building a glass furnace under a tent in an open field on the Hauberg's property. A few faculty, friends, and students from RISD, including Toots Zynsky, were among the original group.[4] Ruth was the first and only woman to teach at Pilchuck for a number of years, although there were many women students. By the end of the seventies, Flora Mace and Joey Kirkpatrick were regulars, returning as faculty and visiting artists.[5]

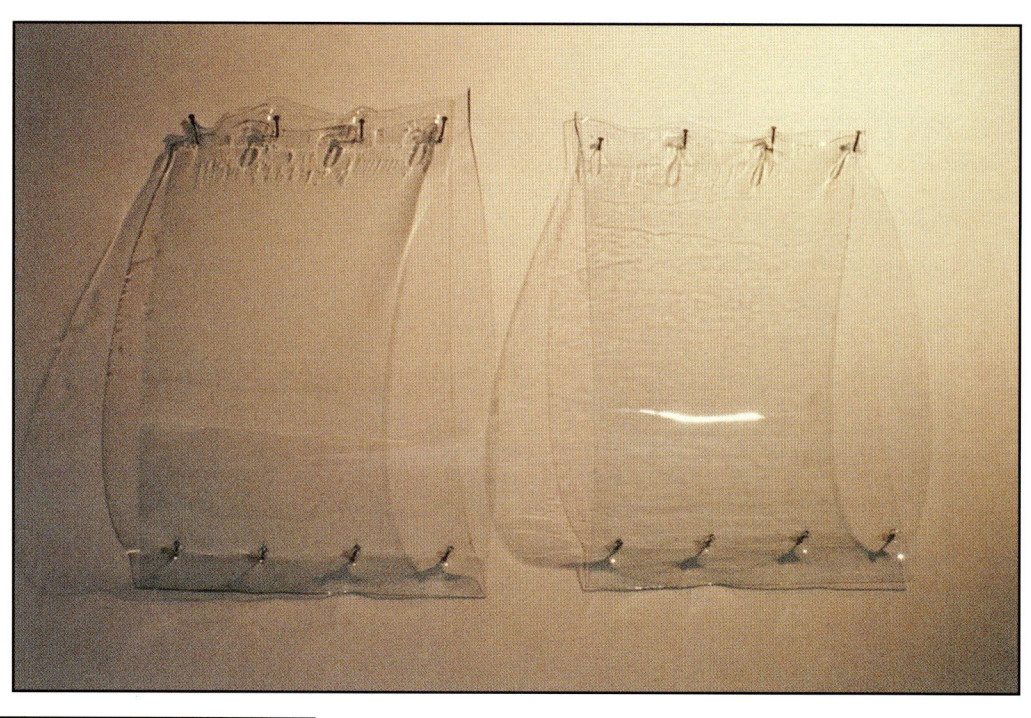

Toots Zynski, *Untitled Wall Piece*, 1972, made at RISD. *Photograph courtesy of the artist.*

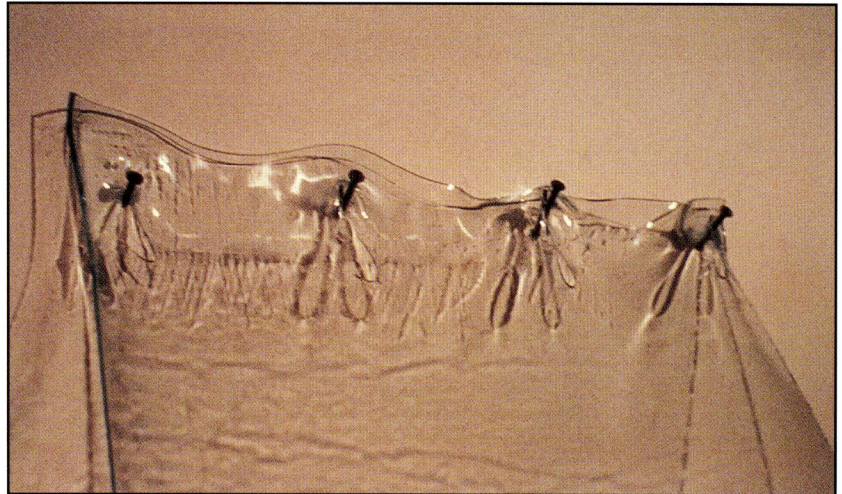

Toots Zynski, *Untitled Wall Piece*, detail, 1972. *Photograph courtesy of the artist.*

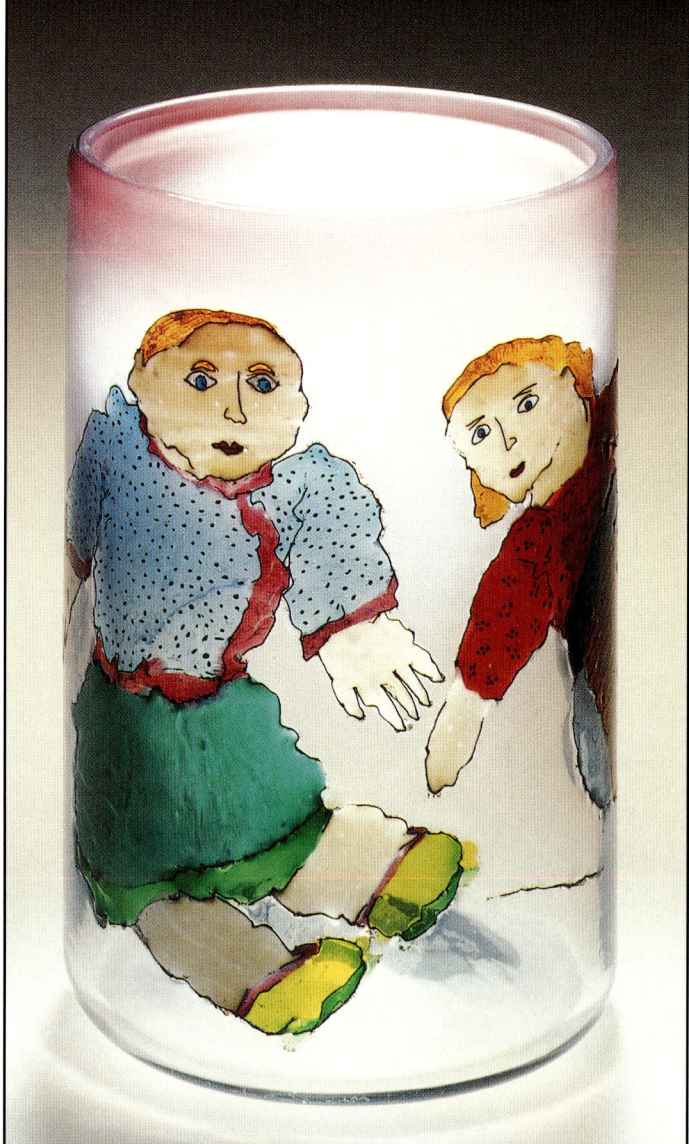

Flora Mace and Joey Kirkpatrick, 1983, *Wishing Well*, 14" x 7", photo: Robert Vinnage. *Photograph courtesy of the artist.*

The Seventies 59

Since the early 1970s Zynsky has enthusiastically explored and experimented with the possibilities of glass in all forms—molten, cold, blown, slumped, cast, shattered, and pushed to the limits of its own and her own creative potential.

Toots Zynski, *Infra red and video series, hot glass/cold plate,* 1973, part of a series of video sound time-release constructions done at RISD with Buster Simpson. Carried on at Pilchuck, the summer of 1973. Photograph courtesy of the artist.

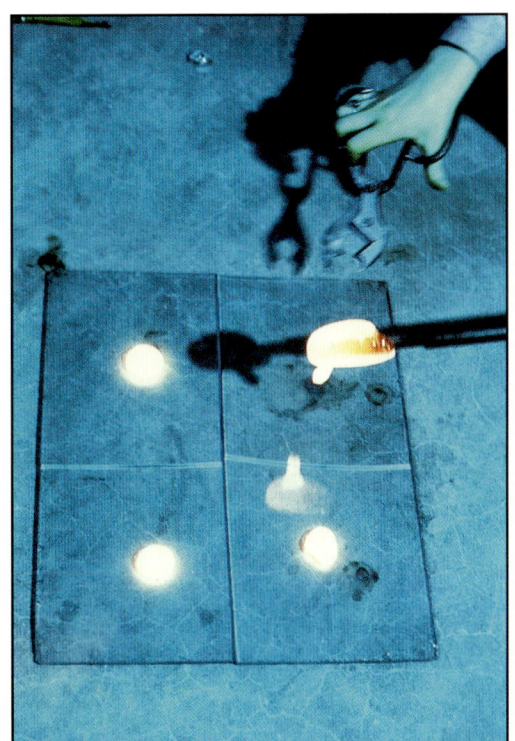
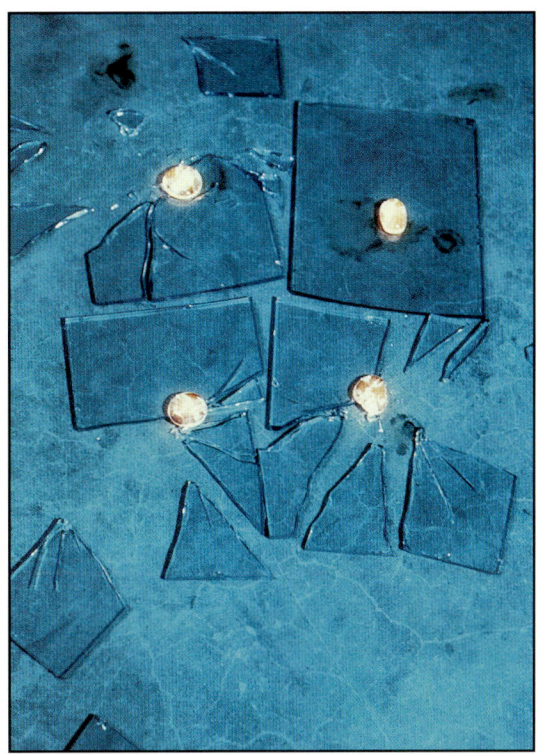
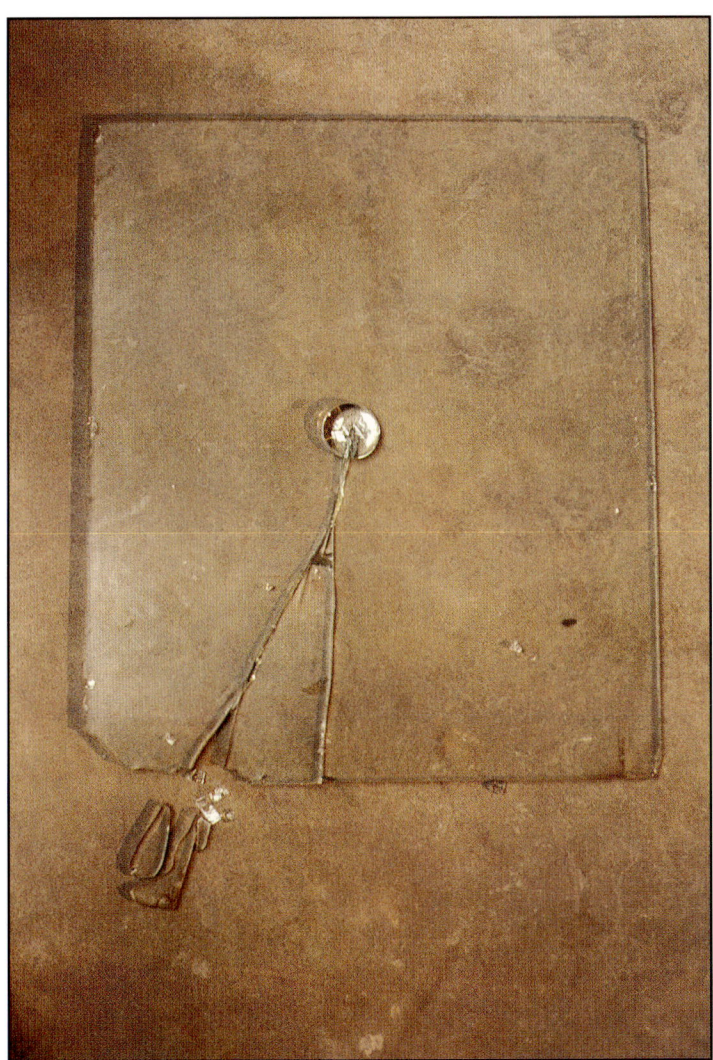
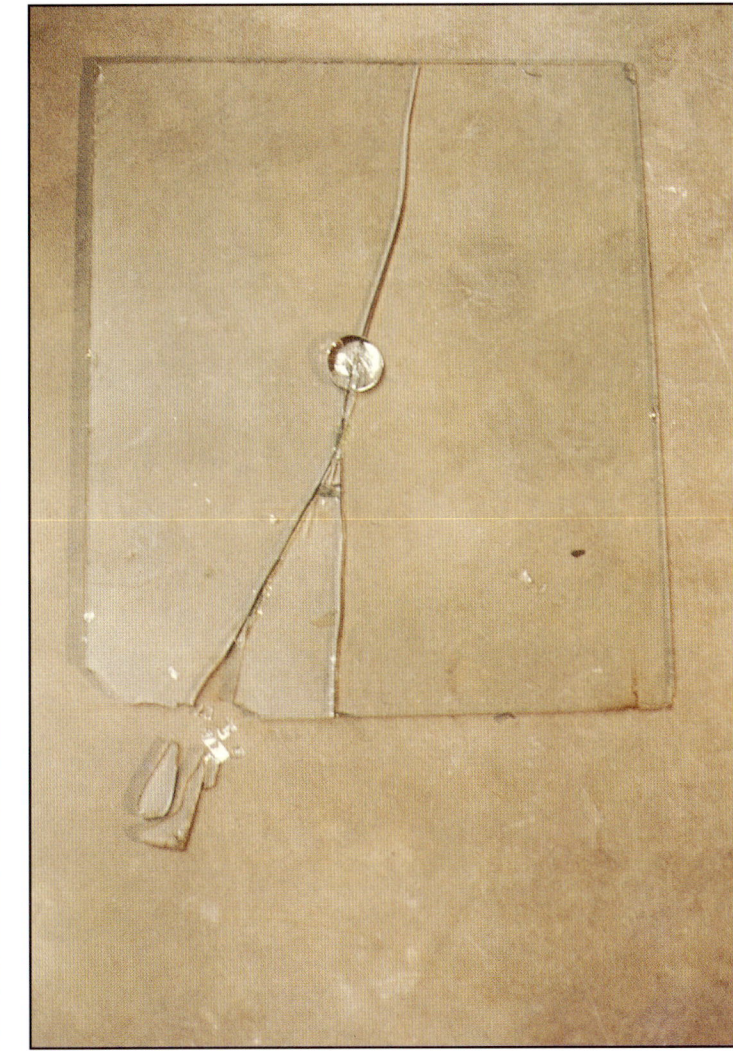

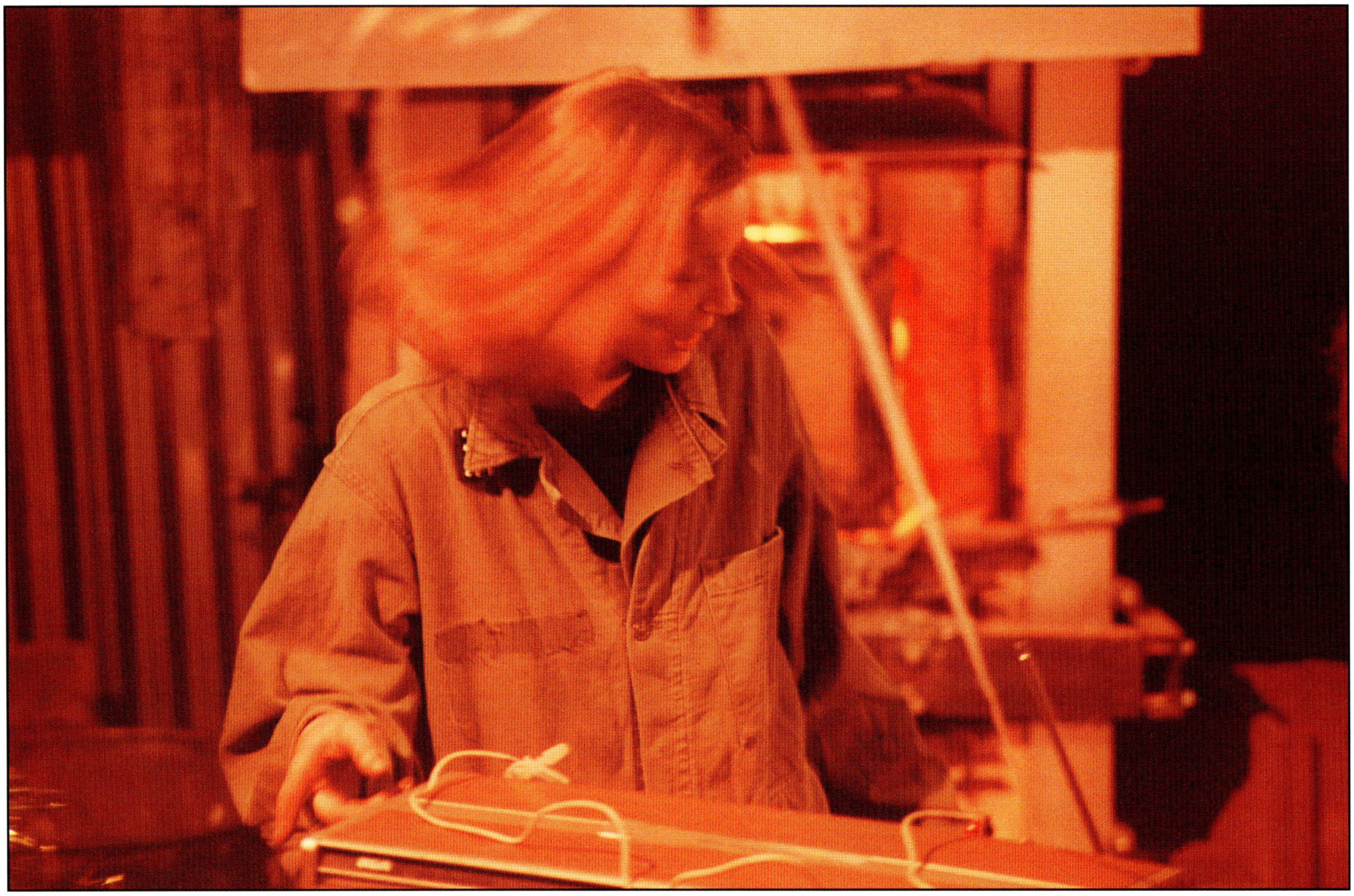

Toots Zynski, *Bound Series #17*, 1979, 12" x 10". Glass and barbed wire. *Photograph courtesy of the artist.*

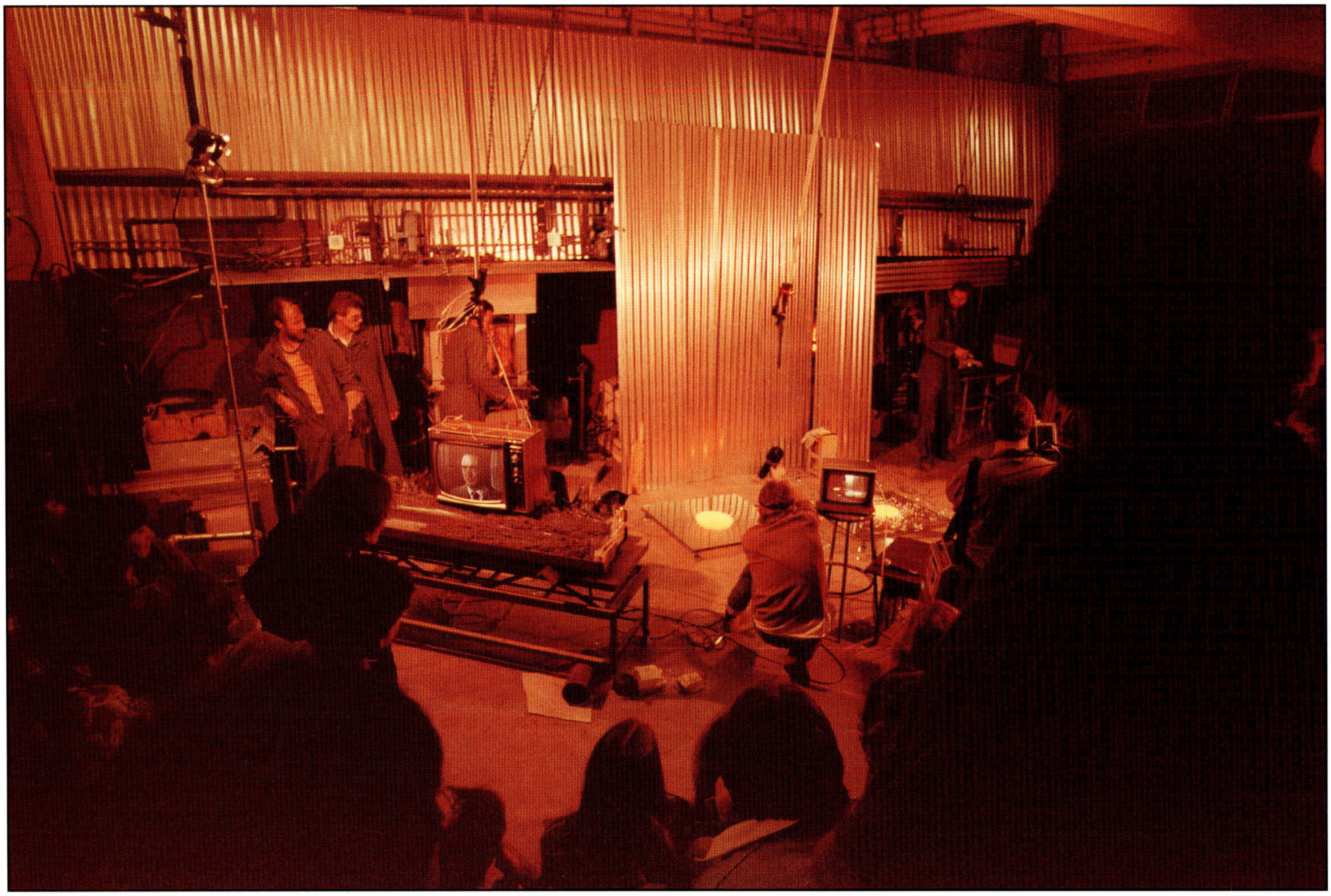

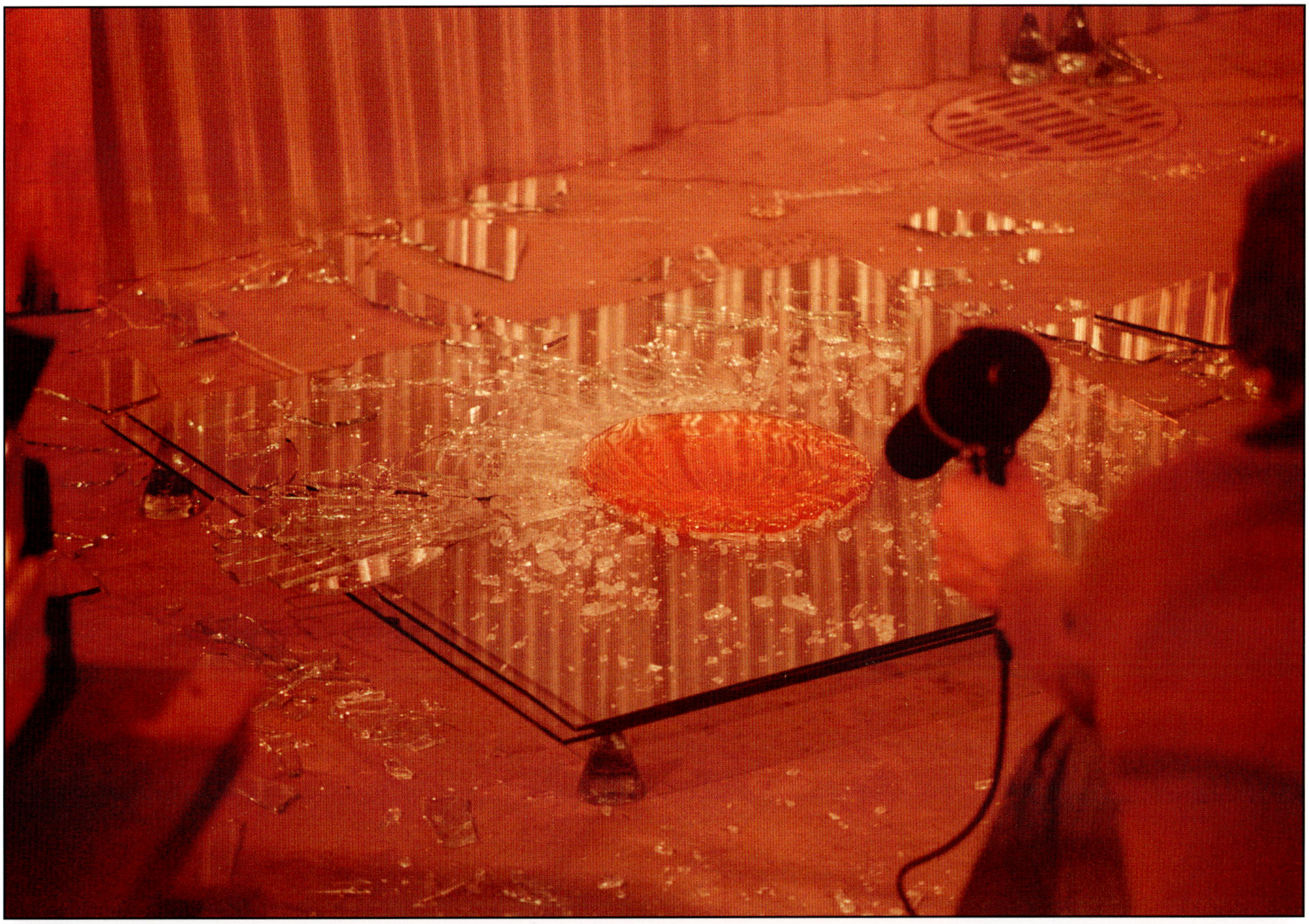

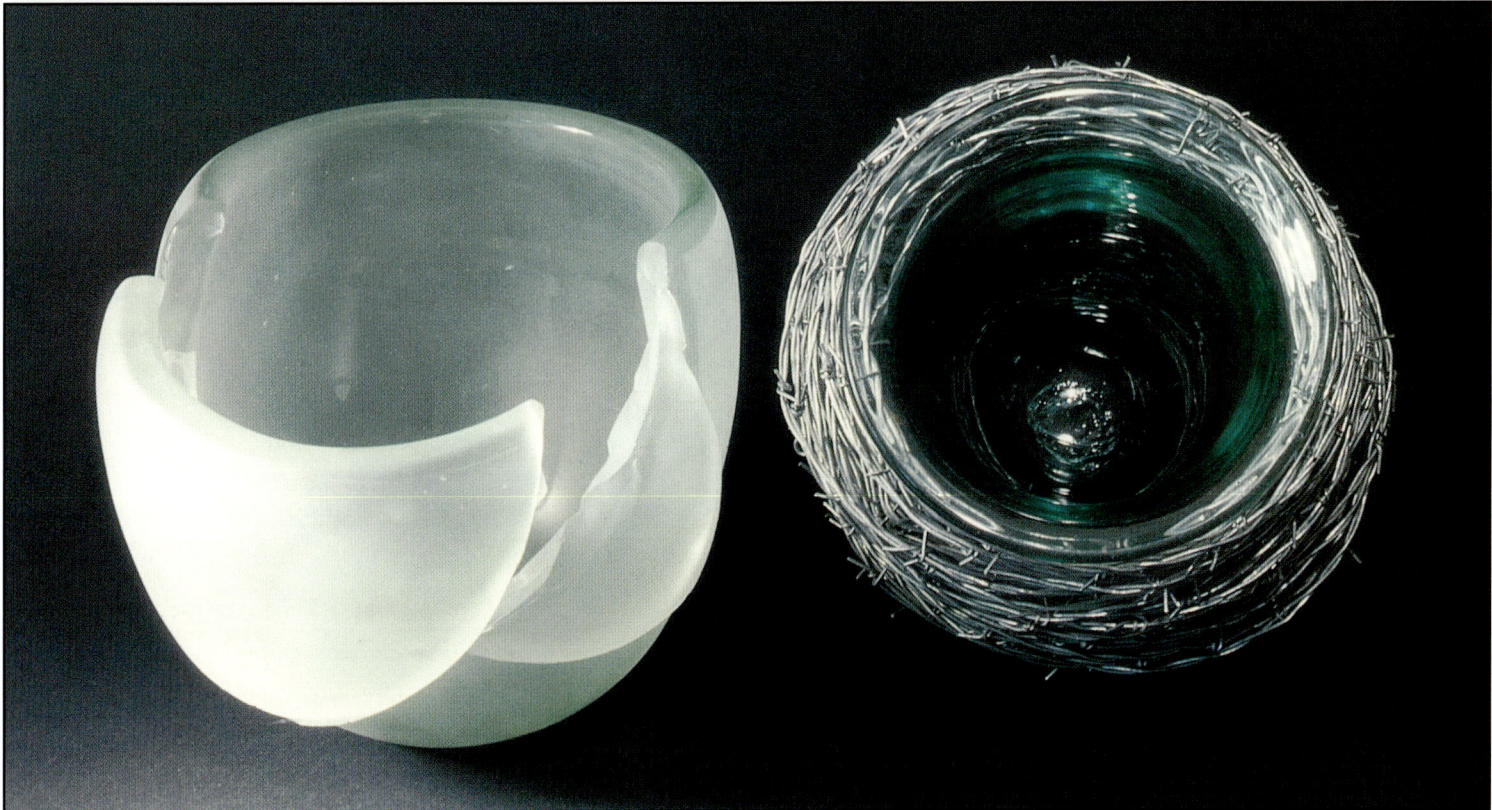

Toots Zynski, part of a series of video sound time-release constructions done with Buster Simpson at the 1981 Seattle Glass Art Society Conference. *Photograph courtesy of the artist.*

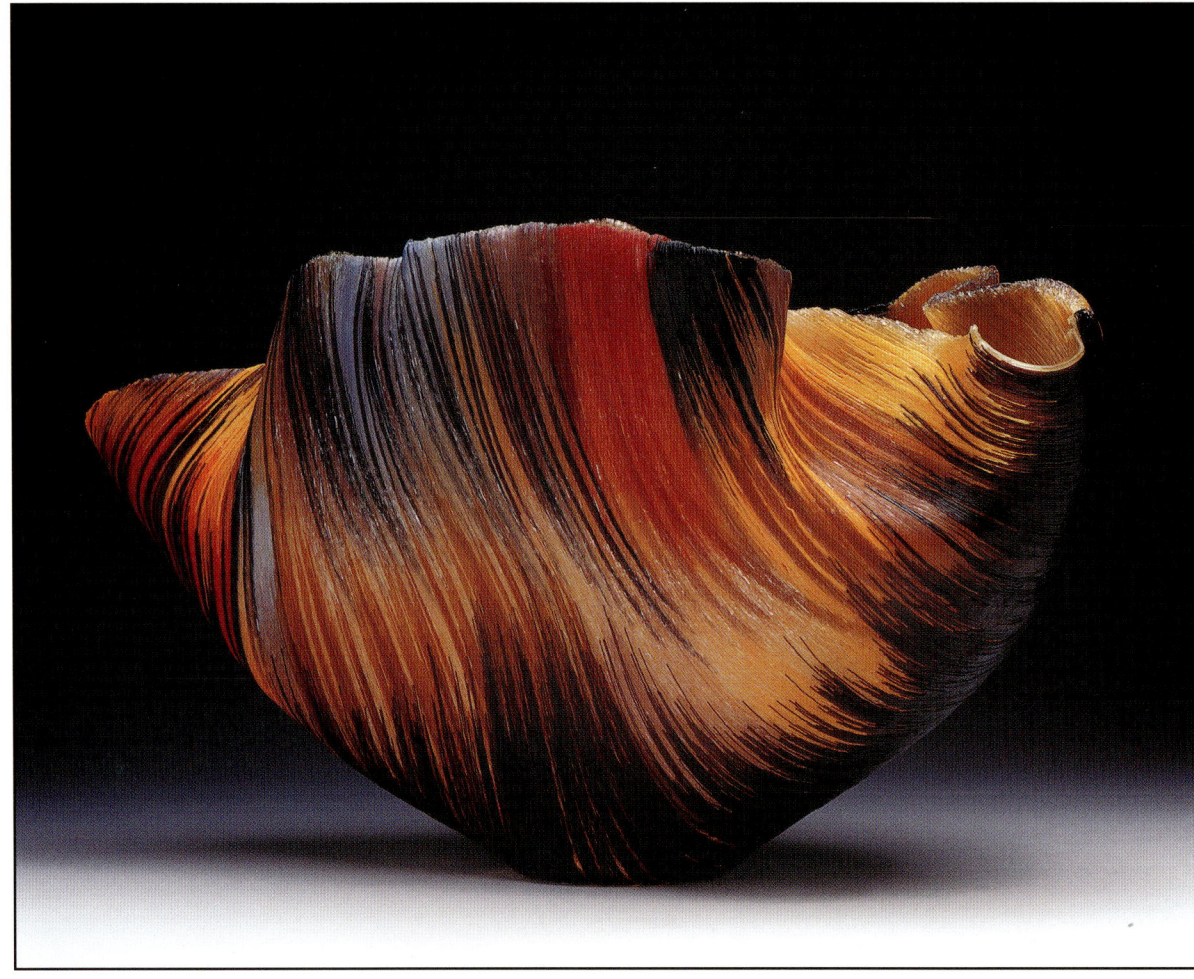

Toots Zynski, Crazy, 2002, 9.5" x 18.5" x 10.5", Filet de verre (fused and thermo-formed color glass threads). *Photograph courtesy of the artist.*

Toots Zynski, Crazy, 2002, detail.

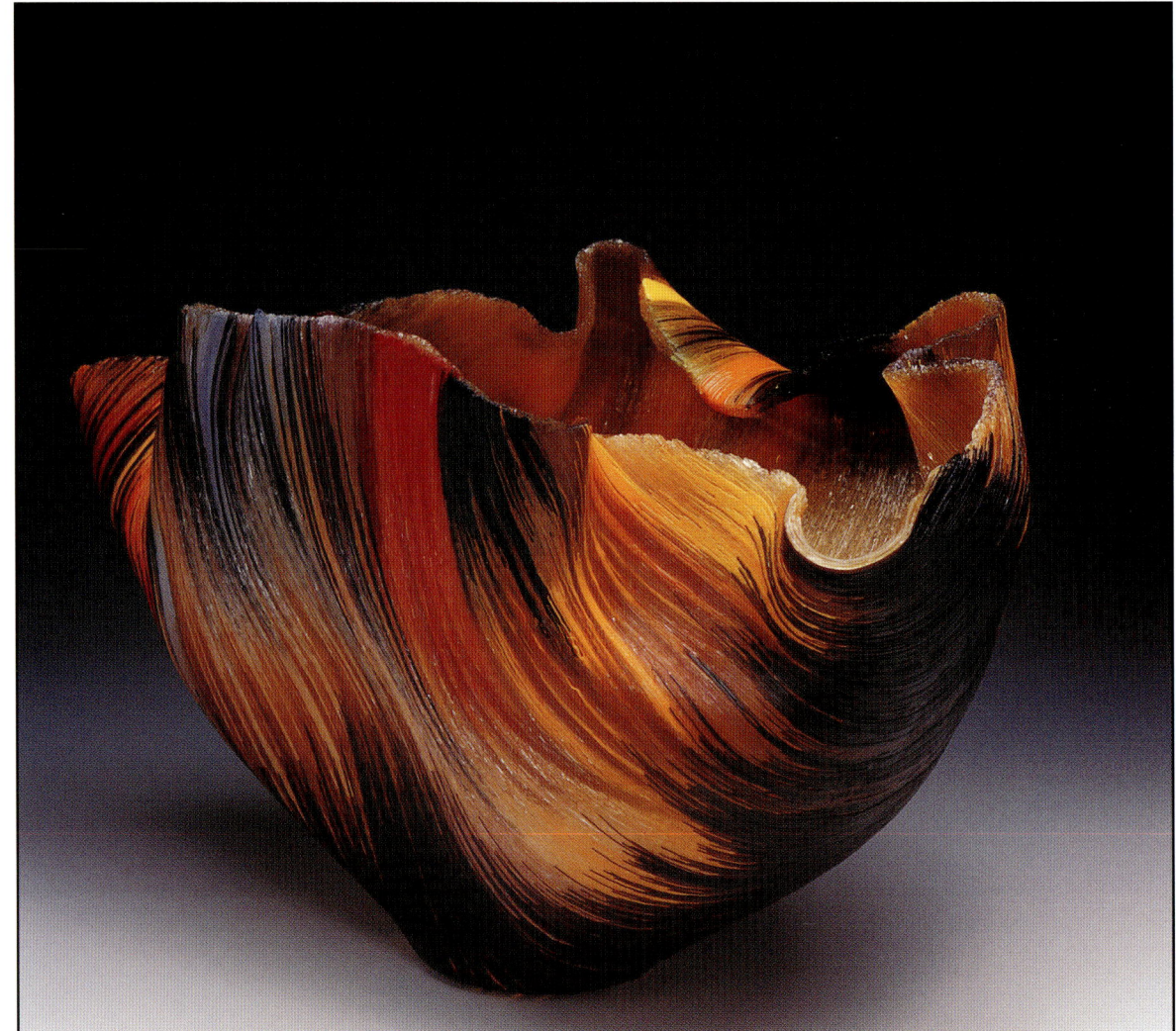

The Glass Art Society was also founded in 1971. A group of glass artists (mostly men) thought it would be a good idea to get together to exchange technical information and have fun. Audrey Handler tells a story from the Society's beginning: "I met Ruth [Tamura] in Toronto at the NCECA conference in 1971. We drove down to the first GAS conference at Penland in Fritz's [Dreisbach] 'Yellow Bus' as we called his van, Ruth and me and Fritz and Michael Taylor and George Thevies and a guy named Bob from Canada. We were stopped at the border coming back into the US and our van was thoroughly searched. The border guard wanted to see Ruth's citizen papers. Ruth responded that Hawaii was a part of the US and she did not need papers."

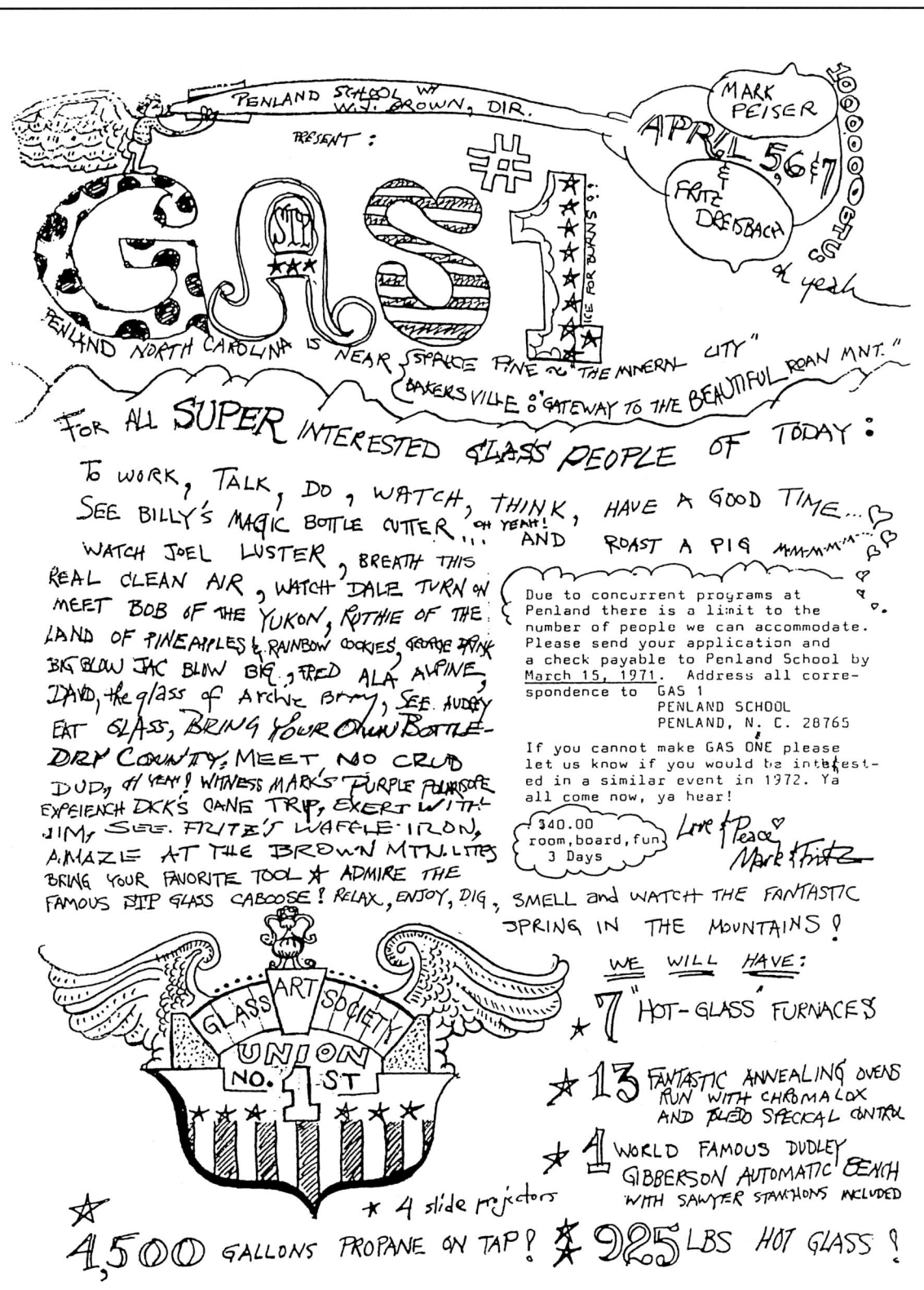

GAS #1 flyer, designed by Fritz Dreisbach and Mark Peiser. Copy courtesy Audrey Handler.

They arrived at Penland, hung out there for a couple of days, blew glass, exchanged information, and decided to do it again the following year. By 1973, when Sylvia Vigiletti joined the group, they had grown to the point of needing organization of information and files. An unofficial tally in 1976 found there were about fifty percent women members. From 1976 to 1984 Sylvia was treasurer and put book keeping in order so that GAS could be eligible for Federal tax-exempt status. Sylvia also had a funny border-crossing story. Years ago, she was coming into the US from Canada with her glass blowing tools. A woman border guard inspecting her car, thinking they might be some sort of weapons, demanded to know what they were and what she was doing with them. In addition to educating the Canadian border guards in its thirty-year history, The Glass Art Society has grown into what is probably the most influential organization of glass professionals in the world. Its journals and newsletters educate thousands of members worldwide; many of them are women.

Glass Art Magazine was founded in 1973 with the January/February issue, to supply information about glass technology and exhibition opportunities to the growing glass art community. Many of the early studio glass artists were involved in writing for the magazine. Ruth Tamura was the editor for blown glass. The December 1973 issue featured an open registry of glass artists. Of the fifty-one entries, twelve were women. The following years' registry was juried; of the 140 entrants, twelve were women. The magazine sponsored an international slide competition titled "Fragile Art '77;" also in 1977 it began publishing a sister publication *Glass Studio* addressed to the glass worker, the artist, craftsperson, student, and the trade.

The Experimental Glass Workshop (now Urban Glass in Brooklyn) also began in the '70s. Its first location was opened in 1977 on Great Jones Street near the New York University's SOHO campus. It was one of the first public access glass studios in the US. Shortly thereafter it moved to Mulberry Street in Little Italy and then in the mid-eighties it moved again to Brooklyn and changed the name to Urban Glass. During the late '70s it published a newspaper titled *New Work*, which covered exhibitions and events for the still young glass art movement. Karen Chambers was a regular writer for the publication and has since gone on to document the development of studio glass in essays and exhibition catalogs. Later, *New Work* became *Glass* magazine and is published now by Urban Glass. Many women established their careers by working and teaching there. In 1980, Toots Zynsky moved to New York and contributed to the founding and development of the second New York Experimental Glass workshop. There she began to further explore and work with hand pulled glass threads, fusing them separately and combining them with blown forms.

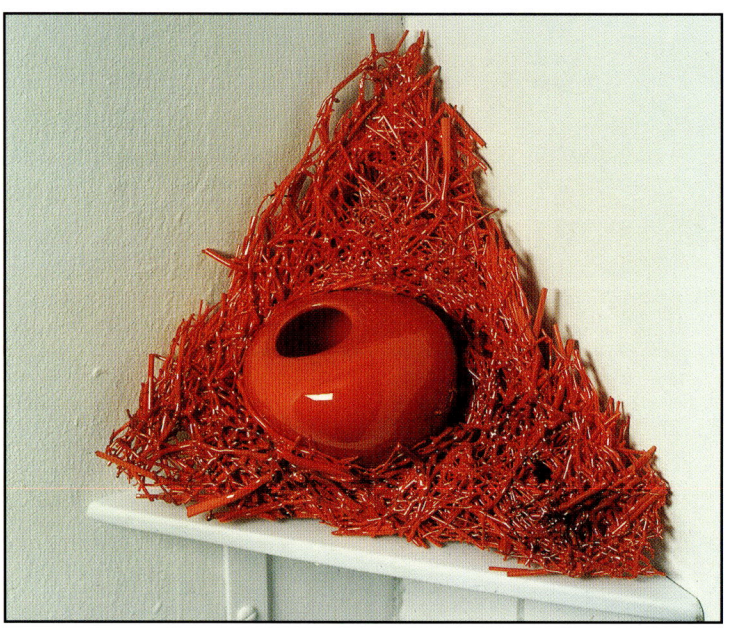

Toots Zynski, *The Guardian*, 1982, blown glass, pulled threads. Photograph courtesy of the artist.

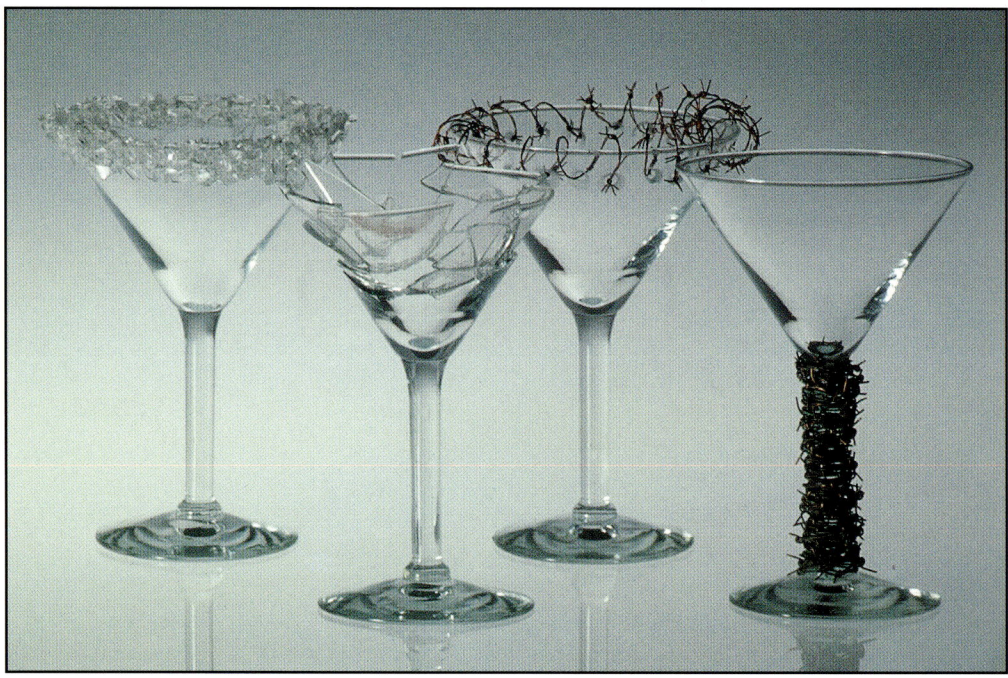

Toots Zynski, *The Coctail Party*, 1981 (made for the late Italo Scanga), Photo: E. Claycomb.

The American Studio Glass Movement influenced many European artists. Rosemarie Lierke, born in Berlin, Germany, began her experience with art by taking classes in painting and enameling at the Werkunstschule, Aachen. During the late 1960s she moved to the United States with her family and took classes with Fritz Dreisbach and Jack Schmidt at The Toledo Museum of Art in 1977 she set up her own lamp-work studio in Germany where she developed her unique craquelè technique. The process was difficult and time consuming; however, it produced glasses which look delicate and fragile, but which are in reality strengthened technically. In recent years Rosemarie Lierke has turned her attention to the study of ancient glass techniques. She discovered that certain ancient glasses were made on a turning wheel, a process she calls "Ancient Glass Pottery."

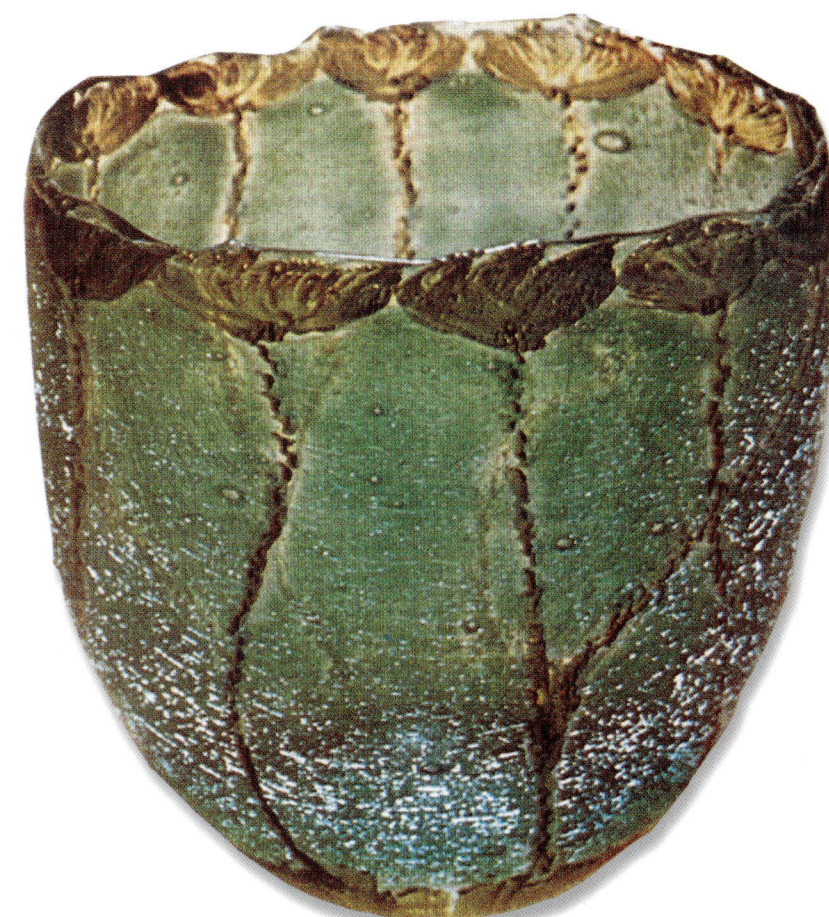

Rosemarie Lierke, *Maigelein*, 1983, 10.2 cm x 5.8 cm, craquele glass. *Photograph courtesy of the artist.*

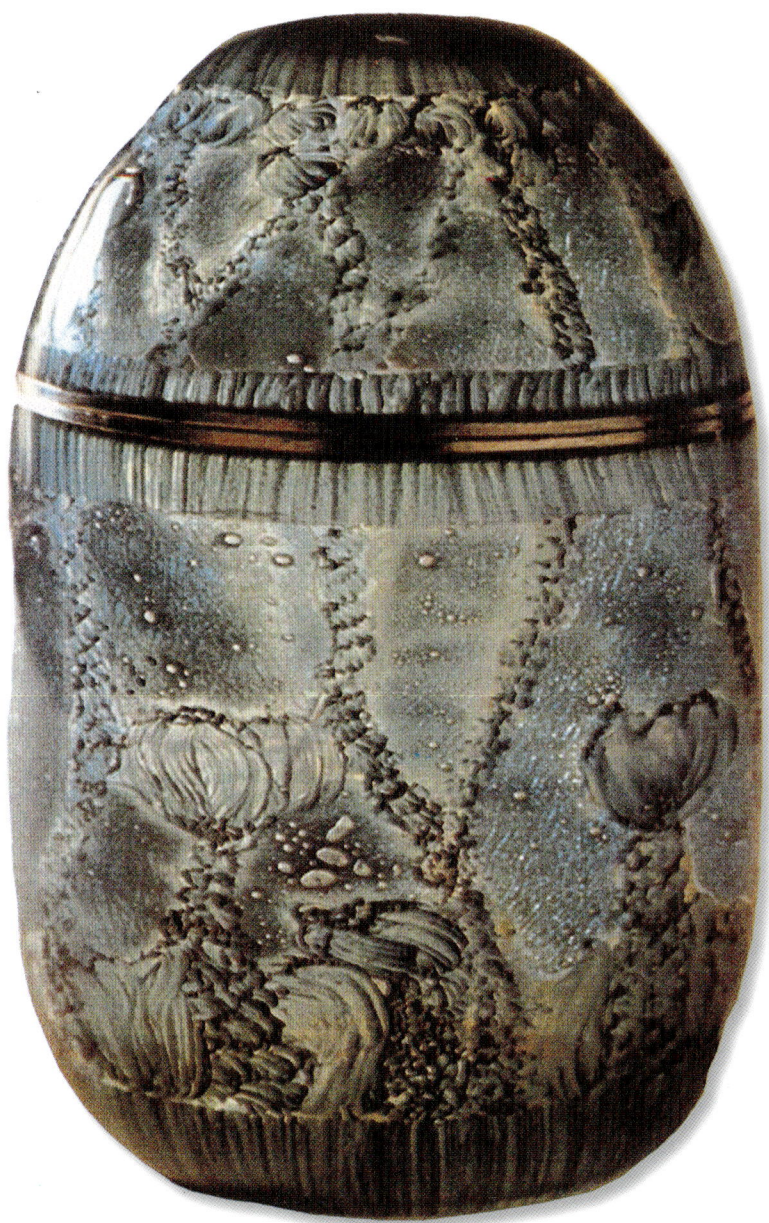

Rosemarie Lierke, *Dose*, 1982, 9 cm, craquele glass. *Photograph courtesy of the artist.*

66 The Seventies

Before the 1970s, objects made from glass were often sold at Craft Fairs and specialty gift shops. A few galleries opened during this innovative decade just to exhibit glass art, including Heller Gallery, formerly Contemporary Art Glass Group, established by Douglas and Michael Heller in New York and Habatat Gallery in Michigan, by Ferdinand Hampson and Linda Boone. Fine craft galleries also began showing studio glass.

Prior to that, the sixties and seventies crafts revival brought back an interest in stained glass. Stained glass windows have been used to illuminate and educate in castles and cathedrals since the Middle Ages. Historically, women had been painting and staining glass, some women in the sixteenth through the nineteenth centuries had even executed and leaded panels for windows. Cappy Thompson carries on the medieval tradition of painting glass today. Modern manufacturing practices for colored sheet glass and the copper foil method of assembly devised by Tiffany has brought about a renaissance of interest for women. Many warm and hot glass artists began by doing stained glass, but very few women stayed with it and grew to compete on an architectural scale. Harriet Hyams has been executing commercial and residential stained glass windows since the early 1970s. Penelope Comfort Starr began her training in stained glass in 1959 and executed many public and private commissions. Gradually, by the mid-1980s, her interest grew more three-dimensional and she began laminating plate glass to build structures. Elizabeth Mears began her career as a stained glass artist and moved on to become a successful lamp worker in the 1990s.

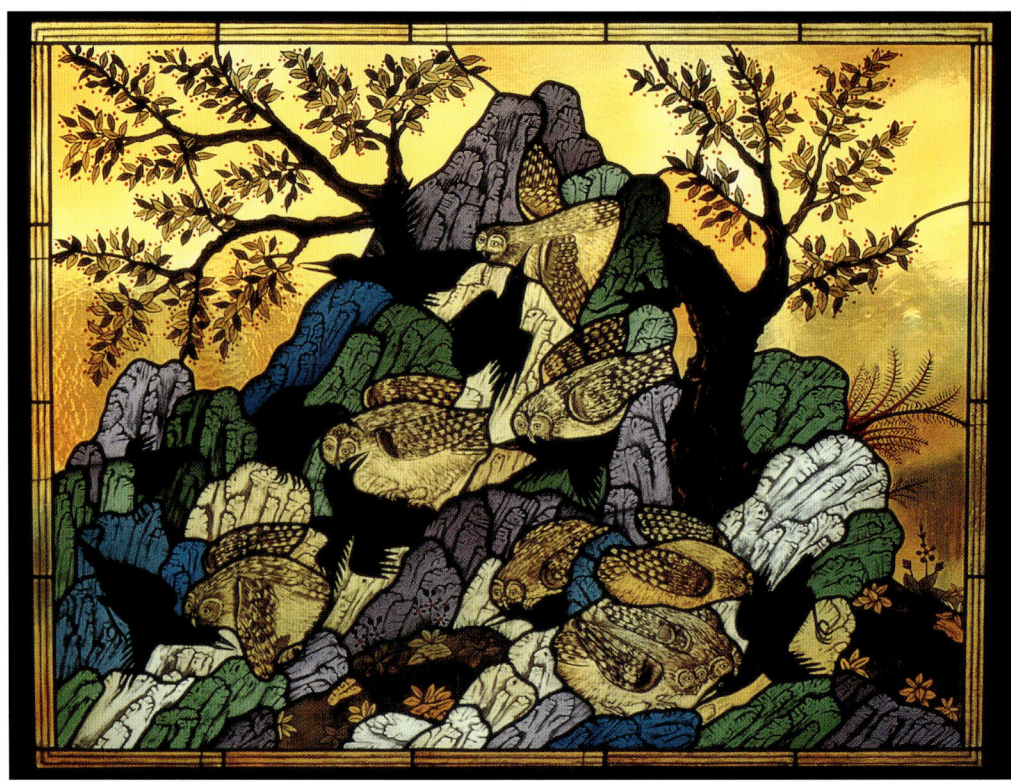

Cappy Thompson, *The Battle of the Crows and the Owls*, 1979, 46" x 61", painted stained glass. Photo: Jeremy Bigwood. *Photograph courtesy of the artist.*

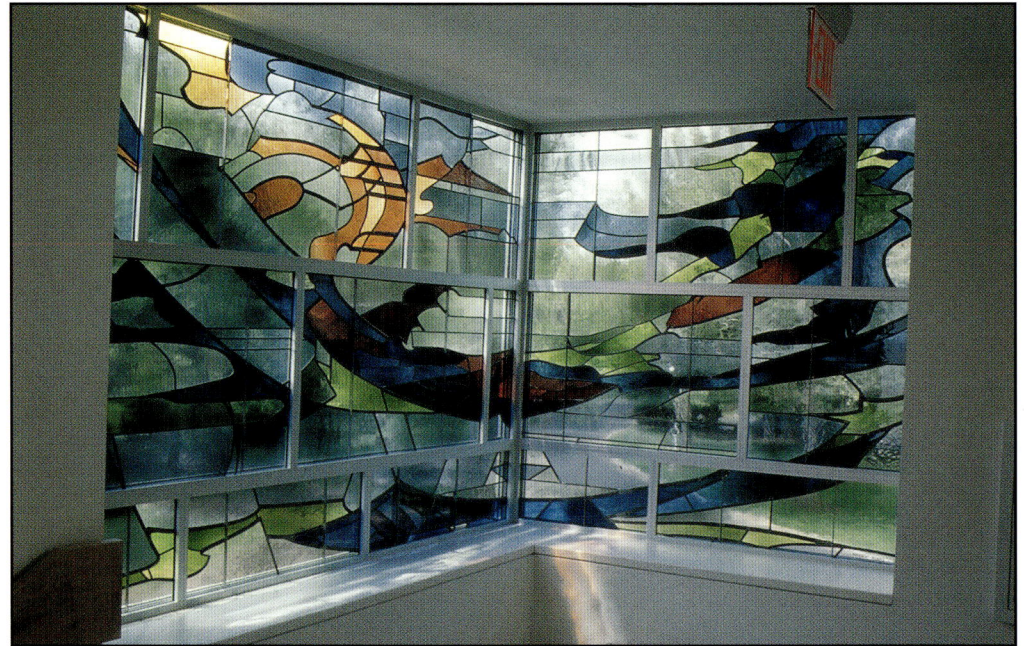

Harriet Hyams, *Resurrection Windows*, 2001, 6' x 9' and 6' x 6', stained glass, Dominion Chapel, Our Lady of the Rosary, Sparkill, New York. *Photograph courtesy of the artist.*

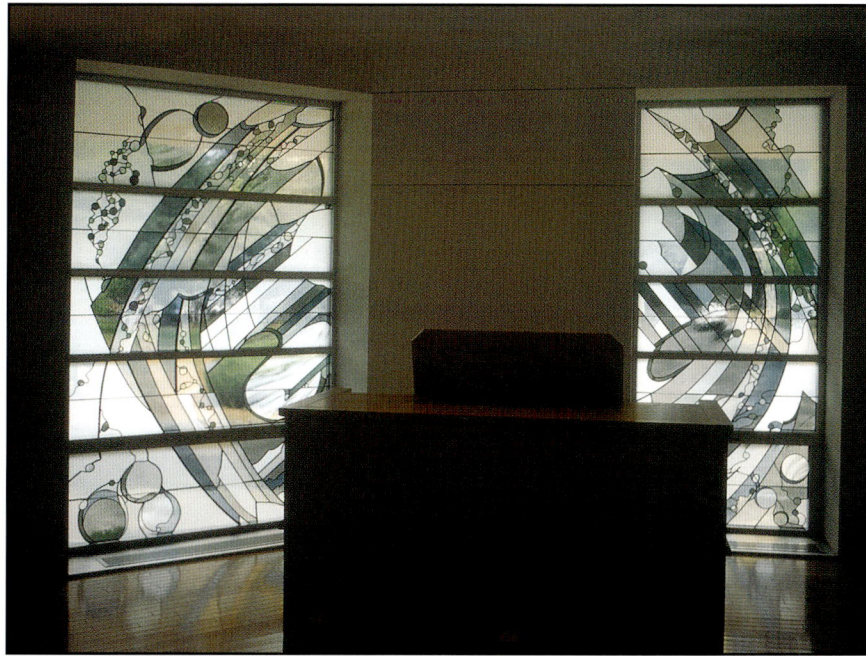

Harriet Hyams, *Choir Windows*, 2001, 9' x 6' and 9' x 4', stained glass, Dominion Chapel, Our Lady of the Rosary, Sparkill, New York. *Photograph courtesy of the artist.*

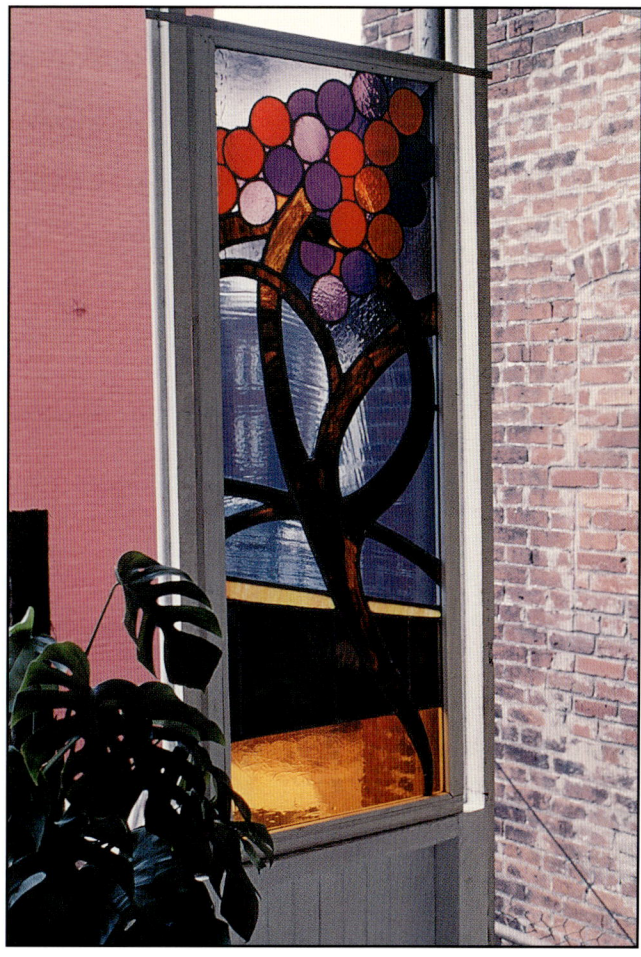

Penelope Comfort Starr, *Magic Grapes*, 1967, 60" x 24", leaded glass, private residence, Washington, DC, photo: *House Beautiful*. *Photo courtesy of the artist.*

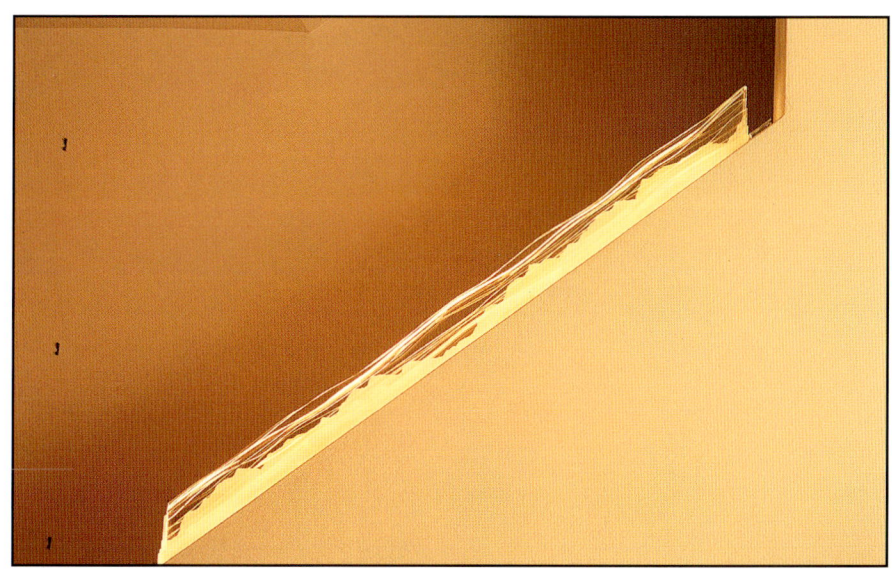

Penelope Comfort Starr, *Stairway Sculpture*, 1991, 4" x 4" x 48" plate glass set into a box balustrade, internally lit, private residence, San Francisco. *Photo courtesy of the artist.*

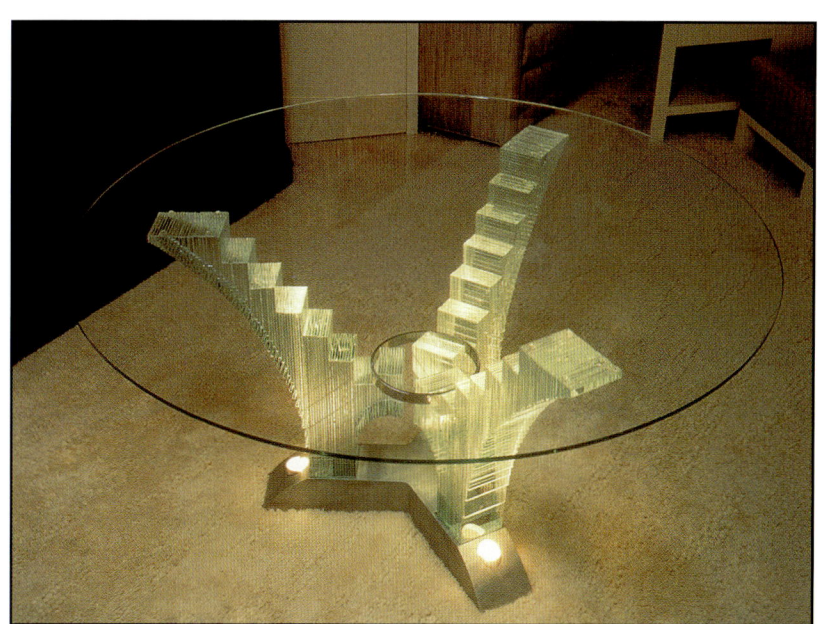

Penelope Comfort Starr, *Dining Table*, 2000, 29" x 54" d, plate glass, lighting, metal. *Photo courtesy of the artist.*

68 The Seventies

Penelope Comfort Starr, *Dining Table*, detail.

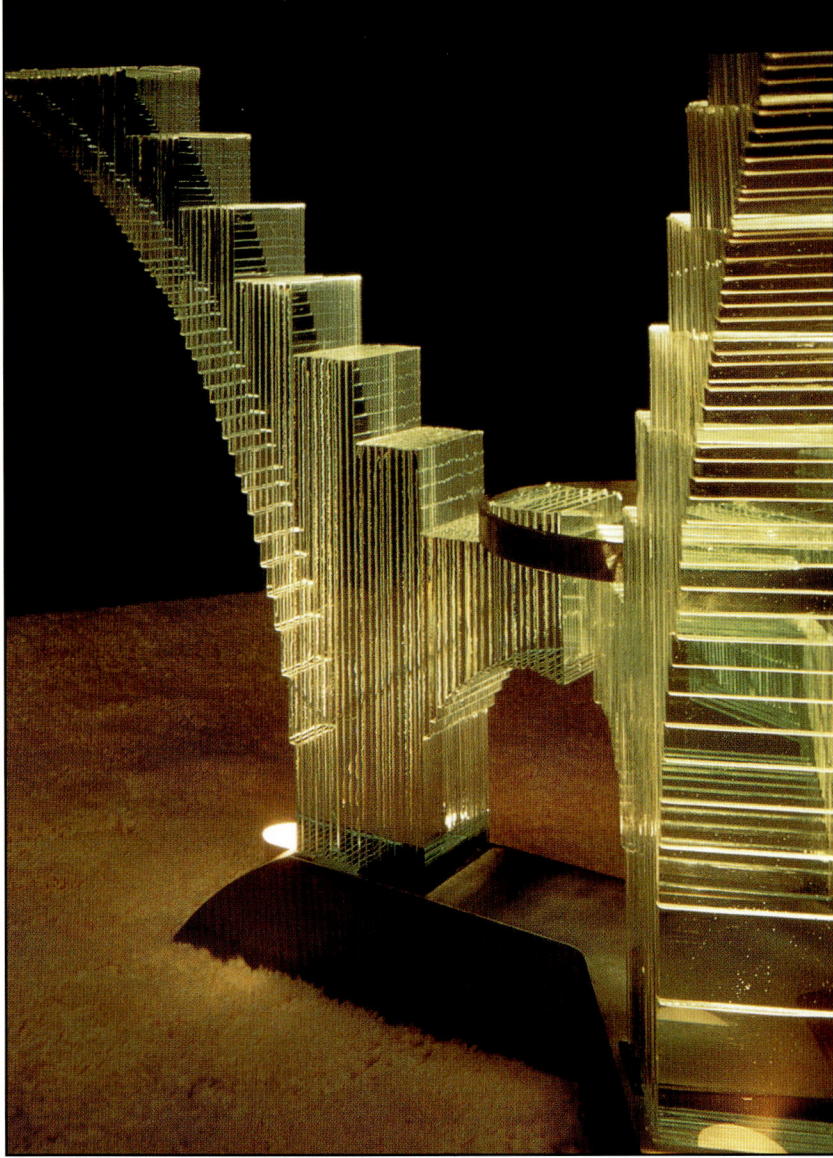

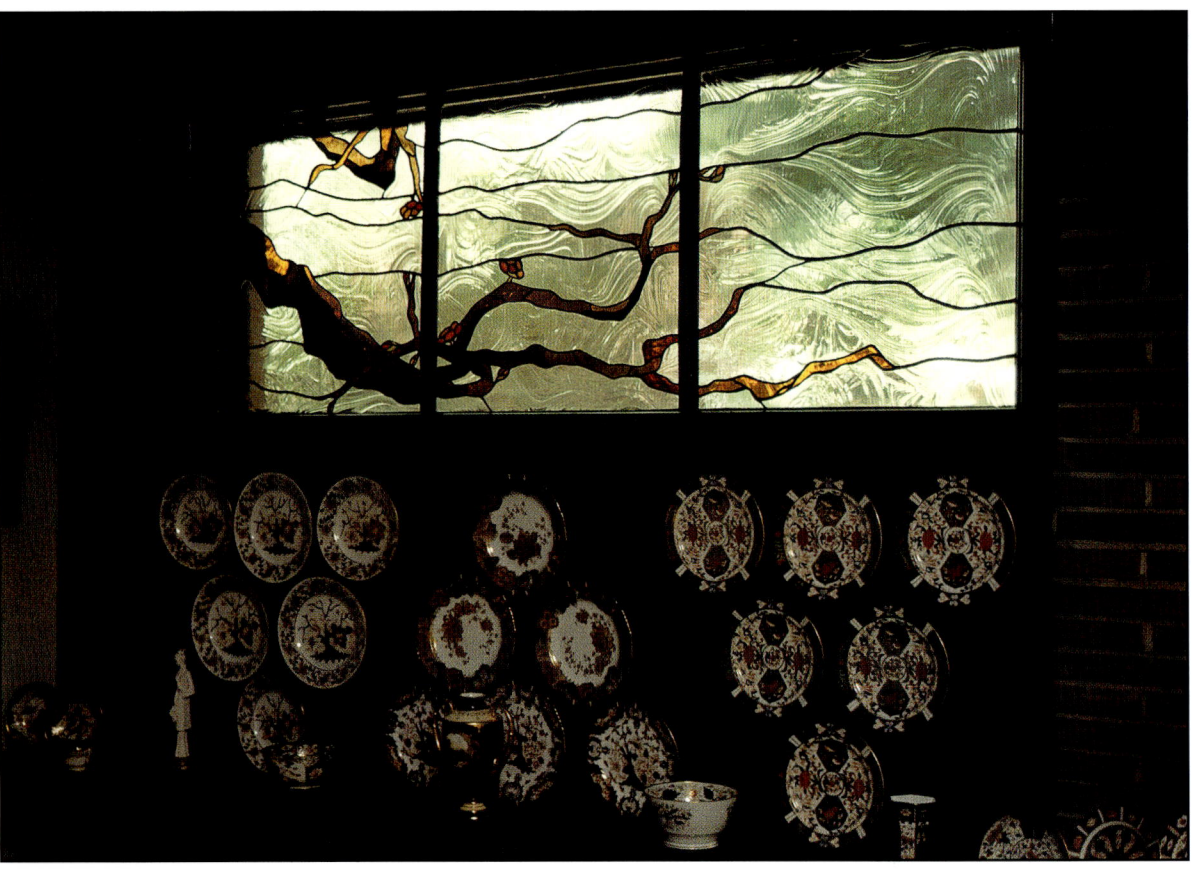

Elizabeth Ryland Mears, *Oriental Limb*, 1984, 36" h x 108", dining room of Kerschner home. *Photo courtesy of the artist.*

By the middle seventies a small number of artists were beginning to look at industrial window glass as a material to make their art. Nancy Mee began using industrial glass when, as a picture framer, she became fascinated by the ever-changing shapes and color of the glass as it piled up in the scrap bin under the glass cutter. Originally a painter and printmaker, she combined her printmaking process with the industrial glass to make sculpture.

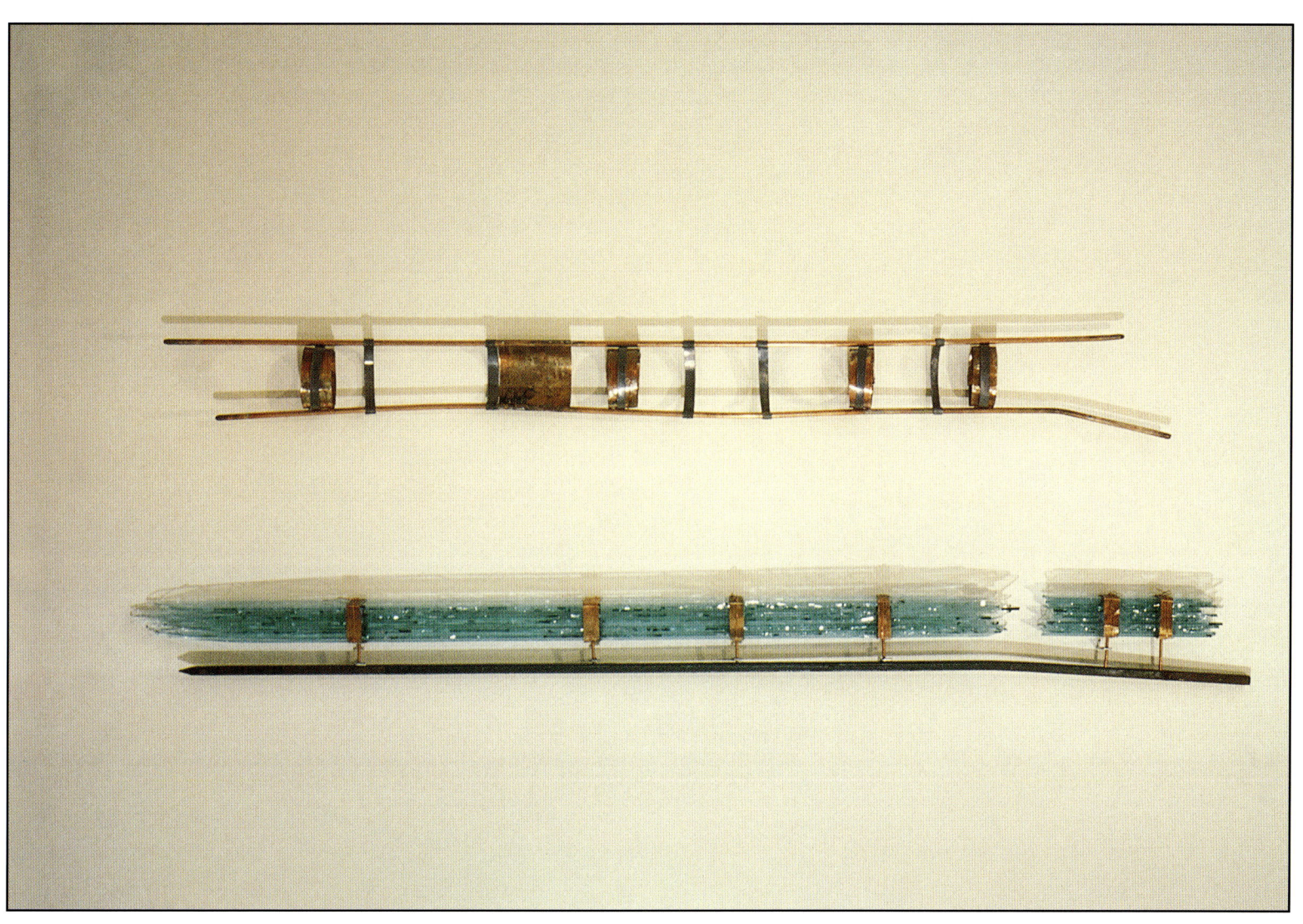

Nancy Mee, *Support*, 1979, 32" x 94" x 7", glass and metal. *Photo courtesy of the artist.*

Mary Shaffer began her artistic life as a painter looking at plate glass as though it were a canvas. It didn't take long for her to become interested in the post minimal concept of process. She discovered she could work with the material in a kiln. She began to heat and manipulate the molten glass into sculptural forms, often combining a metal or wire framework.

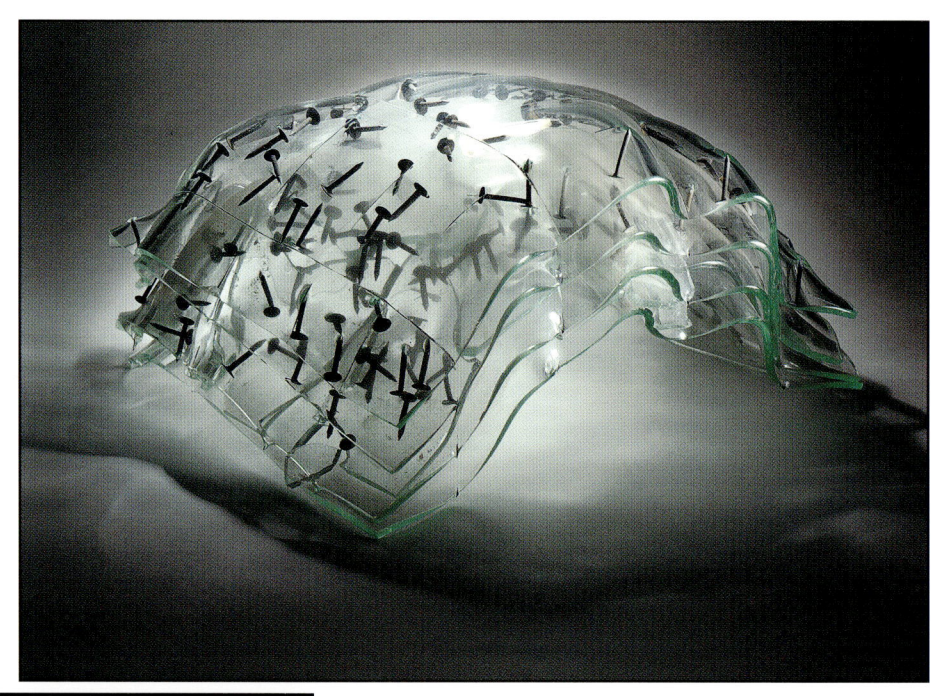

Mary Shaffer, *Nail Pillow*, 1974, 16" x 16" x 10", glass and metal. *Photo courtesy of the artist.*

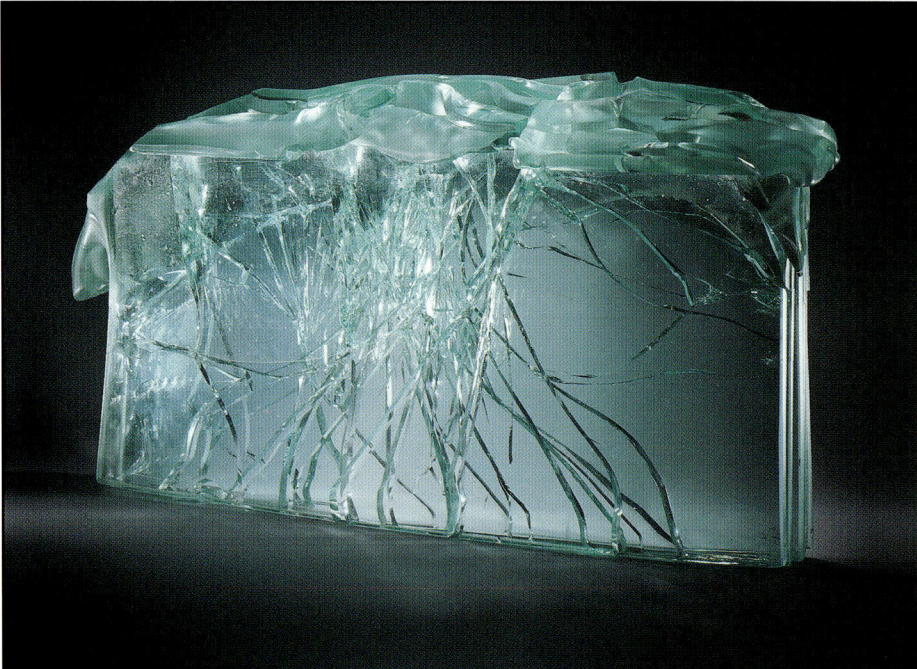

Mary Shaffer, *Elephant Breakage #32*, 11" x 22" x 6", slumped glass. *Photo courtesy of the artist.*

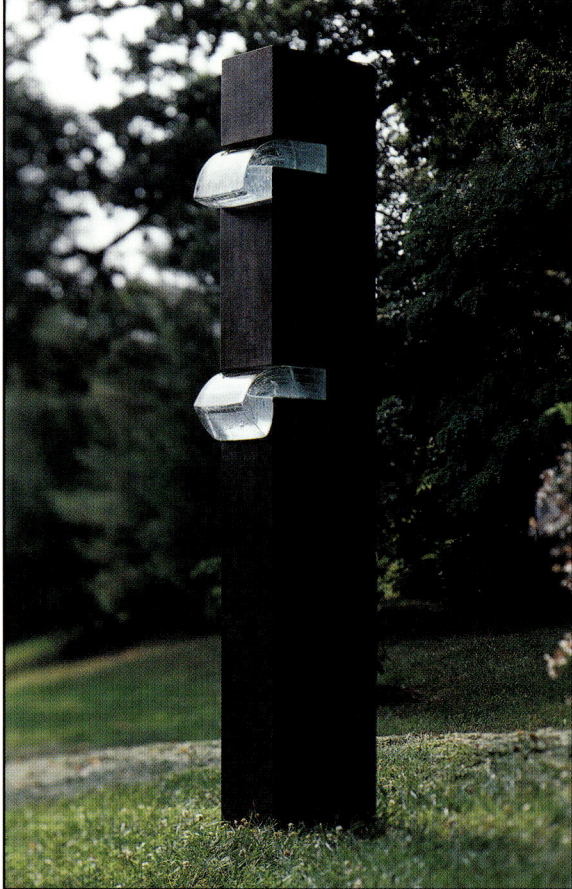

Mary Shaffer, *Mamoure*, 1993, 80" x 10" x 15", bronze and glass. *Photo courtesy of the artist.*

Suzanne Harris was a multi-talented artist who's work ranged from performance art through temporary installations in many materials including glass. She made a large solar measuring device at ArtPark, a summer art colony along the Niagara River in New York State in 1974 and a large earthwork in Battery Park in 1976. Harris considered glass to be stone, much like the ancients did.

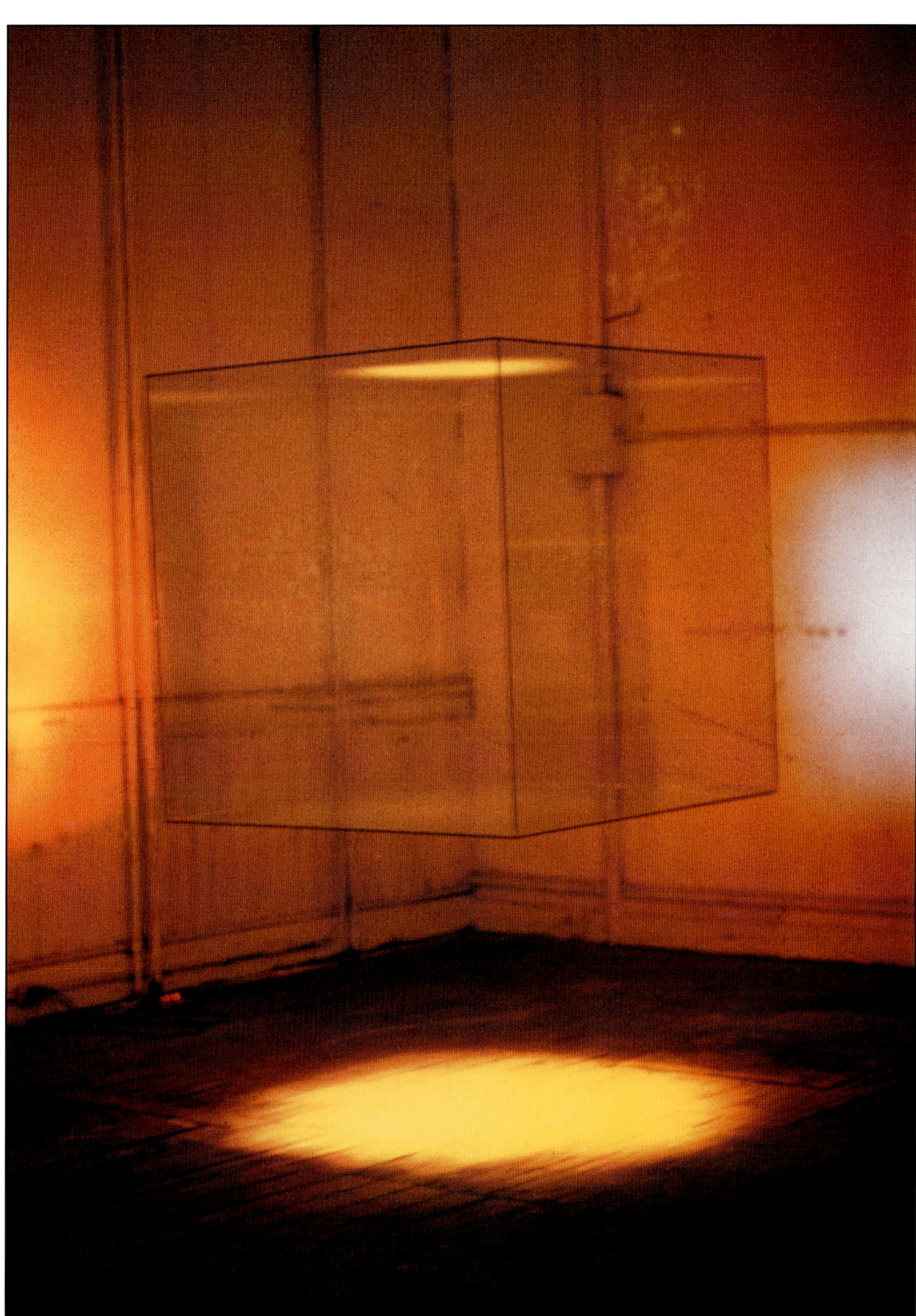

Suzanne Harris, *One for the Won*, 1974, reconstructed in 1998 at Lance Fung Gallery, New York, by Gene Highstein. A plate glass cube hung four feet above the floor. The glass was lit on three sides, by red, yellow, and green bulbs; producing a projected white light. *Photograph courtesy Lance Fung Gallery and Gene Highstein.*

I consider glass, as a material, to be stone. It has a similarity of formative elements, causality, density, strength and weight, with one important special characteristic – transparency. I usually use it in sheet form in the context of the body of my work as follows: (1) Structurally – to build whole forms where transparency is an important factor in perceiving volume and relationship. (2) Cut to a specific size and shape and place (indoors or outdoors) where it acts as a marker for the most prevalent physical relationship of that space. (3) More recently, considering its likeness to stone, I have been experimenting with a casting formula I made up into chunks of very soft glass to carve.

Another statement quoted out of context from a letter Harris wrote in 1976:

Materials speak a language of their own. They must be experimented with in order to make new references between form and the material in which it is made.[6]

Suzanne Harris's life was cut short in 1979. Were she to have continued with her experiments and successfully cast her stones to carve, one wonders what she might have accomplished. Casting as a medium for forming glass at that time was little known to her, so the experiments she was conducting could have proved interesting.

An interest in industrial glass was also growing in Europe. Jutta Cuny Franz, an Austrian sculptor, developed a process to deep carve thick industrial glass plate with the nozzle of a sand blaster.

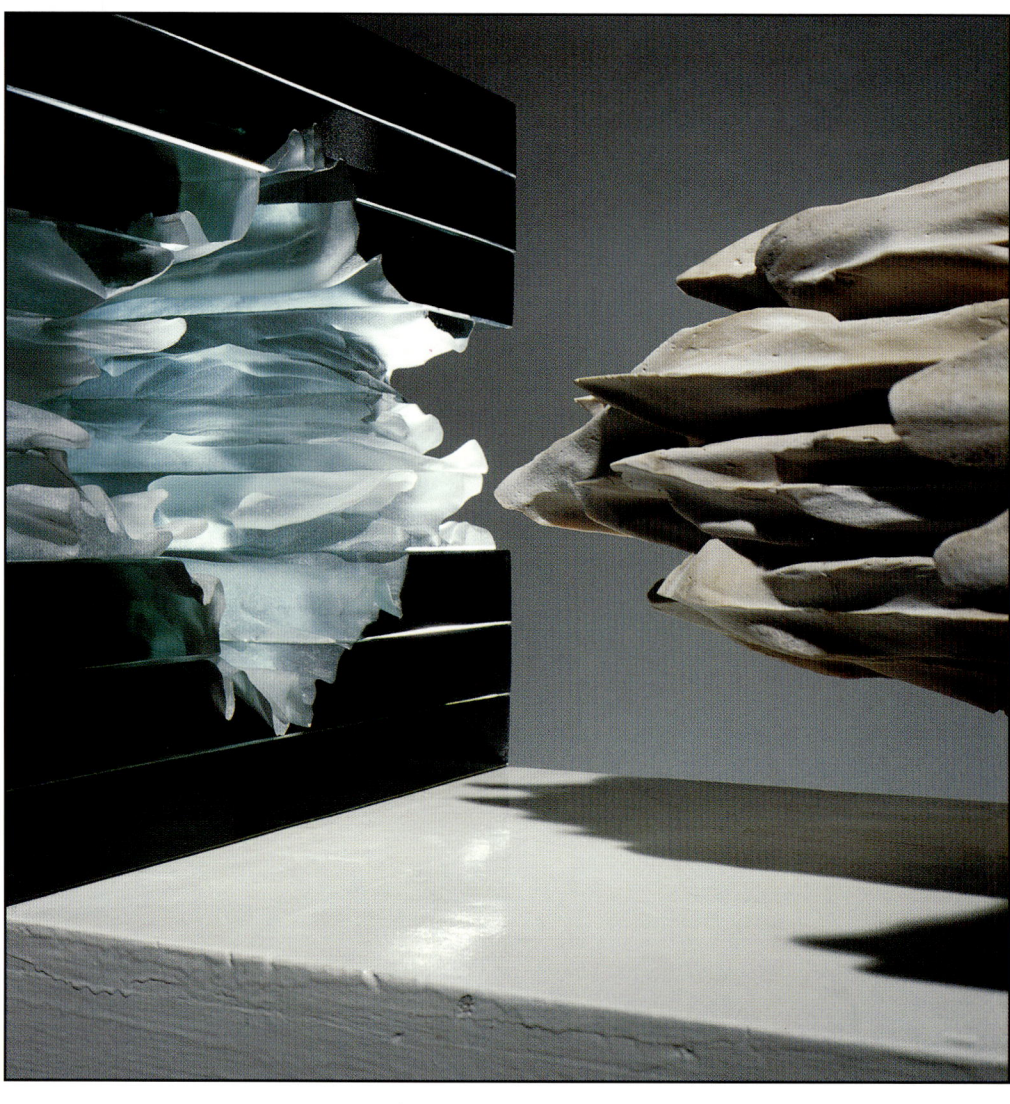

Jutta Cuny, *Grand Affrontment-Penetration*, 1979, 40 cm x 40 cm x 40 cm, glass and polyester resin, photo: Enrico Cattaneo. Photograph courtesy Jutta Cuny-Franz Foundation.

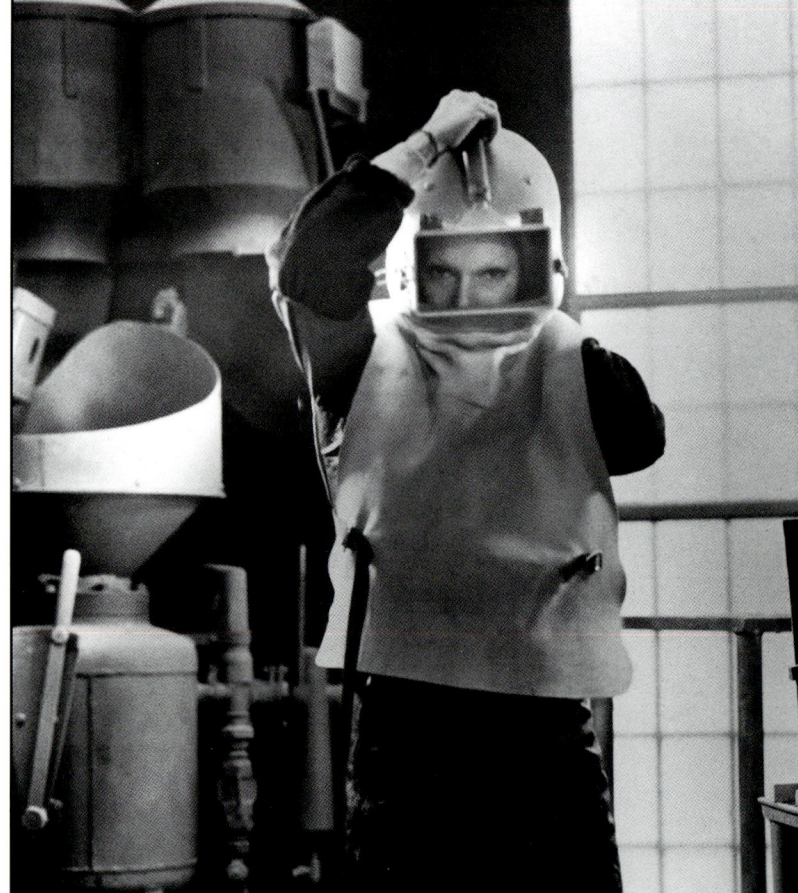

Jutta Cuny, sand blast suit, photo: Enrico Cattaneo. Photograph courtesy Jutta Cuny-Franz Foundation.

"I have since the beginning used the nozzle as a real sculptor's tool, that allows me to shape a precise form on the surface as well as into the depth of the glass, depending on the inclination of the nozzle. The shapes that resulted from this work were extremely natural and organic, a sort of erosion similar to that observed in nature and obtained in this specific case in the studio, by accelerating the process."[7]

My own work began in the mid-seventies with a desire to use glass to cast with like I was using bronze. Not knowing anything about glass at all was both a blessing and an obstacle. I started by using the metal casting techniques I was familiar with to make molds for casting hot glass. Thus began a thirty-year odyssey experimenting with ways to use glass to make my art. Since glass is such a seductive and addictive material, each small success led me deeper and deeper into its grip until I was so ensnared I couldn't retreat. Along the way I learned a lot and made a lot of work. In my travels I learned to use enamels printed on window glass. I also learned how to blow glass, to use a torch to lamp-work, to build equipment, and to grind and polish glass; however, my original intention was to cast glass by using molds to shape my forms, which I still employ today. In that technique I am self-taught. There were few teachers in the seventies and cast glass was not of interest to anyone. It seems hard to believe today because casting is now quite popular.

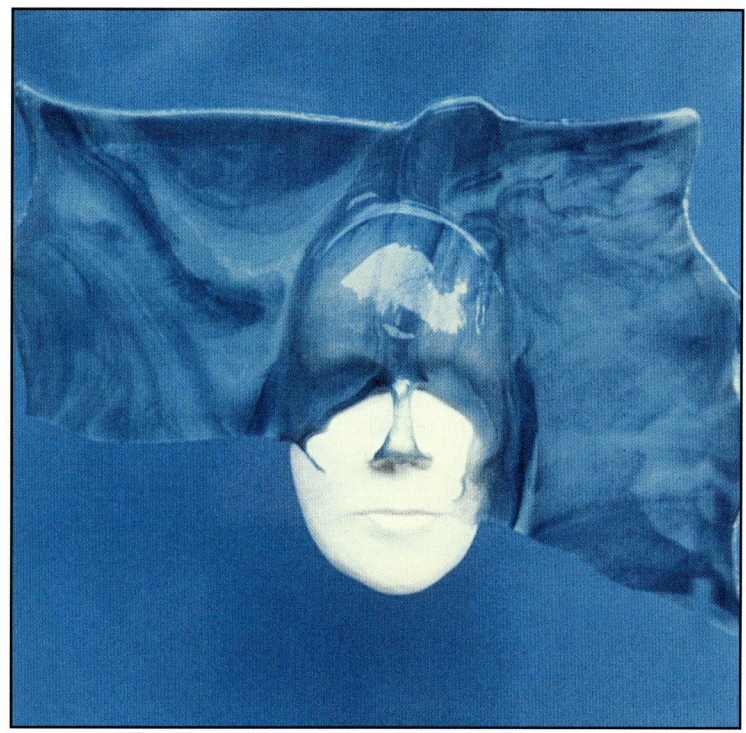

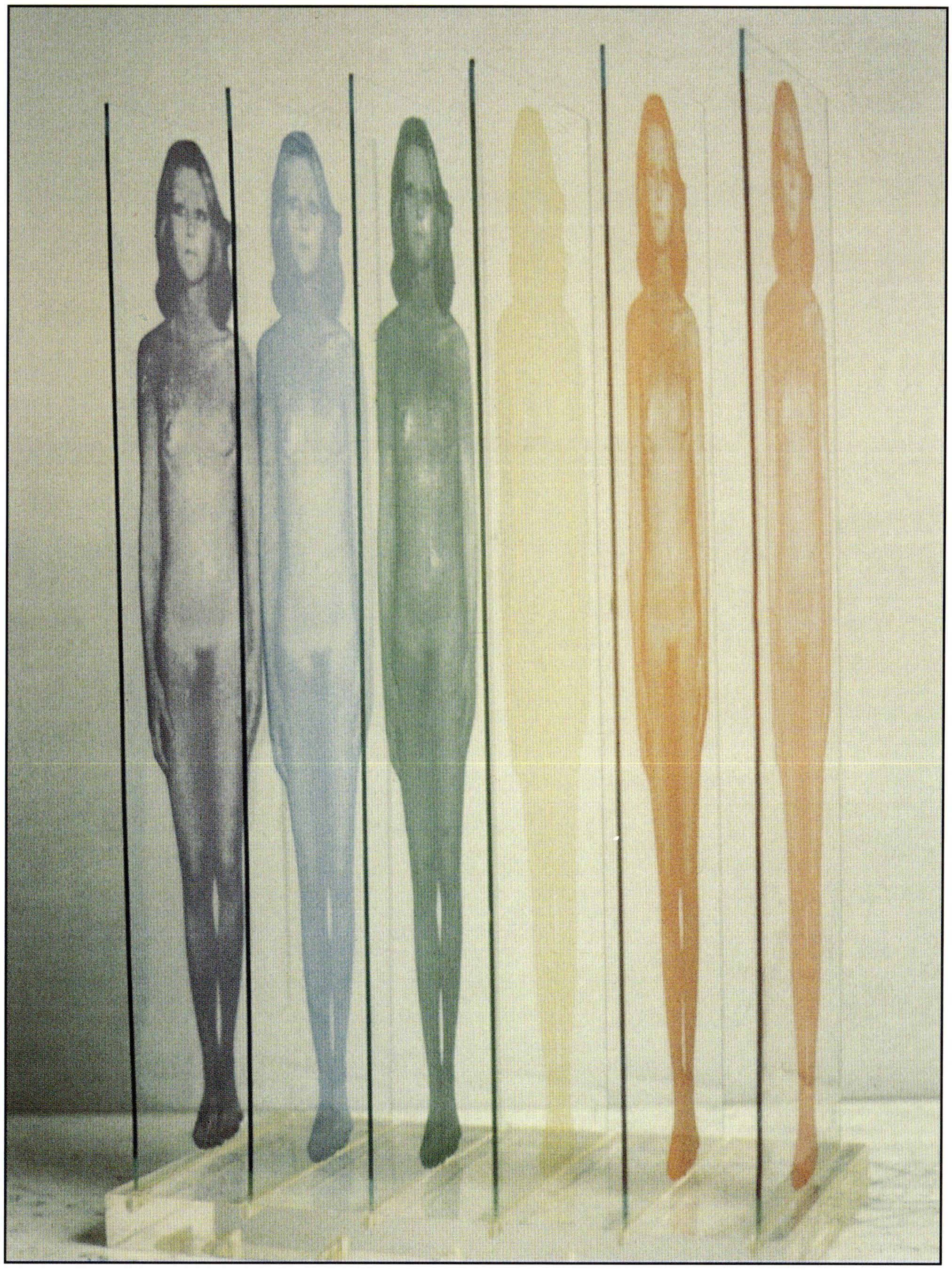

Lucartha Kohler, *Mask*, 1979, 24" x 18", cast glass, fused and slumped overlay mounted on sheet glass. *Photograph courtesy of the artist.*

Lucartha Kohler, *Colors of Consciousness*, 1977, 20" x 12" x 6", photo silk-screen with fired enamels on glass, assembled in Plexiglas base. *Collection Corning Museum of Glass. Photograph courtesy of the artist.*

Lucartha Kohler, *Archangels from Harmony's Realm of Light*, 1990, range from 4' h x 7.5' h, installation 6" x 4' x 8', cast, fused, and slumped glass, assembled. *Photograph courtesy of the artist.*

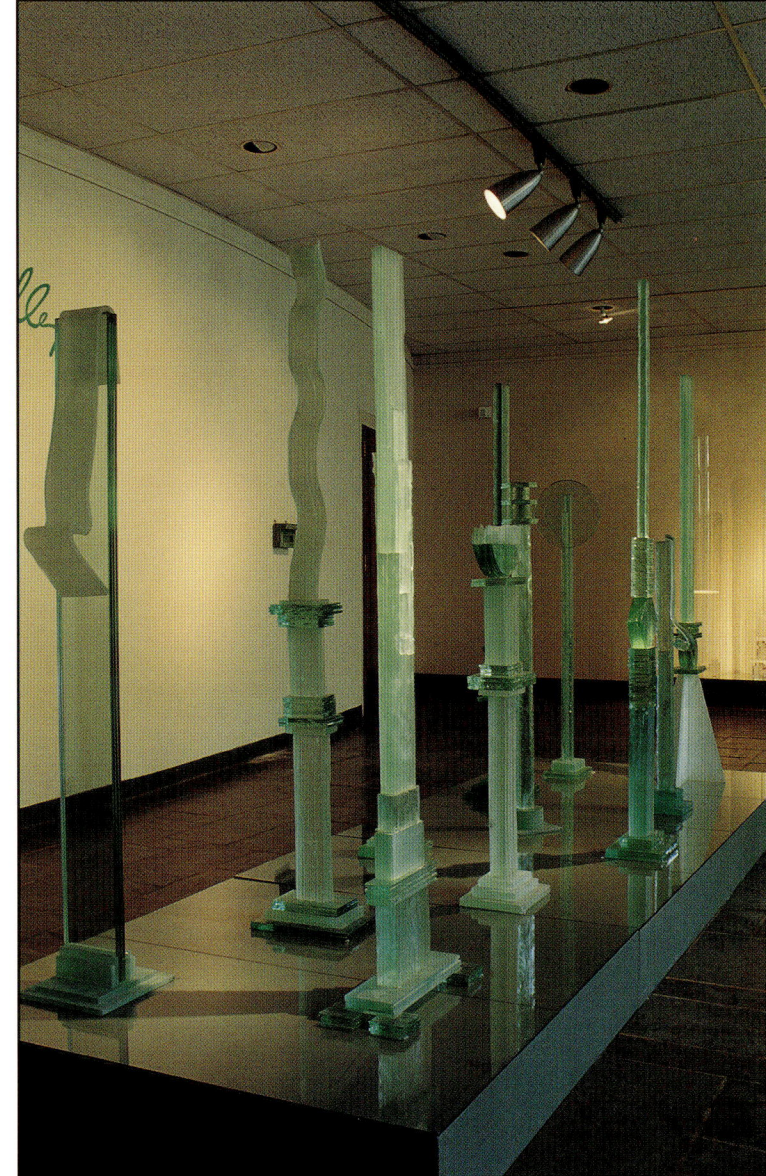

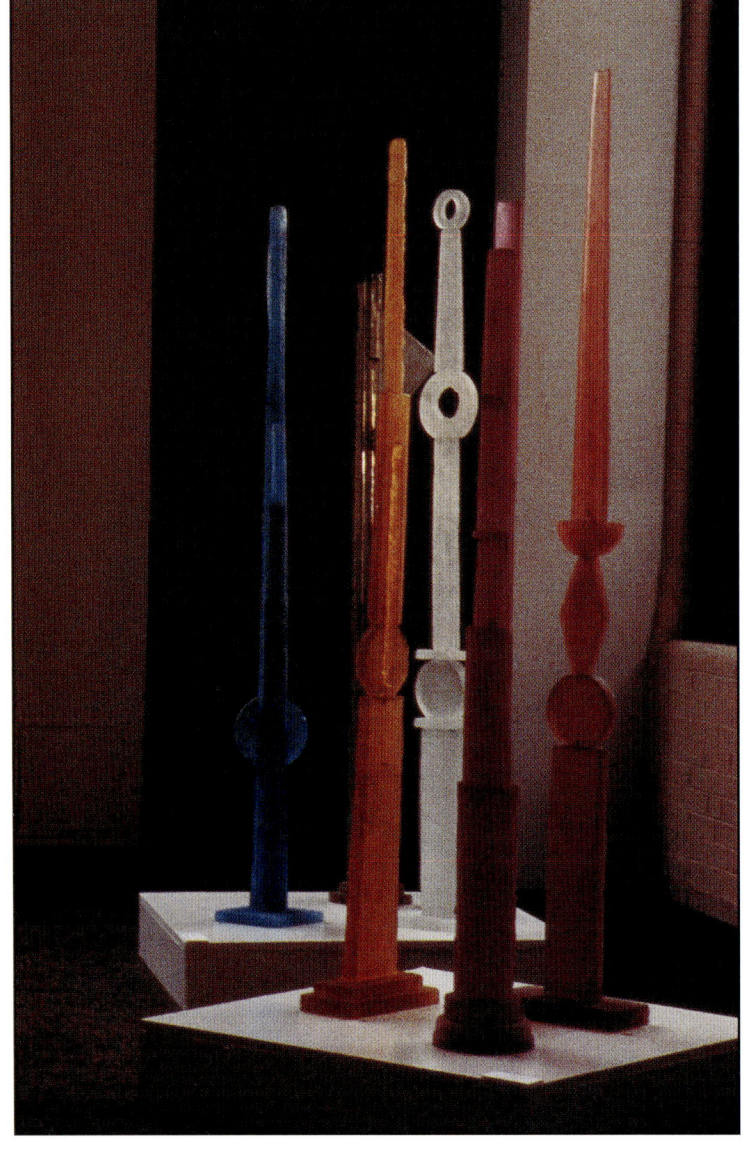

Lucartha Kohler, *Primary Totems*, 1995-97, range from 4' h x 7.5' h, cast, fused, and slumped glass. *Photograph courtesy of the artist.*

The Artists

Cristine Barney

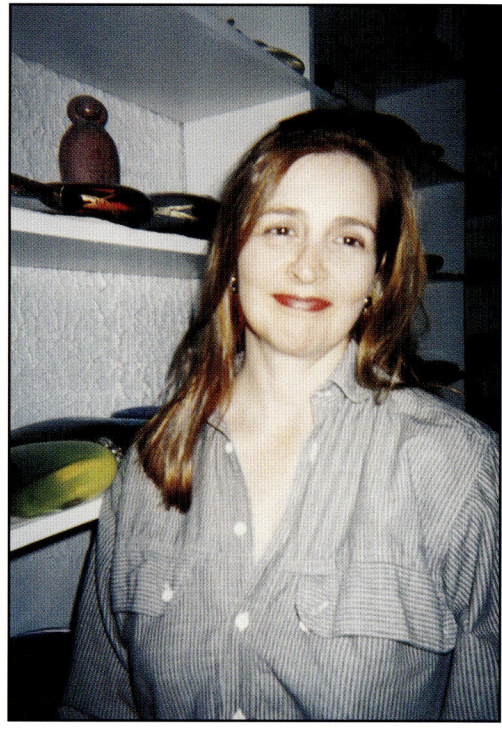

The earliest influences on my work were those of the modern artists following the classic tradition in sculpture: Brancusi, Moore, and Noguchi. After twenty-five years of exploring sculptural form, the classic tradition continues to inform and provide me with insight and inspiration.

I traveled to Venice in the summer of 1984 searching for a teacher. I was looking for information and answers when I visited the Seguso factory. I began to return on a near daily basis. With a feeling of disbelief, I, an American woman, was able to enter one of the fabled glass factories of Murano and could observe for hours without being hustled away. Sure, American men had been given the opportunity to work in glass factories on Murano, but there wasn't equal opportunity for women.

I spent my days at the glass factory and at the end of the summer, Livio Seguso made an amazing offer. He asked me to return! To stay for several years! To learn!

I returned to Venice in 1985 with my previous life in storage and my savings account in hand, hoping to remain as long as possible. What followed was a two-year apprenticeship that required every ounce of tact and grace within my personality to sidestep Venetian jealousies, established rivalries, and traditional male decisions. Livio taught me how to achieve my sculptural ideas in glass. In his teaching, he insisted that I disregard all the traditional Italian techniques that were featured in the surrounding retail shops and concentrate on the discovery of my own relationship with the material. This entailed hours of drawing and hours of watching glass being made in many different studios on Murano. I initiated design projects with several factories and was able to earn money through commissions. My work today is based very deeply on truth to the material and its unique characteristics.

Cristine Barney. *Photo courtesy of the artist.*

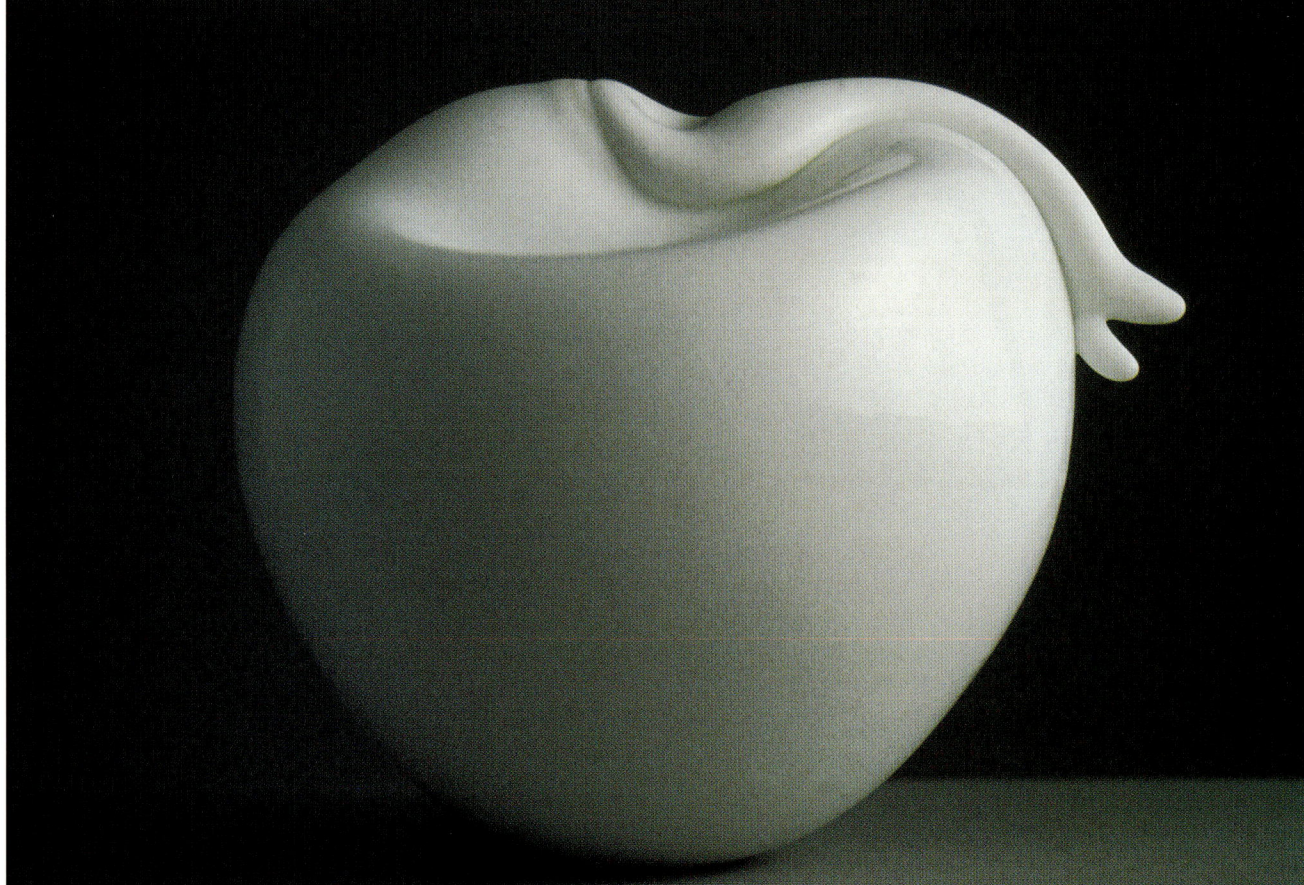

Squod, 1982, 7" x 9" x 9". *Photo courtesy of the artist.*

The Seventies - The Artist 77

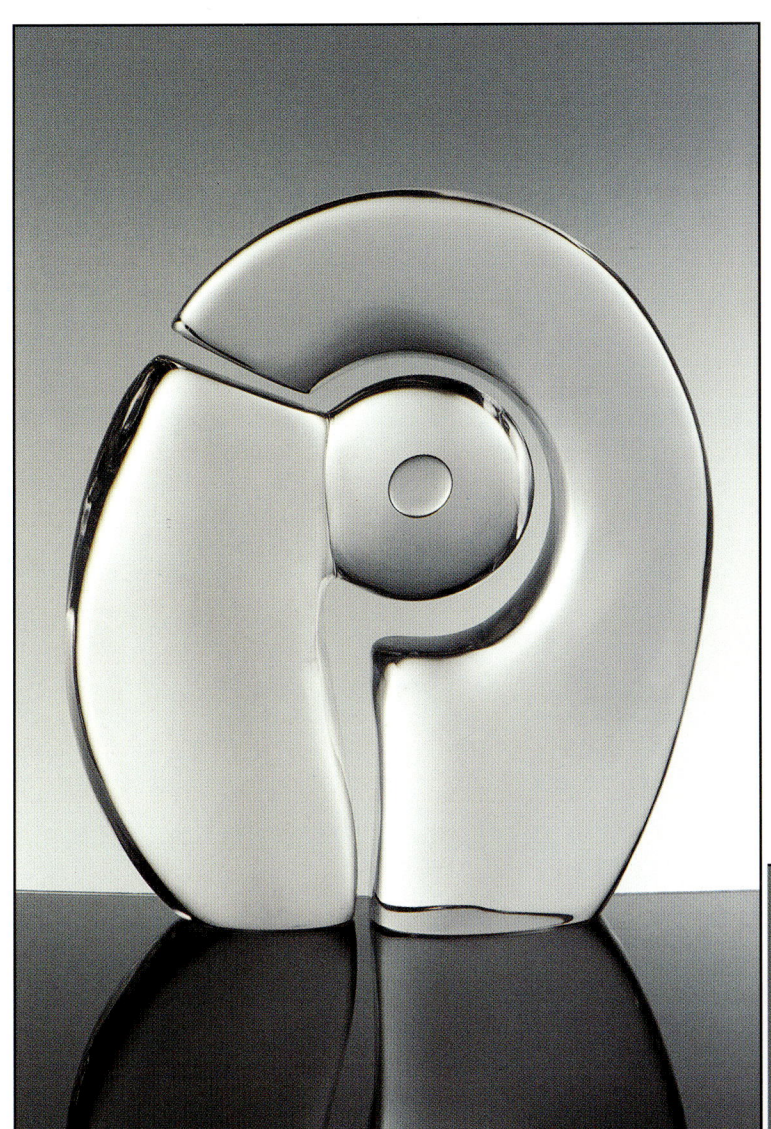

Open Center, 1987, 10" x 9" x 2.5". Photo courtesy of the artist.

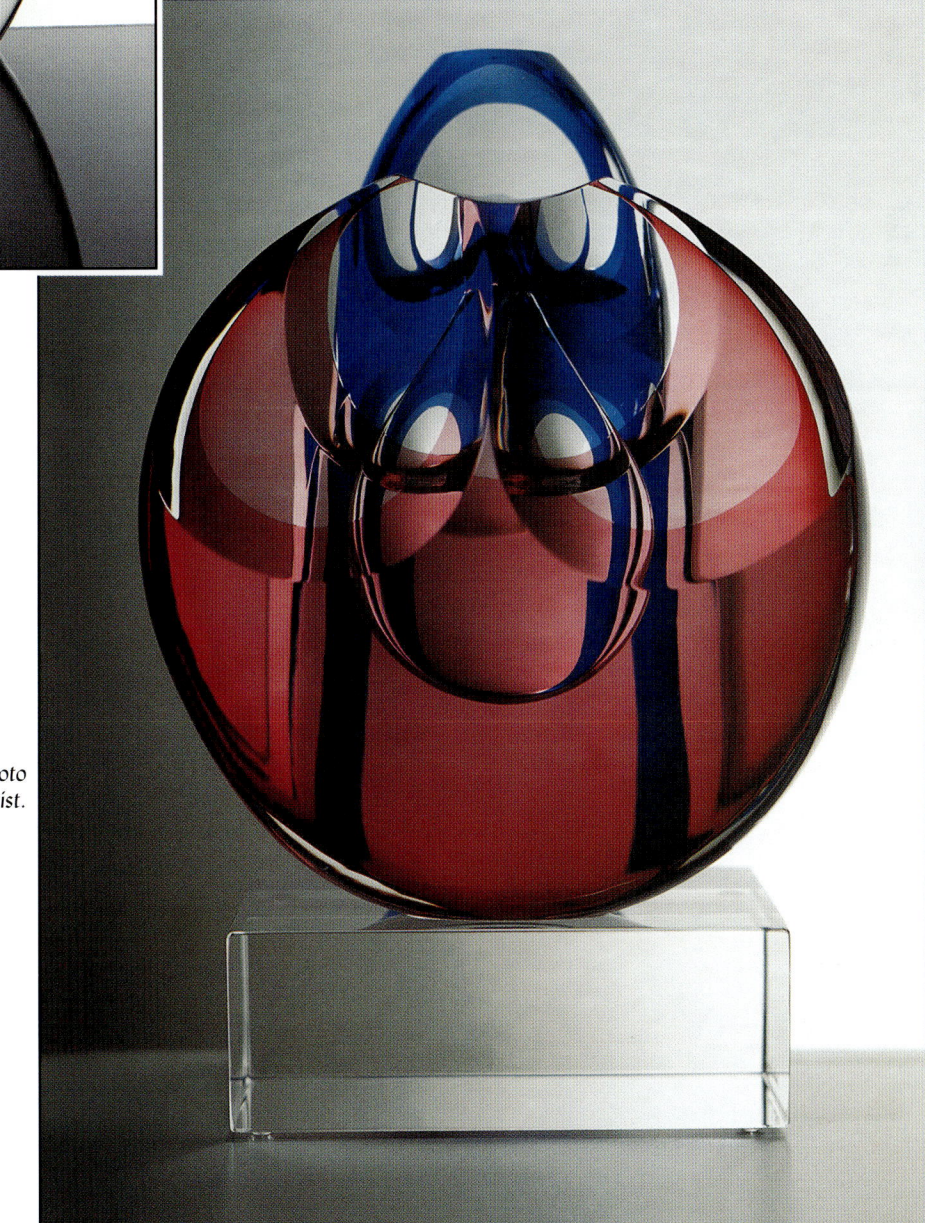

Cobalt Ruby Fusion, 12" x 8" x 5". Photo courtesy of the artist.

Bonnie Biggs

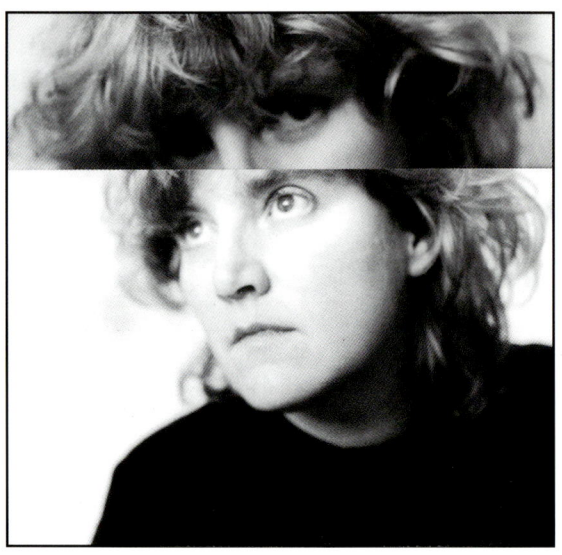

Bonnie Biggs. *Photo courtesy of the artist.*

Opening consciously to the Life Forces of the Universe may take one deep into personally uncharted waters. There are many signs along the way recorded in languages so familiar to the forgotten self.

The remembering is part of our purpose. The image/object making is a tool used to access the remembering – it is sometimes a map or record and sometimes the journey itself – through the layers of space and light.

Glass, existing on the physical plane, is perhaps the most accurate material for describing what one is aware of but cannot fully "see." The ephemeral world of glass – it can serve to hold an image/memory suspended in space for uninterrupted observation and then like some kind of vapor or dense fog hold even space itself.

I work on a extremely wet active surface which is part glass and part inky water. Photo-based images are integrated with the drawings in-between the layers of glass or engraved on the surfaces. The visual dynamics of dimensionally layered imagery, penetrating light, and cast shadow often work to evoke a feeling of pliant movement.

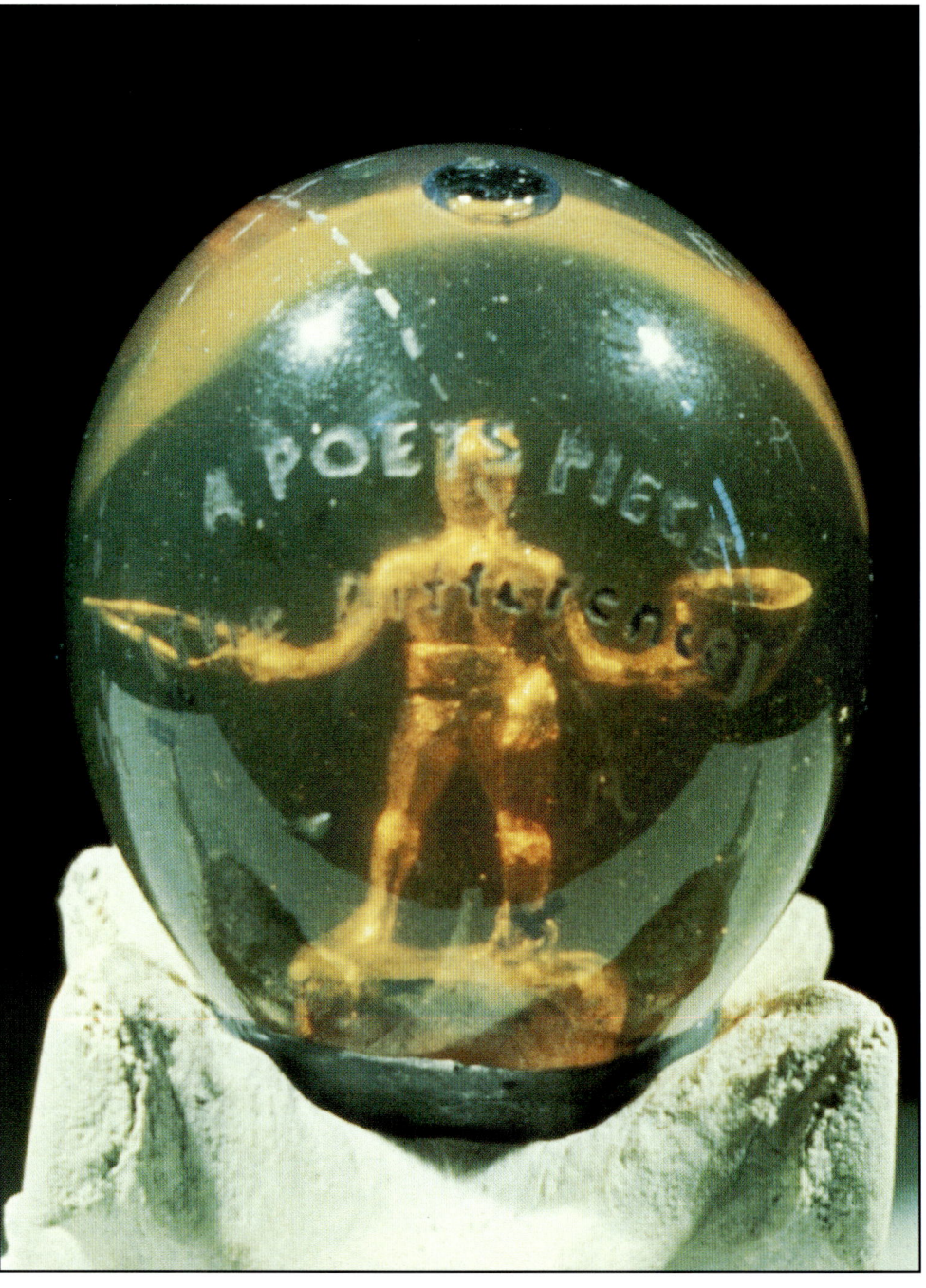

A *Poets Piece*, blown glass-engraved, cast bronze, stand oil, alphabet letter, cast lead, vertebrae, 8" x 4" x 5". *Photo courtesy of the artist*

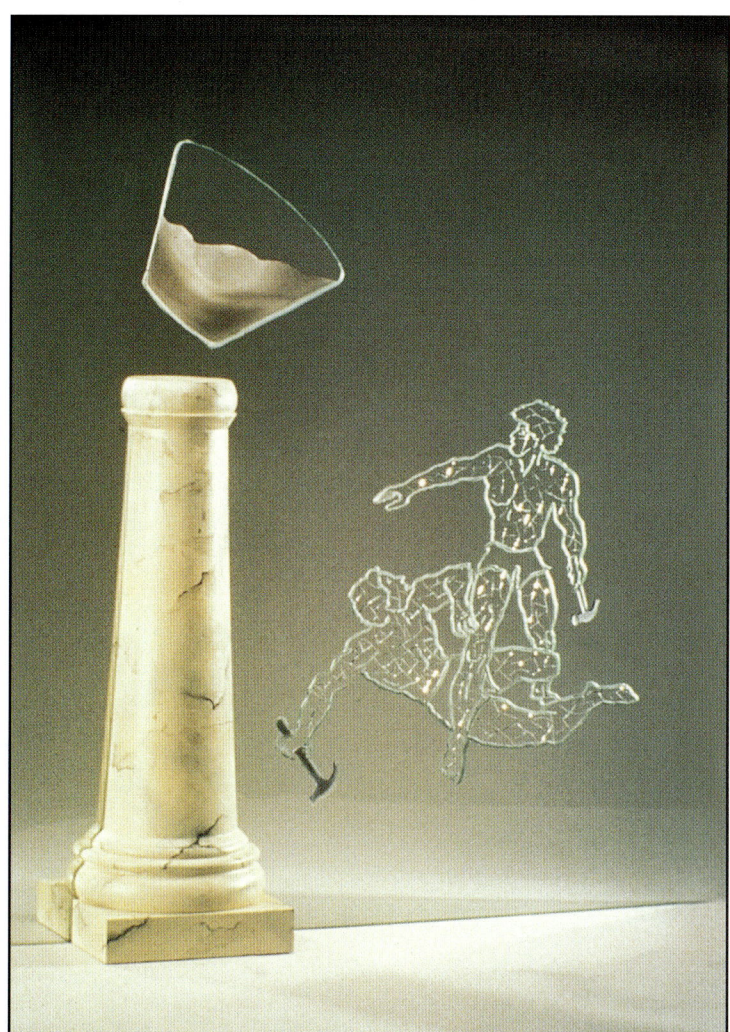

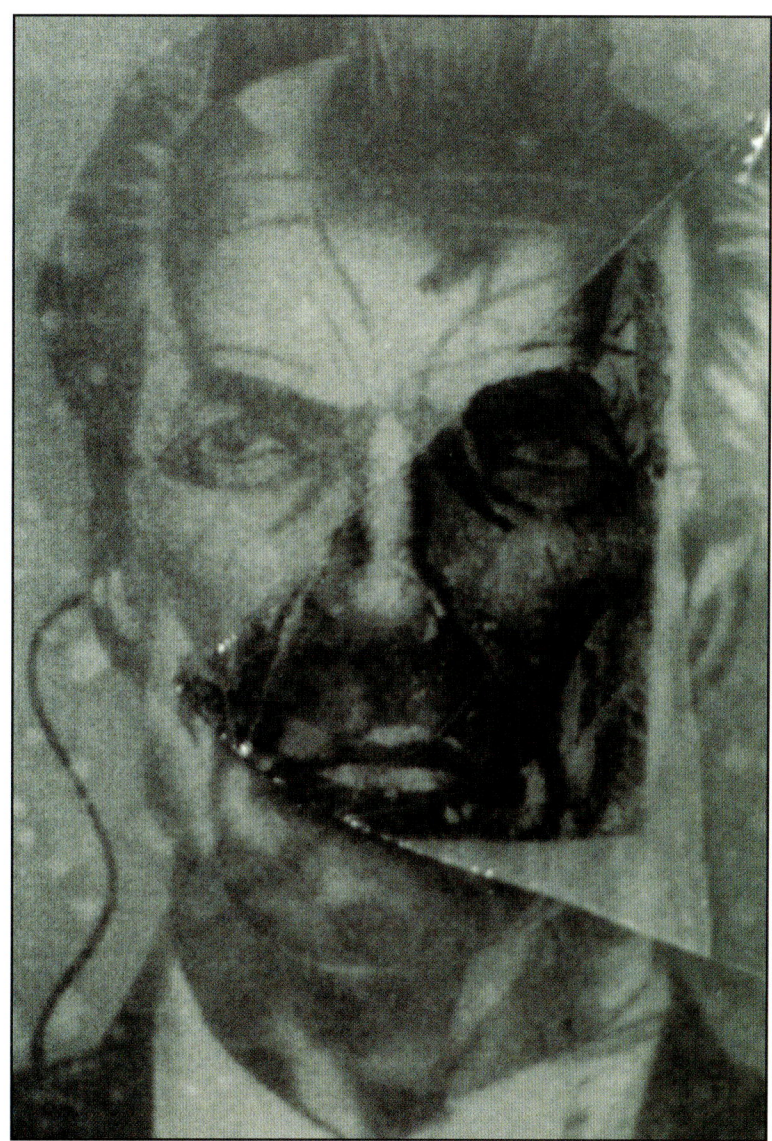

Consciousness Interuptus, 1982, 38" x 32" x 9", pre-laminated glass, sandblasted & cracked, vacu-formed PBV, painted wood. Borofsky/Wagman collection. *Photo courtesy of the artist.*

Double Protection Series: Man with Tie #7, 2002, 10" x 12" x 2', laminated glass with ink wash drawings, acrylic gel lifts, photoengraved surface, painted wood. *Photo courtesy of the artist.*

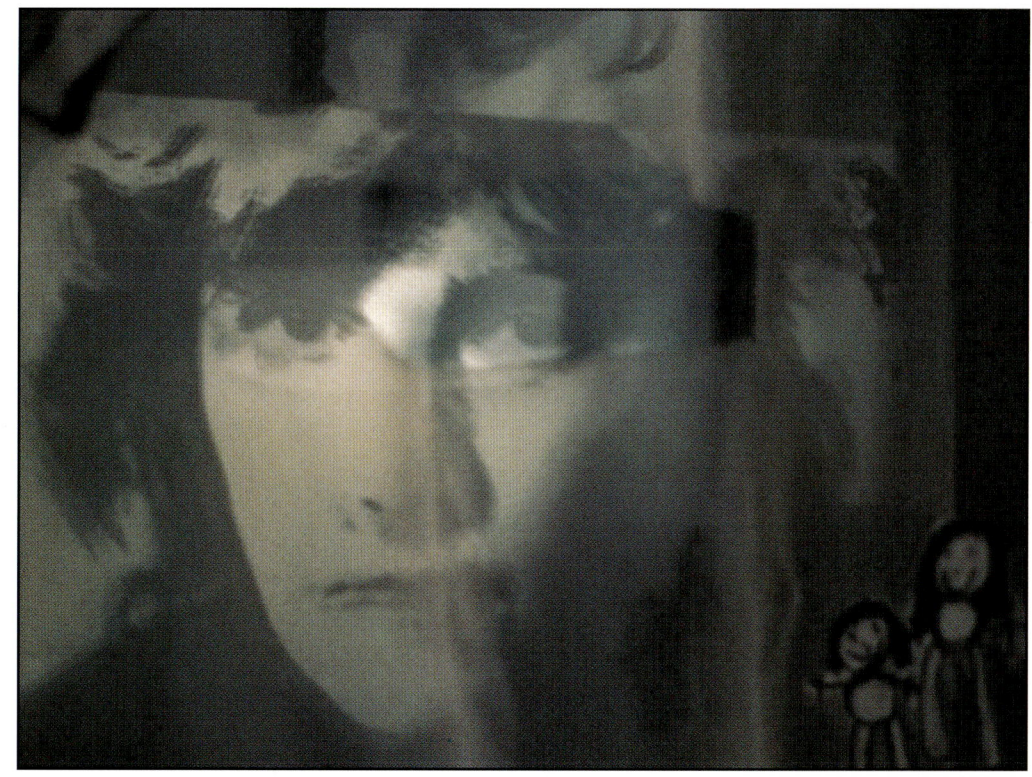

Self Portrait with Spiritual Advisors #4, 2001, 22" x 22" x 6", laminated glass, transfer photo-images, silk, painted wood. *Photo courtesy of the artist.*

Sonja Blomdahl

From the beginning, what I liked about blowing glass was the concentration it required. The process was so demanding that my familiar obsessions about daily life were dispelled...at least until the piece was done.

I have focused on the vessel and find the form to be of primary importance. A vessel holds space and glass holds the light. For me there is still much to explore. The relationship between form, color, proportion, and process still intrigues me.

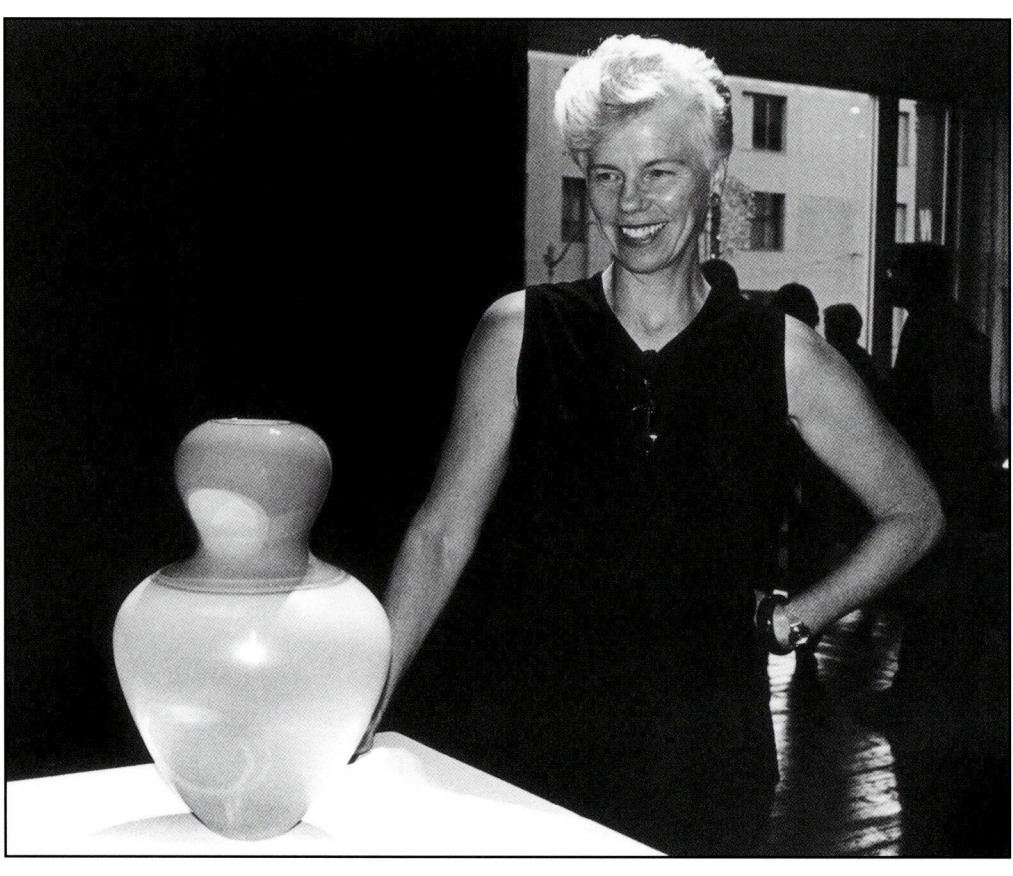

Sonja Blomdahl at William Traver Gallery, photo: Alexandra C. Otto.

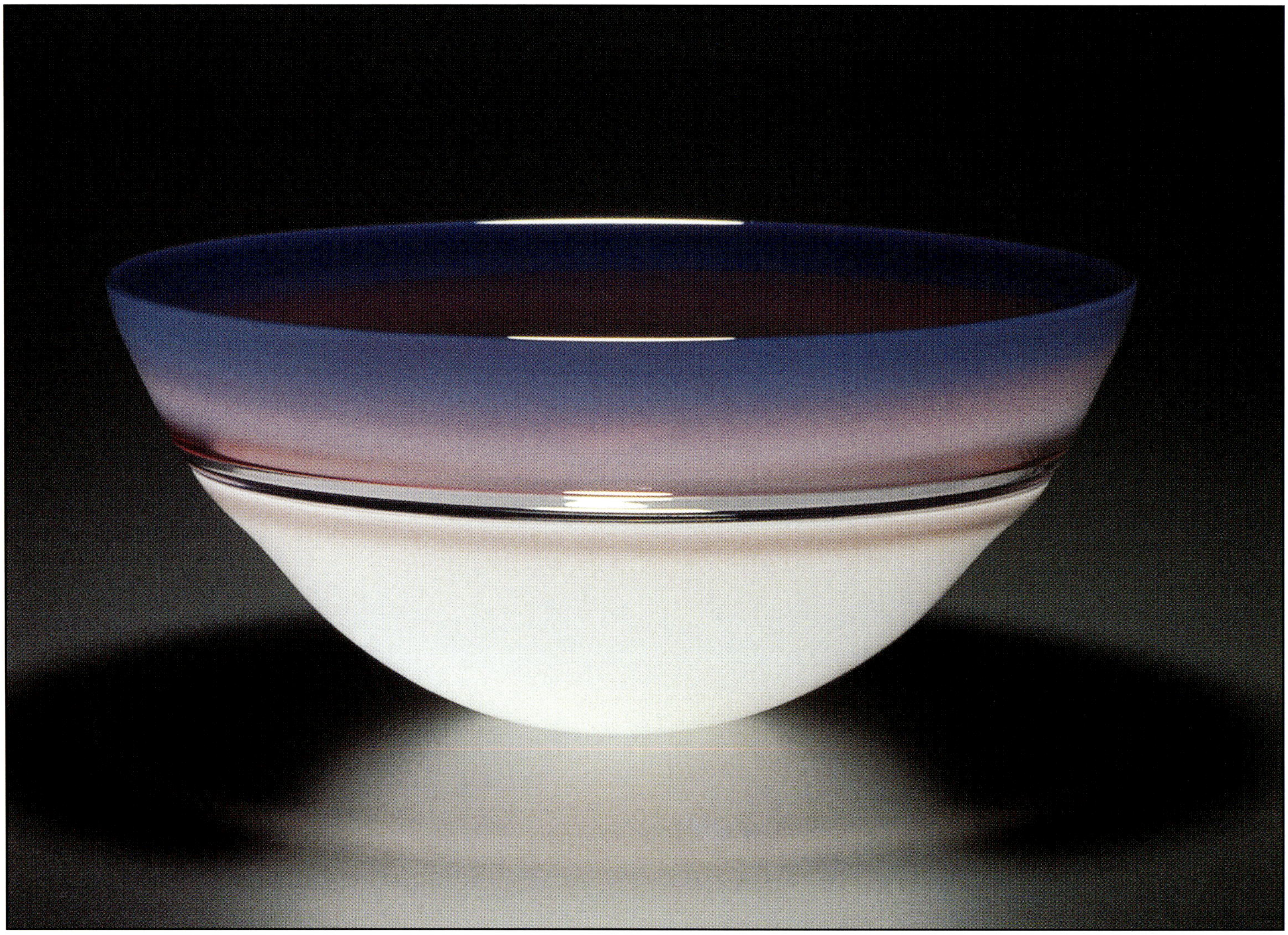

Pink/Violet, 1983, 6" x 13" d, photo: Russell Johnson. *Photo courtesy of the artist.*

The Seventies - The Artist 81

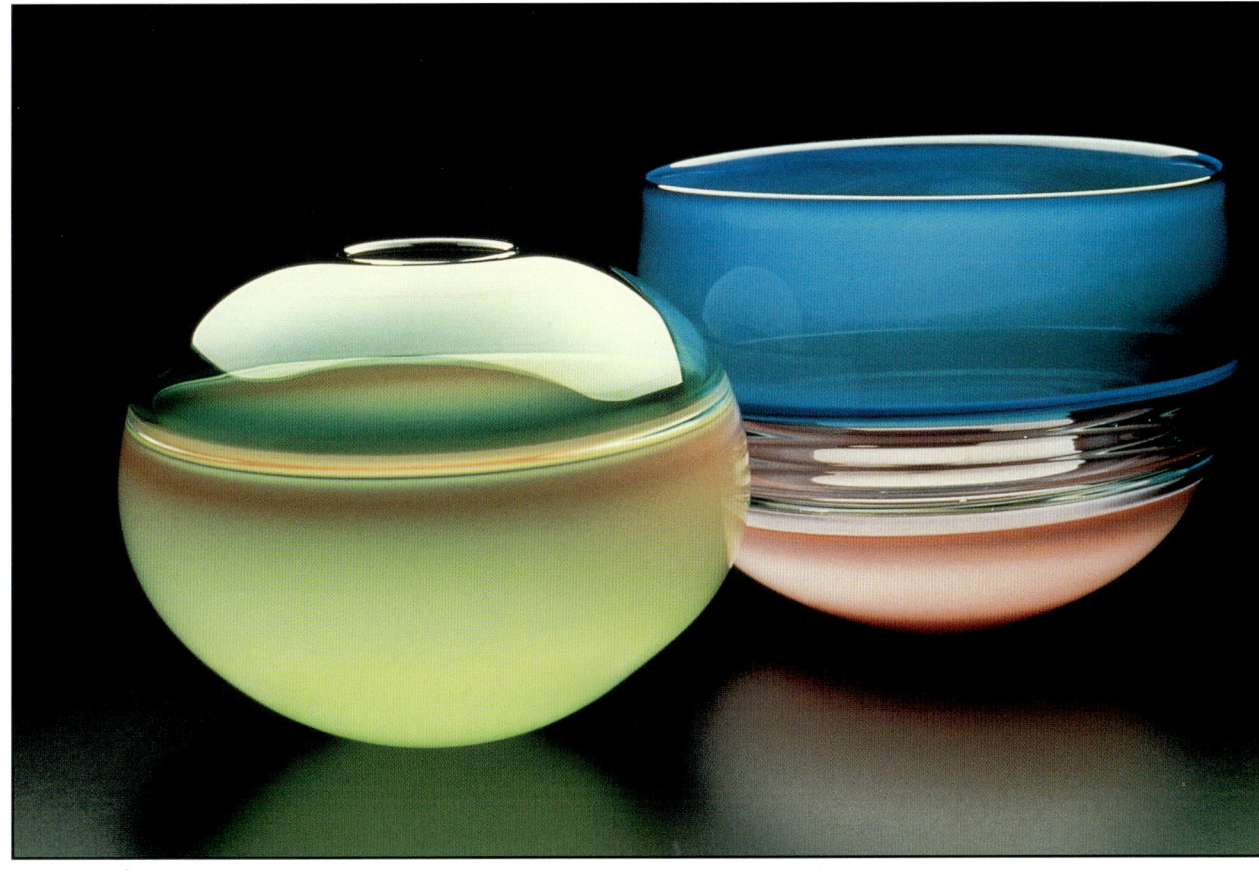

SP4785, 9.5" x 11.5" d & B3285, 9" h x 13" d, 1985, photo: Kevin Latona. *Photo courtesy of the artist.*

B11199, 12.5" x 12" d, 1999, photo: Lynn Thompson. *Photo courtesy of the artist.*

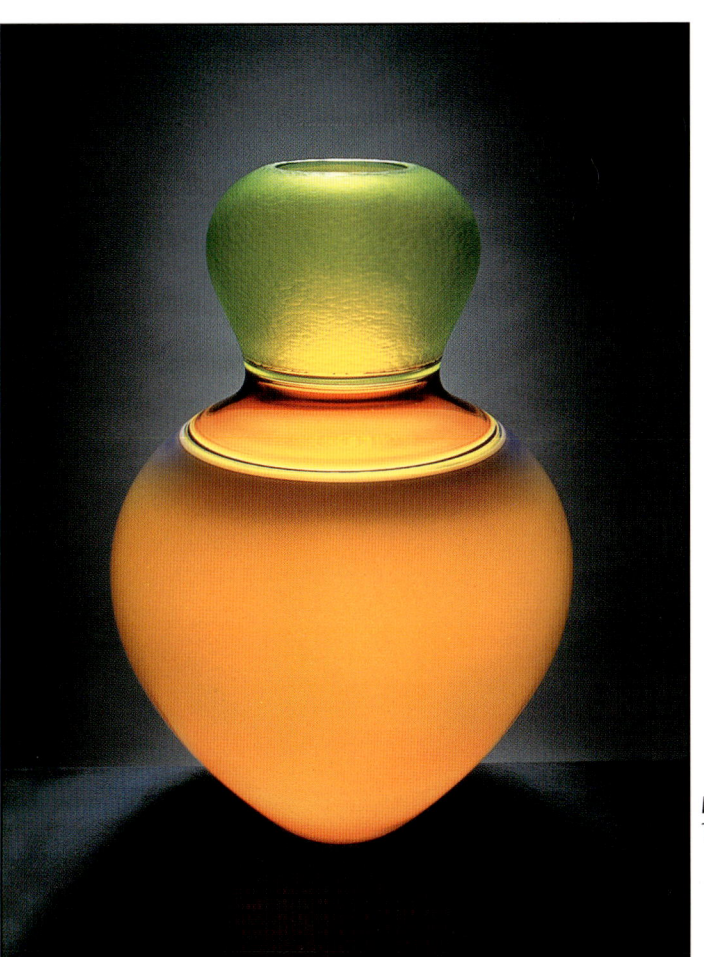

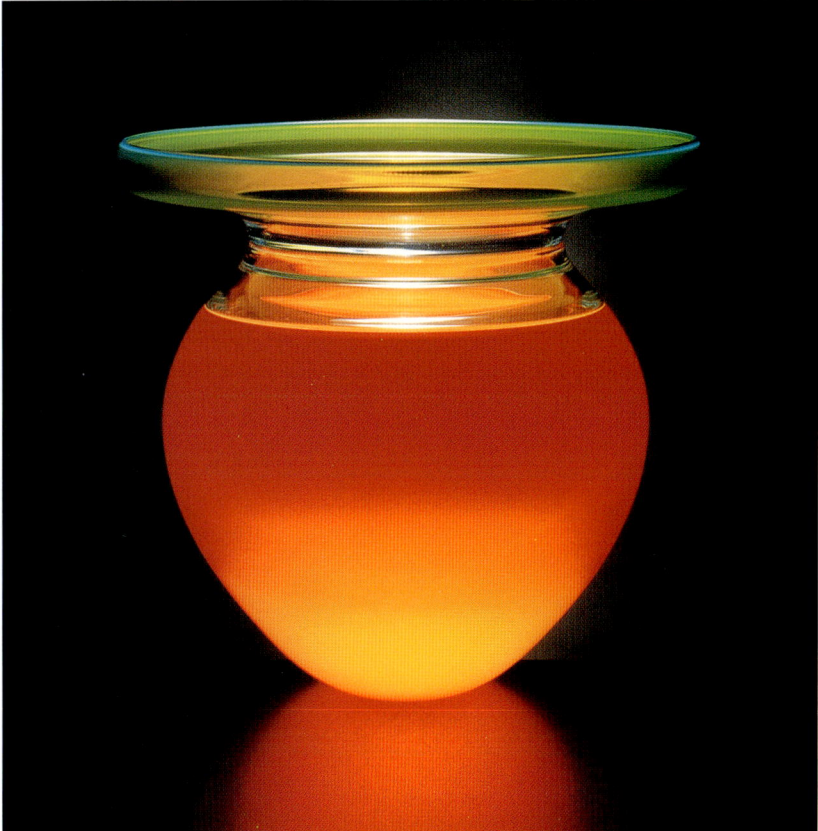

B1401 Battuto Top, 2001, 19" h x 13" d, photo: Lynn Thompson. *Photo courtesy of the artist.*

Rene Culler

The Grail Variations series celebrates humanity; the life journey, and the tenacity to continue and improve.

The topic of the quest for the Grail is the primary inspiration. It is important to note that I do not attempt to "create the Grail." What interests me is the "journey, the search" for perfection which always incorporates creativity. My vertical forms can be seen as figurative in a loose sense. The human body is a container – the heart for emotion, the head for ideas. My work is a unity of the analytical and the spontaneous. I encourage the viewer to see beneath the layers of flesh, myth and history to reveal the purity of thought or feeling suggested by metaphorical objects. The objects are psychological interpretations.

The Grail Variation sculptures began as a whimsy. I wanted to make an object that I considered absurd and appealing. I call these objects sculptures, because they are dimensional, and can serve no function, as by their composition – these often brightly colored stacks of cups and bowls have become rendered useless as functional objects. I am interested in the transformation of these common objects often employed for daily use, into metaphorical "maps" that describe a journey. This work is strongly rooted in Crafts, so I am happy to be a sculptor or a crafts person, the artist who actually fabricates the work. I insist on excellence in my work – the degree of craftsmanship and finish is important to the meaning of the sculpture.

Glass is a changeling material as the plastic material cools in the definition of form. Blown forms evolve through trial by fire or kiln transformation to achieve a "history." Kiln transformation is a process which I developed and is unique to my work. Compositions develop through process, as glass segments are "nested" and fused within the refractory mold. Evidence of process is important to the philosophy of the work, it conveys pathos for what was once or might have been. Transience of beauty and the awareness of mortality are analogous to the fired, textural vessel. Perfection mutates with process. To paraphrase, the French sculptor Auguste Rodin: "There is nothing as beautiful as a beautiful thing ruined."

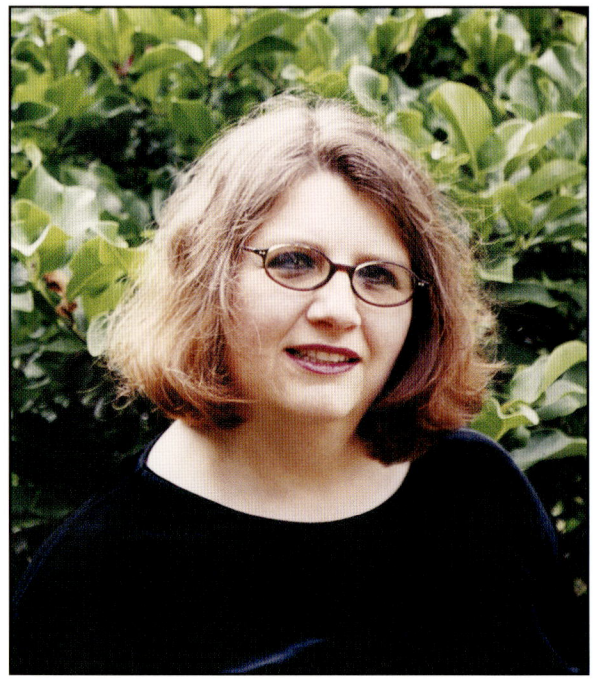

Rene Culler. *Photograph courtesy of the artist.*

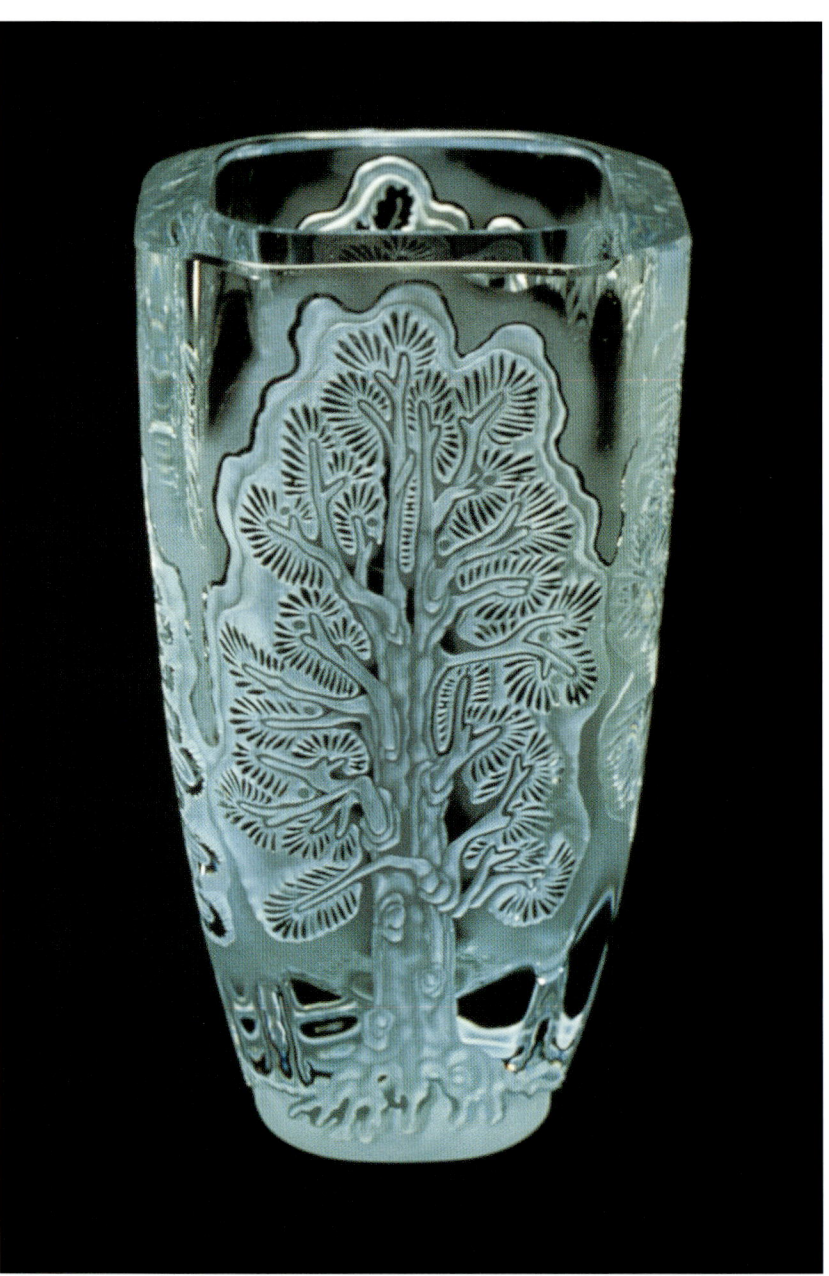

Compass Trees, 1976, 10" x 5" d, Stromberg Swedish Lead Crystal. *Photograph courtesy of the artist.*

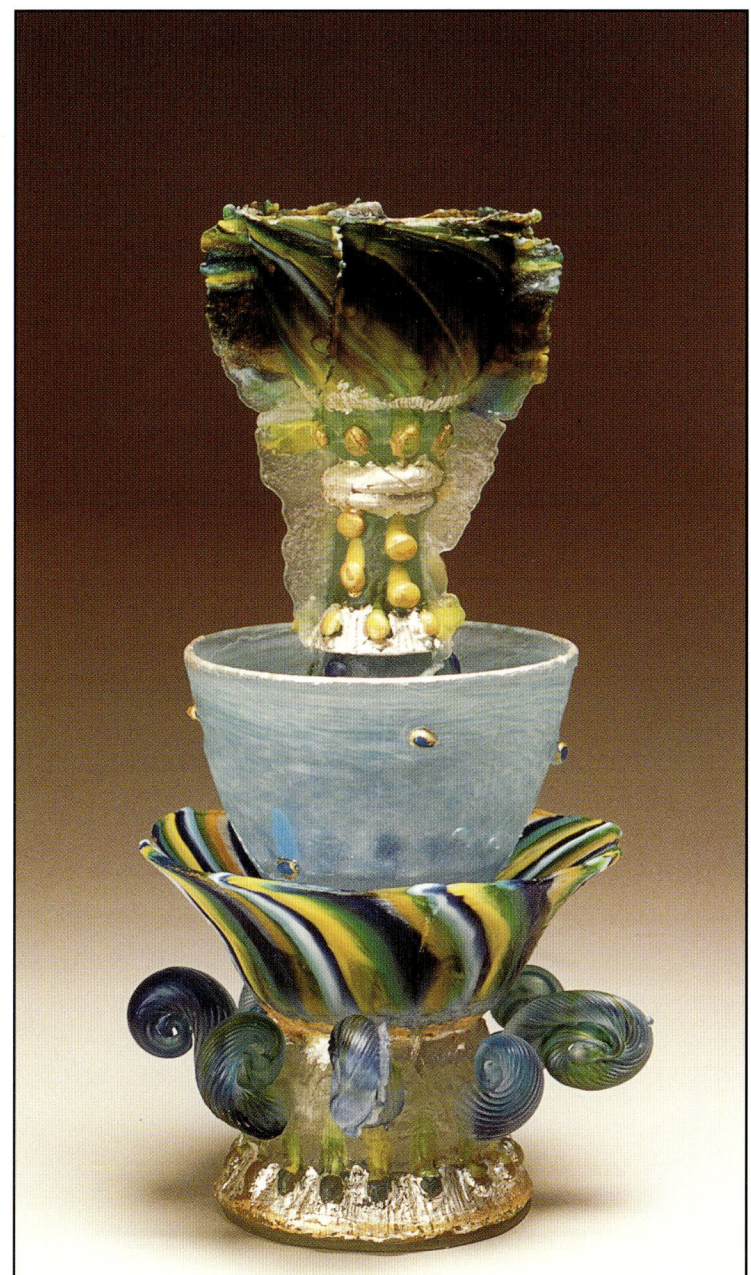

Three of Cups Revisited, 2000, Grail Variation, 28" x 12" d.
Photograph courtesy of the artist.

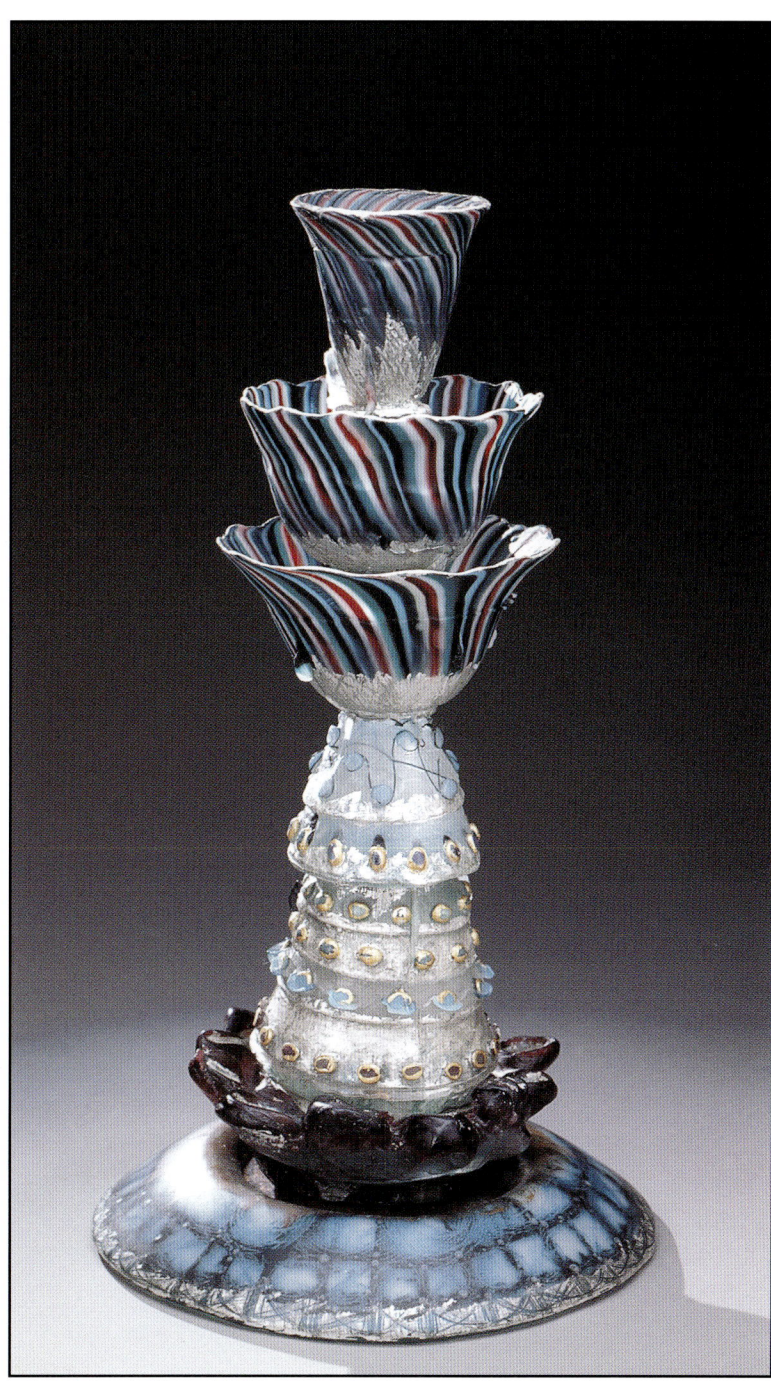

Three of Cups, Past Prime, 2001, 30" x 16.5" d.
Photograph courtesy of the artist.

Diana Hobson

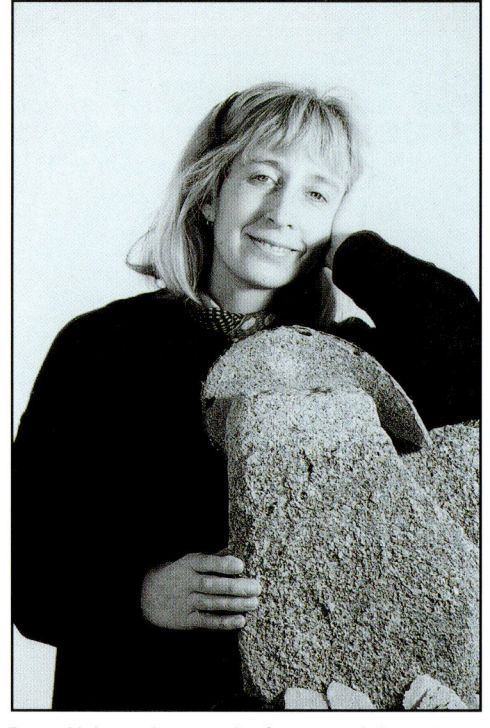

Diana Hobsen photograph. *Courtesy of the artist.*

The creative process has always demanded that I use whatever material and process is necessary to create a piece of work. It is never linear. but within the completion of each work, the seed of the next is gestating.

In 1976 on completing a time piece, where glass was needed to magnify and to be the vehicle for illumination, I had an inspiration. I had worked with enamels (crushed glass layered on to metal) and while working on the timepiece had fallen in love with the light properties of the glass. From these experiences evolved the idea of creating a thin shell of glass by enameling, not on metal, but on a removable former which would leave a very fine form of glass using natural light to create a magic.

Thus began many years of experiment (beginning 1980) into what became Pate de verre. It proved to be a perverse technique which I thoroughly explored and pushed to it's limits and in the last phase introduced other natural materials into it's matrix.

In 1988 I was invited to participate in a workshop sponsored by the Gulbenkian Foundation, where we were asked to experiment with materials new to us. We were given an empty journal to document the process. From this point on, writing became integral to my work, at first for documenting, exploring and focusing my intent. I learned that to explain the work was a barrier to the viewer's experience. Words are such a direct form of communication that an expectation is set up for an experience that the viewer is not always ready for without prior contact with the visual and vibratory content of the physical form. I then found that I had resolved this by beginning to write poetry.

I always begin new work on empty with a very intangible experience.to explore. I found that I was first recapturing this as poetry. This form is a way of programming myself and committing to the process of whatever the experience is I am working with. e.g.. – "Language of Light" evolved from the experience in Lapland of a profound sense of Infinity. I wanted to express something of this feeling in the work.

In 1991 I made the decision to leave the Pate de verre process. It had become too strong an identity which served to stifle my creative and spiritual growth and I returned to where I had begun, with the 'quality of light'

My first work in this New/old form was an exhibition 'Language of Light' at the Butler Gallery, Kilkenny Castle, Ireland, 1996. This was very new work -bronzes of twigs, tree limbs from Lapland and cast glass/light elements. I also produced an artists book as an element of this work. (see quotes) It was very difficult for people who had supported my work to understand this change and to appreciate a much more minimal expression. I moved to California with my husband in December 1998 and this transition into a new form has continued here. My book "Language of Light" was very popular and I began to feel that in order to communicate through the work, ideas and experience that are so intangible, I needed to stage an experience and I began to think about installation.

In 2000 I worked alongside glass artist, Keiko Mukaide and lens based artist, Craig Mackay on 'Elemental Traces', installations in the green houses at the Royal Botanic Garden, Edinburgh. I worked in the primeval atmosphere of the fern house with the tree ferns, glass, light and sound to awaken ancient mind. We also made a small video which I found a very exciting medium and one I feel I could use to effect.

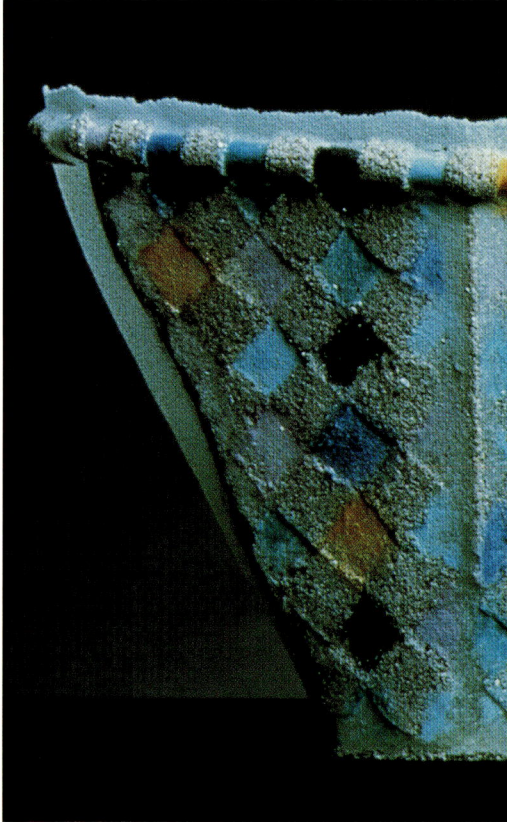

Progressive series no. 5 – Pate de verre 1986 – height 15 cm, lead crystal/beach sand/ceramic glaze stains/colored glass. *Courtesy and photo credit, the artist.*

The Seventies - The Artist   85

Quote by the artist from the catalogue, 'Elemental Traces' for her exhibition at the Royal Botanic Garden Edinburgh in 2000:

'The pattern of a diatom (an ancient single-cell organism) formed from glass rods, nestles in the earth. A vortex of primitive sounds evokes a sense of connection to our primal beginnings'

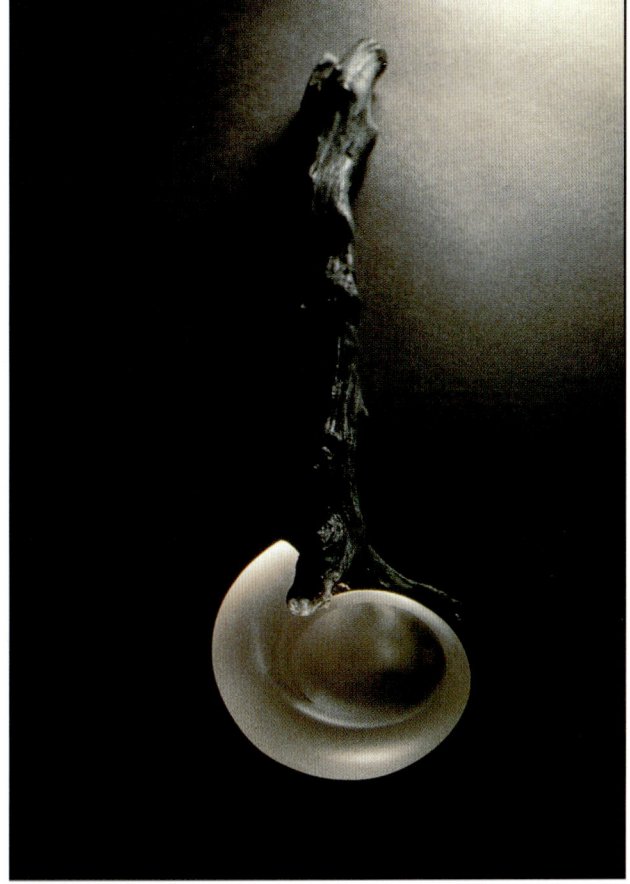

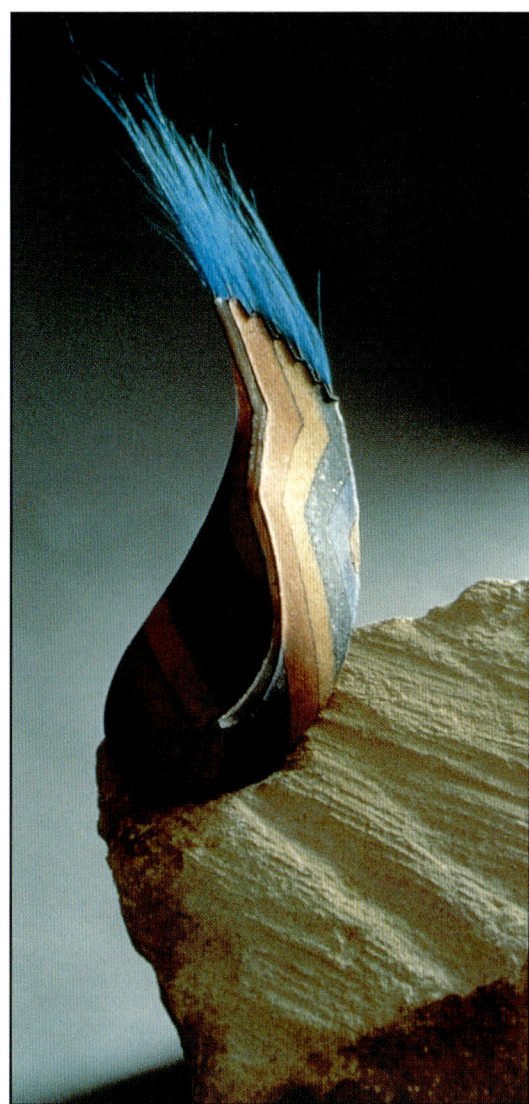

Benu Bird – Pate de verre 1991 – height of piece 28 cm, lead crystal/sand/earth/metal filings/ceramic glaze stain/colored glass. *Courtesy of and photo credit, the artist.*

Talking Stick from Language of Light collection – length 33 cm.

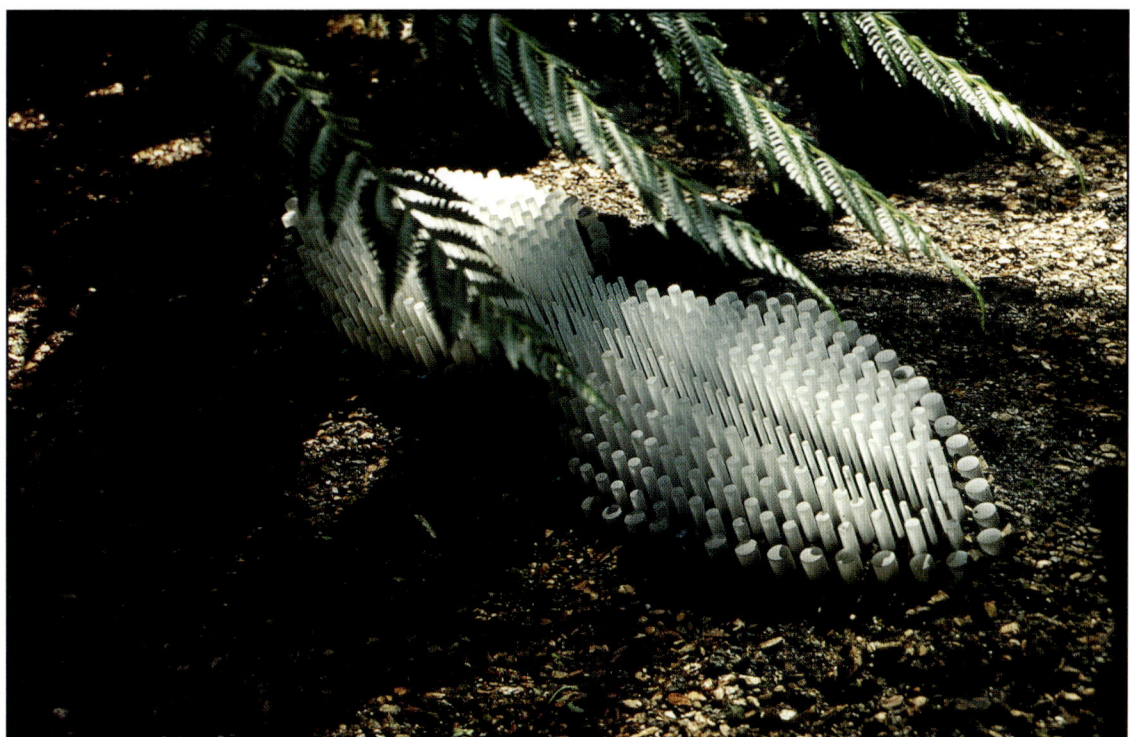

Diatom installation – Elemental Traces, Royal Botanic Garden, Edinburgh, 2000 – length 915 cm, glass rods/earth, situated in the fern house. *Courtesy of and photo credit, the artist.*

Joey Kirkpatrick/Flora C. Mace

Our sculptures are representations of the human figure in relationship to the world and how we "make do" in that world. They express that part of ourselves that has us cut boats from trees, bowls from fruit, hammers from stone. They are about our personal and collective voyage.

The inclusion of the life size head on its side expands our experience to an awareness, recognizing the juxtaposition of ourselves and the natural world. These pieces, in representing a moment of thought, turn us away from our inner selves and celebrate an awakening to our connection and dependence on nature, its cycles and seasons.

The addition of the still life sculptures continue to help us recognize the celebratory aspects of everyday life. They awaken our appreciation of the visual world around us. These works honor our need to live with and preserve nature.

The process we use when making the glass fruit and vegetable Still Life is unique. Our approach evolved out of our experience with the two-dimensional painting tradition. As in painting we have learned to build layers of color on glass forms by sifting colored crushed glass powders onto the hot glass during the blowing process. It was exciting to find a method of "painting" in three dimensions onto blown glass forms that enabled us to create realistic color and textures found in fruits and vegetables.

The Still Life represented here, large in scale, confronts the viewer and awakens our appreciation of the visual world around us. This makes us look outside ourselves and recognize the celebratory aspects of everyday life, our dependence on nature, its cycles and seasons.

Our current body of sculpture, as before, establishes itself within the context of nature but also takes many of its references from imagery associated with what's commonly and historically considered women's work. Using these references and also working with other gender related elements led us to borrow imagery from the world of the domestic. These domestic objects, celebrated as the sacred of everyday life, serve as metaphors that illustrate some of the life experiences in which we access our personal powers and growth. With these forms, to us innately beautiful, we embrace tradition and distinguish ourselves within it.

We add to the borrowed domestic objects of everyday, the paint brush. Through sculpture we describe the brush's ways of use visually, at the same time a metaphor for our creative will, our intentions, and imaginations.

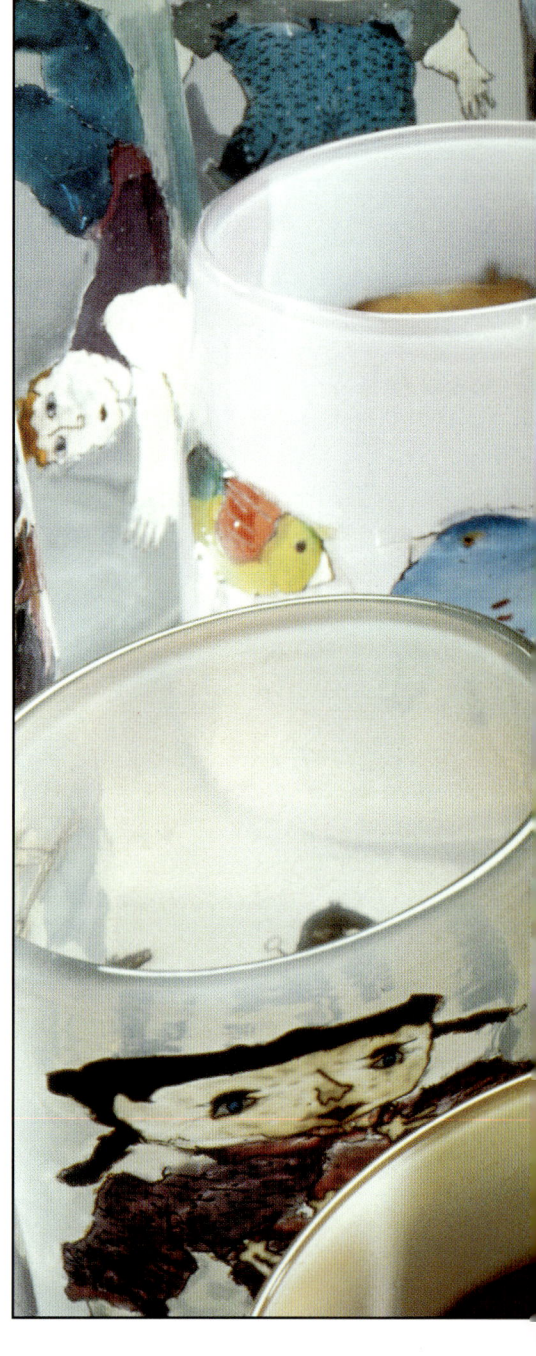

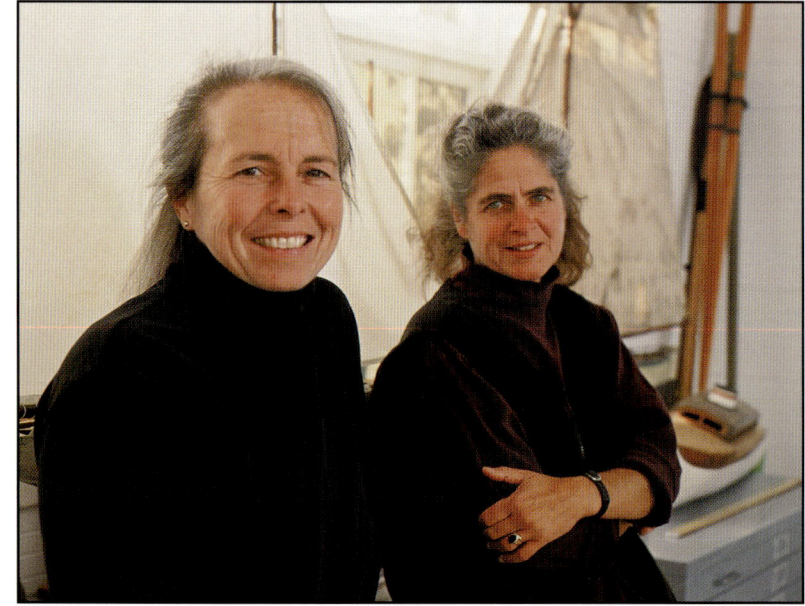

Flora C. Mace and Joey Kirkpatrick. *Photograph courtesy of the artist.*

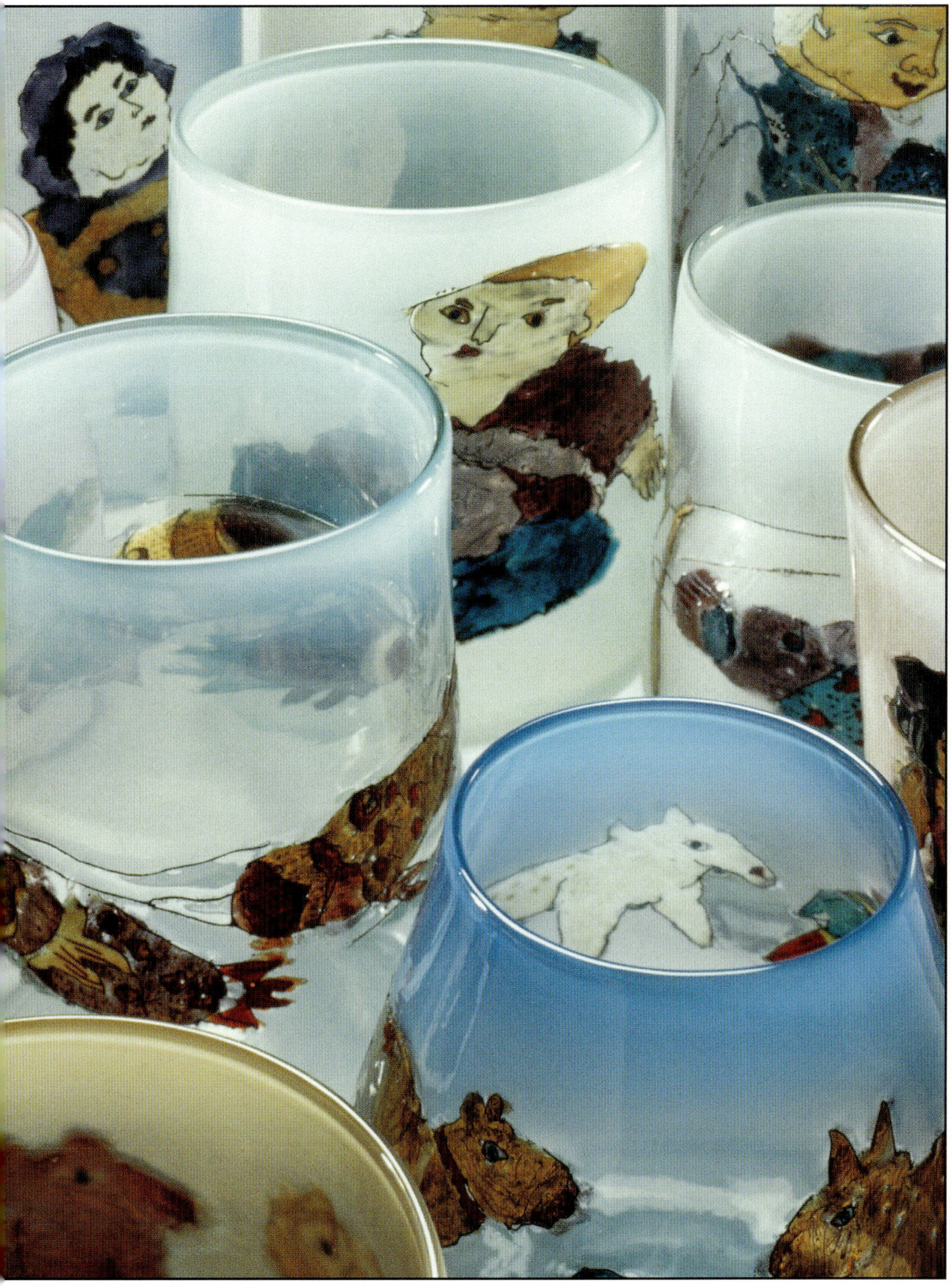

The Seventies - The Artist   87

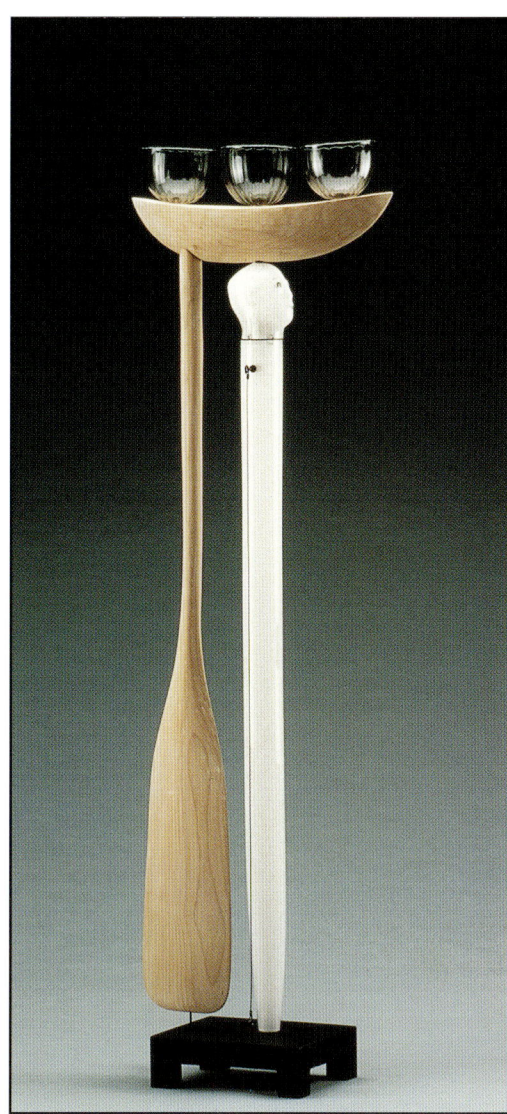

Voyage Carrier, 1985, 55" x 17" x 8", photo: Robert Vinnedge. *Photograph courtesy of the artist.*

Wire and Glass Thread Drawing Cylinders, 1979-1984, photo: Claire Garoutte. *Photograph courtesy of the artist.*

Voyage Carrier, detail.

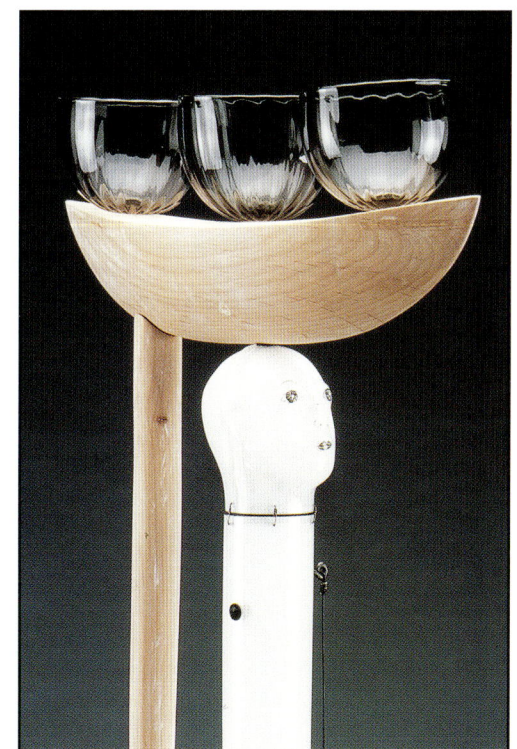

88 The Seventies - The Artist

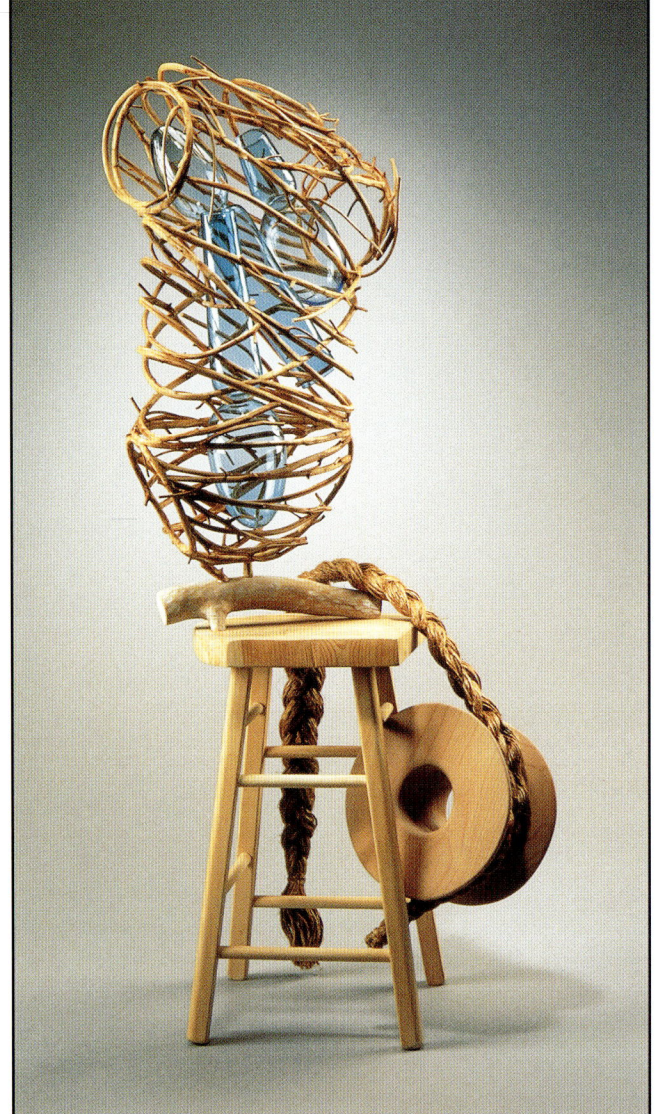

Assembling Memory, 2001, 58" x 25" x 21", Fabricated glass, wood, fiber, steel sculpture, photo: Robert Vinnedge. *Photograph courtesy of the artist.*

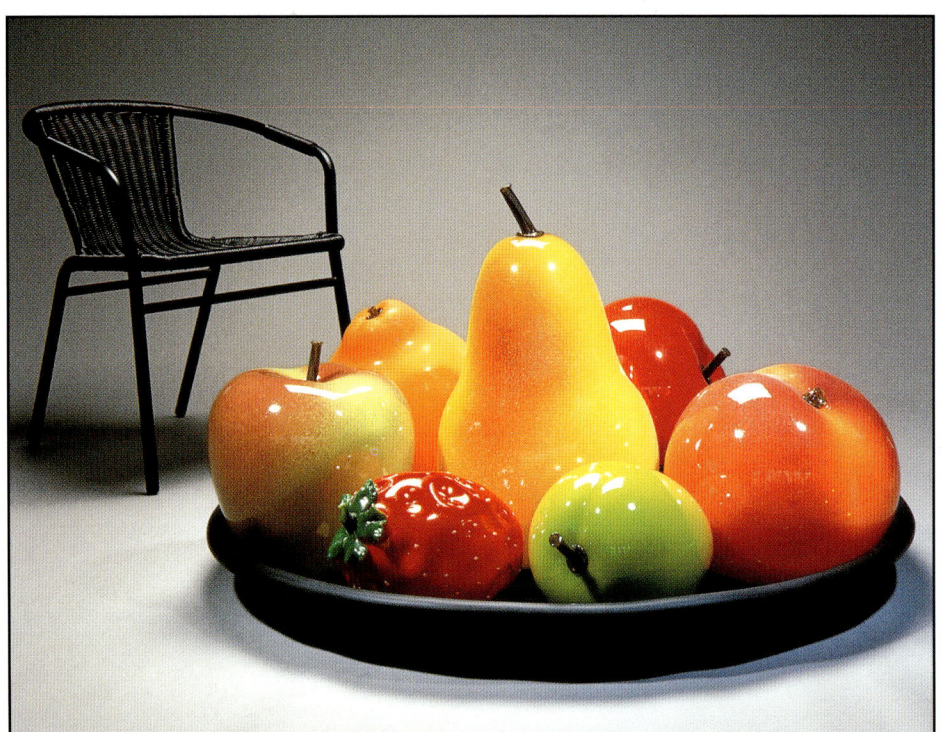

Still Life, 2001, 27" x 45" x 45", hand blown glass fruit forms with crushed glass powders for color, photo: Robert Vinnedge. *Photograph courtesy of the artist.*

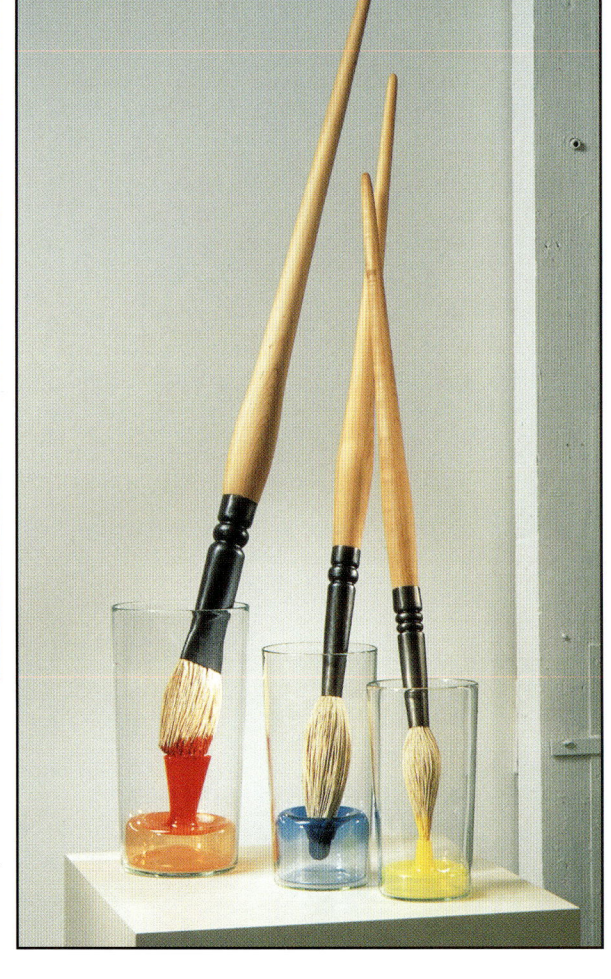

Making Before Meaning, Series Title, Red Brush, 74" x 28" x 11", Glass, wood, fiber, steel, photo: Robert Vinnedge. *Photograph courtesy of the artist.*

Margie Jervis and Susie Krasnican

Two heads are sometimes better than one. We worked collaboratively from 1977-1985. It is hard to imagine how two people can agree when it comes to making art. It seems so personal. Our conversations were not unlike those played out in a single artist's mind. The experience was a fluid mixture of exchanged ideas and tasks. With egos set to the side, the end result yielded more than the two individual contributions.

In the late 1970s, like many working with glass at that time, we explored the vessel form from a "fine arts" perspective. Our aim was to combine painting and sculptural gesture inseparably in the design of these early pieces. In the process, we developed a specific interpretation of glass as a material. It glowed from within.

During the early 1980s our work took a conceptual leap by turning the term "sculptural vessels" sideways to read "sculptures of vessels," a playful notion we decided to take seriously. Perception and expectation became the focus of the work. Two-dimensional vessel silhouettes transformed into three dimensions. The display of the work became part of the subject matter carrying equal weight to the objects themselves. As our work evolved it also became less academic and more poetic. The line blurred between what was real and what was painted. We created whole environments, blending man-made interiors with images of the natural outdoor world, commenting on life as we imagined it.

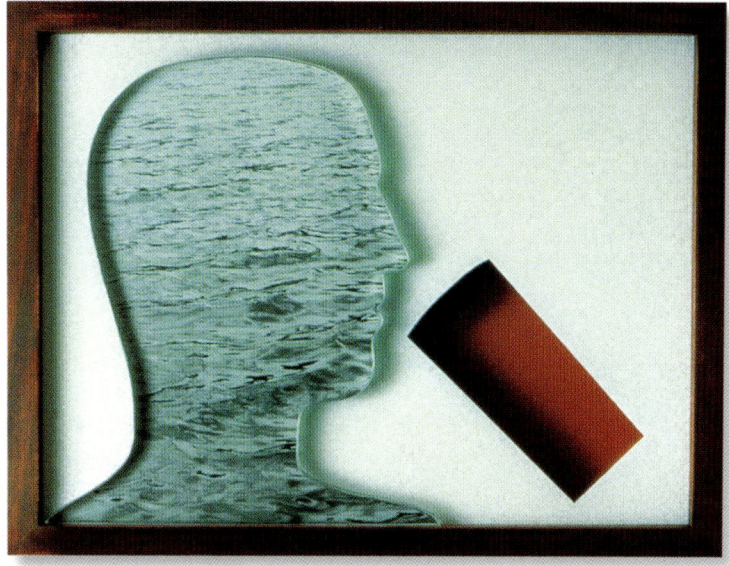

Man Drinking Water, 1985, 12.5" x 16" d x 1.5", glass, wood, photo, and found object. Photograph courtesy of the artist.

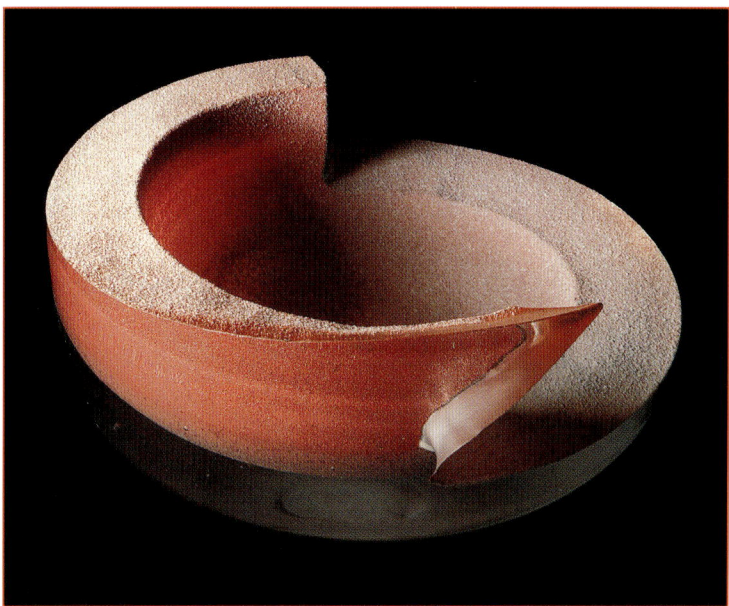

Sharpened Point, 1981, 4" h x 8.5" d, photo: Gary Bogus. Photograph courtesy of the artist.

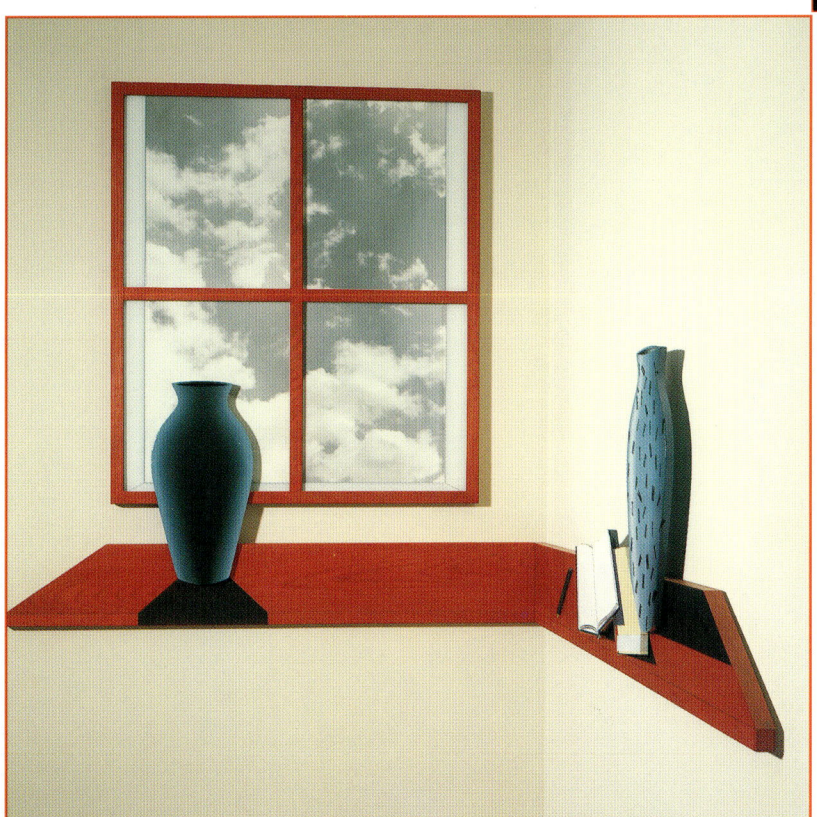

Margie Jervis/Susie Krasnican collabative works.

Abramson Commission, 1984, 44" x 8" x 1.5". Photograph courtesy of the artist.

Margie Jervis

In 1985 I felt that the theater stage rather than the art gallery offered more opportunity to explore using environment as an expressive medium. What intrigued me most, surprisingly, was opera. I found that I loved this archaic, emotive, and strangely beautiful art form. The work I saw was an exciting mixture of technical and conceptual sophistication and passion.

I chose to learn the visual side of opera from the inside out. I first worked in professional scenery production as a painter and sculptor for Seattle Opera and Seattle Repertory Theater. I became the Master Scenic Artist in charge of Seattle Opera's scenic art production staff in 1991. In 1996, when the company initiated a new version of Wagner's *The Ring of the Nibelungen*, the four opera epic, I became the Assistant to the Designer Thomas Lynch and Scenic Art Consultant.

Different from my former experience with collaborative art, opera is more of a collective process. Many disciplines must be completely entwined, although each person has a specific role. When Seattle Opera commissioned Dale Chihuly to design *Pelleas and Melisande*, the technical and construction departments together with the scenic art painters and sculptors, had the unusual challenge of interpreting models made of glass. As the Master Scenic Artist, I contributed my knowledge of both the aesthetics of glass and creative solutions for the stage as we successfully captured the signature qualities of Dale's designs in theatrical materials. For me, when the collective effort is true, there is a metaphor between involvement in the making of art and what I see as the core purpose of the opera performance medium. Art can show us we are individuals, but we are not separate. We all share the arc of emotion, finding the voice within ourselves that will open the hearts of others.

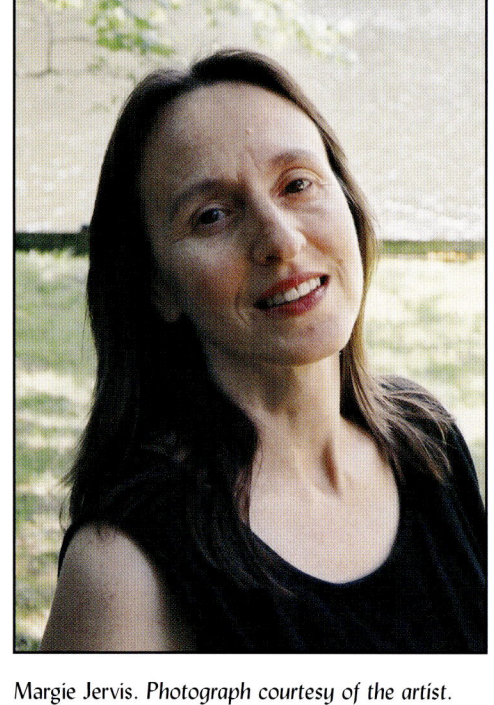

Margie Jervis. *Photograph courtesy of the artist.*

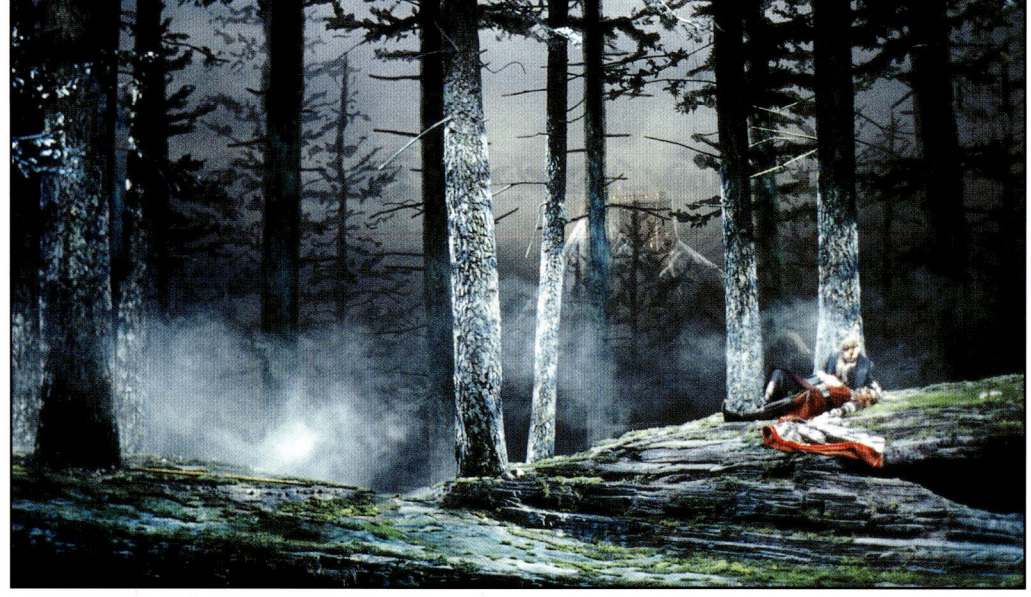

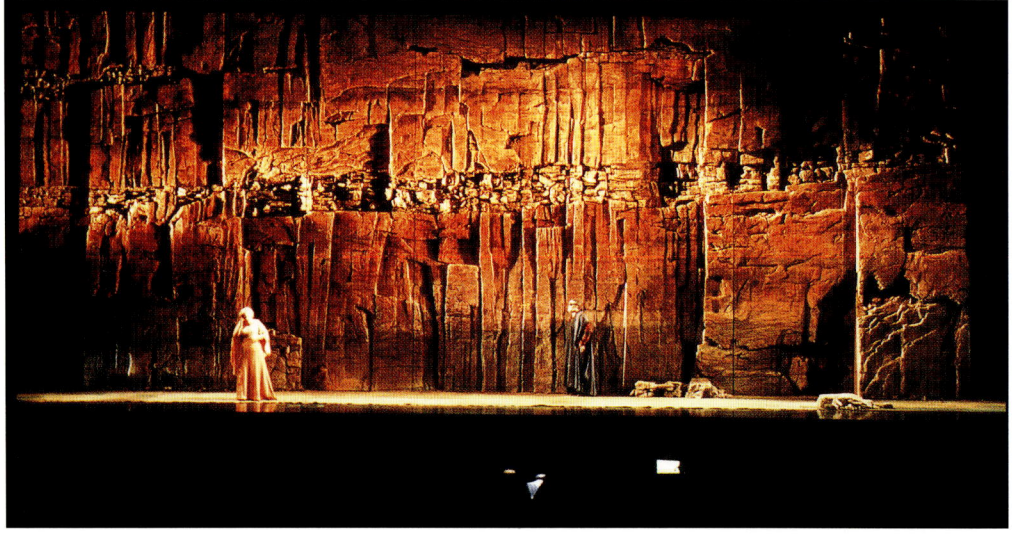

Scenes from The Ring of the Nibelungen, 2001. Designer: Thomas Lynch. Design Assistant and Scenic Art Consultant: Margie Jervis.

The Seventies - The Artist 91

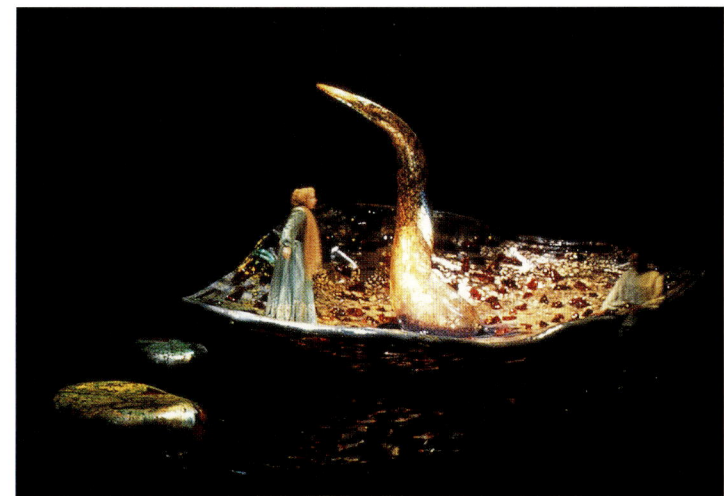
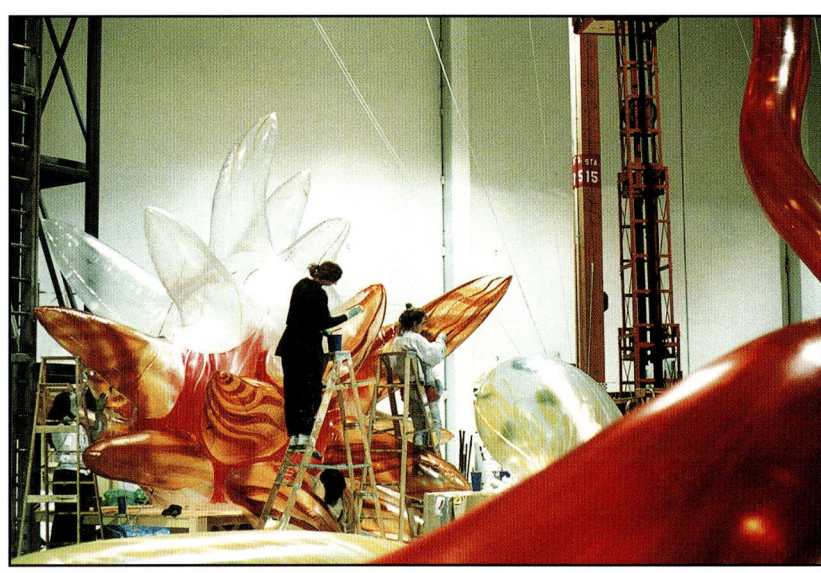
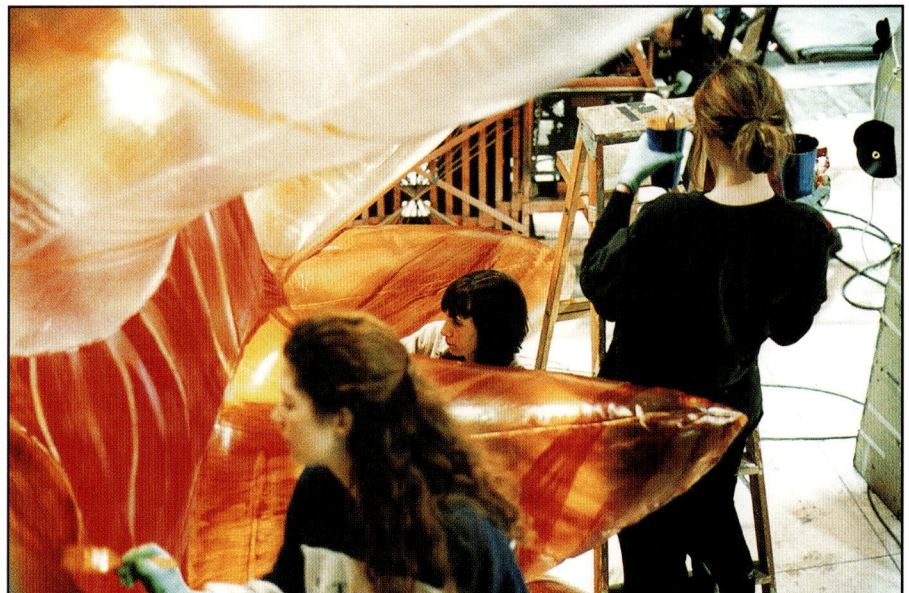

Scene from *Pelleas and Melisande*, 1993, and Artists at work in Seattle Opera Scenic Studio. Designer: Dale Chihuly. Master Scenic Artist: Margie Jervis.

Photo credits (from top): Gary Smith, Rob Reynolds, Russell Johnson, Margie Jervis.

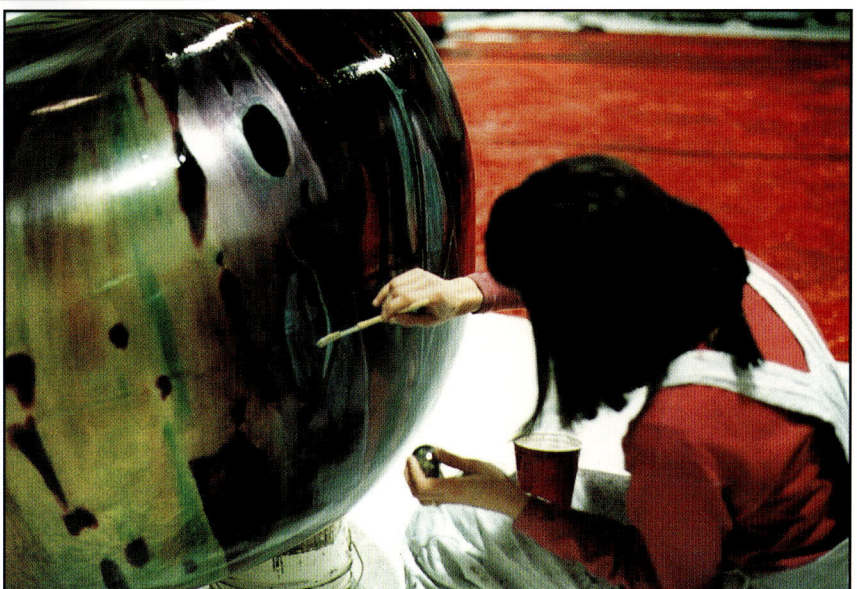

Susie Krasnican

"That's what little girls are made of?"

Society traditionally has conveyed strong messages about gender. In today's world stereotypes about women and men based solely on their sex continue to be re-evaluated.

Here "famous" quotes are re-phrased and posed again as questions. These thoughts were at one time memorable statements of truth. Some still hold true, others seem to be so outlandish that they could never be taken seriously today.

Although there is not one right answer, it is interesting to consider what the next generation of female children will encounter as this evolution continues. It is startling to consider the wonderful and ridiculous legacy of being born a woman.

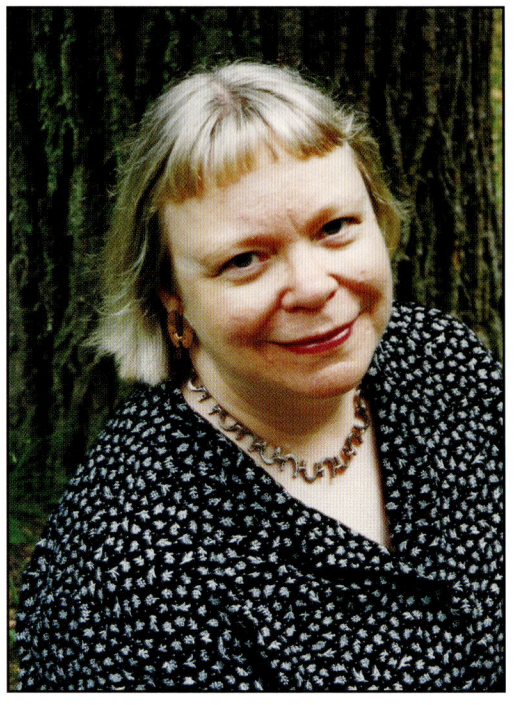

Susie Krasnican. *Photograph courtesy of the artist.*

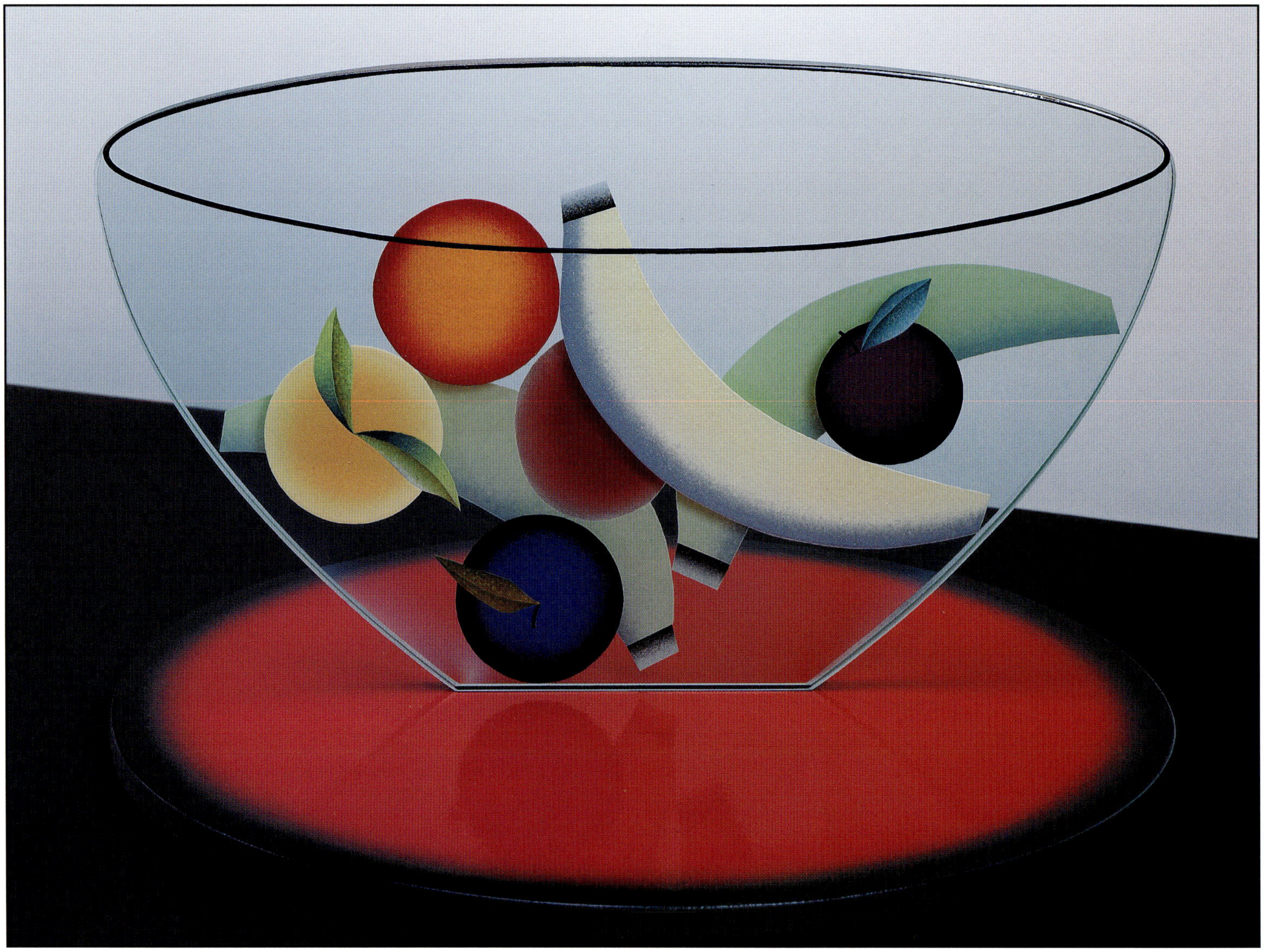

Bowl of Fruit, 1991, 10.5" x 17" d, fired enamels on 1/2" plate glass, photo: Mark Gulezian. *Photograph courtesy of the artist.*

Text *Inside Out*, 2000
(the tortoise or the hare)

If the facts don't fit the theory, change the facts.
Albert Einstein (1879-1955)

The more things change, the more they remain the same.
Alphonse Karr (1808-1890), French journalist, novelist

They always say time changes things, but you actually have to change them yourself.
Andy Warhol (1930?-1987). American artist

The need for change bulldozed a road down the center of my mind.
Maya Angelou (1928-), poet, writer, educator

There is a time for departure even when there's no certain place to go.
Tennessee Williams (1914-1983), American playwright

If you want things to stay as they are, things will have to change.
Guiseppe di Lampedusa (1896-1957), Italian novelist

When you get there, there isn't there anymore.
Gertrude Stein (1874-1946), American writer

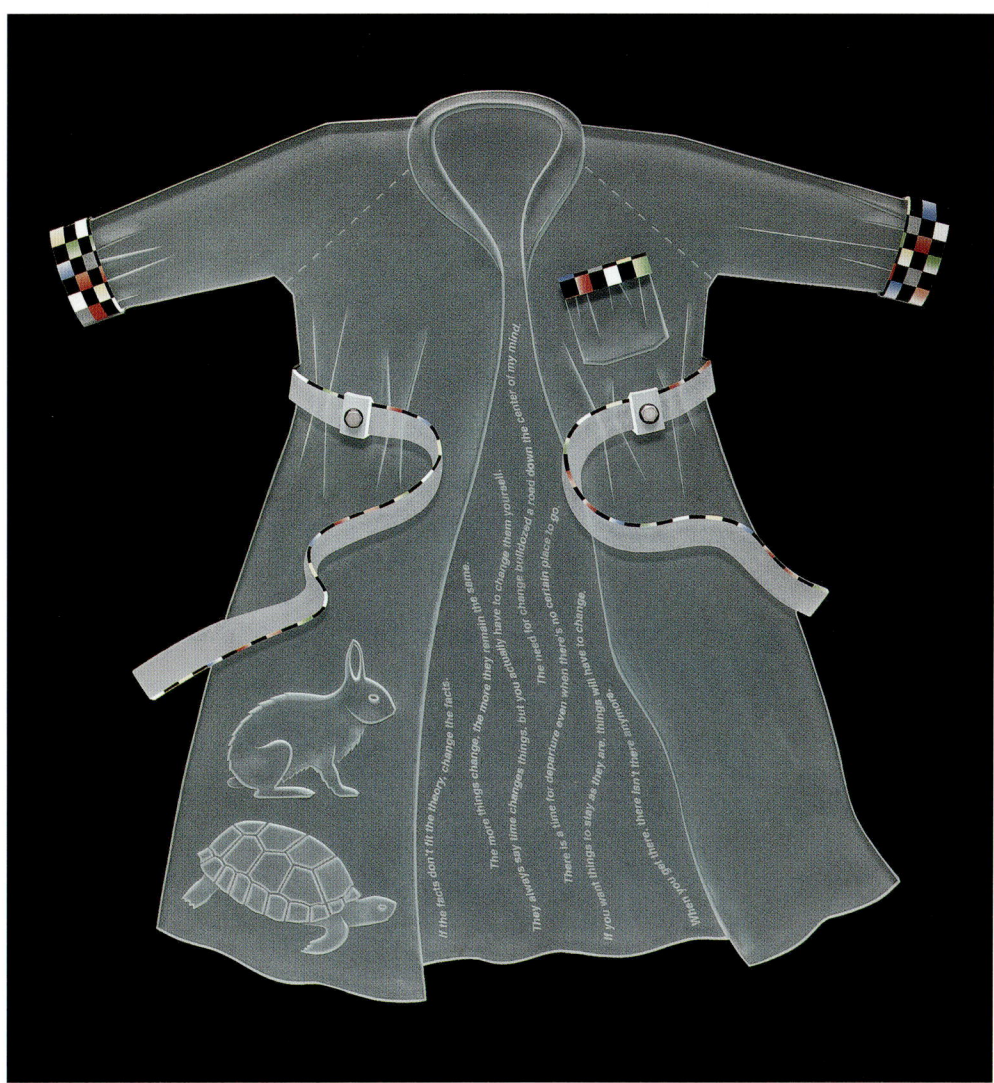

Inside Out, 2000, 25.75" x 25.5" x 1/2", fired enamels on glass, photo: Mark Gulezian. Photograph courtesy of the artist.

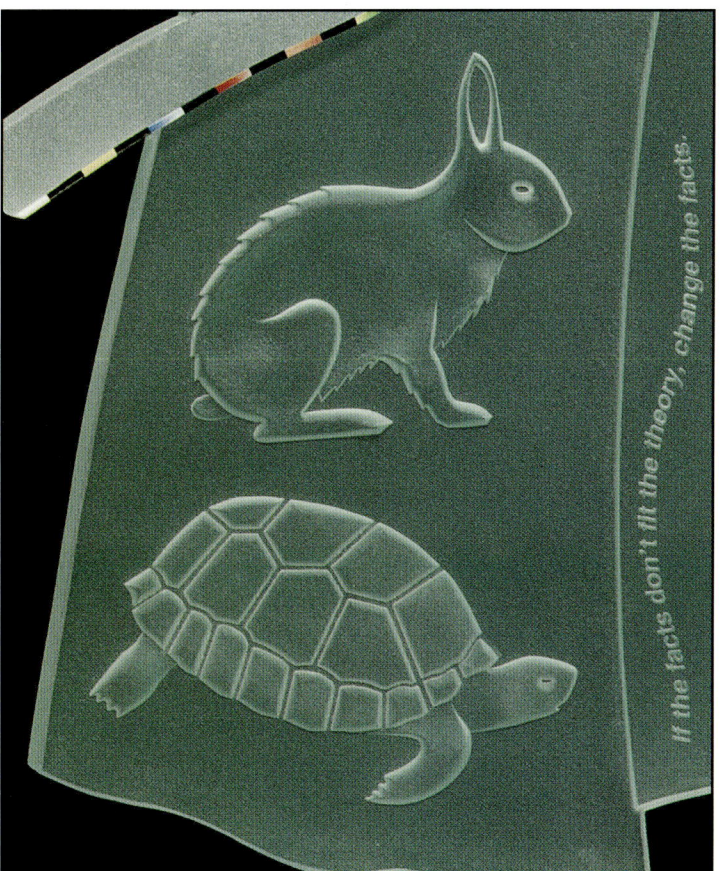

Inside Out, detail.

94   The Seventies - The Artist

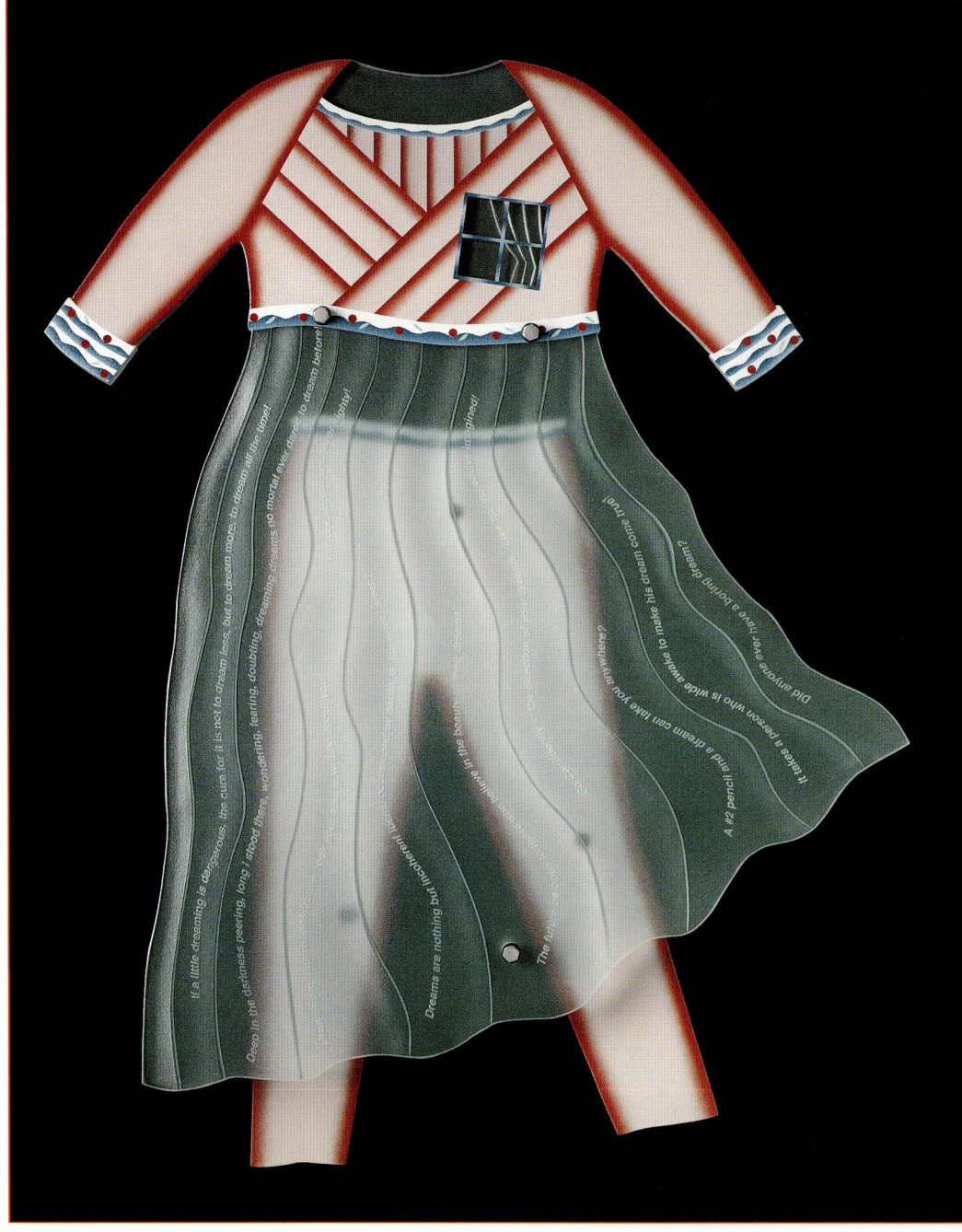

3AM, 2001, 32" x 25" x 1.5", fired enamels on glass, photo: Mark Gulezian. *Photograph courtesy of the artist.*

If a little dreaming is dangerous, the cure for it is not to dream less, but to dream more, to dream all the time!
Marcel Proust. (1871-1922), French novelist

Deep in the darkness peering, long I stood there, wondering, fearing, doubting, dreaming dreams no mortal ever dared to dream before!
Edgar Allan Poe

Dreams are illustrations from a book your soul is writing about you!
Marsha Norman, (1947-), US dramatist

In a dream you are never eighty!
Anne Sexton, (1928-1974), American poet

Dreams are nothing but incoherent ideas, occasioned by partial or imperfect sleep?
Benjamin Rush (1746-1813), US physician, congressman

The future belongs to those who believe in the beauty of their dreams!
Eleanor Roosevelt, (184-1962, American columnist, lecturer, and U.S. delegate at United Nations

Go Confidently in the direction of your dreams. Live the life you've imagined!
Henry David Thoreau, (1817-1862), American writer

A #2 pencil and a dream can take you anywhere?
Joyce A. Myers

It takes a person who is wide awake to make his dream come true!
Roger W. Babson, (1875-1967)

Did anyone ever have a boring dream?
Ralph Hodgson, (1871-1962), British poet

Elizabeth Ryland Mears

My glass leads me
on a journey of creative meditation.

Nestled in the hardwoods of Virginia,
my studio doors open to welcome each season.

The rhythms of nature have become my rhythms.
Deer feast on my plants; birds are my constant companions.
Redwing hawks from their guardian nest
keep a watchful eye and bless my endeavors.
The creek below this adopted land is a place
of solace and protection.
Deer bed down
while spirit children leap stones in the cool wetness.
Dogue Indians lived and hunted here;
Lines of Confederate and Union soldiers ebbed and flowed;
Mammoth hunters stalked prey 11,000 years ago.

These stones and trees
have been witness.
The ground is hallowed by those souls
Who have lived on it
and loved on it
and been nurtured by it.

Their presence welcomes me.
Their spirit is channeled through me
Manifest in my creations.

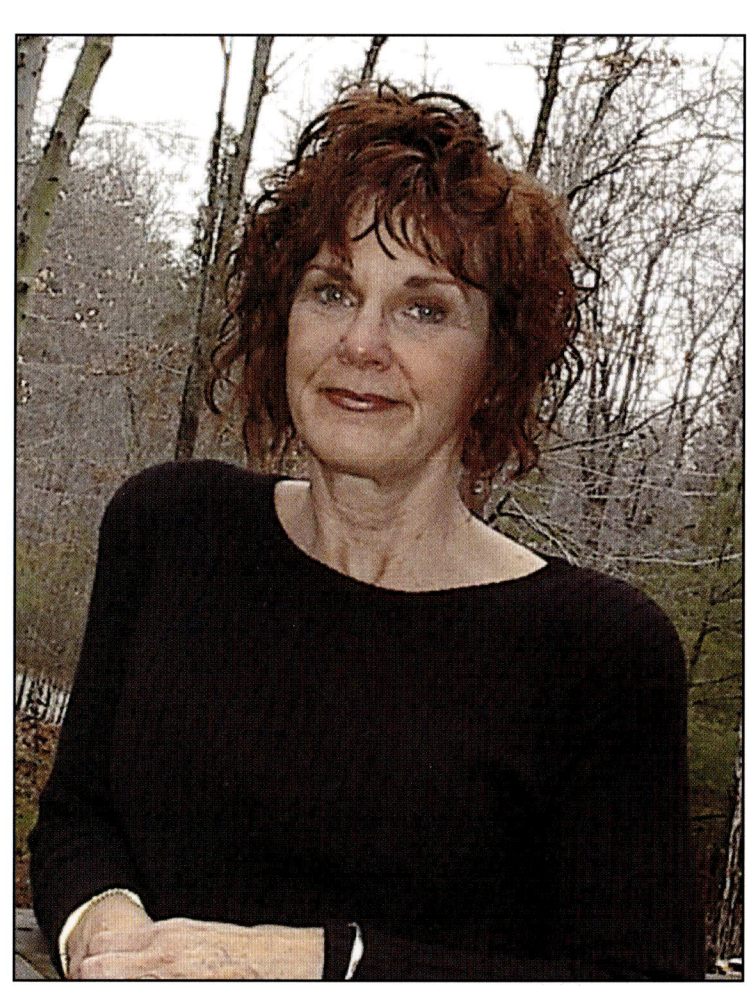

Elizabeth Ryland Mears. *Photograph courtesy of the artist.*

Shelter for her Soul, 2000, 14" x 12" x 12" d, photo: Tommy Elder. Photograph courtesy of the artist.

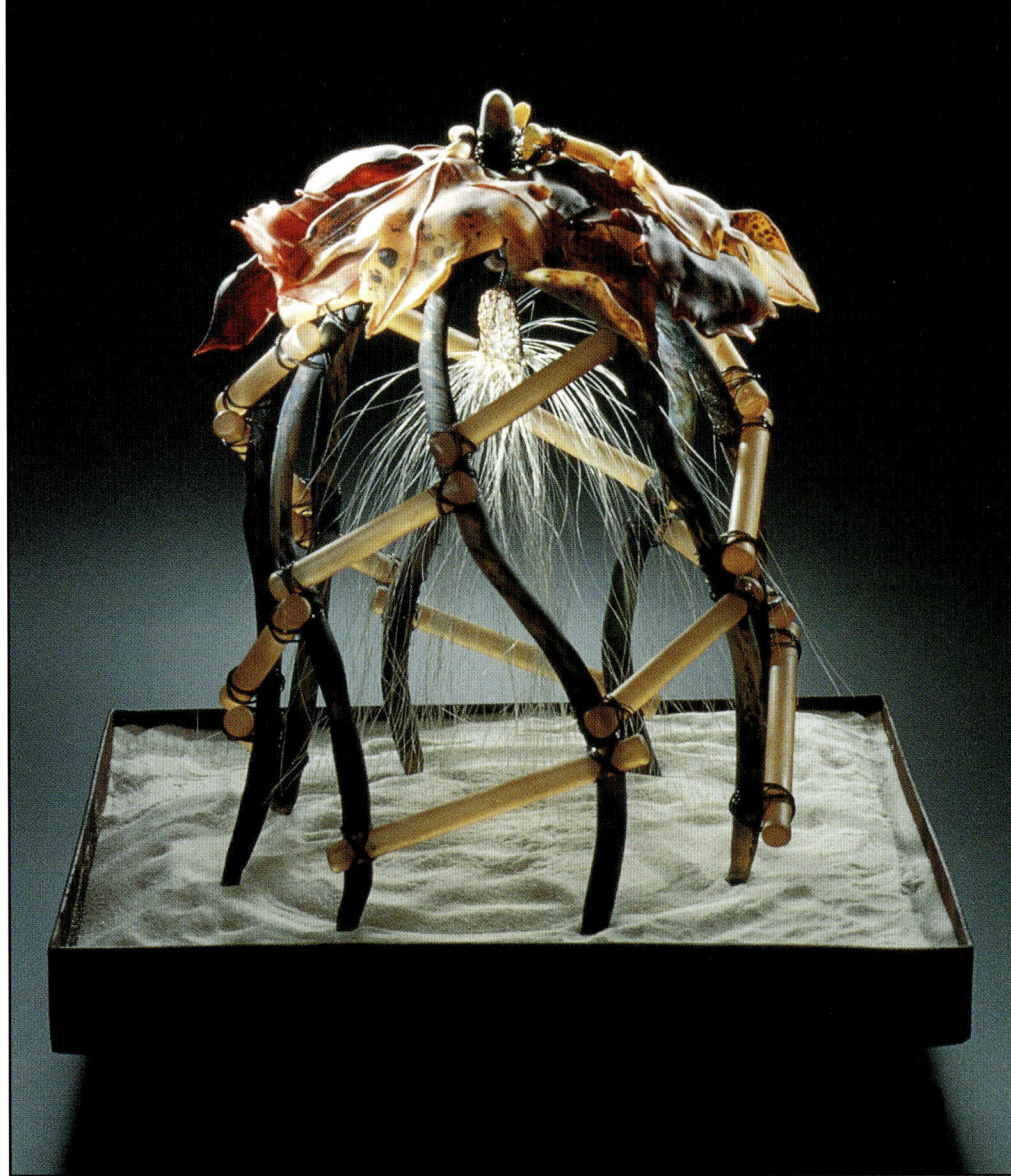

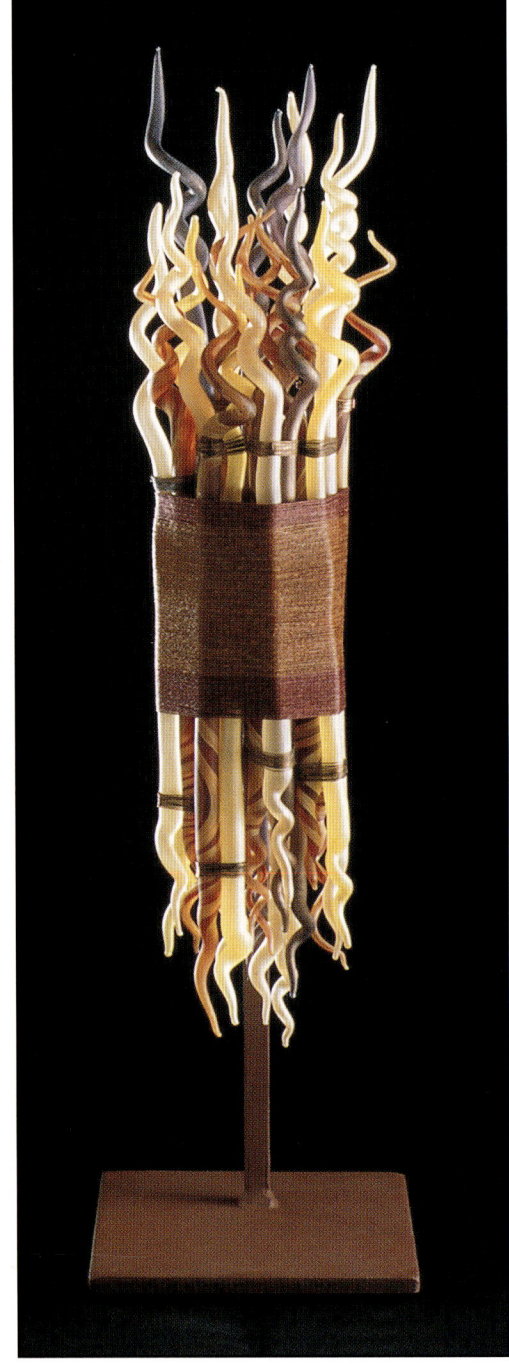

Bundle of Curley Twigs, 2001, 19" x 7" x 5", photo: Tommy Elder. Photograph courtesy of the artist.

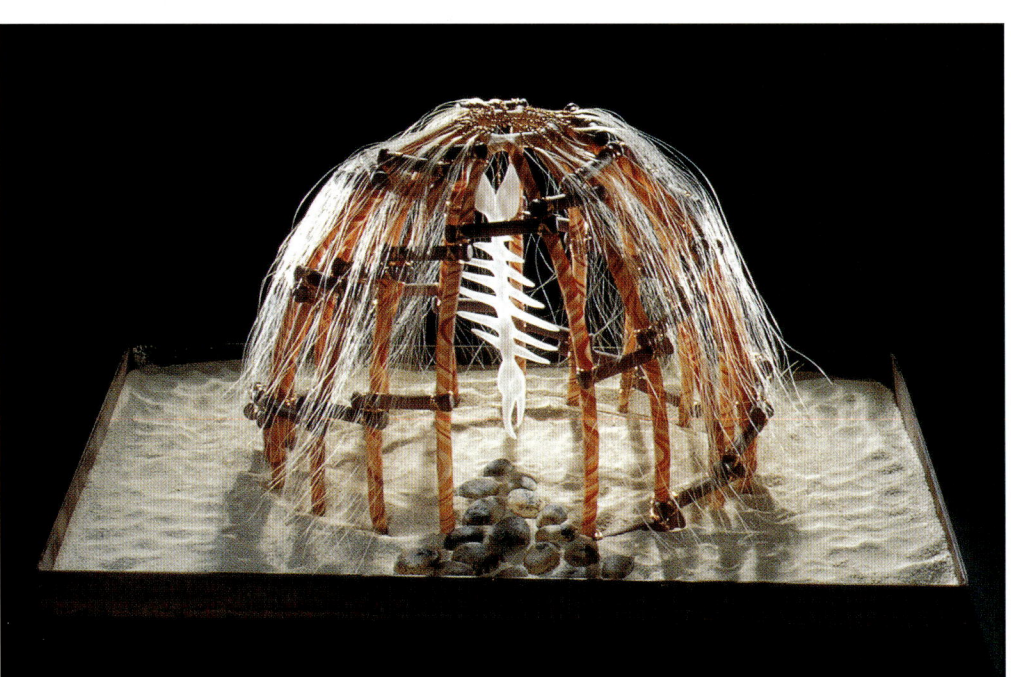

Shelter for Voices From Time Past, 2001, 14" x 24" x 15", photo: Tommy Elder. Photograph courtesy of the artist.

Nancy Mee

Nancy Mee began making art in the 1970s; her early work developed as a result of an interest in medical x rays of the human spine. She was drawn to the plight of disfiguring illness placed in contrast to idealized feminine beauty. Early on, Mee developed a method of applying photographic images of ancient Greek and Roman goddesses to glass to represent classical beauty. The photographic images were sandblasted on glass and placed in steel supports resembling braces.

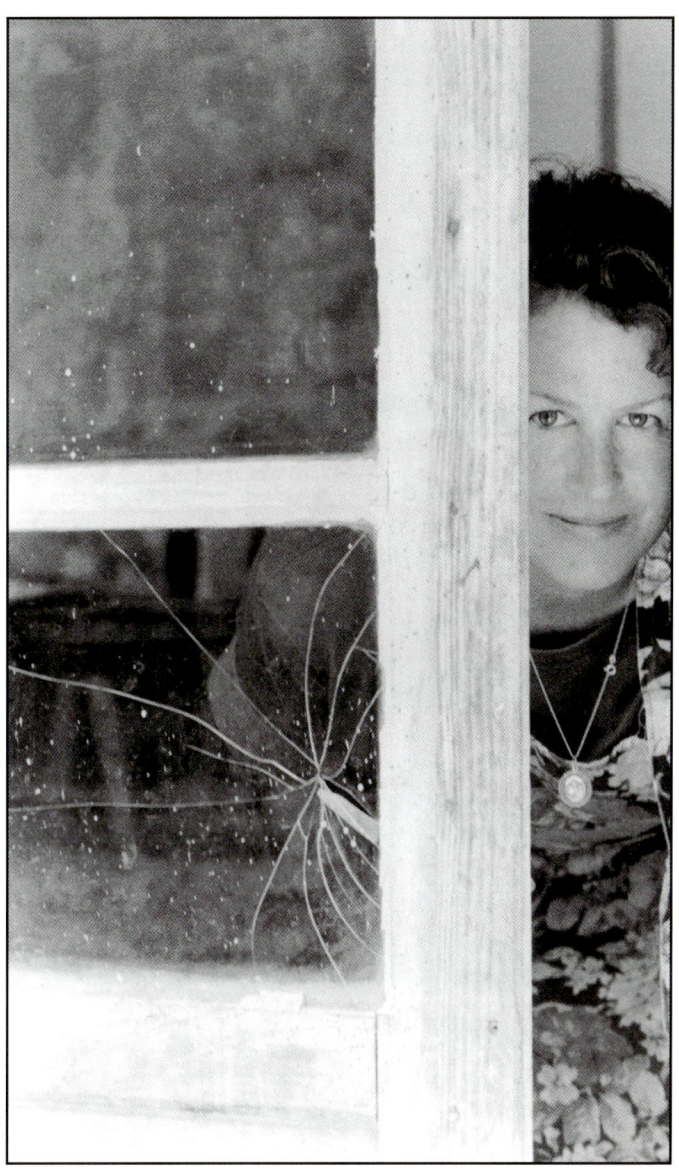

Nancy Mee. *Photograph courtesy of the artist.*

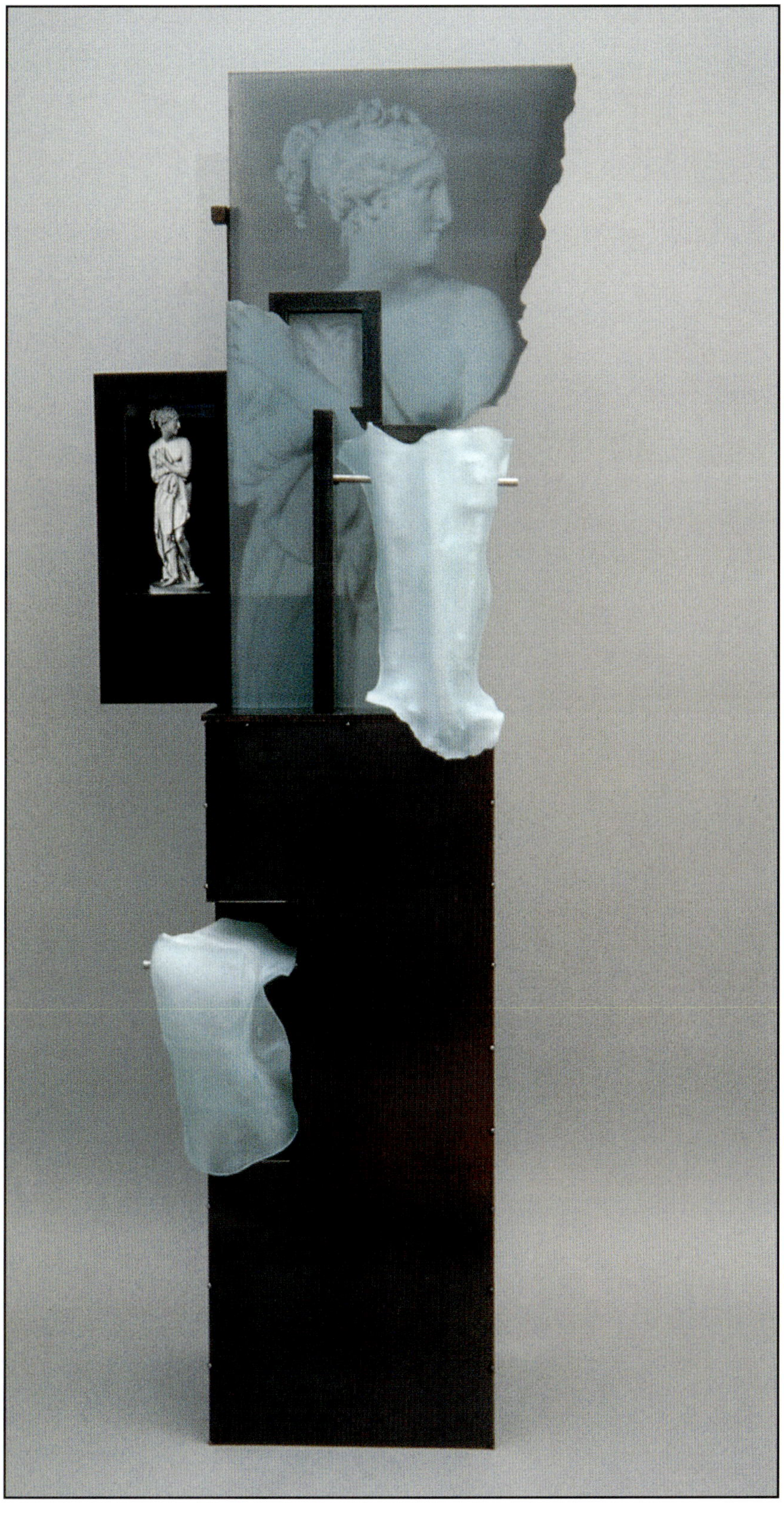

Reconstructing Venus, 1998, 71" x 26" x 18", glass, steel, photo. *Photograph courtesy of the artist.*

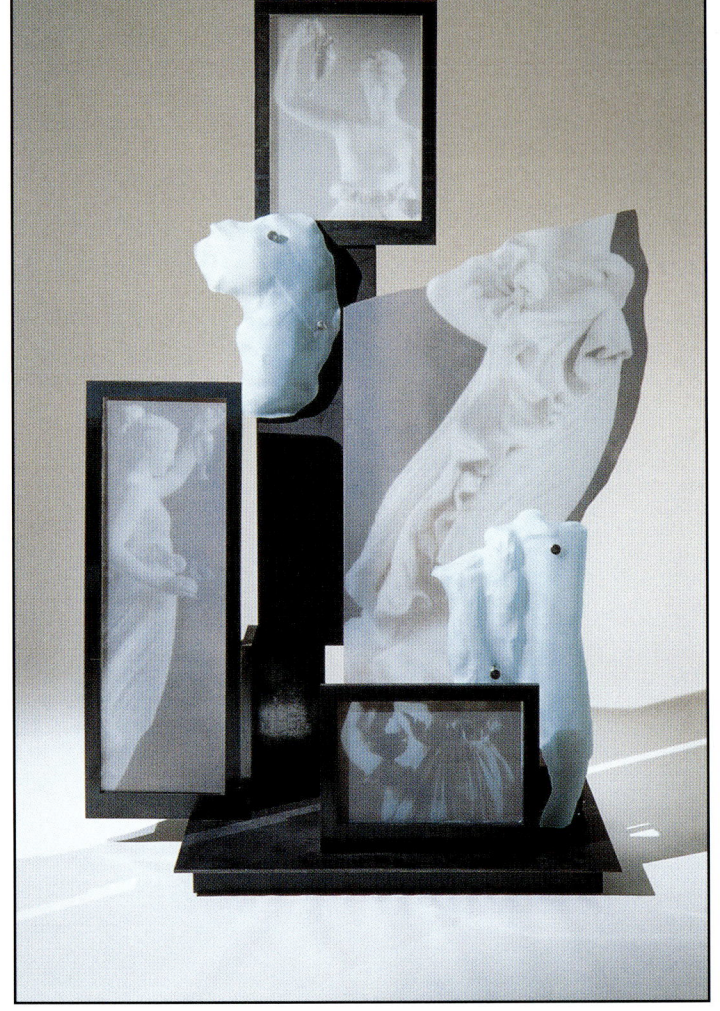

Reconstruction of Ebe, 1999, 82" x 53" x 22", glass, steel, photo-sandblasted glass. Photograph courtesy of the artist.

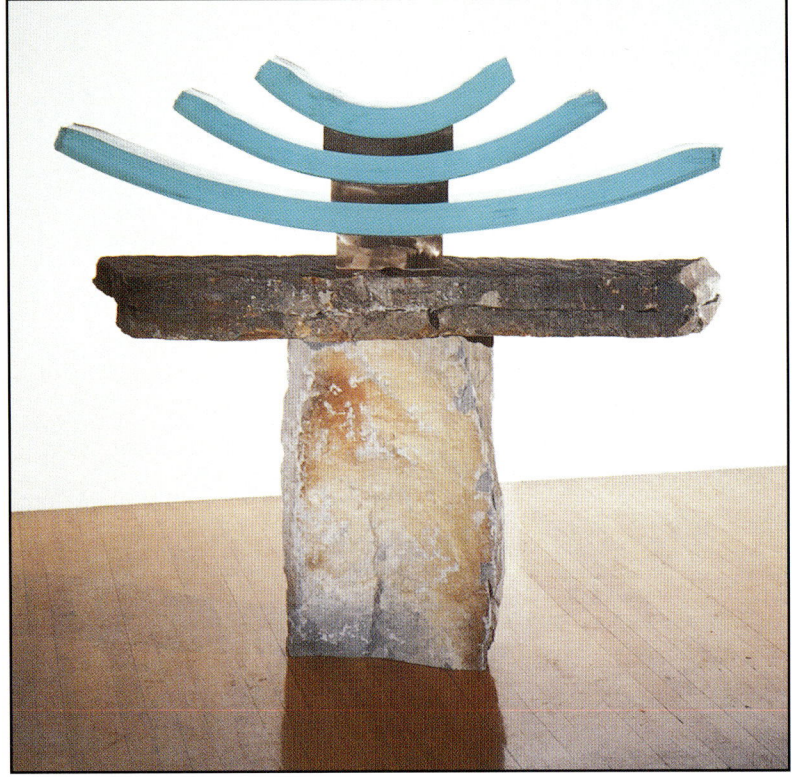

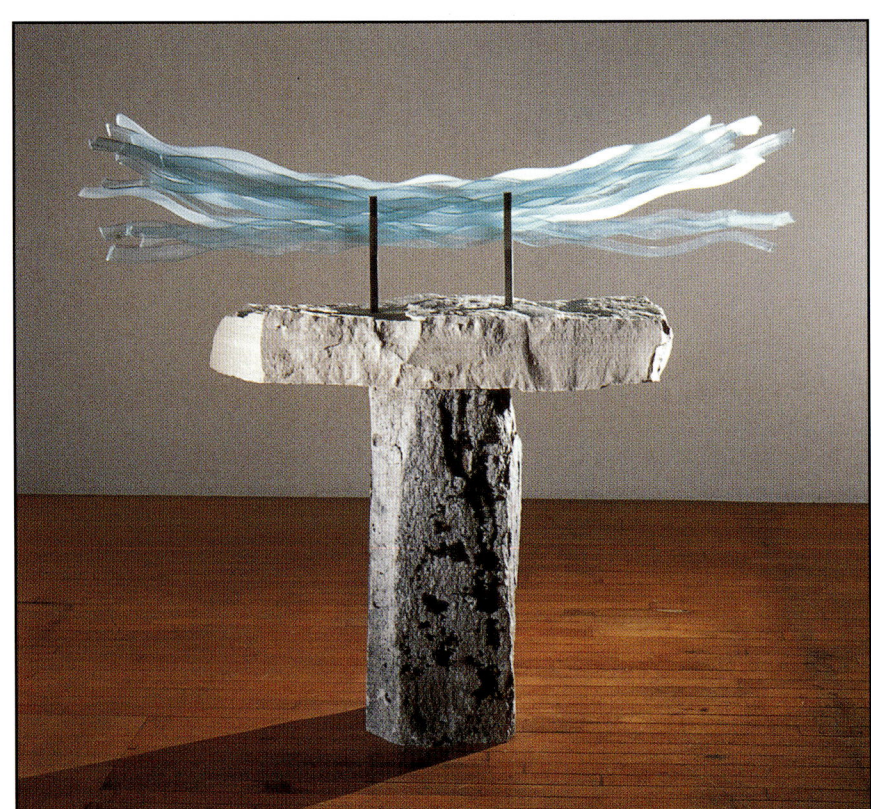

Triple Goddess, 2000, 57" x 65" x 15", glass, bronze, glass. Photograph courtesy of the artist.

Shekhinah Alba, 2000, 54" x 60" x 12", glass, stainless steel, stone. Photograph courtesy of the artist.

Kathleen Mulcahy

Vapors

Vapors is an installation of seven standing metal forms holding clear etched lung-like sacks made of glass with hot attached smaller lower forms that are open or closed The work was inspired by reading about Alchemy and the search for the philosopher's stone or gold, the metaphor for truth. The Alchemists believed that they could distill gold from a certain combination of common elements through heat and evaporation and condensation. They talked about the spirit in the flask. Therefore the alembics or distilling containers had unique and anthropomorphic shapes such as the pelican or two forms twisting. I responded to the idea of the container holding the spirit or breath, creating these spirit forms that in some cases appear to be male and others female.

They are made by two forms joining, one smaller and one larger, and that joining in hot glass is melted to the point of disappearing as the form is blown and swung. The final result is a new form, a form that is just held in a metal stand that mimics the scientific holders for the alembics but on a human scale; a result that is attempting to create a form that is in a moment of transmutation – giving way. The form appears to be breathing, and fluid.

"*Vapors* was inspired by an excerpt of text from *Foucault's Pendulum* by Umberto Eco, *The Breaking of the Vessels*.

> Diotallevi was to talk to us often about the late cabalism of Isaac Luria, in which the orderly articulation of the Sefirot was lost. Creation, Luria held, was a process of divine inhalation and exhalation, like anxious breathing or the action of the bellows.
>
> "God's asthma," Belbo glossed.
>
> "You try creating from nothing. It's something you do once in your life. God blows the world as you would blow a glass bubble, and to do that He takes a deep breath, holds it, and emits the long luminous hiss of the ten Sefirot."
>
> "A hiss of light?"
>
> "God hissed, and there was light."
>
> "Multimedia."
>
> **"But the lights of the Sefirot must be gathered in vessels that can contain their splendor without shattering.** The vessels destined to receive Keter, Hokhmah and Binah withstood their magnificence, but the lower Sefirot, from Hesed to Yesod light was exhaled too strongly in a single burst, and the vessels broke. Fragments of light spilled into the universe, and gross matter was thus born."
>
> (Beginning of chapter 34, p. 185, Ballantine edition, 1990.)

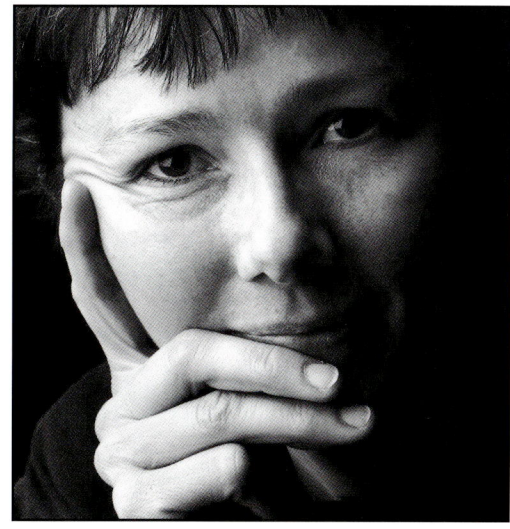

Kathleen Mulcahy photograph.

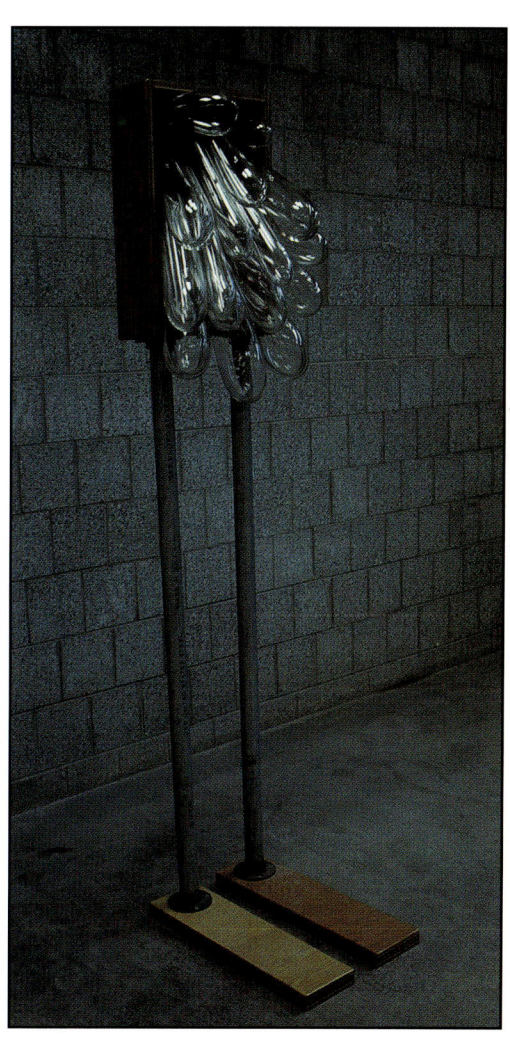

Untitled: self portrait, 1973, 5.5" h x 14" w x 18" d. Photo courtesy of the artist.

100   The Seventies - The Artist

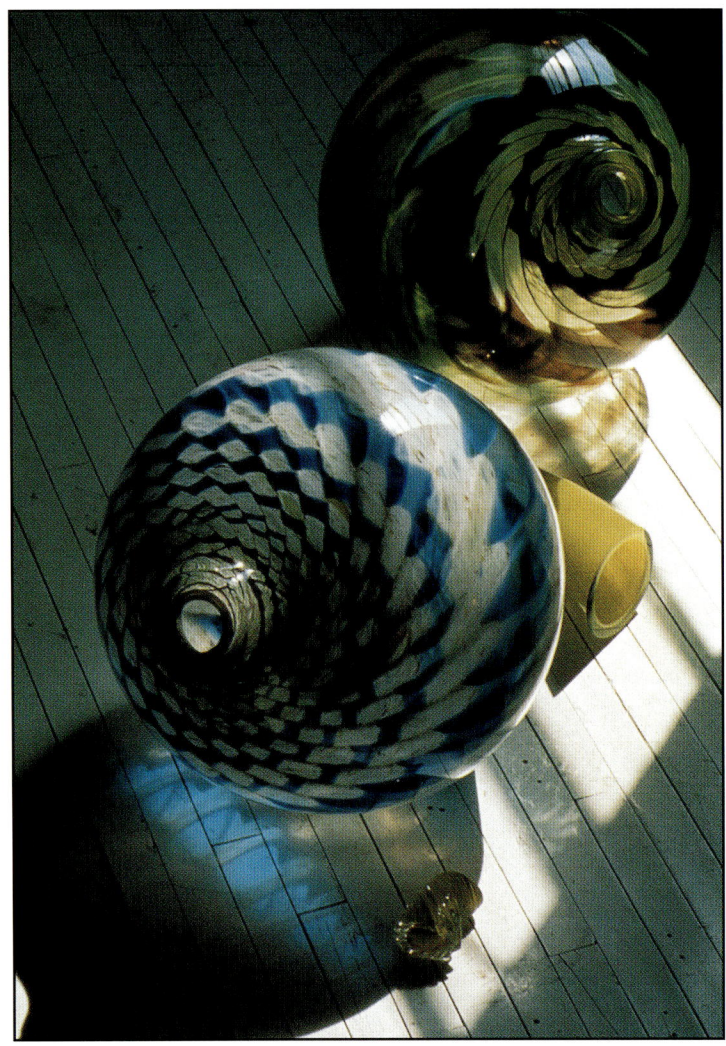

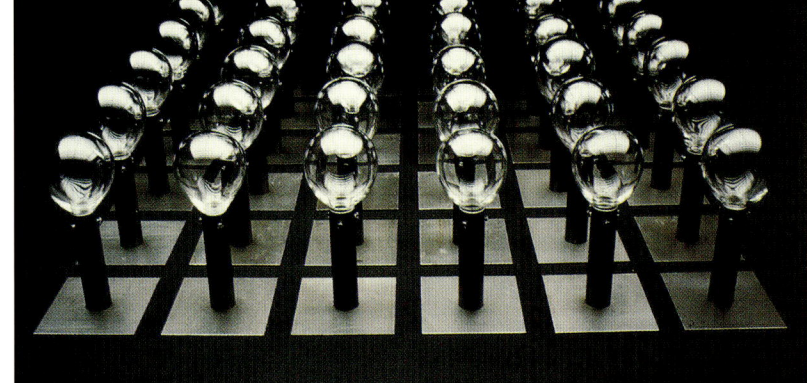

Spinner Installation: Studio, 20" x 22" x 48". *Photo courtesy of the artist.*

Units, 1974, 36" x 36" x 10", 100 units blown glass. *Photo courtesy of the artist.*

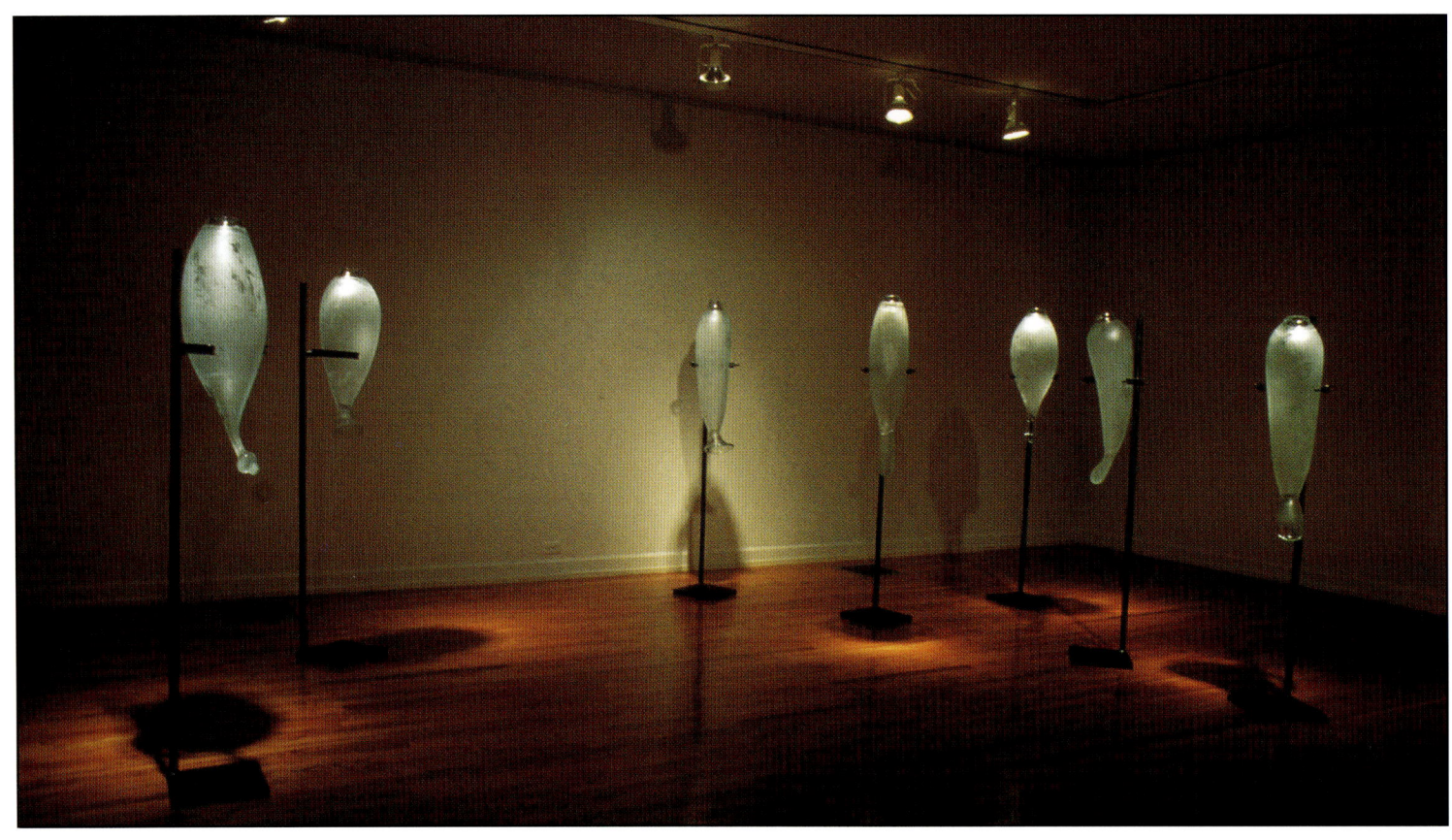

Vapors, 5' h x 15' l x 9' w, blown glass and fabricated metal. *Photo courtesy of the artist.*

Flo Perkins

Flo Perkins has been living and making art in New Mexico for the past twenty years. Her work reflects in-depth investigations of the relationship between blown glass and botanical forms. Through the study of cacti, Flo began to realize how a flower's bud, bloom, and collapse relates directly to the technical process of blowing glass; the bubble, the opening, and the folding. Her cacti and bouquets continue to evolve and assume new shapes and floral forms with each sculpture.

"The Corning Museum of Glass recently acquired *Mazzo Sporgente* (*Leaning Bouquet*), a blown glass, steel rebar, and bronze sculpture, which stands over four feet tall. The sculpture's creator, Flo Perkins, is one of a small group of women artists who began to blow glass in the 1970s. She received a B.A. from Philadelphia College of Art in 1974, and an M.A. from the University of California at Los Angeles in 1981. Her work reflects her experience of nature as a haven from the chaos of daily life.

Best known for the series of colorful glass cacti that she developed over the last twenty years, Perkins began in the 1990s a new series of flower forms that combined glass and metal. Initially experimenting with rebar, she moved onto bronze, steel, and iron for the creation of her large bouquets, lattices, wreaths, and swags. In *Mazzo Sporgente*, Perkins creates a dynamic balance between the innately colorful, fluid glass and the monochromatic, hard metal, conveying a fleeting sense of flowers waving in the wind.

Mazzo Sporgente was selected by staff members of the Corning Museum of Glass on the occasion of the museum's 50th anniversary to celebrate and acknowledge their work during the extensive renovation of the museum complex. Selected by vote, this acquisition was chosen from a group of contemporary glass sculptures and vessels that were preselected by the museum's curatorial staff."

Corning Museum of Glass, 2002

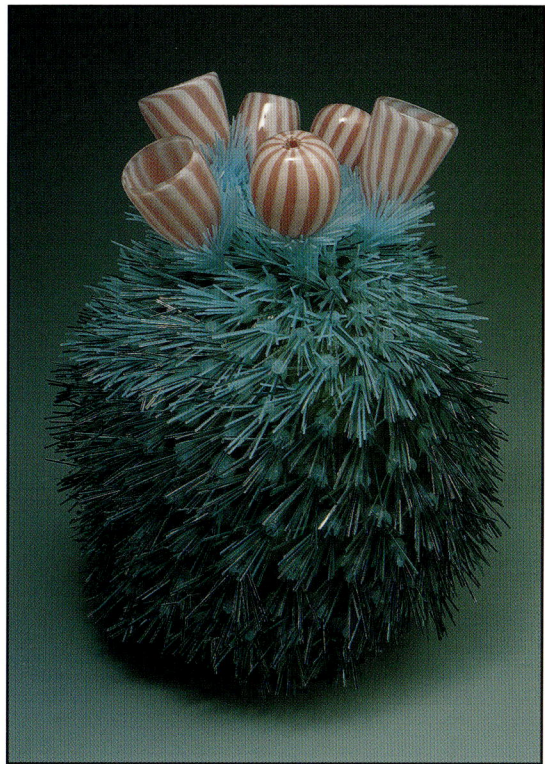

Harbinger, 1986, 15" h, blown glass, photo: Lynn Hamrick. *Photograph courtesy of the artist.*

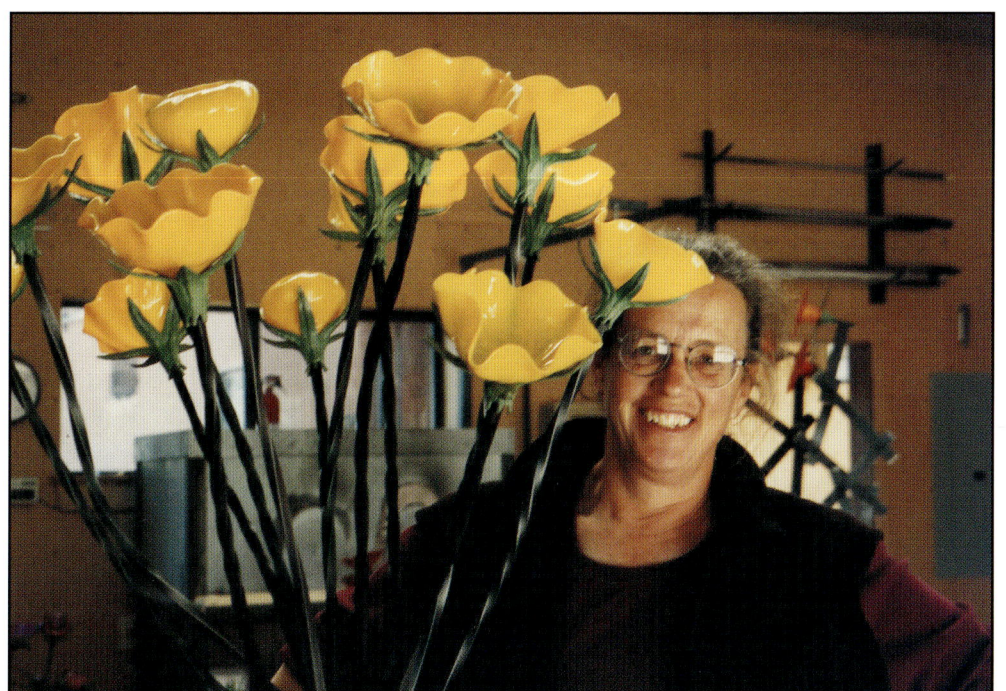

Flo Perkins photograph. *Photo courtesy of the artist.*

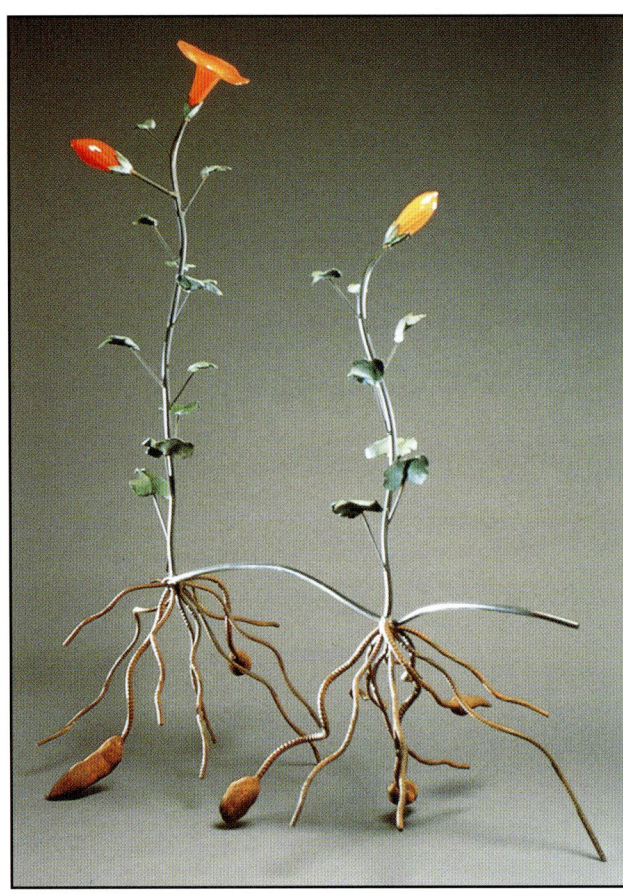

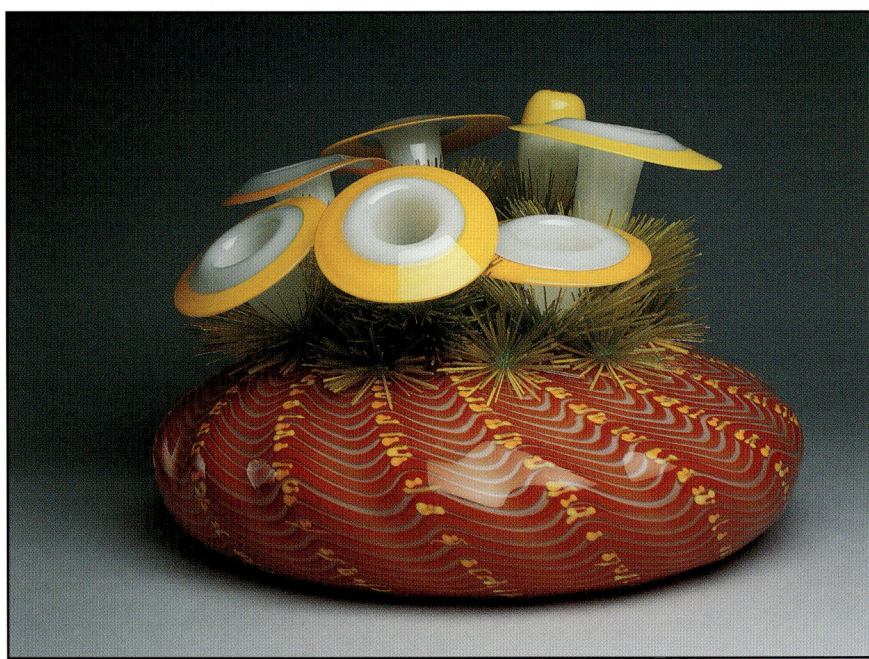

Tuba City Cactus, 1999, 13.5" x 19.25" x 19.25", blown glass, photo: Addison Doty. *Photograph courtesy of the artist.*

Sweet Potato Plant, 1994, 62" x 54" x 28", photo: Addison Doty. *Photograph courtesy of the artist.*

Scelto, 2002, 18.5" x 13" x 13", blown glass, photo: Addison Doty. *Photograph courtesy of the artist.*

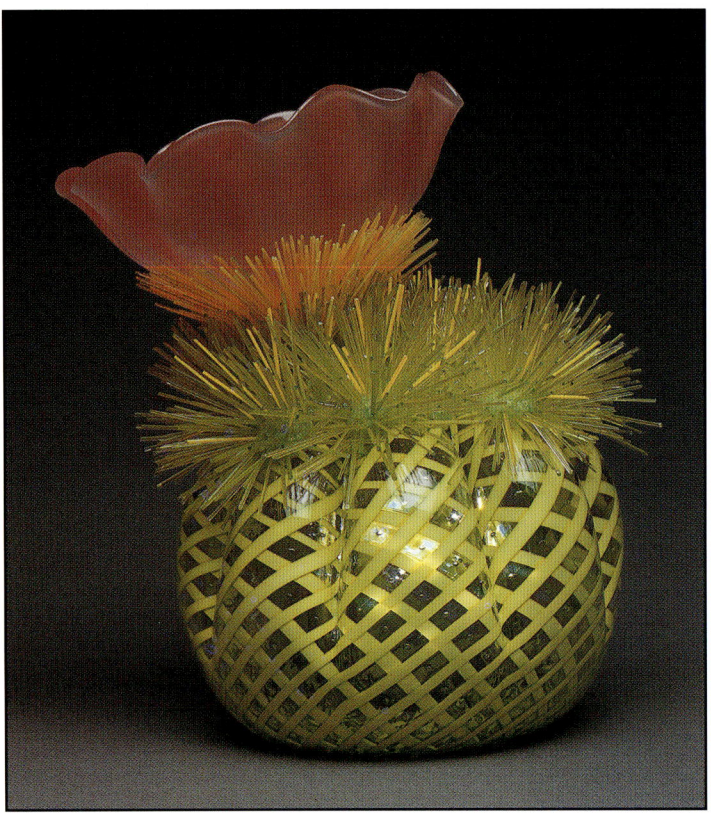

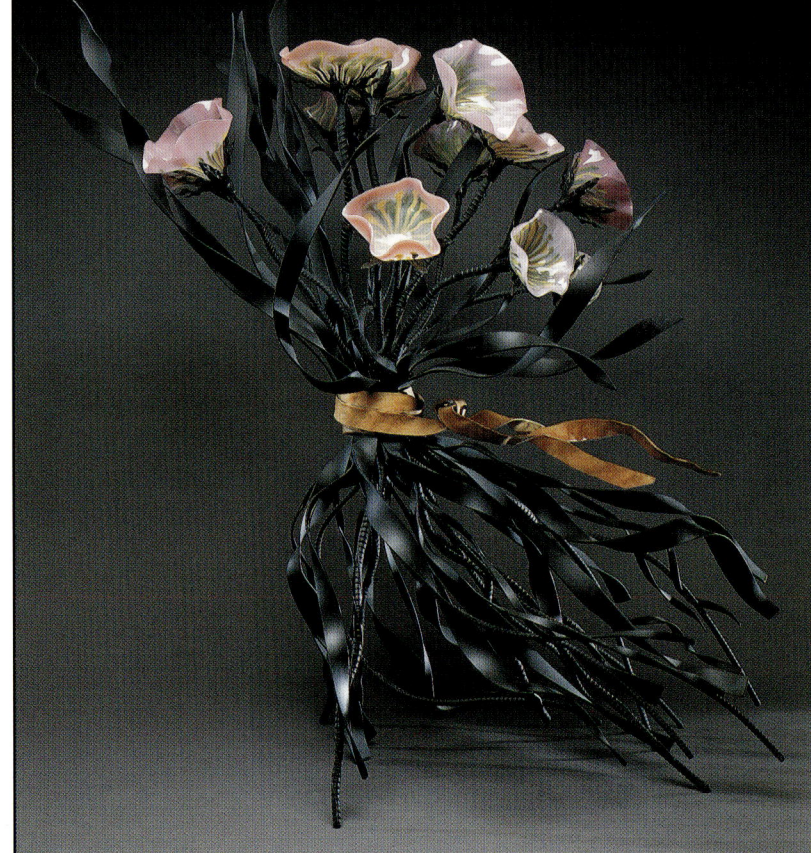

Mazzo Sporgente, 2000, 49" x 47" x 35", blown glass, steel, bronze, Corning Museum Purchase, photo: Addison Doty. *Photograph courtesy of the artist.*

Judith Schaechter

My parents, not artists themselves, accidentally made me an artist by ascribing genius to every scribble I made. My mother kept and labeled everything. Looking through this stuff in college, I was surprised to find out what a case of arrested development I am. I drew dead lions, crying kitties, and Winston Churchill in his coffin. I never thought of myself as an artist and one of the reasons I wanted to go to art school was the lack of either a mathematics and Phys. Ed. requirement.

My involvement with stained glass dates back to whenever it was I got my Lite-Brite™ toy. Later, I made those bake in the oven suncatchers. I took stained glass as an elective in art school (I was a painting major at the time) with Ursula Huth and switched into the Glass Department.

I guess part of the appeal for me is the tedium factor. I don't have too many worthy and profound ideas so each piece needs to take a certain amount of time—this keeps my hands busy and in sync with my head. Ironically, I find my "artistic voice" is liberated only by technical restrictions. Often, the more monotonous and difficult a process, the more exciting I find it. Incidentally, for this reason, I've always found the process of painting intolerable. Nothing is more horrible than a blank canvas and nothing is more easily filled with meaningless "arty" brushstrokes. I went through a phase as a painter when I would gesso over all the superfluous elements—and I would always end up staring at a white rectangle again!

Another reason I stick with stained glass is because I think the raw material is pretty. The uncut sheets of colored glass are really seductive, awesome and unarguably lovely things. Naturally, the temptation to cut and damage all that pristine beauty is too much for me to resist.

Finally, my atheist upbringing accounts for my attraction to the spiritual aspects of transmitted light (plus it was probably an advantage not to have too many preconceived notions about the look and functions of the medium). In the 13th century, Abbot Suger, the designer of St. Denis, said that stained glass was "enlightenment embodied."

The creative process is weird, elusive, and ultimately, probably unknowable. In fact, the more I think I know, the more I am rudely surprised to discover I am clueless! When things go right, I have no grasp of the mechanisms that make inspiration fall in step with the formal elements of art. At those times, I feel "guided by the hand of God" (so much for atheism...). I wish, in the case of abject failure, I was "guided by the hand of Bozo," but those cases seem emphatically my own responsibility.

Sometimes ideas occur suddenly, and sometimes they've lingered for years and years. Ideas are inspired by events in my life, the world, or even other people's ideas that I wish I'd had. The technical process itself generates irresistible challenges, like depicting fire, water or garbage. Often, I let my hands do the thinking. Doodling is an intuitive process and the more distracted I am the better. Radio, television, lectures, and telephone conversations all serve to improve my work. Nothing is more inhibiting than the pressure to come up with some *Brilliant Artistic Idea*. The ideas I get drawing are almost always the best ones—they tend to override any intellectual concepts that seem like good ideas for art. No matter how much I love an idea, I'll sacrifice it for the look of the piece. I believe that in visual art the bottom line "conceptually" is always the aesthetic.

In short, the "idea" is a combination of many ideas and inspirations that are of particularly intense interest to me.

So what is the work about? It would be misleading to speak about its significance as if it came from some kind of master plan or missionary stance. I have no point of view on life that I can't be argued out of in, say, five minutes. I certainly never heard a philosophy so compelling that it merited illustration in stained glass. I don't even have clear narratives in mind. The "story" begins and ends with what you see.

I guess I have no intentions when I approach a project (besides making a piece). Meaning is what happens when it is looked at. My interpretations have no more importance than yours do—if I claim otherwise, I am stealing from the audience.

I think I am a fairly normal human specimen. My interests are not peculiar to me and my thoughts about them not necessarily original (until they become stained glass panels, hopefully). My main interests are sex, death, romance, loss, and violence. I am trying to be as cliché, sentimental, and decorative as possible—not as a strategy for ironic commentary but because this is the stuff that, time and time again, I am obsessed with, in love with, and that I have faith in.

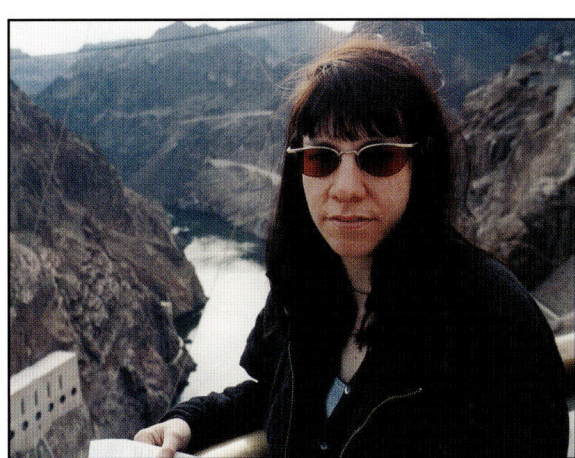

Judith Schaechter. *Photograph courtesy of the artist.*

Primavera, 1987, 24" x 15", stained glass. Photograph courtesy of the artist.

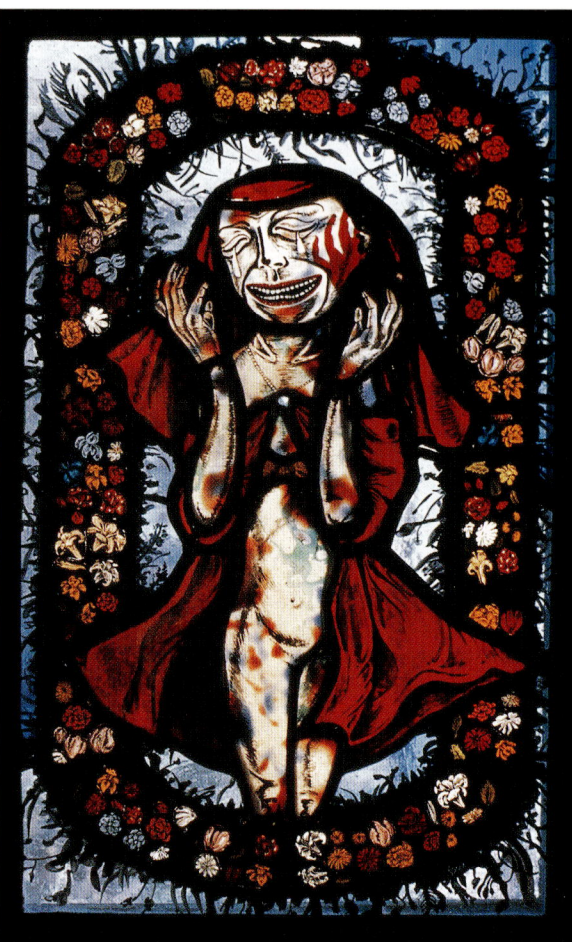

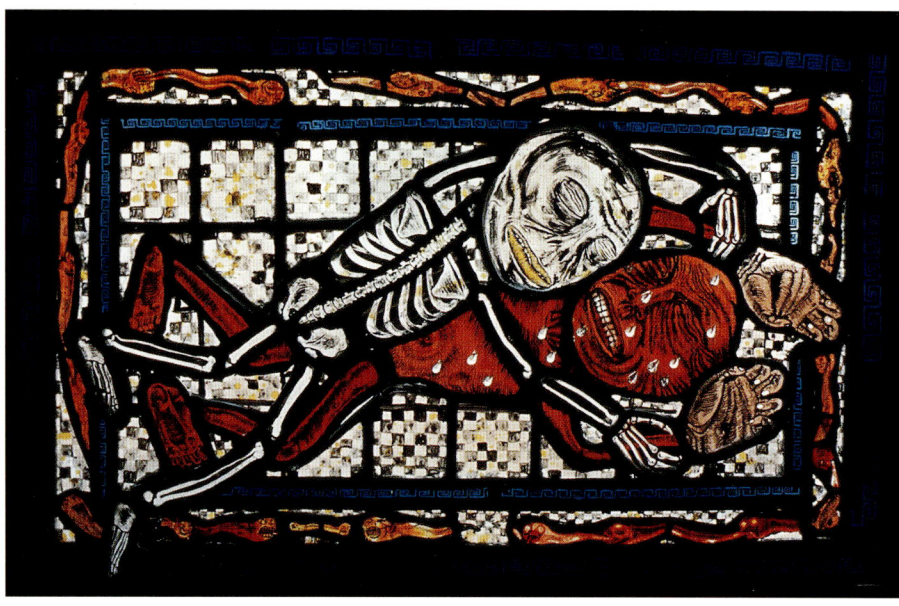

Vide Futentes, 1985, 14" x 24", stained glass. Photograph courtesy of the artist.

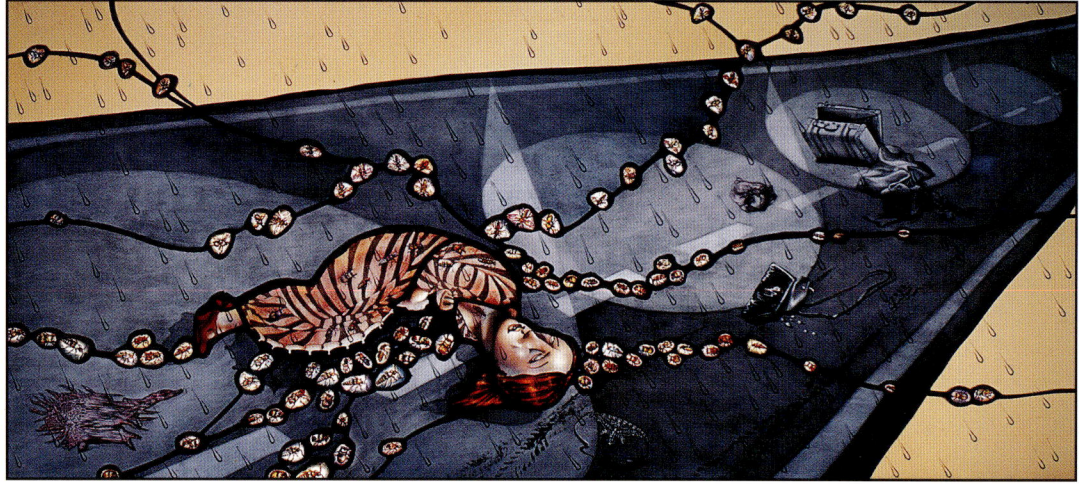

Road-kill Ophelia, 1998, 19" x 41", stained glass. Photograph courtesy of the artist.

Speech Balloon, 1999, 28" x 24", stained glass. Photograph courtesy of the artist.

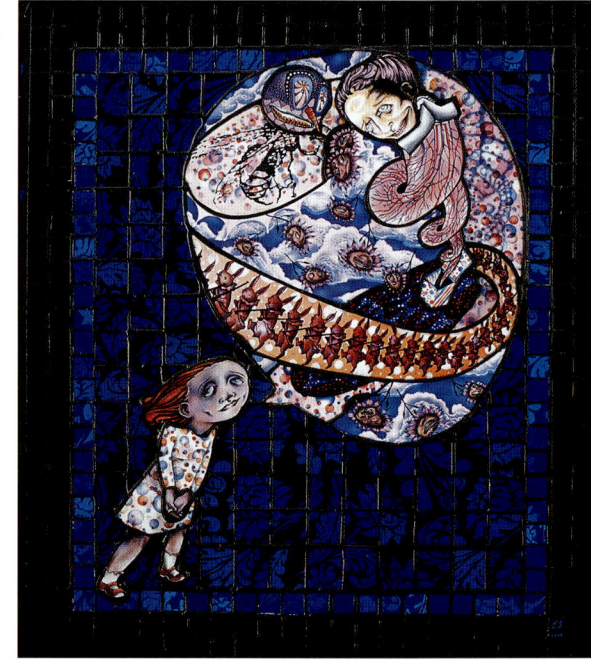

Kathleen Sheard

My love of animals has extended from numerous family pets to a diverse array of exotic inhabitants from far corners of the world. I first visit zoos, wildlife refuges, and National Parks to study the interactions of animals with each other and their surroundings. By observing the animals I gain an understanding that makes it possible to portray the animal in a motionless medium, but still evoke an impression of life, of movement. The soul of the animal resides in the image, giving the viewer a lingering impression of impending motion or action.

I have had the opportunity to travel to Australia and Africa to study some of my subjects in their natural environment. The photographic records of these journeys are my most valued resource in creating my art. By doing research on each subject, I develop a connection with the animal. Using that connection, I make a drawing from my photos, which I transfer to a sheet of glass. I then painstakingly arrange small pieces of glass frit in an initial layer and repeat the process, layering colors upon each other, firing at high temperatures multiple times. This slow process is not exact, and each piece evolves as it is created. The finished piece will not necessarily be a duplicate of my initial conception. This fluidity requires a deep understanding of the subject, allowing me to guide the process, rather than force it to conform to a preconceived idea.

All of my work incorporates the story of the animal. Facts about their lives, their environment, and the threats that they face in their continued existence are facets of a whole that I hope to expose more people to as they view my works.

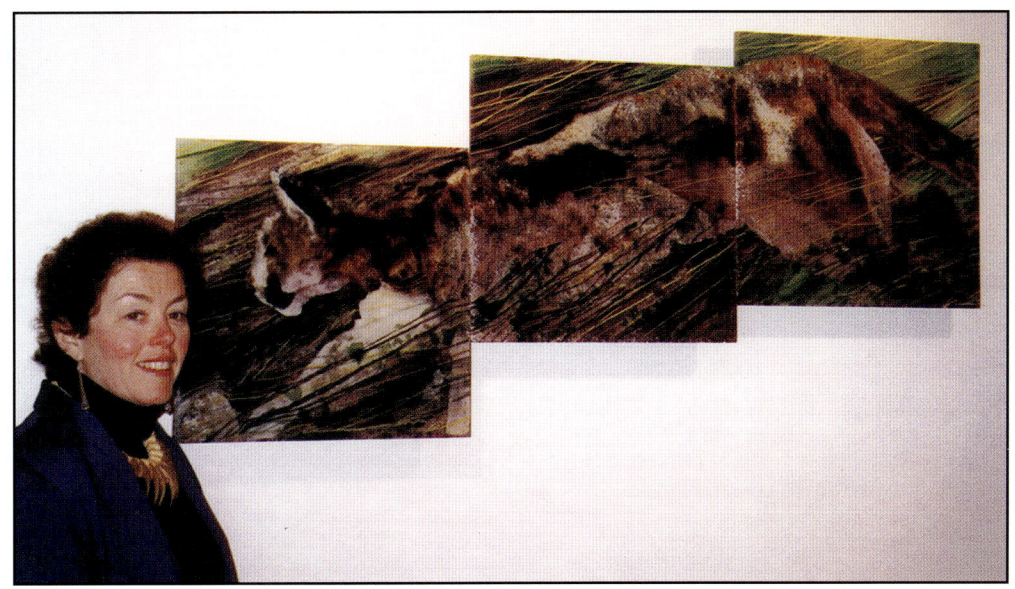

Kathleen Sheard. *Photograph courtesy of the artist.*

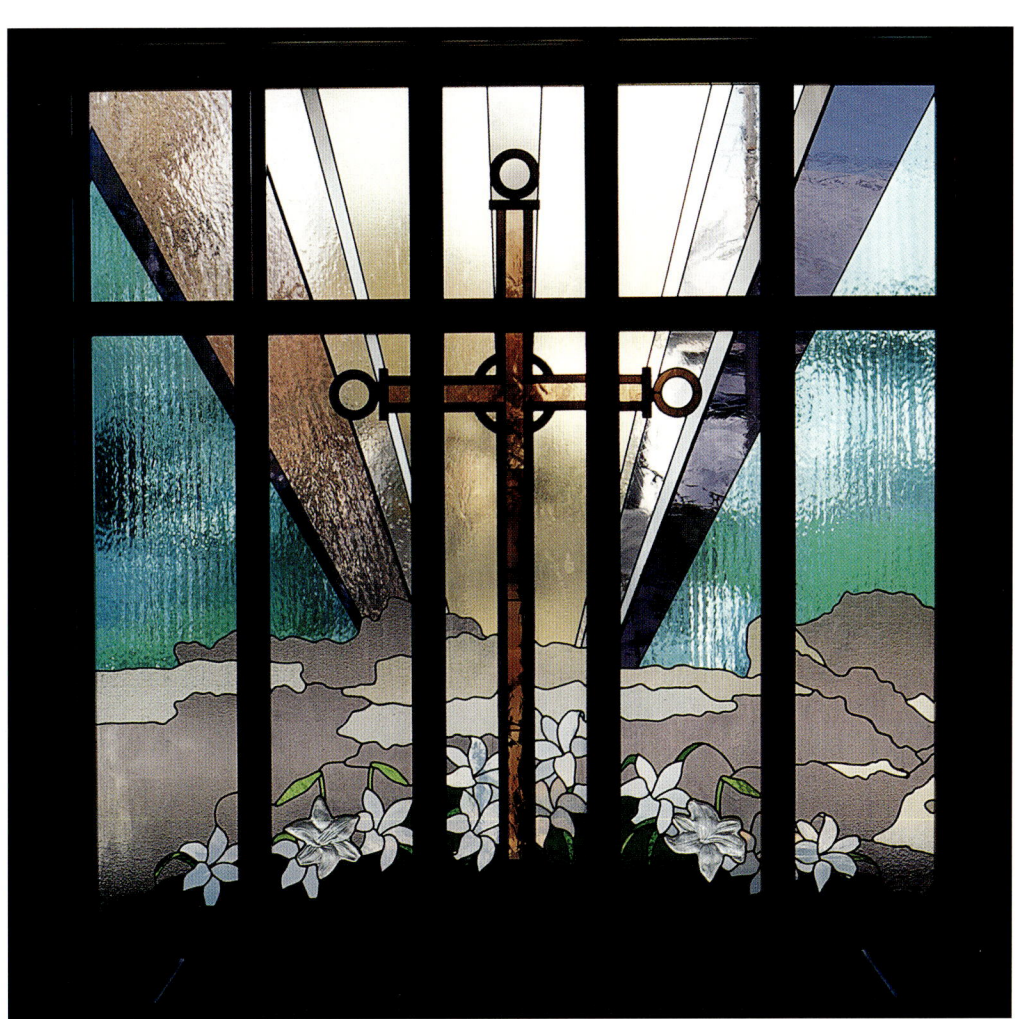

Milwaukee Presbyterian Sanctuary Windows, Milwaukee, Oregon, 1993, 8' x 9', Stained and cast glass. *Photograph courtesy of the artist.*

106   The Seventies - The Artist

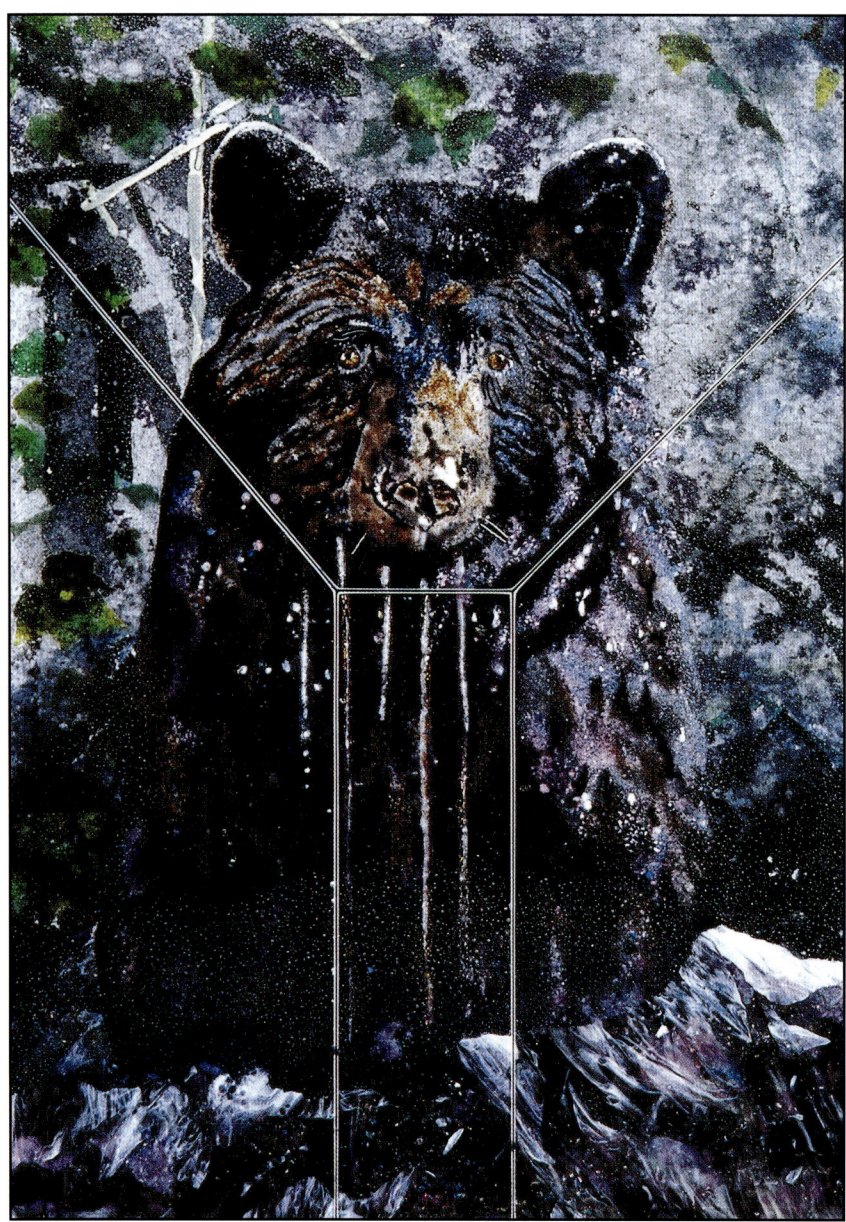

Ursus americanus – Territorial Stand, 2001, 30" x 40", kiln formed glass, photo: Bill BachHuber. *Photograph courtesy of the artist.*

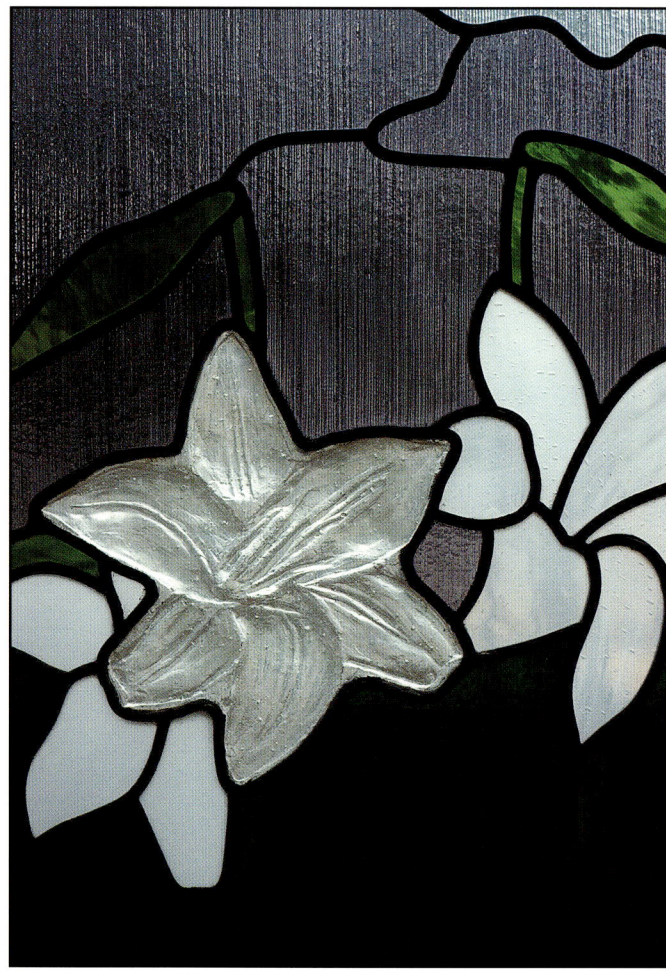

Milwaukee Presbyterian Sanctuary Windows, detail. *Photograph courtesy of the artist.*

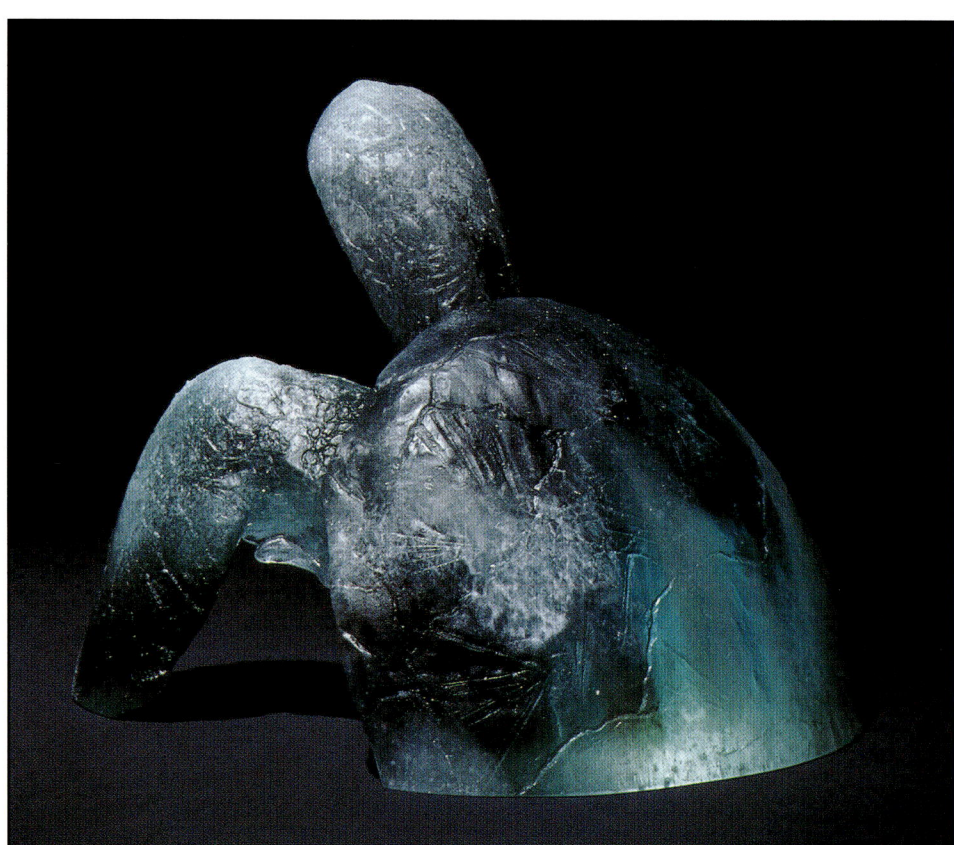

Chelonia mydas-Grandfather, 2002, 14" x 11" x 9", kiln cast glass, Photo: Bill BachHuber. *Photograph courtesy of the artist.*

Molly Stone

My respect and awe of the natural world, the beauty of form and color, and the inner spirit of the moment guide me. I choose to look towards the positive, the beautiful, and the spiritual. I hope that my work reflects joy, as that is how I experience working with glass, and what I find has importance in life.

I love the process of making glass. I love the movement, the focus, and the timing that glass demands. Even after twenty-five years, each day is more rewarding than the last, and I am excited by the potential of what I may make tomorrow. Glass is older and wiser than I, and I learn from it every day.

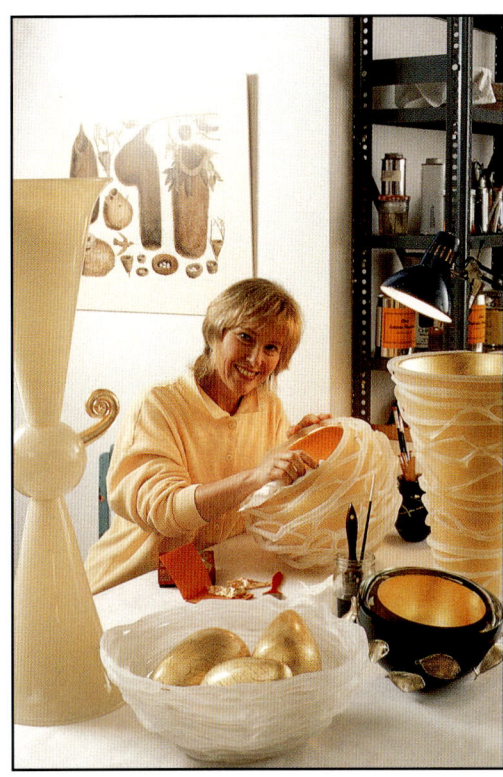

Molly Stone. *Photograph courtesy of the artist.*

Napkin Plate, 1984, 14" d, blown, fused, sandblasted. *Photograph courtesy of the artist.*

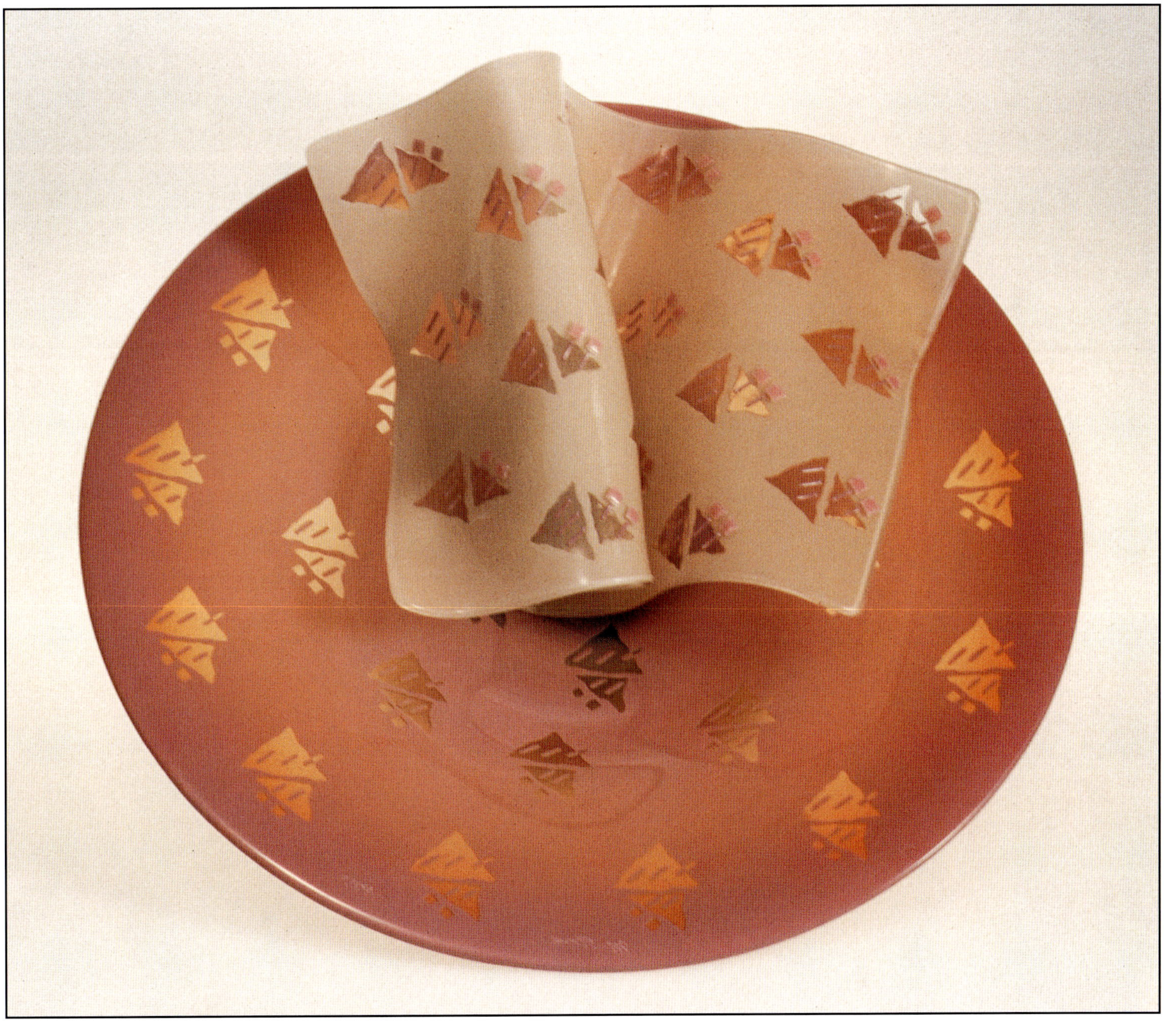

108   The Seventies - The Artist

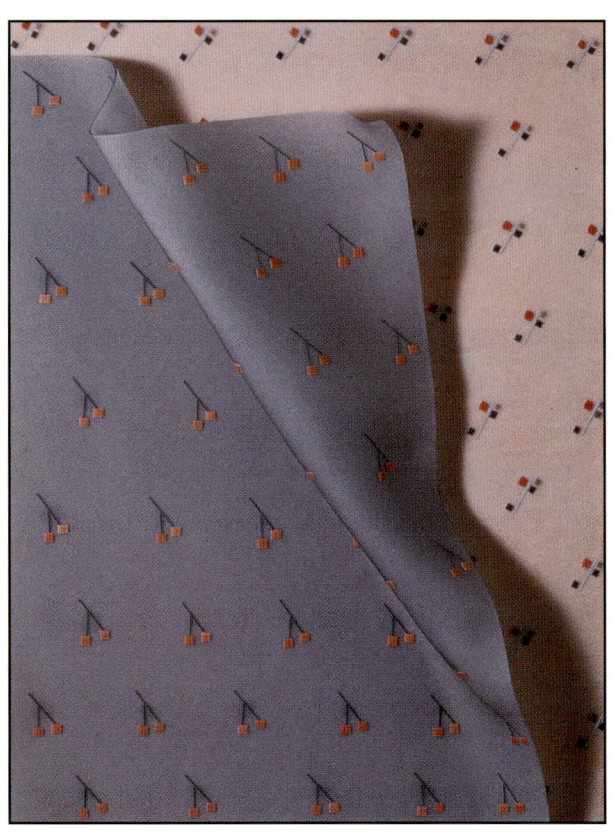

Wall Paper Panel, 1983, 24" x 30", blown, fused, sandblasted. Photograph courtesy of the artist.

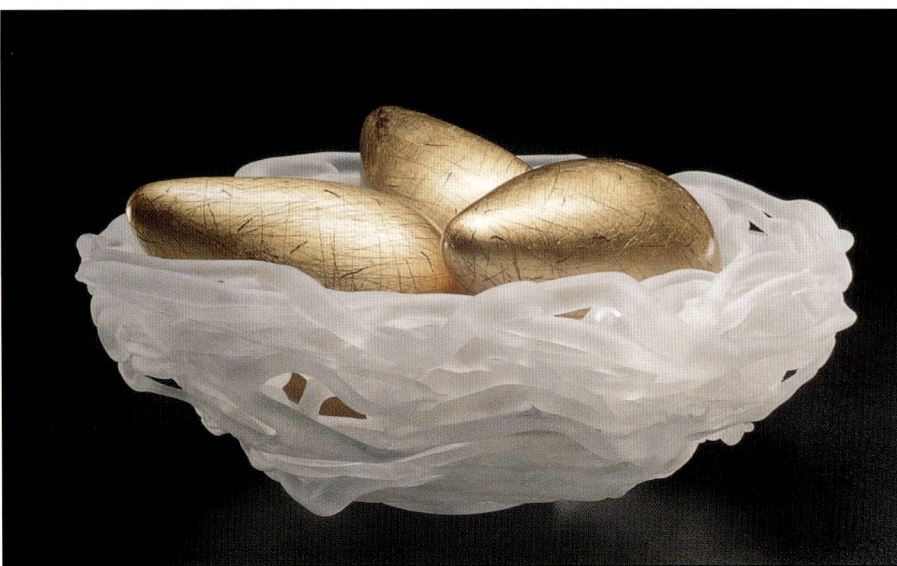

Nest with Golden Eggs, 14" d, blown glass. Photograph courtesy of the artist.

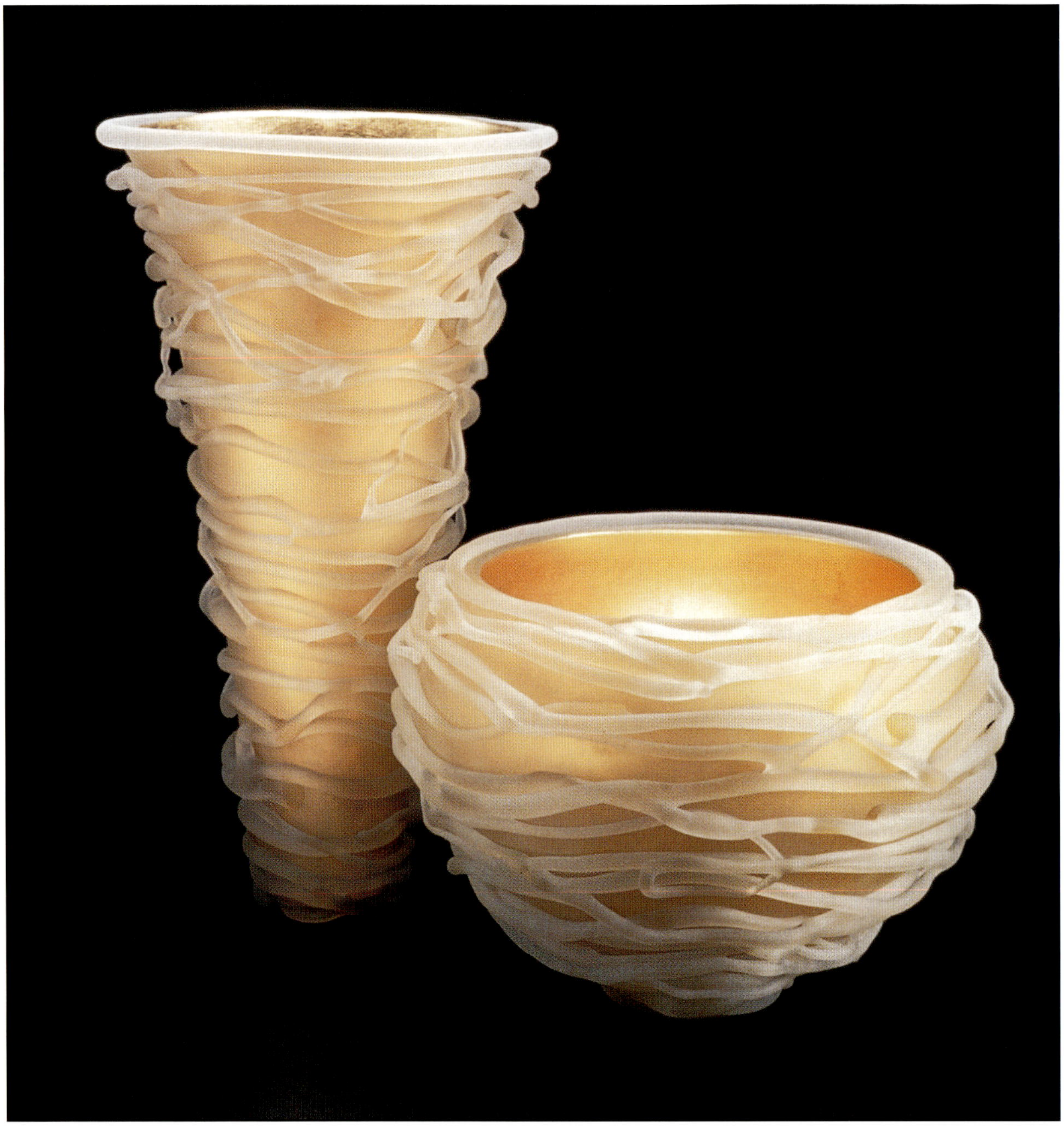

Tornado Series, 1998, 20" x 14" d, blown glass. Photograph courtesy of the artist.

Debbie Tarsitano

A growing number of artists trained as painters and sculptors are joining the glass movement. In response the field of art in glass is developing and expanding its spirit to embrace new visions and possibilities of these artists. I am part of this new movement of formally trained artists who chose glass as their artistic medium. My formal painting and design background, combined with technical mastery of the encasement of flame-work in solid crystal, has led me to create a series of breakthrough artistic statements and visions in my work.

For over twenty-seven years of artistic experimentation my work has progressed steadily, constantly evolving and advancing from simple single flower crystal paperweights to explorations of abstract expressions in glass. My encased flame-work paperweights have been my best known work for years, however my desire to revisit my original design medium of painting has led me to re-think glass encasement techniques from a fine art perspective. I now view each piece of work as an encased flame-worked glass sculpture.

My most recent evolution arises from exploring the world of abstract thought and design. It does not matter to me that the work is glass; art is about the content, the emotion, the quality, and the depth of expression embodied in each piece. My constant urge to innovate has led to such signatures pieces as the Scarlet Dahlia, multi-flowered designs, engraved studies, and recently, my reinterpretation of traditional flame-working techniques such as millefiore and latticino into contemporary glass sculpture.

My latest series of new designs create a powerful, fresh experience by integrating abstraction, sculpture, and the miraculous effect of crystal encasement on flame-work. When I encase a flame-work "painting," I transform the artistic subject into a magnificent sculpture of solid enfolding crystal, presenting new aspects from every viewing direction. I try to involve art lovers personally in my work; provoking them to take what they want from each design by stripping away what is merely decorative to reveal deeper meaning, feeling, expression and beauty. I feel that the young field of art expressed in glass will continue to develop and excite thousands of art lovers. Glass art must enter the mainstream of contemporary art alongside painting and sculpture.

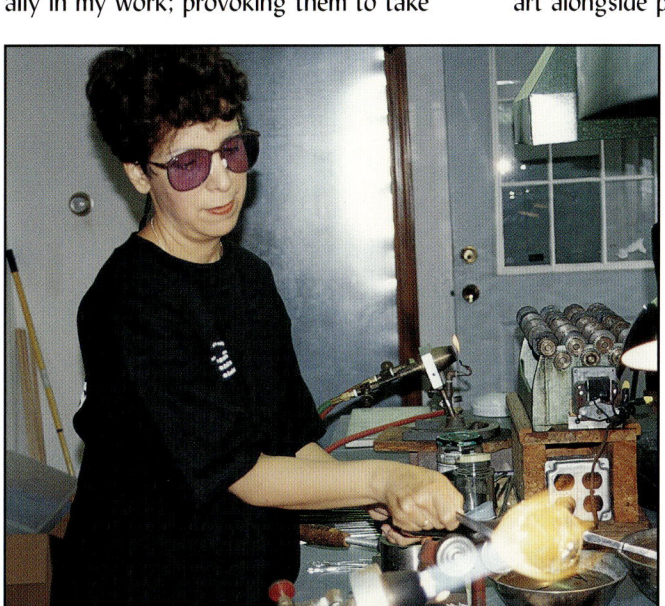

Debbie Tarsitano. *Photograph courtesy of the artist.*

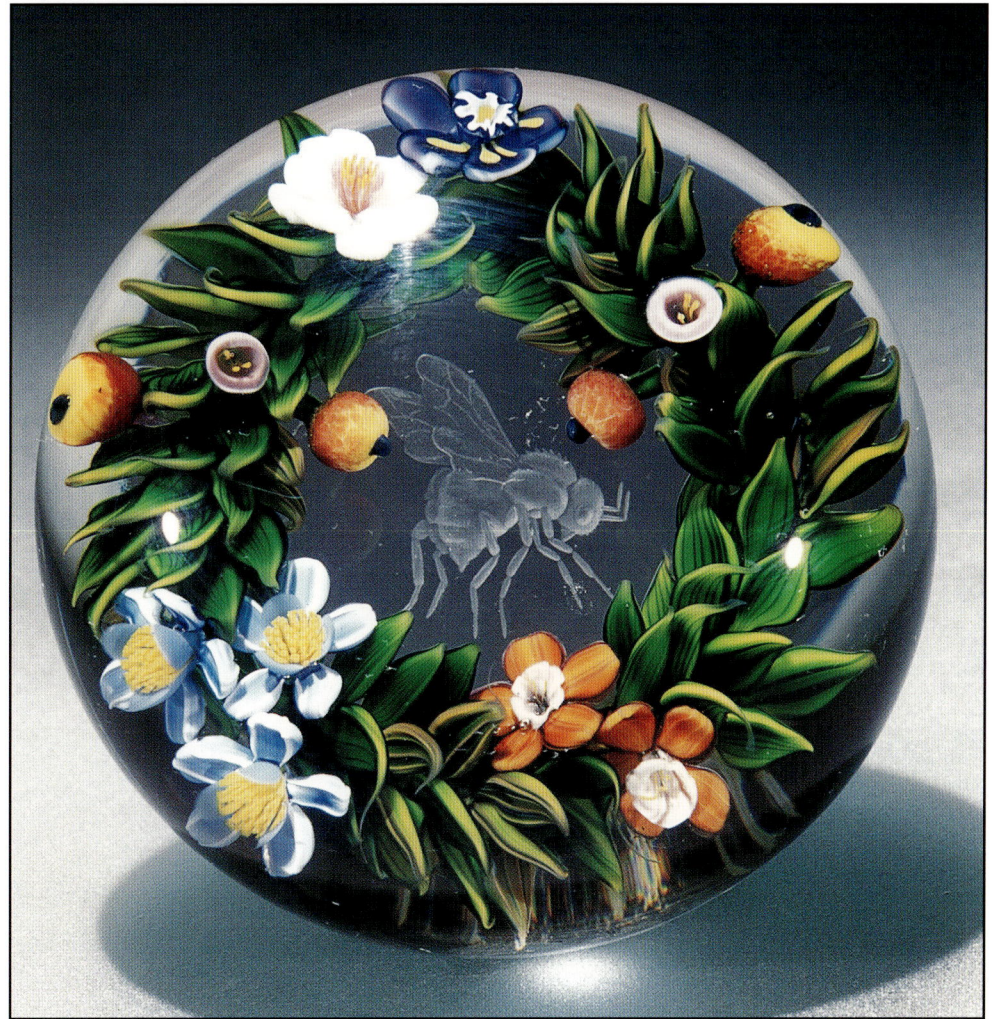

Paperweight, 1985, Max Erlbacher bee engraving, photo: Ned Manter. *Photograph courtesy of the artist.*

110　The Seventies - The Artist

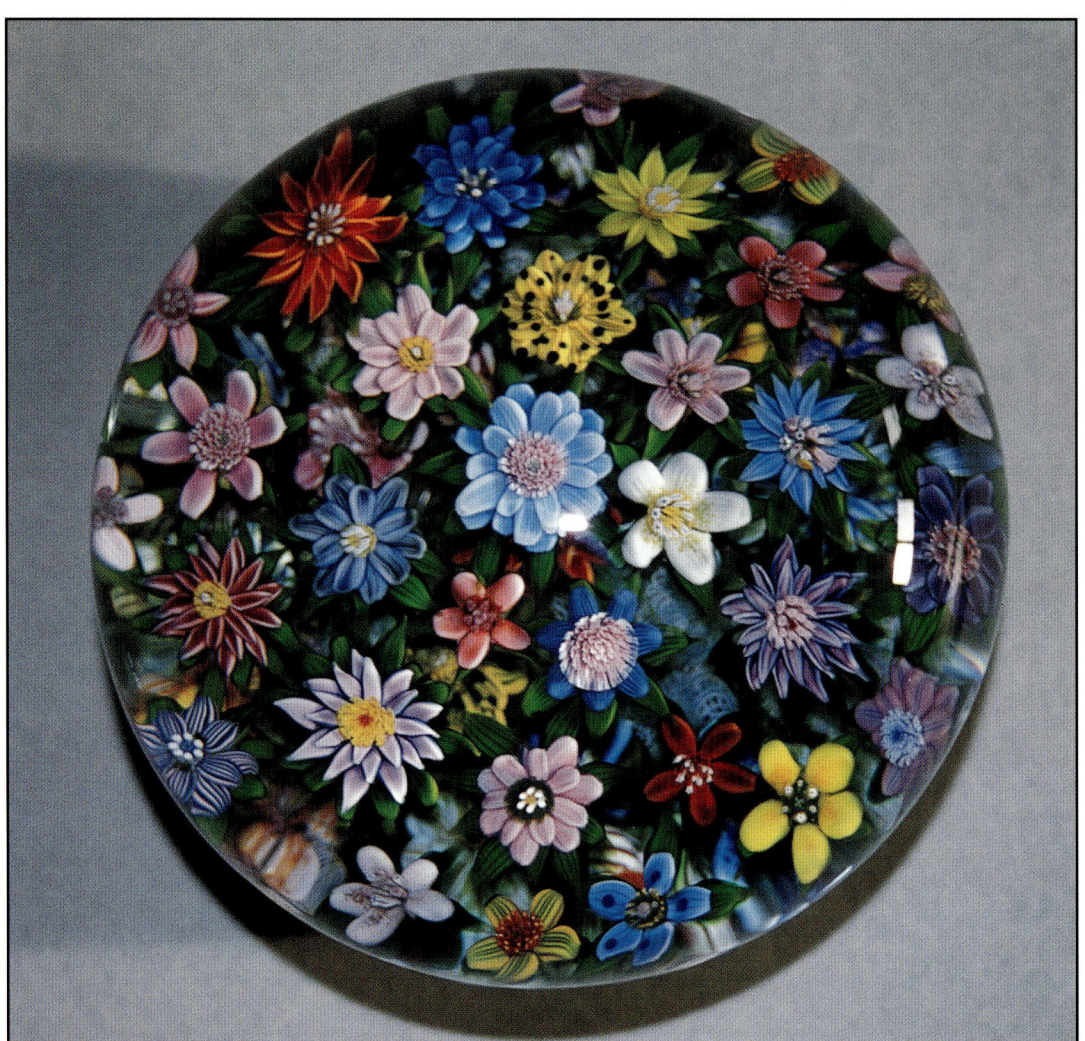

*80 Flower Arrangement, 2001.
Photograph, courtesy of the artist.*

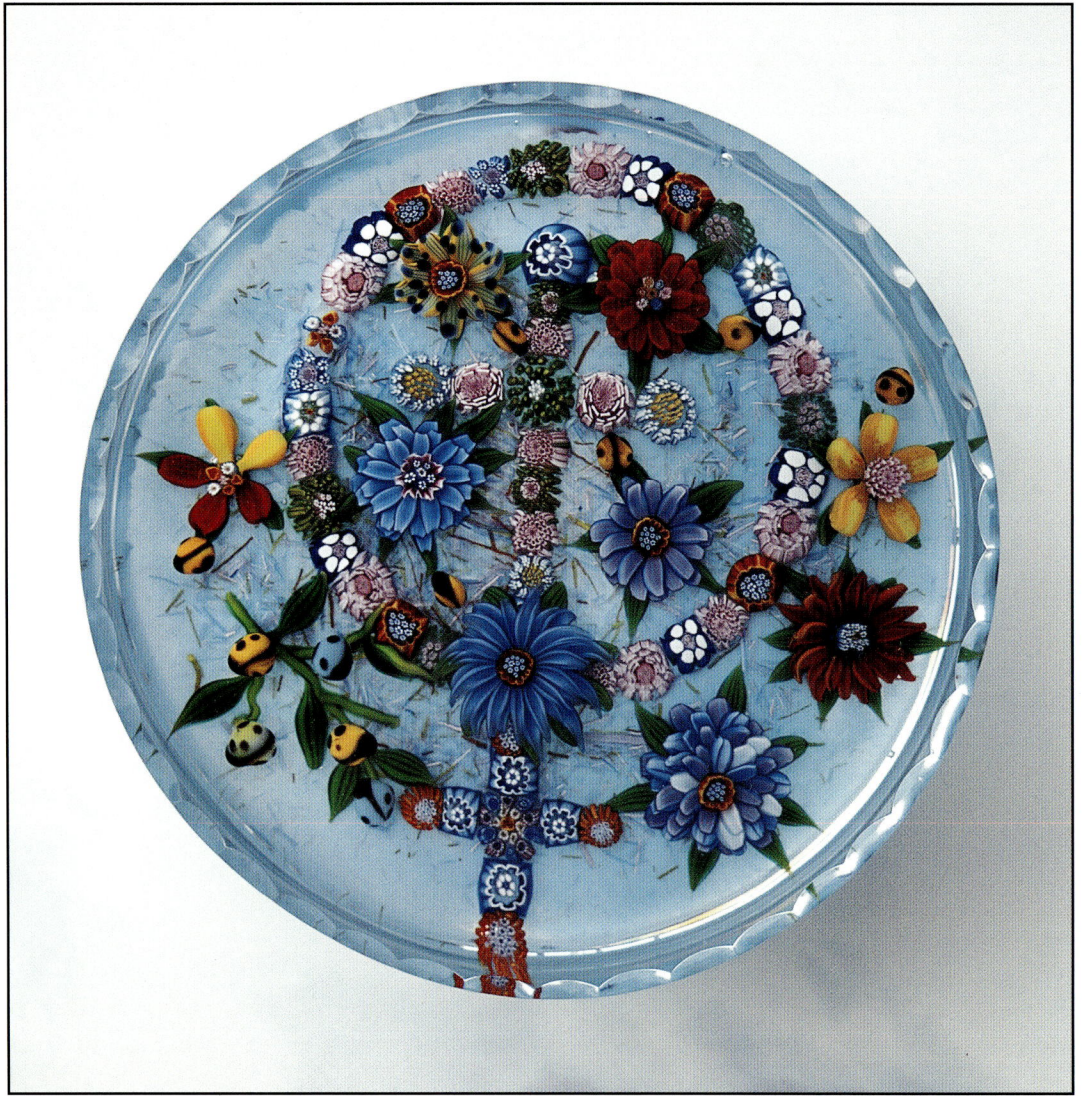

Woman in a Mirror, 2001, 4.5".

Yaffa Todd

I make pieces that I myself would like to live with. My background as a painter led me to relate to clay forms as three-dimensional canvases; when I began blowing glass, the dimensions of motion and flow were added. After some experience, I have found that working in crystal glass allows me to use reflections and two sides of the piece visually interacting, as well as the pure optical qualities of the medium. To achieve these added dimensions, it has become of utmost importance that the basic glass be immaculate and this control has only been reached with years of batch tests and equipment refinement. I use lamp-worked imagery in my new work. Nature is my inspiration. I use nature as an impulse, blending my feelings and fantasies. I add and delete as I deem necessary to achieve a piece that will evoke a feeling of wonder and intrigue.

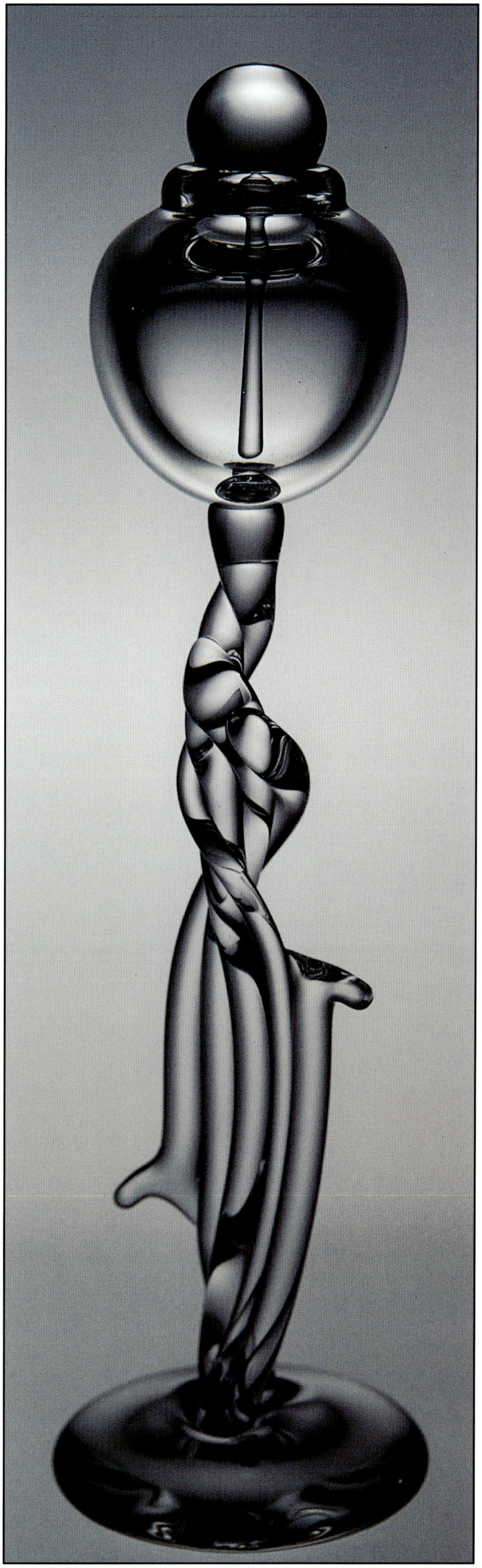

Crystal Perfume Form, 1981, 12" x 4" d, photo: John Littleton. *Photograph courtesy of the artist.*

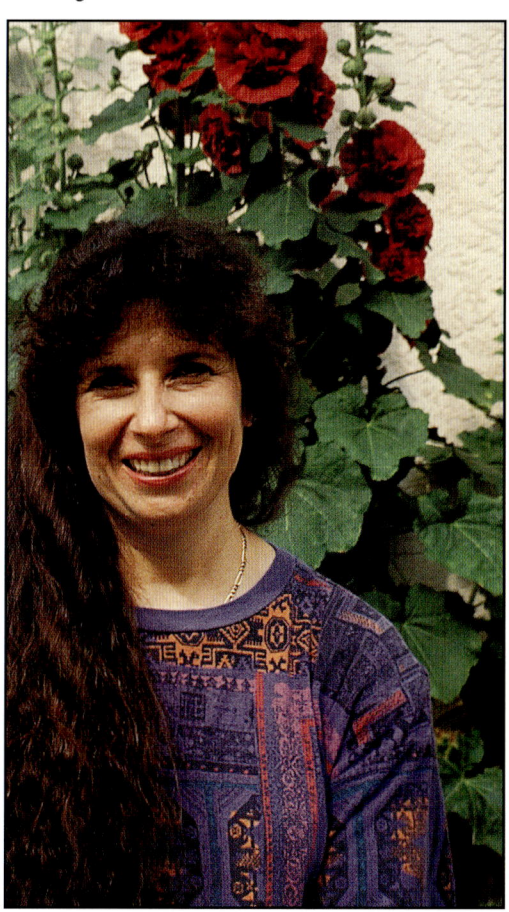

Yaffa Todd. *Photograph courtesy of the artist.*

Close-up: Penland Wildflower Perfume, 1985, 12" x 4" d.
Photograph courtesy of the artist.

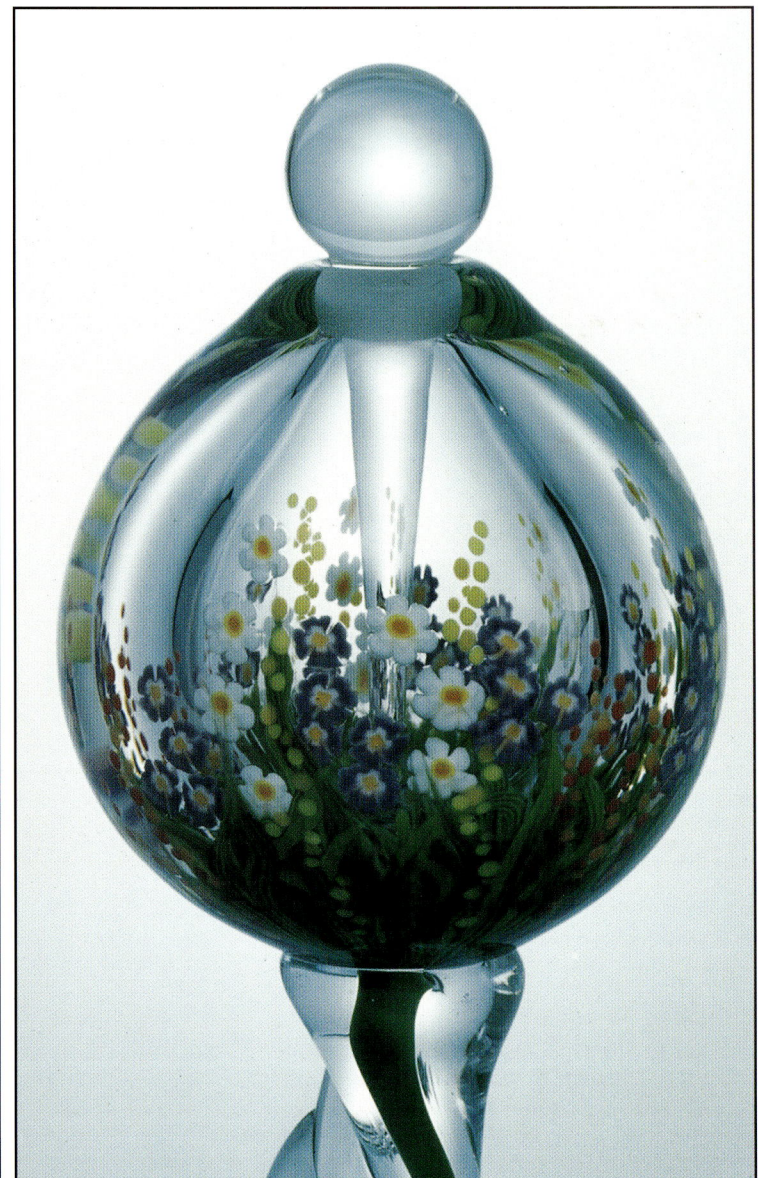

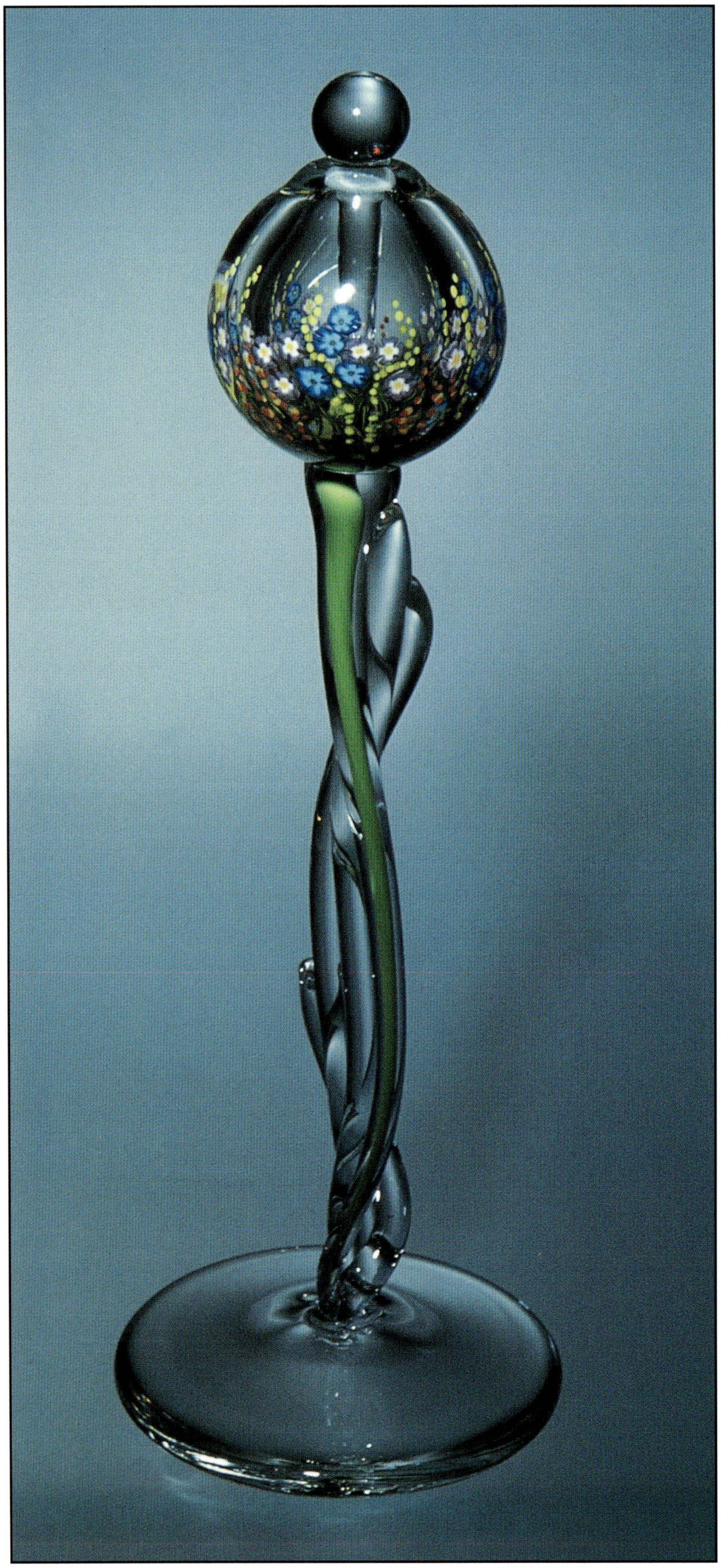

Penland Spring Meadow, 1983, 11.35" x 4" d. Photograph courtesy of the artist.

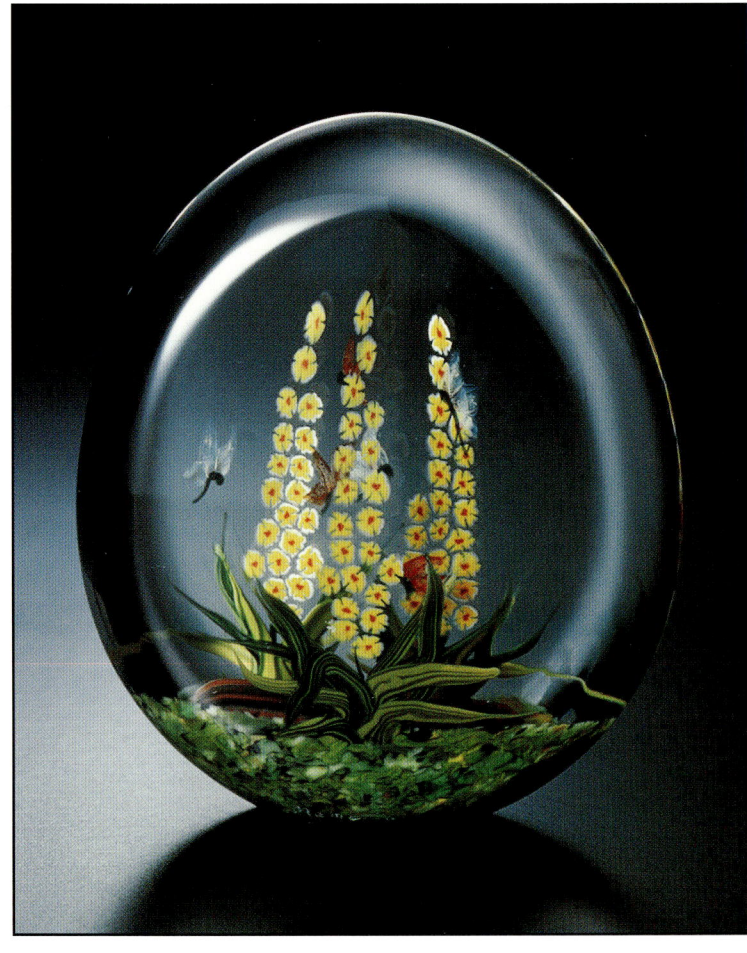

Memories: Yucca & Butterfly, 1988, 4" x 3.25" x 1.25".
Photograph courtesy of the artist.

Ulrica Valien

In my paintings and in my glass, the woman is in the center, in combination with the man and children. In magic and personal experience the stories grow out from reality and fantasy, a mix of longings and everyday life where the man often can be seen as a mix of human and animal, the snake is often the symbol of the unknown and the guard for fears of the dark and unexpected.

It's not the beauty, it's the spontaneous and quick reactions that are the most important to be told.

"Depicted with humor and tenderness, men, women, and animals make their appearances deep in a Swedish forest or in a hectic city jungle. The men may receive their nips. The dunces cap or other derisive attributes are frequently in use. The self-exhibition of the women are rewarded with merciless demascations. Wild animals of various sorts healthily erode every impression of a polite scenario despite the fact the animals may have been inspired by the house cat. But even the house cat Spinnis is more given to observation than to hunting, while preferring the protective warmth of the house, the sharp claws of reality are ever present. The snake crawls away on rather more ambiguous ground, even when its appearance is intended to annoy or to provide a decorative ornament. The scenes are racy and colorful and one can sense the stroke of the brush through the air; the laughter and the anger too."
Mailis Stensman, Art critic

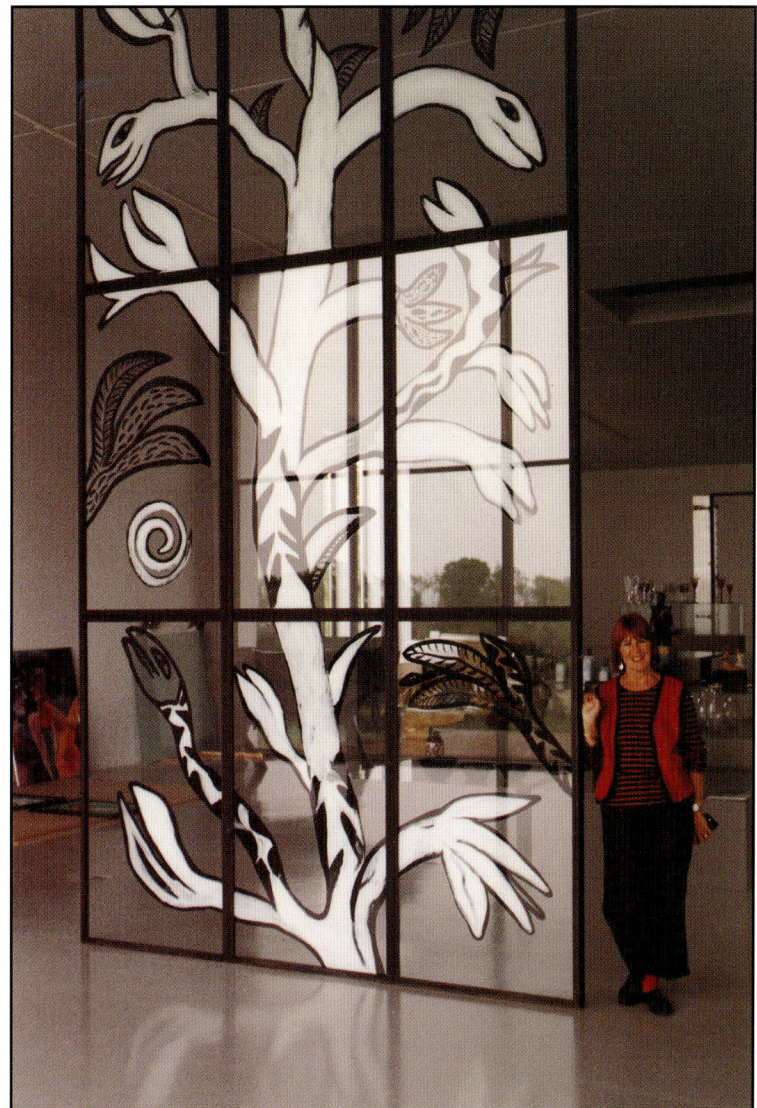

Ulrica Valien at Vida Museum. *Photograph courtesy of the artist.*

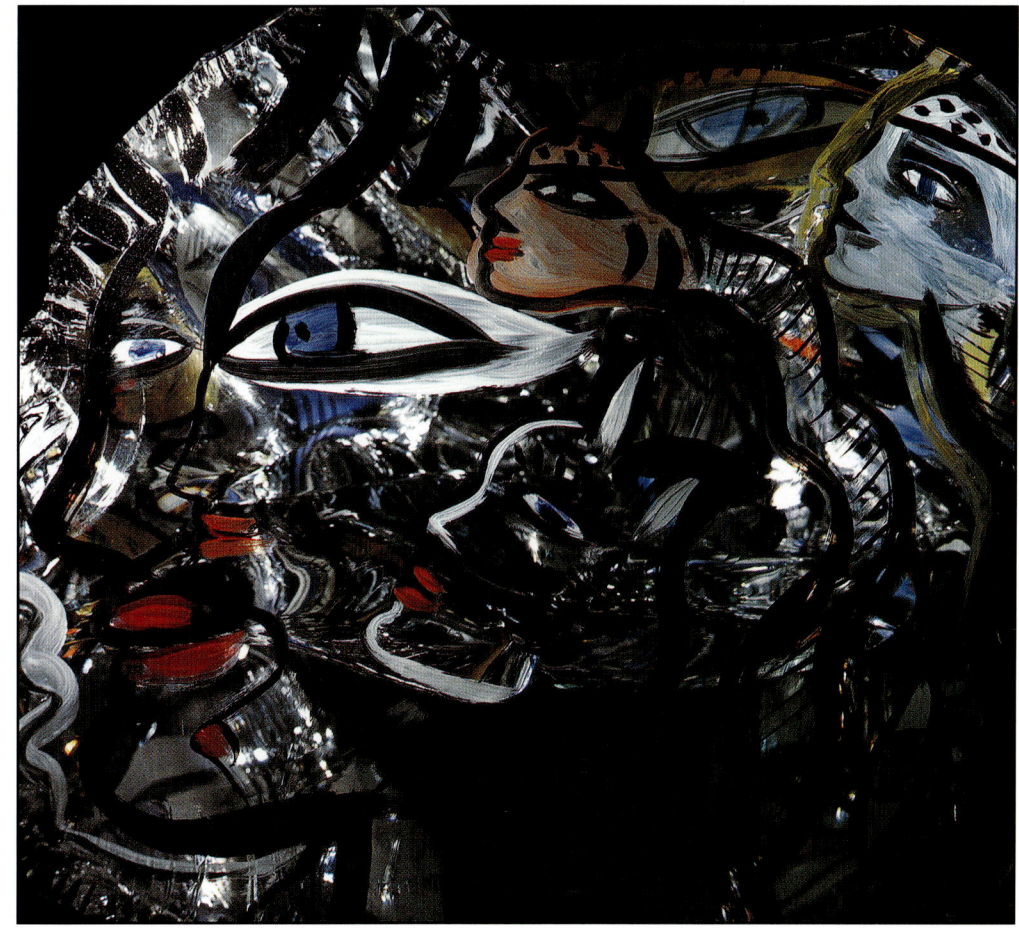

Father-Mother-Sister-Brother, 1978, 450 mm diameter, painted solid 3-D crystal block. Mixed Media, freedom to paint like a watercolor painting in all dimensions. *Photograph courtesy of the artist.*

114   The Seventies - The Artist

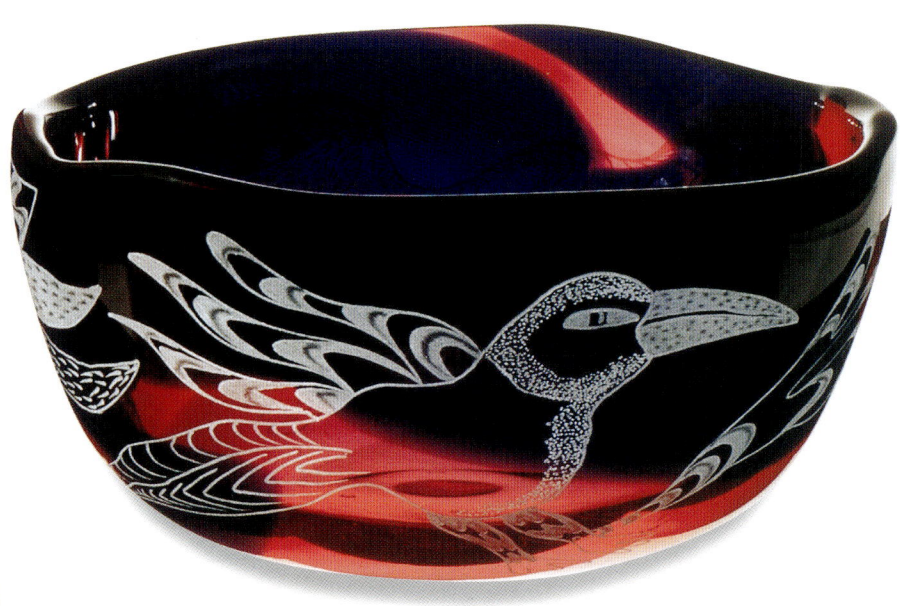

The Bird to Stay, 2002, 400 mm x 250 mm d, blown crystal bowl, unique, engraved, photo: Pelle Wahlgren, Kosta Boda. *Photograph courtesy of the artist.*

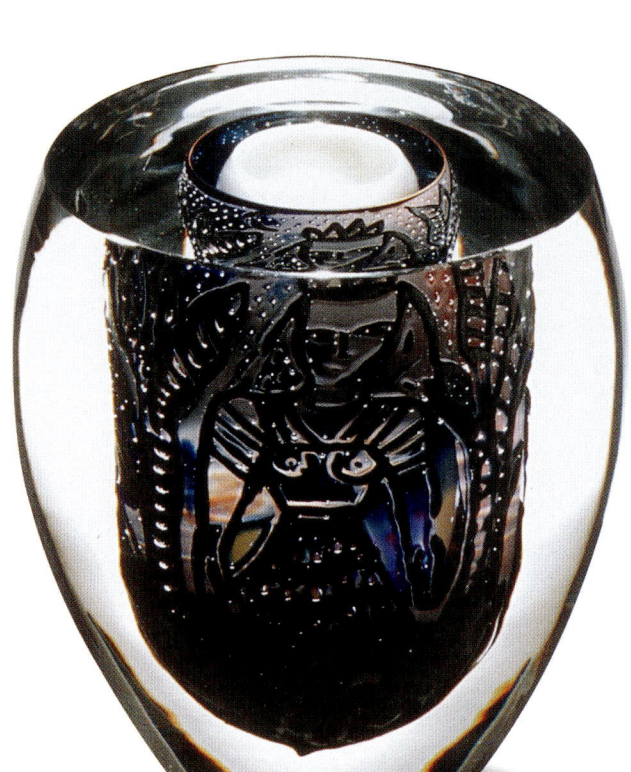

Women for You in Blue Heaven, 2002, 250 mm, unique kabale technique, photo: Pelle Wahlgren, Kosta Boda. *Photograph courtesy of the artist.*

Snakeflower, 2002, 900 mm x 1000 mm, installation at the Vida Museum blown glass with grey color and different patterns.

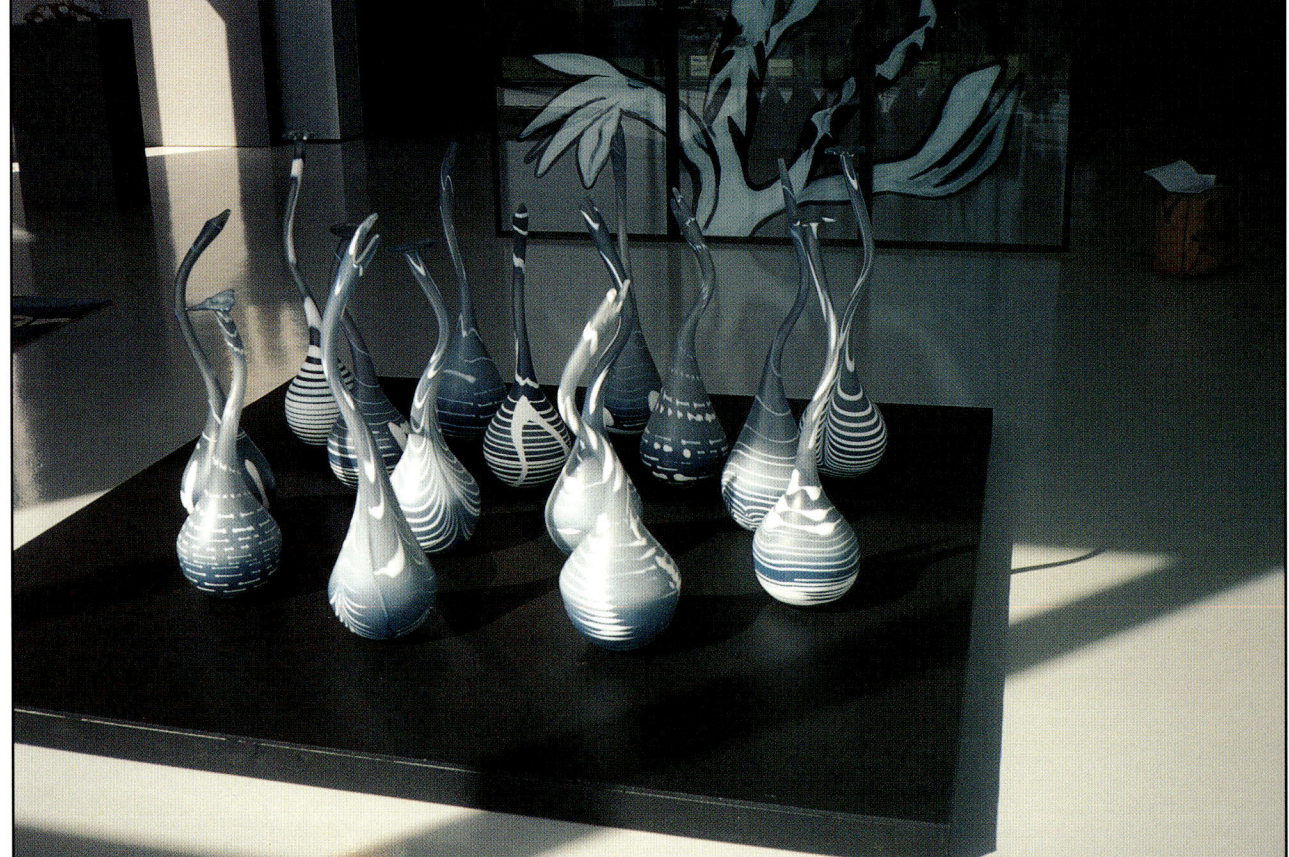

The Eighties

Along with the eighties came the "Reagan Revolution." The ex-movie star/president blamed liberal "big government" for all of America's problems. When he became president in 1981 he brought to a close five decades of government control that began with FDR's New Deal.

In June of 1981 the Center for Disease Control discovered a rare type of pneumonia. In 1982 it was named AIDS, acquired immune deficiency syndrome. A virus that weakened the immune system caused the disease, allowing an infected person to develop incurable infections. By the late eighties it was an epidemic; by the late nineties, thirty-one million people were infected and no cure was in sight.

The nation was slowly recovering from the Viet Nam war. A memorial was proposed and a design by a young architecture student from Yale won a competition to build a memorial to honor the veterans of the highly unpopular war. Maya Lin's design, a simple v-shaped black marble wall set below ground level and engraved with about 58,000 veterans' names was not well received at first because people were accustomed to commemorative statues. Soon though, it became a way families could identify with their loss. Now, it is one of the most frequently visited monuments in our nation's capitol.

The art world was going through severe changes. The idealism of the sixties and the growth and expansion of the seventies was replaced in the eighties by a sense of cynicism. Nostalgia for the "good old days" promoted a trend toward retro everything. The return of classical motifs in art and architecture led to the term "post-modern" which became the buzzword of the decade. The American art market was growing fast: art was becoming an instrument for investment and blue chip artists' prices were skyrocketing. In order to make their work more affordable and marketable to the average person, artists and their dealers published and promoted large editions of lithographs. Collectors, however, began to control the art market. Women became artists, writers, dealers, and curators, but not usually collectors.

The electronic age, begun in the 1950s with giant computers and miniature televisions, finally came into full bloom. TV's, PC's, microwaves, videos, cell phones, and digital technologies all were becoming everyday instruments to simplify life. The tragedy was that through these innocent tools the mass media was gaining control of everyone's personal life.

Public Art became more public as it grew from park monument to major public installations of contemporary ideas, which often invited public participation. Public monies were spent to enhance urban streets and neighborhoods with art. Land reclamation became earthworks leading to Environmental Art. Some cities, led by Philadelphia's mandated percent for art legislation for public buildings, initiated similar legislation. Unfortunately, in the eighties, relatively few women artists had secured these commissions and fewer yet used glass. Ginny Ruffner, known for her whimsical glass art, was awarded several public art commissions in the Northwest.

Athena Tacha, born in Greece, immigrated to the US, where she studied sculpture at the Academy of Fine Arts. She became known early in her career for large-scale public works. *Ice Walls*, made in 1984, is a wall made of glass blocks for the Mary Louise Rasmuson Atrium, Anchorage

Museum of History and Art, Anchorage, Alaska. The artist chose the glass block because of its visual relationship to ice and left the edges unfinished as a reminder of frosty or glacial surfaces.

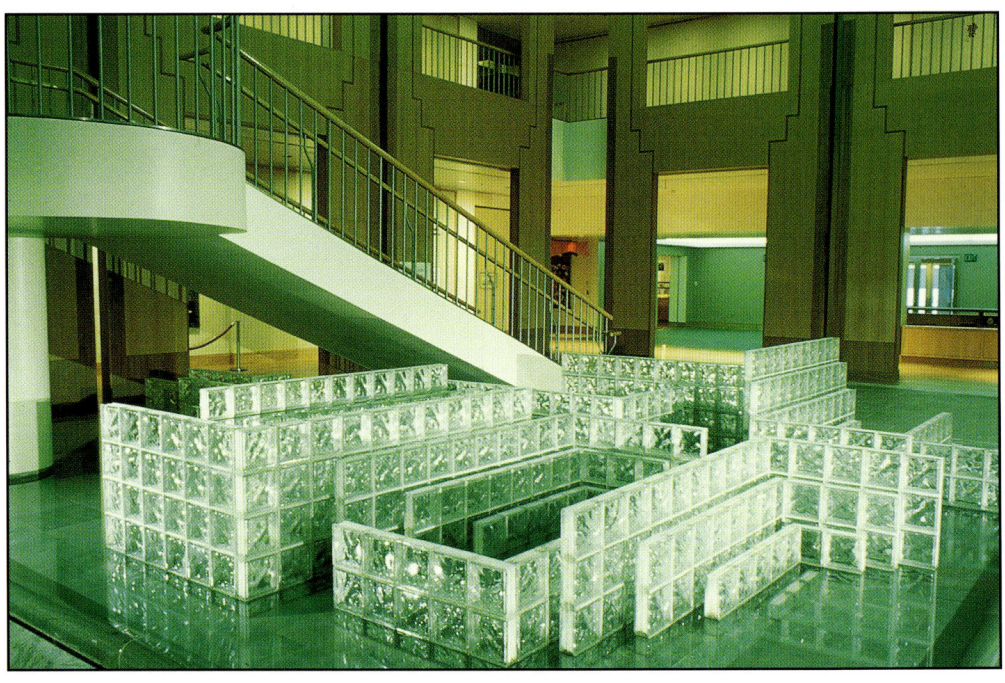

Athena Tacha, *Ice Walls*, c 1984, 4' x 19' x 26.5', Reflecting Pool, Mary Louise Rasmuson Atrium, Anchorage Museum of History and Art, Commission, percent for art program municipality of Anchorage, photo: Chris Arend. *Photograph courtesy of the artist and the Anchorage Museum of Art.*

Niki de Saint Phalle, a French-American, best known for her series of large, playful earth mother forms called *Nanas*, was commissioned to build a glass mosaic fountain at the Schneider Children's Hospital on the grounds of Long Island Jewish Medical Center in Hyde Park, New York, in 1989. *The Magic Tree* is a 10-foot by 20-foot treelike form covered with colorful bits of glass and paint. Enormous snakes spout water from their mouths when the fountain is turned on. Helen and Irving Schneider, generous benefactors and patrons of the arts, commissioned the sculpture.

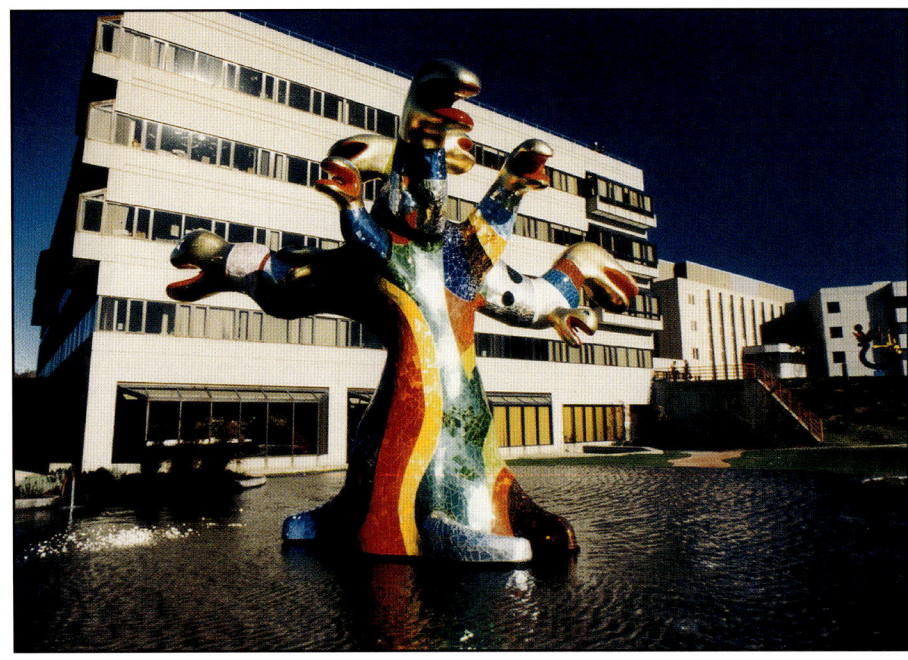

Niki de Saint Phalle, *The Magic Tree*, 10' x 20' d, Schneider Children's Hospital, New Hyde Park, New York. *Photograph courtesy of Long Island Medical Center and Schneider Children's Hospital.*

Niki de Saint Phalle, *The Magic Tree*.

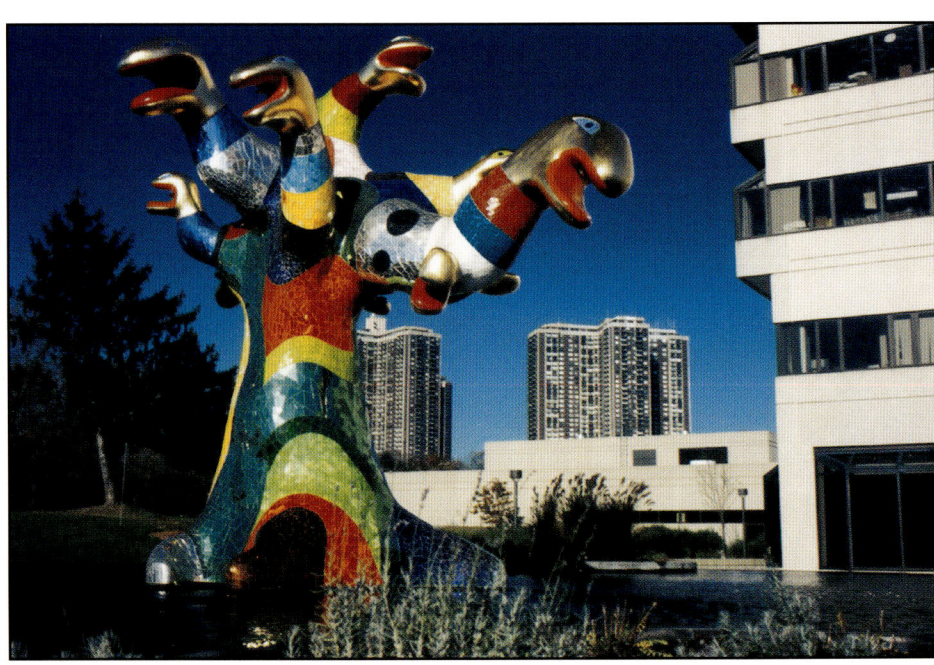

Feminism was gaining strength throughout the eighties, but women were still not afforded enough exhibitions in museums and galleries. The Guerrilla Girls, founded in 1985 to create an awareness of sexism in the art world, donned gorilla masks and took to the streets. They launched a major campaign to make their point in person. In gorilla costumes, they appeared at panel discussions, art openings, and other public art events. In print, via posters, they showed up all over town, naming the galleries who wouldn't exhibit work by women and critics who wouldn't write about them; they focused on the lack of attention paid to women by major museums and the press. Membership in the Guerrilla Girls was and still is anonymous. They feel the secret to their success is their anonymity as there is no opportunity for political gain or reprisal. Names and numbers are a well-guarded secret. Unknown to each other, important museum people, as well as prominent curators and successful artists, could all be members.

THE ADVANTAGES OF BEING A WOMAN ARTIST:

Working without the pressure of success.
Not having to be in shows with men.
Having an escape from the art world in your 4 free-lance jobs.
Knowing your career might pick up after you're eighty.
Being reassured that whatever kind of art you make it will be labeled feminine.
Not being stuck in a tenured teaching position.
Seeing your ideas live on in the work of others.
Having the opportunity to choose between career and motherhood.
Not having to choke on those big cigars or paint in Italian suits.
Having more time to work when your mate dumps you for someone younger.
Being included in revised versions of art history.
Not having to undergo the embarrassment of being called a genius.
Getting your picture in the art magazines wearing a gorilla suit.

A PUBLIC SERVICE MESSAGE FROM **GUERRILLA GIRLS** CONSCIENCE OF THE ART WORLD
532 LaGUARDIA PLACE, #237 • NY, NY 10012
www.guerrillagirls.com

Guerrilla Girls Poster. Courtesy The Guerrilla Girls.

Glass Art had finally come of age and was an official art/craft form, also often referred to as Studio Glass. The experimentation of the previous decade was paying off: young artists just leaving school were exhibiting an amazing amount of technical skill. The older artists were refining their techniques and honing their craft. Women were gaining respect for their tenacity when competing with their male counterparts in all glass techniques and procedures, even when making large heavy works on a blowpipe.

Much of glassblowing is dependent upon teamwork, in some cases women have partnered with other women and sometimes with men to execute work. In either case, many women gained individual recognition as artists. Still, they were finding it difficult to secure teaching jobs in universities when competing with men. The glass ceiling in education was still intact.

A growing number of galleries were opening solely to show this art made from glass. But a question kept recurring: is it art or is it craft, or, better yet, when is it art and when is it craft? The art versus craft topic has been discussed for at least four decades, perhaps even more. The historic traditions of glass making go back thousands of years. Some exquisite examples of beauty and craftsmanship have existed in museums since the Middle Ages. Looking at glass objects within the context of a fine art form is relatively recent. According to Dan Klein, author of *Glass: A Contemporary Art*,

> Every branch of the arts, including what is called "fine art," has its own boundaries. Important conceptual changes in glass have led to a degree of confusion about scope. It was difficult to know where to slot contemporary glass in the hierarchy, where to exhibit it in museums, what sort of commercial galleries to use for shows. There was a basic anxiety that because it was glass it would be viewed and judged in the same light as utilitarian object, that it would not be accorded the status it deserved.[1]

Art critic Kim Levin's topic for the 1984 Glass Art Society Conference in Corning, New York, dealt with art verses craft. Her thoughtful talk "Art, Craft, and Postmodernism" was printed in the 1984/85 *Glass Art Journal*.

> Artists took on worldly responsibilities, got involved with context, tried to merge their art with the world—not in terms of form, but in order to have some effect. Women artists brought craft materials and techniques into their art as a feminist statement. And many male artists did so as a way of rebelling against the sleek sterility and over-specialization of formalist art.
>
> Borrowing from crafts and applied arts was also a way of making a popular statement. Craftwork was less elitist, more accessible. So were utilitarian objects. And because these things had been so neglected by artists in previous decades, they were open areas for innovation.[2]

In 1983, a unique fellowship program was initiated to provide artist residencies for artists working with glass. It was located in the historic glass area of New Jersey. The Creative Glass Center of America (CGCA) was the brainchild of Paul Stankard, a highly respected glass artist from Southern New Jersey. Paul, along with the director of Wheaton Village, Barry Taylor and his wife Gay Taylor, curator of the Museum of American Glass, and with Frank Wheaton Jr., then president and CEO of Wheaton Industries, a privately owned glass company with many divisions manufacturing perfume and cosmetic containers, tubing and scientific ware, pharmaceutical bottles, a tabletop line of houseware items and a plastic division, all with worldwide distribution. The original T.C. Wheaton glass factory was built in 1888 to make patent medicine bottles. In 1970, Frank Wheaton, Jr. built a reproduction of the 1888 glass furnace and a historic Victorian village to house it. Wheaton Village was opened to invite the public to watch glass blowing demonstrations.

Prior to 1982 residencies offered to Paul Stankard, Flora Mace, and a few others, myself included, planted the seed to offer artists the opportunity to make work using the fully equipped glass making studio. Later, a committee made up of artists, curators, gallery directors, and educators met to discuss options that would promote the use of glass as a contemporary art medium. CGCA was established in 1983 within the campus of Wheaton Village for artists to have opportunities to develop ideas and create a body of work with the industrial facilities as a support. The first group contained six fellows, three of those were women: Mary Van Cline, Amy Roberts, and Susan Anton. The first session lasted almost six months; however, subsequent sessions have been modified to three, three month sessions with four fellows per session. The gender distribution since then has remained almost fifty percent women. Since that time many of the female fellows have gone on to highly visible and successful careers.

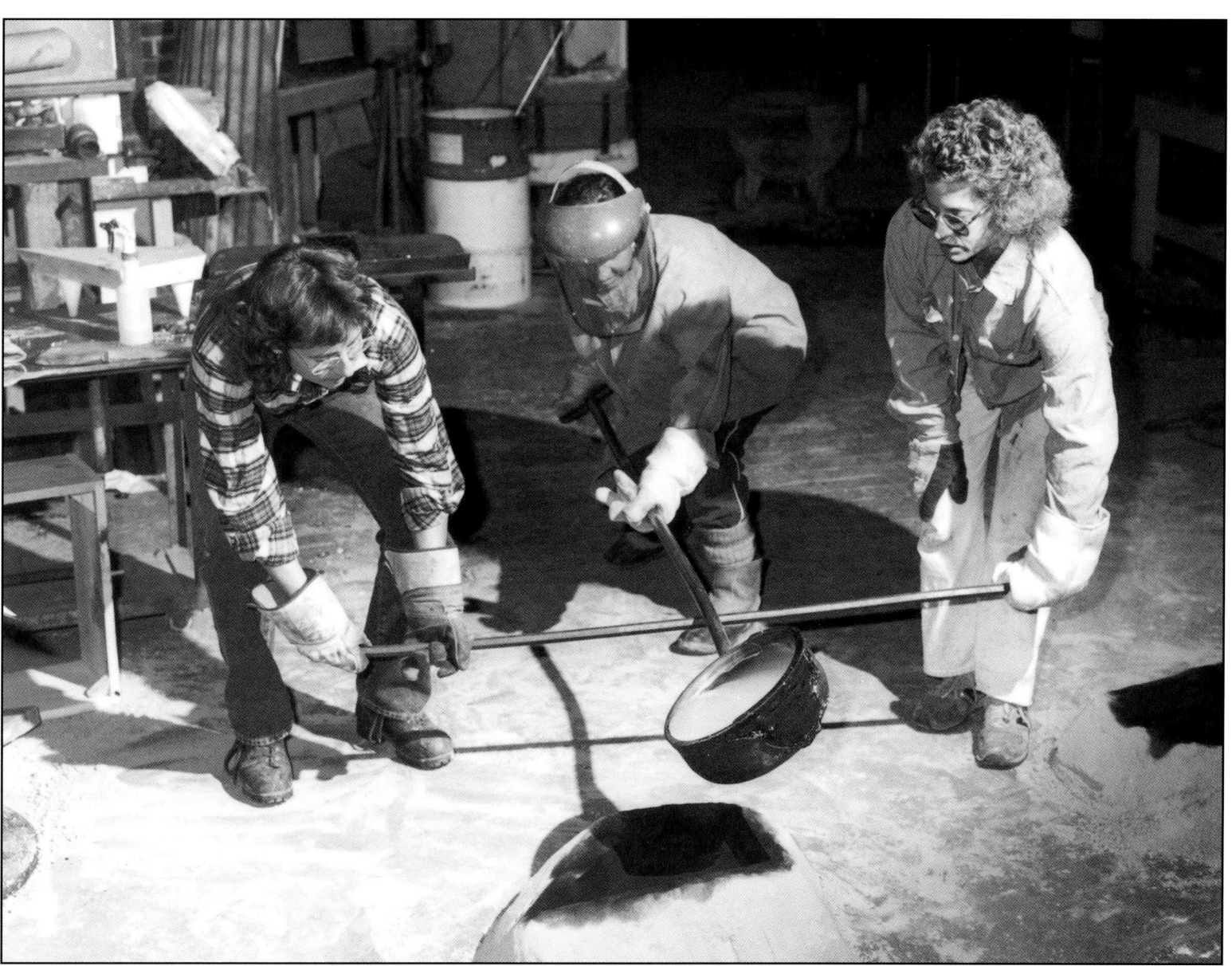

Susan Anton, Mary Van Cline, and Amy Roberts (left to right). *Photograph courtesy of the Creative Glass Center of America (CGCA), Wheaton Village, Millville, New Jersey.*

The art fair concept has been around since the nineteenth century; however, the 1980s saw mega scale block buster art fairs popping up all over the US and Europe. New Art Forms Expo, featuring decorative and applied arts, was born in 1985. Mark Lyman, who now stages "SOFA" (Sculpture, Object, and Functional Art), organized it. Looking through the 1989 catalog, I was surprised to find only a dozen women represented by galleries exhibiting glass.

By the 1980s Pilchuck Glass School was an established institution. The list of faculty, visiting artists, artists in residence, and alumnae reads like a who's who in the world of glass art and includes many women. In 1983 Pilchuck began an artist in residence program, inviting artists from other artistic disciplines to experience glass. Nancy Mee and Lynda Benglis were the first women selected. Charles Parriott, a Seattle glass artist and Pilchuck regular, states in Tina Oldknow's book *The Pilchuck Glass School*, "My prediction is by the year 2000, Pilchuck will become a woman's art colony…Almost all of the staff are women, the…director is a woman, the faculty is at least half women, the students are at least two-thirds women, the visiting artists are almost all women. It's the direction of glass." He also adds, " The macho myth in glass predominates, — because males are more powerful glassblowers. But they're not more powerful artists."[3]

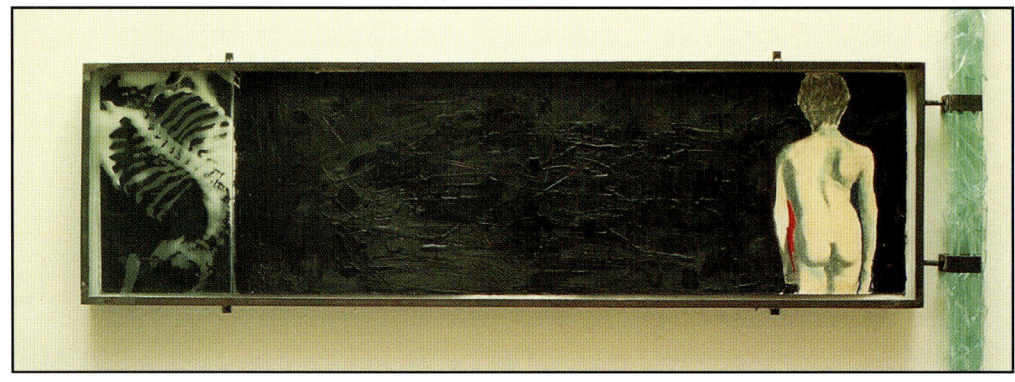

Nancy Mee, *Deform*, 1985, 42" x 53" x 2", Xerox transfer, etched glass, encaustic glass, steel. *Photograph courtesy of the artist.*

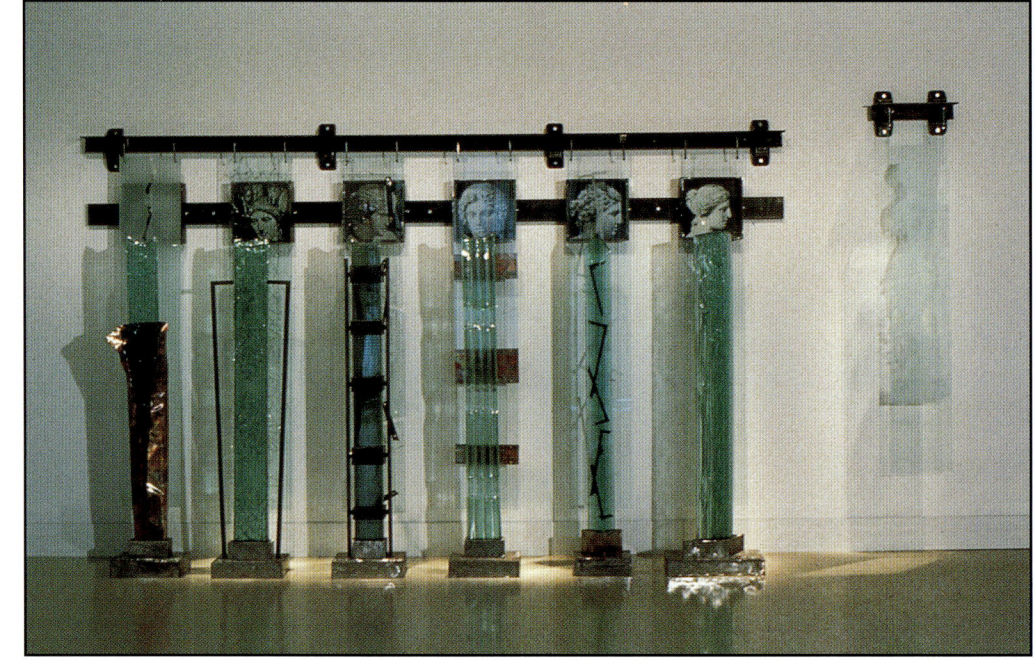

Nancy Mee, *Seven Beauties*, 1987, 156" x 84" x 16", mixed media. *Photograph courtesy of the artist.*

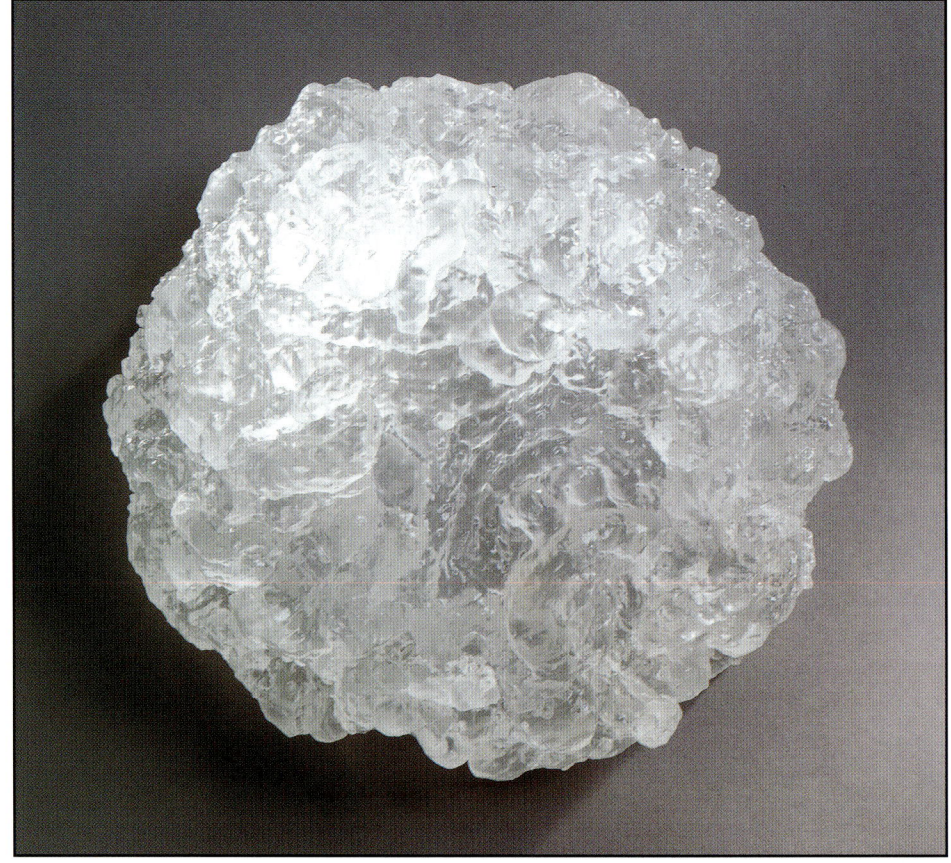

Lynda Benglis, *Untitled*, 2001, 12" x 12" x 6.5", Crystal (glass), photo: Queseda/Burke. *Photograph courtesy Cheim & Read, New York.*

The Artists

Tina Betz

In the lace-like, flame-worked glass sculptures I reproduce identifiable common objects to point out their sculptural qualities. I wish to create metaphorical associations using imagery that is, by appearance, fragile and precious, yet in actuality very strong. Therefore the seemingly fragile way a piece is built and appears is appropriate to the ideas behind the work. The material speaks to the idea and the idea speaks to the material. I wish to celebrate femaleness, family, and nature in my work.

Technically speaking, these flame-worked sculptures are created by cutting plate glass into strips, then pulling them into thin strands in a flame. The strands are manipulated and fused together with a hand torch. The sculptures are created free form as if they were three-dimensional drawings in glass. Although fragile looking, the forms are quite durable because their repeated patterns create an architectonic structure.

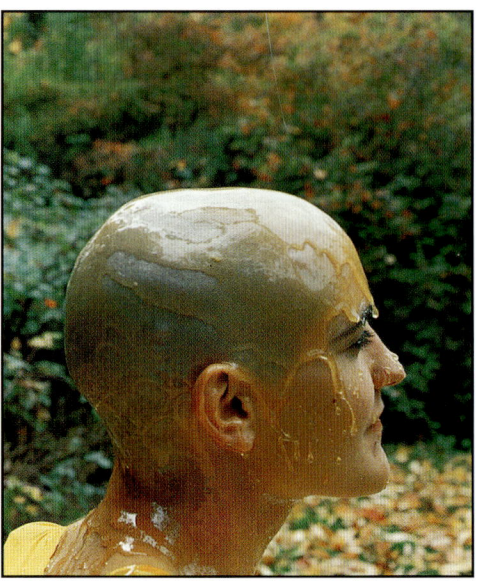

Tina Betz photograph. *Courtesy the artist.*

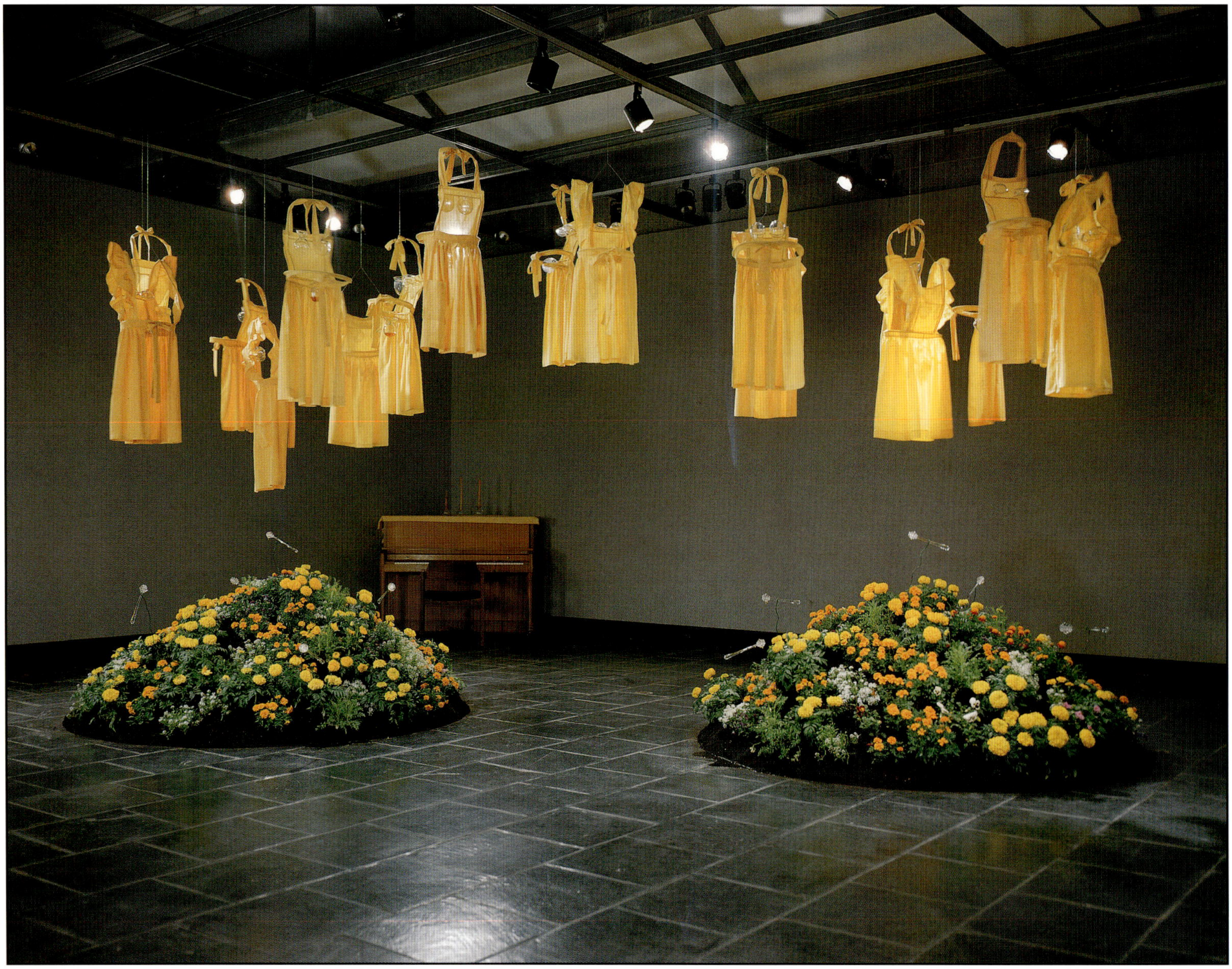

Infinite Cycle, 1992, 10' x 22' x 20', fabric, flowers, steel, glass, earth, piano, and honey. *Photograph courtesy of the artist.*

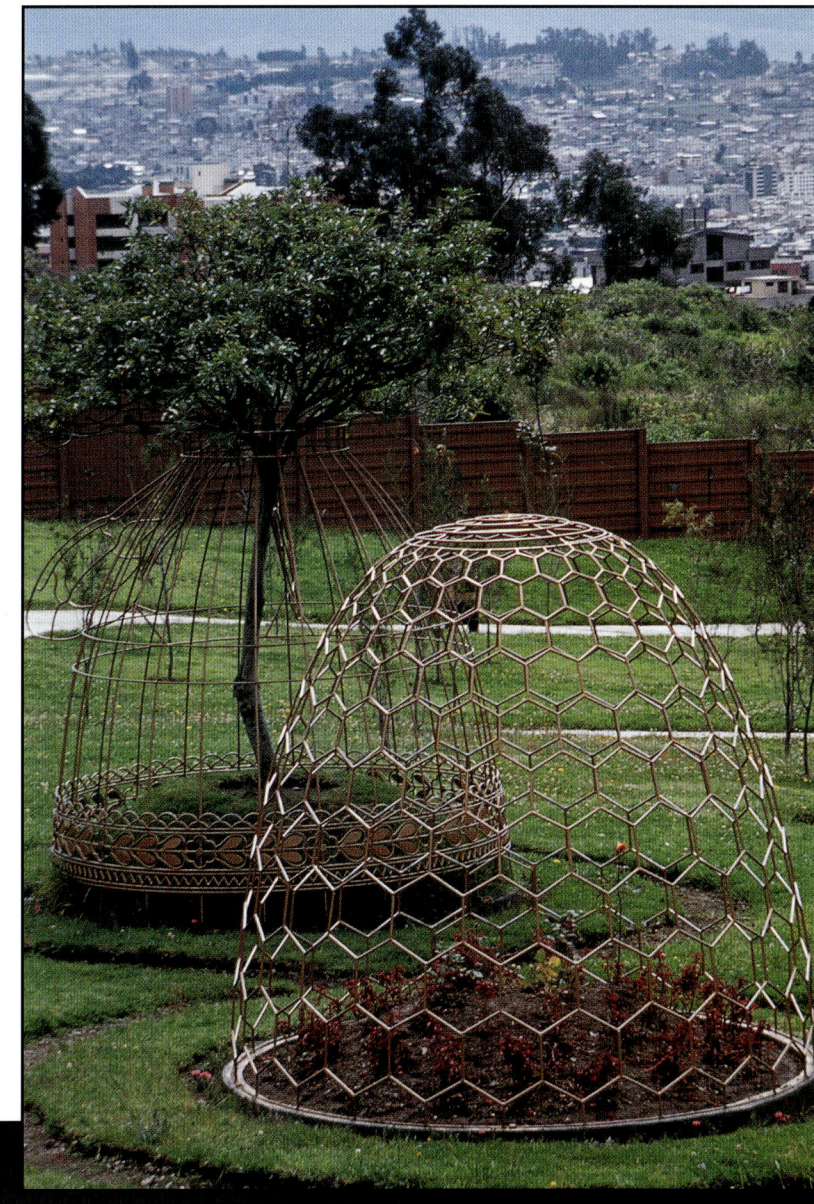

Women's Work, public commission, Quito, Ecuador, 12' x 34' x 16', welded steel, tree, and plants.

Ruby Sandals with Wings, 2001, each, 4" x 9" x 3", flame-worked glass. Photograph courtesy of the artist.

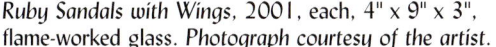

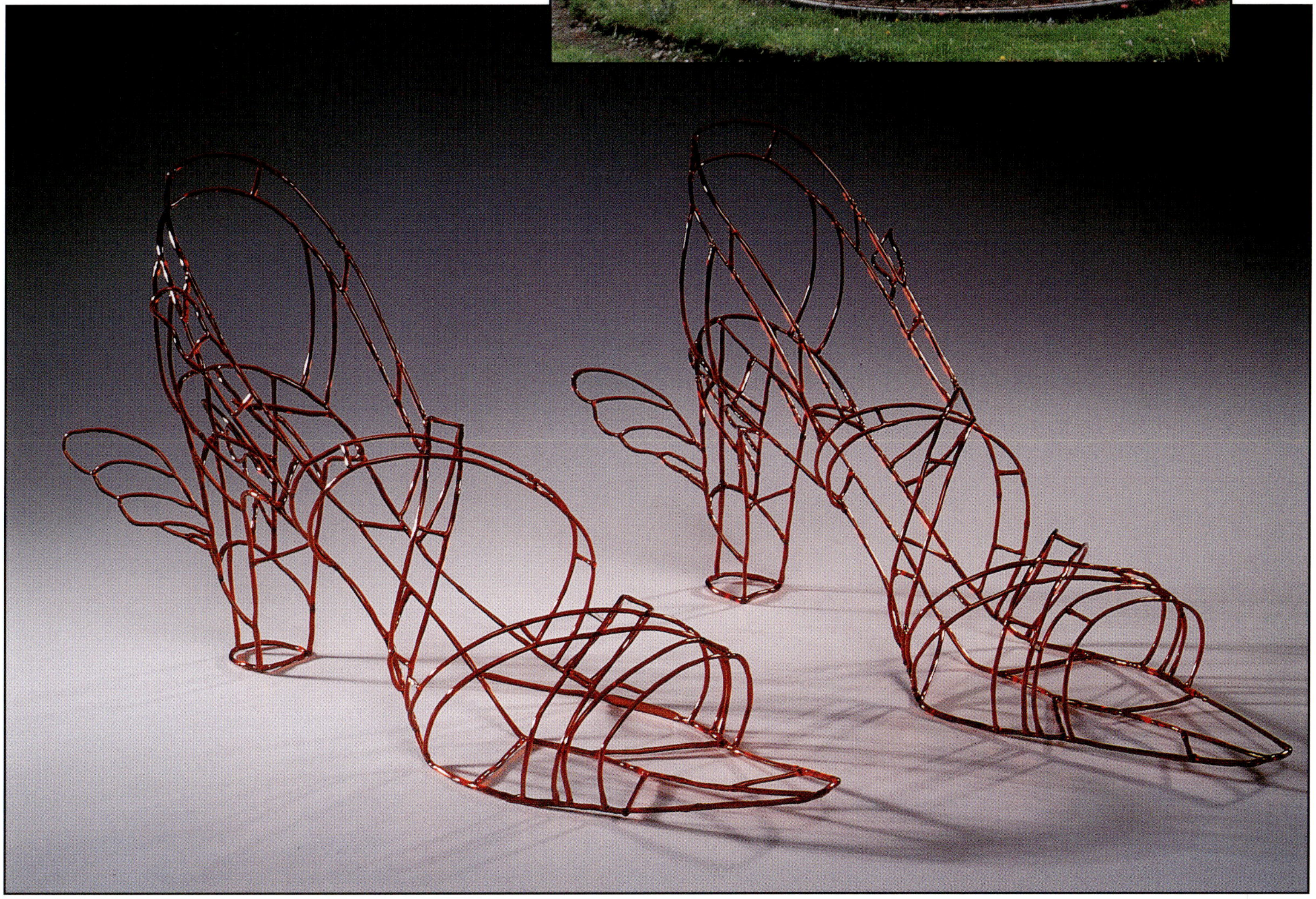

124 The Eighties - The Artist

Jody Bone

Jody Bone creates cast glass pieces, many are of primitive head or mask shapes. The pieces are usually one-of-a-kind; occasionally some are a limited edition. They are set in a variety of bases, ranging from carved wood to stone.

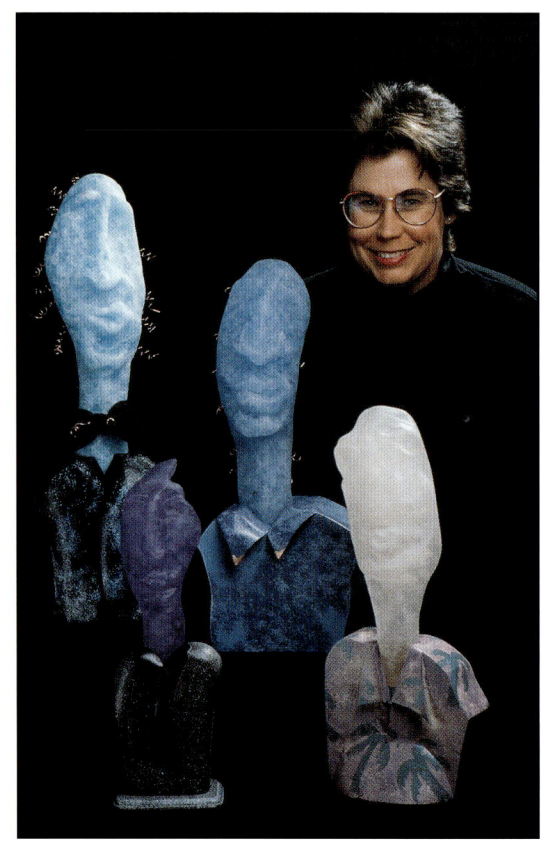

Jody Bone with heads. *Photograph courtesy of the artist.*

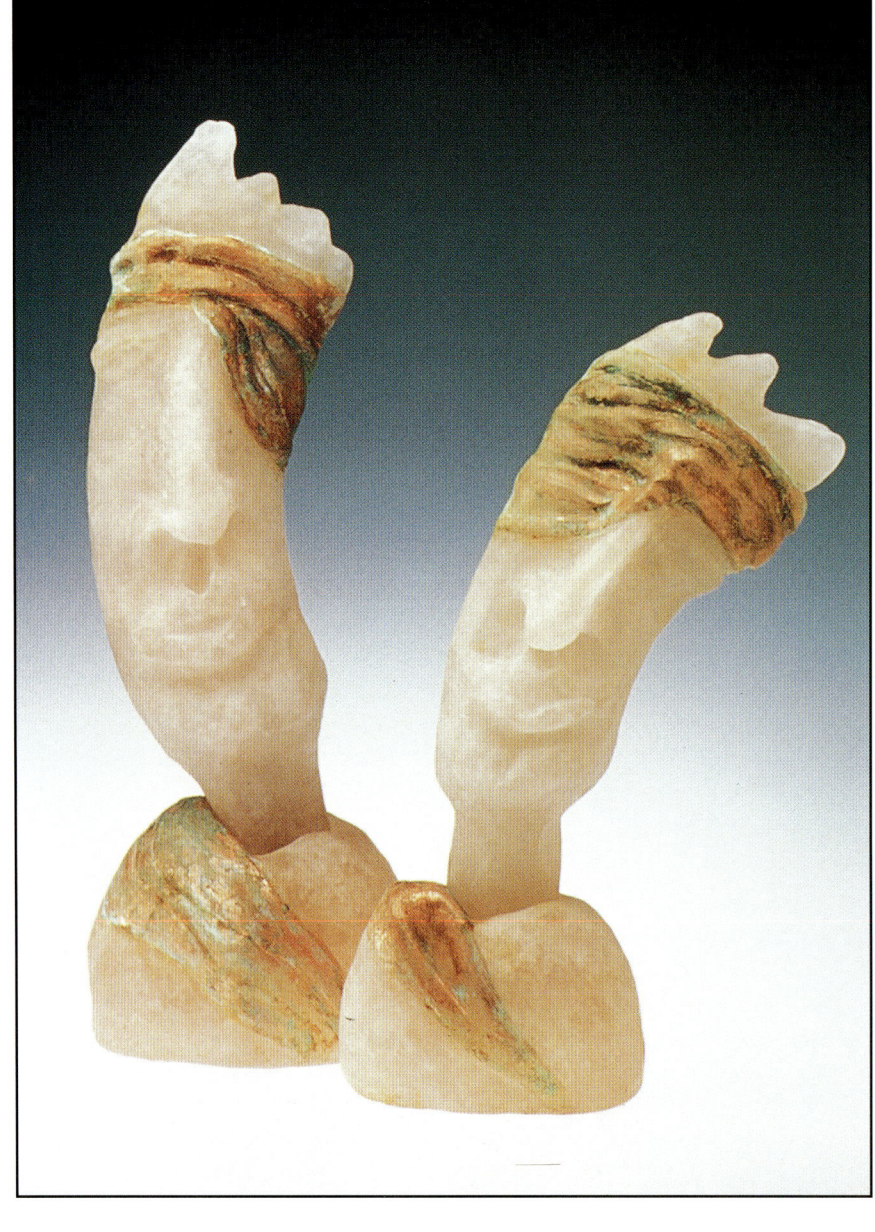

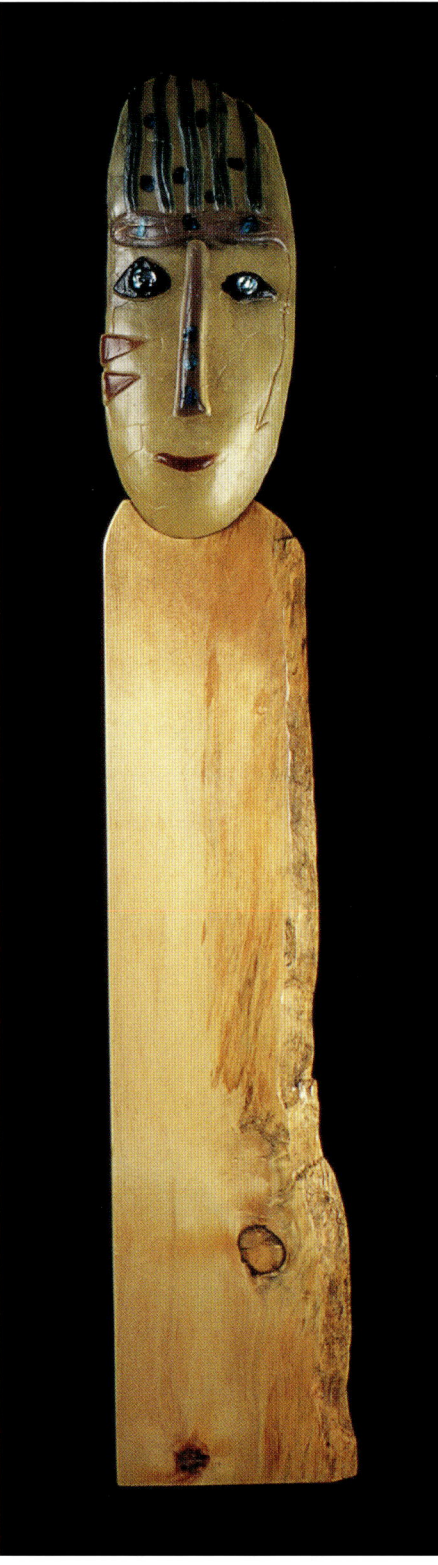

N.W. Native, 2001, ca. 30" h. *Photograph courtesy of the artist.*

Two Friends, 1986, 27" x 24". *Photograph courtesy of the artist.*

Anna Boothe

I come from a strong matrilineal line of accomplished crafters and from an upbringing visually peppered with ancient Middle Eastern and East Asian references. As an employee, I have spent much time "playing-out" the decorative art gene in the guise of a traditional French/Italian pastry chef in Philadelphia and later on as a cake sculptor and illustrator (using whipped cream modeled with a palette knife).

My vessel castings tie together these aspects of my background with my training as a sculptor and user of glass. I view the frit or traditional pate de verre casting process I use to create the forms as a type of permanent baking. The technique's resultant translucent sugary fused glass allows light to hold imagery, as if floating in space, and provides me with a medium through which I am able to diffuse emotional, dream, and pragmatic experiences into one layered montage.

For example:

> *Sugar-Bearers* refers to the "in-service" characteristic of motherhood.
> *Core Gathering* evolved from the need for replenishment.

My earlier and more recent figurative sculpture refers to my ongoing ontological inquiries. Each modified and augmented female form searches for context. Each grouping of parts provides a specific set of psychological boundaries. As an artist, I work to question the relevance of and reactions to these fabricated situations. In a humble manner, I suppose that I am creating icons to promote my own sanity and personal growth.

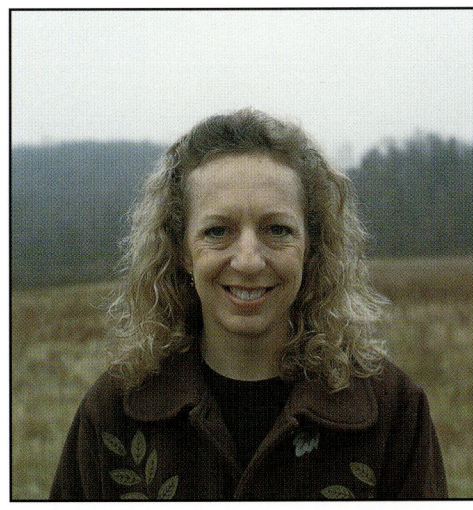

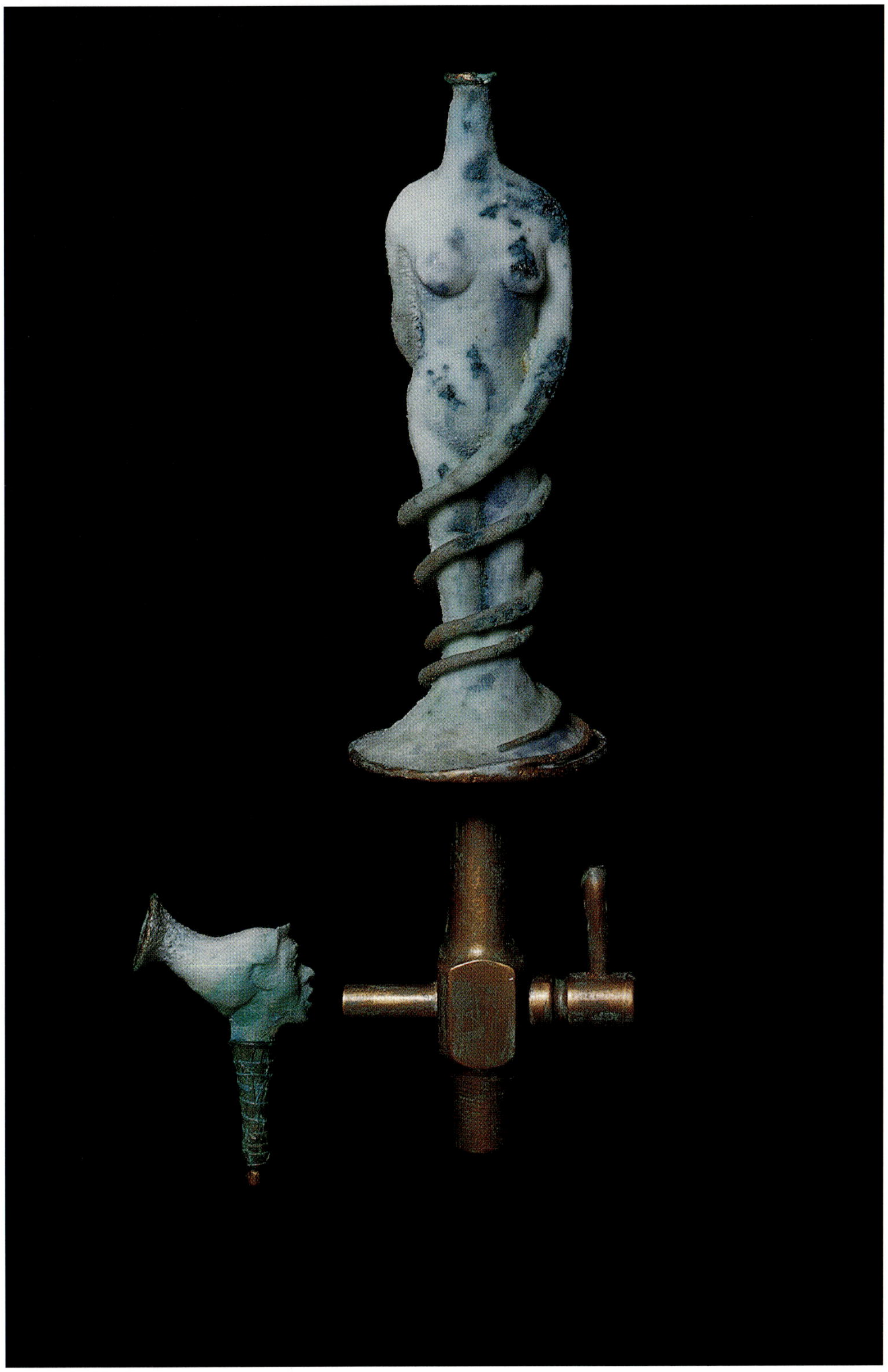

Anna Boothe. *Photograph courtesy of the artist.*

Divining the Dark, 1991, 17" x 7.5" x 3.5", glass (kiln cast), wood, copper paint, photo: Eric Mitchell. *Photograph courtesy of the artist.*

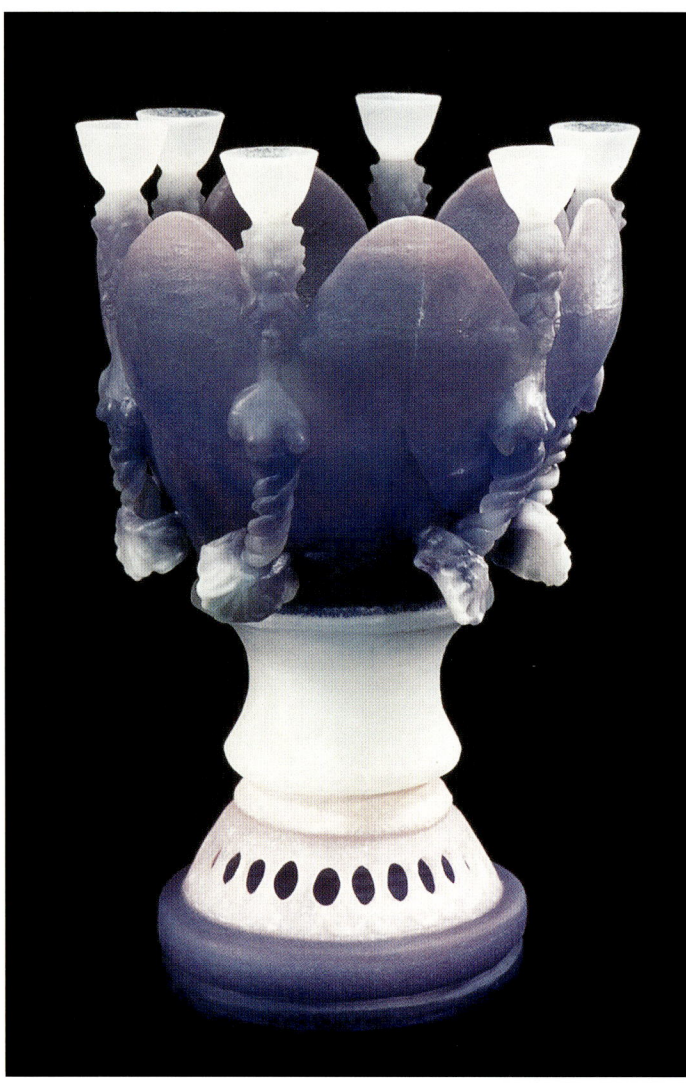

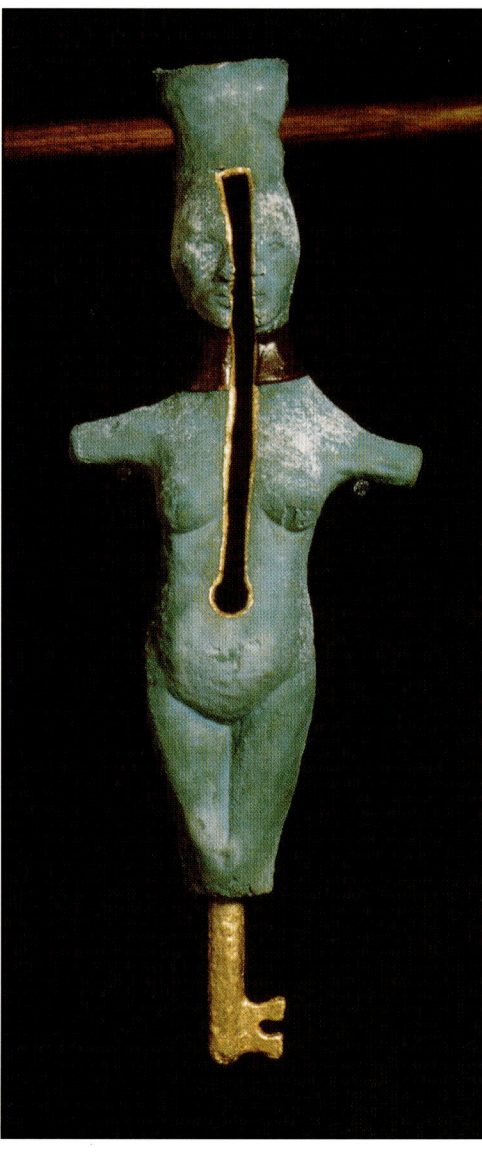

Fish or Cut Bait, 1991, 23" x 13.5" x 4", glass (kiln cast beads), gold leaf, wood, photo: Eric Mitchell. Photograph courtesy of the artist.

Lightning Dancers (Core Gathering), 2001, 28" x 18" d top, 11.5" d bottom, glass (pate de verre), photo: Bruce Miller. Photograph courtesy of the artist.

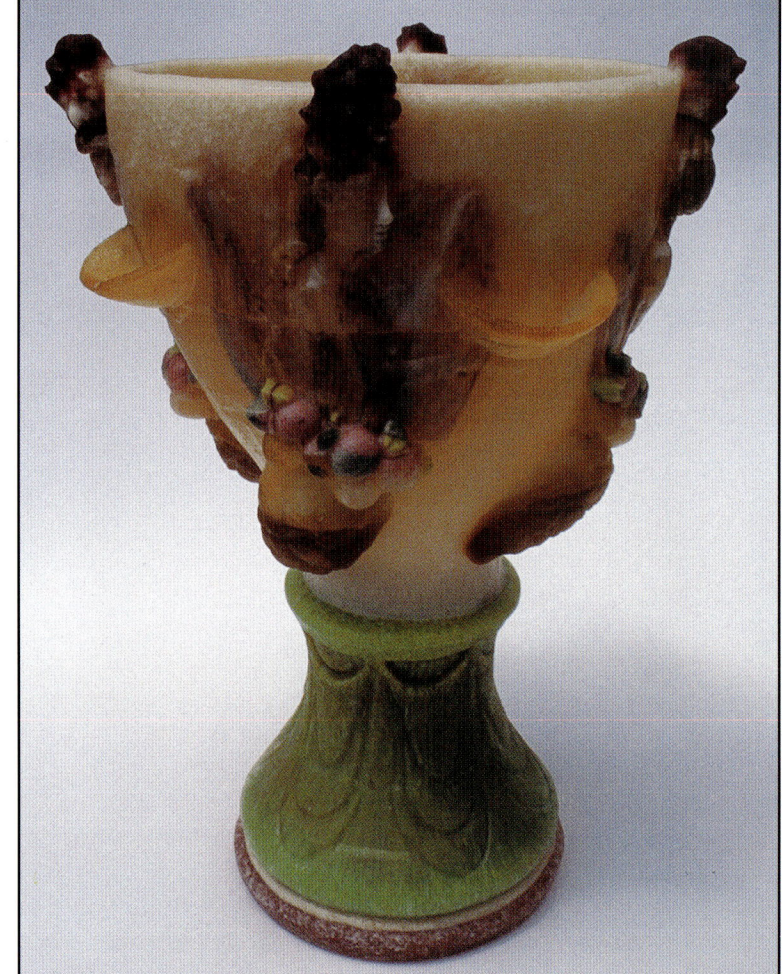

Sugar-Bearers, 2000, 22" x 15.5" d top x 9.5" d bottom, glass (pate de verre). Collection: Corning Museum of Glass, photo: and photograph courtesy of the artist.

Ruth Brockman

My work is an extension of my curiosity and intuition. With nature as my source of inspiration I discover answers, which provide me with greater understanding and meaning.

My work deals with birth, death, transformation, and rebirth. The prevalent theme has been the interrelationship of all living forms, their spirits, and vital connections with man. This is a crucial time for human beings to become aware of the devastation being manifested on this planet. It is my theory that human beings need to reconnect with the spirits of nature to change behavior patterns and become more holistic.

An utmost concern is to raise awareness and reconnect man's consciousness today to the web of life. I try to incorporate these issues and concerns in my work.

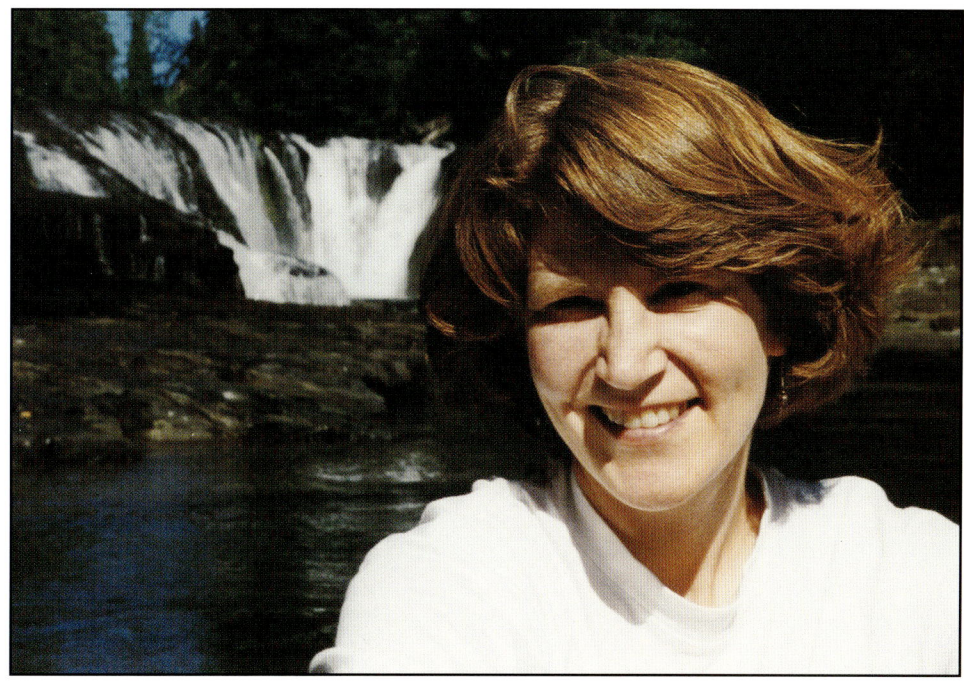

Ruth Brockman. *Photograph courtesy of the artist.*

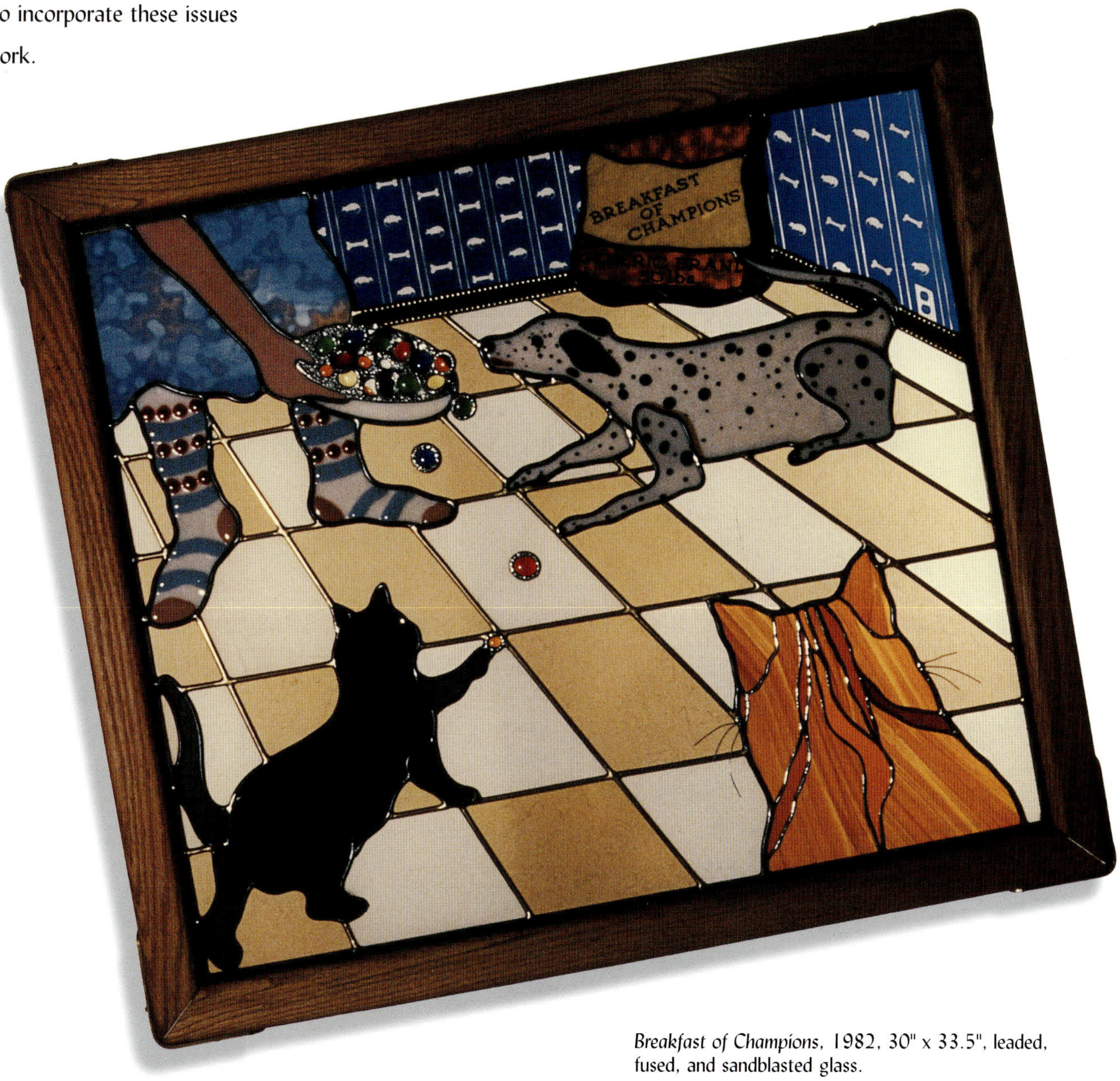

Breakfast of Champions, 1982, 30" x 33.5", leaded, fused, and sandblasted glass.

128   The Eighties - The Artist

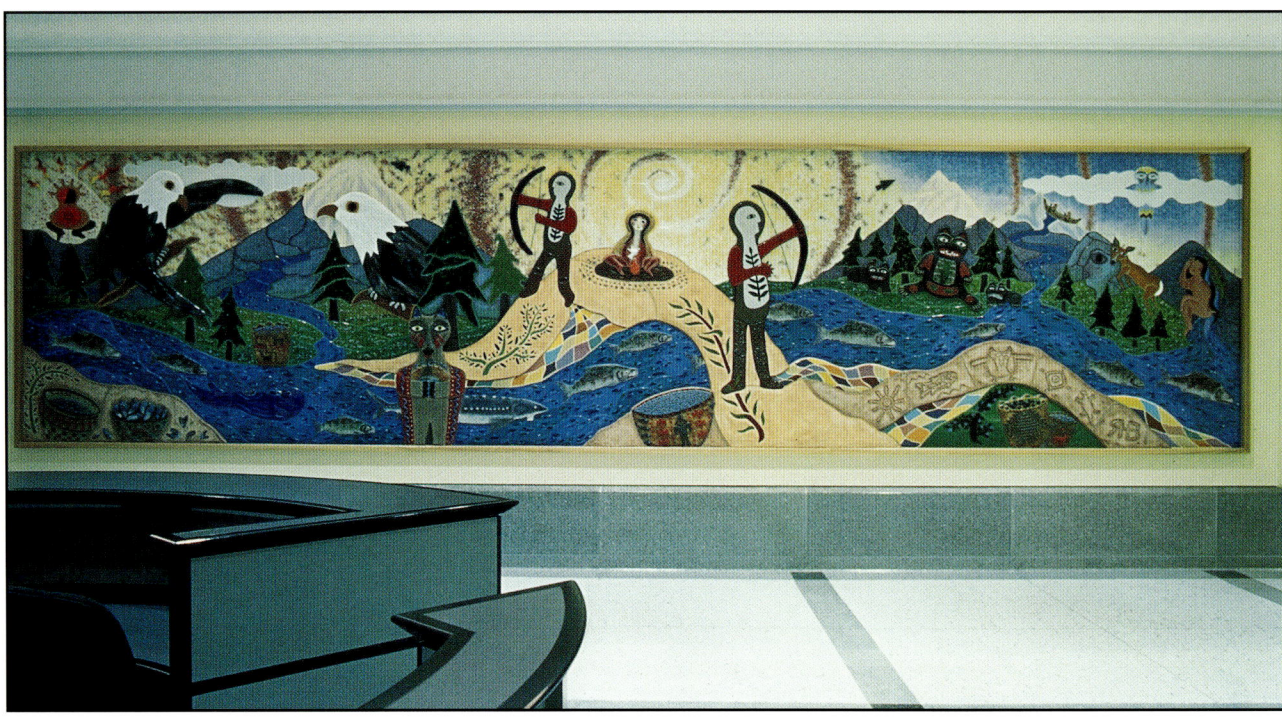

The Bridge of the Gods, 1992, 6' 6" x 26' 5", kiln cast and fused glass, cement, Portland State Office Building, photo: Roger Schreiber. *Photograph courtesy of the artist.*

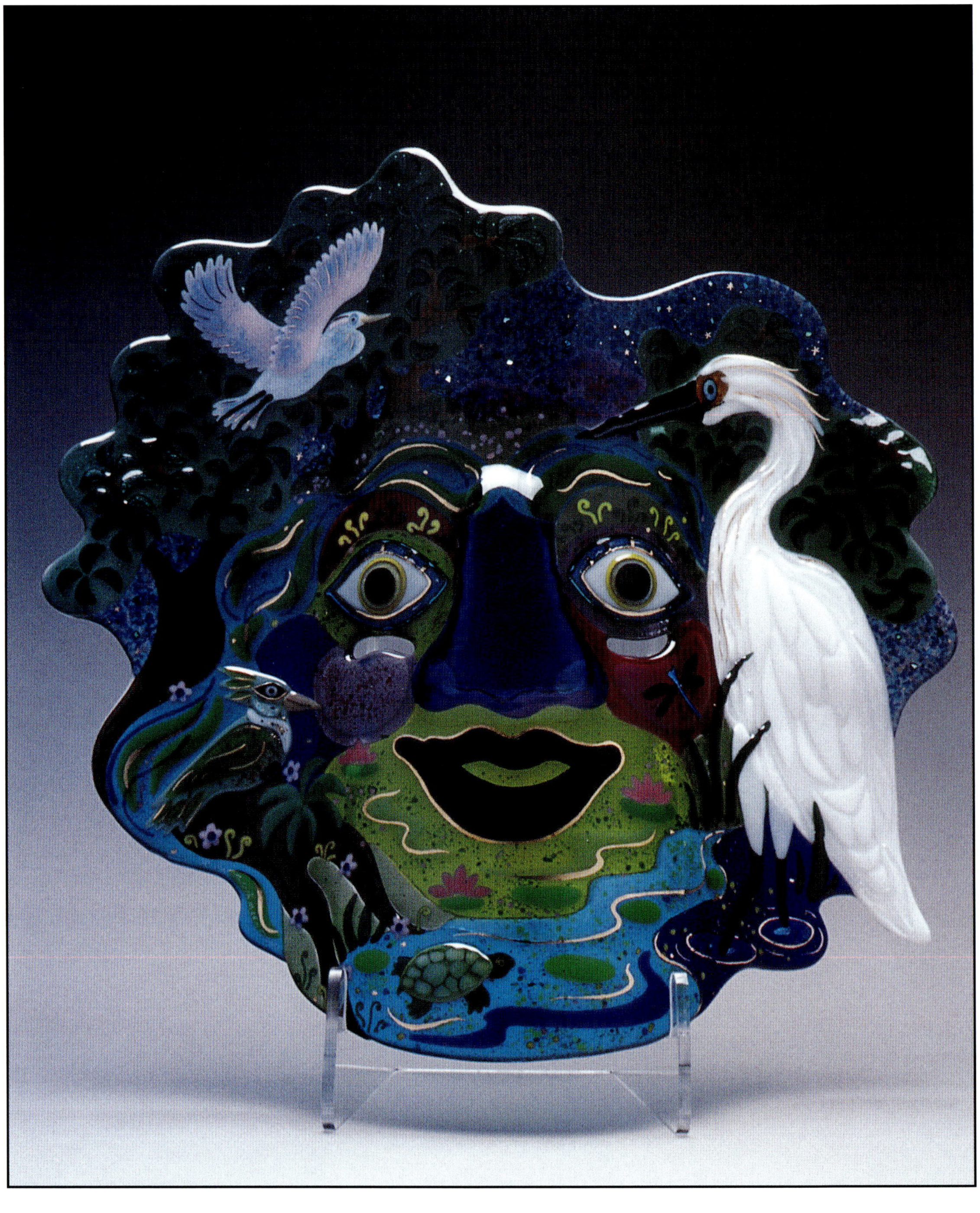

Aves De La Laguna, 2001, 18" x 18" x 6", fused and slumped glass, photo: Bill Bachhuber. *Photograph courtesy of the artist.*

Carol Cohen

My work uses epoxy paint, ordinary window glass, and sometimes wood bases to hold and space the layers of painted glass.

What slides of my work may not convey is that these assemblages and stacks of painted window glass hold the illusion of actual three-dimensional forms, images of objects (such as teapots, shoes, and fish) that change perspective as the viewer moves around or up and down; which images disappear when the viewer is edge-on to the glass layers.

I invented the technique in 1982 in order to solve design problems of my stacked steel bar sculpture three-dimensionally. But the solution, at first using Plexiglas layers, was so interesting in itself that I decided to commit myself to developing it into artwork.

When I began to develop the technique I wanted to restrict myself to representational imagery because I felt abstractions would be too easy in this technique. Much of the imagery I chose involved objects one would want and expect to touch, such as telephones, wineglasses, and cups, in order to establish a tension between the "touchableness" of the actual object and the non-tangibility of the image painted on the layered sheets of glass.

In order to know exactly where to put the paint on each layer of glass, I devised a Rube Goldbergesque "contour device" that allows me to take the needed outline (for each separate layer) from an actual object or a model I make, such as a clay figure. This enabled me to avoid learning to use a computer with its 3-D programs. I have managed to avoid using a computer ever since, except for ATMs at banks. I think if they designed a personal computer that presented me with fifty dollars every time I pushed the right keys (like ATMs), I would definitely become computer literate.

Using glass was new for me in 1982. I had to invent my own techniques because I thought there were only two artists using glass: me, and Larry Bell. In 1987 I felt the work was ready to be seen, and so I took two pieces to a New York gallery and found out that hundreds of artists were working with glass, in hundreds of ways. (None, thank heavens, in my way!)

Although glass is an interesting and challenging material to make art out of, I chose it for practical reasons: it is cheaper than Plexiglas, harder, less electrostatic, and easier to cut by simple scoring-and-breaking. It is also beautifully green when stacked in layers, and surgically sharp-edged. But I paint on glass because I cannot paint on air.

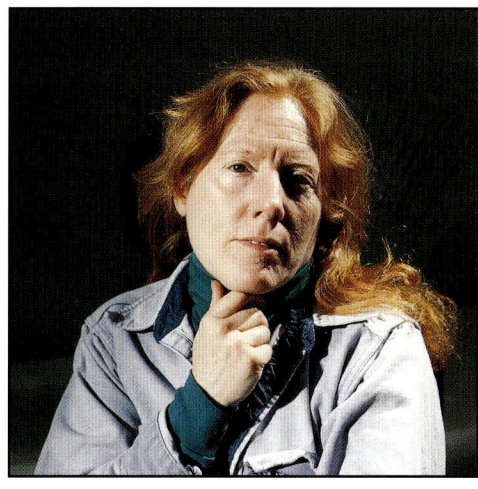

Carol Cohen. *Photograph courtesy of the artist.*

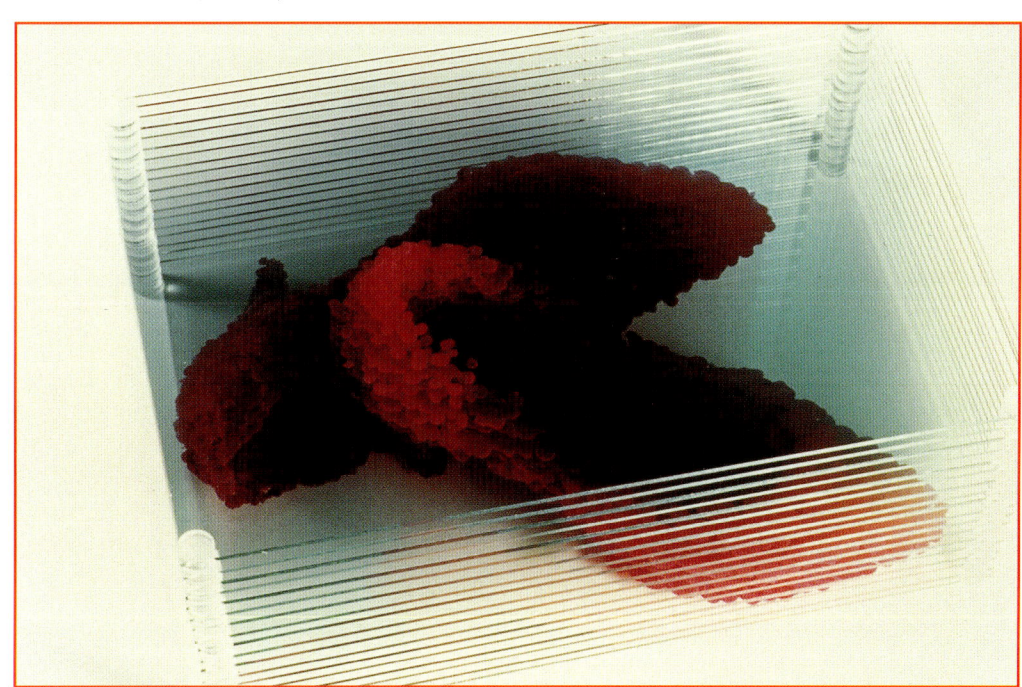

Red Shoes, 1987, 5" x 12" x 8", stacked, painted glass. *Photograph courtesy of the artist.*

130　The Eighties - The Artist

X-d Out, 1987, 10" x 9" x 13", stacked, painted glass. *Photograph courtesy of the artist.*

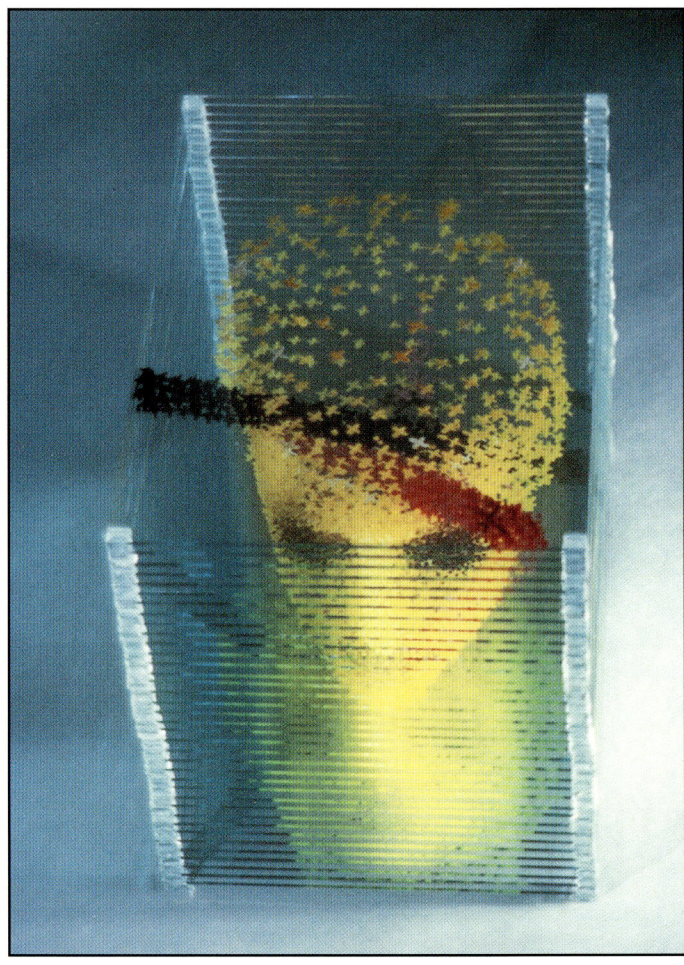

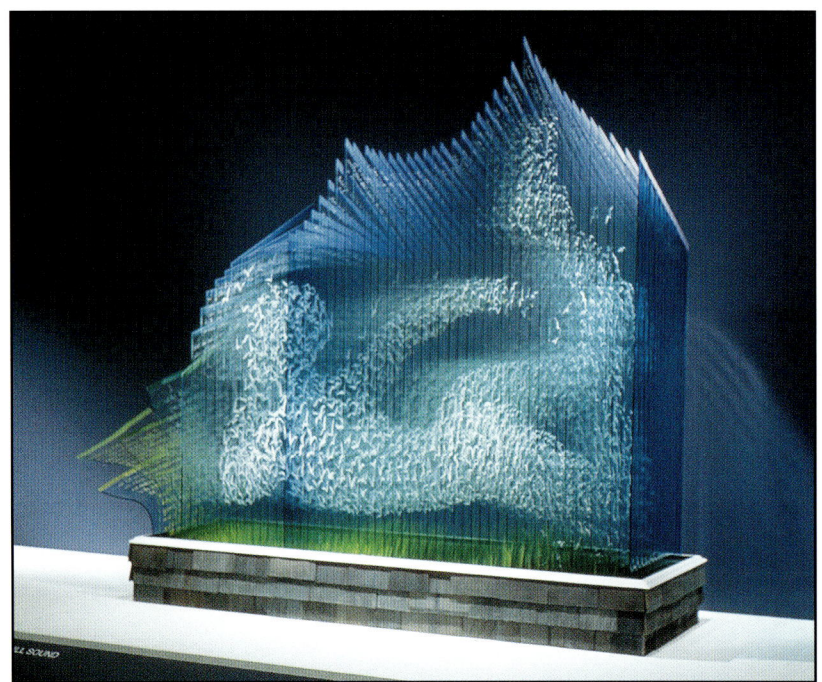

Little Compton, 1997, 60" x 72" x 20.5", glass, paint, wood. *Photograph courtesy of the artist.*

Josephs Coat, 1999, 38" x 40" x 13", glass, paint, wood, metal. *Photograph courtesy of the artist.*

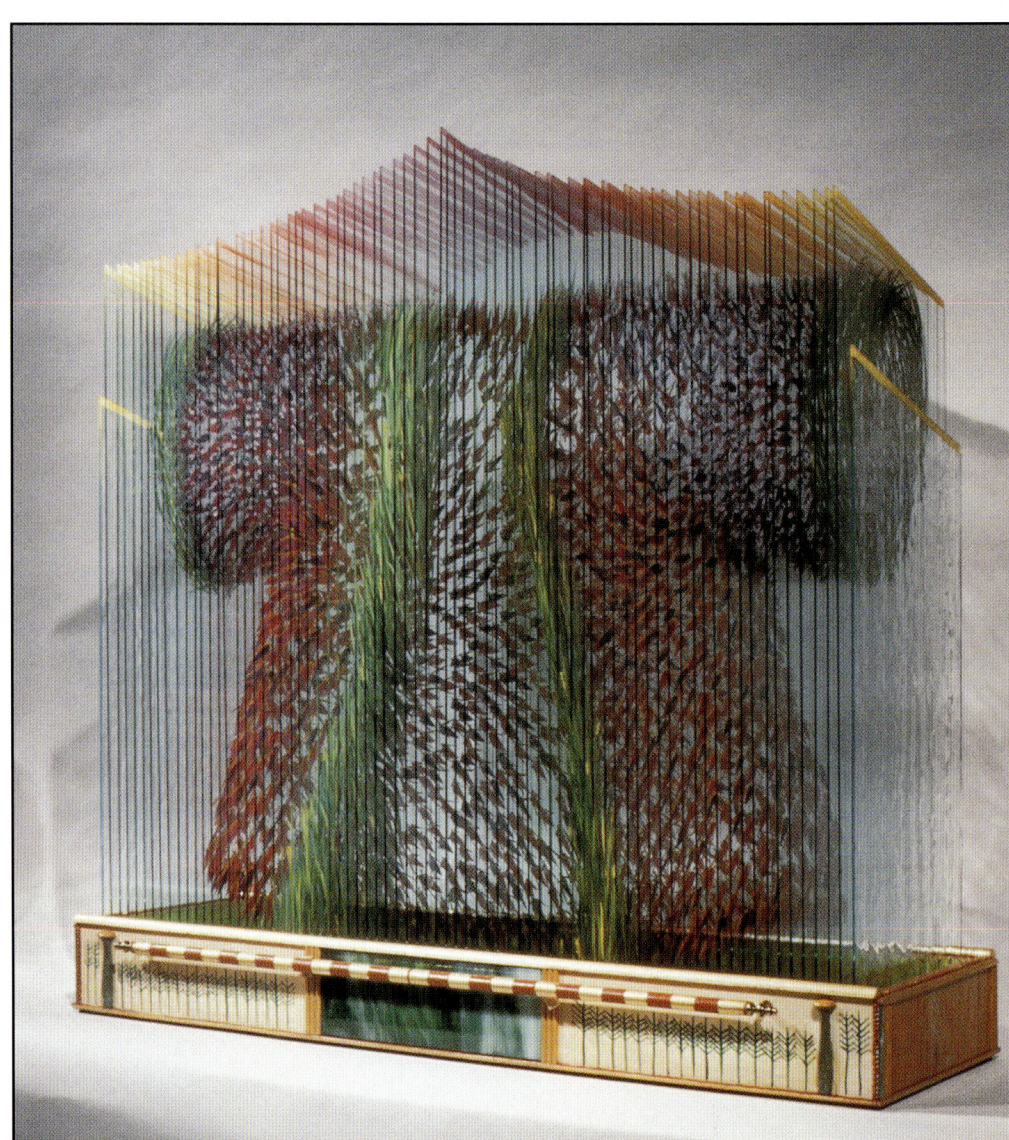

B. Jane Cowie

My work is symbolic of moments of vulnerability and isolation. The glass figures I make are transparent, still, bound, entrapped or fixed. If their bindings are removed they are exposed, vulnerable, isolated. Shadows that born ominously are the thoughts and memories that cannot be shaken off, only hidden or temporarily forgotten.

I use the suitcase as an indicator of place, of a temporary home, something to return to, something to hide next to or lean on for strength. For me the suitcase contains the hopes, dreams, and desires that are collected and carried along with fears, doubts, and insecurities.

House bricks suggest the notion of home, a place of questionable security, a tenuous sanctuary. A house can protect you from the world, but it can also entrap you. A home can become a kind of personal prison that is self-imposed, or imposed by the intimate other.

Walls can provide an unreal sense of comfort.

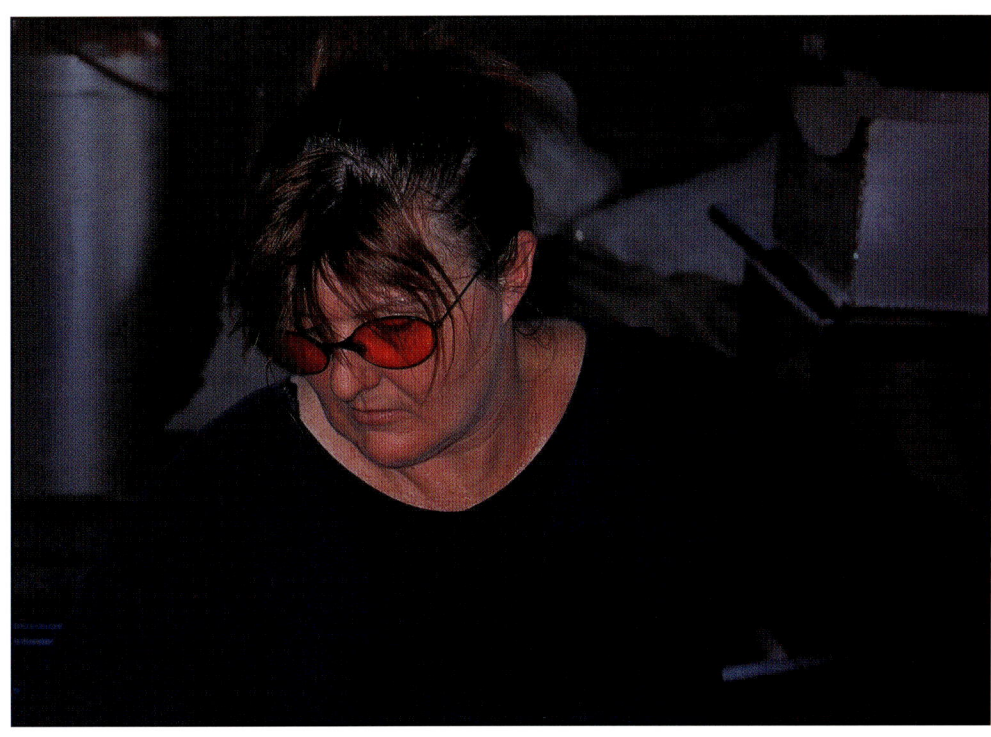

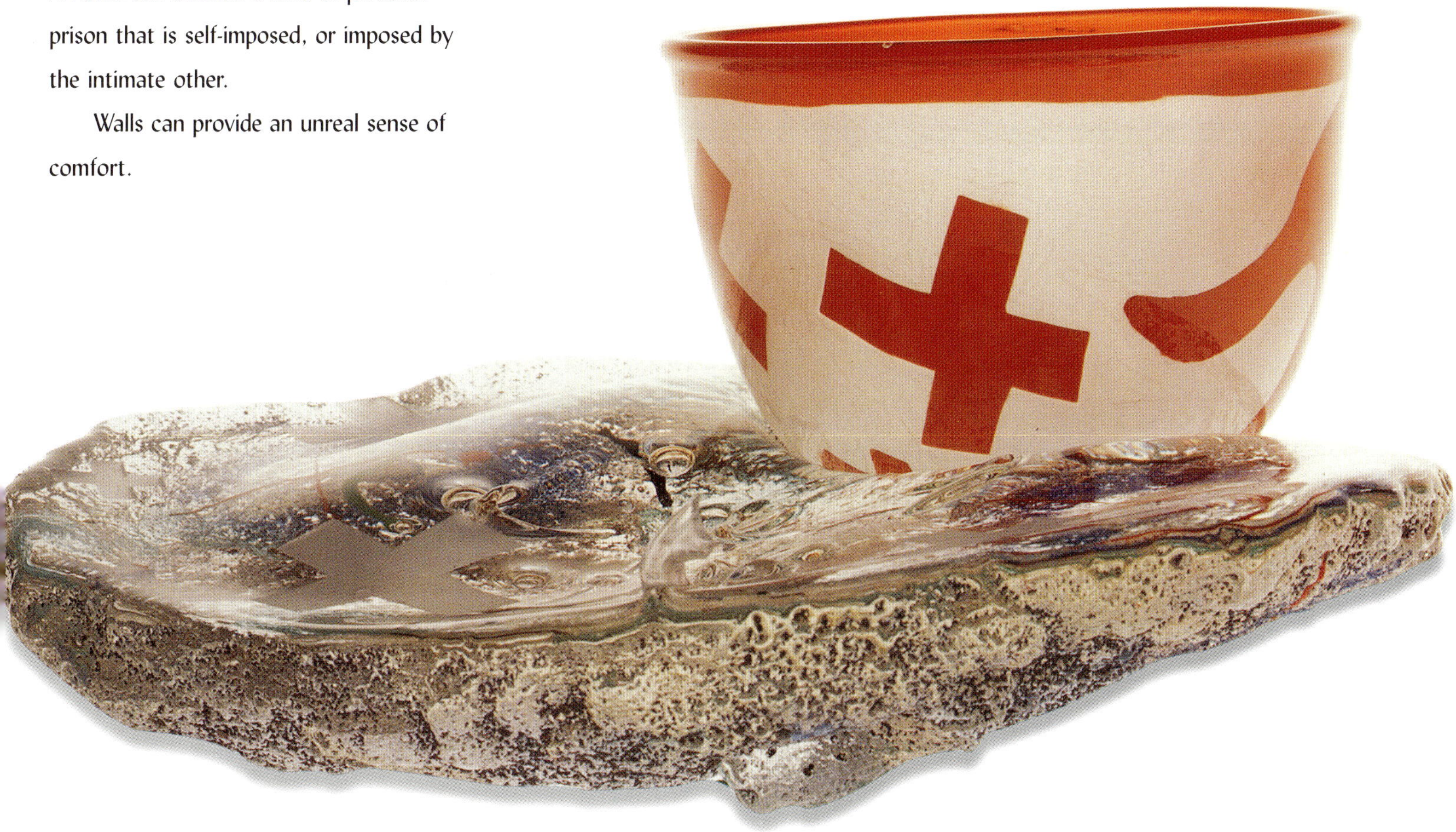

B. Jane Cowie. *Photograph courtesy of the author.*

...*reaching out*..., 1989, 205 mm h, Blown and cast glass hot joined, sandblasted. *Photograph courtesy of the artist.*

132   The Eighties - The Artist

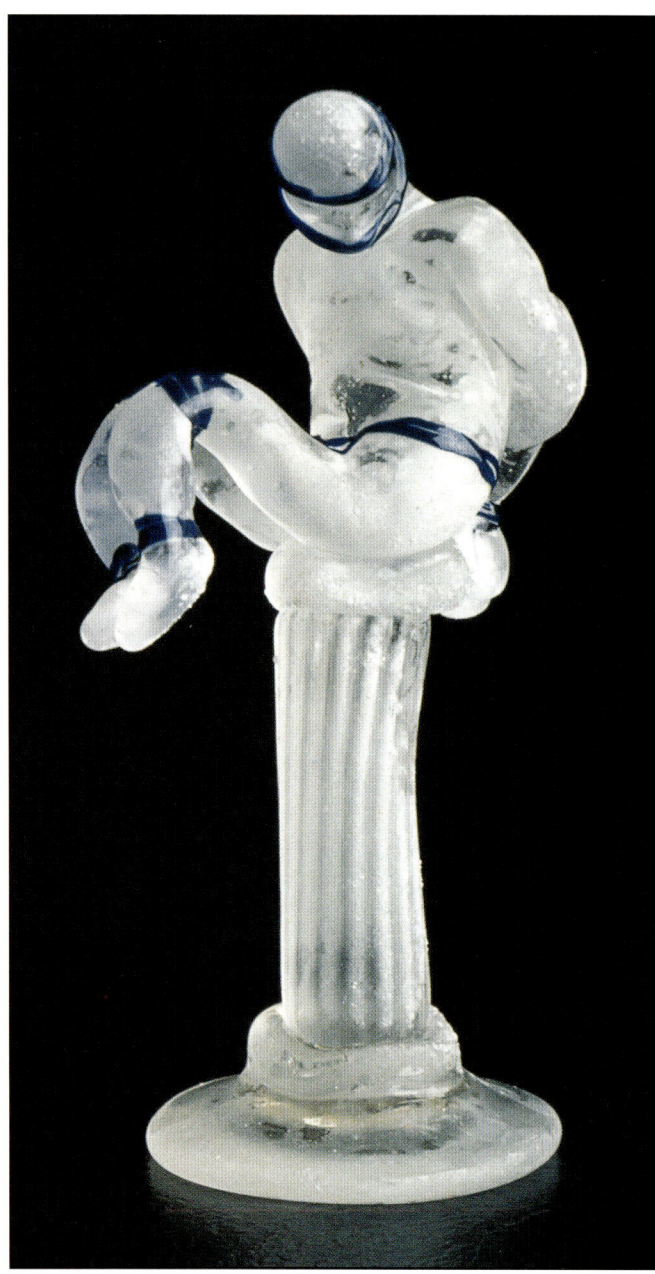

Enticed, 1993, 280 mm, hot sculptured glass. Photograph courtesy of the artist.

Untouched, 2001, 200 mm, hot sculptured glass and mixed media. Photograph courtesy of the artist.

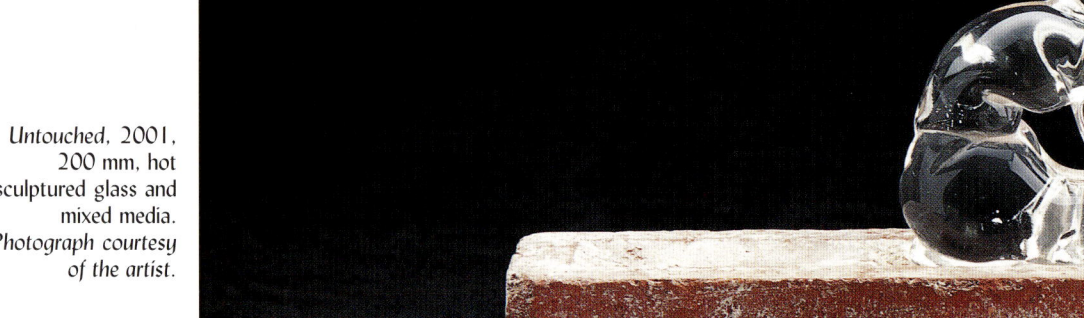

Keke Cribbs

I started working in glass in 1980. I was attracted to its ability to transmit light and its versatility as a two-dimensional or three-dimensional material. The fact that color can be an inherent quality of glass and that one can use so many different techniques for surface decoration, or creating imagery within the glass, results in a magical material unlike any other.

On the other hand, glass is limited to some extent by its fragility, and it can be somewhat unforgiving when trying to form it. For that reason, I have found it very important to use other media in conjunction with glass in order to fulfill my creative intent. I have used fiberglass, wood, metal, and clay as supports for my sculptural, mixed media pieces, and I continue to experiment with other materials.

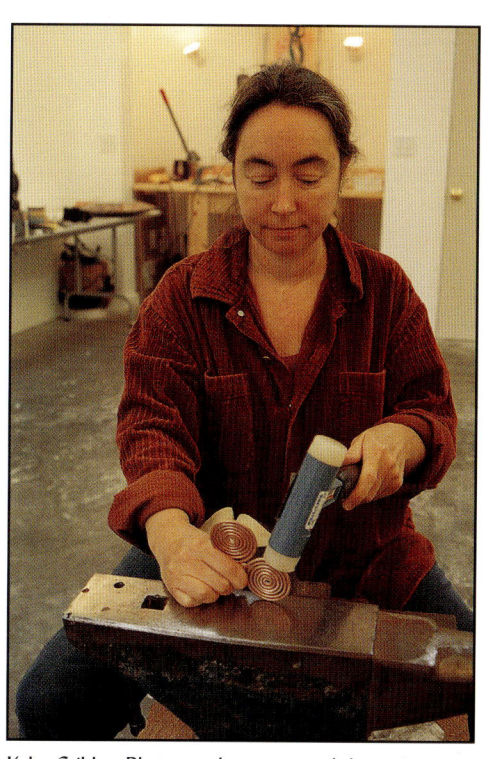

Keke Cribbs. *Photograph courtesy of the artist.*

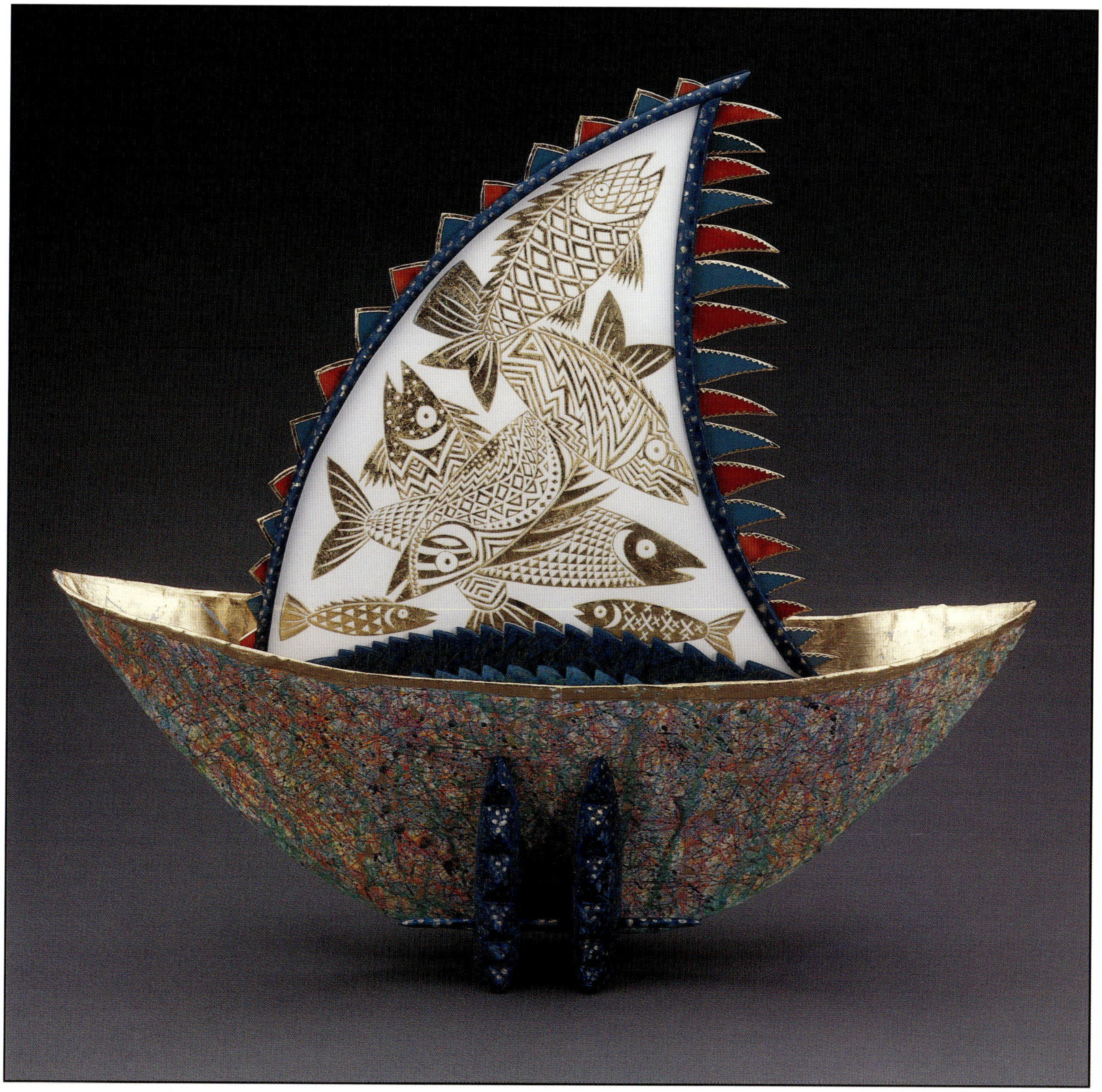

Sailing to Byzantium, 1986, 28" x 29" x 8", sandblasted flash white on clear glass with gold leaf, papier-mâché, wood. *Photograph courtesy of the artist.*

134   The Eighties - The Artist

Blue Bird, 1996, 30.75" x 31.25" x 2", reverse painted glass with oil paint, engraved and sandblasted, painted wood frame.

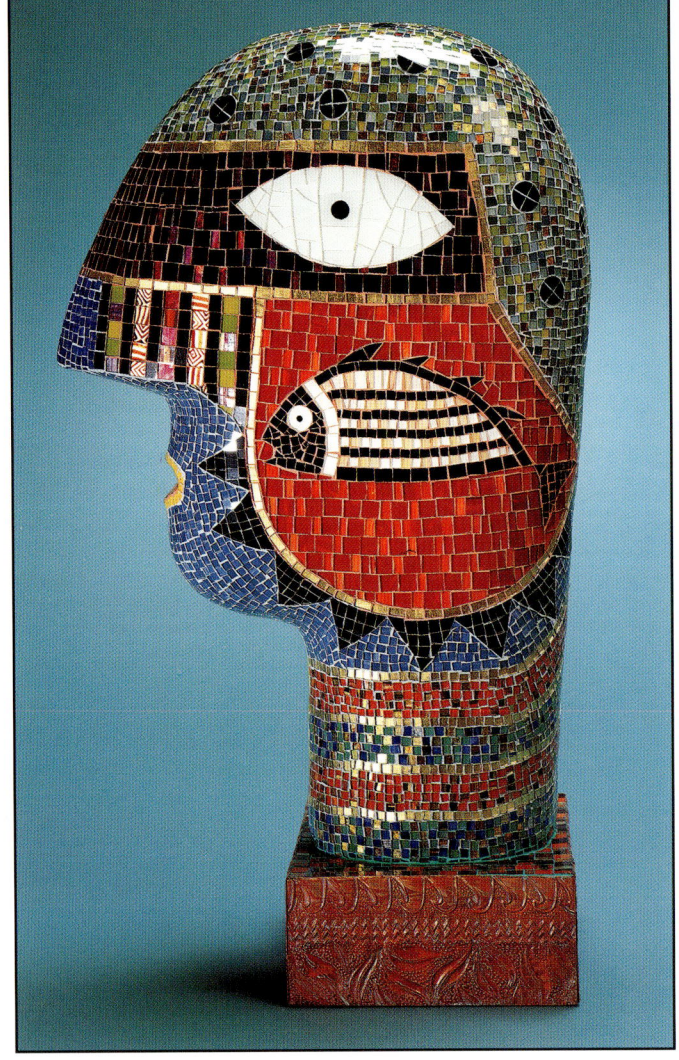

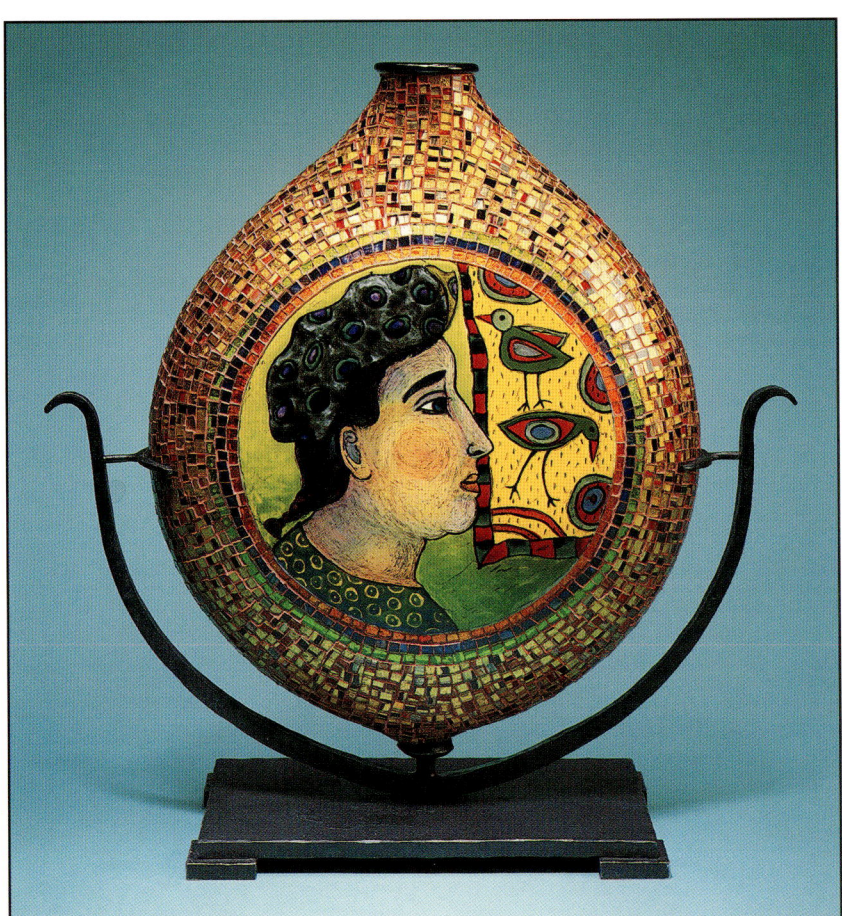

Guillaume, 2001, 27" x 16.5" x 9", reverse painted fired enamels on glass, cut into mosaics, mounted on hybresized concrete form, copper repousser. *Photograph courtesy of the artist.*

Varia, 2002, 18" x 17.5" x 6.5", reverse painted fired enamels, slumped, and cut into mosaics, mounted on blown glass form, steel base. *Photograph courtesy of the artist.*

Laura Donefer

I love being a woman! When I met hot glass for the first time and was allowed to touch it, I fell in love with being a woman all over again...

How best to describe how I feel from the inside out than with a material so unabashedly sensual, so molten, so hot without any excuses! Glass to me is the essence of the female in her purest form, and it is a privilege to work with. How lucky am I! Glass is everything that I strive for; glass never has to apologize for the way it behaves! Glass married to colour is life itself, glass clear and cool are the constellations above, glass bound to metal is the perfect relationship we all long for, and glass hot out of the tank is unimagined erotic love. If you were to look inside my secret self, there would be a furnace of hot-honey-horny "help me mama" glass!

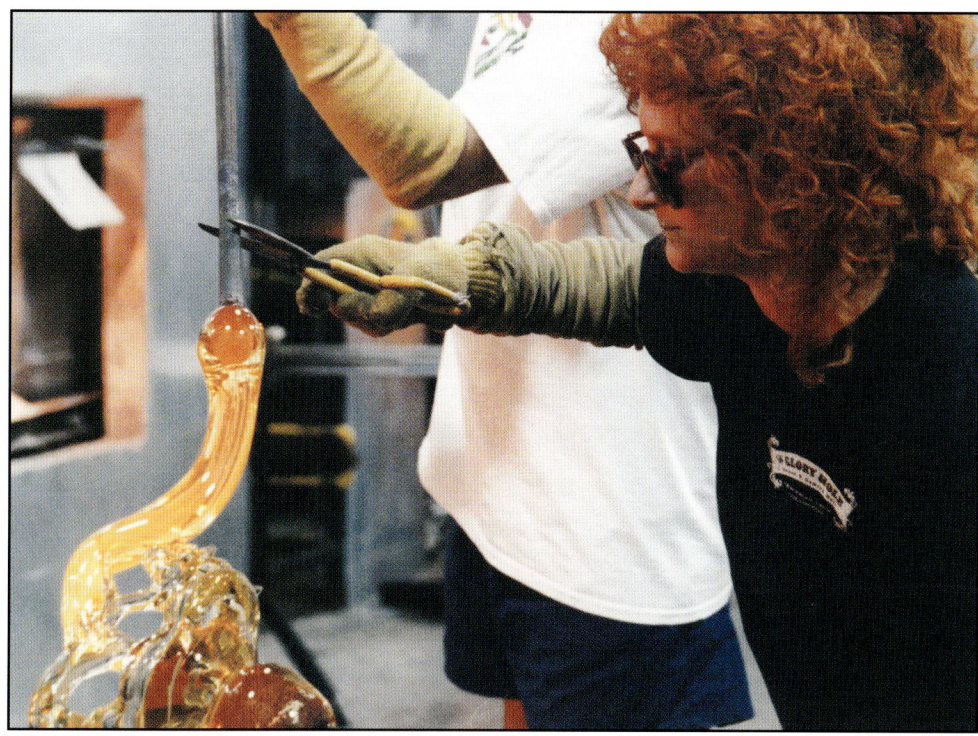

Laura Donefer. *Photograph courtesy of the artist.*

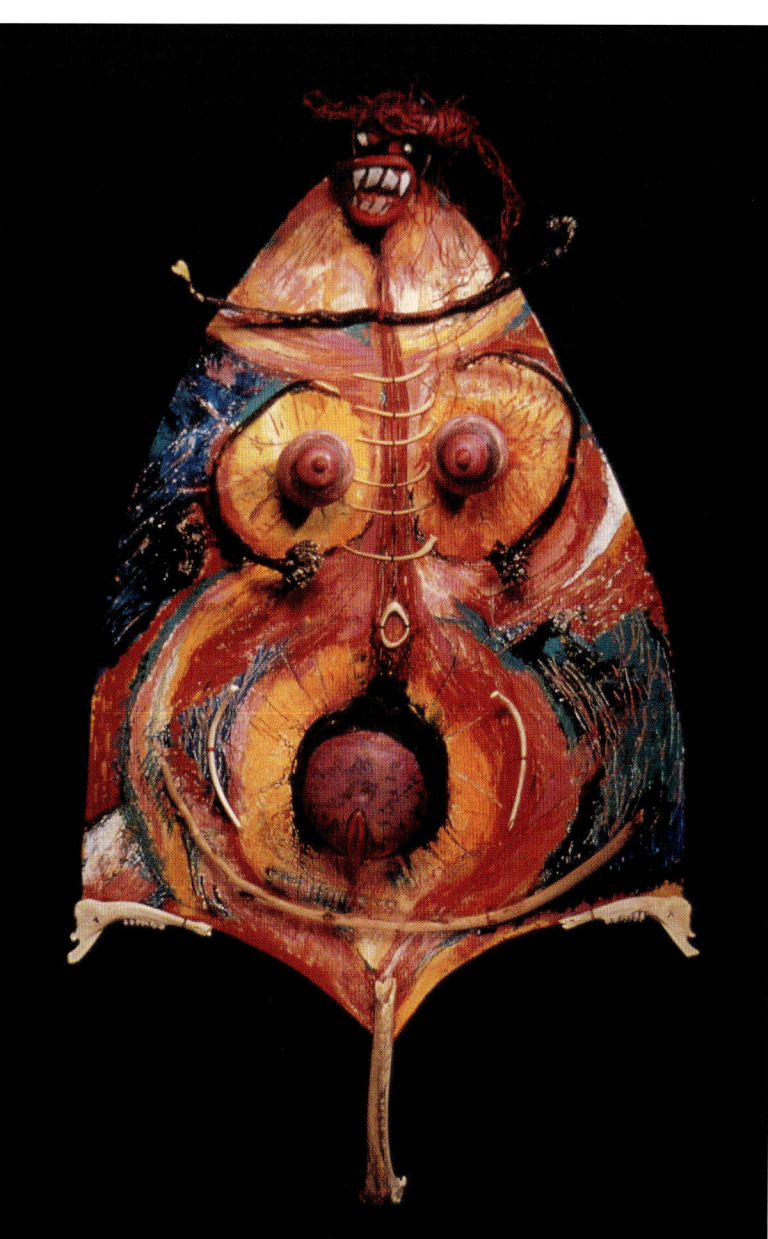

Kali-Black Mother Time (Shield Series), 1986, 5' x 5' wall piece, blown glass body parts, mixed media. *Photograph courtesy of the artist.*

Heat
Heart
I am flammable.
Sometimes I want to warn,
"Watch out, one small spark and I'll ignite"
Bursting so full of
Life, Love, Vision, Touch,
I am always about to go up in flames.
Maybe that is why
I crave
Working with hot glass-
It helps to harness
All my heat
To the pulsing heart of creation.

136 The Eighties - The Artist

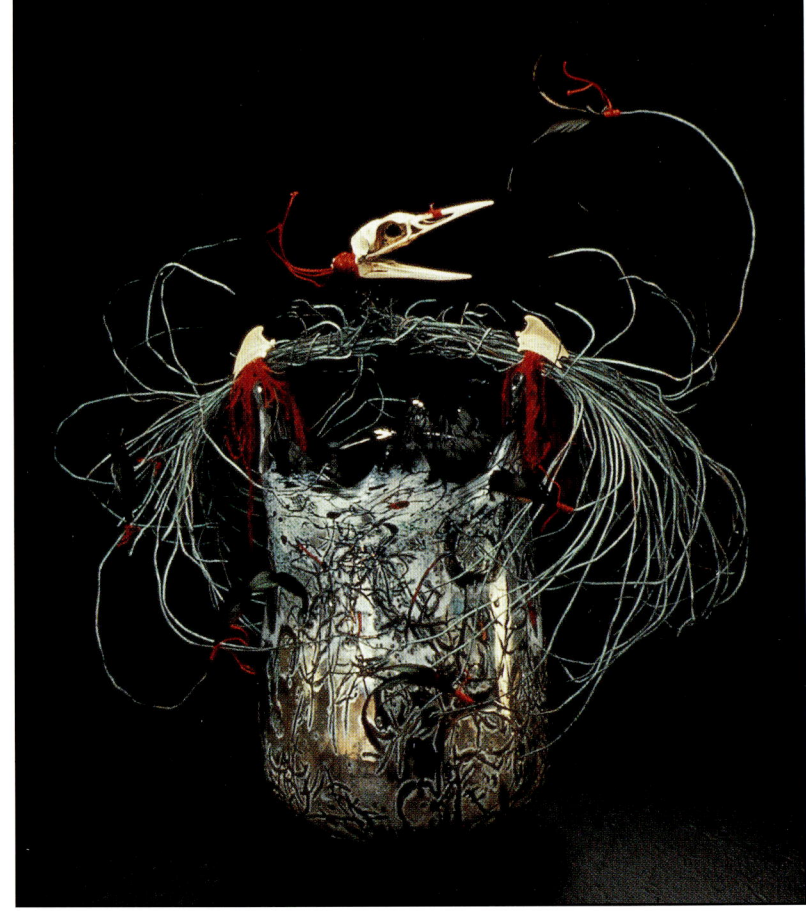

Blue Heron Witch Pot, 1986, 25" x 25", blown glass with copper in surface, mixed media. *Photograph courtesy of the artist.*

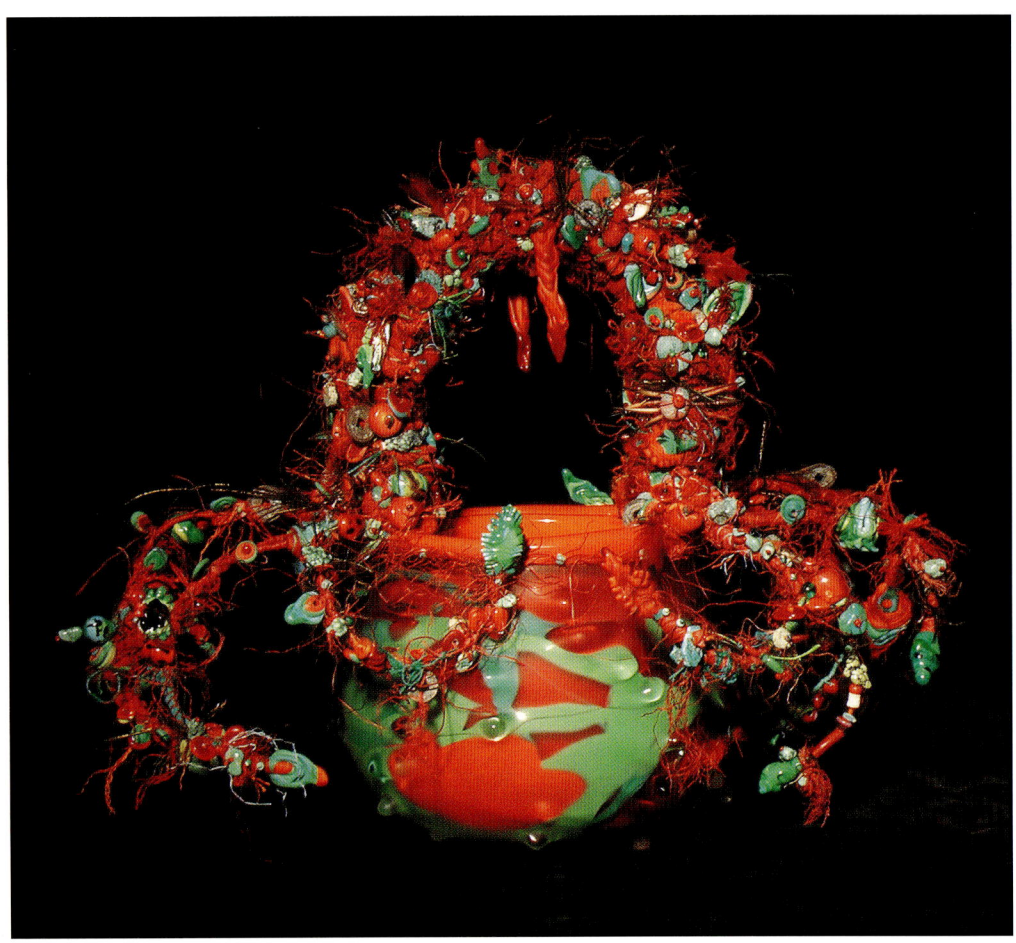

Virgin (Earth-angel Series), 1998, 28" x 6", solid worked hot glass. *Photograph courtesy of the artist.*

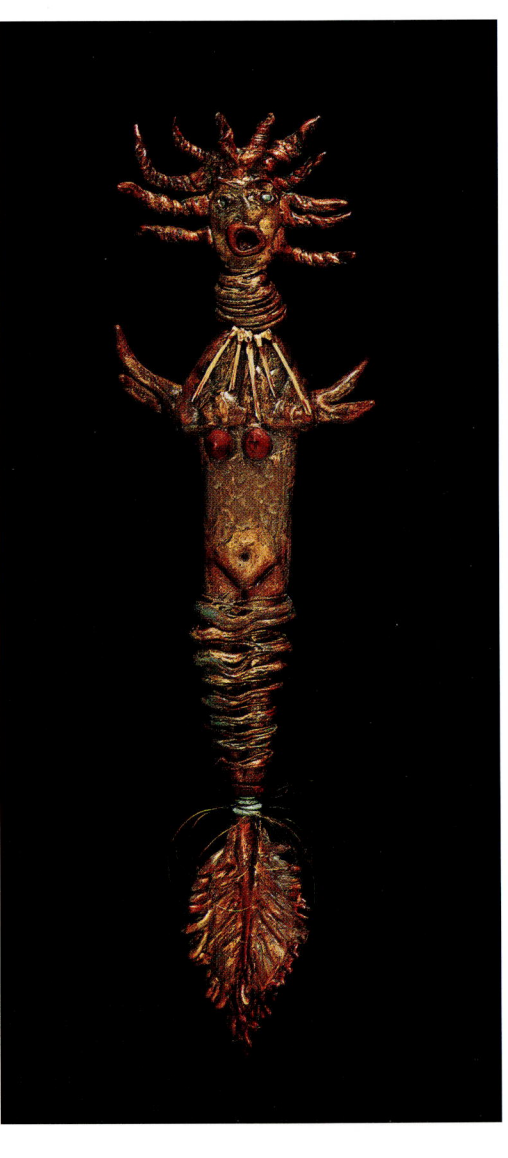

Bonnechance JUJU Amulet Pot, 2002, 25" x 30" x 12", blown glass with glass torch worked jujus and mixed media. *Photograph courtesy of the artist.*

Susan Edgerley

Exploring glass in relationship with other materials has allowed me, over the past eighteen years, to develop a personal and richly textured visual dialogue which explores themes of identity, community, existence, and the human condition. Glass with its enticing transparency yet solid impregnability remains a seductive and elusive medium full of contradictions:

> fragile, solid, hard, strong
> transparent, translucent, opaque
> fluid, soft, malleable
> colorful, clear
> tactile
> hot, warm, cold
> sharp, smooth, rough, textured
> mirror, reflect, refract
> brittle, break, shatter

What better material with which to express the diversity and complexity of human existence: its power, its mystery, its beauty, and its pain. Glass is the fragile metaphor with which I can ponder, struggle with, and create those things which live inside of me.

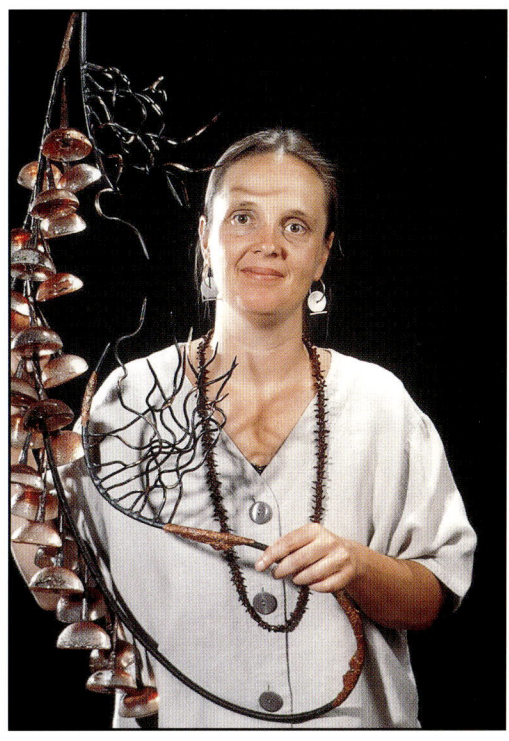

Susan Edgerley. *Photograph courtesy of the artist.*

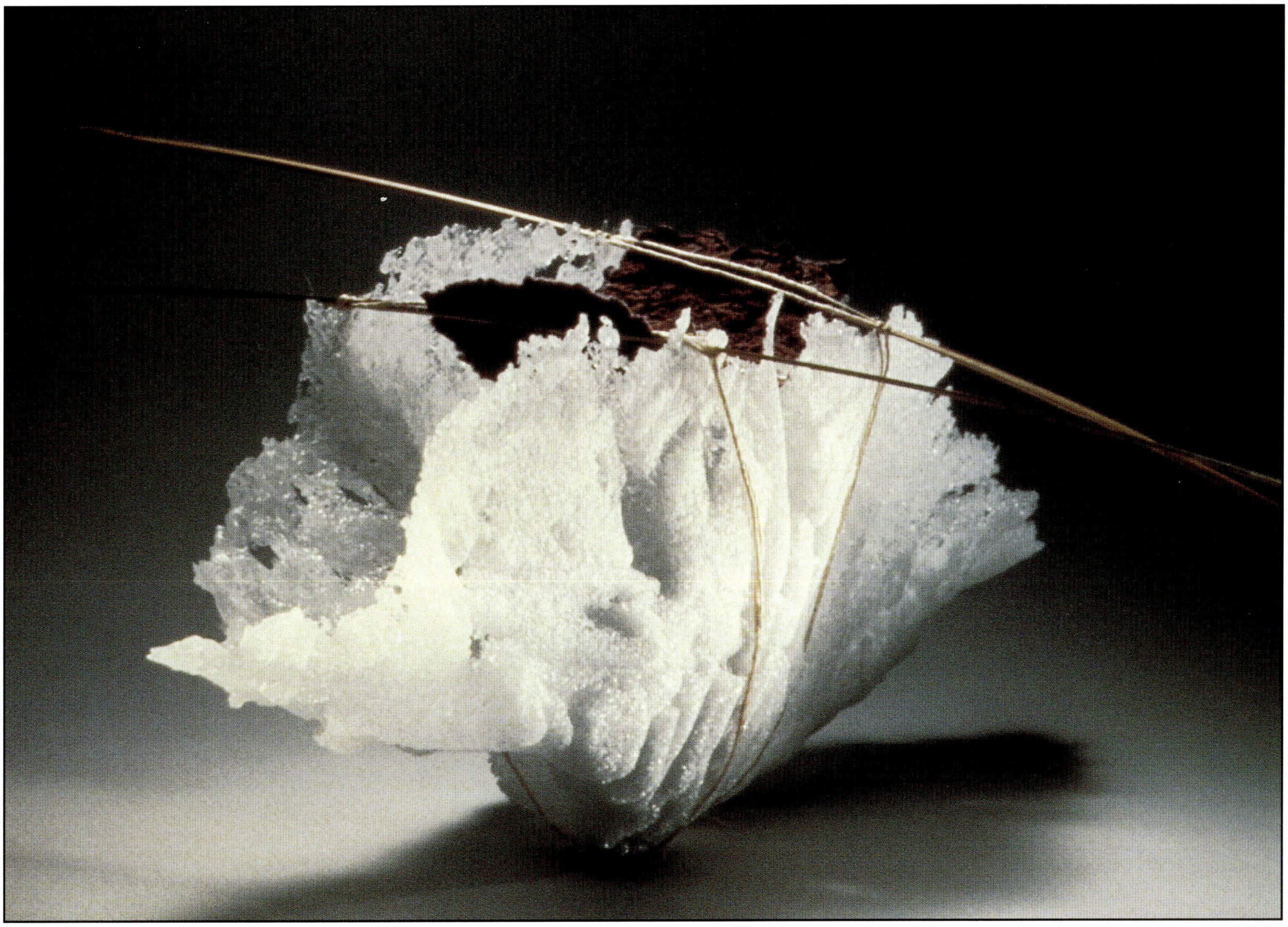

Fleeting Glimpses, 1985, 17" x 17" x 20", fused glass frit handmade paper, bamboo, sea grass. *Photograph courtesy of the artist.*

From the One, 1999, "From the seed sower series," 78" x 60" x 5", 30 element wall installation, sandcast glass, copper, wood, photo: Jocelyn Blais. *Photograph courtesy of the artist.*

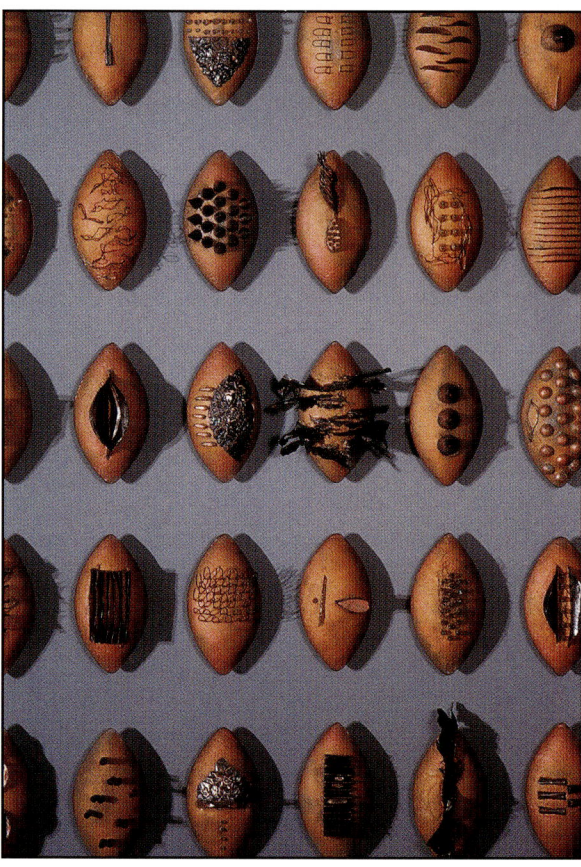

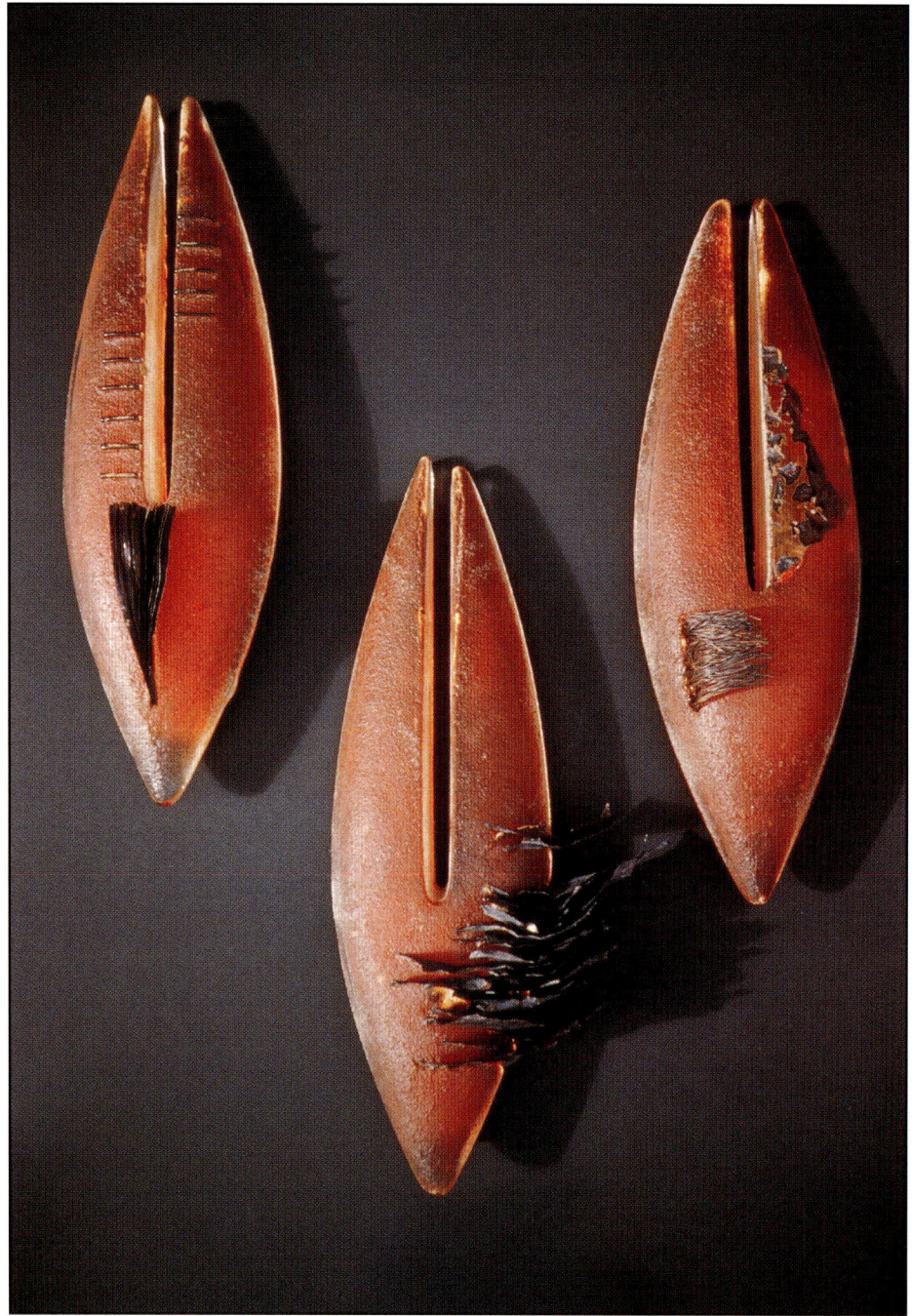

Pods, 1998, "From the seed sower series," 37" x 32" x 4", 3 element wall installation, sandcast glass, copper, wood. *Photograph courtesy of the artist.*

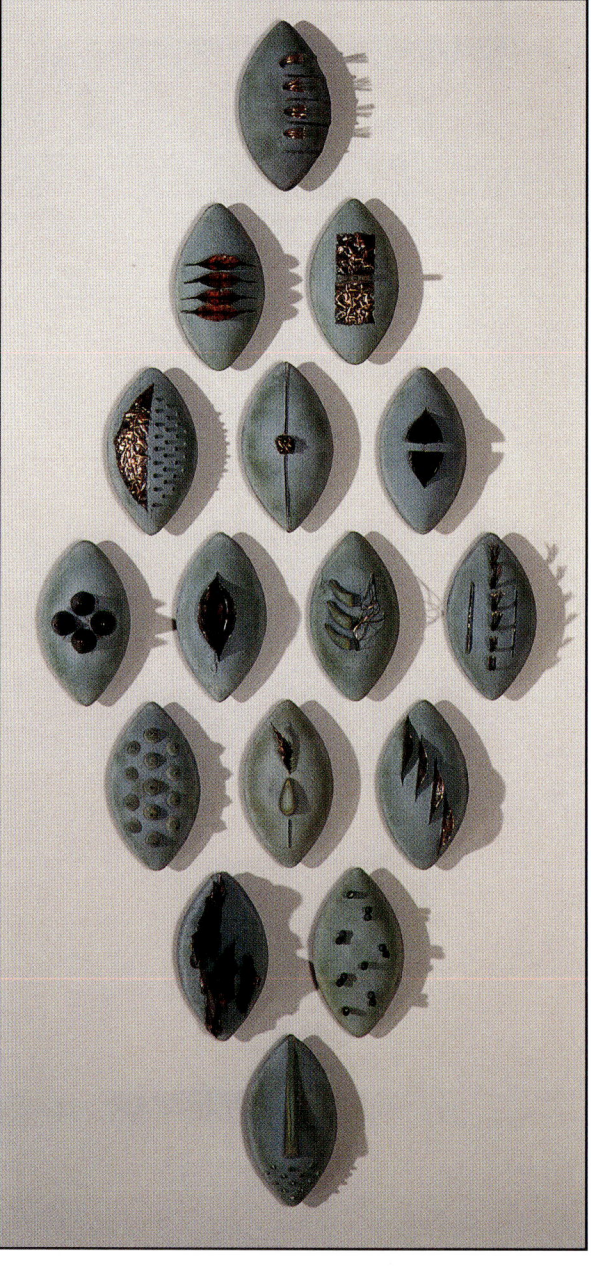

From the One, Series VI, 2001, "From the seed sower series," 80" x 35" x 5", 16 element wall installation, sandcast glass, copper, wood, photo: Jocelyn Blais. *Photograph courtesy of the artist.*

Irene Frolic

The work of Canadian artist, Irene Frolic, is noted for its emotional impact and for its exploration of the human condition. She draws on the power of her life experience and echoes the relationship of an urbanite with the land.

"My sculptures have been concerned with the crust of things: with the link between the psychology of the human face and the geology of the enduring rock of our land. Glass has served me as the perfect metaphor and medium, because it is made by fire: the fire that animates our soul and that forms the center of our earth.

In my latest sculptures I have begun to explore other aspects of my chosen material. I have decided to go to the heart of the matter. Not the time scarred surface, but what is at the center, the essence, the form within."

Irene maintains a studio in Toronto. Her work is in numerous private and public collections in Canada, the United States, Mexico, and Europe.

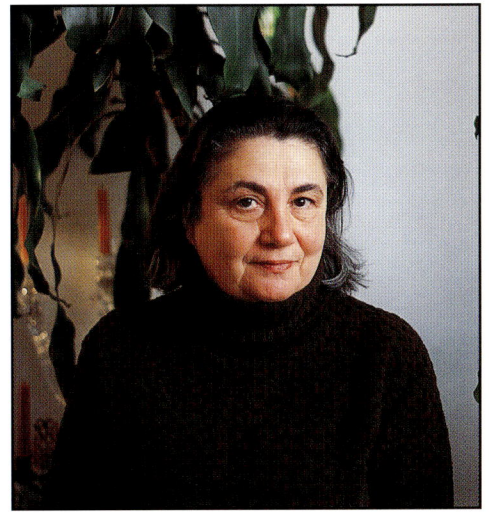

Irene Frolic. *Photo credit: Adam Frolic.*

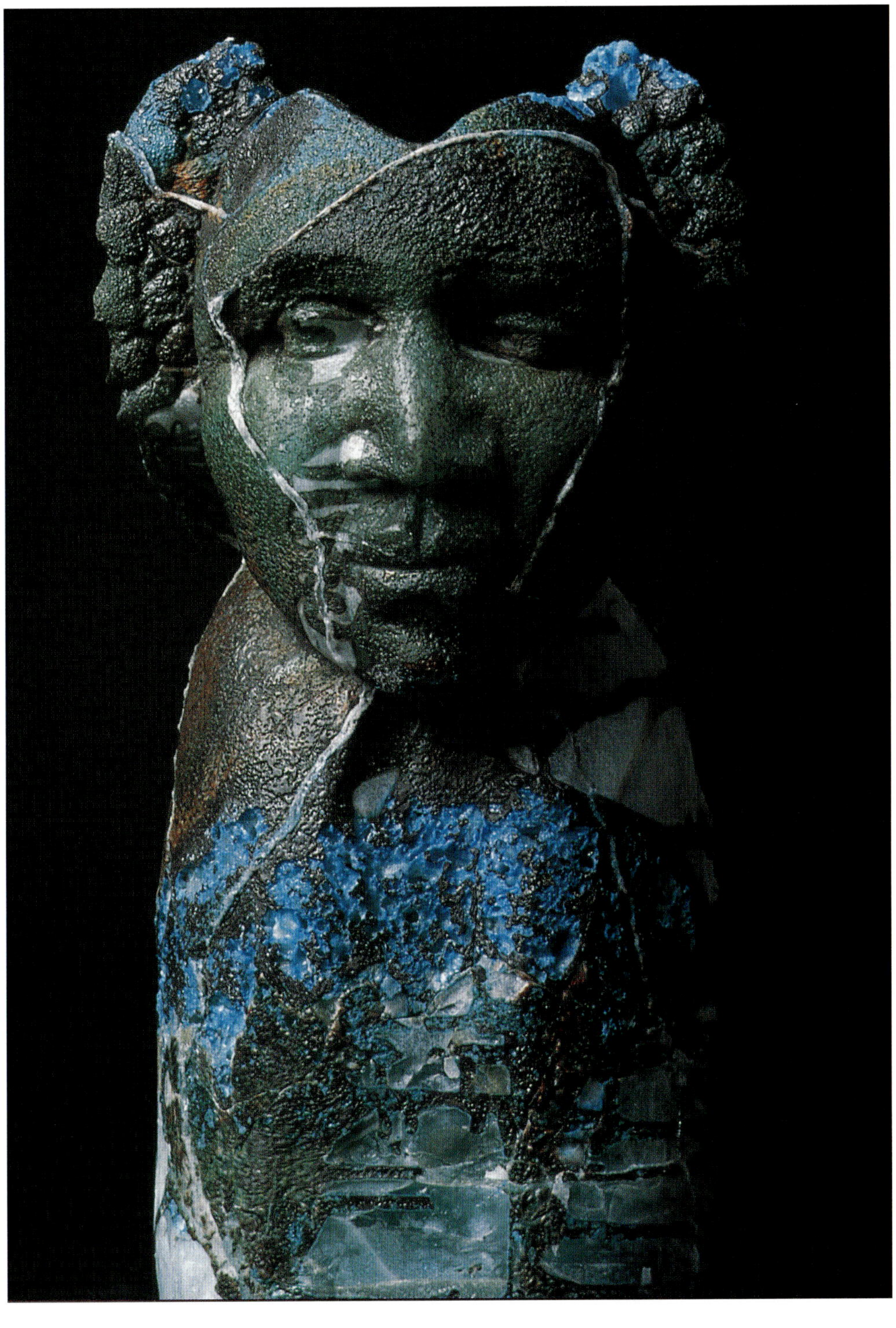

Songs of Experience: II, 1992, 16" x 10" x 8", Kiln Cast Glass. *Photograph courtesy of the artist.*

140   The Eighties - The Artist

Tree Mother, 1997, 14" x 8" x 8", Kiln Cast Glass.
Photograph courtesy of the artist.

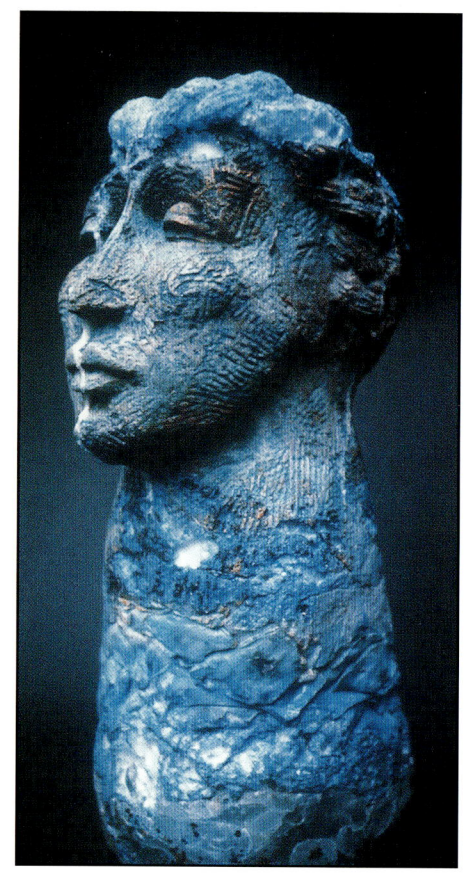

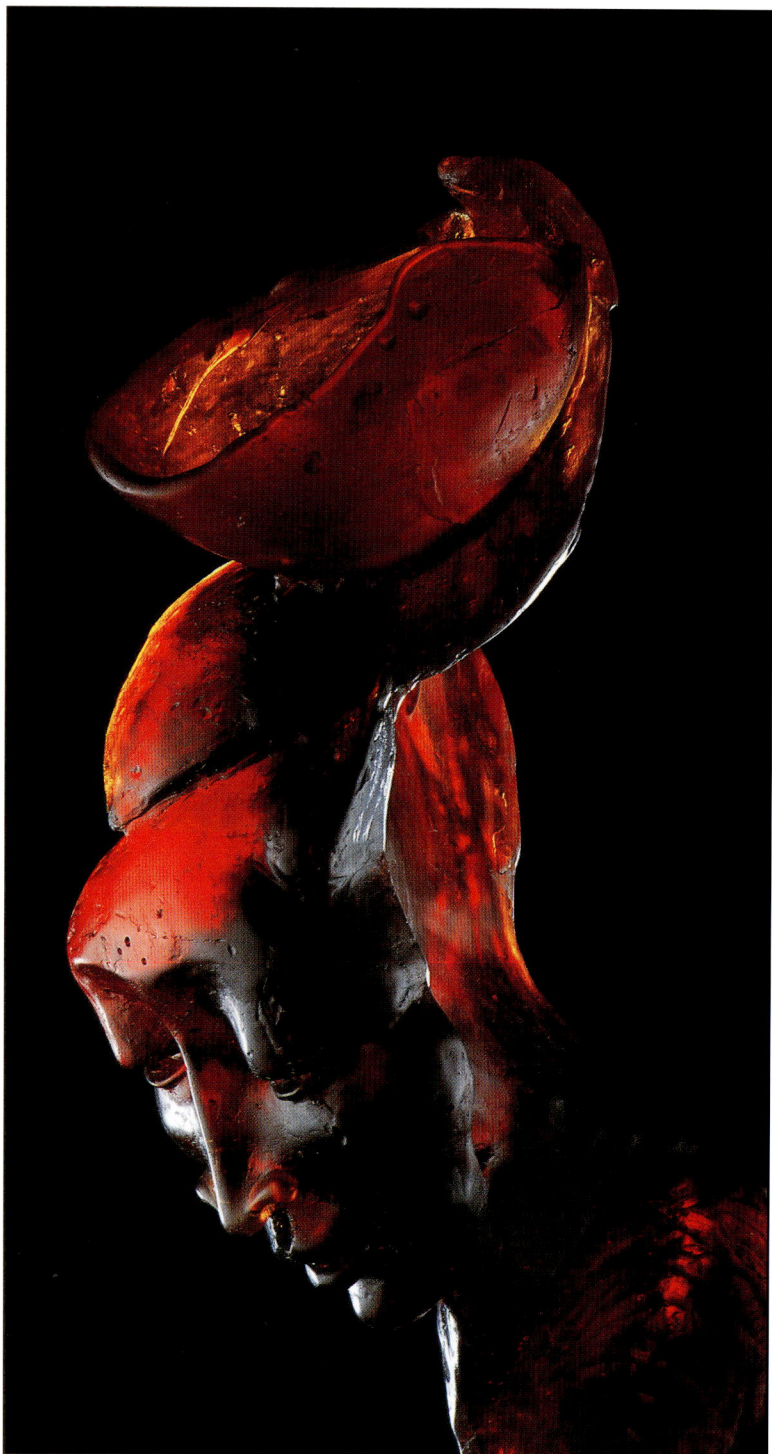

Botanic Series: Orchid (detail), 2002, 24" x 10" x 12", Kiln Cast Glass. Photo: Peter Tang. Photograph courtesy of the artist.

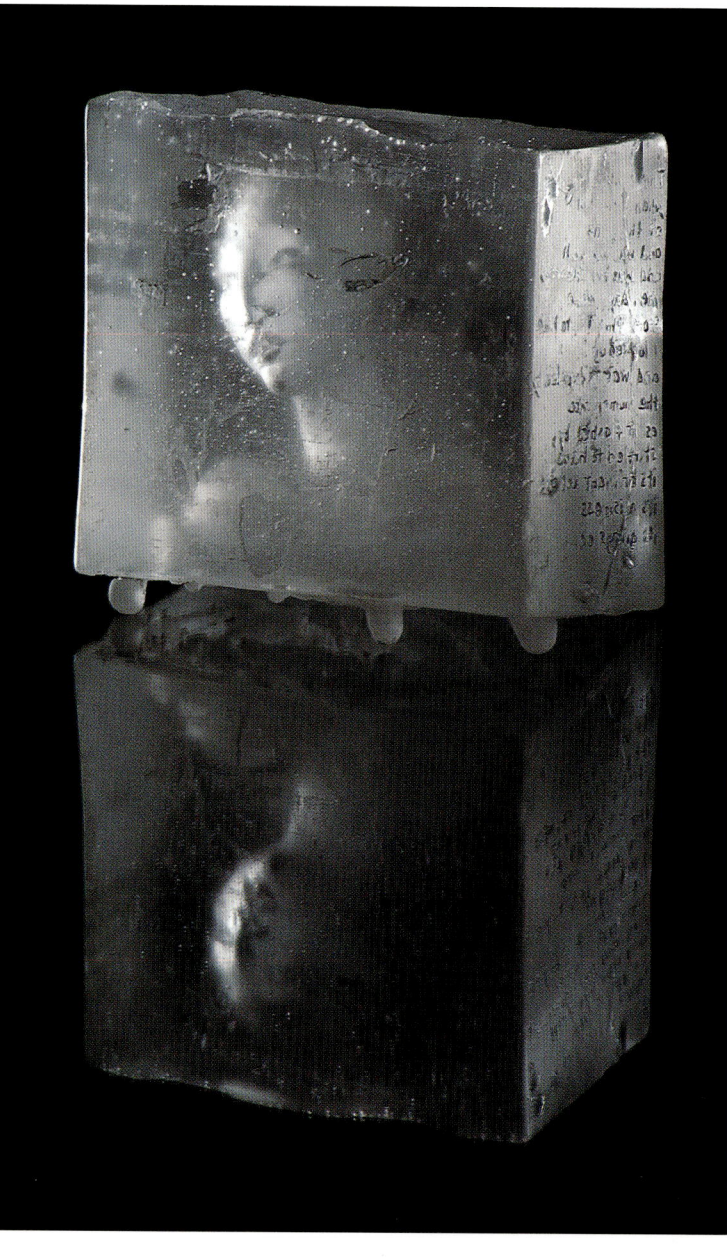

Gone Within: I, 2002, 6" x 4" x 3", Kiln Cast Glass.
Photo: Peter Tang. Photograph courtesy of the artist.

Robin Grebe

My work is made from kiln cast glass. It incorporates elements of slumped plate glass, enameled images, and the occasional carved wood or brazed metal element. The pieces are figurative, with influences from folk art, Islamic, and Indian miniature paintings. While not self-portraits, the pieces are autobiographical.

The figurative element, which is the main form of the sculpture, acts as the setting or canvas for which the images exist. The images become metaphors for psychological and/or physiological states of being. It is these "states of being" that tell autobiographical tales of my life. They tell of changes, of artist's struggles and conflicts, of parenthood and growth processes, and the acknowledgement of decomposition and death. They help me understand my relationship to the world.

It is important to me to use autobiography as a format in my work because it aids in self-knowledge. However, it is equally important to examine common or archetypal conditions that help link ourselves to all of humanity.

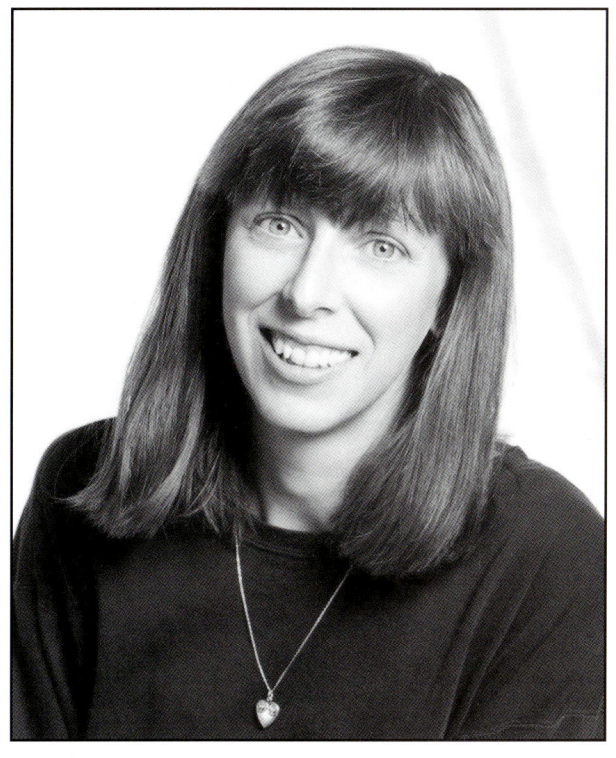

Robin Grebe. *Photograph courtesy of the artist.*

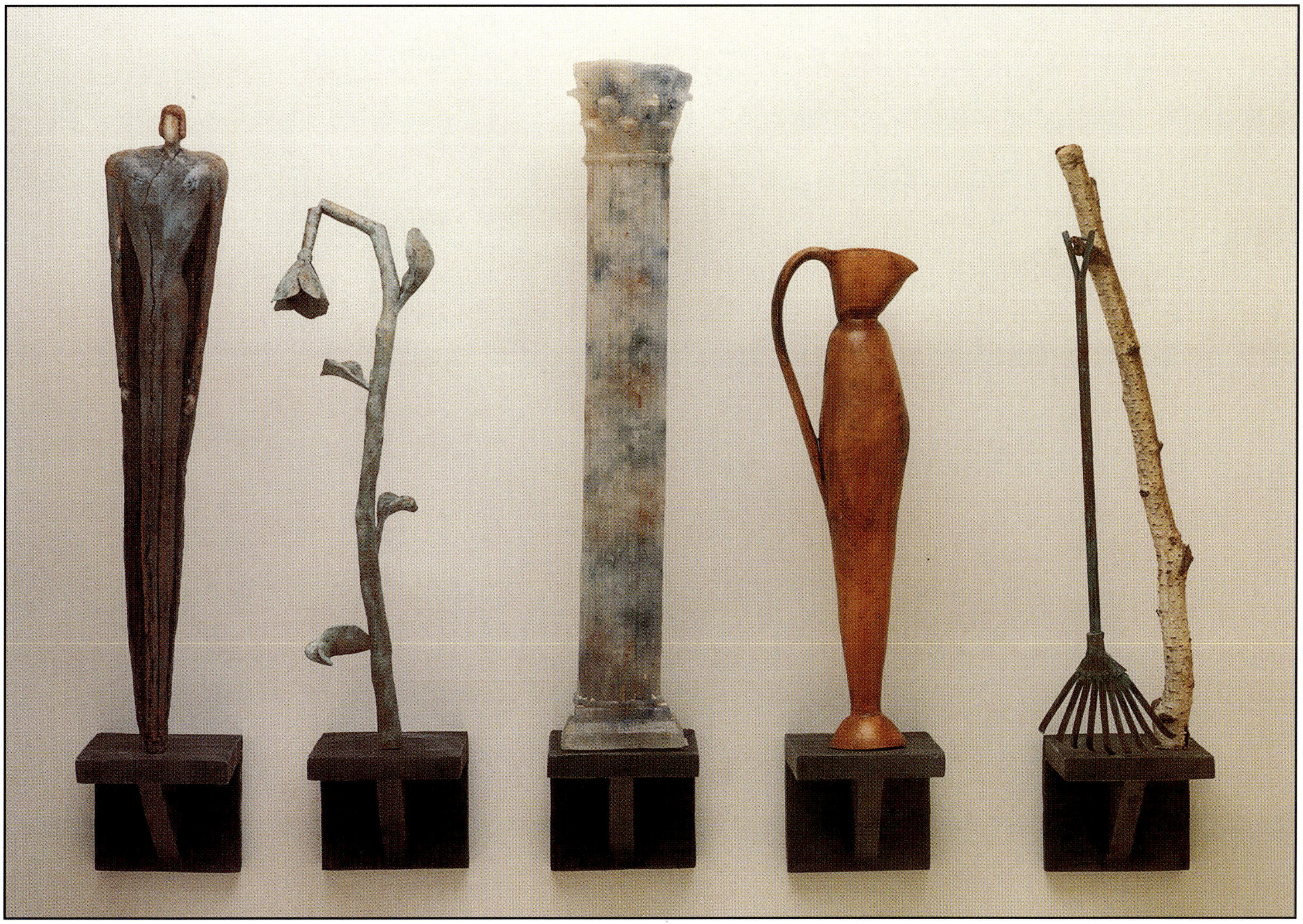

Daily Rhythms, 1988, 38" x 27" x 7", glass, wood, ceramic, copper, birch. *Photograph courtesy of the artist.*

142   The Eighties - The Artist

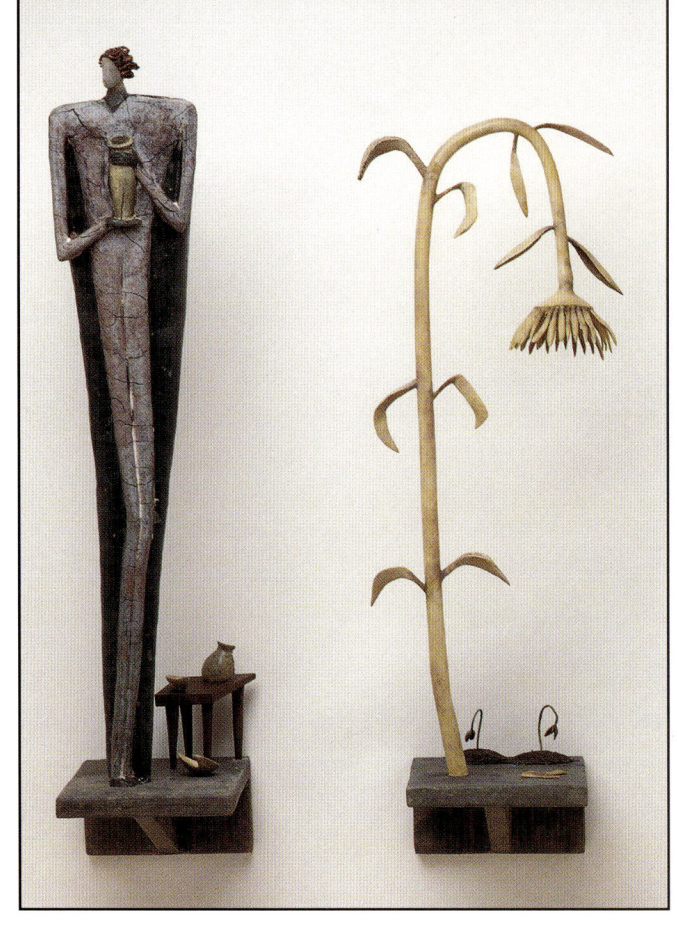

Necessity of Loss, 1989, 34" x 22" x 9", glass, wood, ceramic. *Photograph courtesy of the artist.*

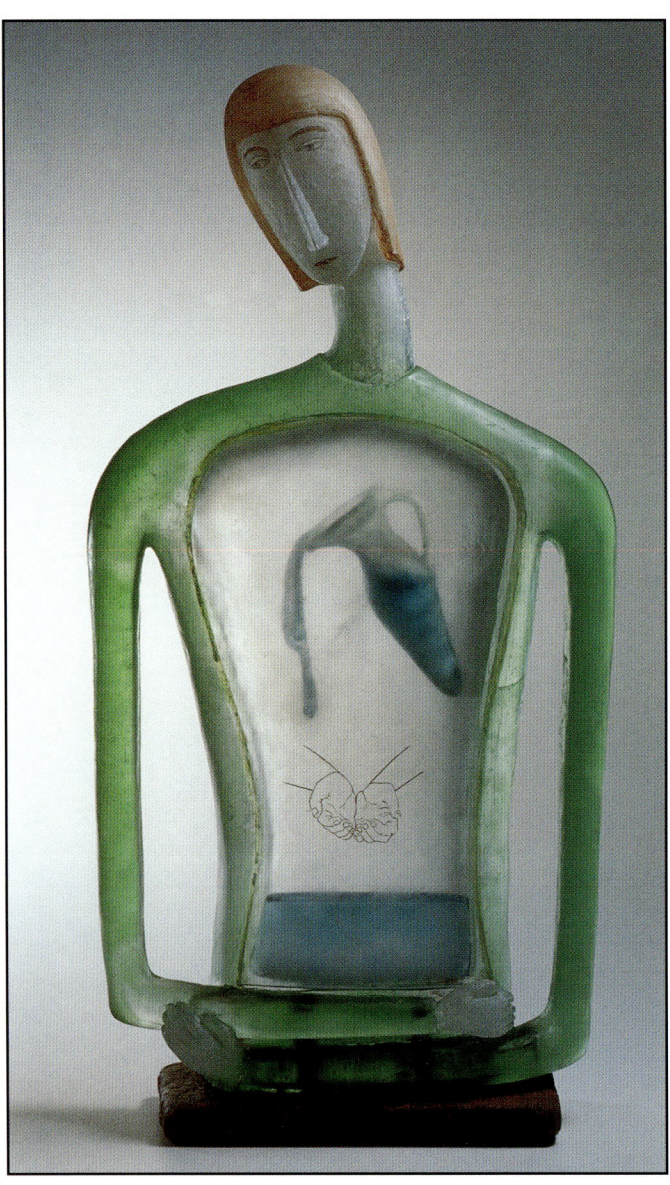

Ablution, 2000, 36" x 18" x 6", cast and slumped glass, copper paint, stone base. *Photograph courtesy of the artist.*

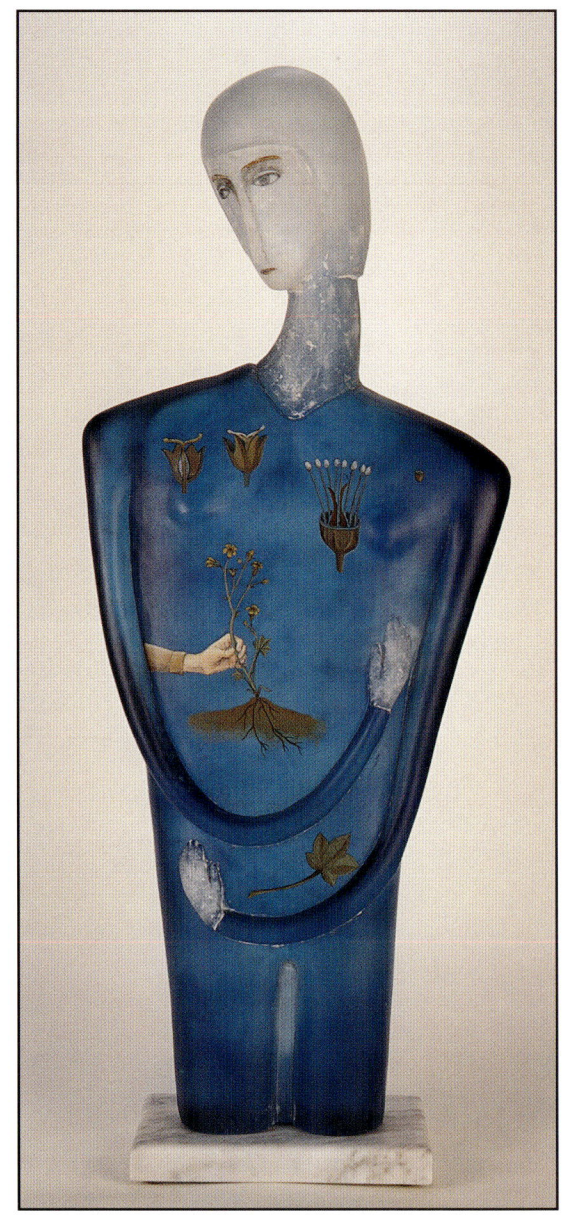

Random Moment, 2002, 32" x 13" x 6", cast glass, paint, marble base. *Photograph courtesy of the artist.*

Shari Hopper

I have been totally involved with glass since 1969. It is a material that opens up so many artistic possibilities. Being a part of the Glass Movement, and Glass Bead-making Movement has given me the opportunity to travel, which gives inspiration to my bead-making.

My beads are lamp blown using borosilicate and neon tubing. The clear glass becomes a blank canvas to explore the decorative techniques I enjoy: painting with enamels and lusters, engraving, sandblasting, acid etching, mirroring, applying decals, and filling my beads with objects and textures to express a theme.

I use an innovative new technique involving taking photographs and making them into my own photographic decals which I fire onto my glass beads. This allows me to put a lot of content into my work. I like the additional challenge in designing my beads into one-of-a-kind pieces of wearable art.

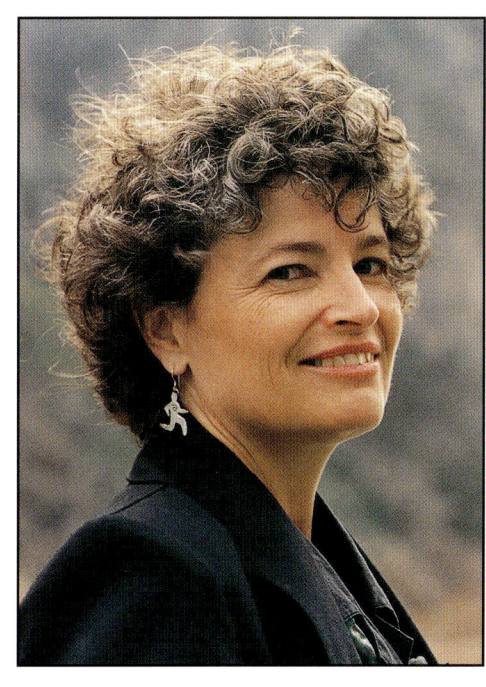

Shari Hopper. *Photograph courtesy of the artist.*

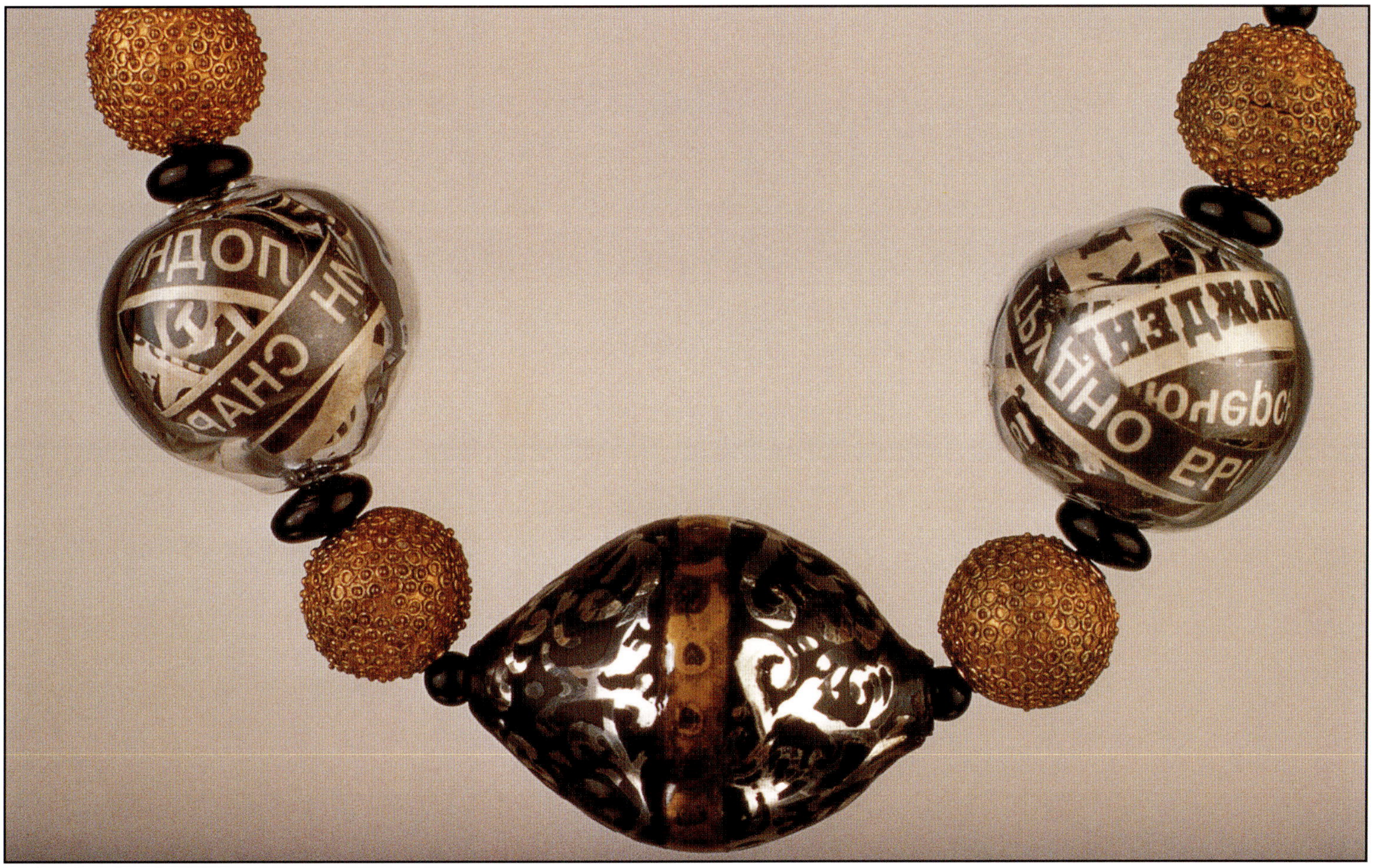

Russian Fantasy, 1996, Lamp blown soft glass, 2 filled with Russian paper text, center bead inspired by Fabergè eggs, gold luster, black enamel with mirroring inside. *Photograph courtesy of the artist.*

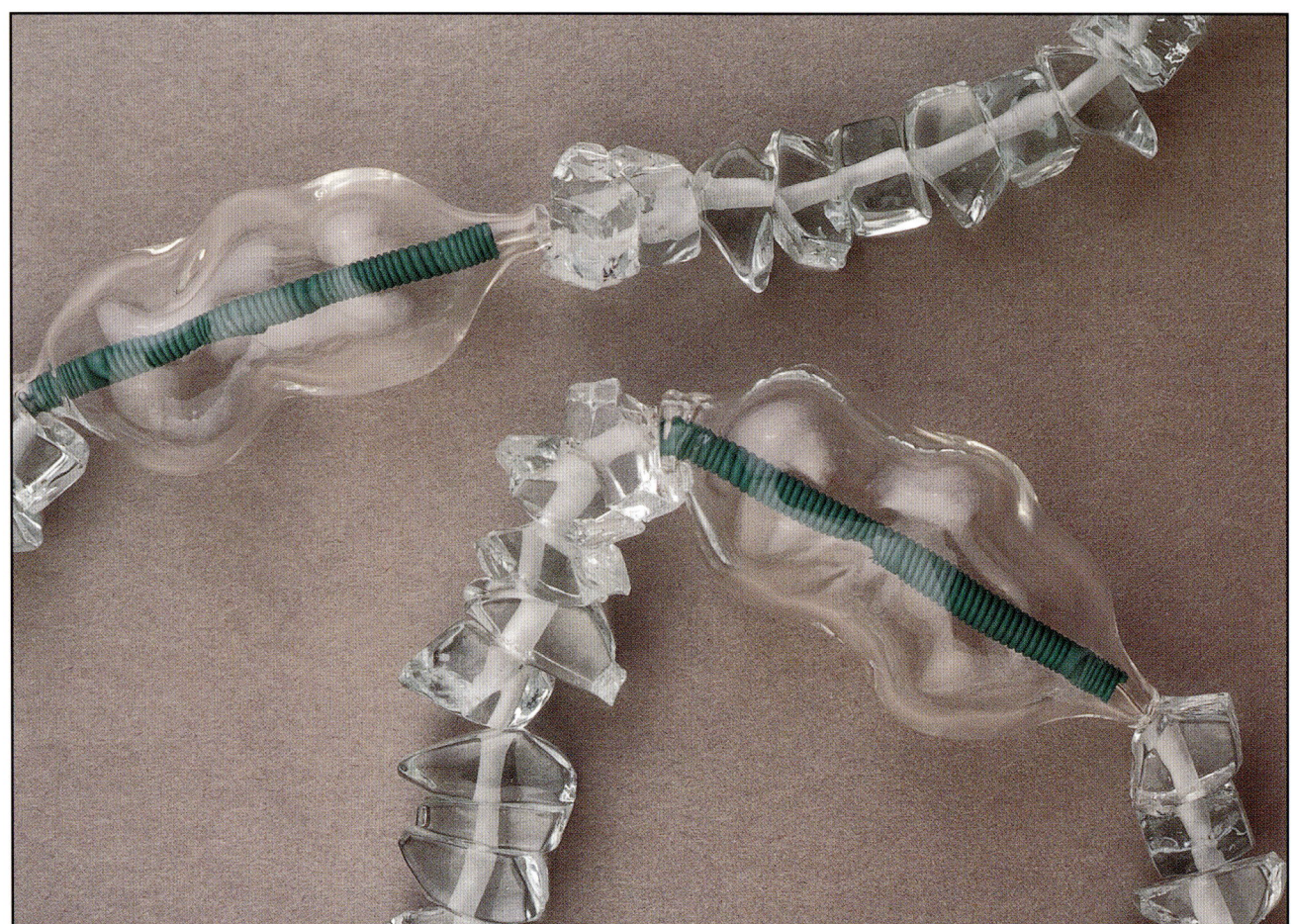

Safety First, 1998, Lamp blown borosilicate amorphous beads with shower door safety glass broken and drilled. *Photograph courtesy of the artist.*

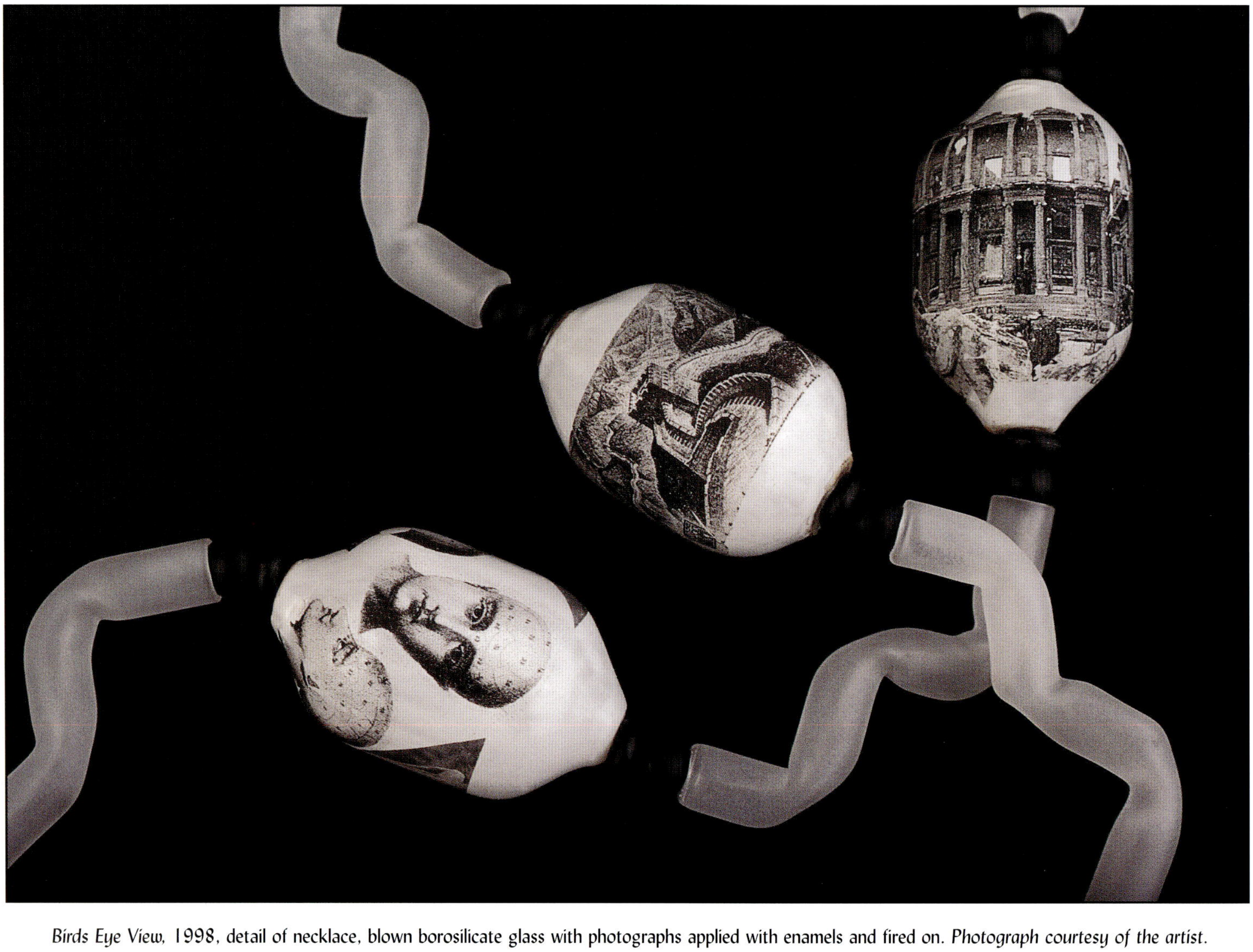

Birds Eye View, 1998, detail of necklace, blown borosilicate glass with photographs applied with enamels and fired on. *Photograph courtesy of the artist.*

Dinah Hulet

Today there is a quiet renaissance taking place – a resurgence of interest in the ancient and intriguing technique of figurative murrine or mosaic glass. As one of only a small group of contemporary glass artists involved in the creation of these highly complex miniatures, I draw my inspiration from the mosaic glass of the ancient Alexandrian glassworkers of the first century BC/first century AD, as well as from the incredible miniature murrine portraiture of the nineteenth century Venetian glass artist Giacomo Franchini. The constant element that exists in all of my work is the concept of an image that is made up of, and contained within, the glass itself.

With this mosaic glass technique I seek to create portraits in glass which capture the emotion, life, and mystery that is seen in the faces of the people around me. Everyone is intimately familiar with the human face – the entire world is reflected in the eyes of man. Looking into the face of another person, being drawn in by their eyes and then establishing a narrative with them – that is what motivates my work with glass. My goal is to challenge the viewers to establish their own relationship with the face that I present to them – to develop their own personal narrative.

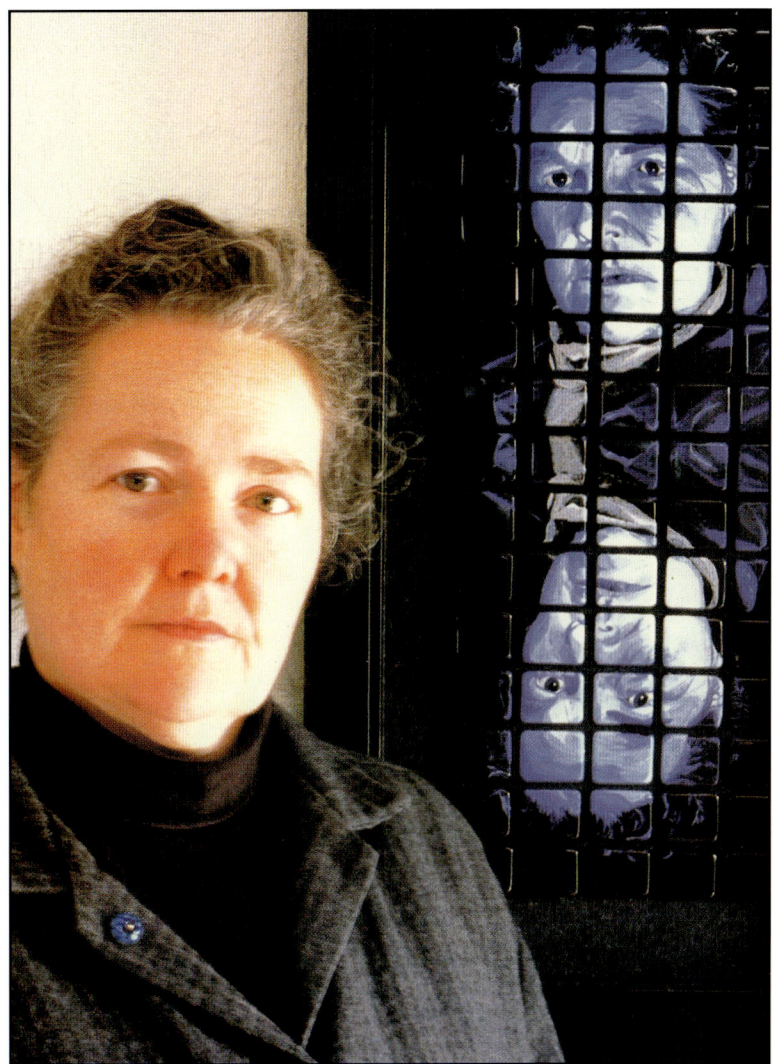

Dinah Hulet. *Photograph courtesy of the artist.*

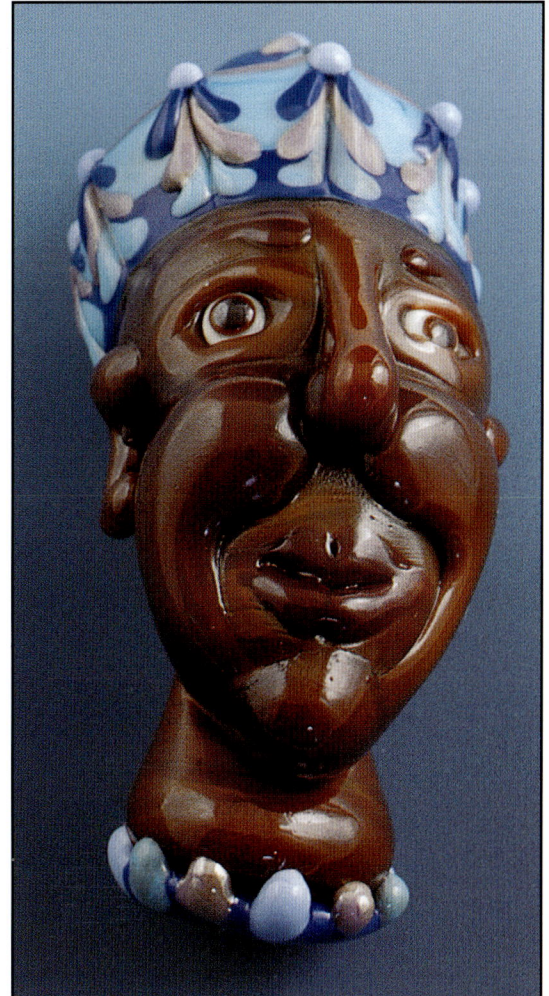

Portrait Bead, 1990, 1.75" x 1", Lamp-worked glass, Photo: Patty Hulet. *Photograph courtesy of the artist.*

146　The Eighties - The Artist

Just Clownin' Around, 1990, 5" x 5", Lampworked glass. Photo: Patty Hulet. *Photograph courtesy of the artist.*

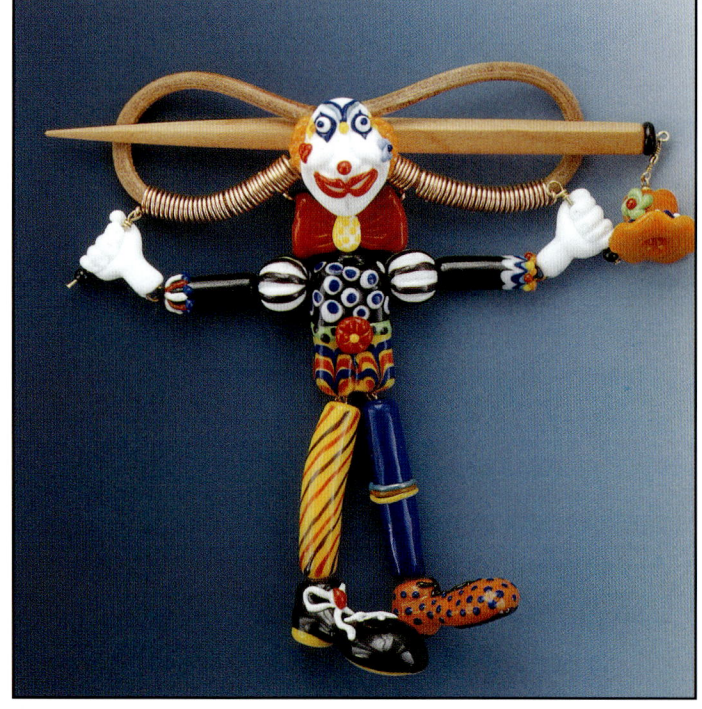

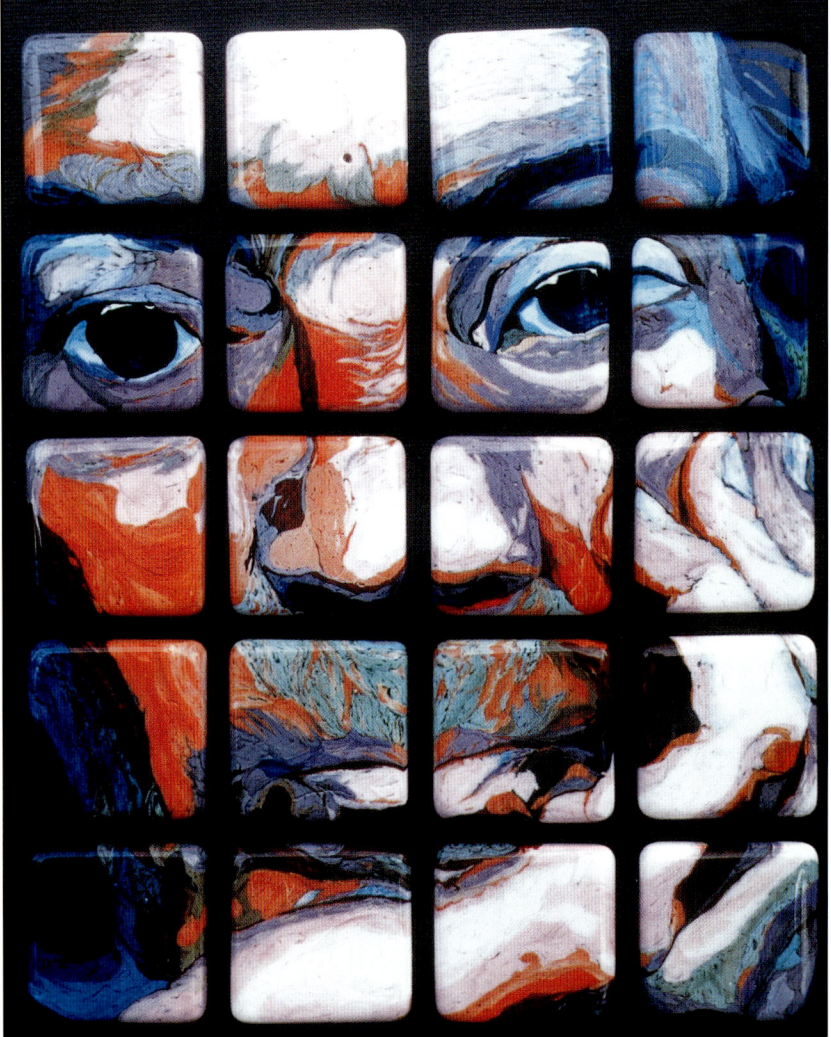

Jim's Wife, 1998, 40.5 cm x 35.3 cm x 3.8 cm. Photo: Patty Hulet. *Photograph courtesy of the artist.*

...a man called George, 1998, 12" x 17" x 1.5". Photo: Patty Hulet. *Photograph courtesy of the artist.*

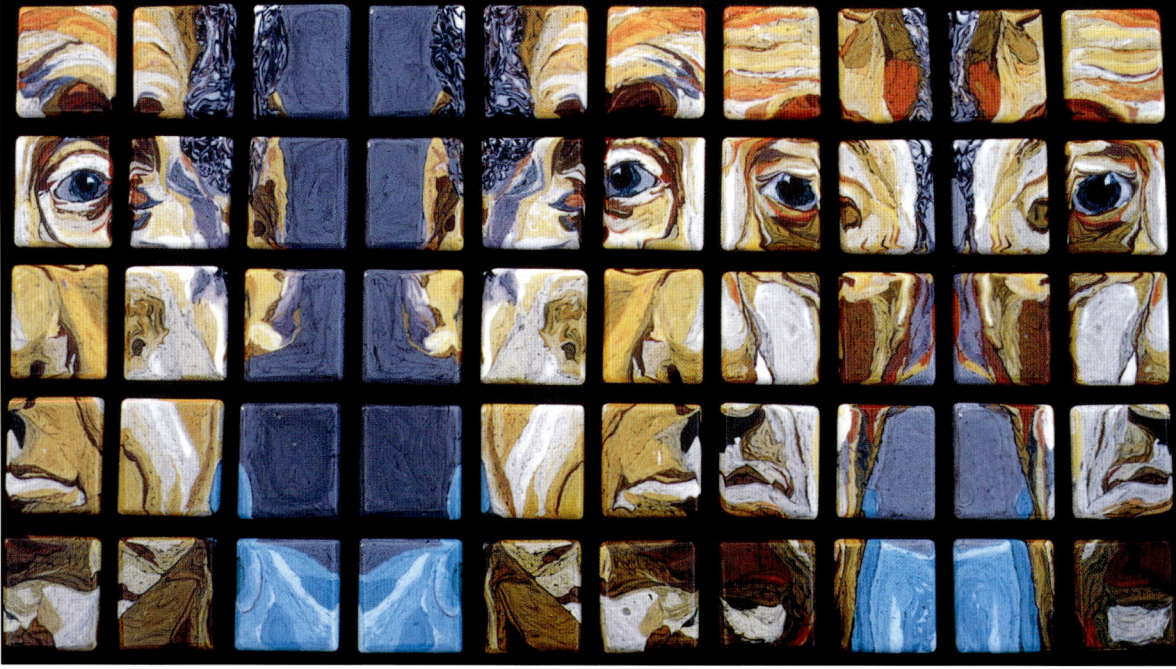

Judy Jensen

Many influences inform my work, but travel has always been prominent. When I'm planning a trip, the planning includes extensive research from many sources, including the film, art, history, and literature of the country of interest. My course is occasionally diverted by this research. For instance, in 1999, I began planning a trip to Nepal which was to take place in 2001. During the early itinerary planning, it was evident that the three most logical connections to Kathmandu were from New Delhi, Hong Kong, or Bangkok. Since I was going that far I thought I may as well have a stopover in one of these three cities. I originally considered New Delhi, as Indian miniatures have long been an interest of mine.

However as I researched Bangkok, I became so interested in Thailand, I eventually went there instead of Nepal, with a five-day stopover in Hong Kong. The painting A Calendar of Good and Evil Days was influenced by drawings from my Nepal research combined with images of objects I later collected in Hong Kong (a silver meat fork) and Thailand (the Burmese puppet head and blue bowl). However, the idea for the calendar came from an exhibit in Greenwich, England, which included a Balinese calendar depicting good and evil days. I liked the ambiguity of the imagery. It was difficult to distinguish the good from evil days, as all had monsters in them.

While in Thailand I was stunned by the astonishing snakes forming the entrance to almost every Buddhist temple. The contrast between the Buddhist view of the snake as the protector of Buddha and the Judeo-Christian view of the snake as the tempter and defiler was striking. I examined the contrast in the painting Caduceus. On the snakes undulating body, I placed images of different serpentine aspects of the caduceus, the ancient symbol of healing; the DNA double helix; a natural science illustration of a crane eating a snake; the Buddhist snake-as-protector; and the snakelike spermatozoa. The snake's tongue and tail are formed by bits of carved wood I found in Thailand.

With Eclipse it was both the seen and unseen aspects of the object and its barrier (the earth, in the lunar eclipse, and the moon in the solar eclipse) that interested me. I wanted to do a painting that combined eros with romance, as in Indian erotic miniatures. The eighteenth century knife on the work, I bought on Portabello Road in London. For years I've been collecting things when I travel, using them mostly as visual references for paintings. But after I'd painted this knife on the bottom glass panel, I decided I wanted the texture of the real object, so I included it.

Somerset Maugham once said "Art, to be reckoned with as a force in civilization, must teach tolerance." I feel it is through travel we recognize our shared humanity.

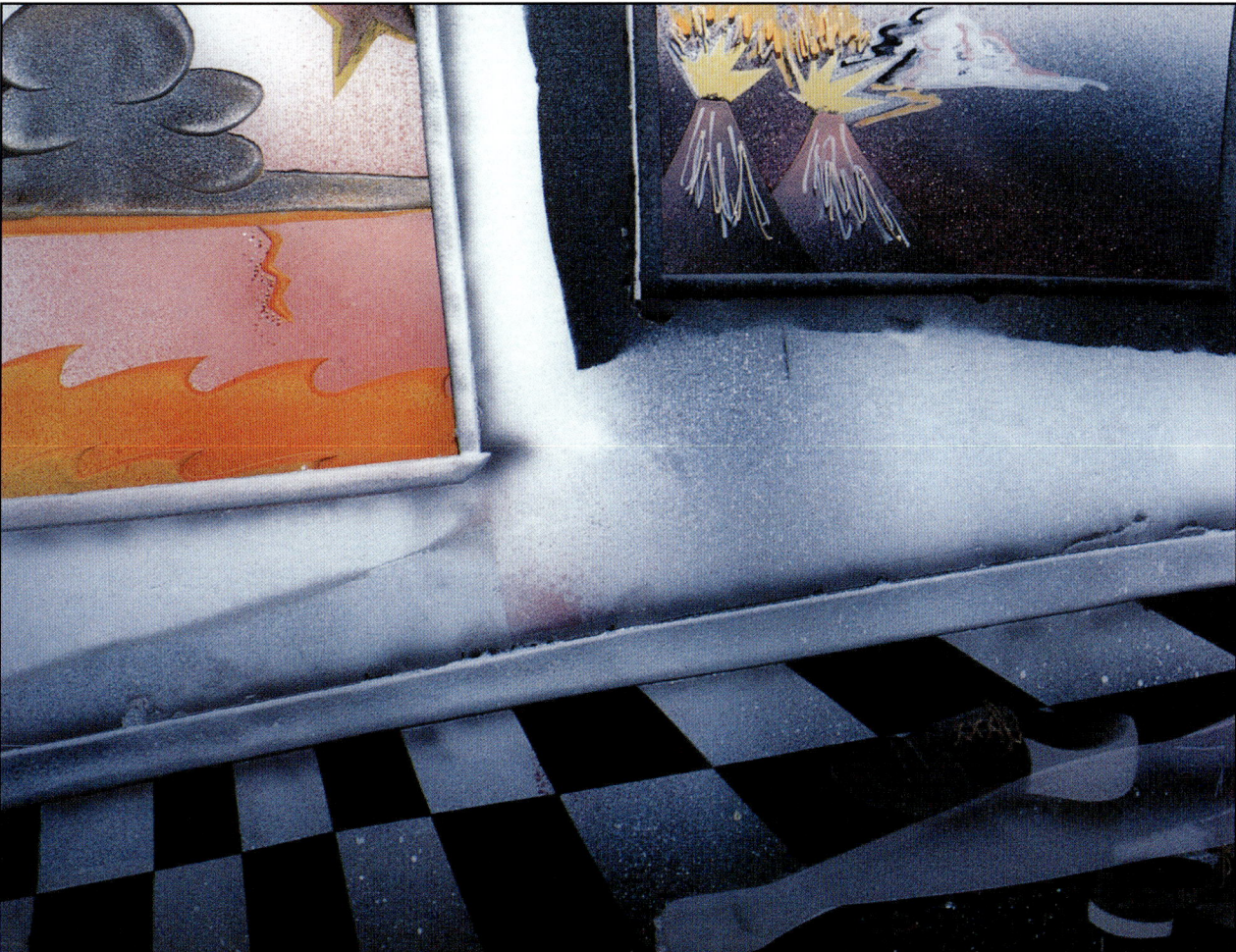

Cryptic Sleep, 1984, 11" x 9", reverse painting on glass. Photograph courtesy of the artist.

148   The Eighties - The Artist

Eclipse, 2001, 40" x 17", reverse painting on glass. Photograph courtesy of the artist.

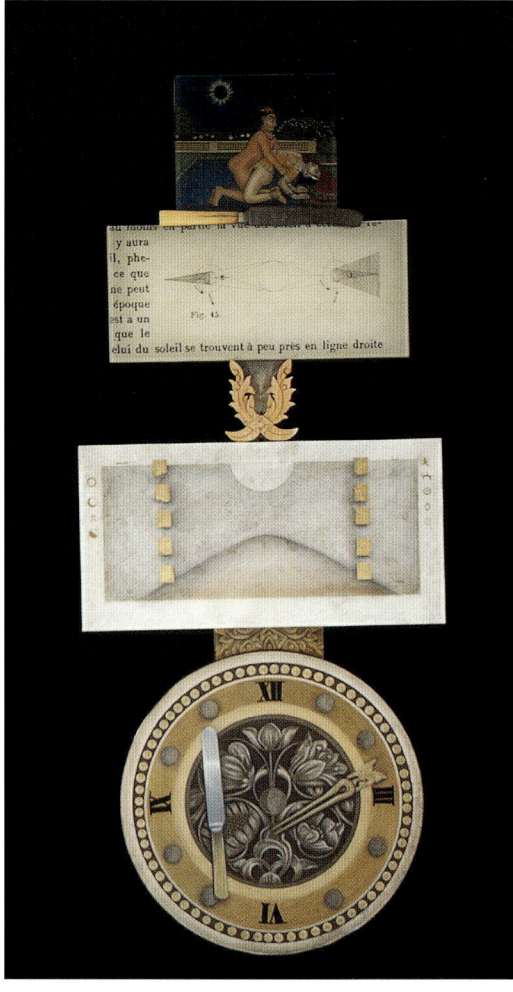

Caduceus, 2001, 18" x 44", reverse painting on glass. Photograph courtesy of the artist.

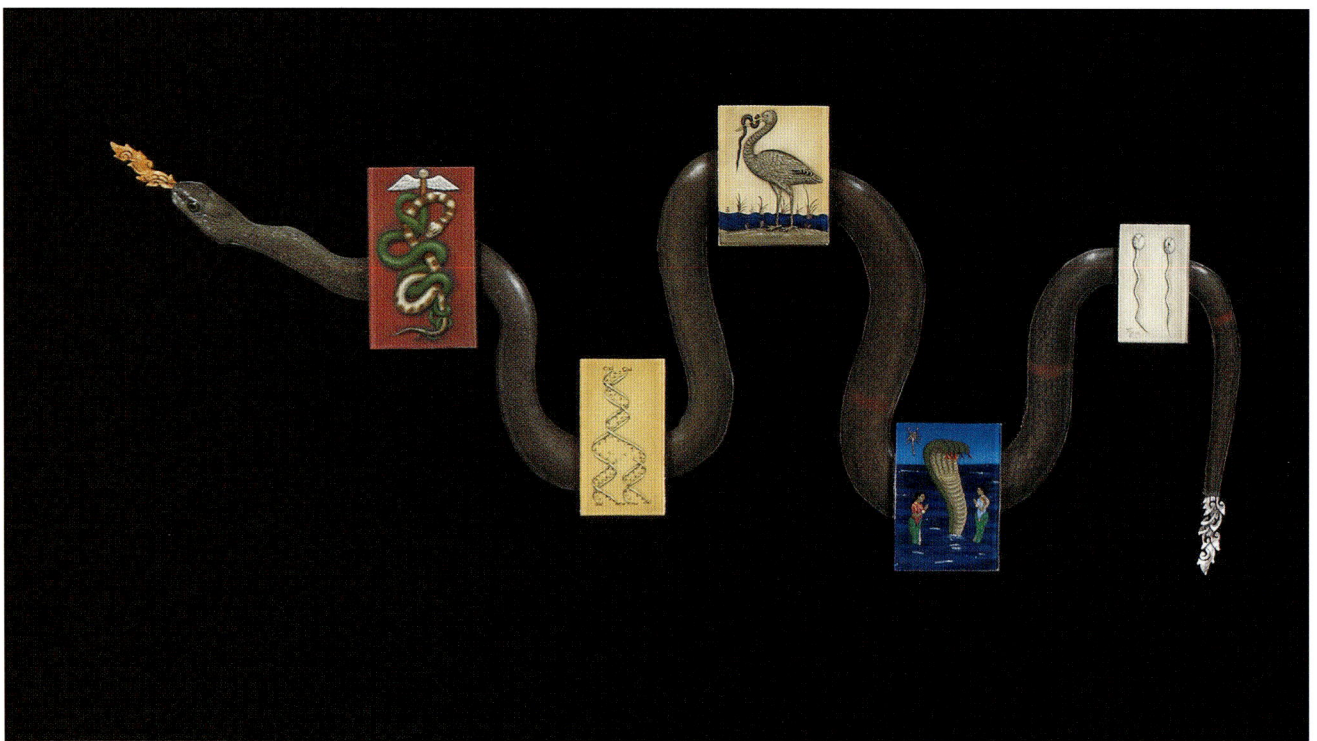

A Calendar of good and evil days, 2001, 14" x 58". Photograph courtesy of the artist.

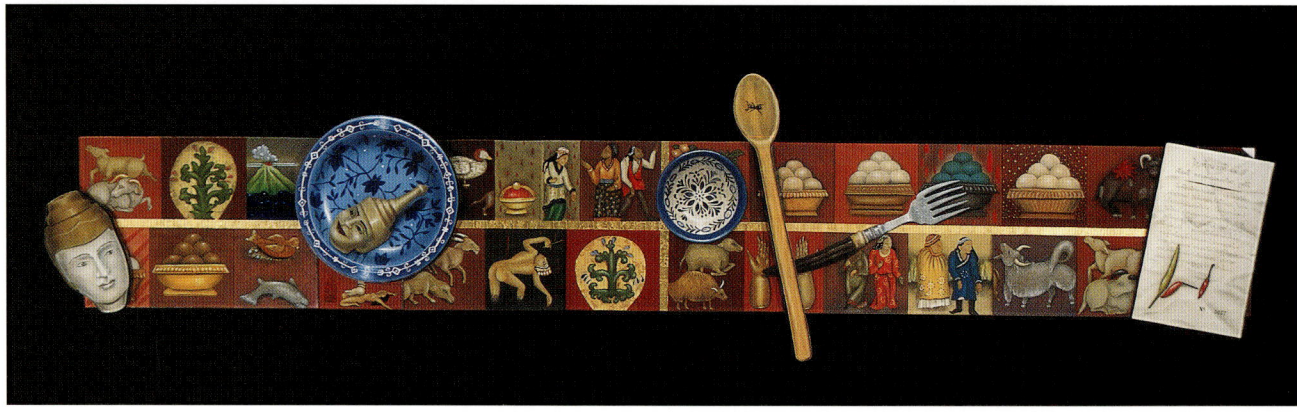

Sabrina Knowles
Jenny Pohlman

Ceremonial Bird Pots

The Ceremonial Bird Pot series originated with two separate forms, adorned pots and the female bird form, both of which we were working on before our first African trip. Affirmation of our pots came with our first encounter with African storage pots made out of clay and earth by the women who used them. They are kitchen utensils and what we enjoyed most was seeing the form, the same form we chose to create without really knowing why.

Our female bird form was derived from a 5000-year-old stone sculpture found in Hungary. We have exaggerated her tapered waist and full form. She represents to us women in the warrior stage of life, women like Nehanda of Zimbabwe who worked to right wrong. And though we were working on this form prior to our African travel, we did not know how to properly display her. In Harare, Zimbabwe's capitol, we came upon an adorned pot topped with a sculpted clay female form. The pot was used for divination by the tribal healers.

Four weeks after our journey we envisioned our bird form on our adorned pots. The Ceremonial Bird Pot series was born. Each of our pots tells a story through the bird, her gesture, color, and adornment.

The inspiration for the adorned head forms originated from head forms for our female birds. We witnessed authentic tribal dancing in Zambia during a journey in 1997. The Masked dancers became spirits from another world as they imparted morals and history and folklore to their audience. We feel these pieces are empowered with energy and spirit before they leave our studio and present themselves to the viewer.

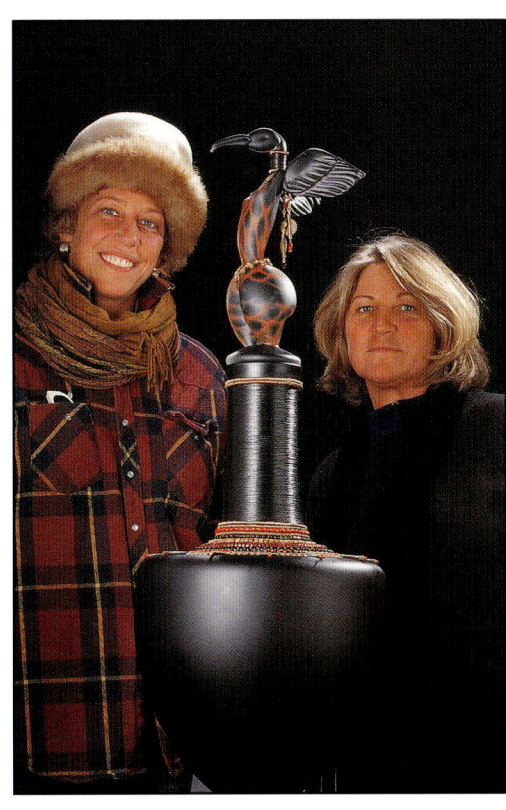

Sabrina Knowles/Jenny Pohlman, photo: Russell Johnson. *Photograph courtesy of the artists.*

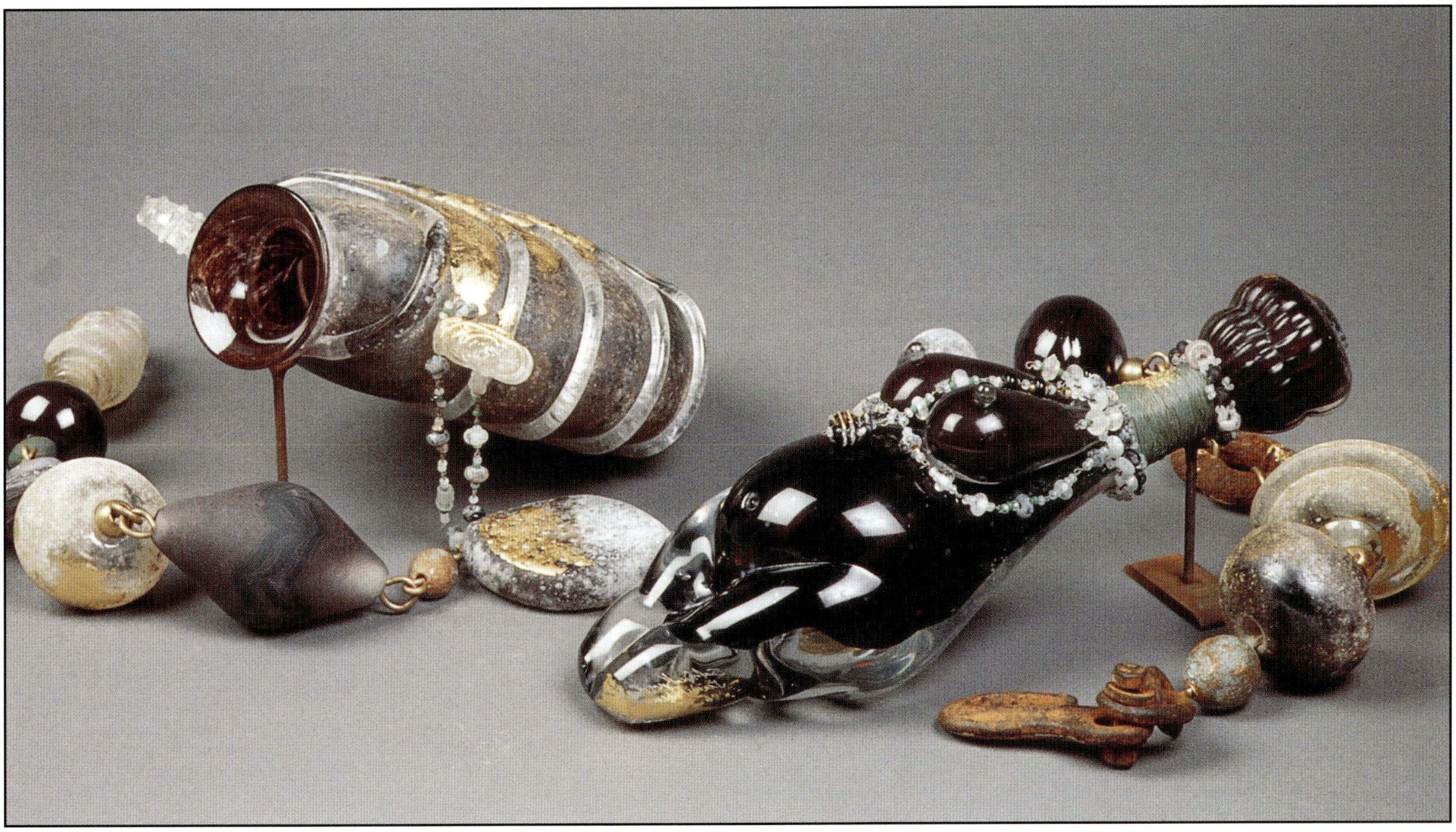

Columbia Street Ruins, 1991, 14" x 36" x 16", hot worked glass figure, beads, blown vessel, photo: Mike Seidl. *Photograph courtesy of the artists.*

150   The Eighties - The Artist

Mweya, 2001, 72" x 17" x 12", Glass, metals, found objects, photo: Russell Johnson. *Photograph courtesy of the artists.*

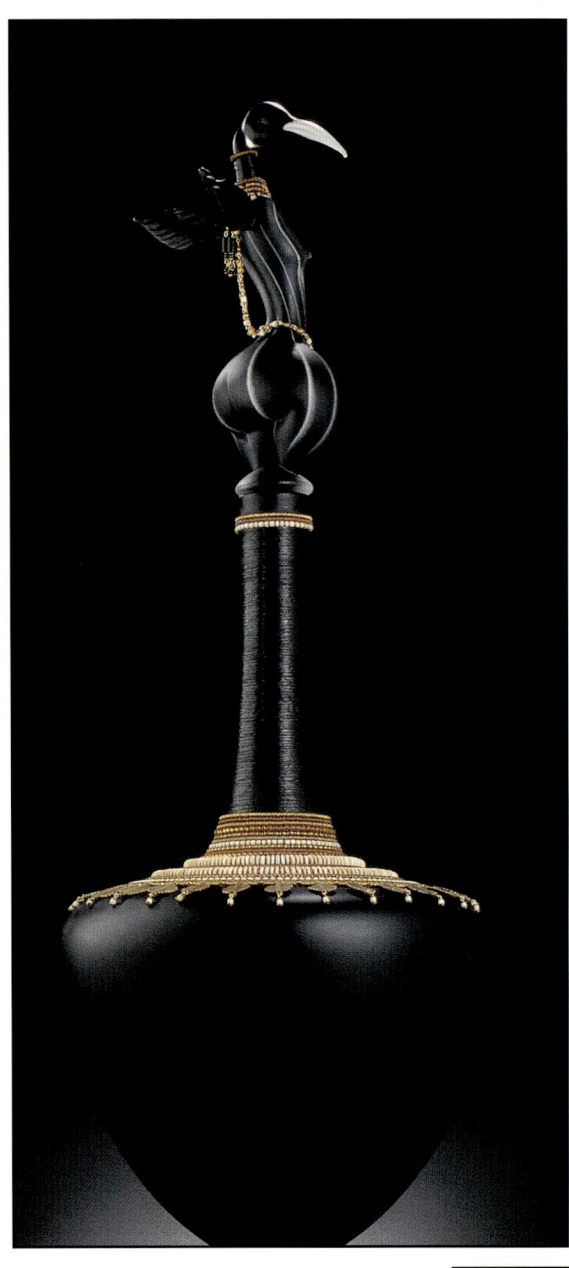

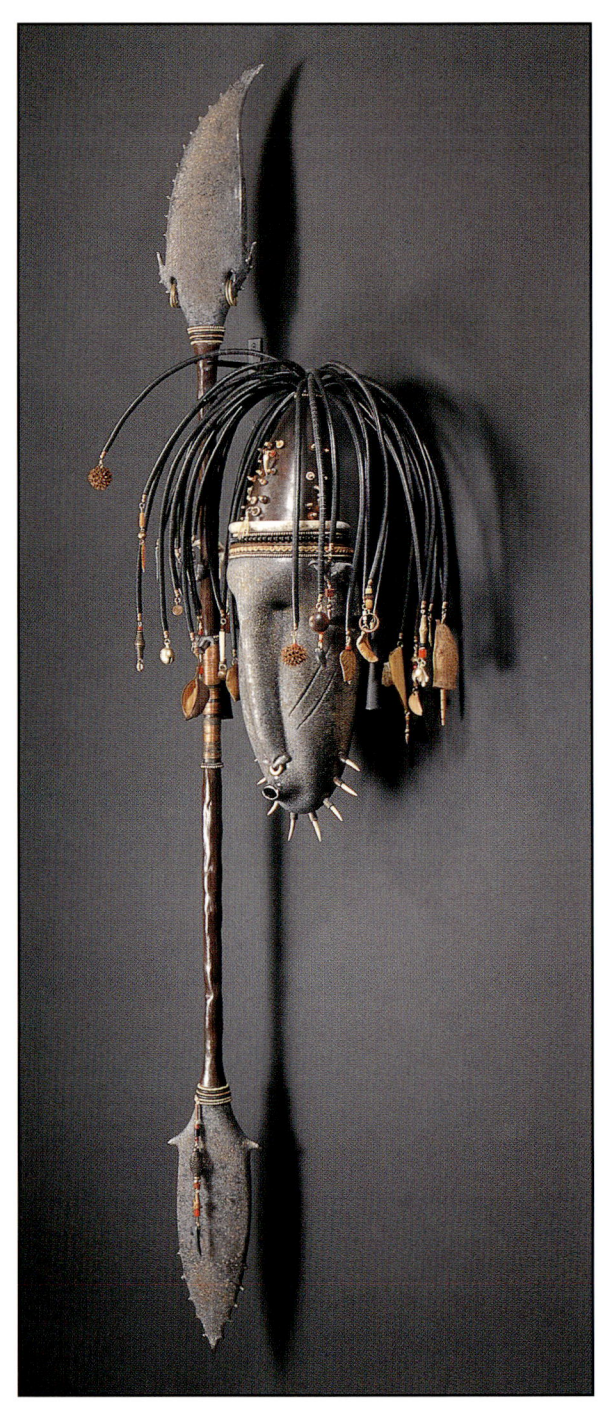

The Enchantress, 2001, 38" x 13" d, glass, glass-beads, photo: Russell Johnson. *Photograph courtesy of the artists.*

Enchantress detail.

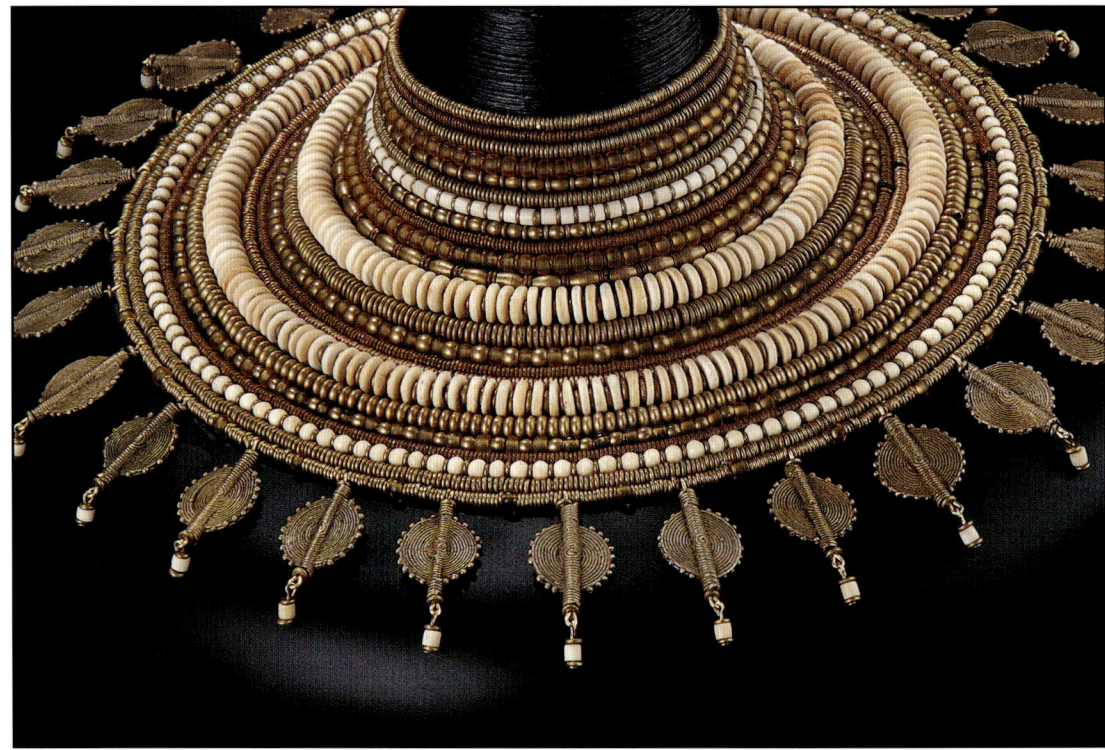

Maria Lugossy

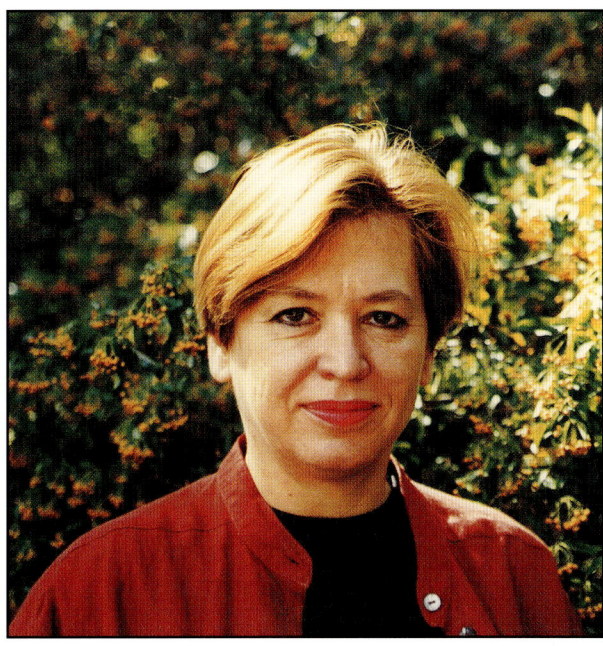

The primordial and inexhaustible energies of Nature form the materials that determine the created world since the beginning of Time. The stones, the minerals, the crystals, and the like are the faithful guardians of that primeval state from which the traces of various happenings may be followed up. This kind of contemplation fills me with awe, even piety; but beyond this, it is important that the currents of my own inner sentiments continue to form materials, continue where Nature left off if you will, recognizing the peculiarities of outer formative forces.

Let therefore the materials form, in this case glass already resulting from human knowledge, as though they were created by water, ice, or even various erosions.

My inner intention is the parallel identification of my collaborative efforts with Nature: for this constitutes my credo in the existence of creation.

Maria Lugossy. *Photograph courtesy of the artists.*

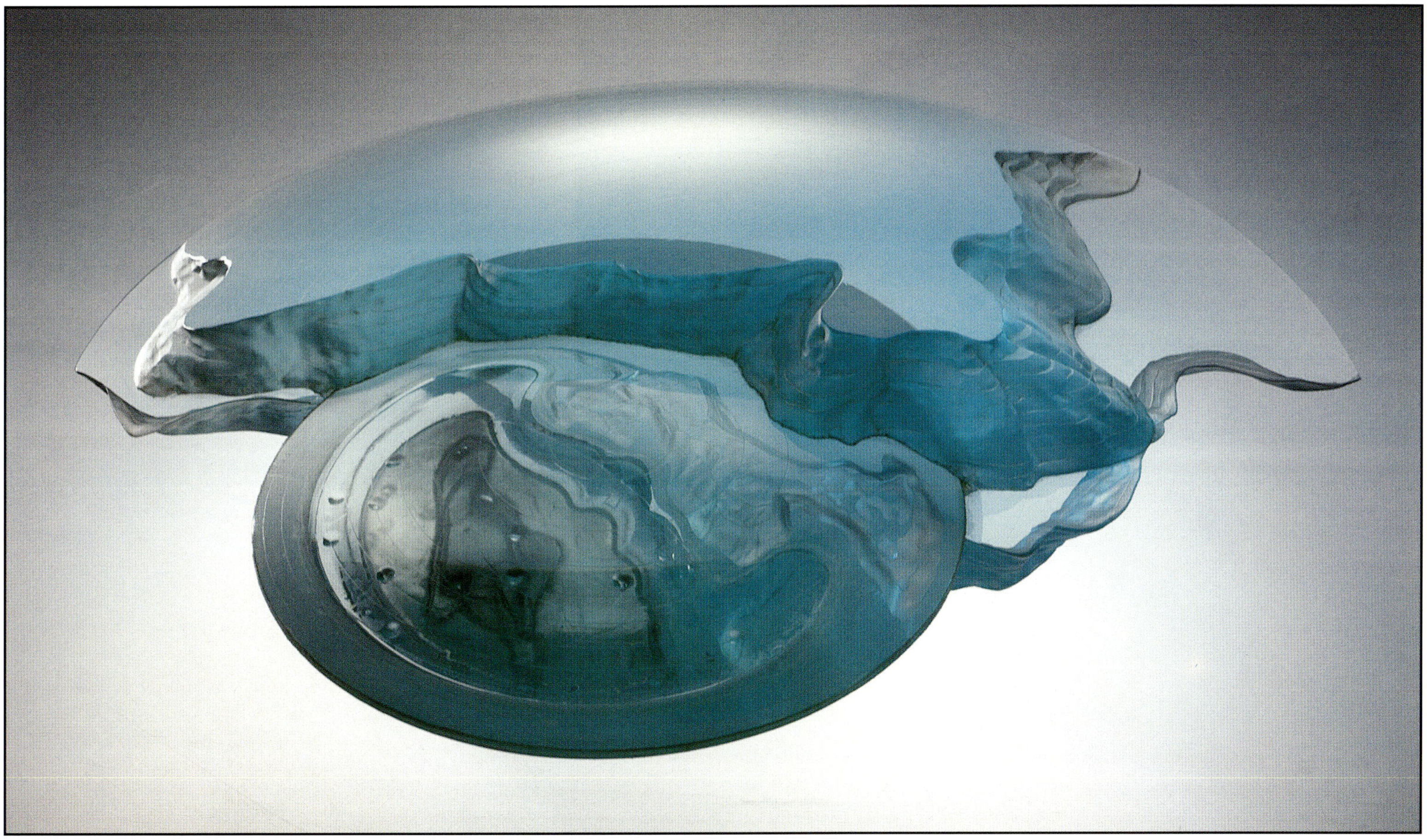

Kozmogenesis, 1986, 14 cm x 68 cm x 60 cm, Laminated, glued, sandblasted, polished, mercury (quick silver) included. *Photograph courtesy of the artist.*

Primary Rock, 1988, 18 cm x 52 cm x 36 cm, Laminated, glued, sandblasted, polished, (smaller lenses included). *Photograph courtesy of the artist.*

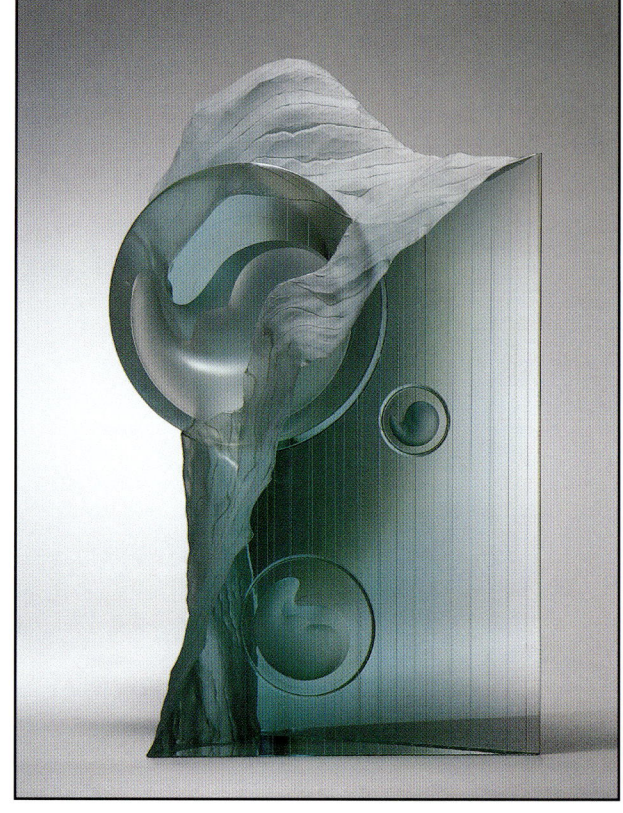

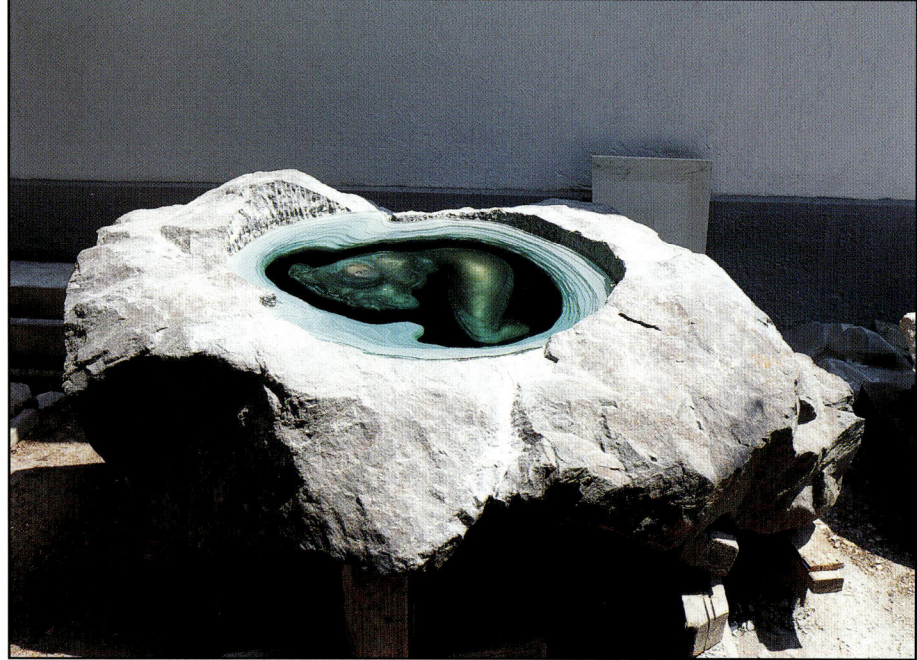

Rhea, 1996-2000, 230 cm x 130 cm x 100 cm, Life-size cast bronze female torso included in laminated glass block placed into granite block. *Photograph courtesy of the artist.*

Genesis, 1998, Laminated, glued, sandblasted, polished (smaller lenses included). *Photograph courtesy of the artist.*

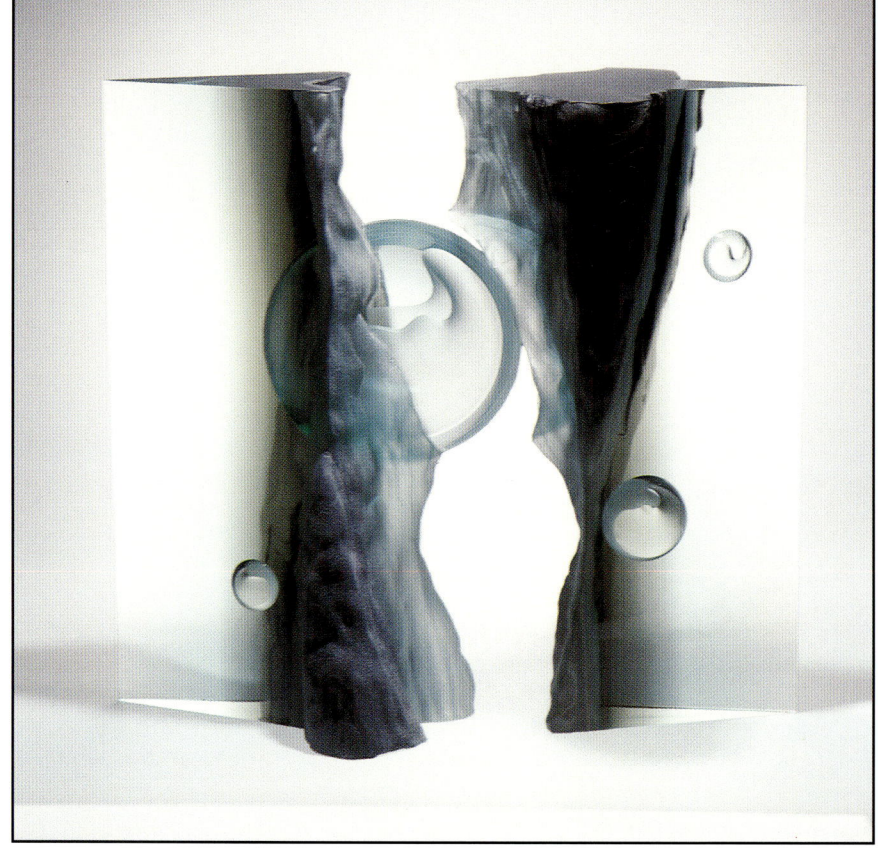

Linda MacNeil

Glass as a material has unique qualities which attract me. I respect its raw beauty. The many types of glass I use, from vitrolite (an industrial opaque plate glass which was made in a wonderful range of colors) to transparent lead crystal glasses, allow me to explore its changing characteristics. It can be highly polished and reflective, or softly translucent and glowing. My forms may be hard edged and mechanical, or abstract and organic. Recently I have been experimenting with pate de verre glass, mixing powdered glass colors with clear crushed glass, melting these mixes in refractory molds. The resulting pieces have hundreds of small bubbles, which bring light to the interior of the piece. The endless possibilities with glass continue to attract me.

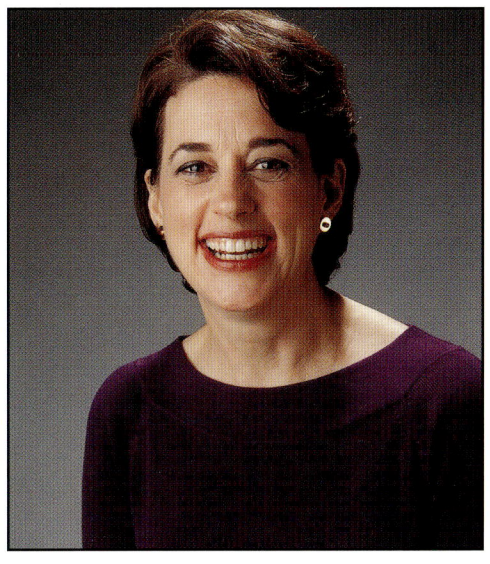

Linda MacNeil, photo: John Carlano. *Photograph courtesy of the artist.*

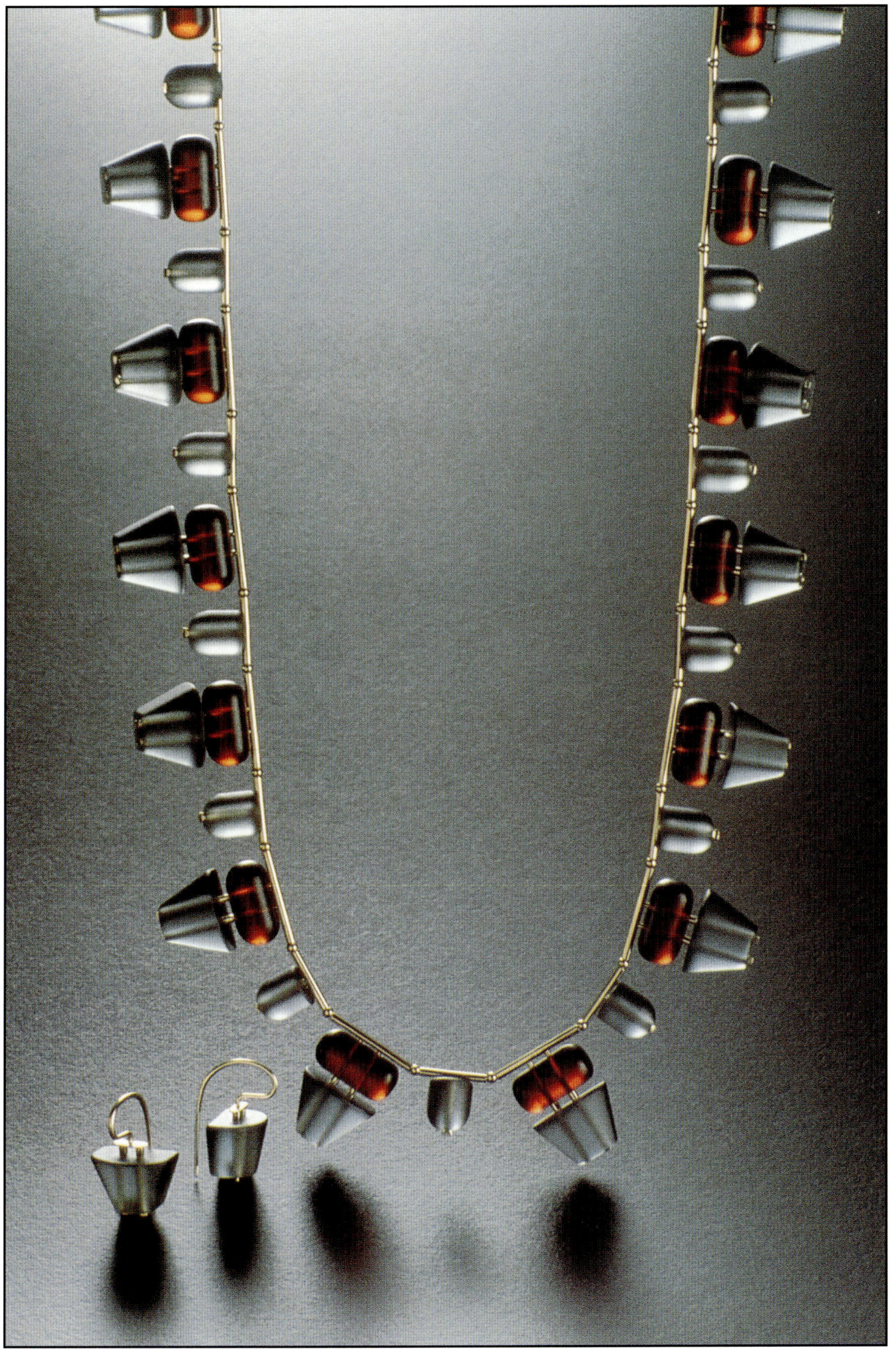

Lucent Lines Series, 1983, 9" d, Acid polished smoky grey and brown transparent glass, 14k gold tubing, with earrings, photo: Susie Cushner. *Photograph courtesy of the artist.*

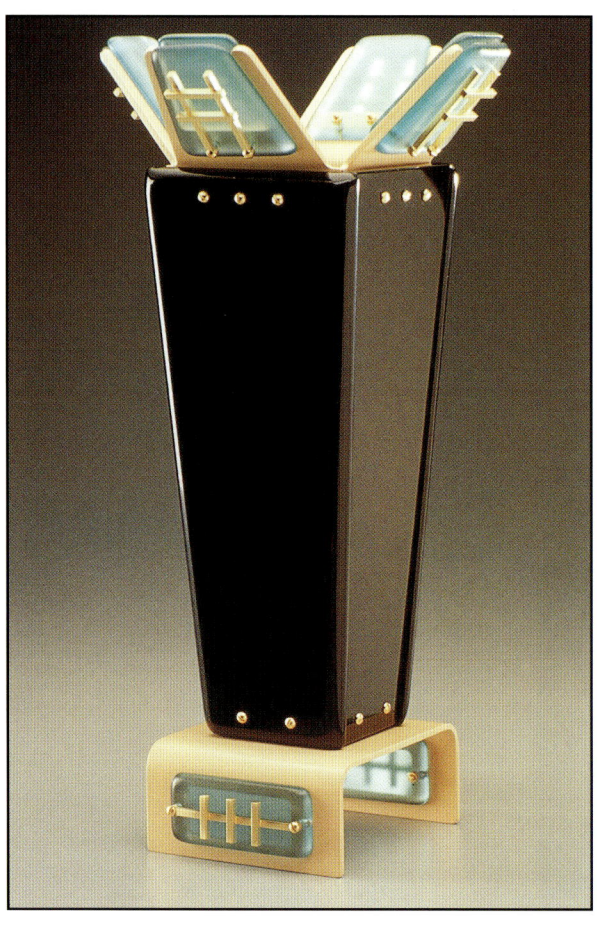
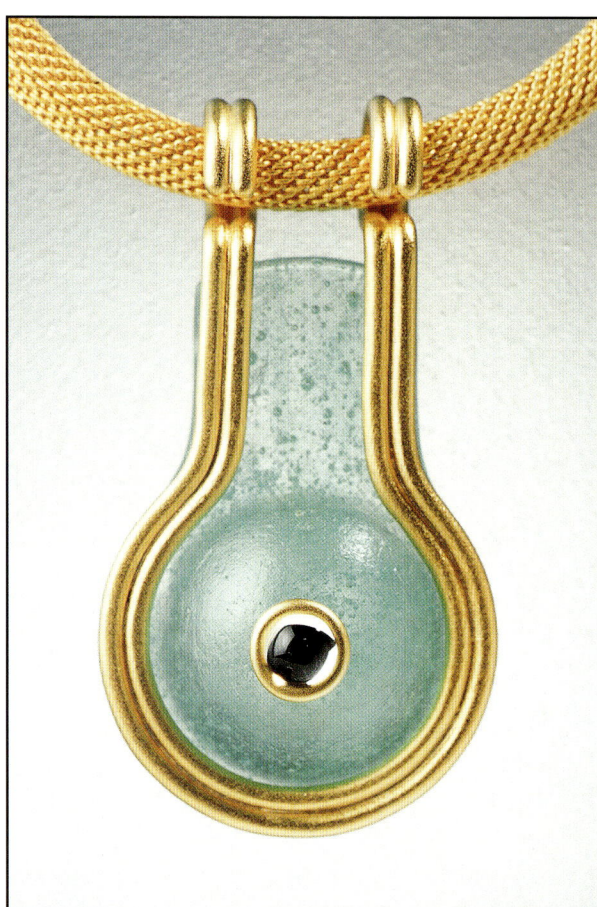

Plate Glass Vase, 1984, 15" x 6" x 6", Gold plated brass. *Photograph courtesy of the artist.*

Mesh Necklace, 1994-98, cast glass patè de verre, mirror detail, 24k gold plated brass. *Photograph courtesy of the artist.*

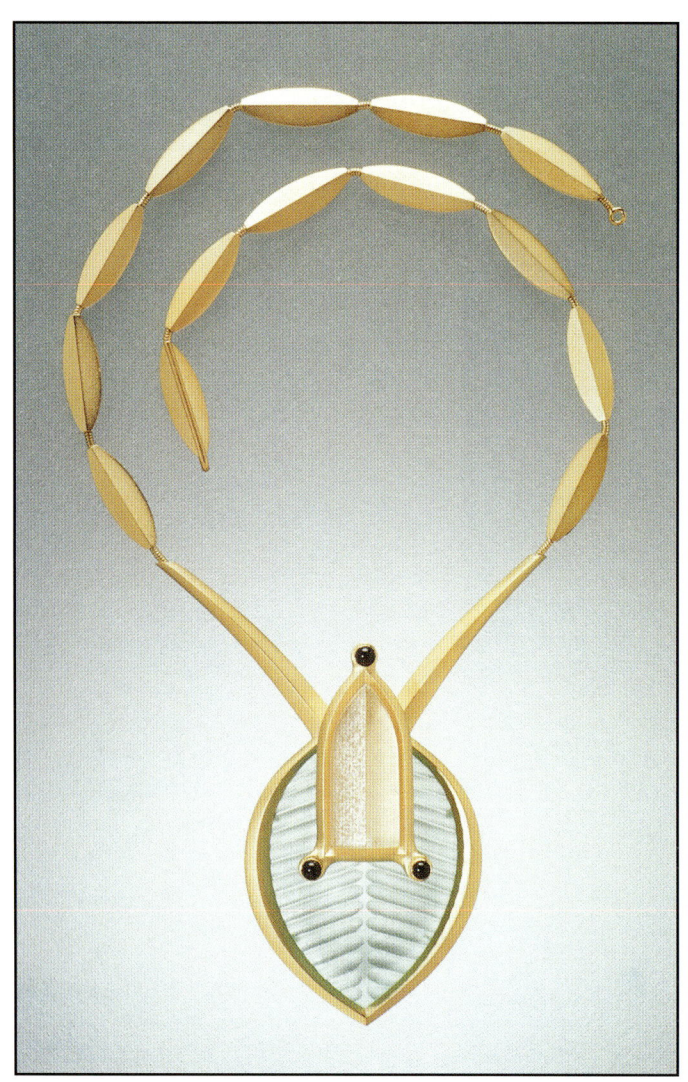
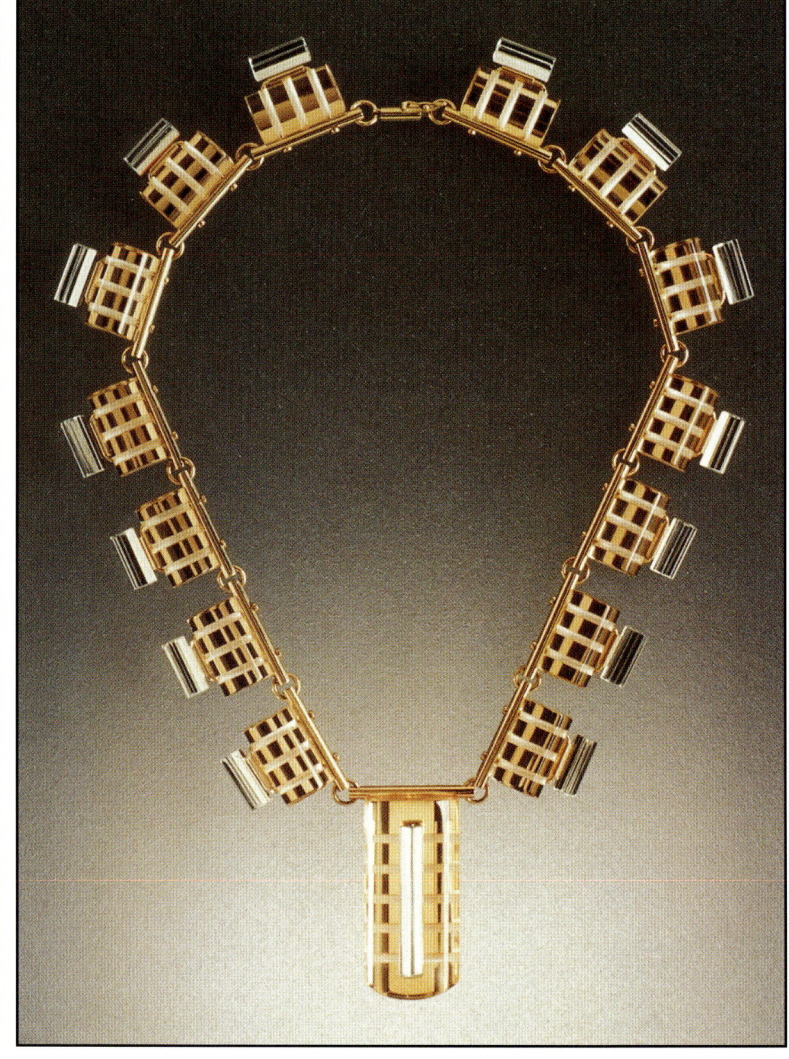

Good Fortune, 2000, Pendant, 3", Acid polished transparent green and clear glass, 24k gold plated brass, onyx detail, photo: Bill Truslow. *Photograph courtesy of the artist.*

Lucent Lines Series, 2000, 7" d, Optical glass with mirrored details, 14k gold, photo: Bill Truslow. *Photograph courtesy of the artist.*

Jackie Pancari

The two main aspects I am addressing through my work are light phenomenon and sensual experience. It is love of the sensual qualities of glass combined with the fascination for all aspects of light. The elemental physical properties of glass are what excite me the most. Some of these properties are its hot and fluid qualities, its refractive properties, its magnification and reductive properties. Glass speaks clearly about light. Its simplicity is complex.

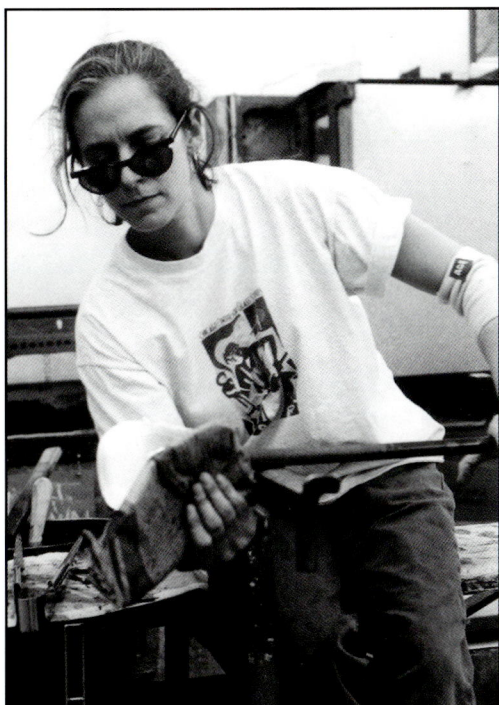

Jackie Pancari. *Photograph courtesy of the Creative Glass Center of America.*

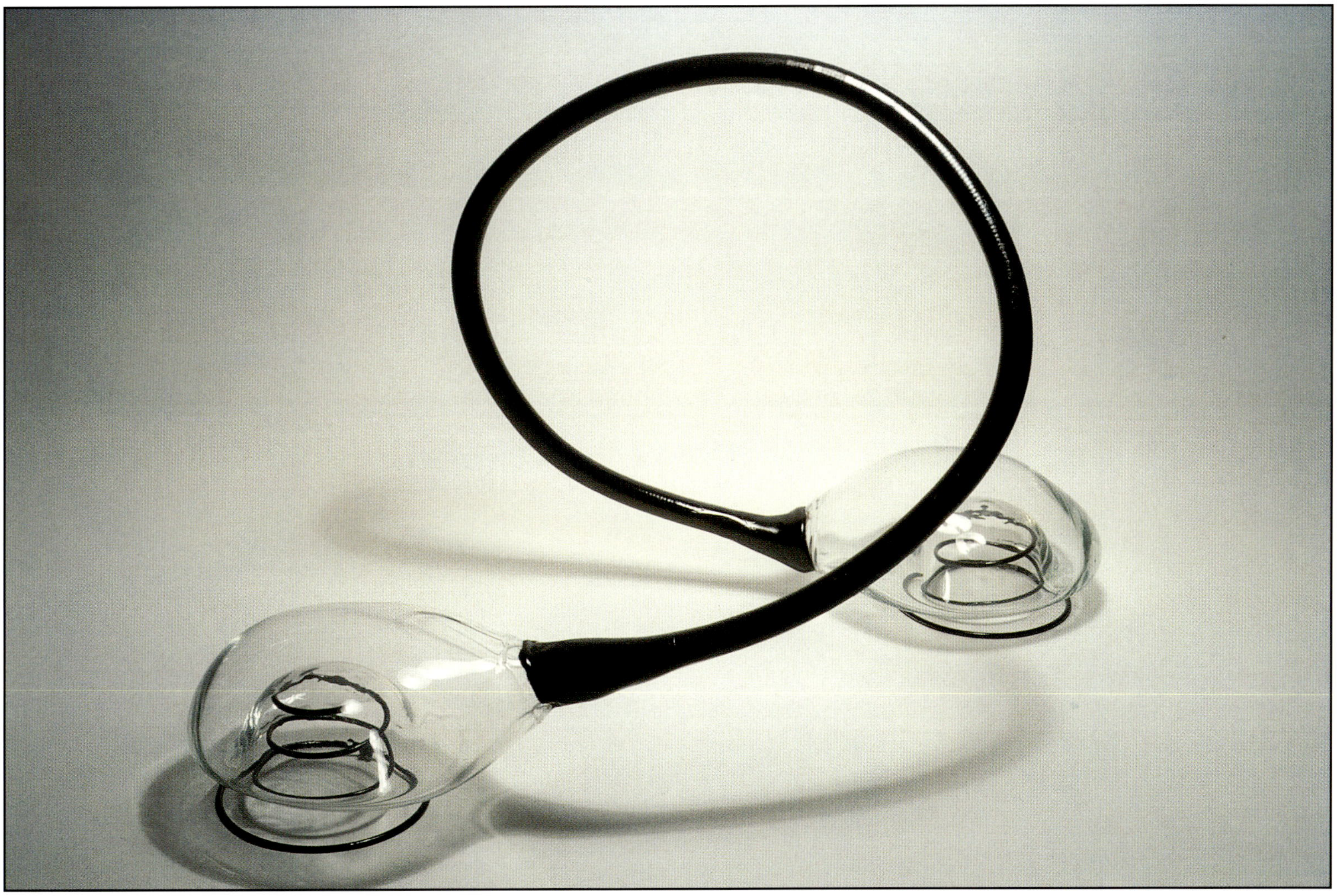

Bounce, 1983, 15" x 26", blown glass, encased wires. *Photograph courtesy of the artist.*

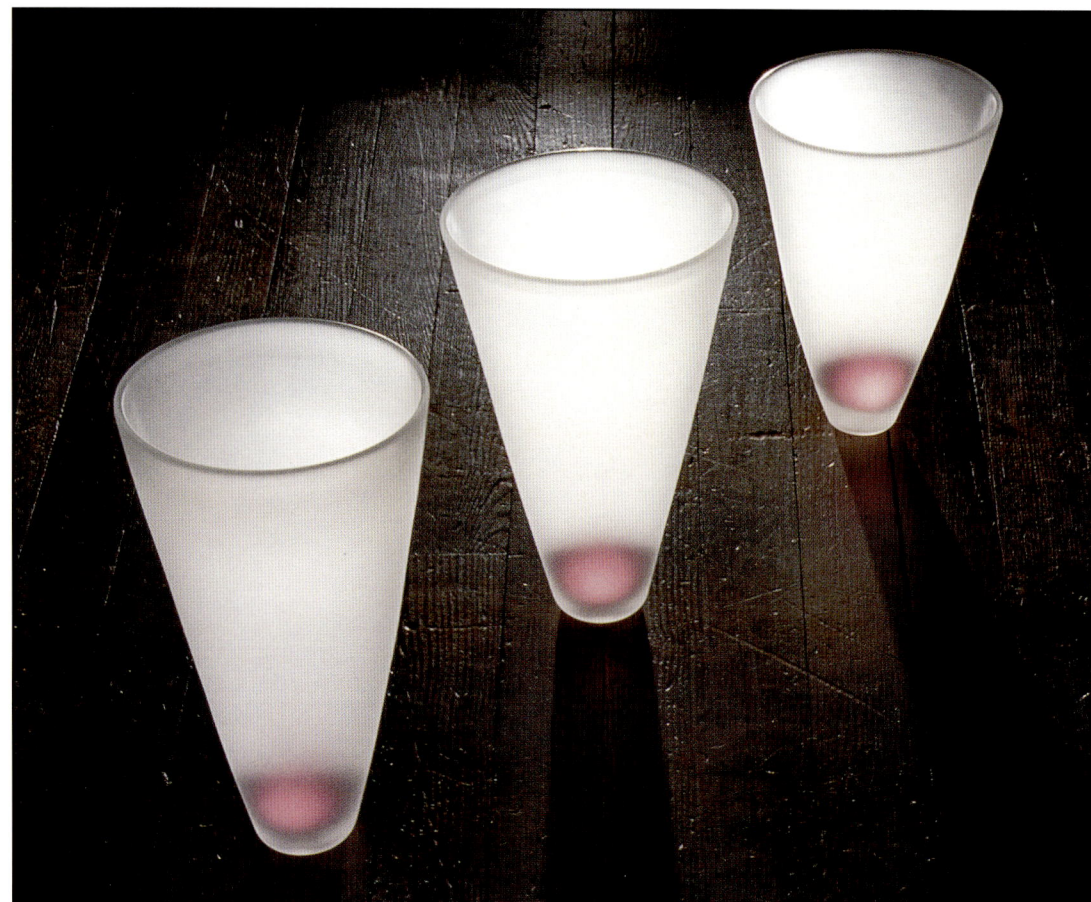

Light Cones, 2000, three pieces, each 18" x 10", Frosted blown glass, neodymium spheres. *Photograph courtesy of the artist.*

Perfectly Round, 2000, Blown and solid glass, water. *Photograph courtesy of the artist.*

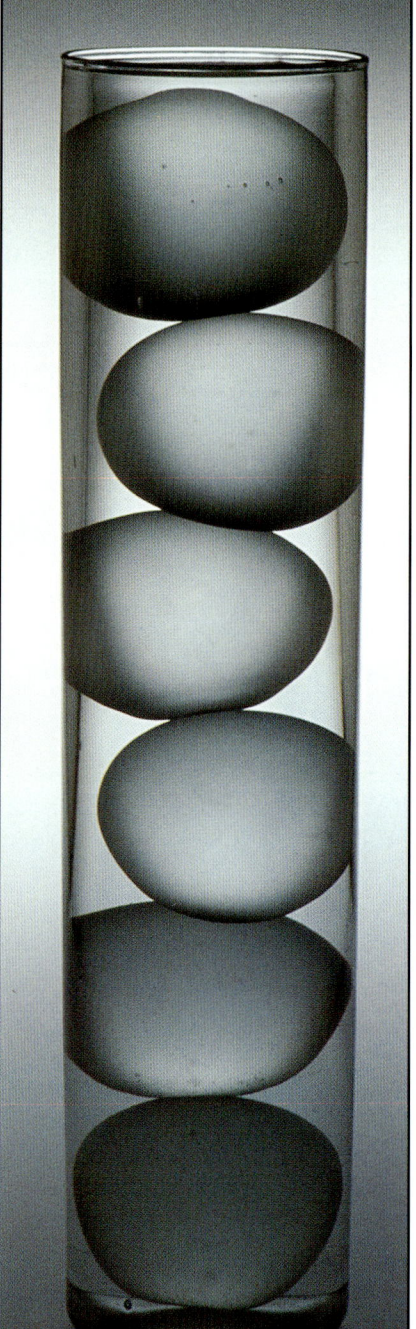

Sally Prash

Sally Prash is a rare artist with both advanced technical skill and the creativity required to make works of art. She has a Bachelors Degree in Fine Art in Glass and Ceramics and a Certificate in Scientific Glass Technology. Perhaps, even though she enjoys making her artwork and approaching complex laboratory apparatus, her greatest fulfillment comes from teaching.

Her current work is characterized by the combination of her technical skills and a strong art esthetic. She is well known for her goblets made with coiled stems that bounce when handled. A strong believer in feminism, she uses her work to express her frustration with an industry traditionally dominated by men.

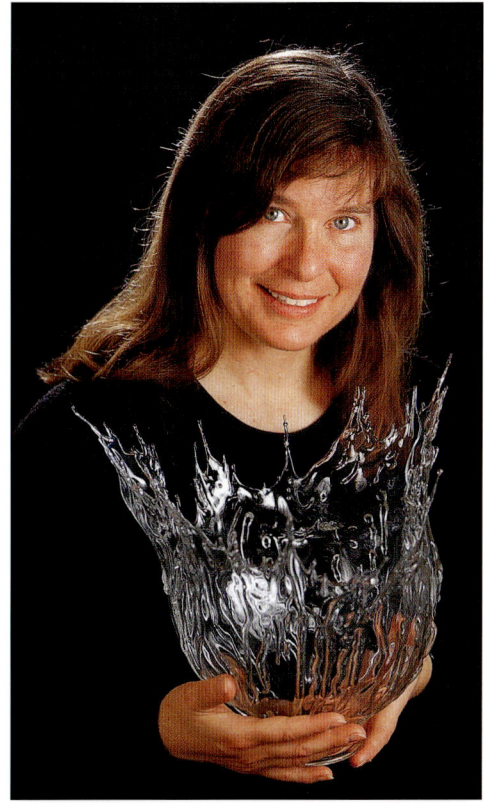

Sally Prash, photo: Tommy Olaf Elder.

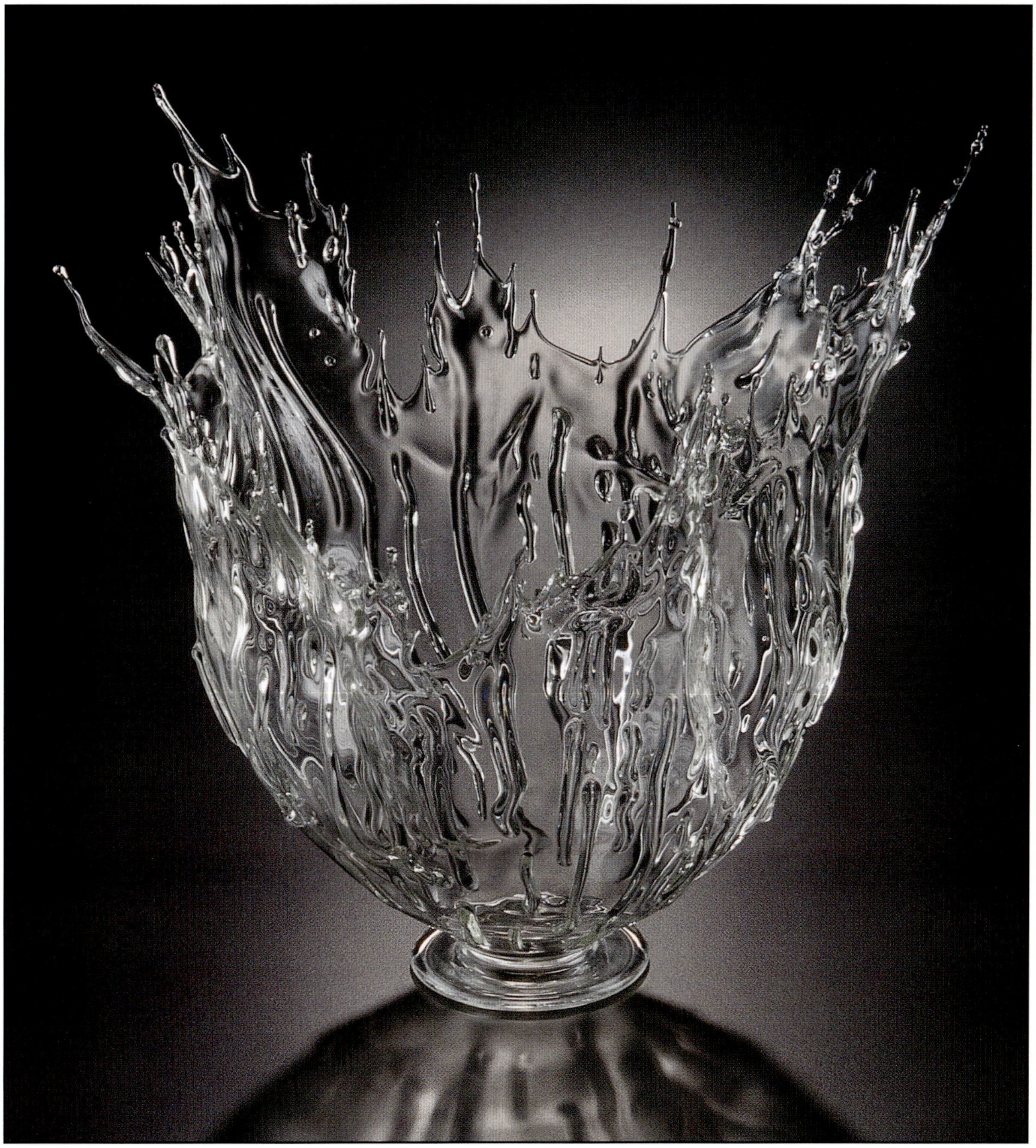

Splash, 2000, 12" h x 12" d, photo: Tommy Olaf Elder. *Photo credit the artist.*

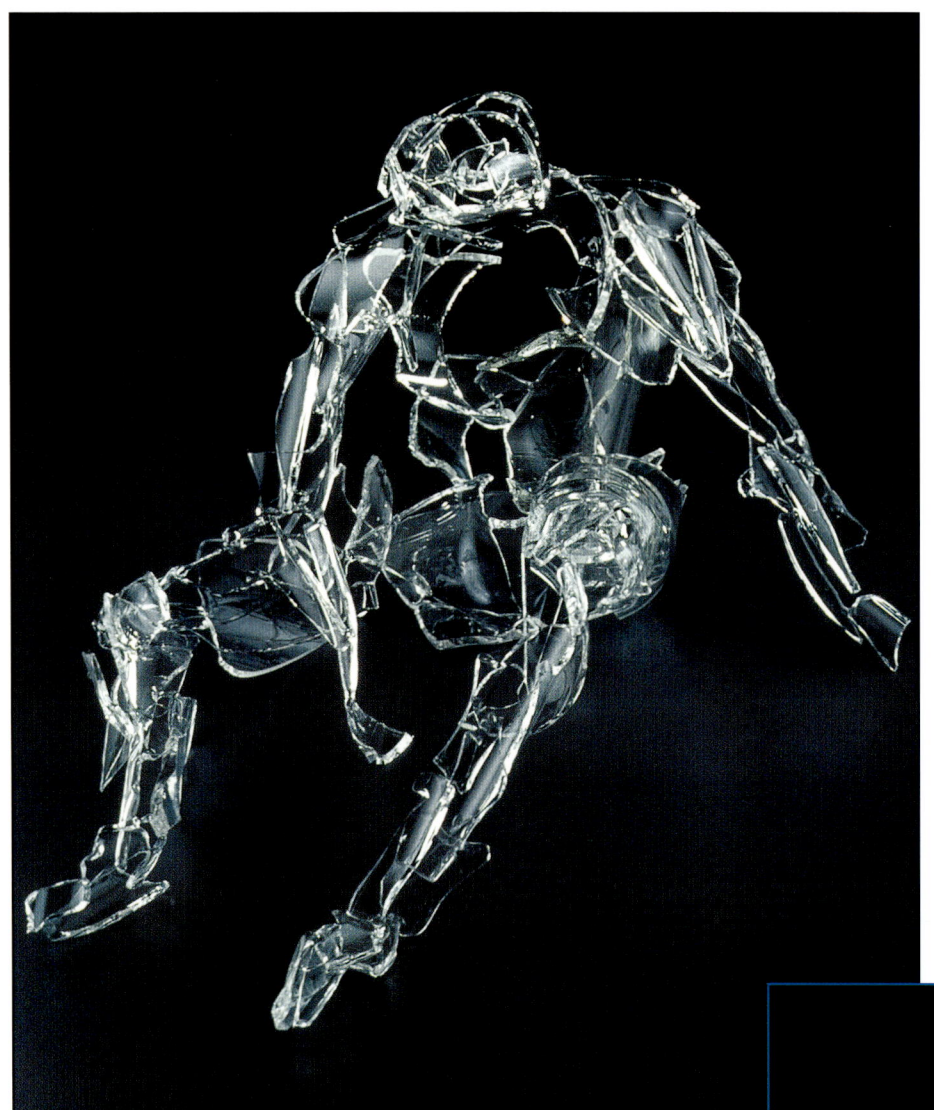

Shattered Shell, 1992, 40 cm x 25 cm, photo: Tommy Olaf Elder. Photo credit the artist.

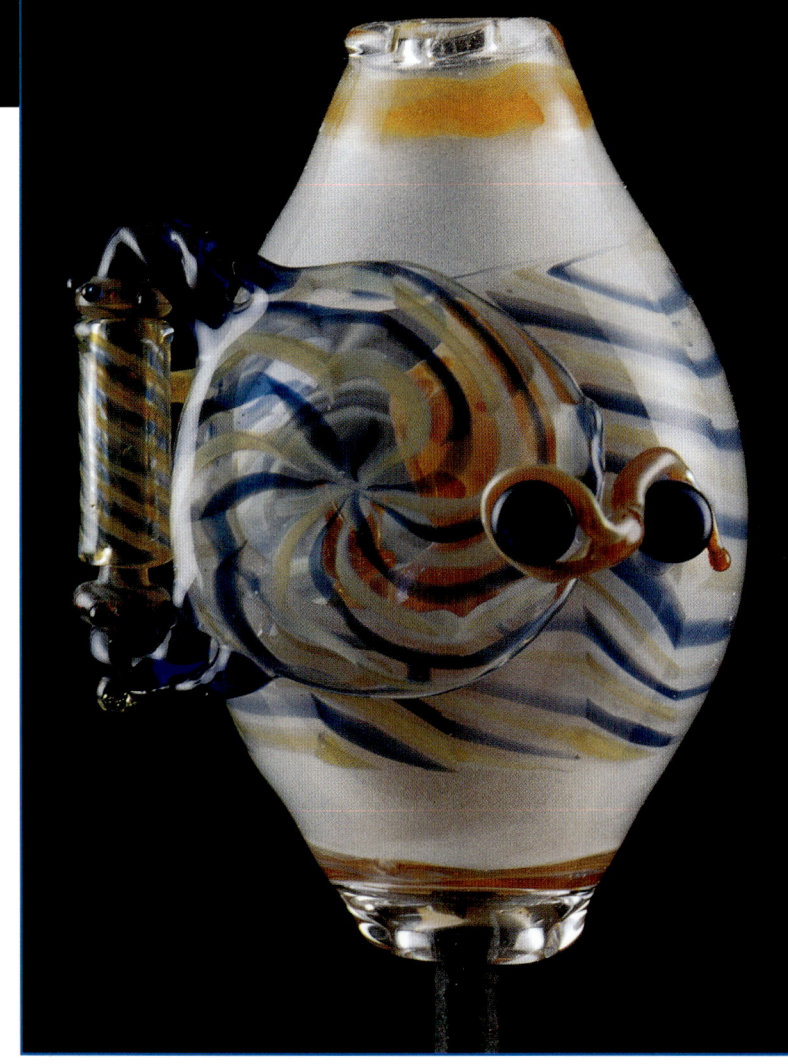

Hinged Bead with a little person asking for Peace Inside, 2002, 41 mm x 31 mm, photo: Tommy Olaf Elder. Photo credit the artist.

Amy Roberts

My work incorporates molten glass and plate glass with mediums such as wood, copper, and sticks. I am interested in combining elements and placing them in relationships that express unique qualities and associations. My work, in essence, is concerned with revealing layers of myself to viewers.

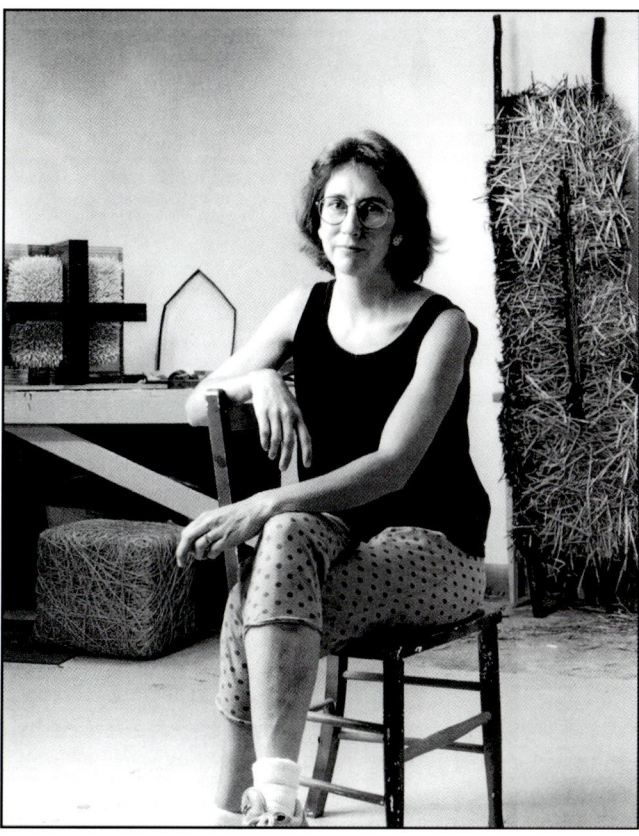

Amy Roberts. *Photograph courtesy of the artist.*

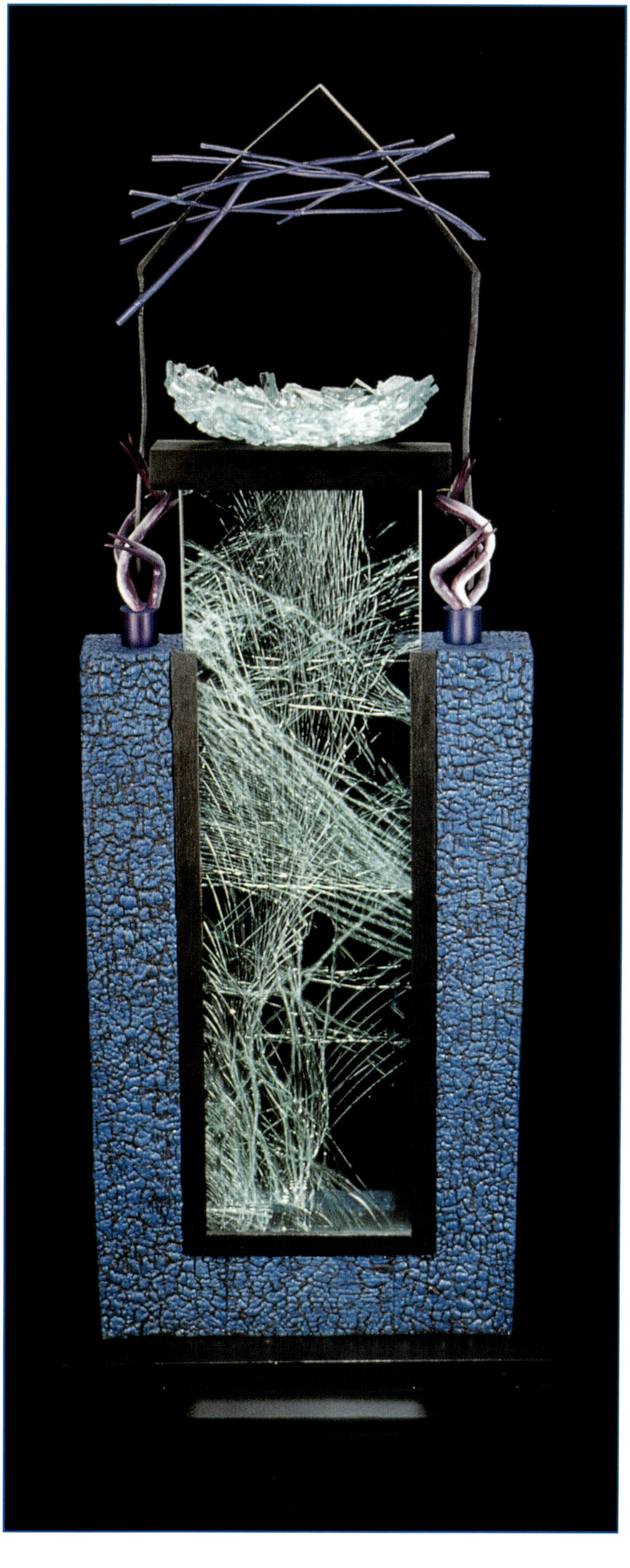

Transcendence, 1990, 52" x 20" x 8", glass and mixed media, photo: Kevin LaTona. *Photograph courtesy of the artist.*

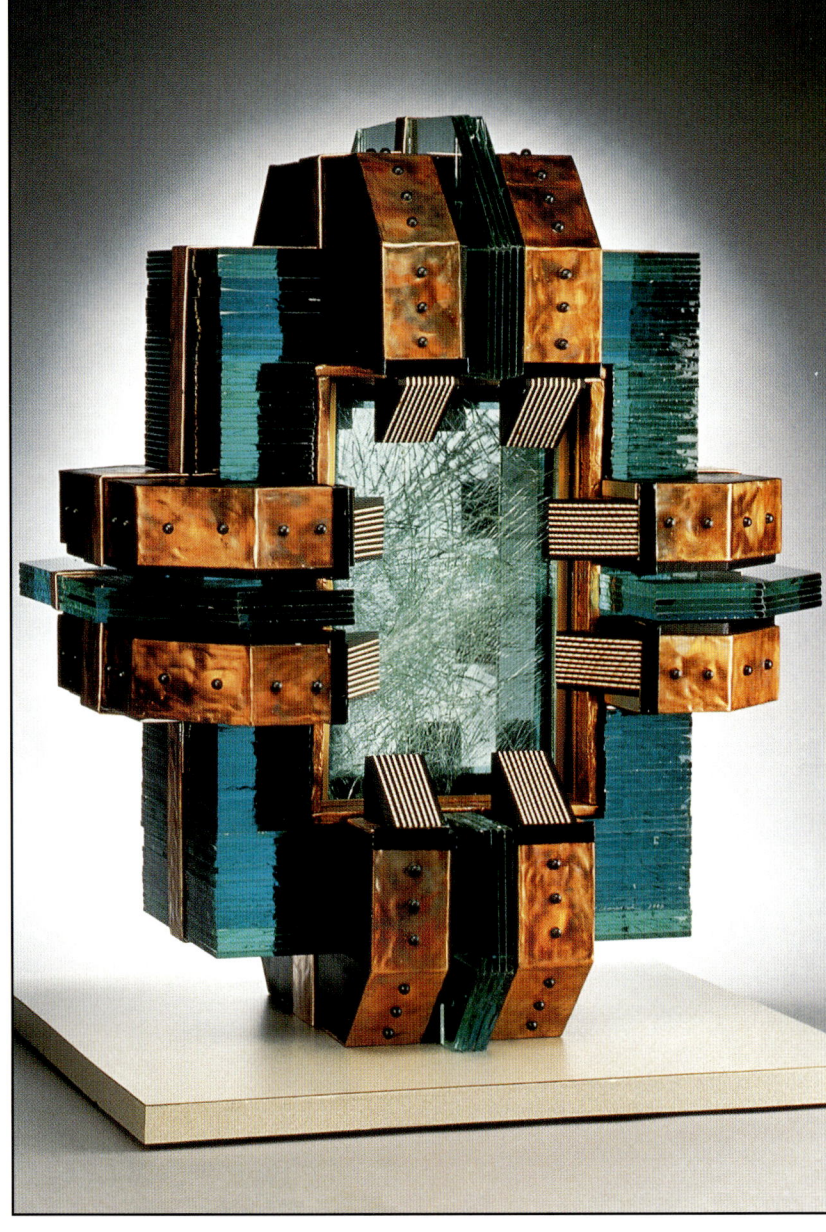

Portal, 1994, 30" x 26" x 20", glass and mixed media, photo: Kevin LaTona. Photograph courtesy of the artist.

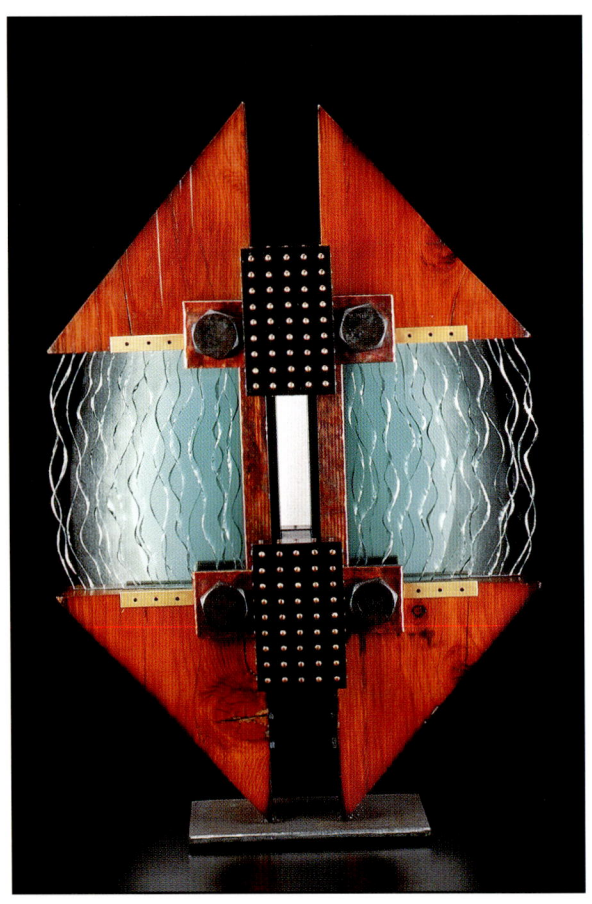
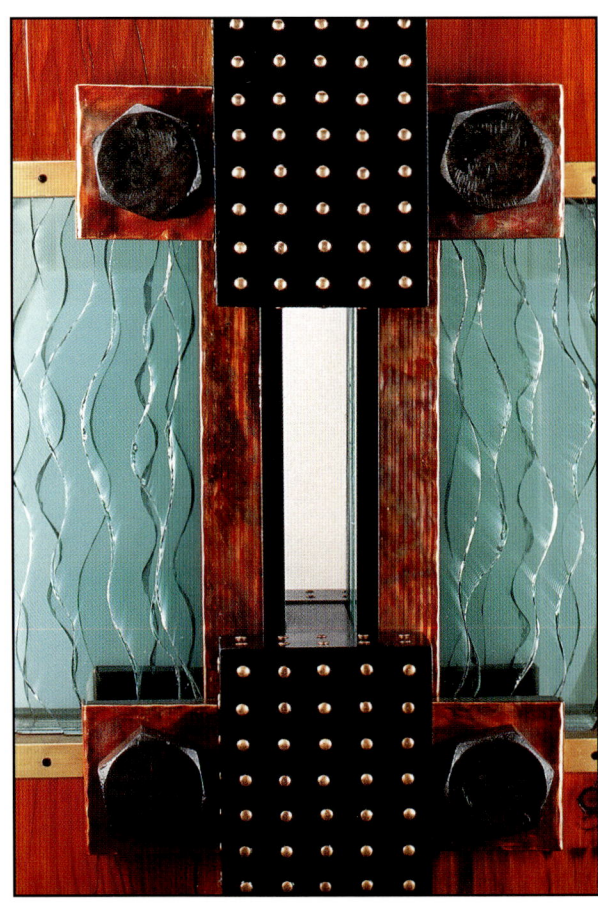

Left: *Core #2*, 1995, 36" x 26" x 9", Glass and mixed media, photo: Roger Schreiber. Photograph courtesy of the artist.

Right: *Core #2* detail.

Linda Ross

Currently, I am examining ways that nature is portrayed within the context of kitsch from the Victorian Era through modern times. I am particularly interested the unique identities of objects in Western culture, and how those objects have evolved from handcrafted means to large-scale mass production. Ordinary objects found in the home and yard speak to interesting issues of class, religion, and race within our American culture and consumer society. My art explores the parallels and differences between art and artifice, nature and industrial fabrication. My pink flamingo sculptures for example, explore my interests in both natural history (that of the bird itself) and the lawn ornament that serves as a plastic cultural icon. The flamingo is simultaneously exotic and majestic, as well as tacky and in bad taste. My work is not a critique of consumerism per se, nor is it a form of revised Pop Art. Rather, my art reflects the spontaneous creativity generated by what I consider to be odd and intriguing "urban anthropology."

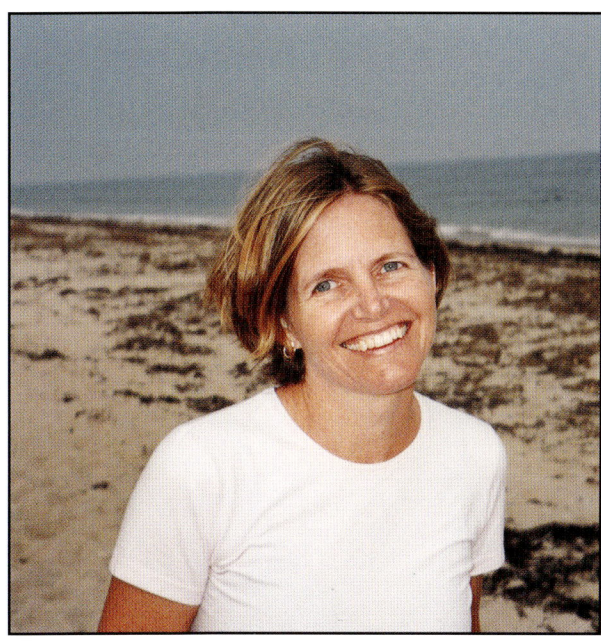

Linda Ross. *Photograph courtesy of the artist.*

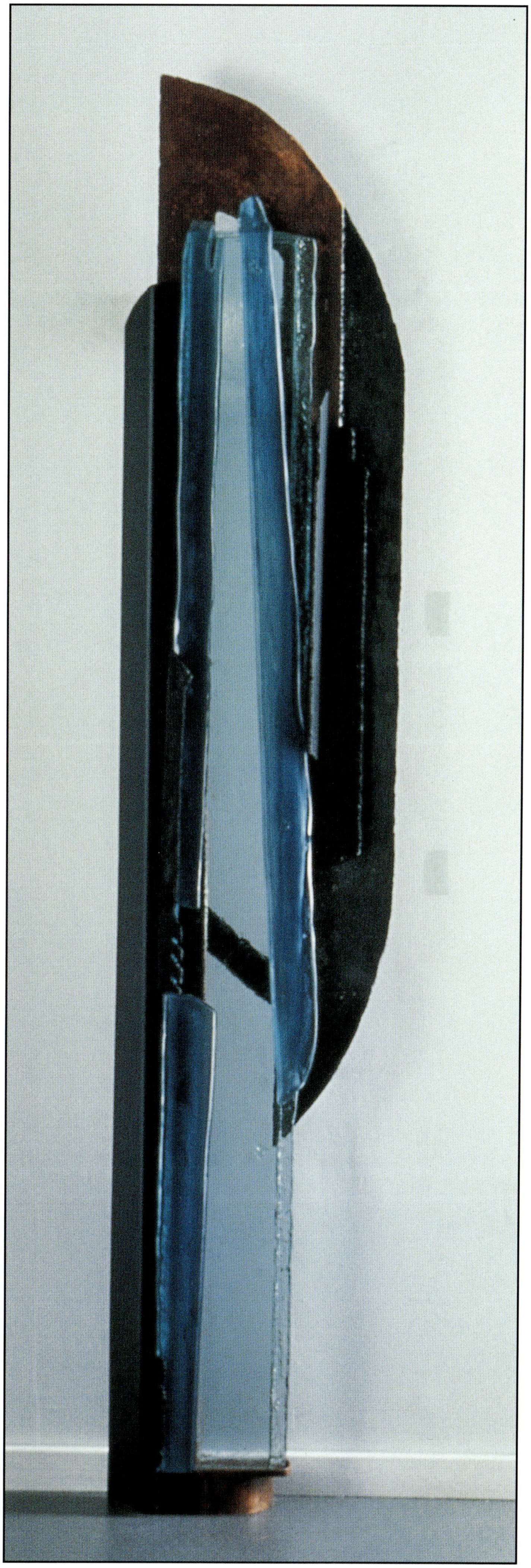

Parthenon, 1989, 87" x 19" x 5", Glass and Steel.
Photograph courtesy of the artist.

162 The Eighties - The Artist

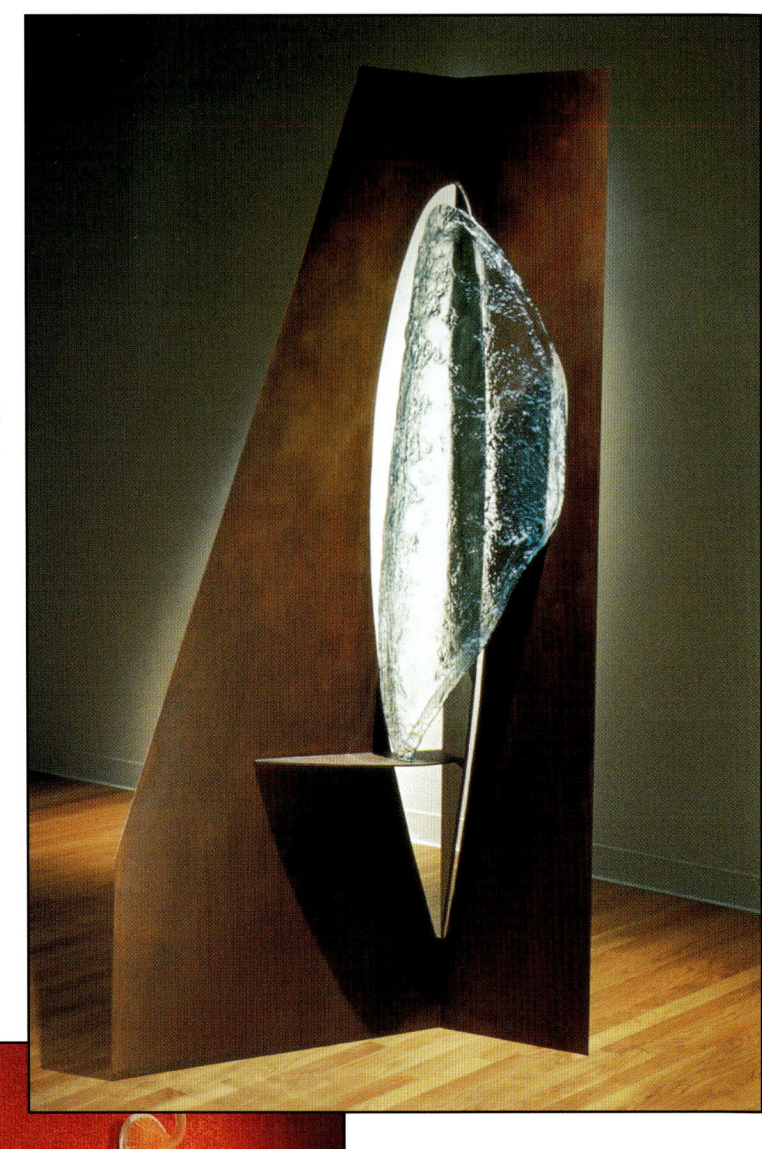

Echo, 1993, 84" x 42" x 18", slumped glass and steel. Photograph courtesy of the artist.

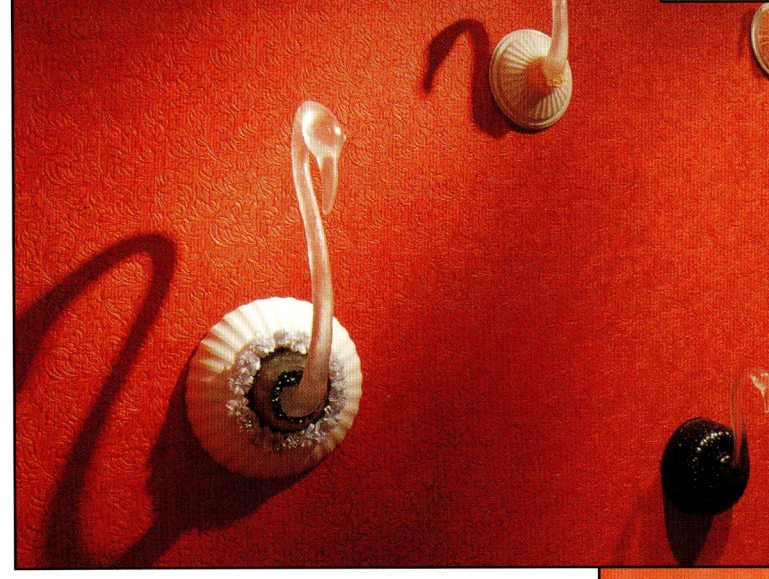

Flamingo Parlour, 2001, Dimensions variable, Glass, plastic, wallpaper. Photograph courtesy of the artist.

Flamingo Parlour detail, golden, 9" h x 9" w x 16" d, cast glass.

Ginny Ruffner

"I believe in beauty and art's potential to transmit as well as teach it. Teaching about beauty makes us self-aware, and cognizant of the less than beautiful, as well as makes us think about the true nature of beauty (beyond superficial prettiness). That's what I want to achieve in my work; beauty that makes you think."

"Where do my ideas come from? Mostly, I notice them in a corner of my consciousness, waiting for the music to start. Some are wallflowers and require a little coaxing; some are dancing fools jitterbugging across the synapses, flailing their skinny double-helix arms, shaking their light bulb heads and screaming, 'make me, make me…' They are all flirts. And when they get together in that ambidextrous dance palace between the ears, the results are like a dating service from Mars."

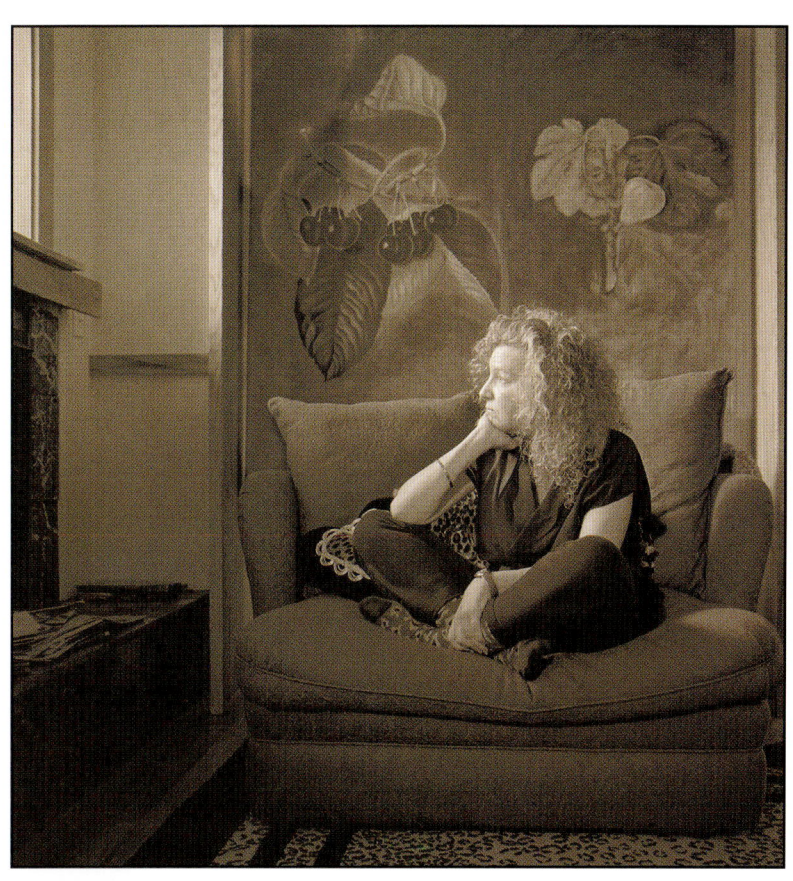

Ginny Ruffner, photo credit: Davis Freeman. *Photograph courtesy of the artist.*

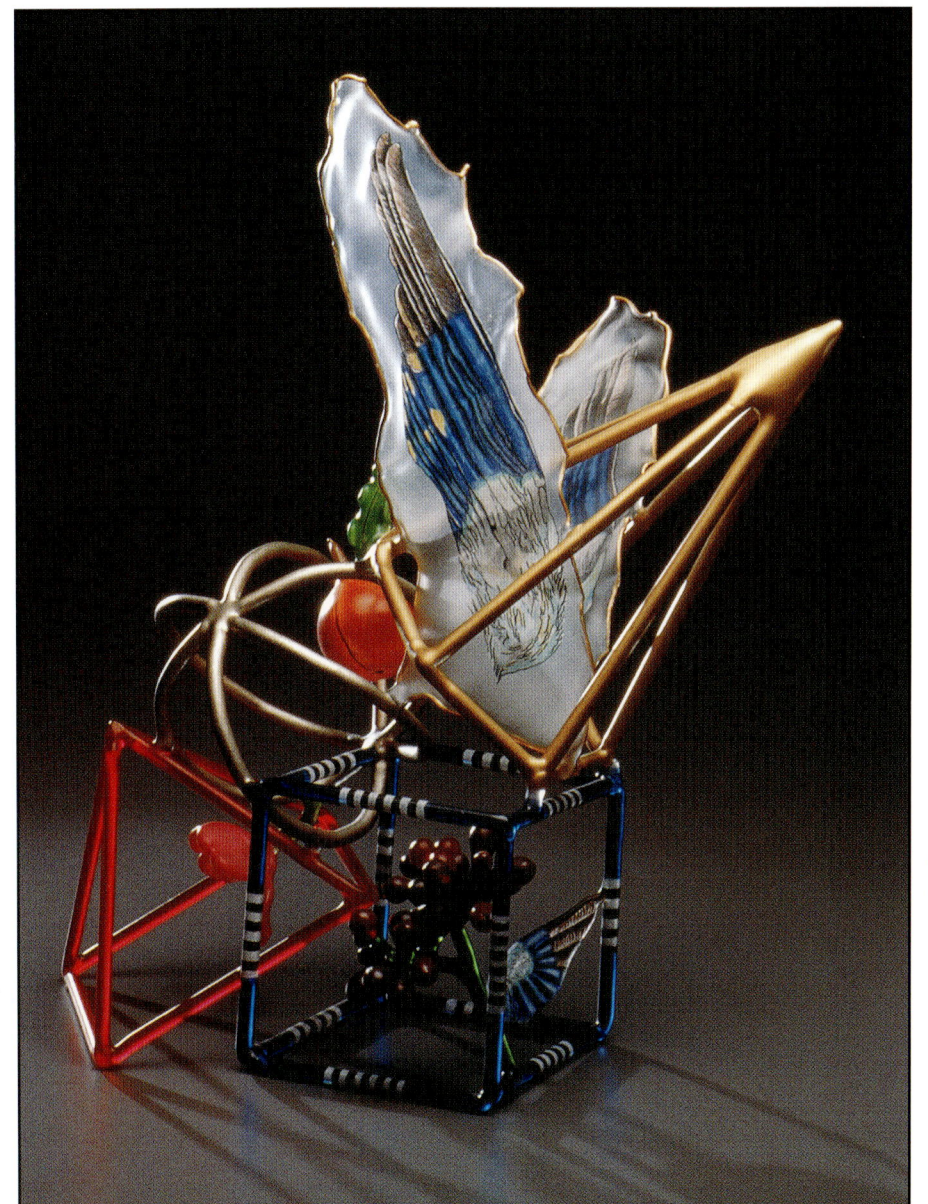

On the Wings of Geometry, 1994, 22" x 26" x 12", glass and mixed media. *Photograph courtesy of the artist.*

164   The Eighties - The Artist

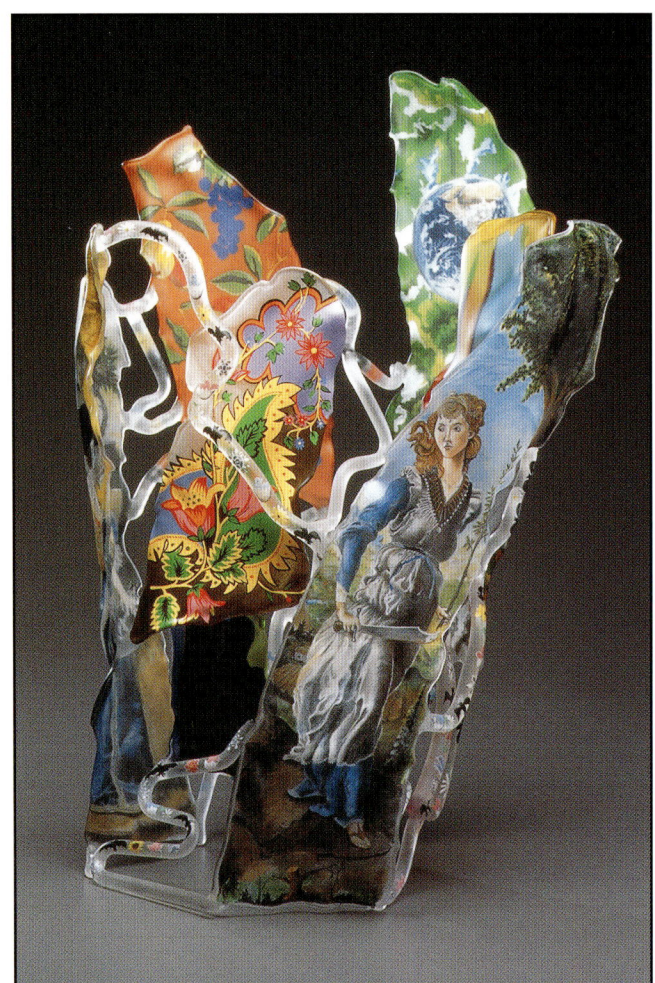

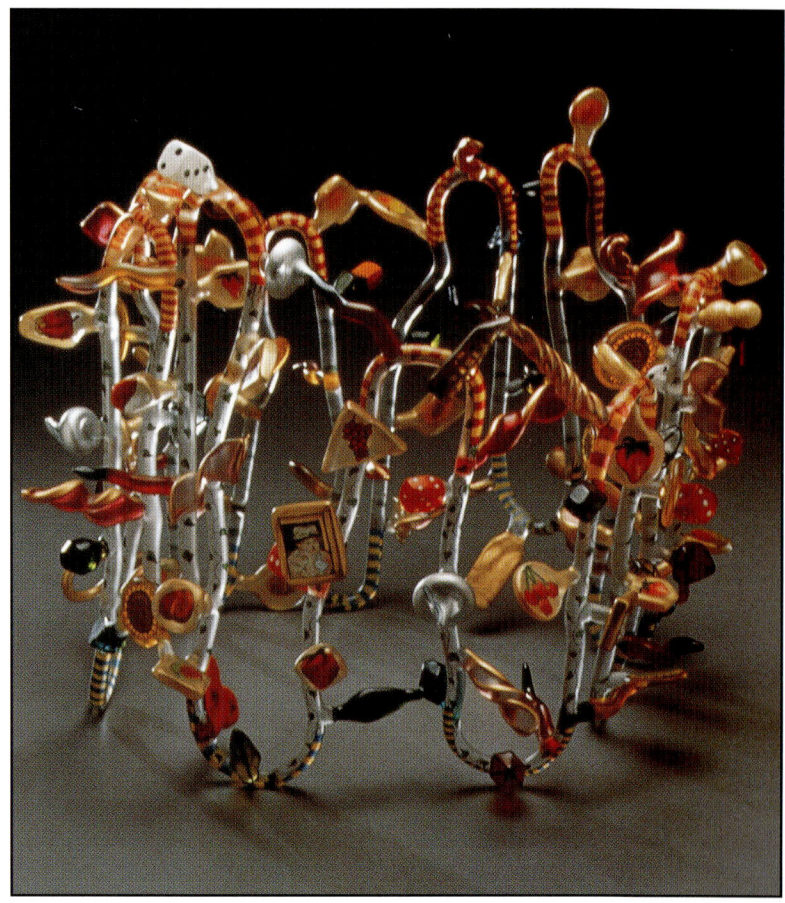

Viewing the Seasons, 1994, 24" x 15" x 13", glass and mixed media. Photograph courtesy of the artist.

Circuitous Path, 1994, 19.5" x 22", glass and mixed media. Photograph courtesy of the artist.

The Basso Profundo Aria of Roots, 2002, 86" x 50" x 36", Bronze, stainless steel, and glass, photo: Mike Seidl. Photograph courtesy of the artist.

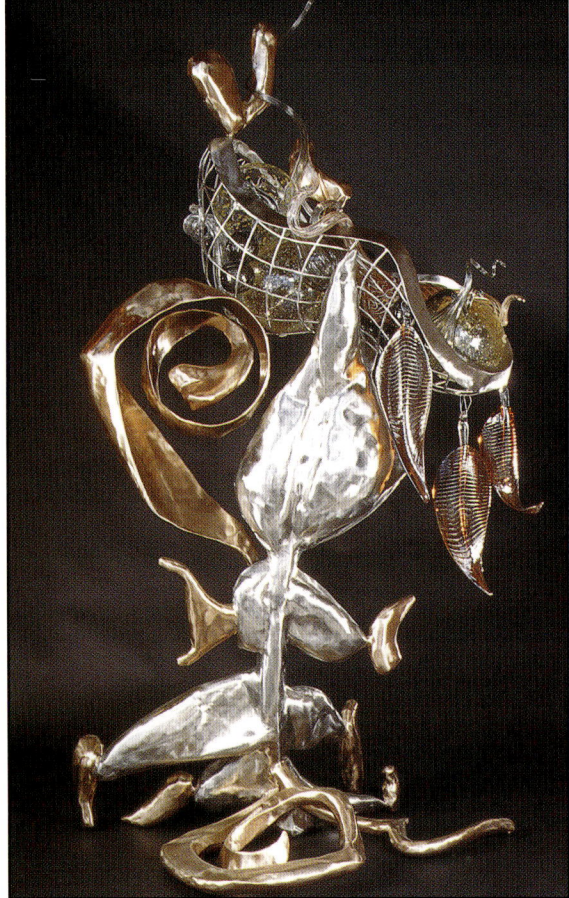

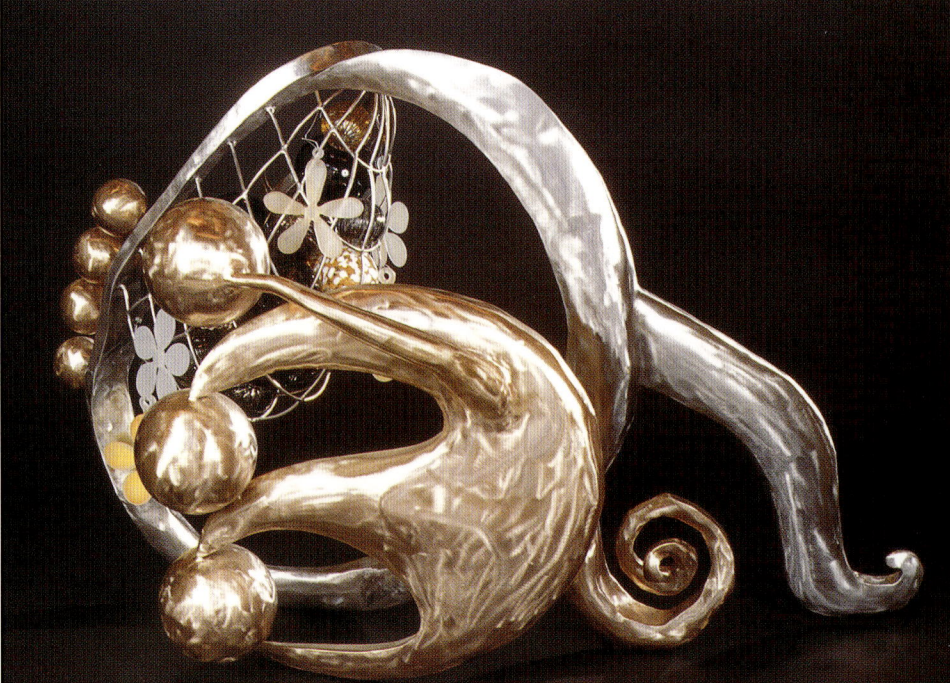

Crab Nebula with Floral Stars and 7 Planets, 2002, Bronze, stainless steel, and glass, photo: Mike Seidl. Photograph courtesy of the artist.

Lisabeth Sterling

The images in my engravings and paintings are much like lucid dreams on glass. I explore symbolic uses of narrative imagery. I exercise some conscious control, but if I intellectualize the process or the image, the magic ends.

My work is in part an avenue to self exploration—an opportunity to get to know the workings of my subconscious—but it is also a collection of images from the stories of the collective unconscious.

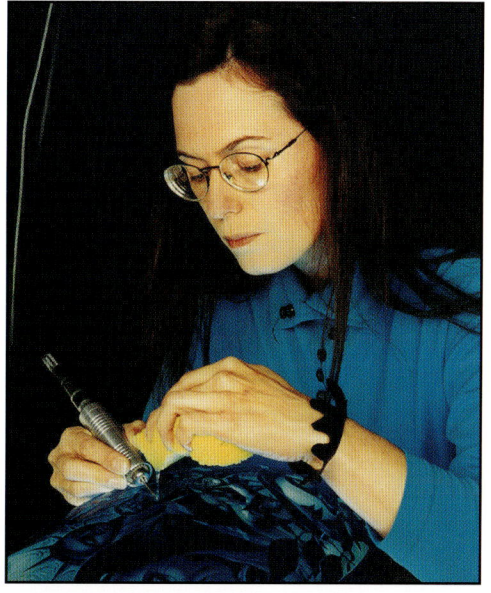

Lisabeth Sterling, photograph: Robin Sterling Brewer. *Photograph courtesy of the artist.*

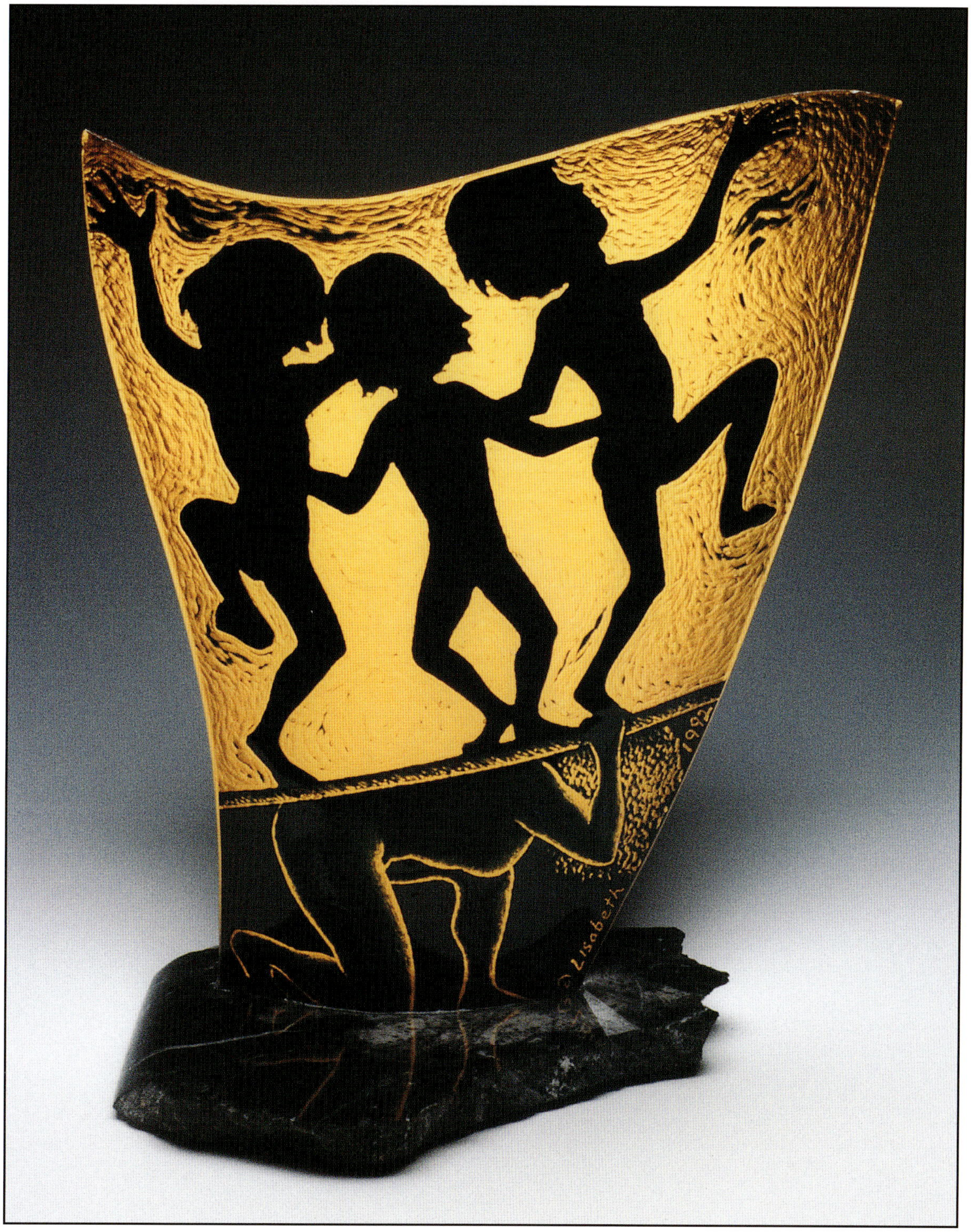

Motherhood, 1992, 8" x 7" x 4", engraved glass, photo: Robin Sterling Brewer. *Photograph courtesy of the artist.*

166   The Eighties - The Artist

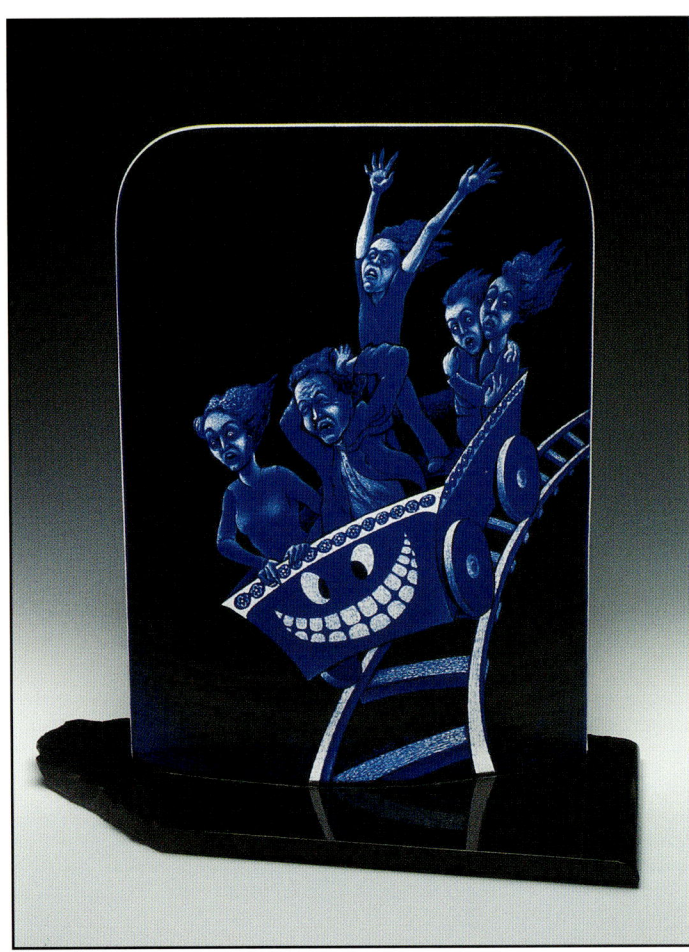

Life on an Emotional Roller Coaster, 1993, 12" x 12" x 6", engraved glass, photo: Robin Sterling Brewer. *Photograph courtesy of the artist.*

A Face in the Crowd, 2002, 11.25" x 5.5" d, engraved, photo: Roger Schreiber. *Photograph courtesy of the artist.*

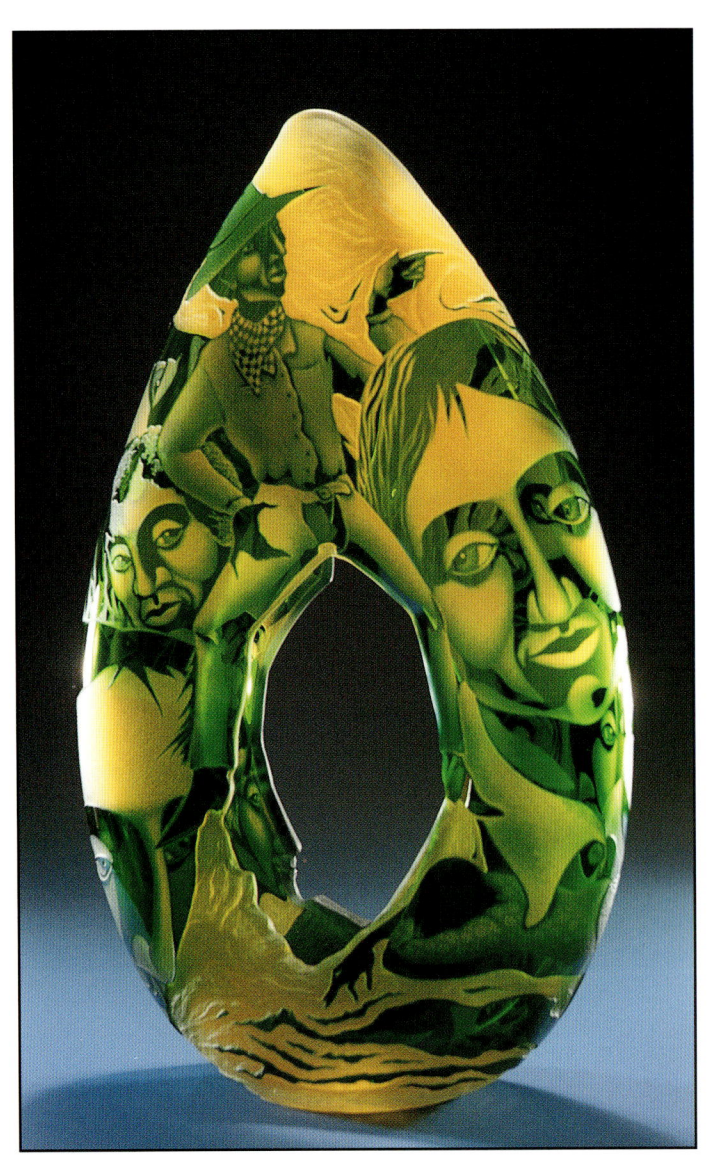

Ridin' and Shootin', 2000, 13" x 8.25" x 2.5", engraved. *Photograph courtesy of the artist.*

Raquel Stolarski-Assael

In 1980, by mere coincidence, I designed my earliest piece of carved flat glass and that was love at first sight. After twenty-two years of working with this precious material, my passion is still growing. Why? Maybe because it implies an ongoing experiment and challenge; or it keeps my curiosity fueled with its many secrets yet to discover; or is it that glass' unique qualities open doors to create an unlimited variety of artworks. Perhaps it is the uncertainty that accompanies the process of the making, where one never really knows what will come out, but there is an ever-present expectation of the unexpected. It could also be the combination of play, imagination, pleasure, and pain inherent to creation. For these reasons and others time will further disclose, I can't keep my mind and hands off of glass. And truly I must confess, I'm addicted to it.

I have devoted all this time to flat glass and cold working techniques; a drop in the sea of possibilities to produce glass art. Never the less, this realm is so vast that I've only scratched its surface. At the beginning I treated the glass plate as canvas, carving and painting its surfaces. Slowly I got rid of the edges and started constructing interrelated flat figures, on different planes. On a further stage and having at hand excellent adhesives, lamination was possible and thus sculpture came about. Sand carving is my main technique. The pieces are like jigsaw puzzles; I construct each of the multiple individual parts and then put them together; be it an abstract or a figurative composition. The entrails of a sculpture are made up by the combination of clear and colored glass together with other elements such as metal, internally carved and painted surfaces, bark paper, obsidian, flower petals, and voids between sheets.

A glass sculpture is a space of light occupied by landscapes. Layers and layers of transparency encase elements and colors that comprise a figure. Its surfaces interact, creating depth, volume, and illusory spaces within, an effect exclusive to glass and reminiscent of the submarine and cosmic spheres. What an artist can do with glass has no limits. This noble material exposes both skin and soul of a sculpture, by letting the eye caress its multiple interiors. But above all, glass is a substance dreams are made of...

My work is a journey through a diversity of figures, whose common denominators are luminosity and the voluptuous interplay between inside and outside. It includes large-scale elements incorporated with the architecture, functional and sculptural objects.

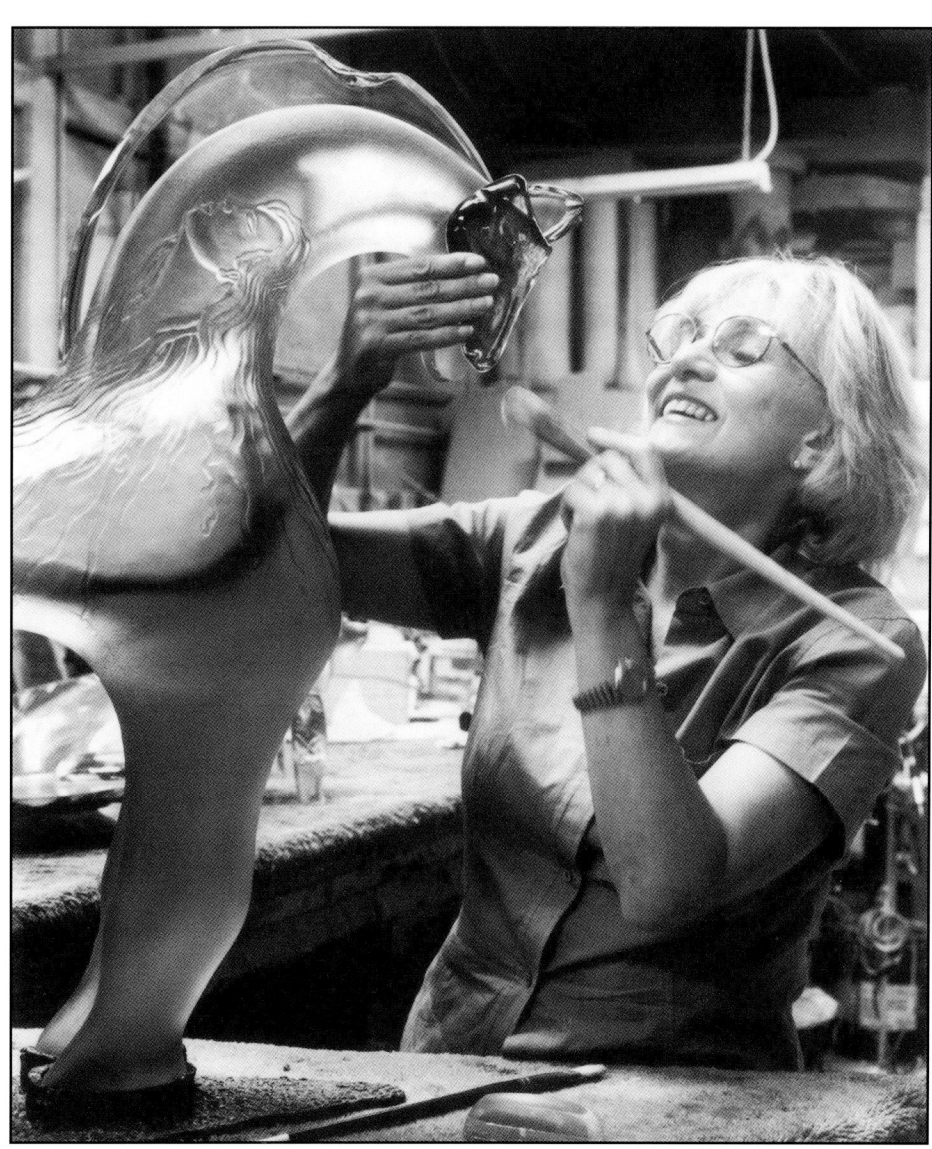

Raquel Stolarski-Assal. *Photograph courtesy of the artist.*

168 The Eighties - The Artist

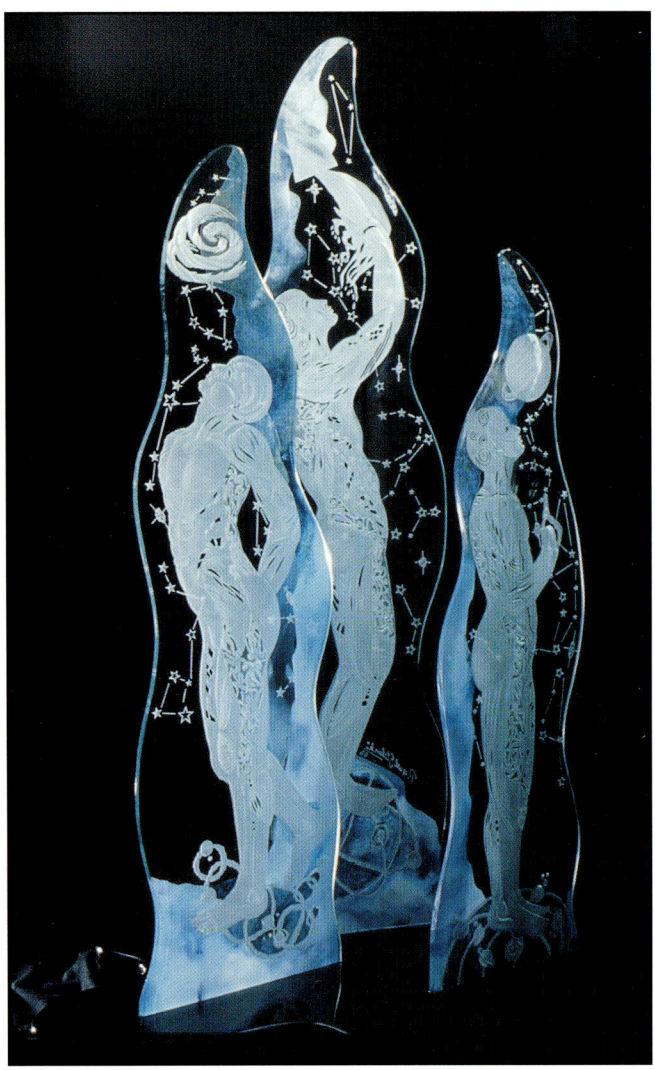

Awe at Creation, 1989, 61" x 44" x 30.75", sand carved and hand-painted, mixed media, plate glass on lacquered wooden base. Photograph courtesy of the artist.

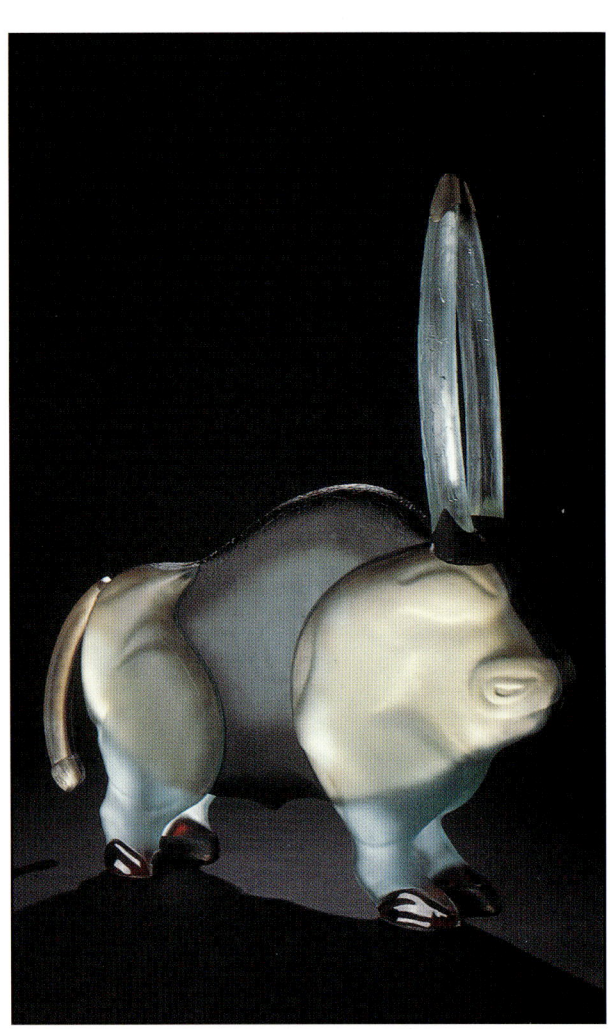

Tlatoani (The Master, Aztec), 1999, 48" x 32" x 20", laminated, sand carved, acid dipped plate glass—clear and colored with metal inclusions; and polished glass on marble base. Photograph courtesy of the artist.

Taurus, 2002, 25.5" x 22.75" x 4.5", Laminated, sand carved, and acid dipped plate glass—clear and black: with copper inclusions; carved and polished red mirror: metal. Photograph courtesy of the artist.

Cappy Thompson

As a painter, I combine two ancient lineages in my work—that of the Medieval artists who painted on stained glass and that of the Greek artisans who painted clay pots. And like them I paint pictorial narratives.

My work is pulled in opposite directions by the panel and vessel forms. Stained glass is an architectural medium with a long history as a public art form. It belongs to the collective. The vessel exists on an intimate scale, relating to the individual in its form and function. This conflict finds expression in my work as a desire to communicate broadly on the one hand and an impulse to go deeply into the personal on the other.

In college, in the early seventies, I was drawn to stained glass as a perceptually compelling medium driven by light. I realized that if I wanted to paint on it, I would have to teach myself *grisaille*–the medieval technique of gray tonal painting on glass. This technique involves painting and firing vitreous paints onto glass. First the black line work—called tracery—is painted onto the glass surface and permanently fixed by firing. Then a wash of black paint—called a matt—is applied over the tracery and subtracted by specially shaped bristle brushes. The tonality and patterning (modeling) created by this subtractive process is then fixed by firing.

My first panels were heavily influenced by the art of the medieval period from many cultural sources—Hindu, Pagan, Judaic, Buddhist, Christian, Islamic. I loved the naive naturalistic content and emotional expressiveness of that period. I began to design and paint panels based on the narrative content of European mythology fables and folk tales, drawn in oblique projection, with jewel-like colors.

I worked in stained glass for twelve years. Then in 1987, during a summer job at Pilchuck Glass School, I was handed a large transparent blown-glass bowl to paint and saw immediately—like the Greeks of antiquity—that a vessel combining cylindrical and spherical forms is a nearly perfect structure for painted narration. The glass vessel is a separate world for the story, and its transparency allowed the painting to become sculptural, seen from one side through to the other, changing as the viewer circumambulates the structure.

This was the beginning of a thirteen-year period of vessel painting that continues in the present. I spent several years working in black and white captivated by the compositional possibilities of images drawn on the vessel form. Gradually, I came to appreciate how the qualities of blown glass, colored vitreous paints, and the metaphors hidden in the vessel form could bring more meaning to my work.

As a metaphor, the vessel can represent various objects and functions deeply embedded in our Psyches and culture. For example, concepts such as internal/external, center/rim, surface/interior, boundary/territory, open/closed, above/below, background/foreground, male/female, container/content, world and self – to name a few oppositions. The form itself is made from molten sand and constructed by the application of breath and turning – allegories for creation, the planetary bodies, and time. The ability of glass to hold space, color, and light suggests the spiritual qualities of transparency, translucence, and transcendence.

About ten years ago I found myself moving away from existing mythological narrative and toward compositions that drew upon images and themes from my

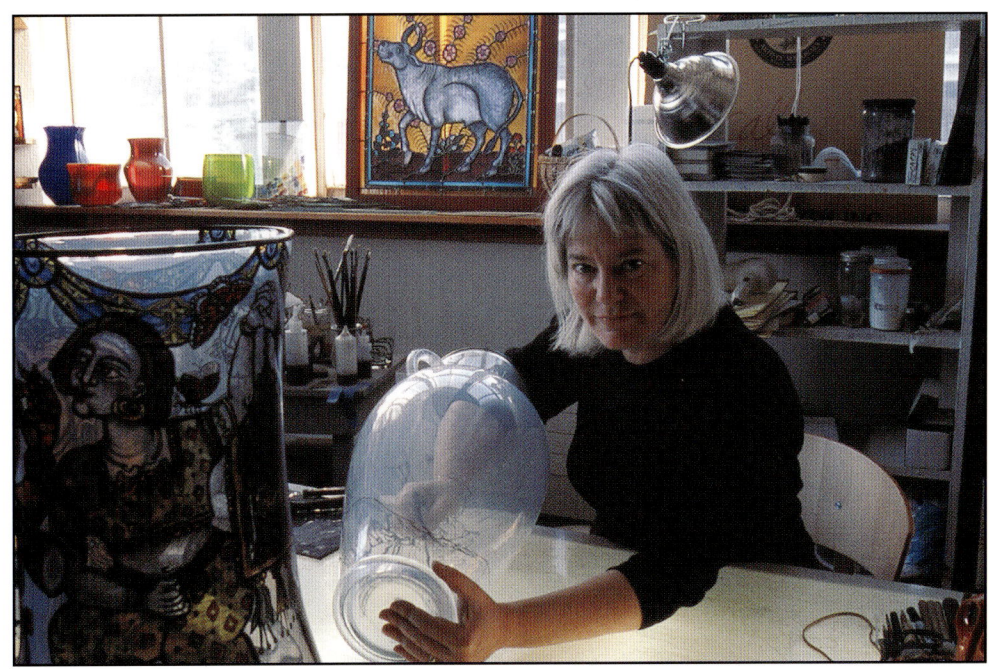

Cappy Thompson, photograph: Joanne Petrina. *Photograph courtesy of the artist.*

personal life. Elements would drift up and assemble into picture-poems that seemed to have a life of their own. I began to "read" these works as reflections of the spiritual and psychological issues in my life. I painted members of my family and myself in a kind of autobiographical fantasy, working with the mytho-poetic materials of my life. I cast myself into scenes from various world spiritual traditions.

I am currently working on the largest project of my career – one that brings me full circle back to stained glass – a Painted window-wall measuring thirty-three feet by ninety feet for the new south concourse at Seattle International Airport. Entitled *I Was Dreaming of Spirit Animals*, it pictures a couple sleeping high in a tower-house. Behind them is the arc of the night sky, shining with seventeen animal constellations of the Northern Hemisphere across the sky, winged horses (Pegausu and Equilius) draw a chariot bearing the Sun and Moon, who sprinkle stars upon the dreamers and travelers below.

This project incorporates into a stained-glass composition what I have learned from vessel painting. The fabrication method allows me to float the imagery upon an expanse of color laminated onto plate glass The building becomes a vessel, and stained glass washes the space with the brilliance of colored light.

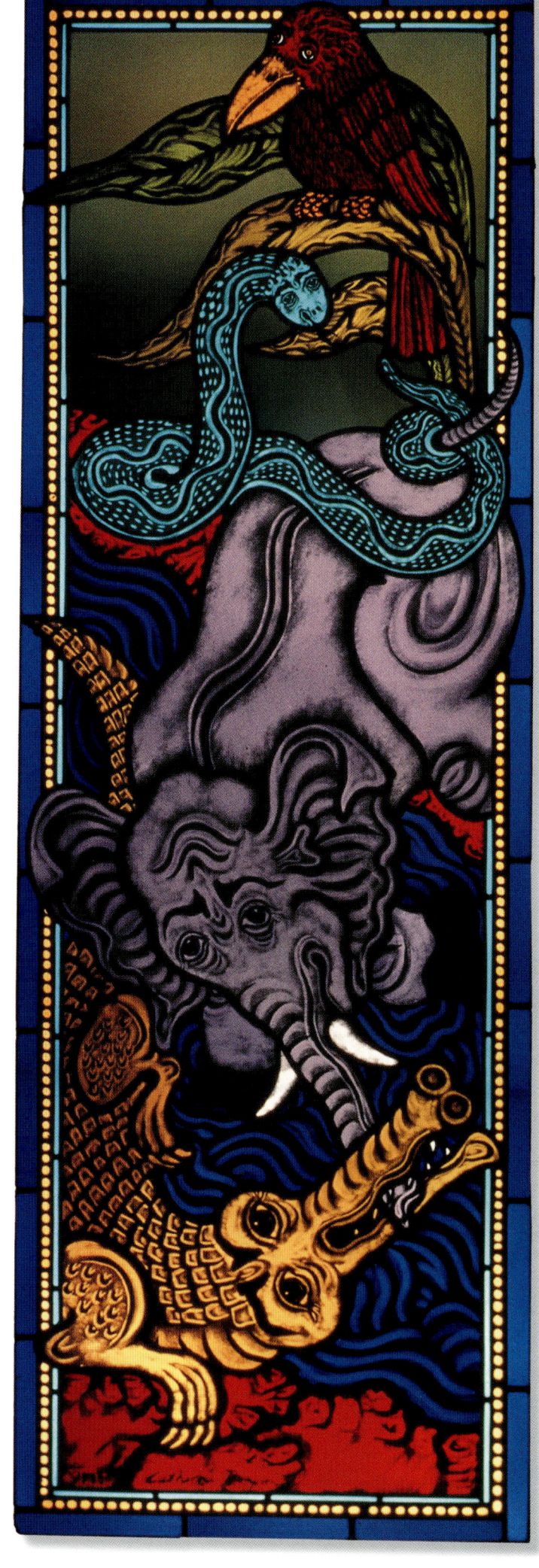

The Elephant's Child, 1989, 76" x 26", painted stained glass, Mountlake Terrace Public Library, Mountlake Terrace, Washington, Commissioning agency, Mountlake Terrace Arts Commission, photo: Michael Seidl. *Photograph courtesy of the artist.*

The Eighties - The Artist   171

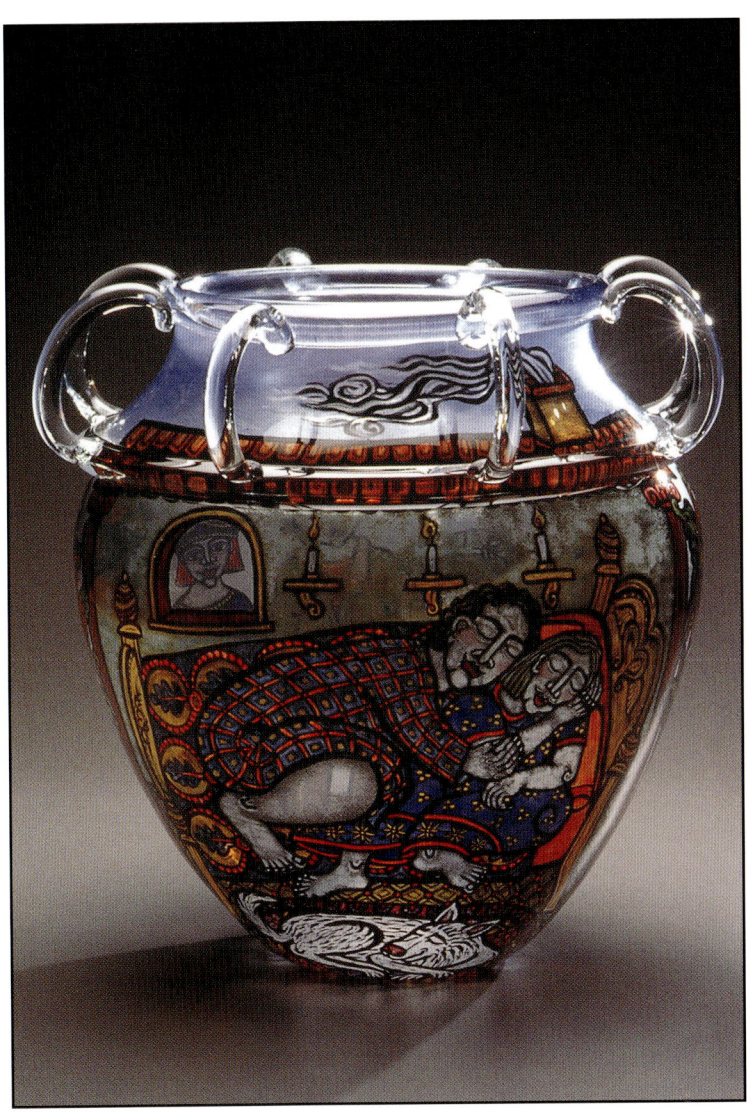

Lovers Dreaming a Dream, 1996, 16" x 16" x 16", vitreous enamels reverse painted on blown glass. Photo: Michael Seidl. *Photograph courtesy of the artist.*

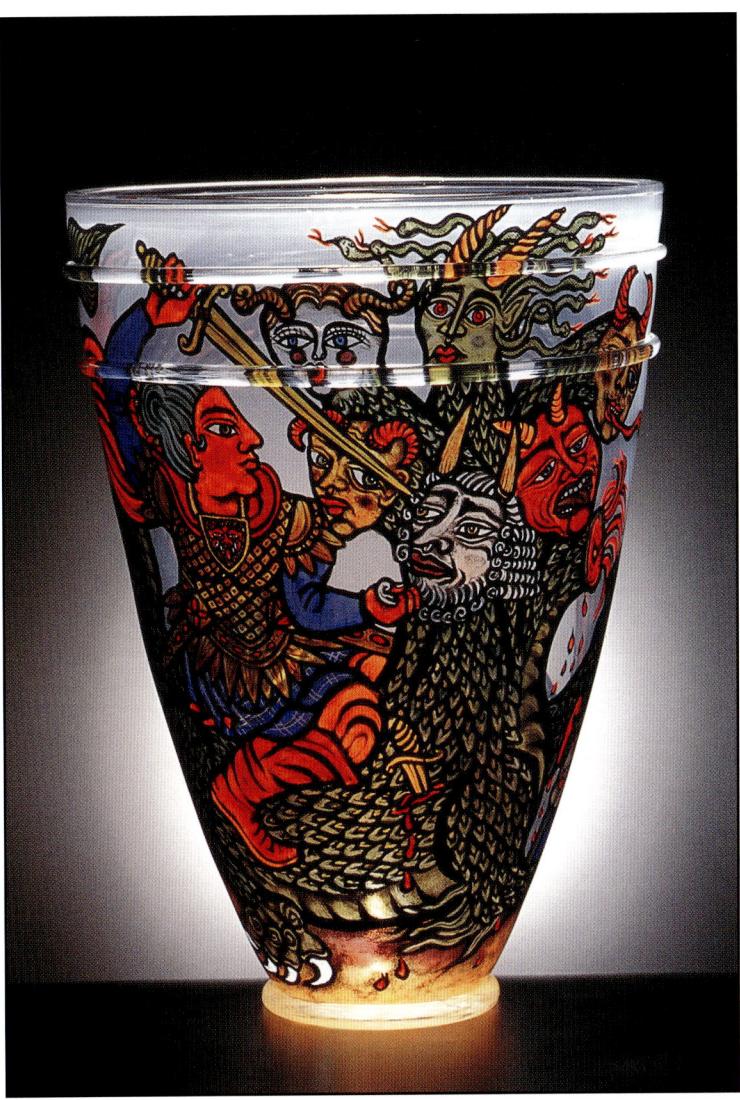

I Do Battle with My Evil "I"s on the Ground of Being, 2000, vitreous enamels reversed painted on blown glass, photo: Russell Johnson. *Photograph courtesy of the artist.*

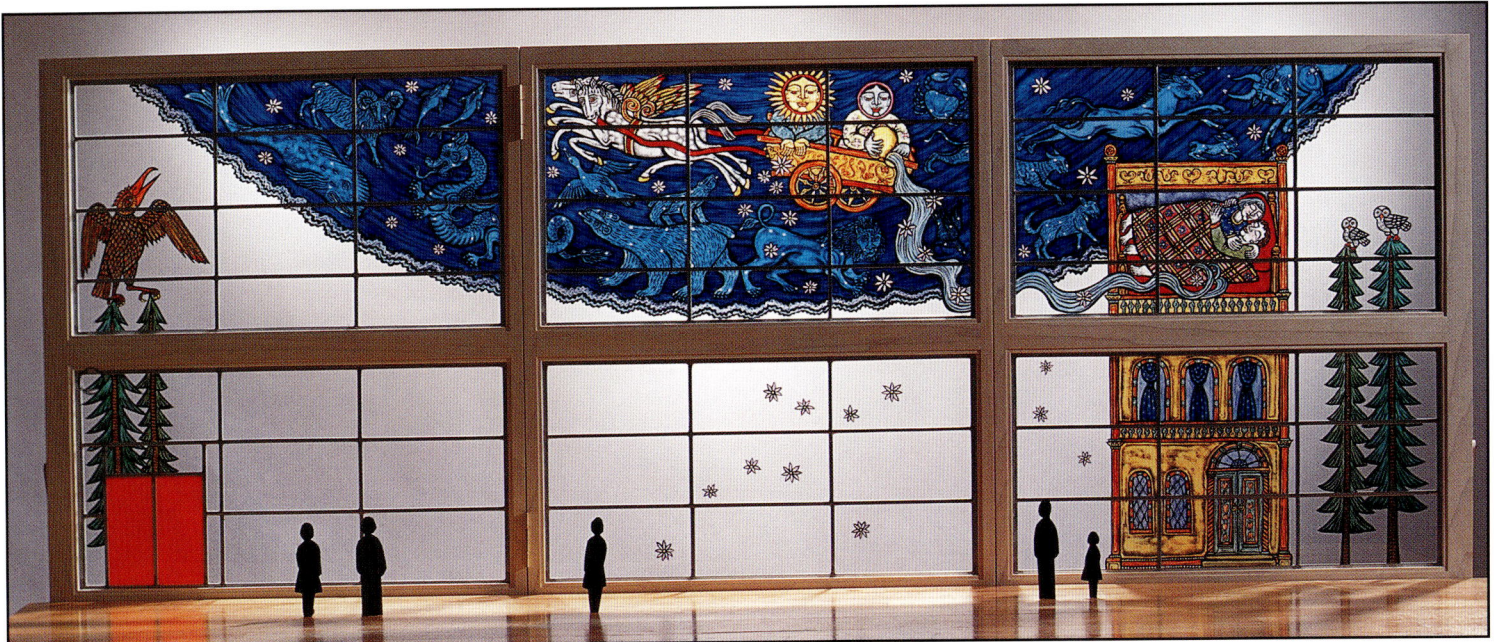

I Was Dreaming of Spirit Animals..., 2000, scale model for insulated glass window-wall for new concourse terminus at Sea-Tac International Airport, to be installed in 2004. Fabrication method for wall: Vitreous enamels painted on float glass with reverse-laminated stained glass. Fabricated at Derix Glass Studios, Taunusstein-Wehen, Germany, 2002. Commissioning agency Port of Seattle, photo: Russell Johnson. *Photograph courtesy of the artist.*

Pamina Traylor

My work expresses oppositions through form, material, structure, and finish—exploring how people learn to demonstrate power and manifest vulnerabilities and fears. I have often used wrapping or binding to depict these ideas. The use of these techniques may have been influenced by early childhood experiences, watching my Japanese grandmother as she wrapped food and gift items, taking the time and care to create something both beautiful and functional. I have since become very interested in Japanese packaging techniques and architectural forms.

I am intrigued by certain dichotomies: strength/vulnerability, protection/confinement, and freedom/need, and the way we find our point of balance between them – if, in fact, we do. My most recent body of work explores these dualities with respect to language and how we learn. I am curious about the way language and its subtext influences our values. The ideas are loosely based on writings of twentieth century psychoanalyst Jacques Lacan and his discussions of language and desire. He states that "the function of language is not to inform, but to evoke," which, for me, holds true for sculpture as well.

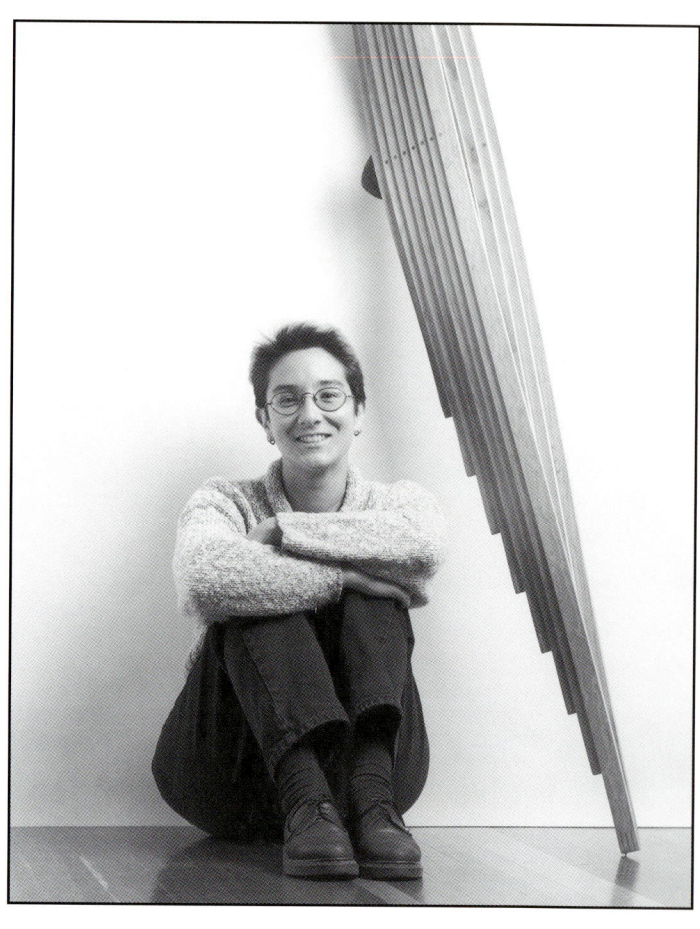

Pamina Traylor, photograph Kallan Nishimoto. *Photograph courtesy of the artist.*

Mesonephric Ridge, 1997, 14" x 32" x 18", glass, wood, twine, photo: Lee Fatheree. *Photograph courtesy of the artist.*

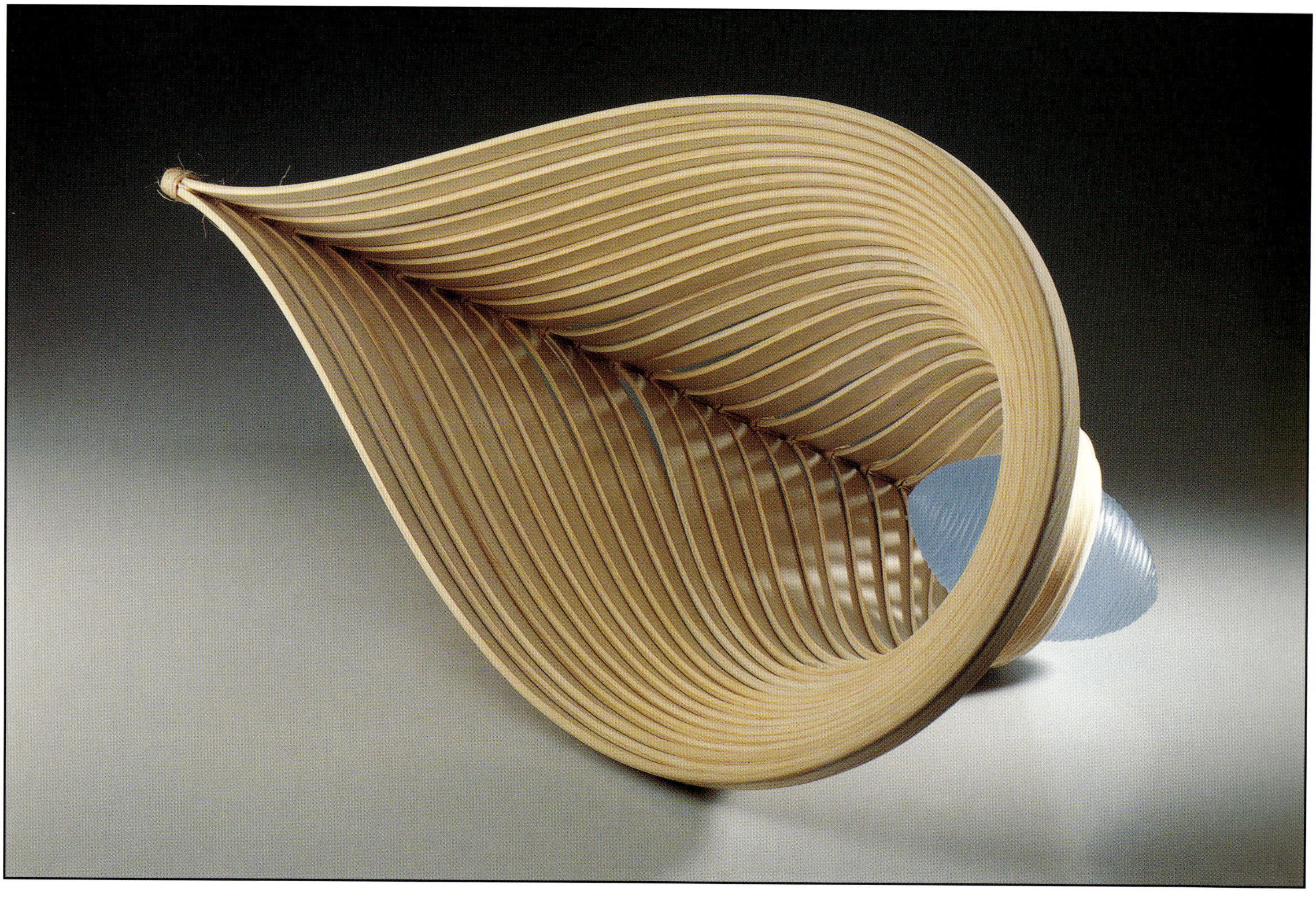

The Eighties - The Artist 173

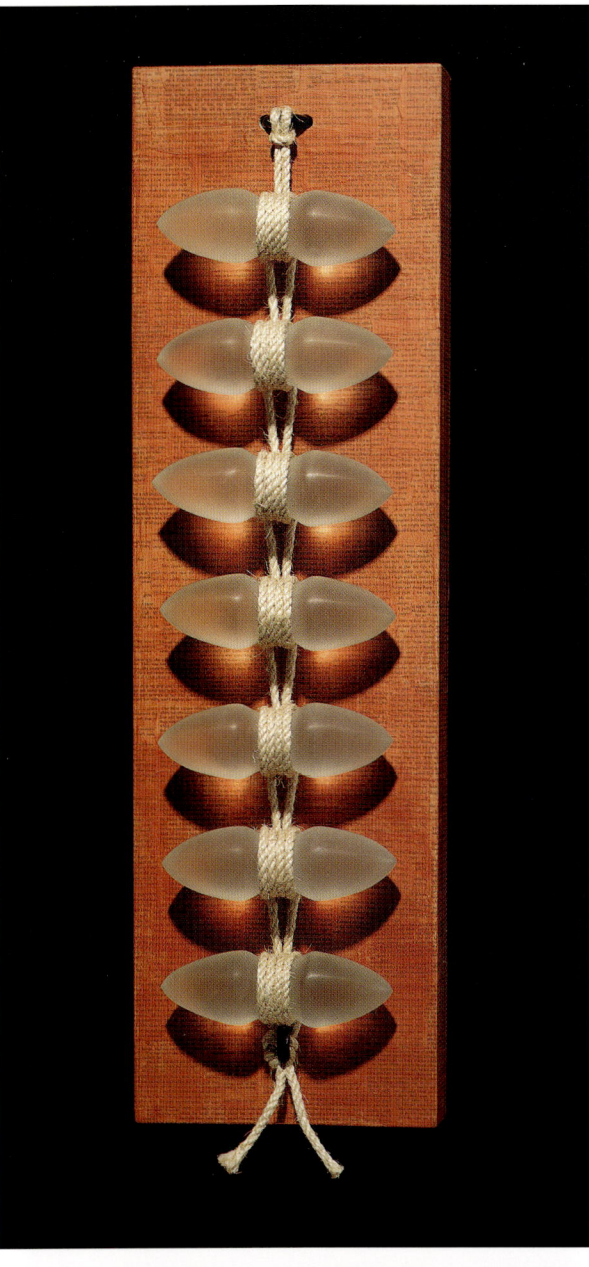

Taught, 1997, 38" x 11" x 6", glass, mixed media, photo: Kallan Nishimoto. Photograph courtesy of the artist.

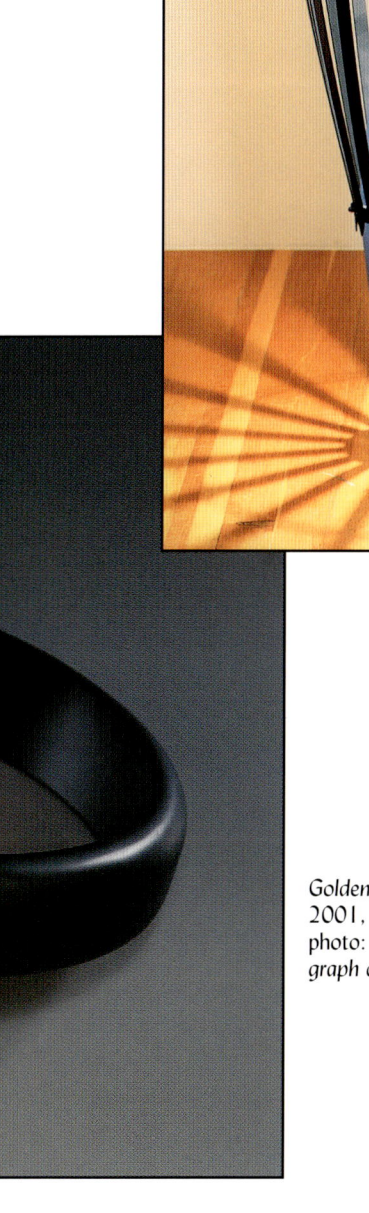

Focus, 2000, 76" x 15" x 15", Glass, steel, light, photo: Kallan Nishimoto. Photograph courtesy of the artist.

Golden Topaz (Engaging Series), 2001, 9" x 17" x 11", Glass, steel, photo: Kallan Nishimoto. Photograph courtesy of the artist.

Dana Zamecnikova

July 10, 2000

At the edge of this ugly, gray, most magnificent city, again the bread falls with the buttered sided down. Angry husband/angry dog, the Universal Black Madonna, a lovely friend dying slowly of drink: Kacka's horse is lame, mother is on the telephone, the basement floods, the computer crashes, say a prayer for the beloved white rat (not mouse). One joking, screaming woman ties it all together. The "stolen souls that catch on my line" are added like the chains around her neck. They are lost window reflections and glimpses at a journal let open to a certain page. You and I are invited to sift through the layers, hours, confrontations, and memories of her-my-your grandfather. D.Z. shows you almost everything.

© copyright Susanne K. Frantz, Prague
Catalogue: *Dana Zamechnikova*

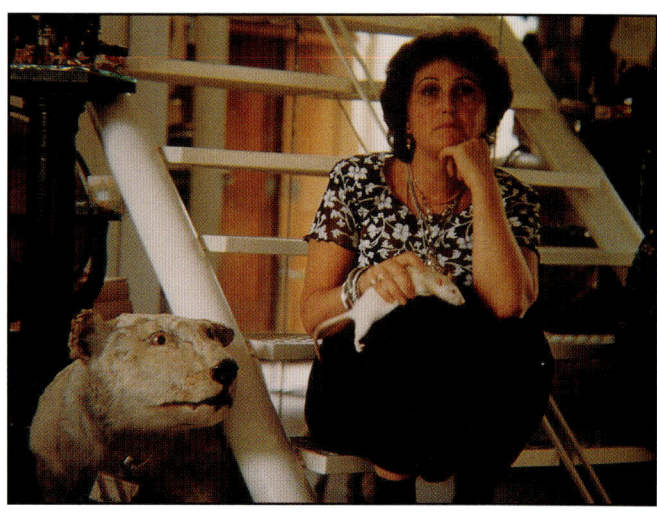

Dana Zamechnikova. *Photograph courtesy of the artist.*

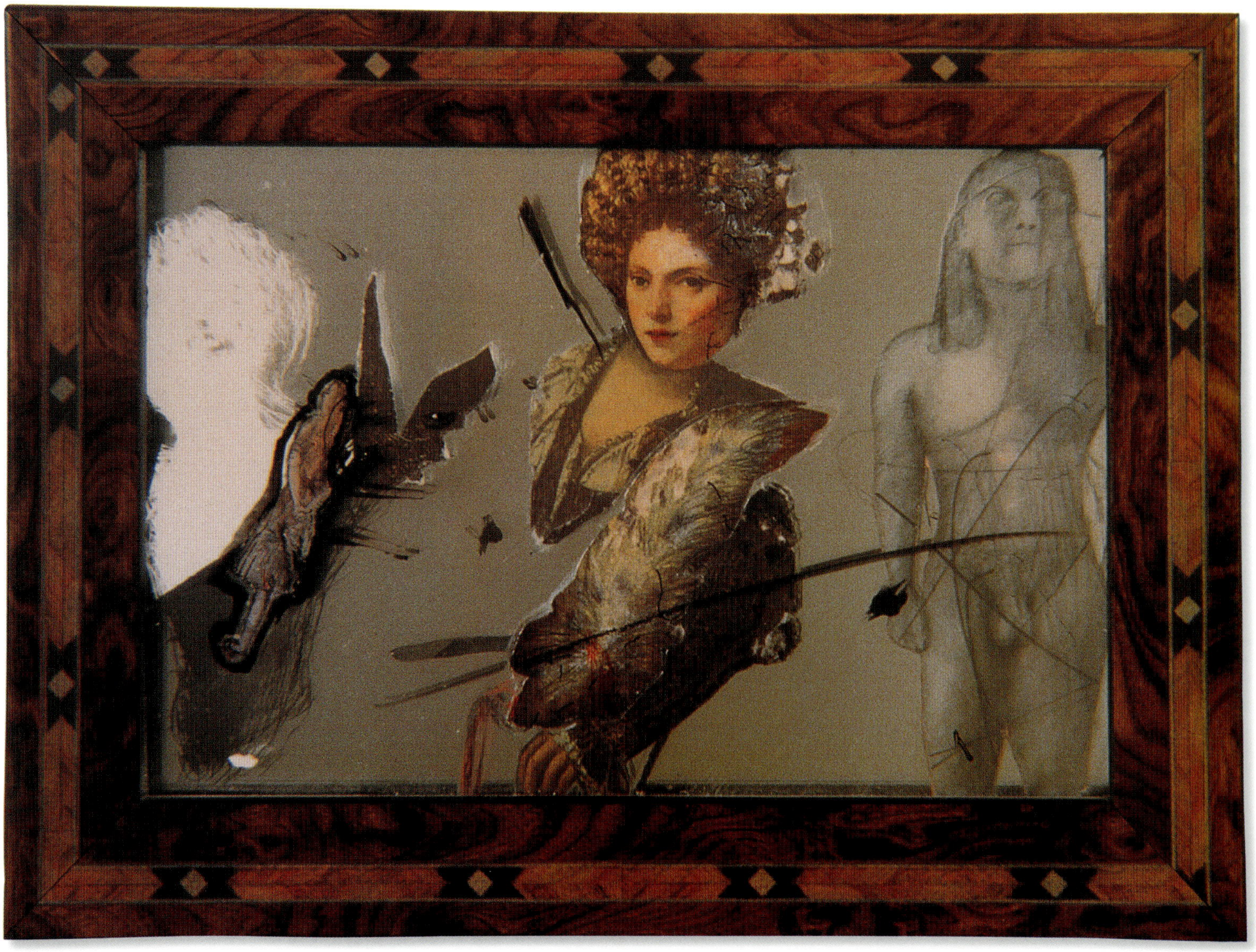

Woman Jinonice, 1995, acid etching, painting. *Photograph courtesy of the artist.*

The Eighties - The Artist   175

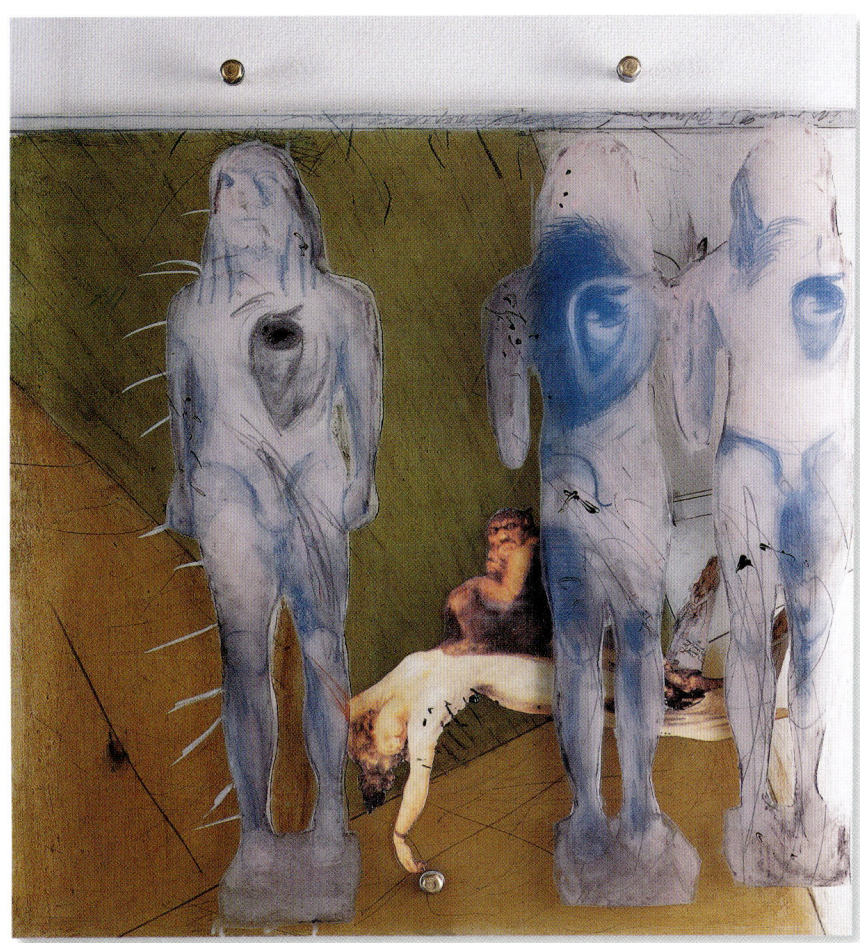

Kouros, 1995, 33 cm x 30.5 cm x 3.2 cm, acid etching, painting. *Photograph courtesy of the artist.*

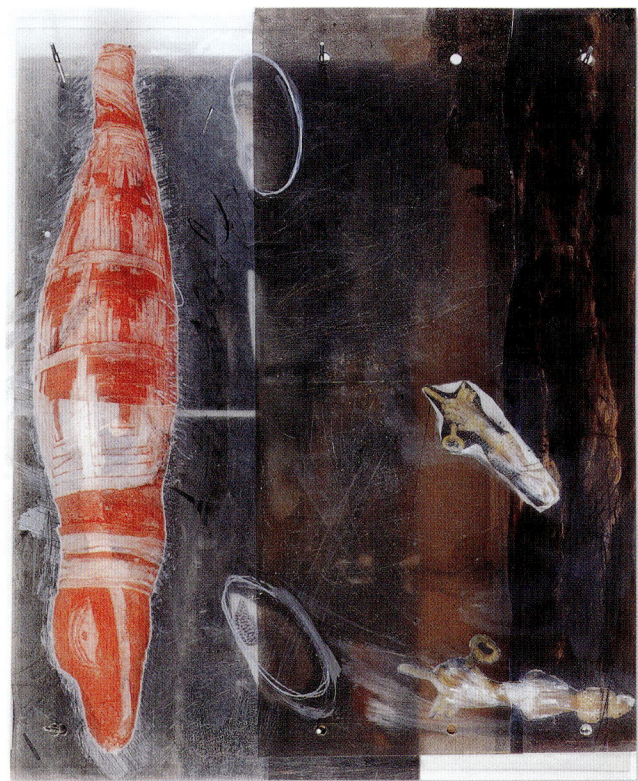

Dalmacie/Sea, 2000, 113 cm x 84 cm x 17 cm, acid etched, painted and digitally enameled glass, metal. *Photograph courtesy of the artist.*

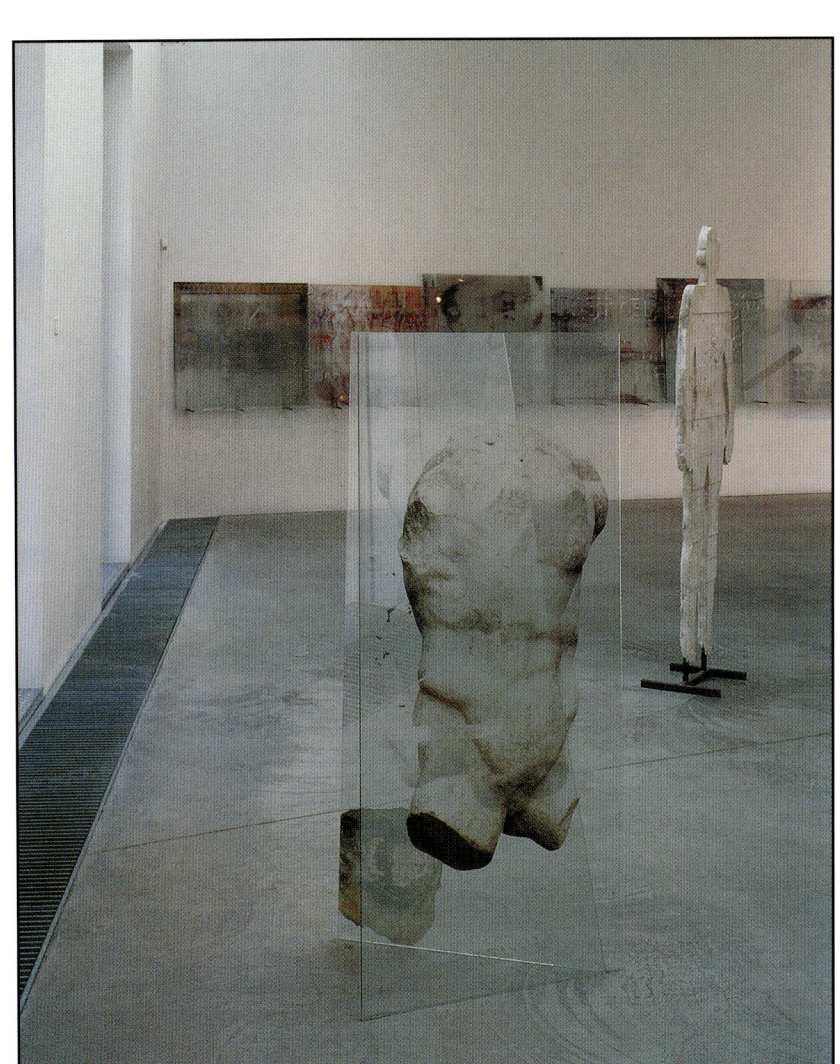

Installation, Kampa Museum, Praha, 2002. *Photograph courtesy of the artist.*

A. (Foreground) *Torso/Conversation with a dog*, 1992, 160 cm x 180 cm x 80 cm, acid etching, painting and digital print on slumping glass.

B. (Background) *Intimacy*, 2001, built from 12 objects, ca 135 cm x 110 cm x 17 cm / 135 cm x 1500 cm x 17 cm, Acid etching, painting and digital print on slumping glass, metal brackets.

The Nineties

The nineties and another war, this one called Desert Storm, was launched against Iraq and its Dictator Sadam Hussein. This war saw the largest deployment of women military personnel in American history, probably the largest group of fighting women since the Amazons of Greek mythology. Throughout the decade, the US found itself acting as arbitrator, enforcer, and peacekeeper with troops stationed in many troubled countries. At home, violence seemed to dominate the news. Meanwhile the economy was doing well; the stock market reached an all time high and the art market was growing fast. A whole new breed of savvy collectors was intent upon acquiring an excess of worldly goods including studio glass.

The concept of the Internet was introduced as early as the seventies, but it was complex and limited to a few supercomputers. By 1993, the first commercial software was available to put the web within reach of everyone. By the end of the decade, the web had reinvented just about every aspect of doing business, shopping, research, communications, and medicine. It also spurred a plethora of new visual technologies, and introduced the era of digital photography, both as a marketing tool and as an art form.

Male artists were the primary beneficiaries of the growing number of newly affluent glass collectors. The prices of glass objects skyrocketed, much like prices of paintings and sculpture did in the New York art market of the 1970s. There were more women climbing the success ladder now, but relative numbers still did not reflect the growing ratio of women working in all of the glass techniques. Just as there were women gallery owners and dealers in the crafts and fine arts like Helen Drutt and Ruth Snyderman in Philadelphia, Theo Portnoy in New York, and Linda Farris in Seattle; so were there early women glass art dealers: Sandra Ainsley from Canada, Ruth Summers from Los Angeles, Anne O'brien with Sally Hanson from DC, Kate Elliot from Seattle, Bonny Marks, Chicago, and Ellie Miller from New York. All achieved success by promoting their glass artists to the glass collecting public (some of whom were women). Many women now occupied powerful arts administrative and curatorial positions. Gay Taylor, director and curator of the Museum of American Glass since the 1970s, helped develop the museum's collection of early American glass and established the museum as a showcase for contemporary glass art. Davira Taragin, was until recently curator of nineteenth and twentieth century glass at the Toledo Museum of Art in Toledo, Ohio, until recently. Tina Oldknow not long ago replaced Suzanne Franz as curator of contemporary glass at the Corning Museum of Glass in Corning, New York.

The Glass Art Society held a series of discussion groups at its twenty-fourth annual conference "Pacific Currents" in Oakland, California. Dr. Susann Moeller reports in *Neues Glas* on the results of the session, which she chaired, held within the conference titled "Currents in Women's Glass."

Prior to the conference, the above session had occasionally been referred to as Babes in Glass. Though humorous at first glance, it bears noting that language signifies concepts and images that in this case and at second glance connote more than a humorous nickname.[1]

The focus of the discussion among the women present (about fifty) revolved around the desire for a better support system among them and the need to take responsibility for creating opportunities among themselves in addition to a need for women glass artists to take responsibility for creating opportunities for themselves and to campaign for equal access to grant monies. In the mid-nineties, when this session took place, the glass ghetto was still dominated by men who set the mark for exhibition policies and aesthetic criteria as well as technical standards. Today we have seen enormous growth in attitudes and opinions away from the gender bias of the past. Women are getting many more exhibition opportunities and teaching positions in universities affording them the recognition they deserve. The glass ceiling, still evident to some extent in big business, seems to be slumping a bit in the glass world.

By the last decade of the twentieth century, schools were producing MFA's in almost every discipline and specialty you could imagine, including glass art. During the 1980s many more women were hired by schools than in previous decades to teach glass courses, a few were chosen to head or chair a department. By the early '90s the number of women faculty and students was equal to men, if not greater in many universities. In this new millennium even more women are securing top positions in important glass schools and universities. Beth Hylan, an important asset of the Rakow Library of the Corning Museum of Glass and an important help to many glass artists over the years, has even caught the glass making fever.

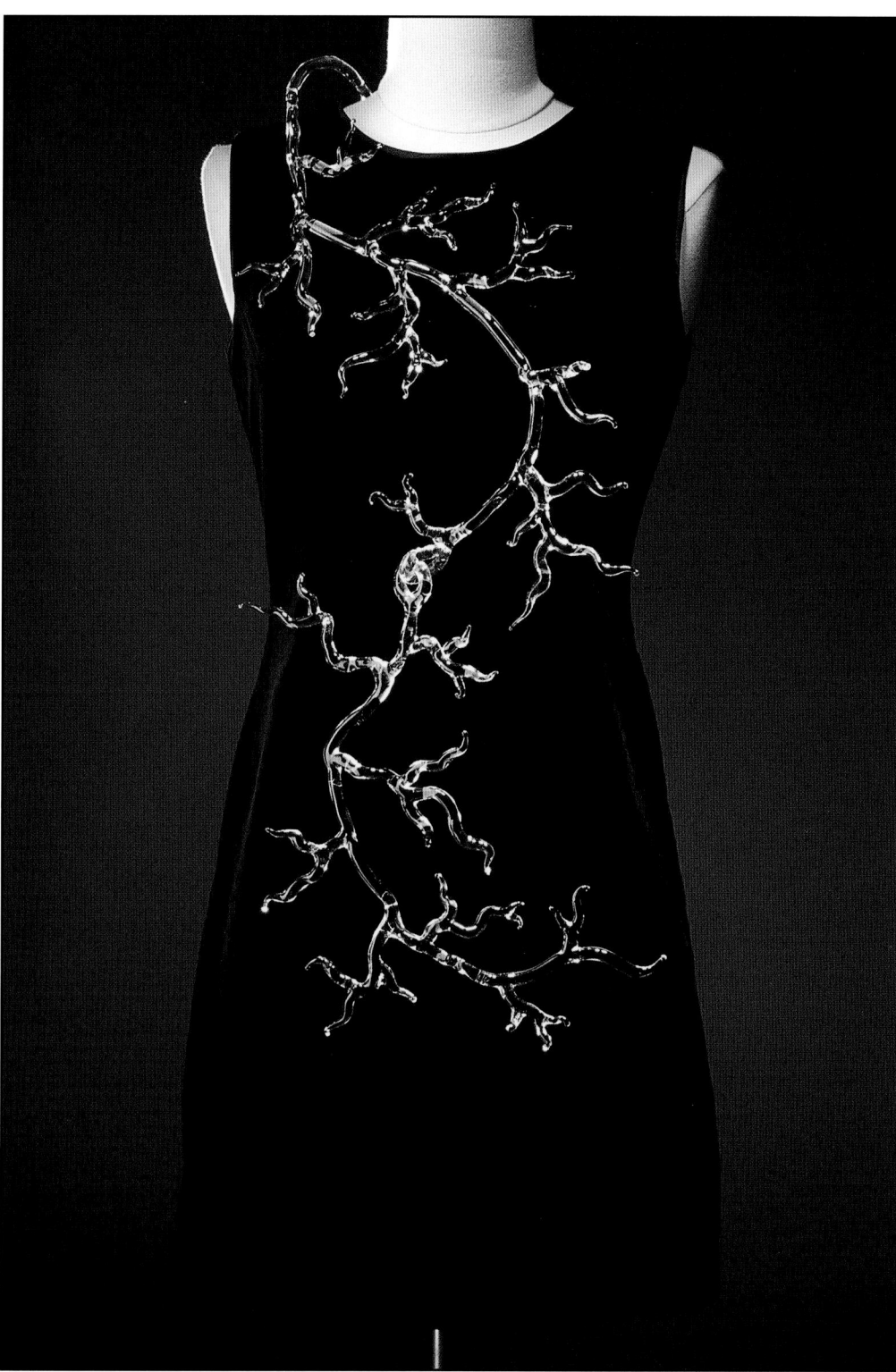

Beth Hylan, *Branches*, 2001, (glass dress), borosilicate glass. Lamp-worked on velvet dress. *Photograph courtesy of the artist.*

Another development belonging to the decade of the nineties is the growth of independent glass schools, many founded or directed by women, some of whom are also accomplished glass artists. The Studio of the Corning Museum of Glass in Corning, New York, was developed and is now directed by Amy Schwartz. Kathleen Mulcahy raised three million dollars to found and house the Pittsburgh Center for Glass. Pilchuck has had several women directors and currently Pike Powers is artistic director. A new glass school in Turkey, The Glass Furnace, is directed by a woman, Lale Basirir, who is currently learning to blow glass.

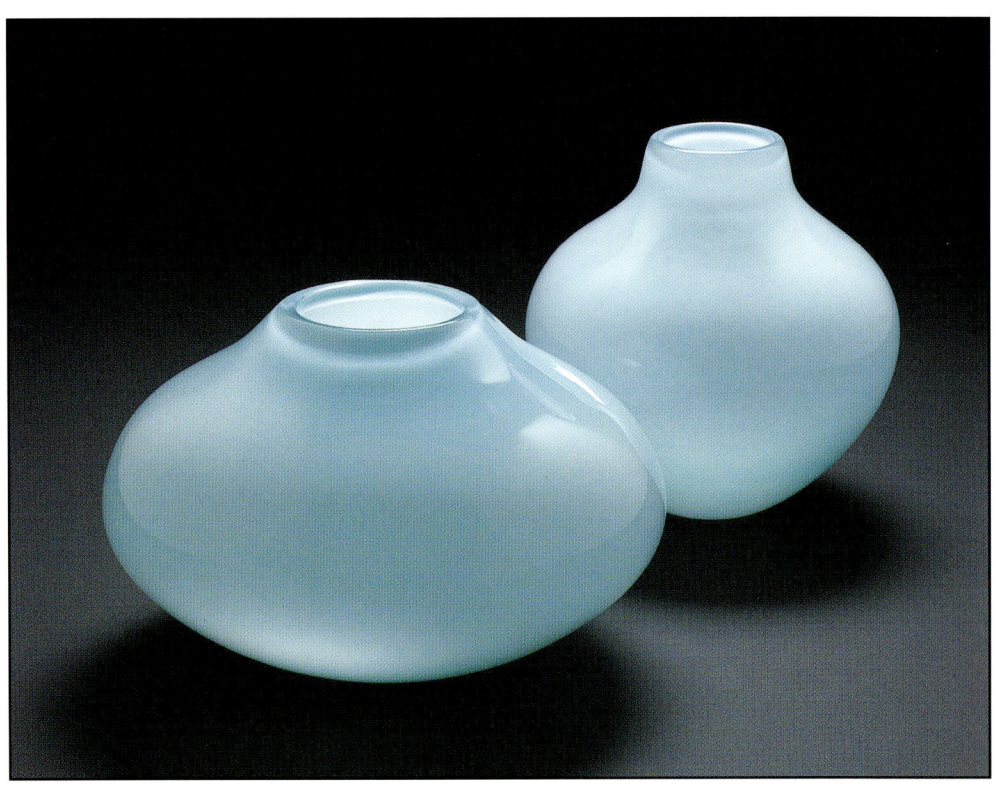

Amy Schwartz, Vases, 2001, assorted sizes, blown glass. *Photograph courtesy of the artist.*

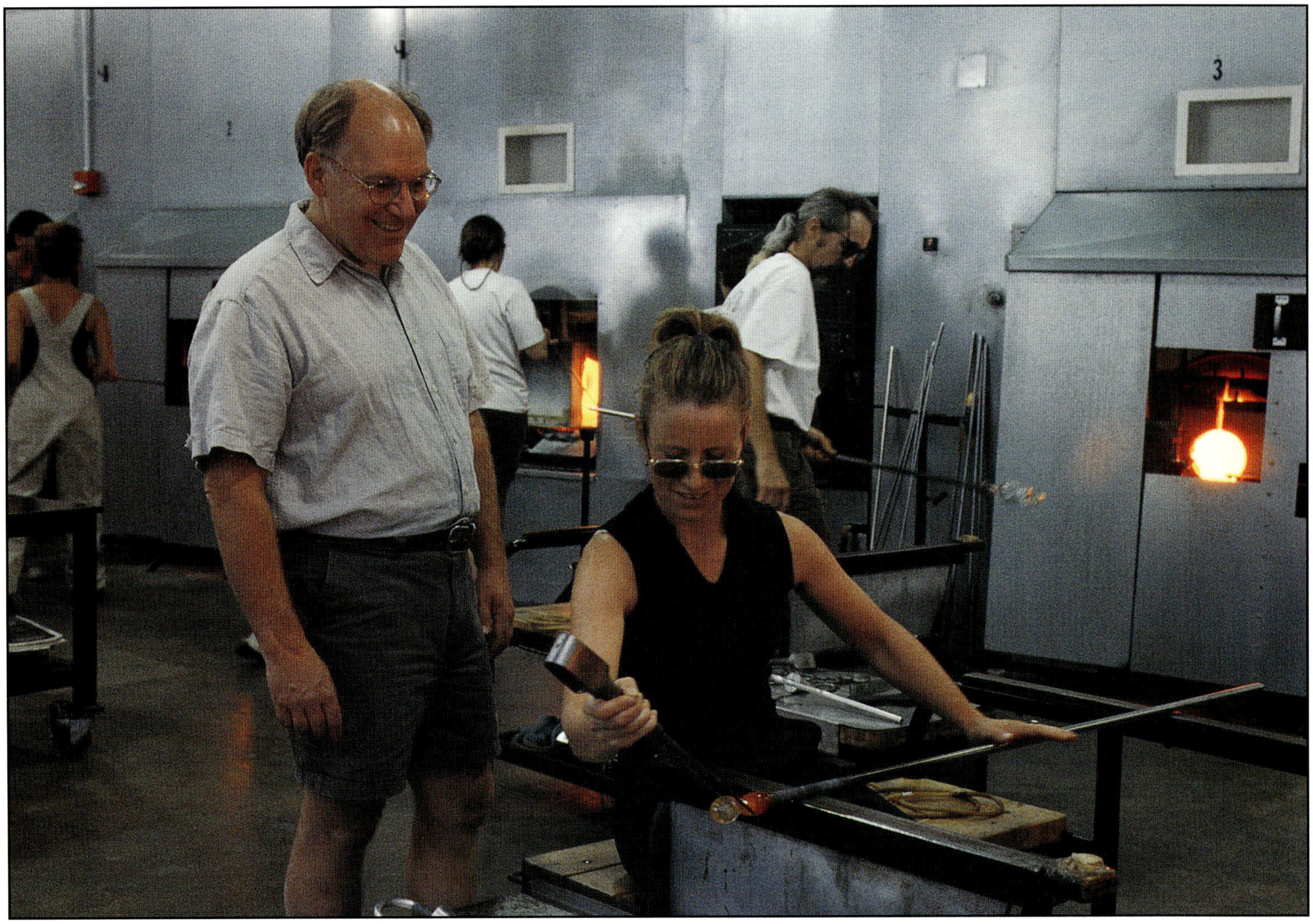

Amy Schwartz, Head of the Studio: Bill Gudenrath teaching an in-depth Venetian glass blowing class to a student. *Photograph courtesy of the artist.*

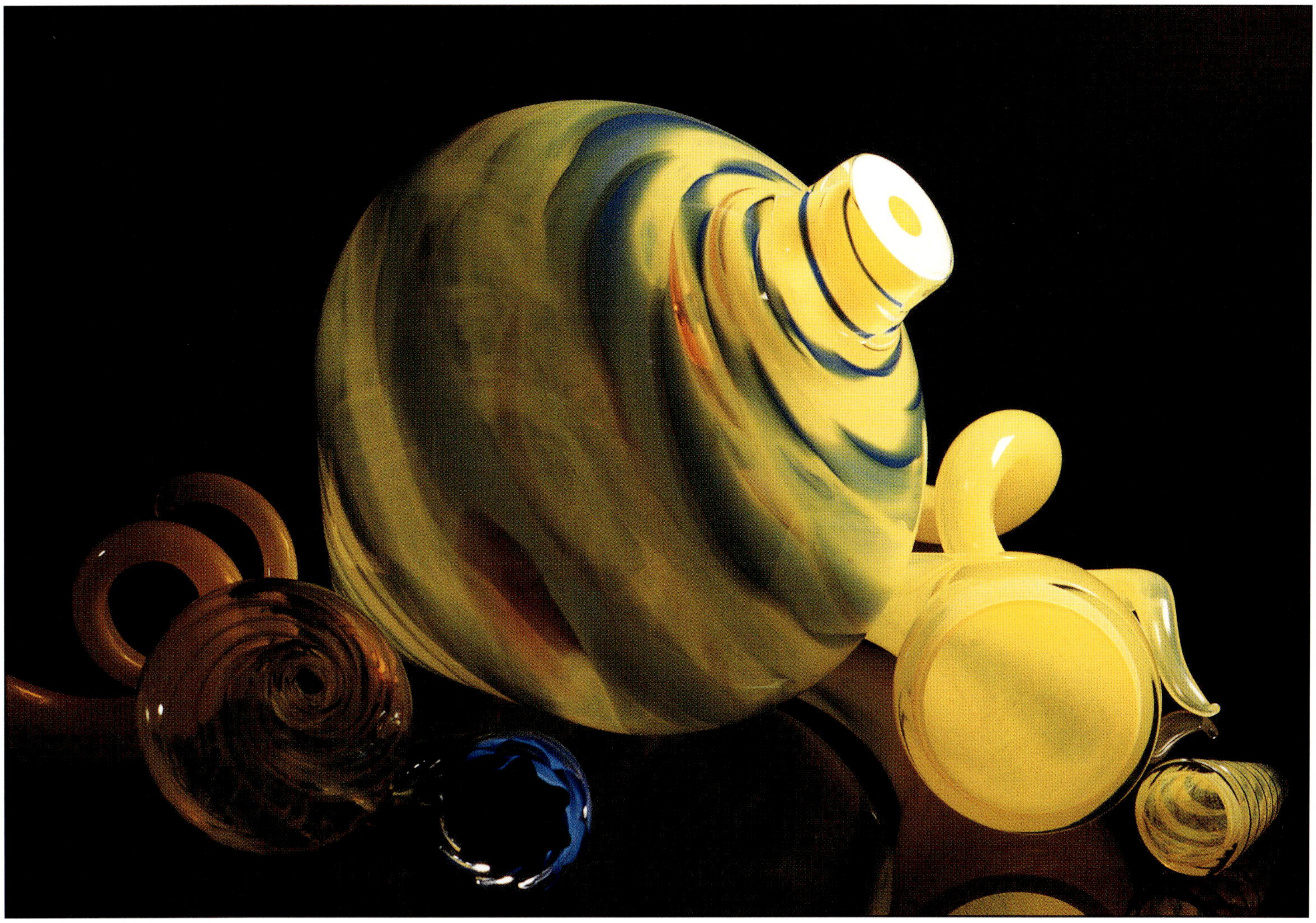

The Nineties 179

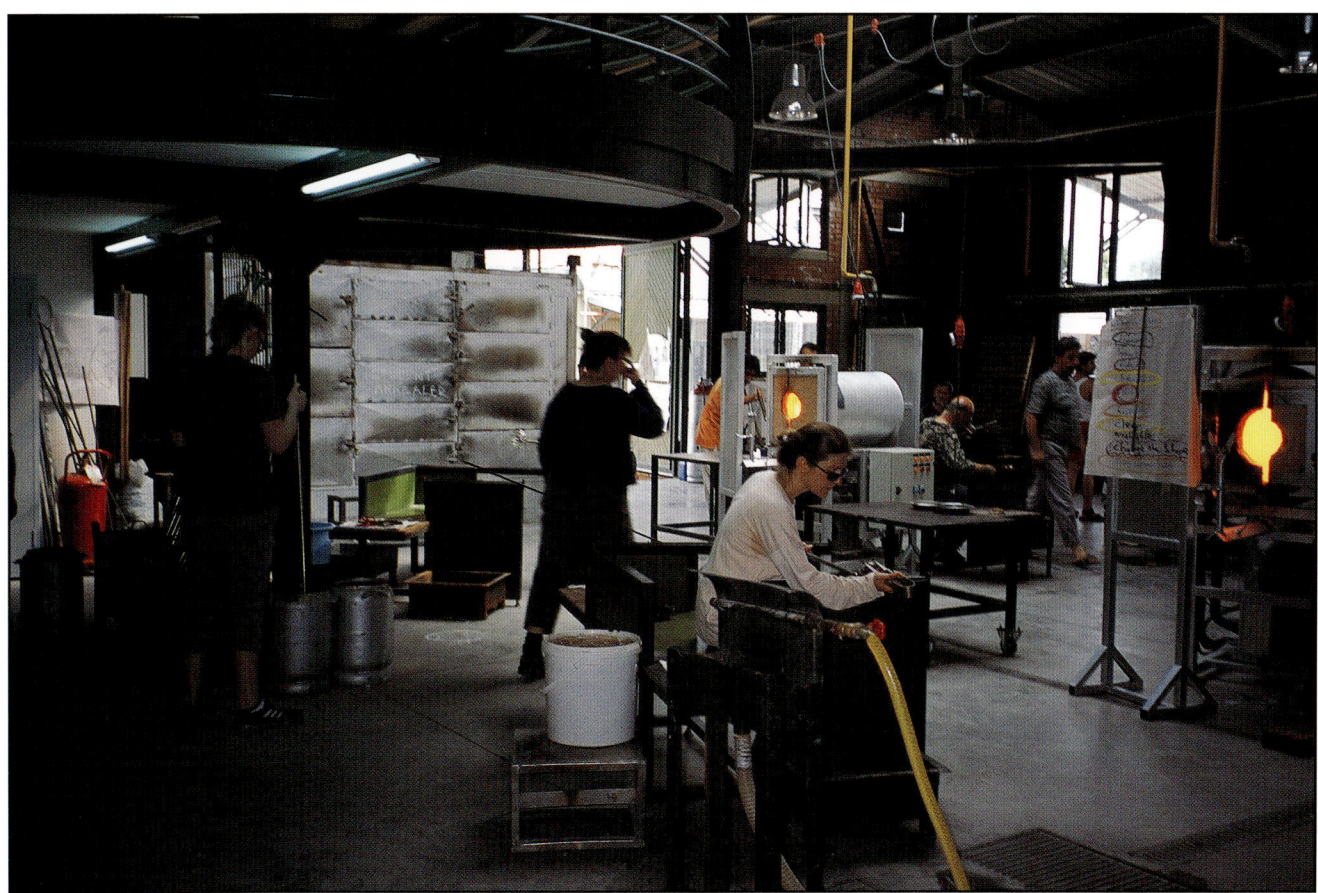

Kathleen Mulcahy, Golden Spinner Group, 24" x 30" x 24", Commission for the Heinz History Center. Photograph courtesy of the artist.

Lale Basirir, blowing glass, The Glass Furnace School, Istanbul, Turkey.

Today there are a few foundations granting money exclusively to women artists. In Philadelphia, The Leeway Foundation, established in 1993 by Linda Alter to support women in the arts, has a sculpture/crafts category of awards that rotates with other art disciplines every few years. Stained glass artist Judith Schaechter was the recipient of an award in 1999. The Jutta Cuny Franz Foundation was established in 1983 in her daughter Jutta Cuny's memory. Its biennial awards are presented to a select group of young women under forty who have achieved a level of excellence and whose work falls into the realm of fine arts. Maria Lugossy was the first to be honored.

Women today have many opportunities to apply for and get grants, residencies, and fellowships. I believe for the first time in history women's artwork is judged for its merit alone. Glass galleries are beginning to show many more under-recognized and emerging women artists.

During the early nineties there were a number of thematic group exhibitions featuring the work of women. Amy Morgan, of Morgan Contemporary Glass, a relative newcomer to the list of Glass Galleries operated by women presented as one of her first exhibitions a show titled "For, By and About Women." Dr Helmut Ricke curated an exhibition in 2000 in collaboration with the Jutta Cuny-Franz Foundation titled "Spirited Approach: Women Glass Artists Today" at the Kunstmuseum in Dusseldorf, Germany. Many fine art galleries, including some top New York galleries, are now showing art made from glass. In greater numbers, critics, curators, and museums are also paying attention to artists who use glass.

During the 1980s Pilchuck Glass School invited a number of established artists not familiar with glass to explore glass blowing with the help of gaffers (glass blowers). The project was successful and as glass making can be very addictive, those that tried once usually came back for more. Many of the early participants returned to Pilchuck or found other opportunities to incorporate glass in their work. Pilchuck's artist residencies were not limited to women although women seemed to be especially attracted to the material. Maya Lin, the architect and sculptor who created the Viet Nam Memorial in Washington DC, was a Pilchuck artist in residence in 1994. She had used glass in some of her public art installations. When the Wexner Center for the Arts in Columbus, Ohio, offered her a visual arts residency in 1993 to create a site-specific work, she chose to fill spaces in several areas outside the building with shattered glass. *Groundswell* is made up of forty-three tons of shattered safety glass, the type of fragments you find scattered all over sidewalks in urban areas.

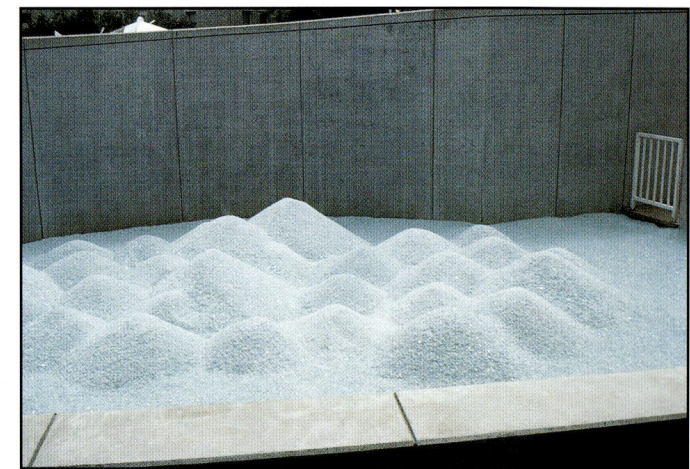

Maya Lin, *Groundswell*, 1992-1993, tempered safety glass, Permanent Installation, commissioned by the Wexner Center Foundation, Installation view at the Wexner Center for the Arts, photo: Darnell Lautt. *Photograph courtesy of the artist.*

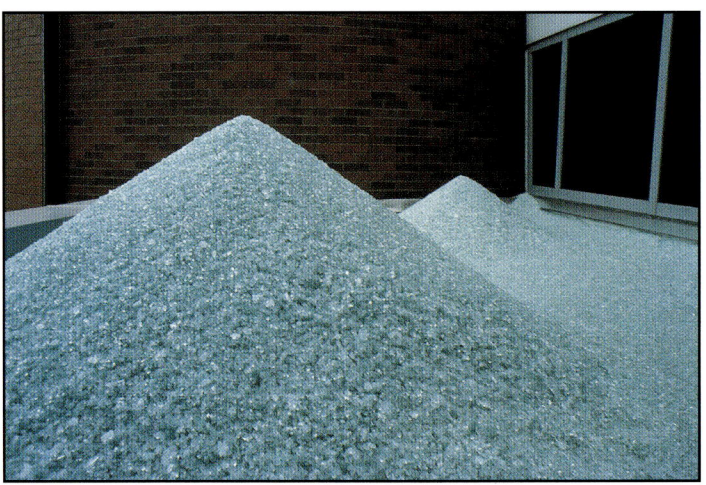

Maya Lin, *Groundswell*, detail.

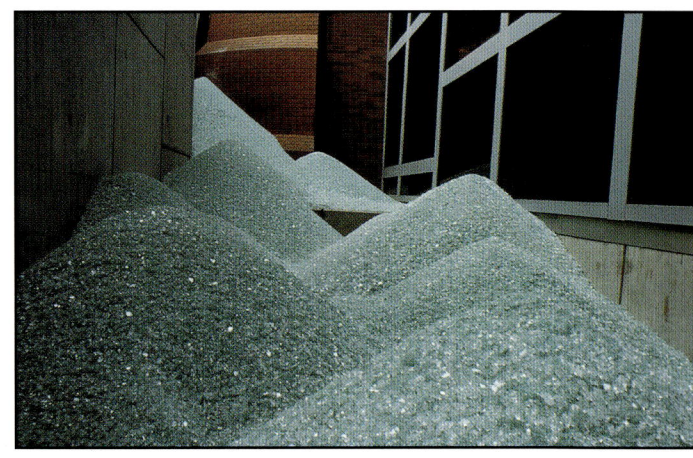

Maya Lin, *Groundswell*, detail.

Kiki Smith was invited to Pilchuck in 1993 and returned again in 1994. She uses glass to express a concept or an idea and where the glass comes from or who makes it has no consequence.

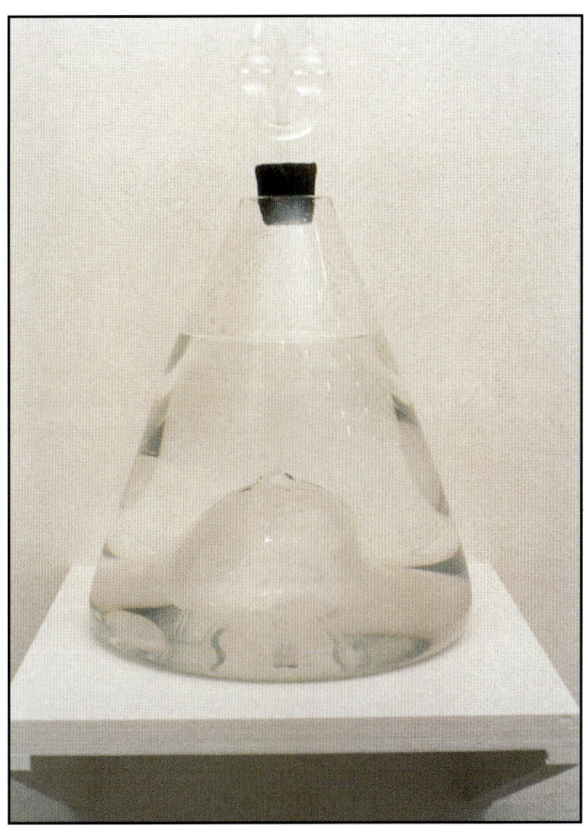

Kiki Smith, *Untitled* (breast jar), 1989, Glass, 18" h. *Photograph courtesy of the artist.*

Kiki Smith, *Nests*, 3" x 6.5" to 5" x 8" x 8", 10 units each approximately, Installation dimensions variable. Photographed by Ellen Page Wilson. *Courtesy of Pace Wildenstein.*

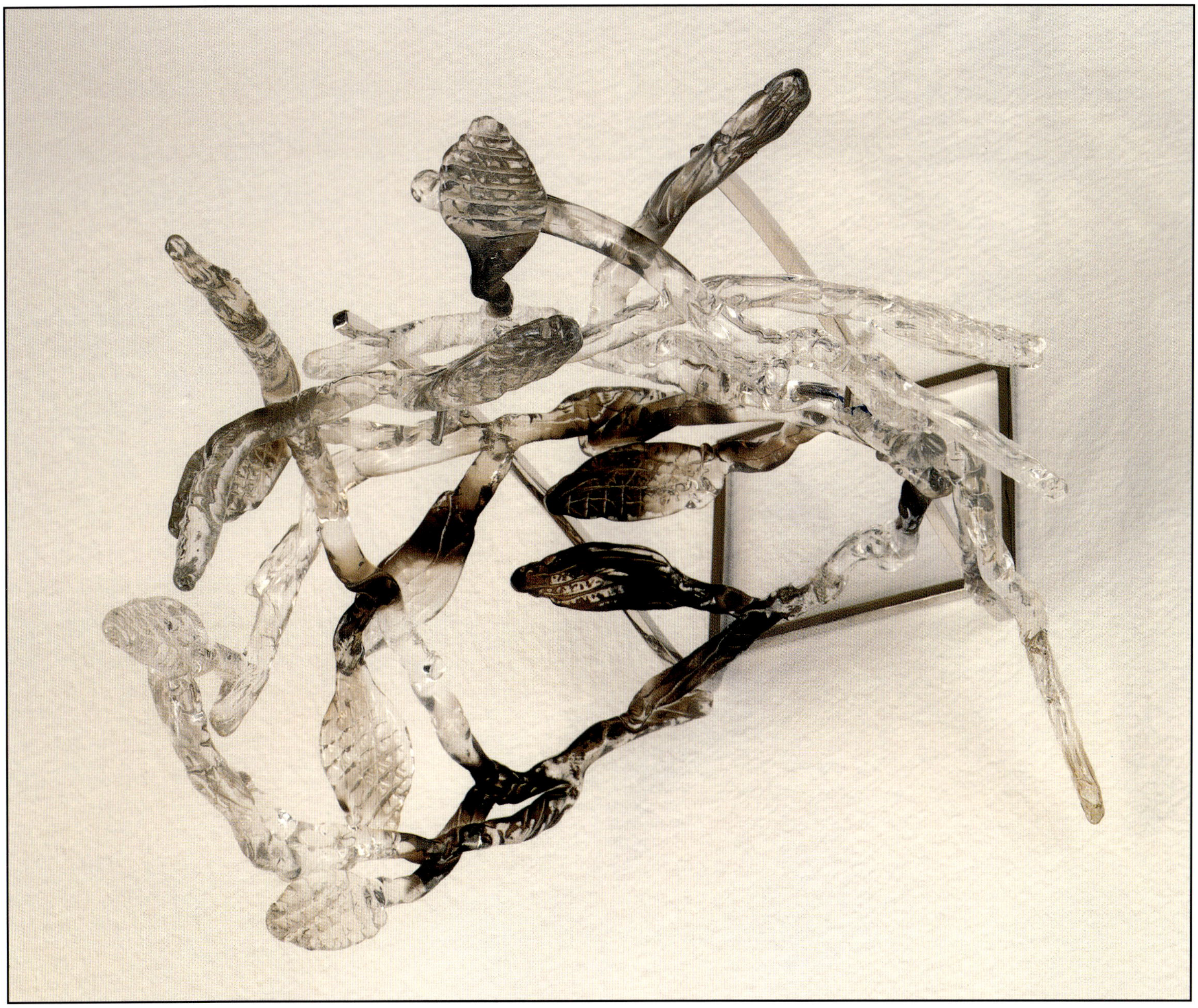

Other venues encourage artists to explore glass. CIRVA, an international research center for glass and the visual arts in Marseilles, France, invited Betty Woodman, a celebrated potter, to come and create a body of work in glass. Her exploration of the material and the realization that she would not be able to model her shapes directly allowed something quite different from her usual manipulated contours and multi-colored glazes to emerge. While keeping with the forms of her ceramic work, she chose to concentrate on the blown vase as her primary form and use the contrast between transparency and translucency. "Drawing on the transparent body of the vase motifs, which then sandblasted, become translucent and play with the pattern of the handles in translucent *pate de verre*. Betty Woodman engages in a game of deconstruction and reconstruction of the shape, which in essence remains equivalent to her pictorial treatment of ceramic."[2] A team of gaffers that included Jeff Zimmerman and Lino Tagliapietra blew the vase forms. The handles were cast.

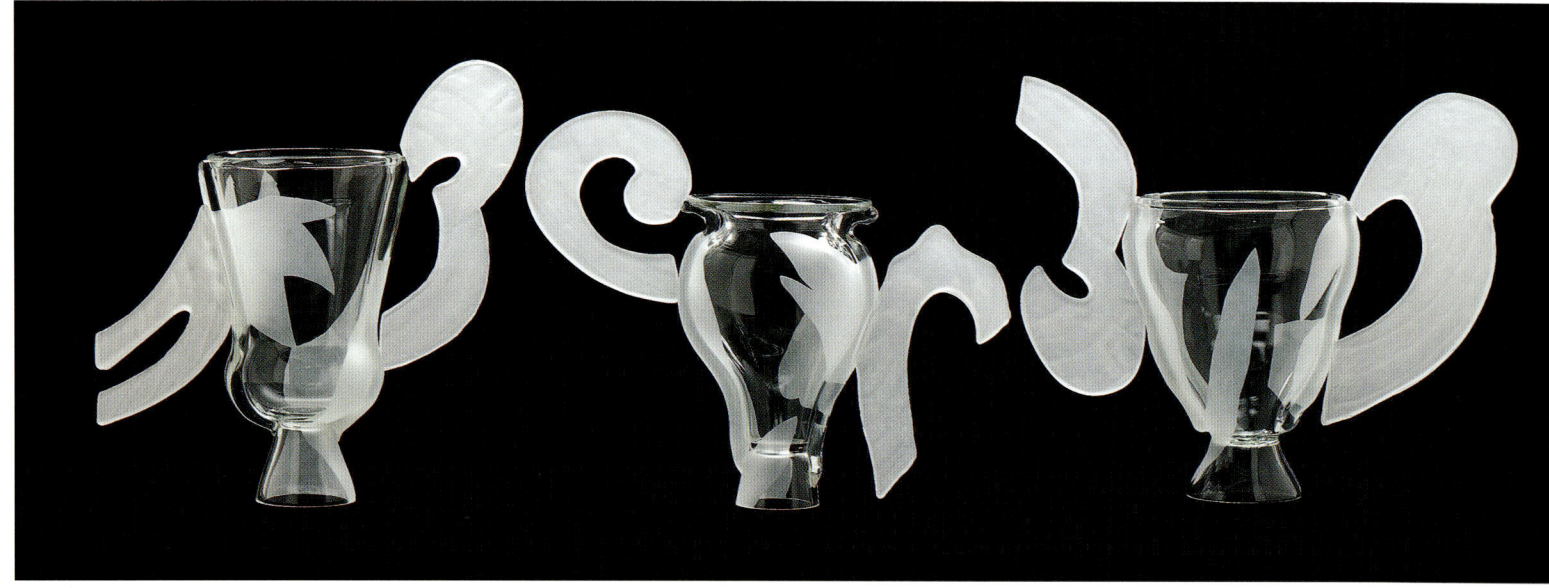

Betty Woodman, *Triptych B*, 1993-1996, 52.5 cm OH, glass: blown, applied, assembled, sandblasted. Photograph courtesy of The Corning Museum of Glass, Gift of the Ben W. Heinman family, 98.3.15.

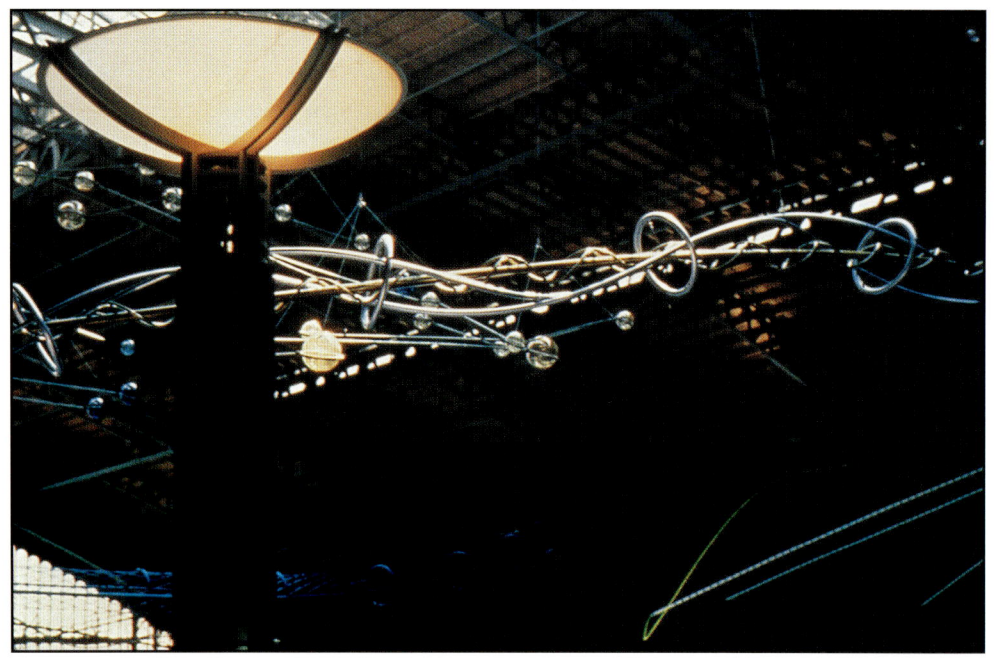

Judy Pfaff, *Cirque, Cirque*, 1995, Installation Pennsylvania Convention Center, 250' x 210' x 20', aluminum, steel, automobile lacquer, and glass. Photograph by Larry Salese. *Courtesy of the Pennsylvania Convention Center.*

Judy Pfaff, a high profile New York artist has been combining materials with an irreverent attitude since 1975 when her work was shown at the Whitney Biennial. She was a Pilchuck artist in residence in 1989, 1990, and 1991 and has used glass in her large-scale public installations since then. In the early nineties she was invited by the Pennsylvania Convention Center Authority in Philadelphia to submit a proposal for the new convention center.

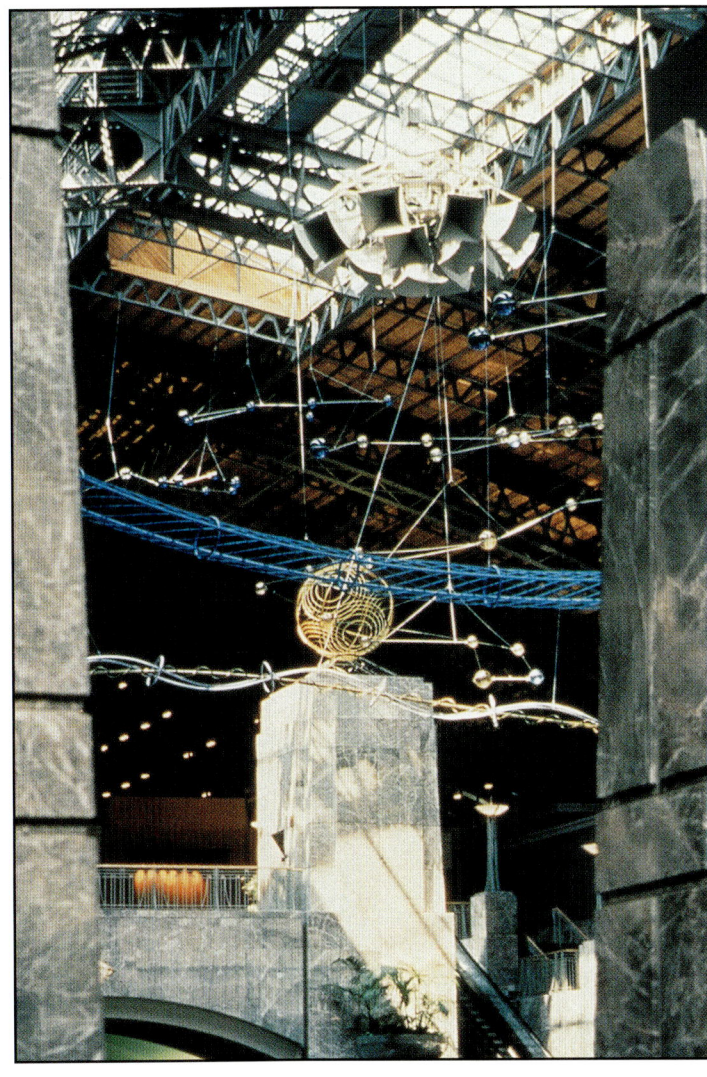

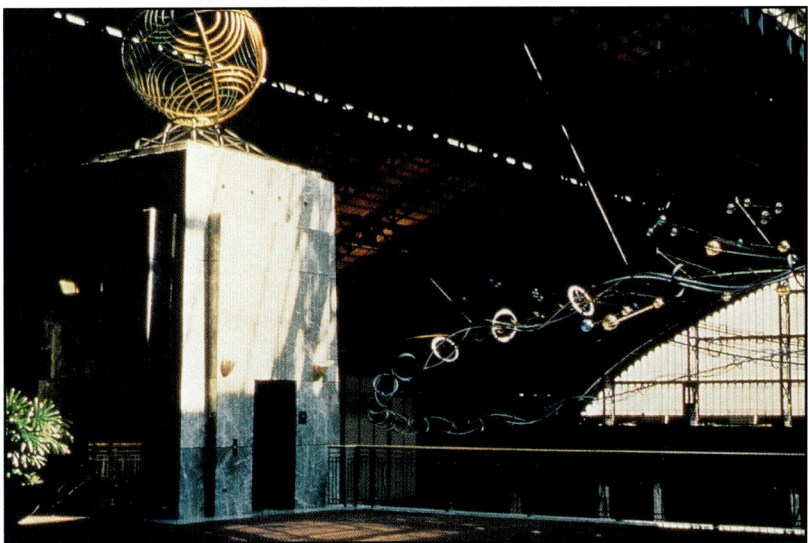

Judy Pfaff, *Cirque, Cirque*, 1995, Installation Pennsylvania Convention Center, 250' x 210' x 20', aluminum, steel, automobile lacquer, and glass. Photograph by Larry Salese. *Courtesy of the Pennsylvania Convention Center.*

Judy Pfaff, *Cirque, Cirque*, 1995, Installation Pennsylvania Convention Center, 250' x 210' x 20', aluminum, steel, automobile lacquer, and glass. Photograph by Larry Salese. *Courtesy of the Pennsylvania Convention Center.*

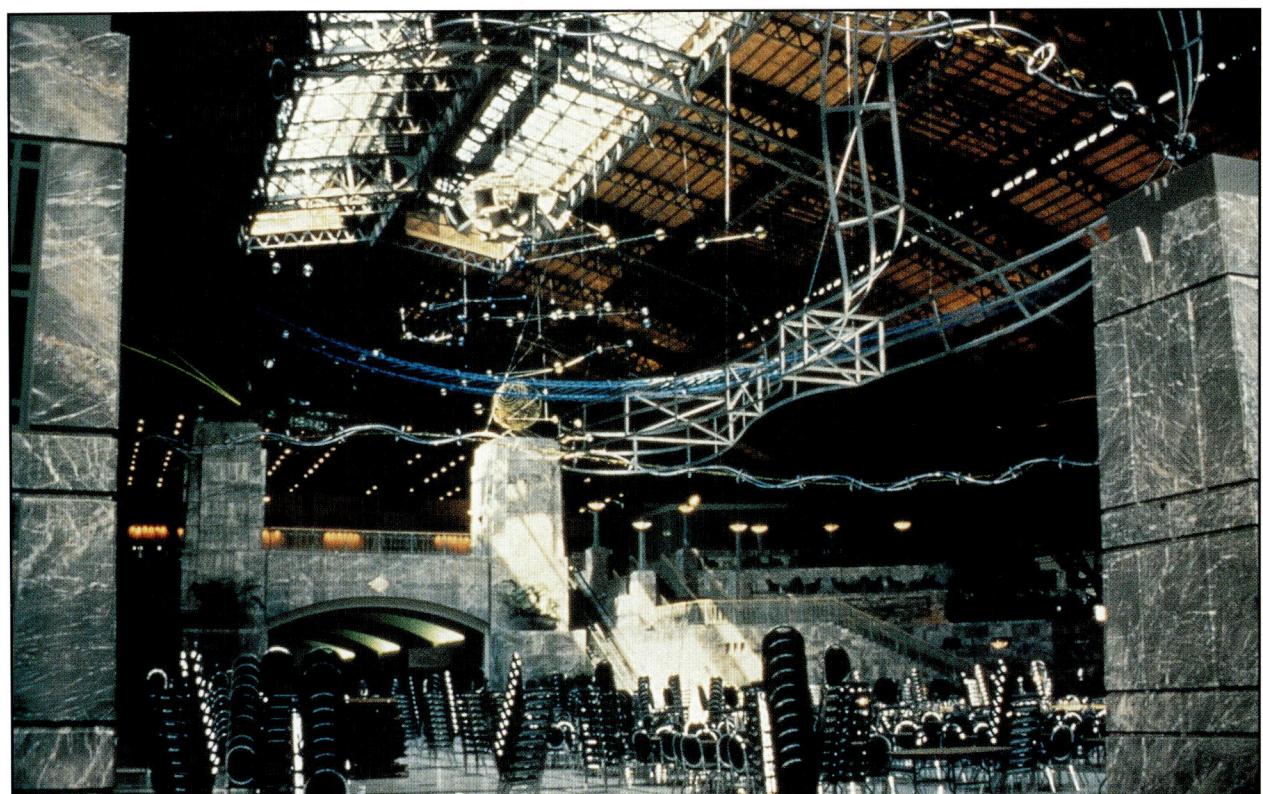

Judy Pfaff, *Cirque, Cirque*, 1995, Installation Pennsylvania Convention Center, 250' x 210' x 20', aluminum, steel, automobile lacquer, and glass. Photograph by Larry Salese. *Courtesy of the Pennsylvania Convention Center.*

184　The Nineties

Lynda Benglis has always followed her own vision and incorporated many craft materials in her work. Her hands on approach to art making leads her to use whatever means required to achieve her end result. Critic Mathew Kangas questions in a *Glass Magazine* article about her work, "With all her subsequent interest in ceramics and glass, is it time to re-categorize Lynda Benglis as a closet craft artist?"[3]

Louise Bourgeois, the grand dame of women artists, often uses the fragility of glass. Once glass is cracked, damage can never be hidden. She feels this fragility is analogous to human relationships. When there is a break, it remains there forever. She also likes the transparency of glass because nothing is hidden and there are no secrets.

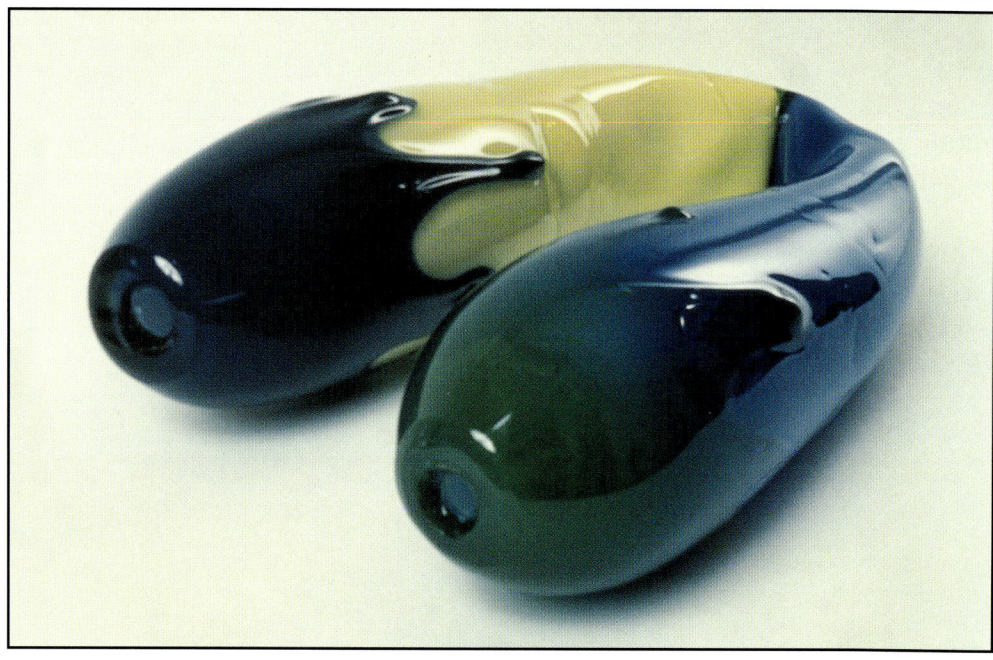

Lynda Benglis, *Praha*, 1997, 5.5" x 20" x 13", Unique hand-blown sculpture made at the Ajeto Syudio, The Czech Republic. *Photo courtesy Dorfman Projects, New York.*

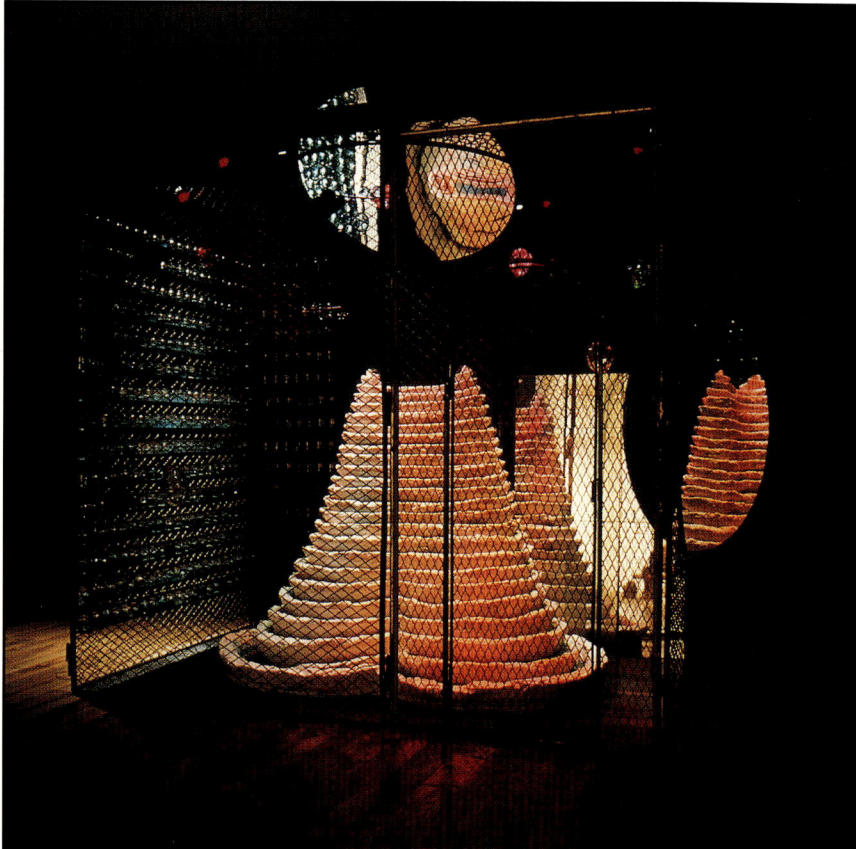

Louise Bourgeois, *Cell XV (For Turner)*, 2000, Steel, Painted Aluminum, Mirrors, Glass, Water, and Electrical Light, 108" x 120" x 68". *Courtesy Cheim & Read, New York, Photo: Christopher Burke, or, Colin Harvey.*

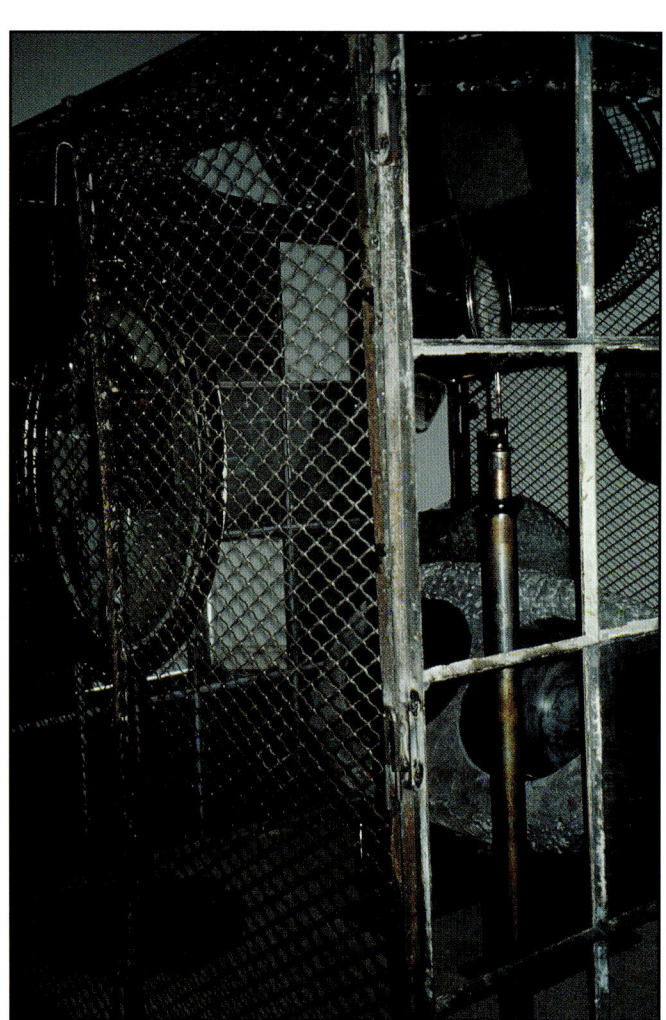

Louise Bourgeois, *Cell (eyes and mirrors)*, 1989-93, 93" x 83" x 86". Collection Tate Gallery, London, *Courtesy Cheim & Read, New York, Photo: Peter Bellamy.*

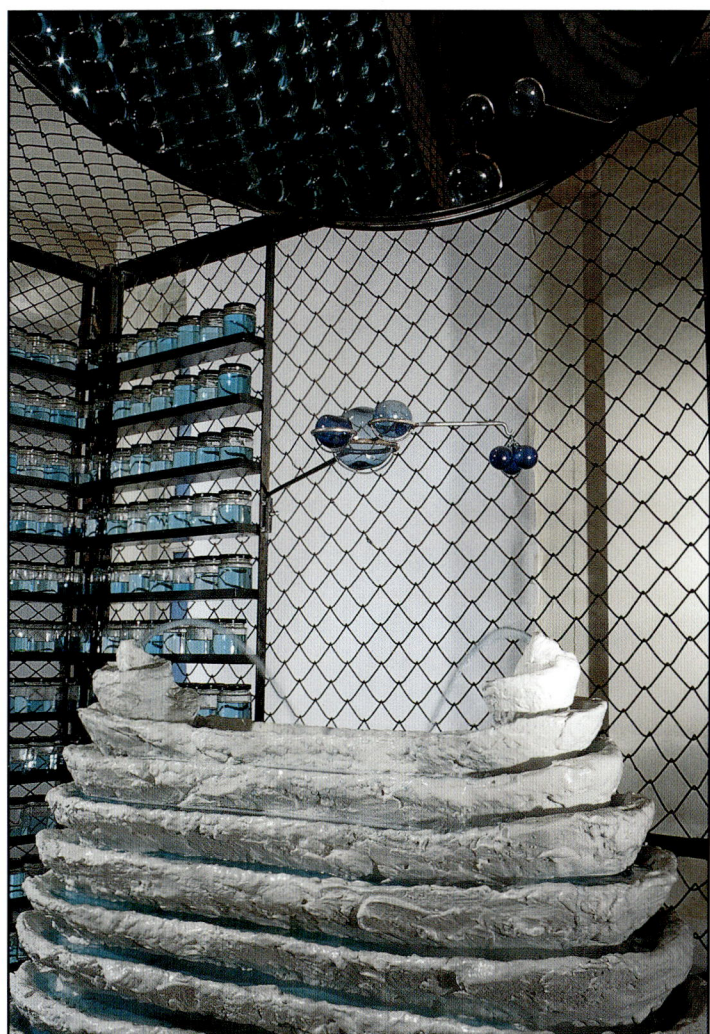

Louise Bourgeois, *Cell XV (For Turner)*, 2000, detail.

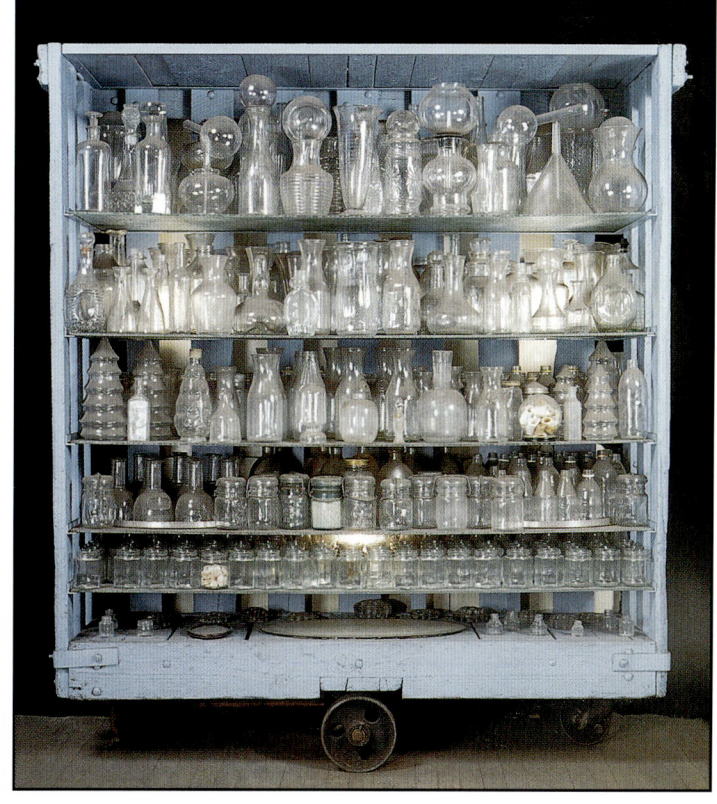

Louise Bourgeois, *Le Defi IV*, 1994, 73.5" x 65" x 24", Painted wood, glass, mirror, and mixed media. *Courtesy Cheim & Read, New York, Photo: Christopher Burke.*

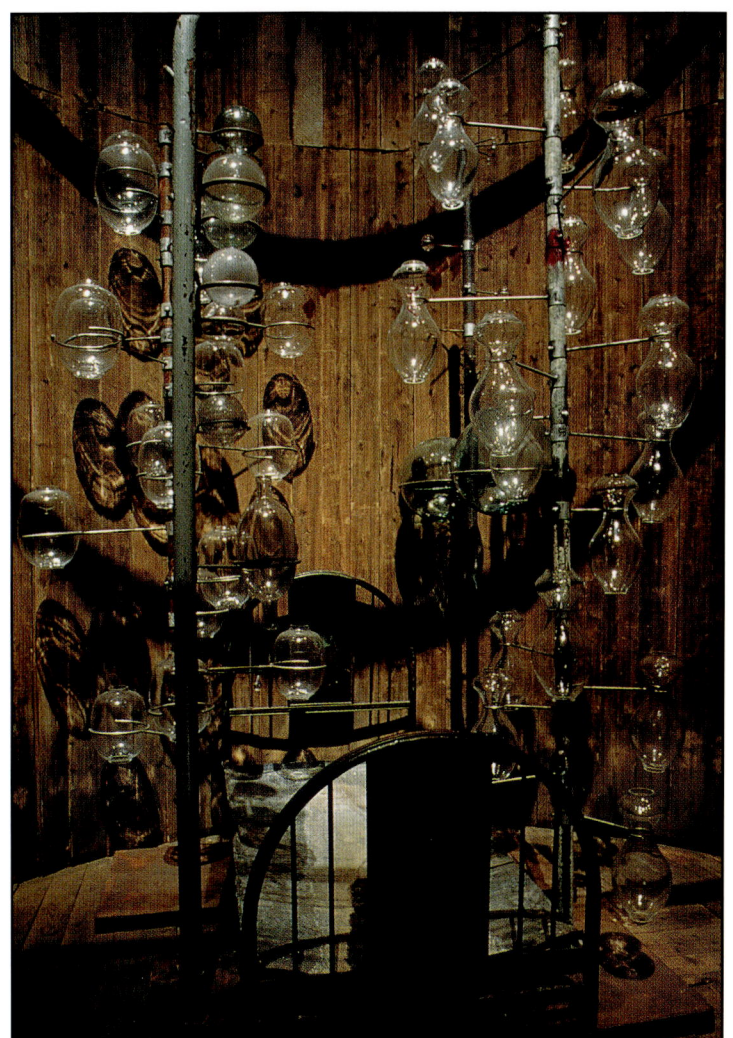

Louise Bourgeois, *Precious Liquids*, 1992, 167.5" x 175.75", Wood, metal, glass, alabaster, cloth, water. *Collection Musèe national d'art moderne, Centre Georges Pompidou, Paris, Courtesy Cheim & Read, New York, Photo: Frèdèric Delpech.*

Women are still working today in factories and as designers. I began this book with women working in glass throughout history. Since most of the history of glass has to do with objects that had a function, their manufacture was executed in what we call today factories. Throughout the 2000 years since Roman times women have had a tough time competing in male terrain. A few women have been recorded as having actually blown glass or worked in a factory in the past. Or, even in the case of painting and assembly of stained glass windows, some have had hands on experience. A few women in history were cutters and engravers, but most were designers. Today, with big automated factories making glassware there are thousands of women employed in jobs that men used to do, still, probably even now at lower wages. Some factories that hand make glass today are employing women. Steuben Glass Works in Corning, New York, has employed Judy Galo as a gaffer for twenty-five years. Uoboros Glass Company in Portland, Oregon, has a women gaffer, Alexandra Farnham, who blows their "frack" and "streamers" to be included in the flat glass sheets they manufacture. A hand blown glass factory in Turkey has a woman designer who also blows glass (totally unheard of in the past), Guilfidon Ozmen.

A number of designers from other fields have become attracted to glass. Dorothy Hafner began her artistic life as a ceramic designer producing work in her own studio. She went on to design successful pieces in the prestigious Rosenthal China Company's Studio Line collection. In the '90s she turned her attention to glass.

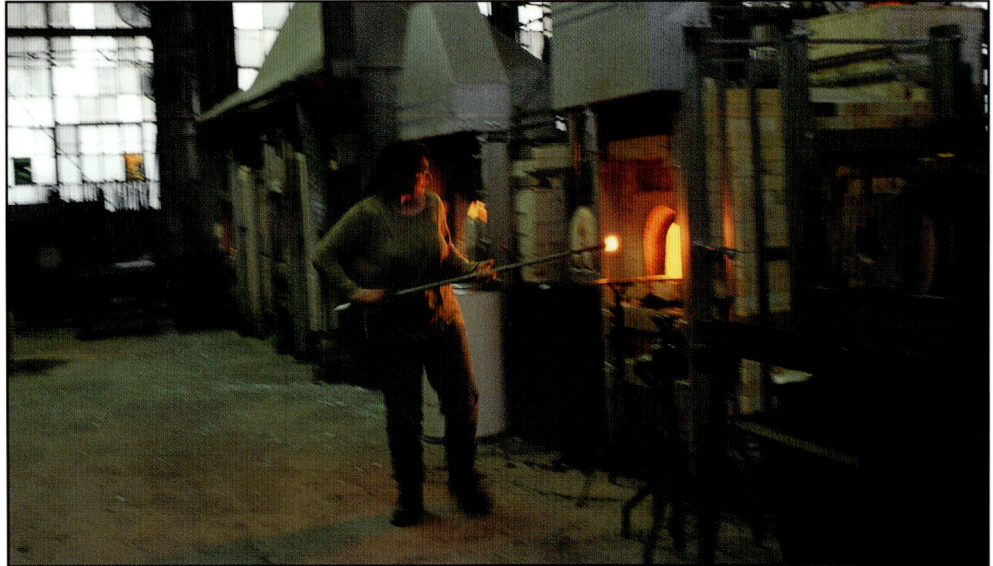

Alexandra Farnham, *blowing frac*, Uroboros Glass Factory, Portland, Oregon. *Photograph courtesy of the author.*

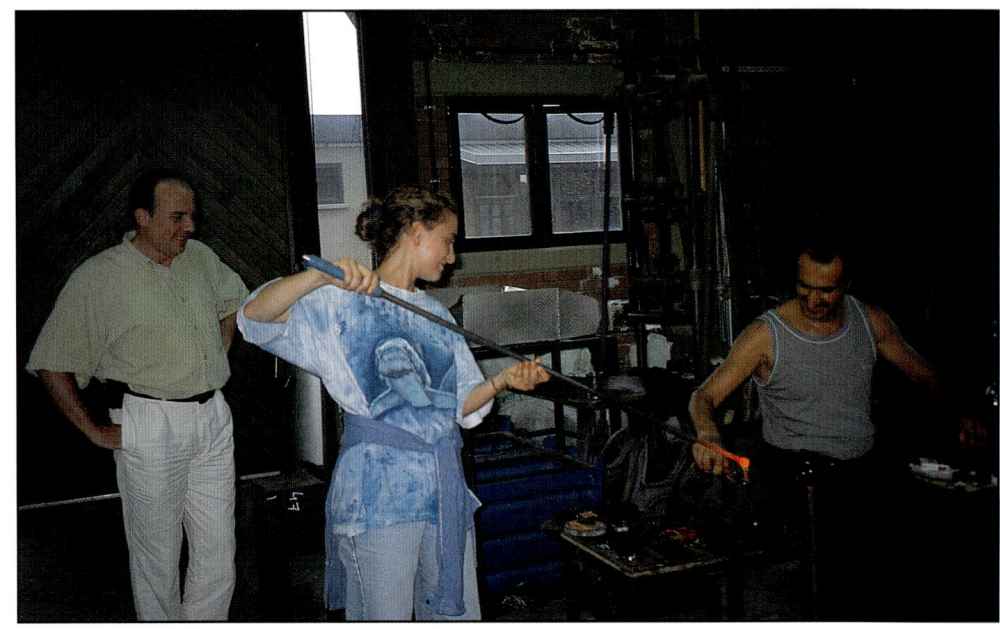

Gulfidan Ozmen, blowing glass, The Glass Furnace Factory, Turkey. *Photograph courtesy of the author.*

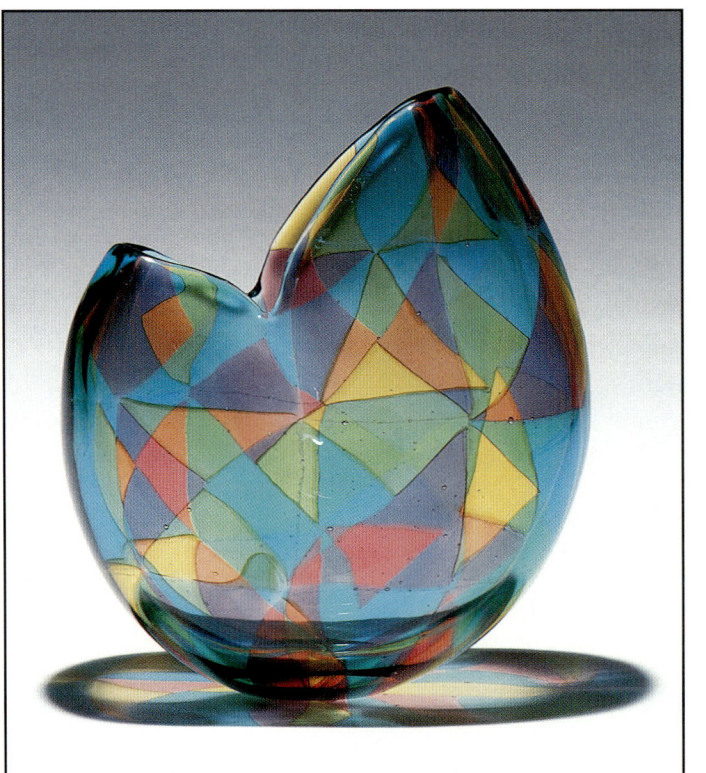

Dorothy Hafner, *Sky Diamond*, 1994, 12" x 9" x 5", fused and blown glass. Photo: James Dee. *Photograph courtesy of the artist.*

Swedish glass factories have a history of employing women glass designers. Some came to design trained as artists, others from an industrial design background. Ulrica Valien studied painting, ceramics, and glass at the National College of Arts, Crafts, and Design in Stockholm. She went to work as a freelance designer for Kosta Boda in 1972. Since that time she has had many successful designs in production. Her designs for other companies in other media include china and porcelain, paper products, textiles, children's books, five airplanes for British Airways, and two cows.

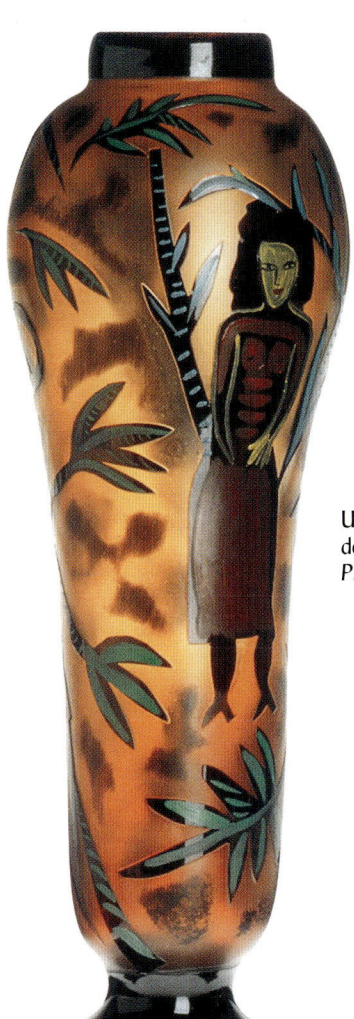

Ulrica Hydman Vallien, *Prinsess*, 1984, unique design, photo: Pelle Wahlgren, Kosta Boda. *Photograph courtesy of the artist.*

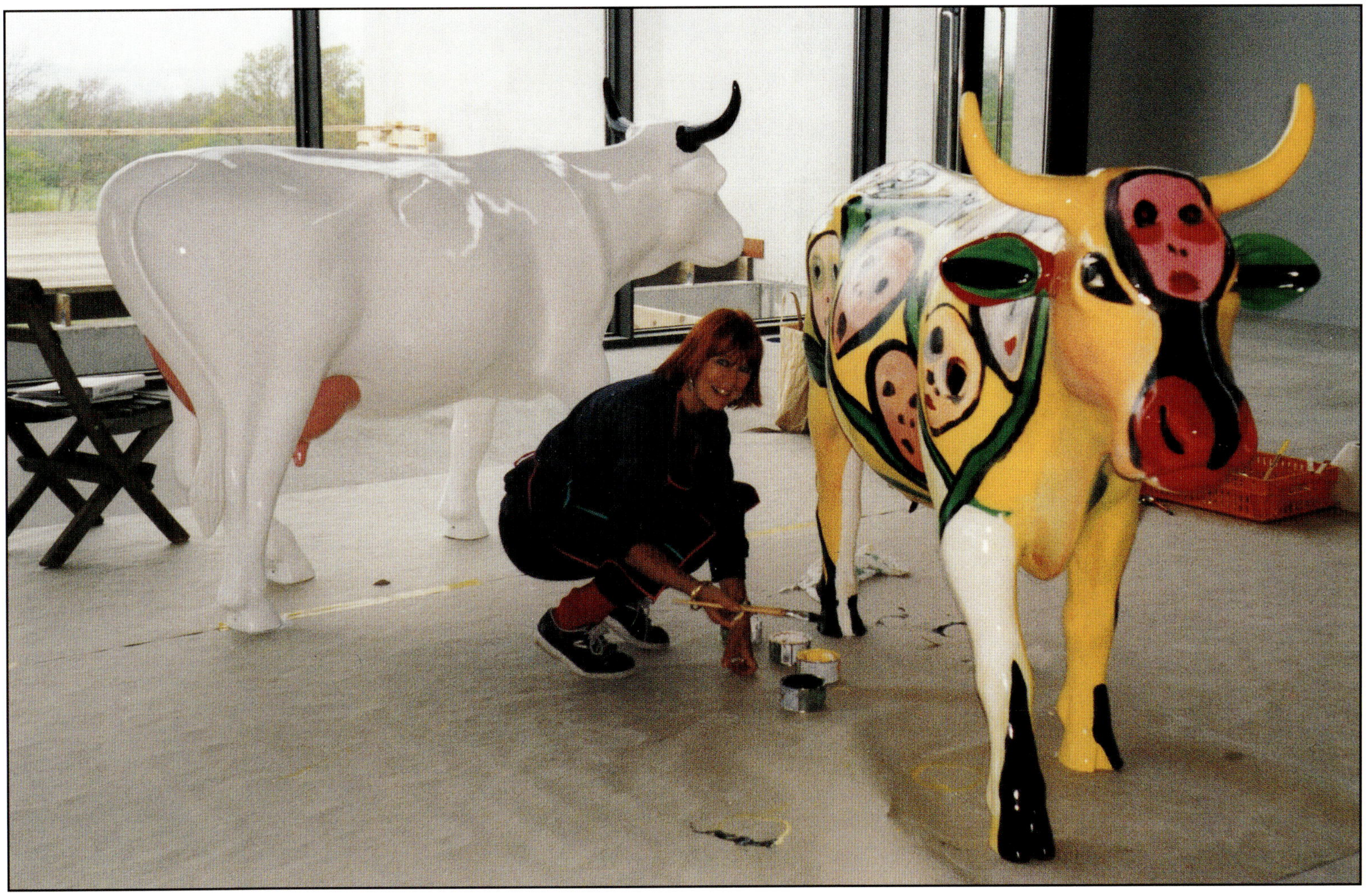

Ulrica Hydman Vallien, Ulrica painting cows. *Photograph courtesy of the artist.*

An issue that is paramount in many women's lives is that of motherhood. Some of the women coming to glass early on did so after their children were either grown or at least out of diapers. Some decided not to have children. Today women are attempting to "have it all" by working and raising children at the same time. There is a new breed of men these days who work to support the creative efforts of women: men who are taking an active part in child care and offering emotional and career support for their female partners and colleagues. In addition, there is a new breed of women who are talented, self-reliant, confident, strong, and determined who are beginning to serve as role models for their younger sisters. Jessica Julius is one of them.

Because there are so many artists who began working in glass in the decade of the nineties I will only include a few examples here. Look around in galleries, in magazines, and on the Internet and you will find them in ever increasing numbers.

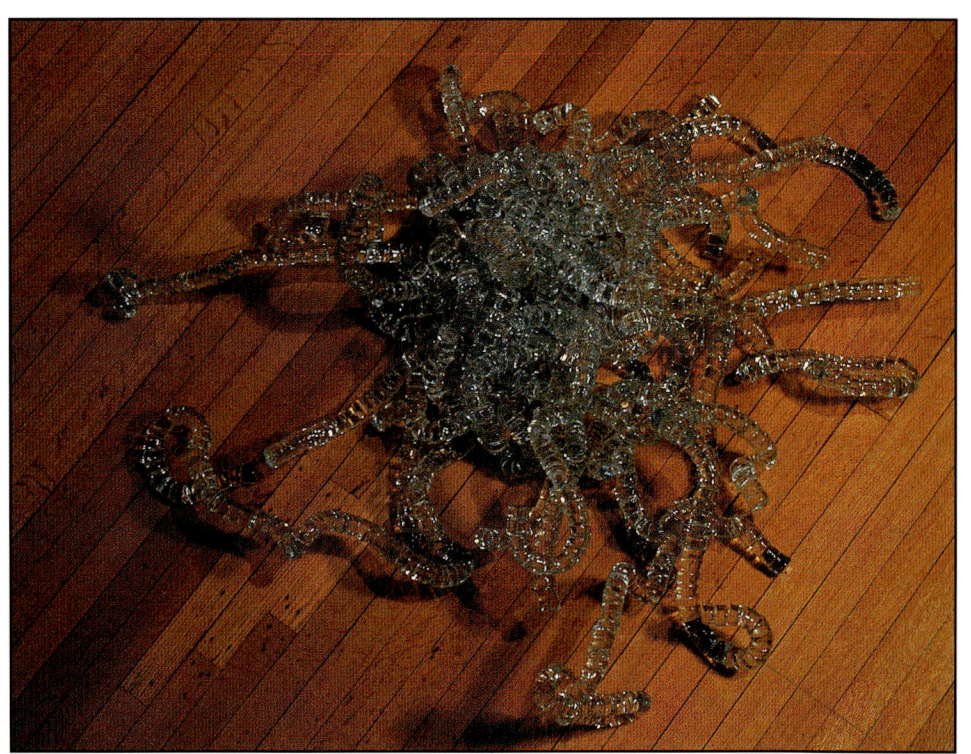

Jessica Julius, Untitled, 2001, 12" x 18" x 12", hot worked glass. *Photograph courtesy of the artist.*

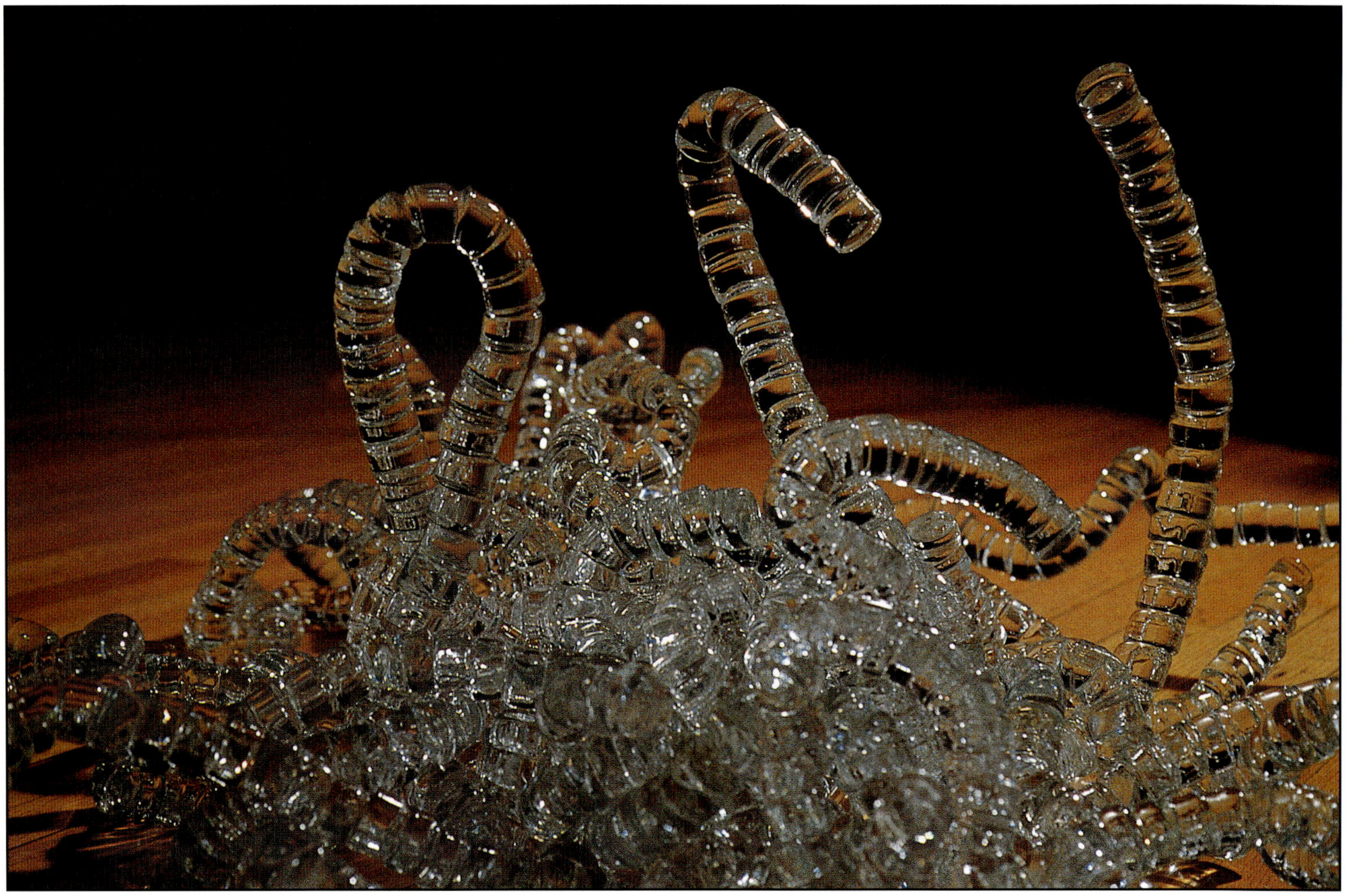

Jessica Julius, Untitled, detail.

The Artists

Robin Cass

I see my sculptural work as an ongoing research project into how people experience the physical world, relate to one another, and perceive their own existence and mortality. When making work, I look to the natural sciences, early industrial forms, and psychology for inspiration. While I use a variety of materials, glass is often at the heart of each piece. I have been seduced by its ability to take on such a wide range of forms, subtle textures, colors, and qualities. The spontaneity of working with molten glass inspires me and leads to unique forms that serve my ideas. Glass is unique in its potential translucence, which is rich with metaphorical associations.

My current works, Divers and Travelers, are meant to suggest scientific models of the psyche. They are suspended at or above eye level and rotate of their own accord. These forms are meant to appear organic from a distance, only revealing their mechanical construction upon close inspection. Each piece in this series has a diatom-like nucleus of blown glass that has been entirely enclosed by progressive layers of metal or glass. These delicate carapaces can be seen as both protective and restricting, and obscure the innards of each piece to various degrees. On one level, these works refer to the psychological constructions people develop around their essential selves in order to function in the world.

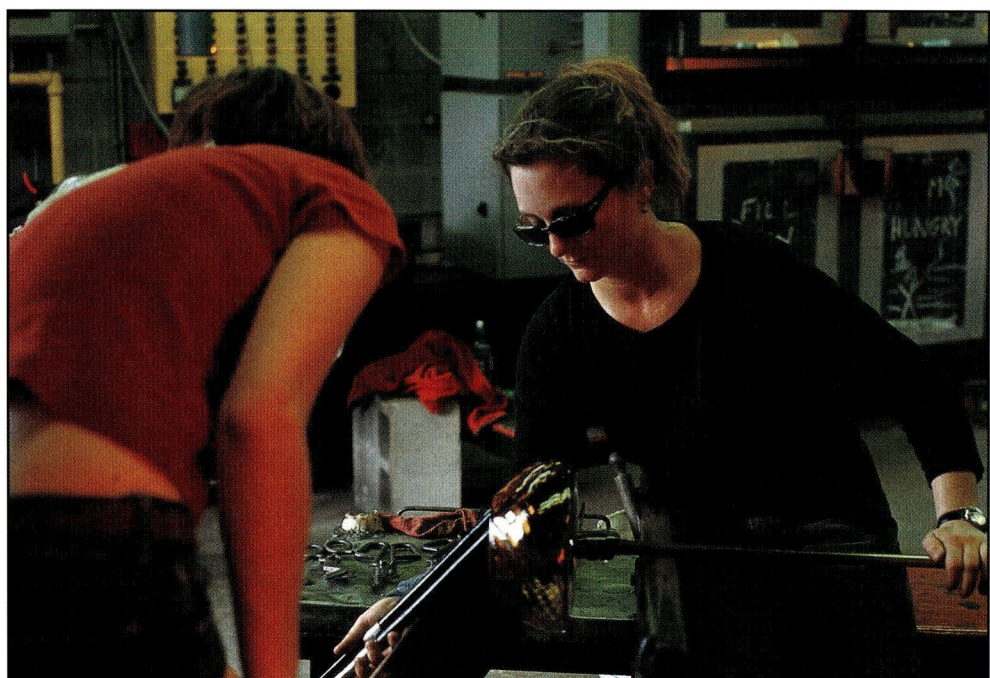

Robin Cass. *Photograph courtesy of the artist.*

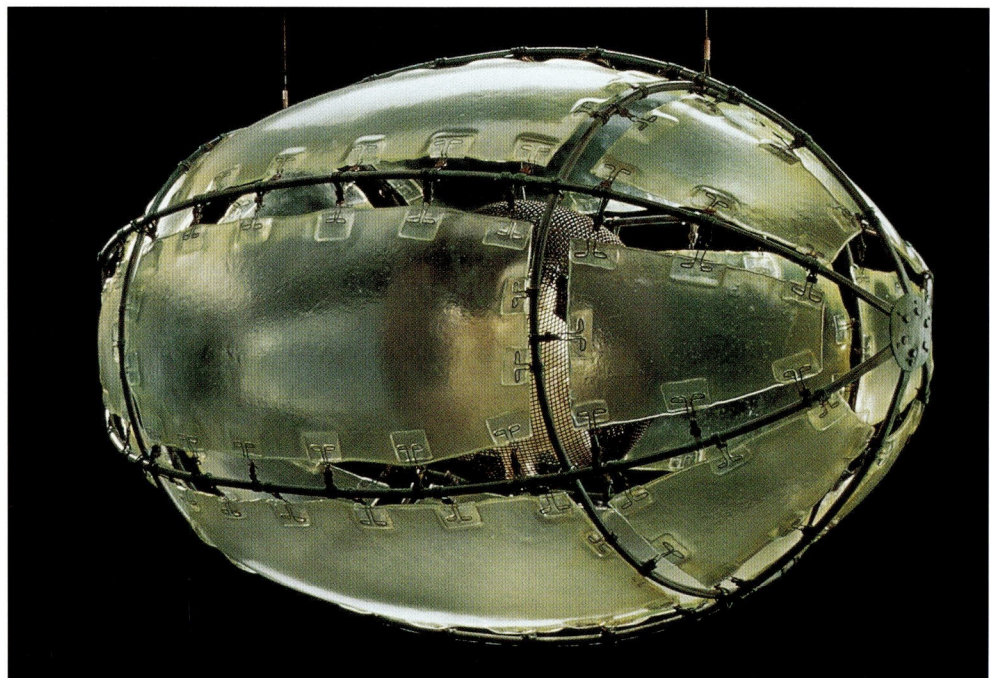

Traveler, 2000, 28" x 22" d, slumped, fused, and blown glass; copper, brass, and steel mesh. Photo: Bruce Miller. *Photograph courtesy of the artist.*

I would like to elicit a number of associations and responses with each piece on a cerebral as well as visceral level. I try to raise questions and present possible realities that involve the viewer in a state of intellectual reflection as well as sensory engagement.

Opposite page:
Traveler, detail. Photo: Bruce Miller. *Photograph courtesy of the artist.*

The Nineties - The Artist   191

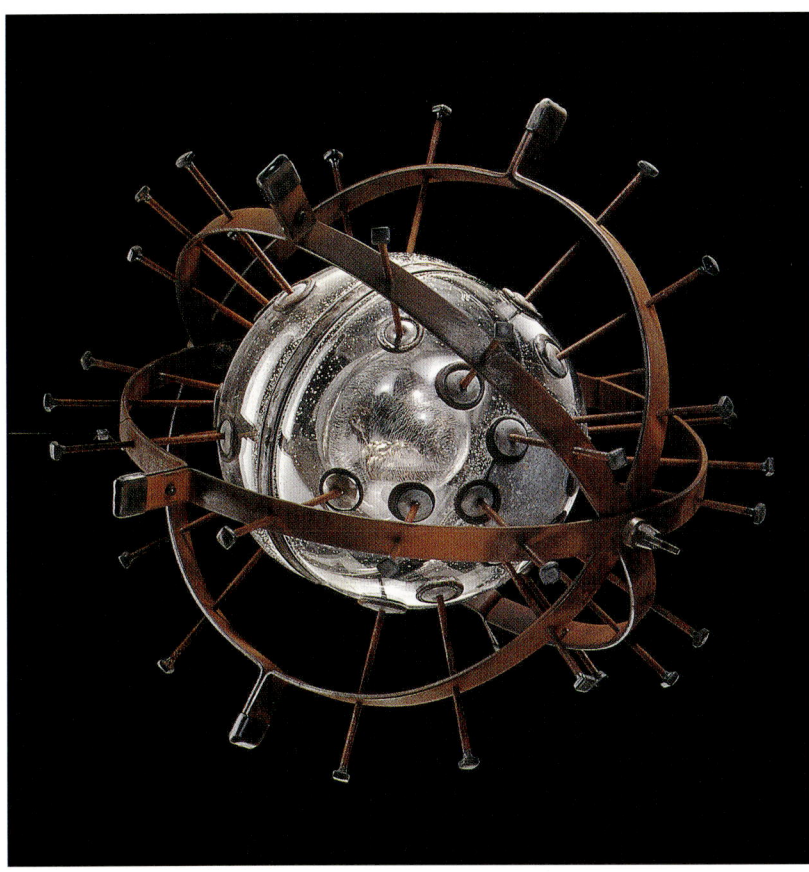

Diver VIII, 2000, 20" x 24", blown and engraved glass, steel, lead, and rubber. Photo: Bruce Miller. *Photograph courtesy of the artist.*

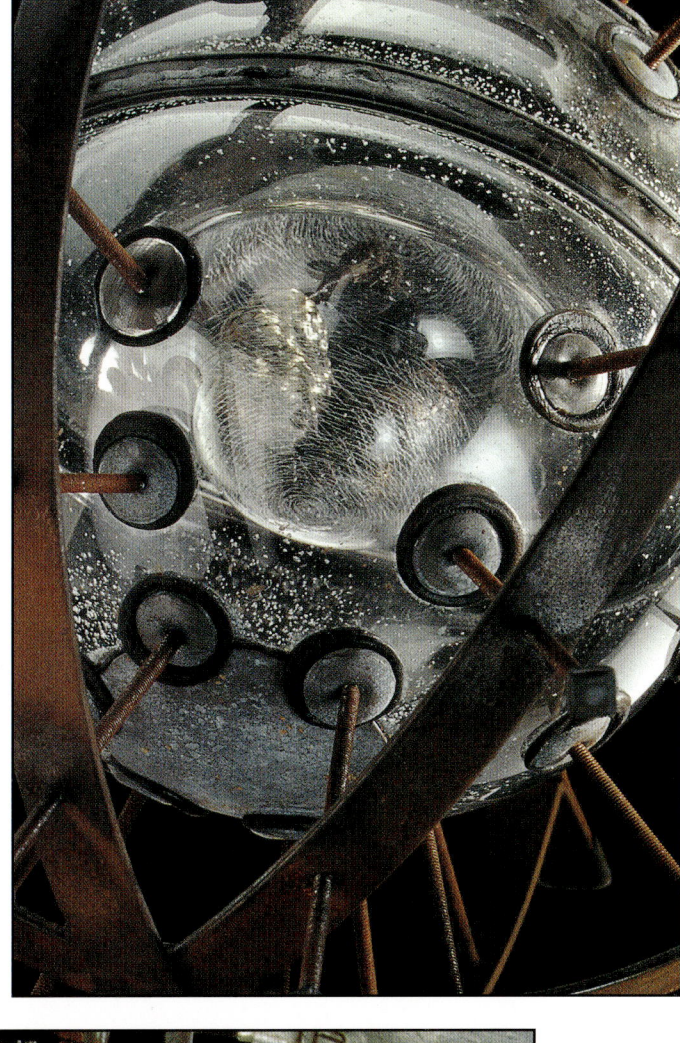

Diver VIII, detail. Photo: Bruce Miller. *Photograph courtesy of the artist.*

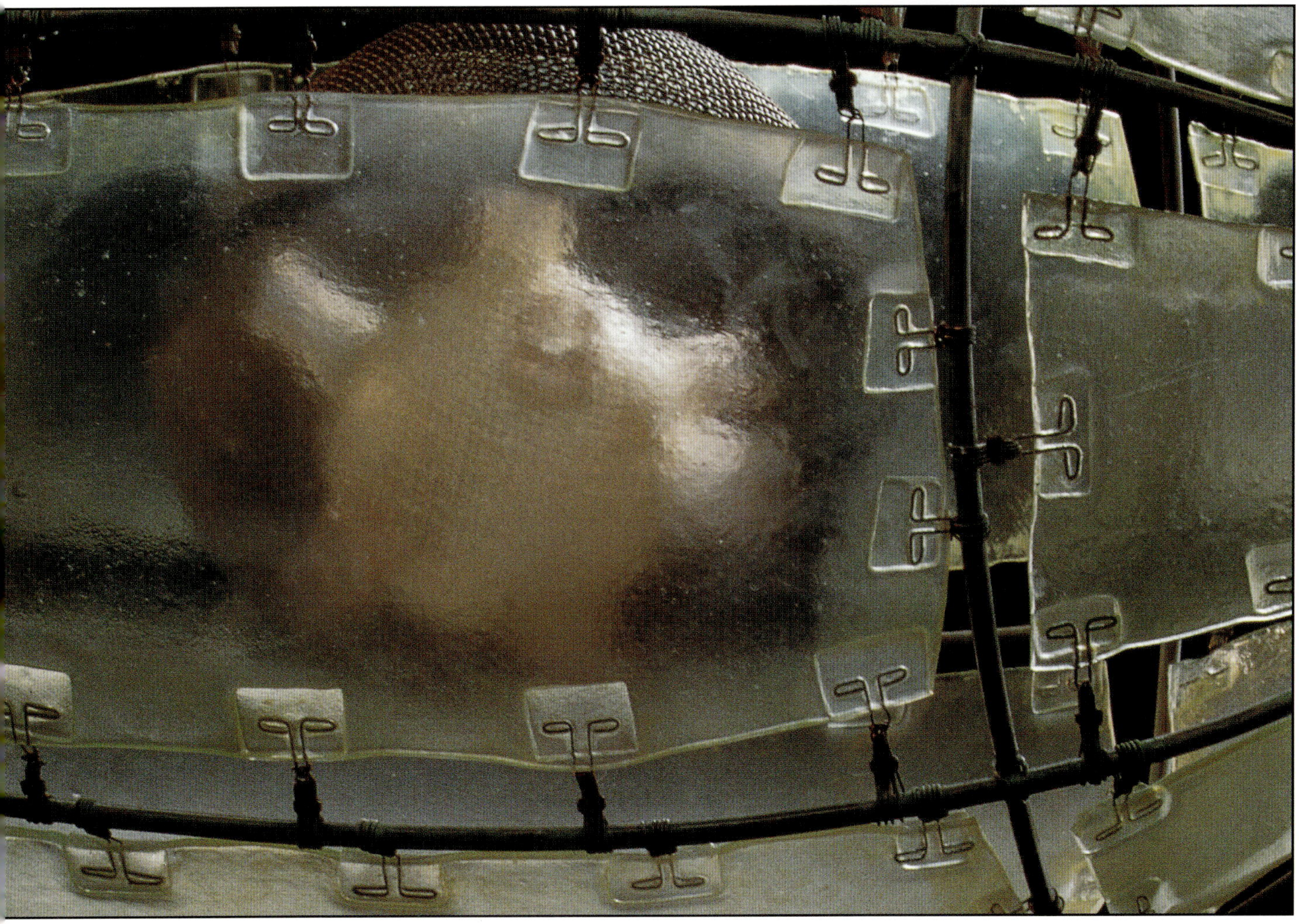

Dorothy Hafner

In 1993 I turned to glass after a strong fifteen-year career in ceramics. I had just been scuba diving on the Great Barrier Reef and returned with a passion to explore aspects of transparency and reflection as they impact on image, form, and color.

By complete serendipity I became reacquainted with glass and in it found the perfect medium for my painterly imagery.

With my vessels I hope to create "paintings in the round" where the imagery and colors change as one walks around each piece. Different vantage points offer completely new combinations of foreground and background colors and shapes.

With the panels, I build layer upon layer of flat transparent shapes, fusing them together only when

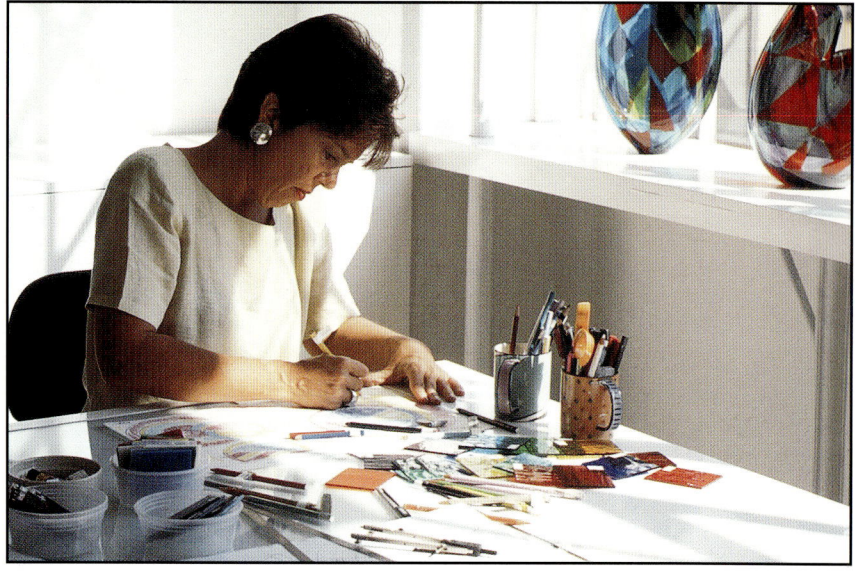

Dorothy Hafner. Photo: George Erml. *Photograph courtesy of the artist.*

I feel satisfied that I have achieved a similar density of illusory imagery. My sources now are vast and wide, but mostly are my responses to music, scientific imagery, and the varied landscapes to which I travel.

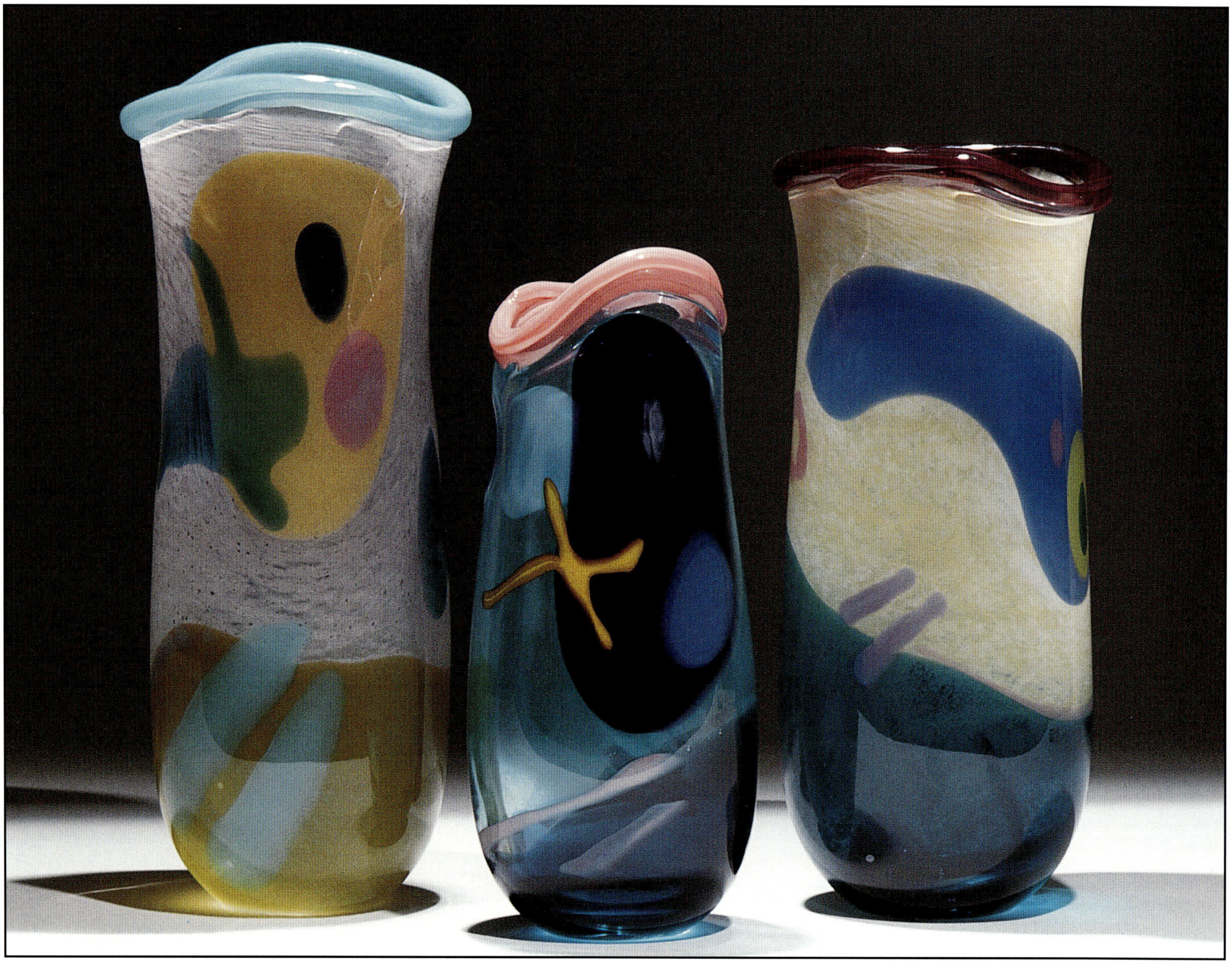

Dreamscapes, 1993. Left to right: 19" x 6.25" x 5"; 15" x 6.25" x 4.5"; 17" x 6.5" x 5". Fused and blown glass. *Photograph courtesy of the artist.*

The Nineties - The Artist 193

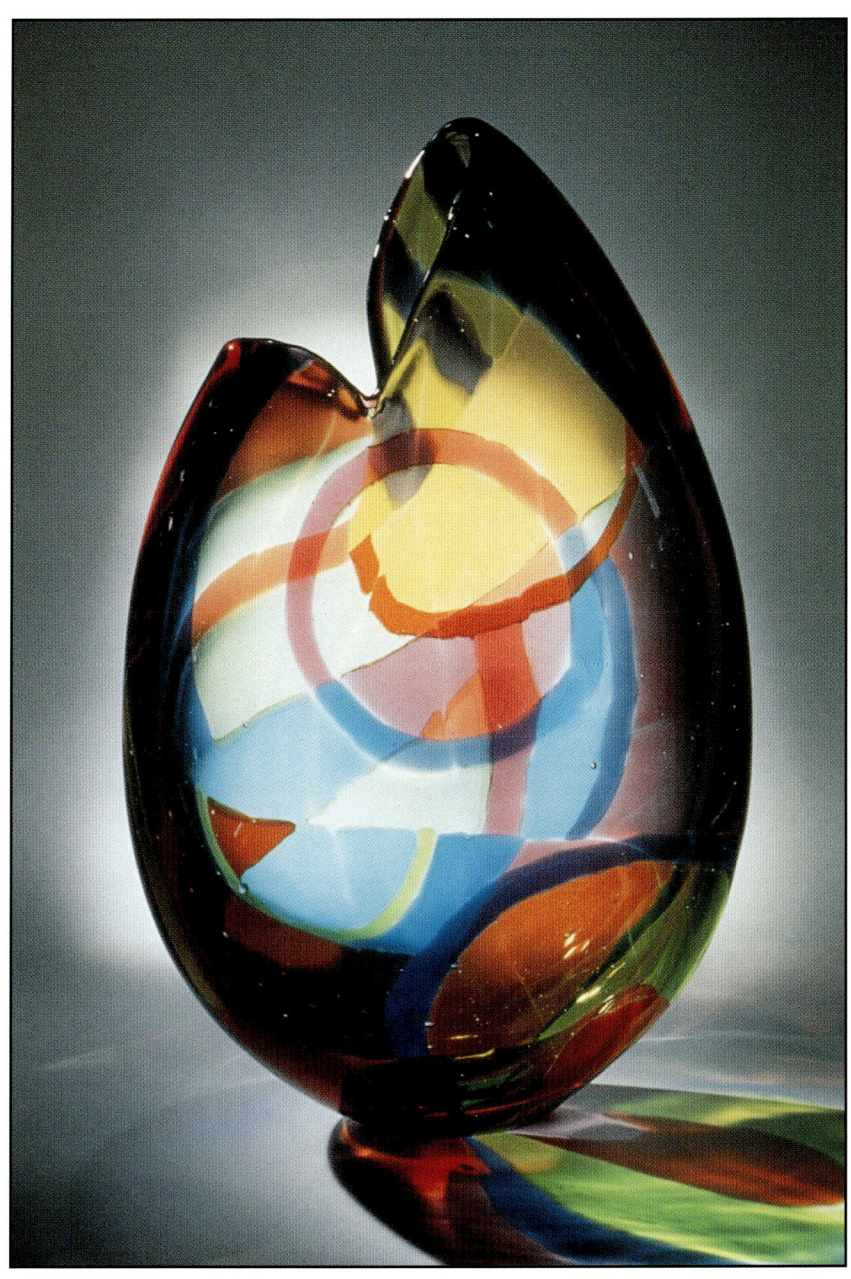

Ring Toss, 1995, 17.5" x 10" x 4", fused and blown glass. *Photograph courtesy of the artist.*

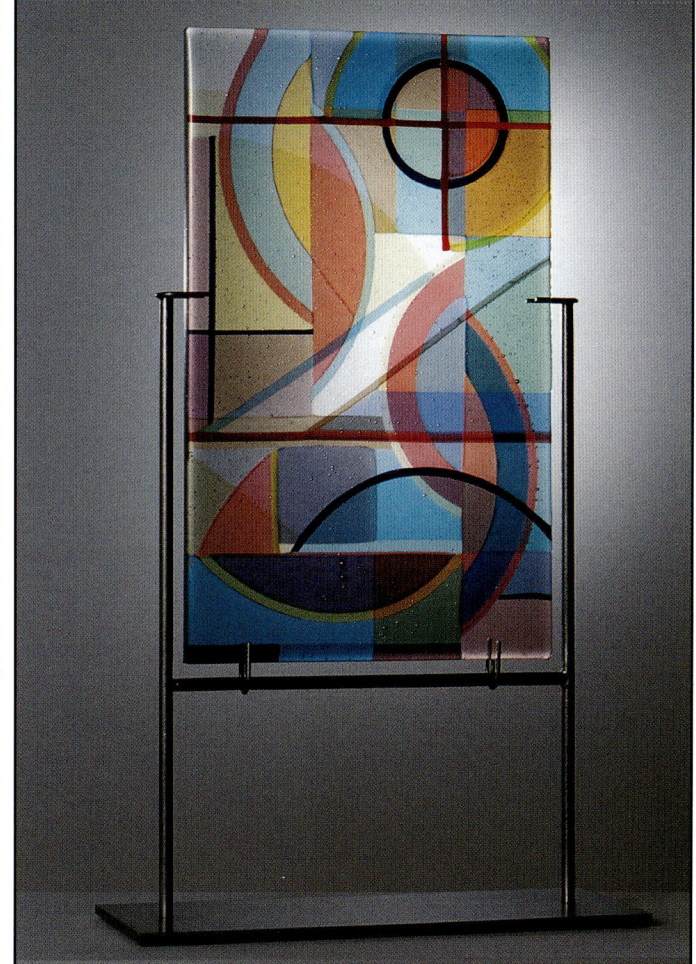

Twins, 2002, 24" x 14" x 6" with stand, fused glass, stainless steel. Photo: George Erml. *Photograph courtesy of the artist.*

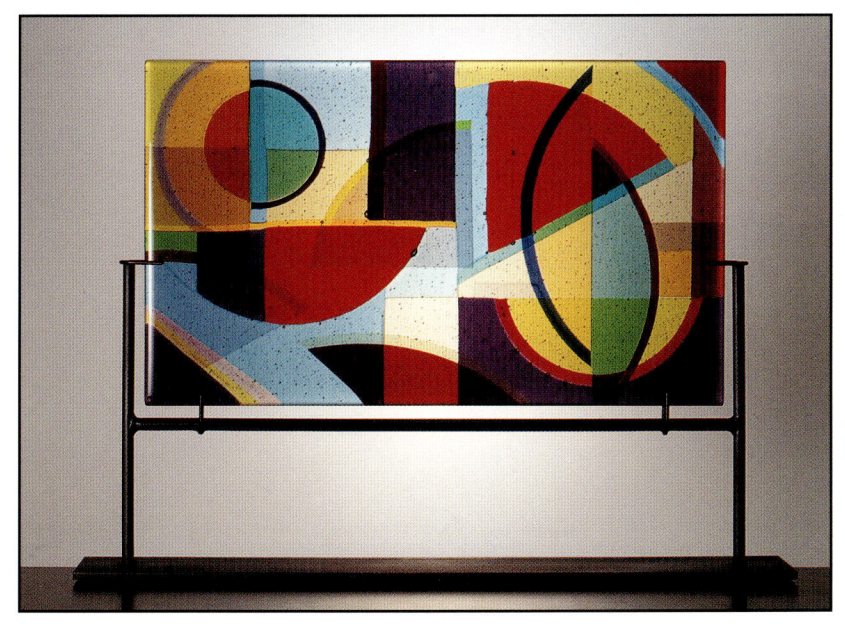

Quick Set, 2000, 15" x 20" with stand, fused glass, metal. Photo: George Erml. *Photograph courtesy of the artist.*

Beth Hylen

I'm intrigued with glass. It was part of my childhood: I watched with my father as glowing gobs of optical glass shot through a massive machine; entered the elegant, sparkling Steuben Shop with Aunt Tillie; and observed lamp workers creating fanciful animals.

In my role as a librarian doing reference and book acquisitions at The Corning Museum of Glass, Rakow Research Library, I am immersed in the art and history of glass. The experience is an incredible opportunity to talk with researchers, students, and artists about their work, as well as absorb ideas from artists who visit CMoG and participate at the Glass Art Society. I disseminate what I've learned to people worldwide. I even got to handle ancient glass – the iridescence flaked off on my fingers.

Eventually, I wanted to try different techniques so I would understand them more fully. In 1987 I began to explore glassmaking, starting with stained glass and fusing with local artist Nancy Gerbasi; then continuing with furnace work at New York Experimental Glass, Horizons, Studio Access to Glass, and with friends. At CMoG's Studio I tried pate de verre and developed my lampworking skills. I have been a teaching assistant at the glassmaking schools Urban Glass, Pilchuck, and Pittsburgh Glass Center.

I learned to melt and shape borosilicate glass (Pyrex) at the torch with Sally Prasch, who conveys the power of precise techniques and an ability to communicate ideas and Susan Plum, who delves into emotional and spiritual expression.

Recently, I have been exploring line and gesture as wearable sculpture. I am fascinated by sinuous Art Nouveau lines; tree branches silhouetted against the sky; icicles; and diagrams of old Masters paintings where gesture can carry your eye through a painting.

My work conveys movement – flowing, organic. I enjoy the moment when glass is between being molten and frozen into shape, when it responds to my touch and the heat of the torch.

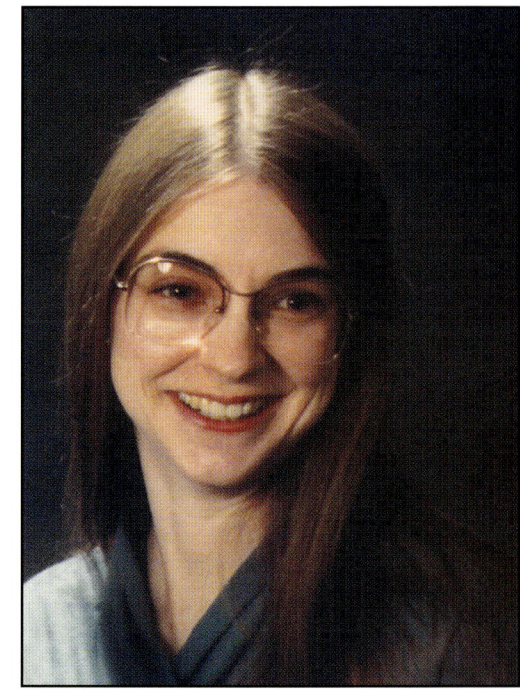

Beth Hylen.

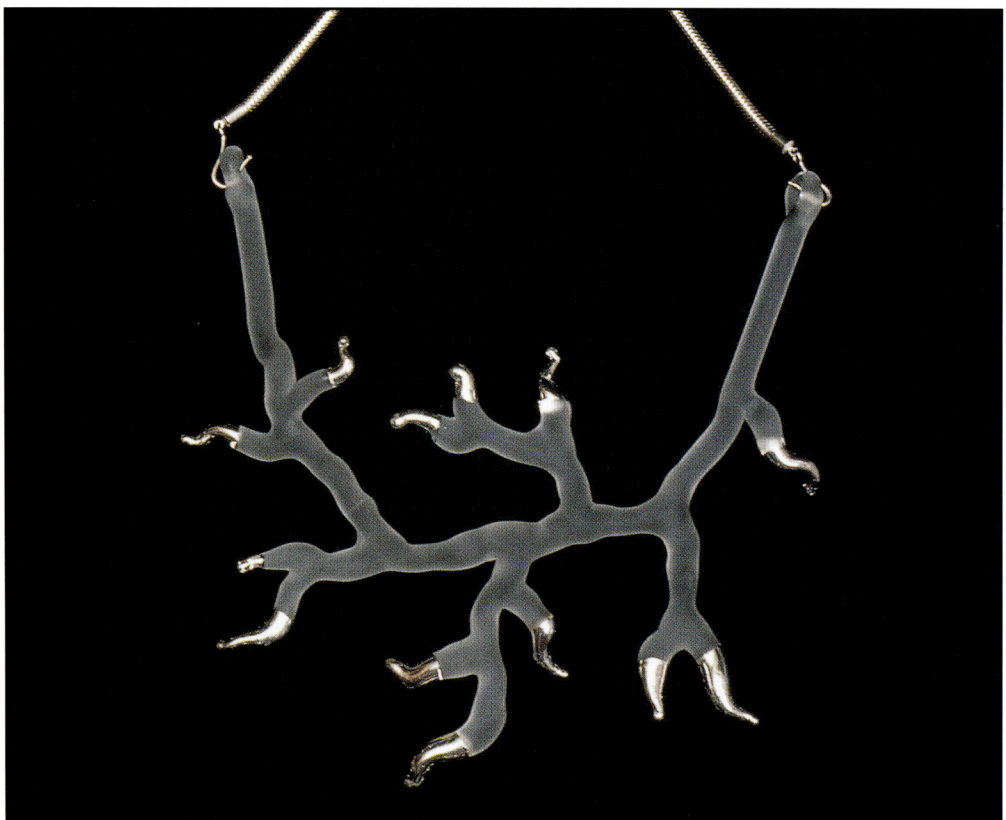

Frozen Spring necklace, 2001, 7" x 8", lampworked borosilicate glass with sterling silver (chain collaboration with Karen Kreiger). Photo: Dan Neuberger. *Photograph courtesy of the artist.*

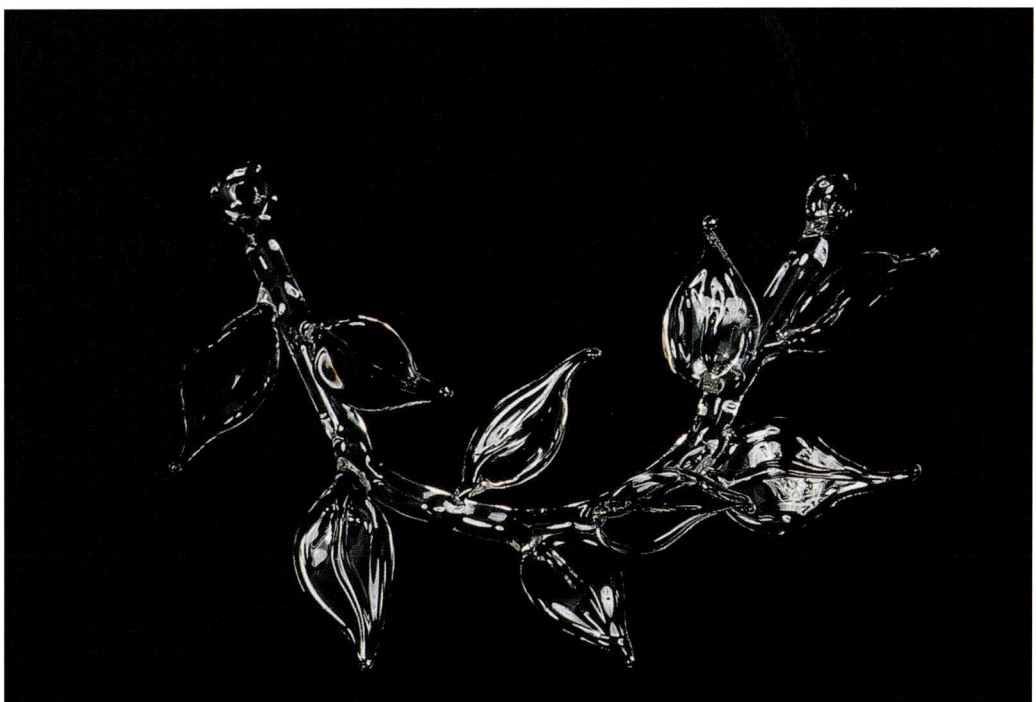

Blossoming, 1999, 7" x 7", lamp-worked borosilicate glass. Photo: Dan Neuberger. *Photograph courtesy of the artist.*

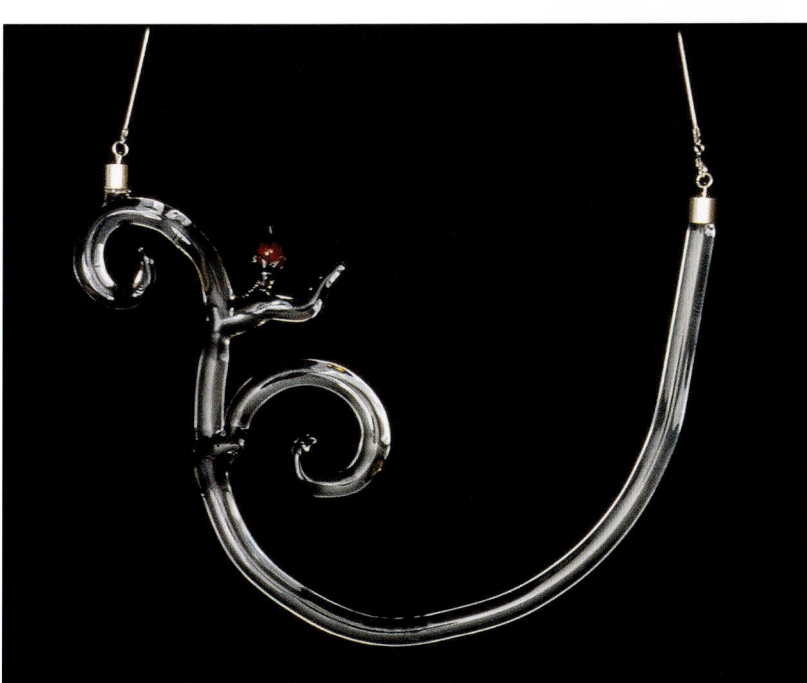

Budding, 2001, 7" x 7", lamp-worked borosilicate glass and sterling silver. Photo: Dan Neuberger. *Photograph courtesy of the artist.*

Budding detail.

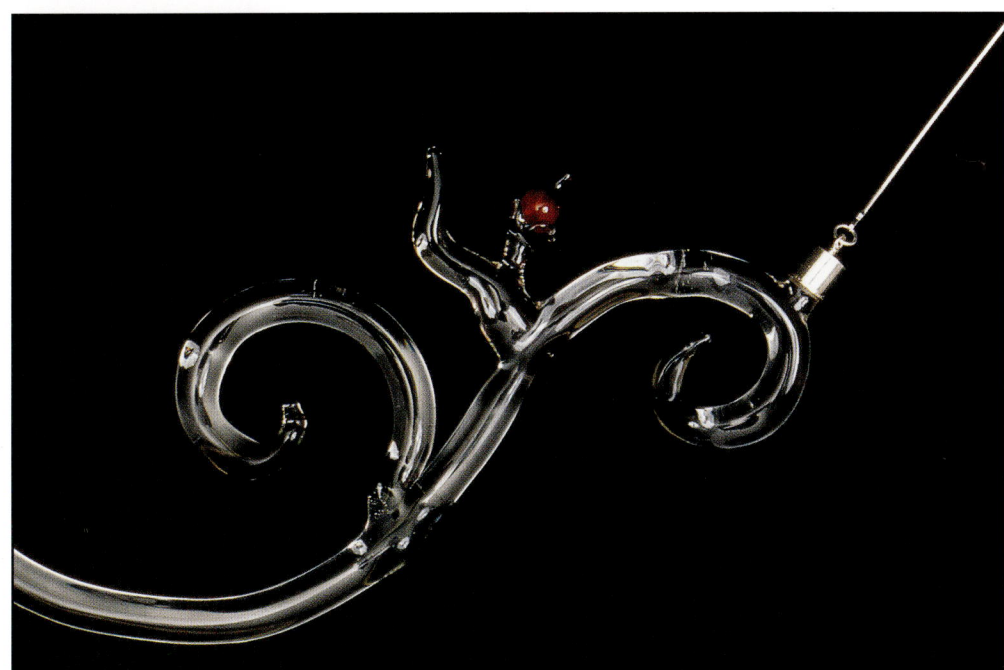

Karen Lamonte

In our society clothing both protects the individual and projects a persona. It is a non-spoken language through which we communicate. It is armor and costume, plumage and camouflage. Clothing separates public from private space. Rendered in glass, clothing becomes a window to the interior, where the impression of the human remains. One can glimpse the ephemeral inner form through the protective outer shell. I am exploring this non-spoken language.

I use clothing as a metaphor for identity and human presence. I believe we have two skins that outline and define who we are. One is our natural skin, but we obscure and conceal it beneath clothing which is a Second skin, our social skin. In both my prints and sculpture I use transparency to expose what is normally concealed. It is an exploration of what lies below the surface.

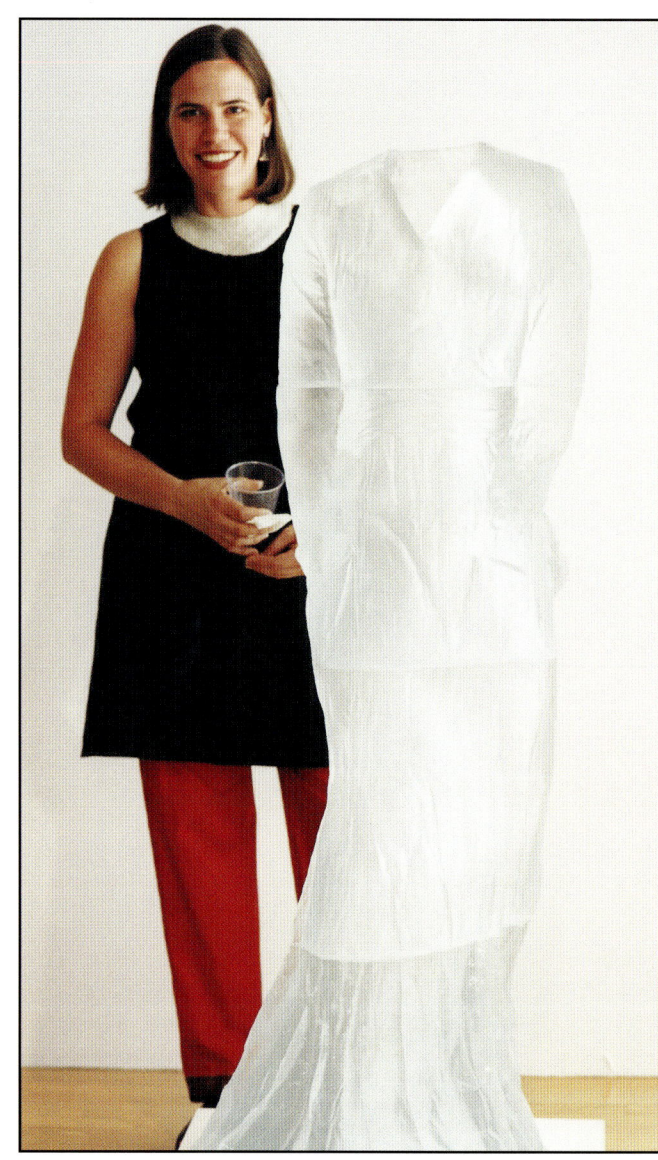

Karen Lamonte. *Photograph courtesy of the artists.*

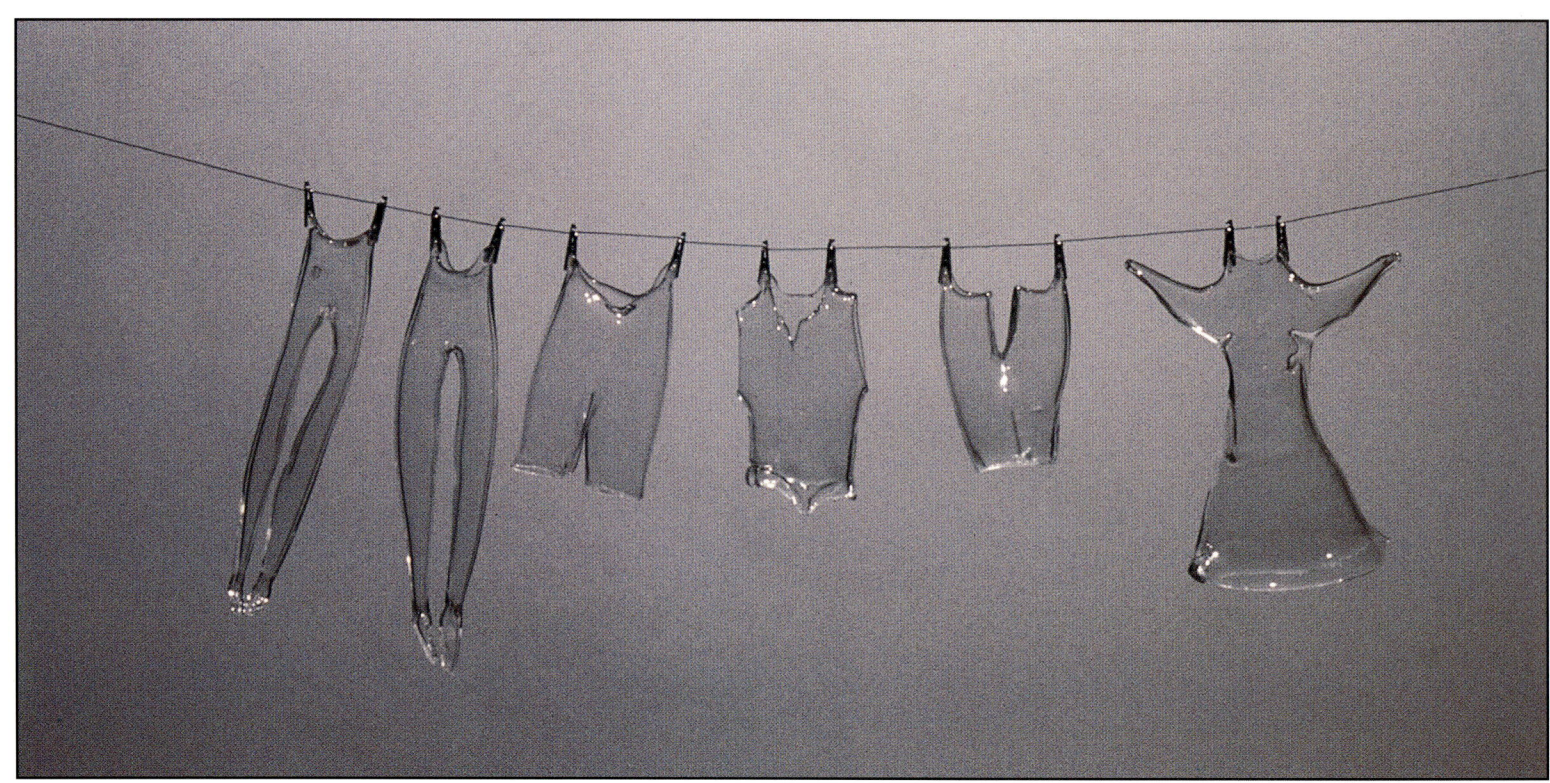

The Emperors New Clothes, 1995, 10" x 48" x 3", blown glass. *Photograph courtesy of the artists.*

The Nineties - The Artist 197

Jester and Queen, 1995, blown and enameled glass. Photograph courtesy of the artists.

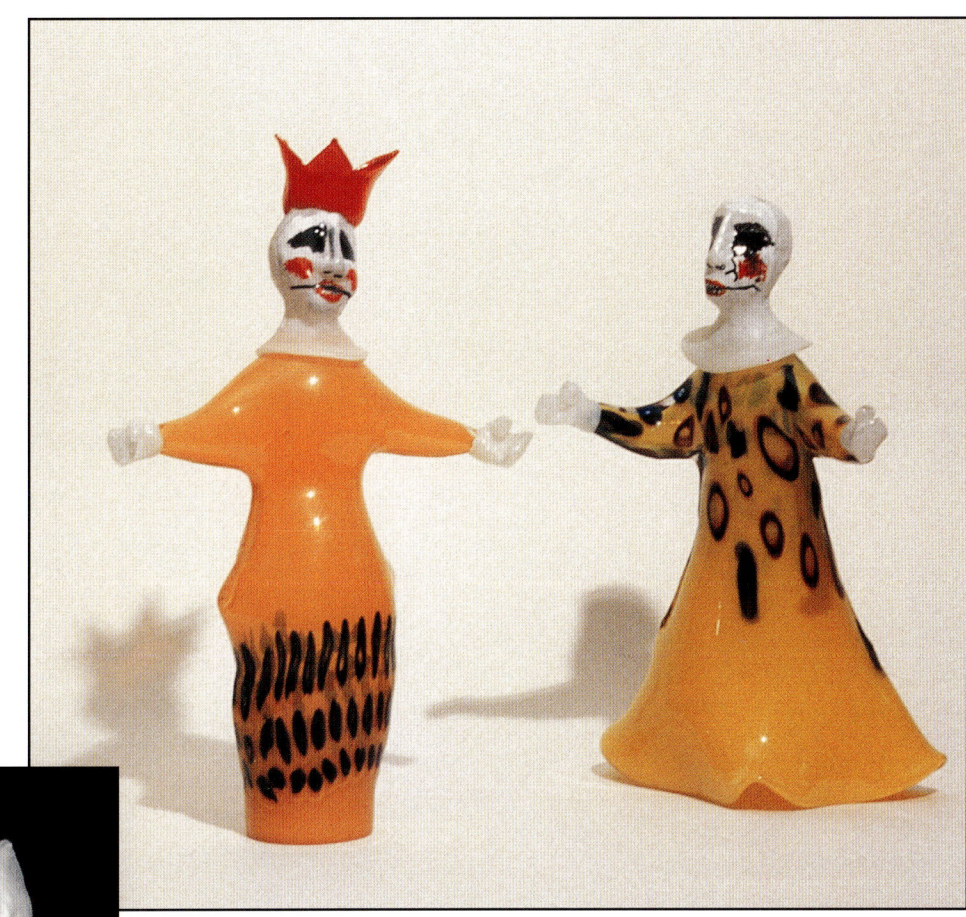

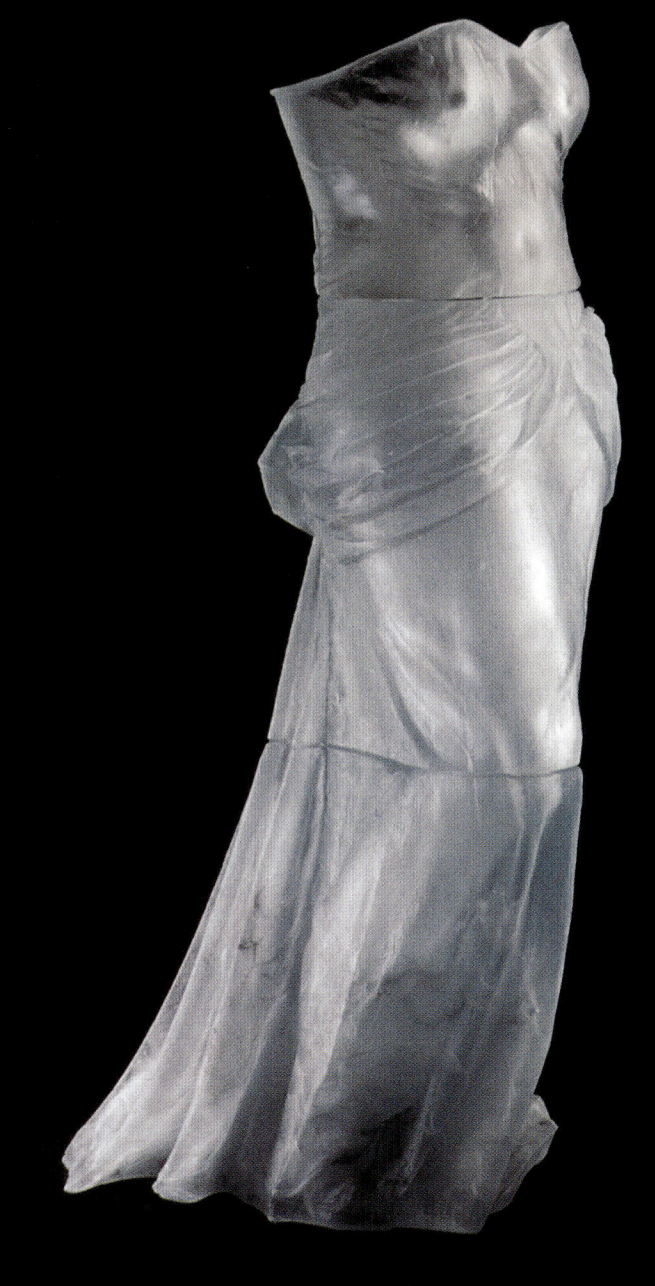

Dress 6, 3/4 front, 2001, 51" x 17" x 24", cast glass. Photograph courtesy of the artist.

Beth Lipman

I recreate still life paintings in hand sculpted glass. The works are inspired by still life paintings of Dutch, American, and Italian origin and date from the seventeenth to twentieth century. Most paintings are chosen for their content and composition, and, in some cases, as a souvenir of an experience. Most contain symbols of wealth and prosperity. Some paintings have symbolism that has evolved over time.

The use of glass creates a tangible third dimension, capturing the painting's polished quality. Its transparency suggests an ideal form, the essence of an object. It is timeless, constant. It makes permanent objects that are perishable. There is a direct parallel between the tradition of still life painting and art made from glass. During the sixteenth and seventeenth centuries, still life paintings were considered of secondary importance to paintings of political and religious genre. Art made from glass has been seen as subordinate to painting and sculpture.

The still life goes far beyond the mere recording of objects. Our universal need for food and drink, our common knowledge of life's transience, the beauty found in every object, are as relevant today as in the seventeenth century.

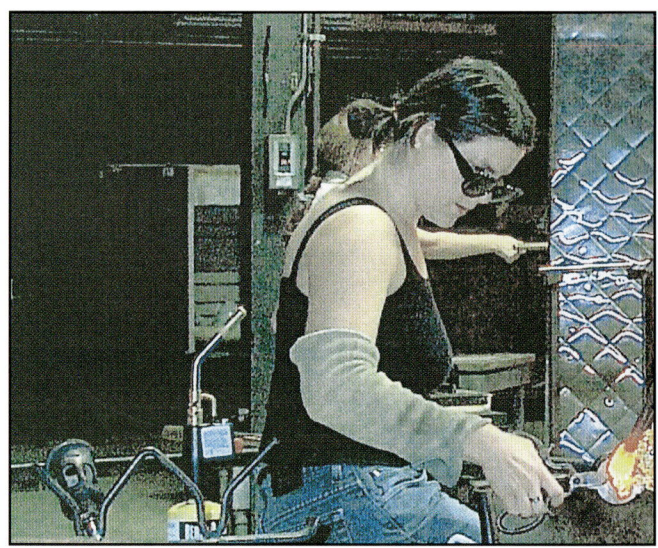

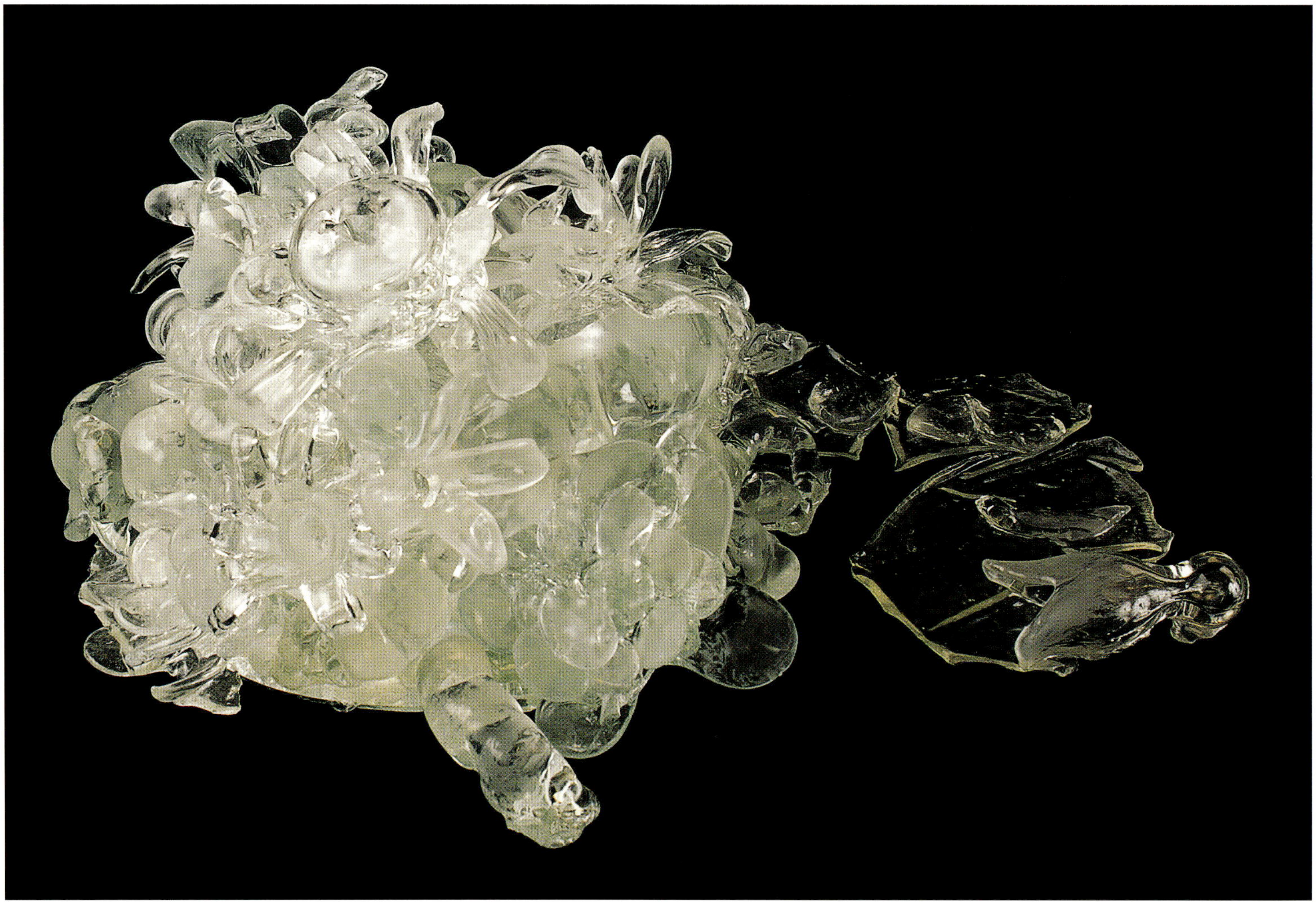

Beth Lipman. Photo: John Marselis. *Photograph courtesy of the artist.*

Flowers and Feces, 1996, 15" x 26" d, glass and mixed media. Photo: Aaron Igler. *Photograph courtesy of the artist.*

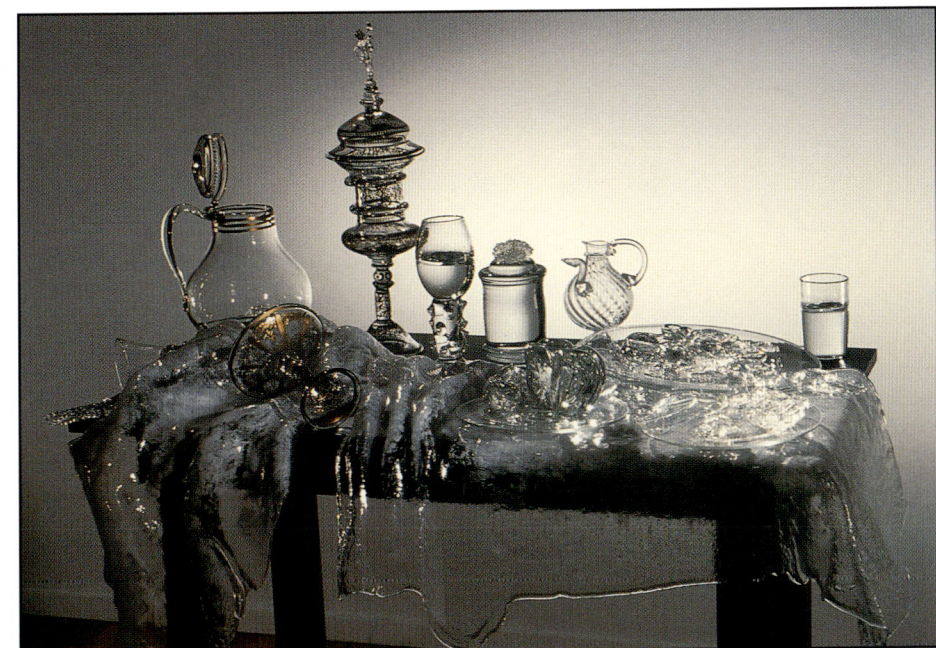

Stilleven (after Willem Claesz Heda), 2001, 3.5' x 2.5' x 1.5', glass and mixed media. Photo: Eva Heyd. *Photograph courtesy of the artist.*

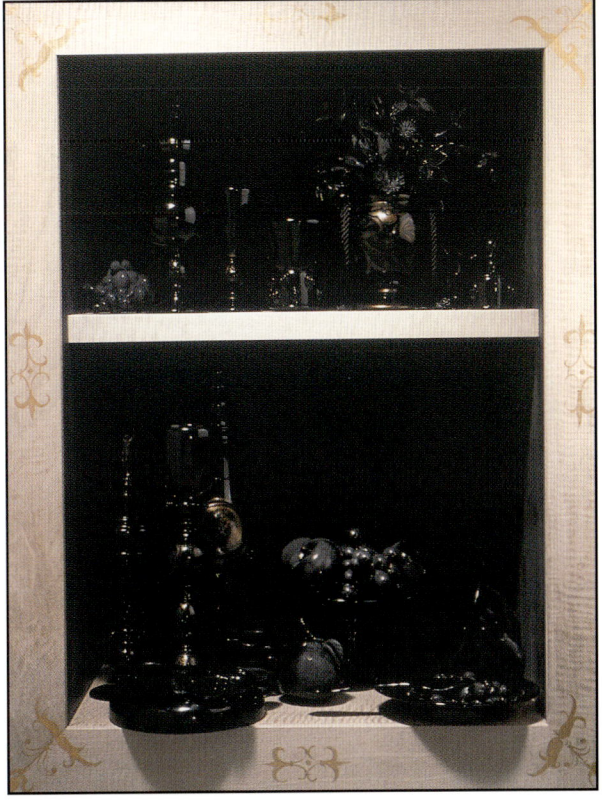

Cupboard Picture with Flowers, Fruit, and Goblets (after Flegel), 2002, 3' x 2.5' x 1.5', glass and mixed media. Photo: Eva Heyd. *Photograph courtesy of the artist.*

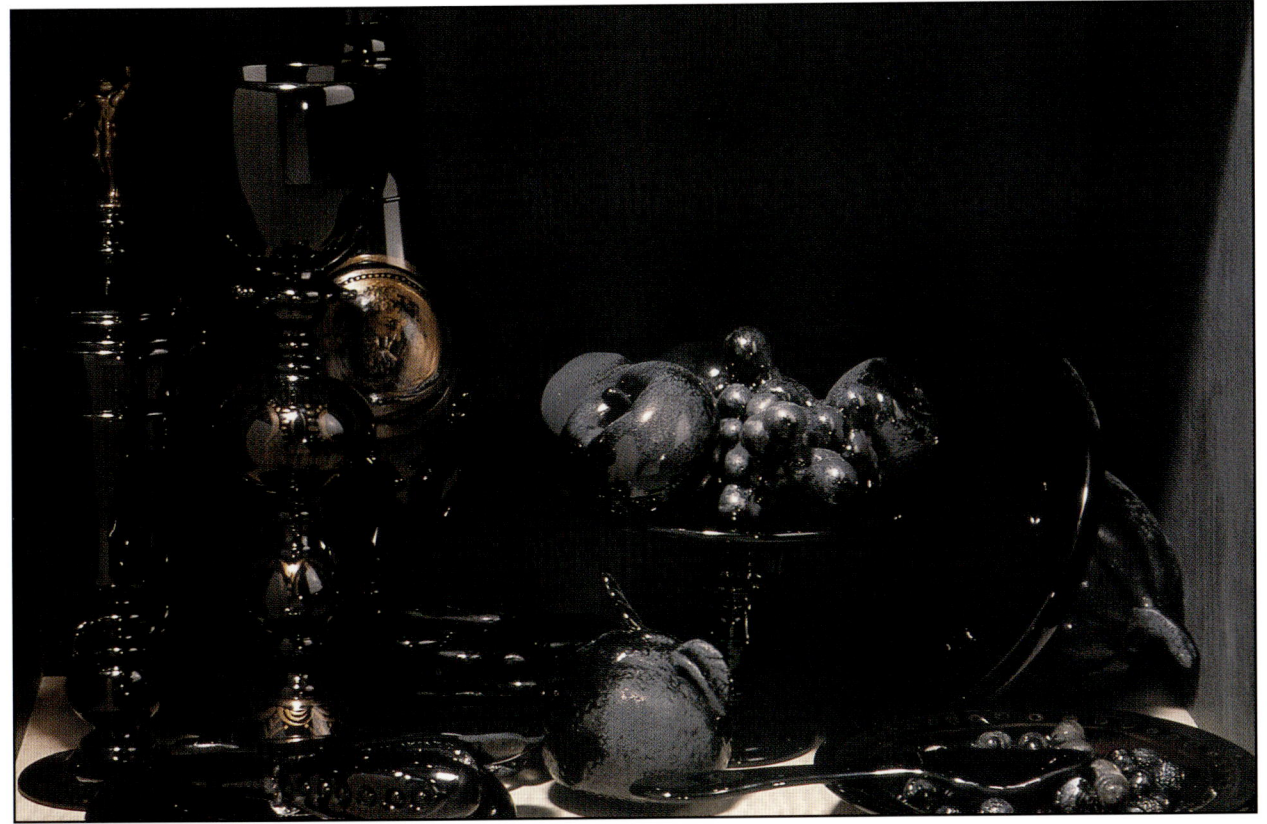

Cupboard Picture with Flowers, Fruit, and Goblets detail.

Kristina Logan

Kristina Logan uses her keen color sense to create compelling combinations. To an object of lusciously colored pate de verre – often suggestive of food, such as marmalade or cherries – she will add beads that are both decorative and functional, used as feet, finials, and handles. Logan's pieces bring endless pleasure to all fortunate to behold them.

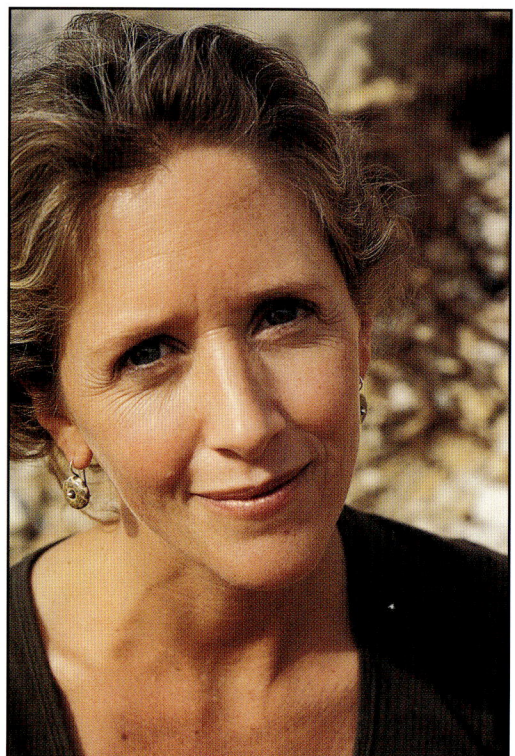

Kristina Logan. *Photograph courtesy of the artist.*

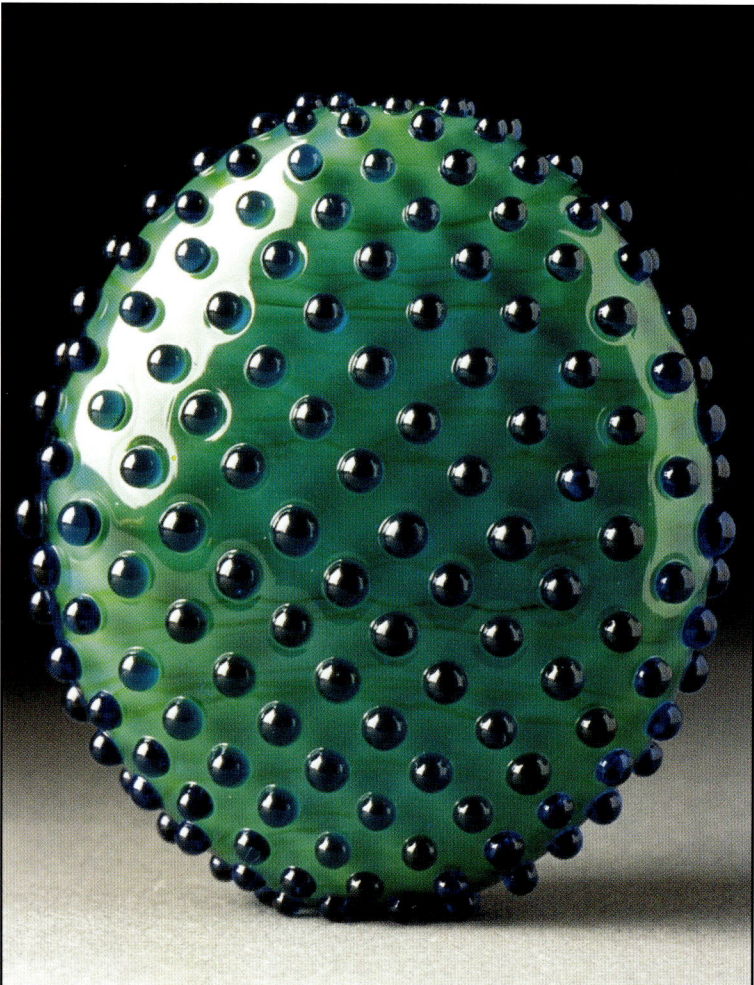

Cactus Bead, 1997, 1.75" x 1.5" d, lamp-worked glass. *Photograph courtesy of the artist.*

Ivory Disc Bead, 1997, .5" x 2.15" x 2.15" d, lamp-worked glass. *Photograph courtesy of the artist.*

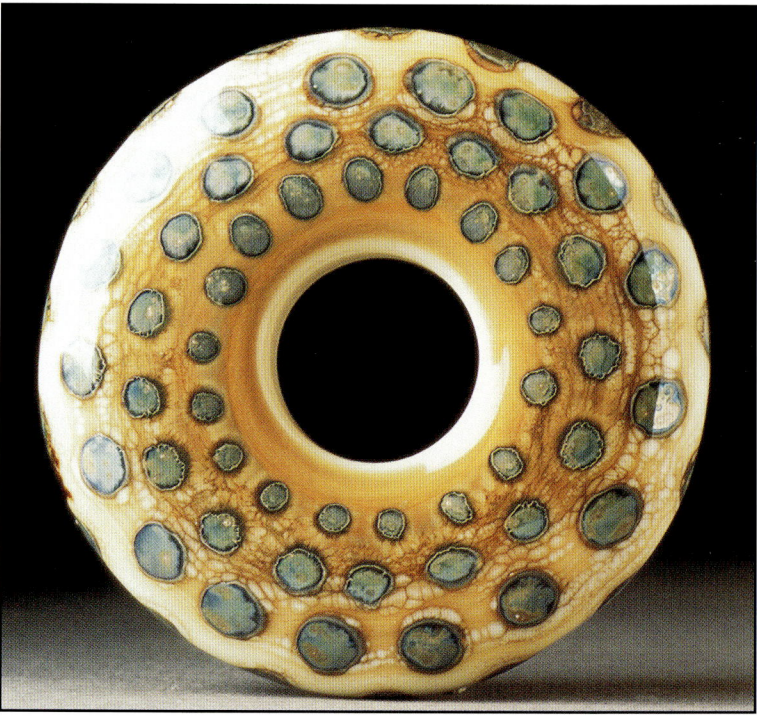

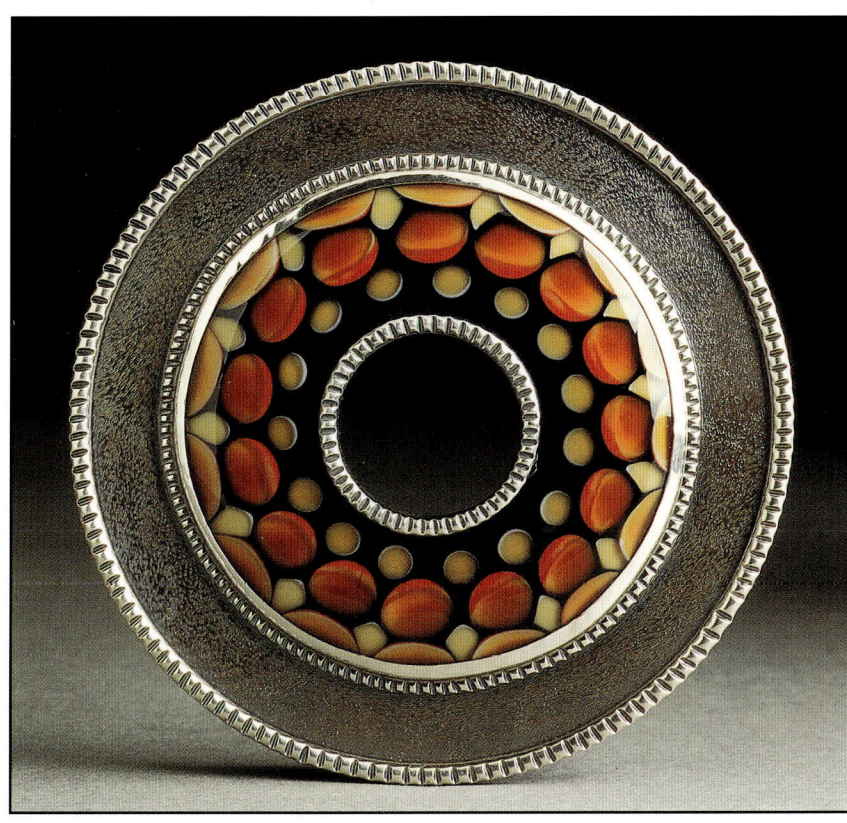

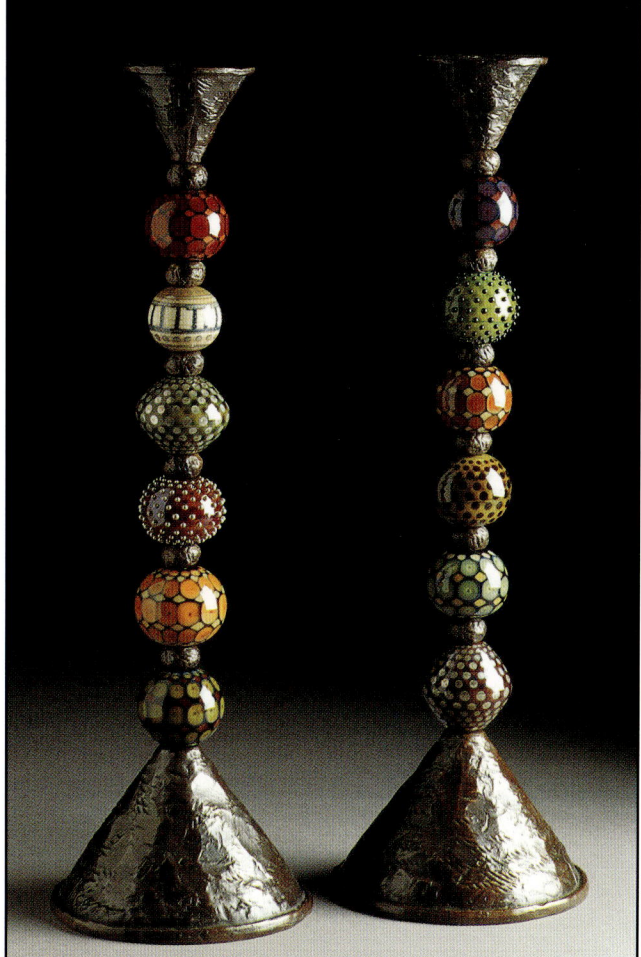

Pendant/Brooch, 2001, 5" x 2.75" d, lamp-worked glass and silver. Photograph courtesy of the artist.

Candlesticks, 2001, 13.5" x 4.5" d, bronze and lamp-worked glass. Photograph courtesy of the artist.

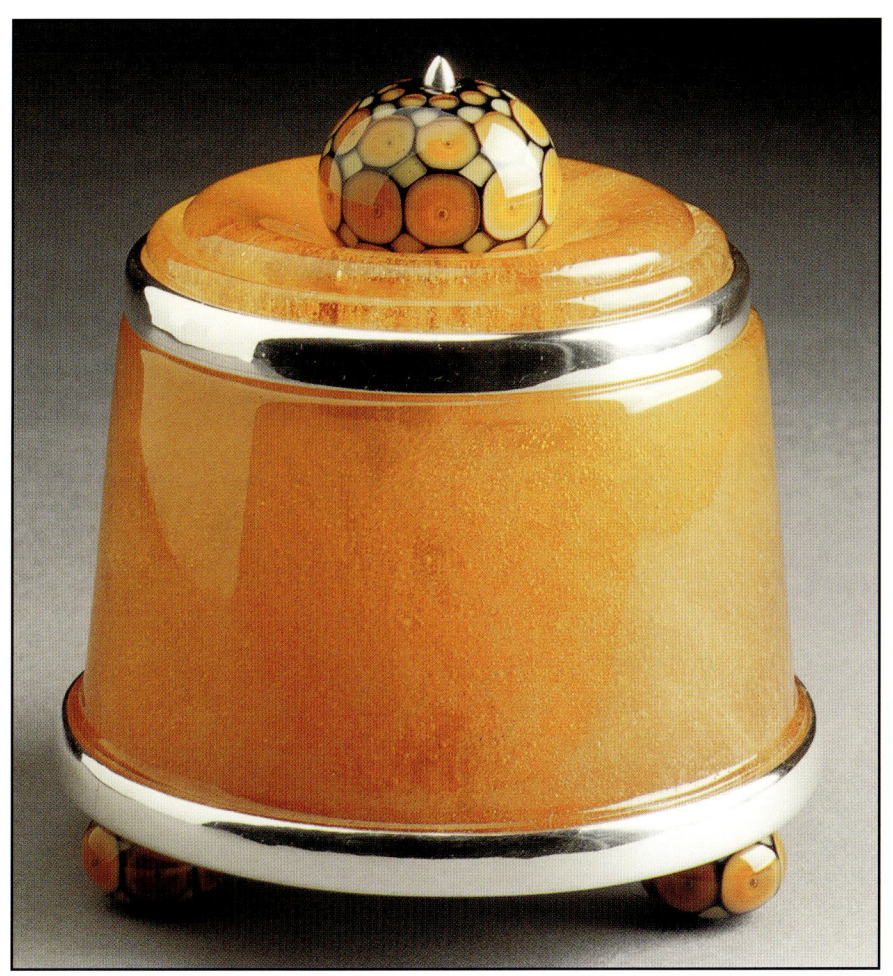

Amber Box, 2002, 4.5" x 4" d, pate de verre and lamp-worked glass, sterling, and fine silver. Photograph courtesy of the artist.

Amy J. Schwartz

In my work as a glass artist, I aim to make forms that are elegant and functional. Rich color is very important to the work. Carved and engraved vessels are the next step in my work.

In my work as an advocate for artists and students using glass, I strive to create a state of the art environment that is friendly and supportive at the Studio of The Corning Museum of Glass. I work hard to provide opportunities for artists through scholarship and residency programs, by inviting top-notch artists and expert craftspeople to teach in the facility, and by putting artists together with people and materials that might help expand their work and their visions.

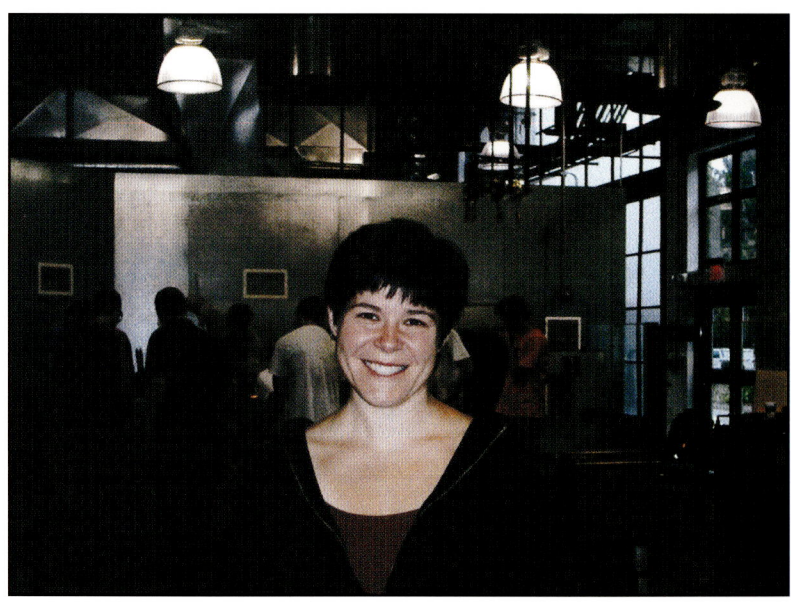

Amy J. Schwartz in The Studio of The Corning Museum of Glass. *Photograph courtesy of the artist.*

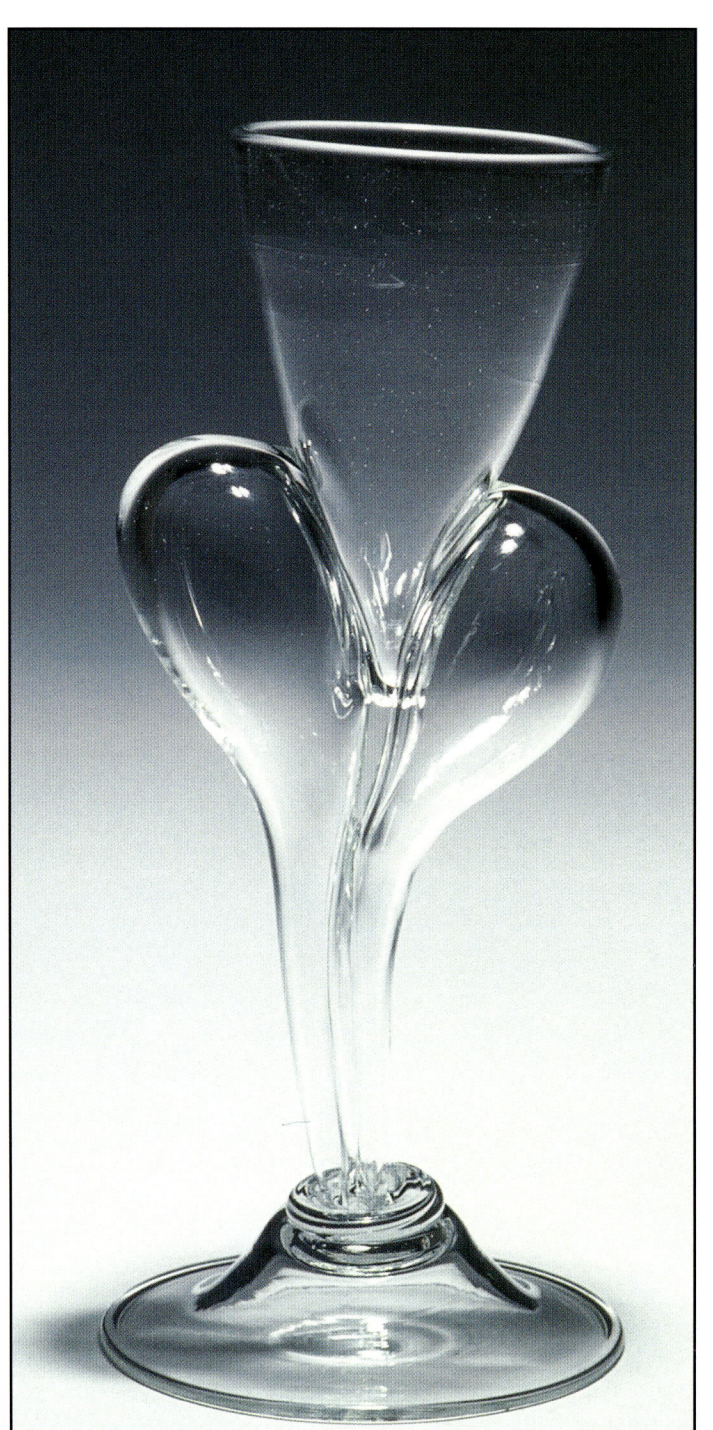

Goddess Goblet, 1994, blown glass. Photo: Dennis Murray. *Photograph courtesy of the artist.*

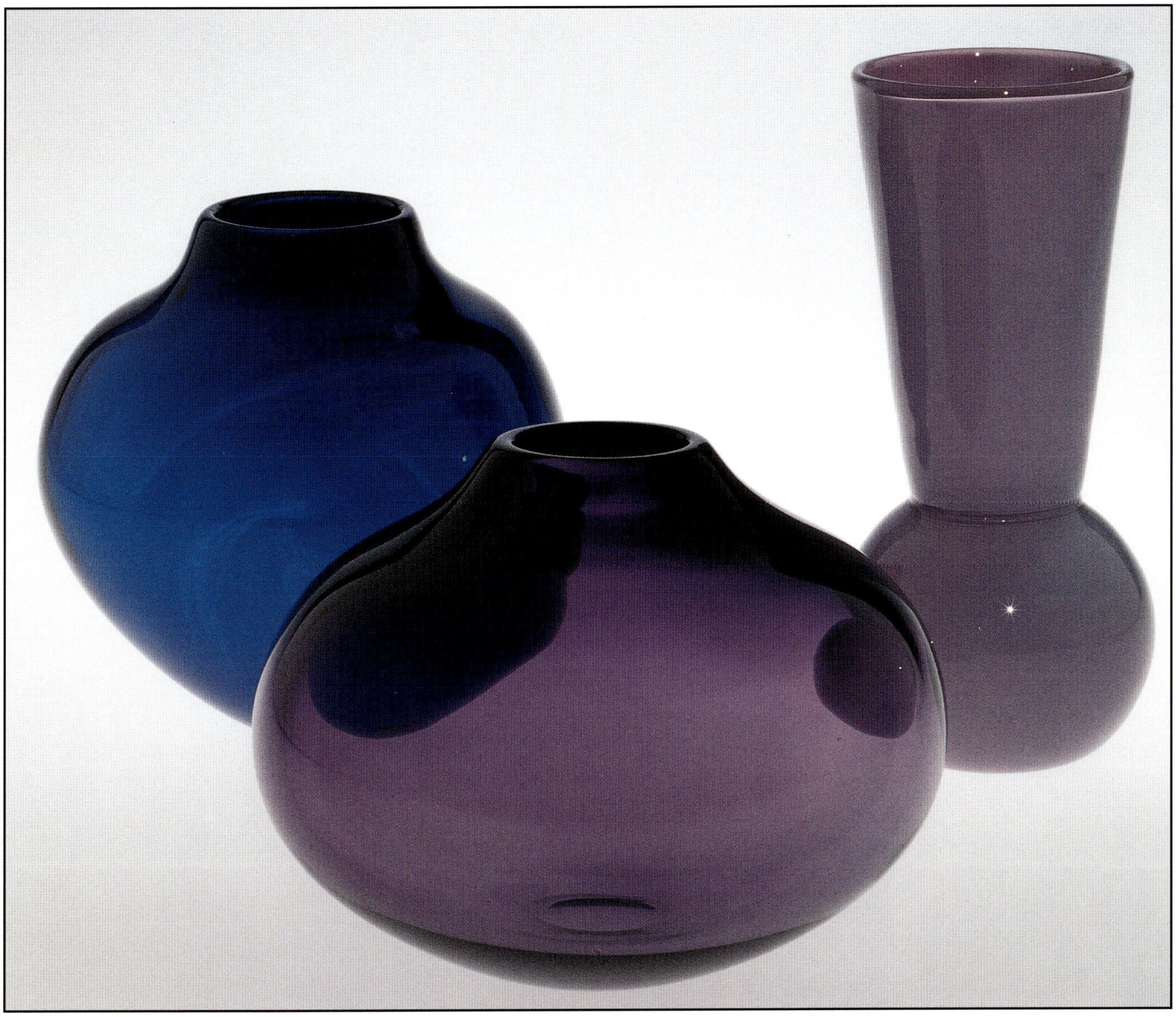

The Nineties - The Artist   203

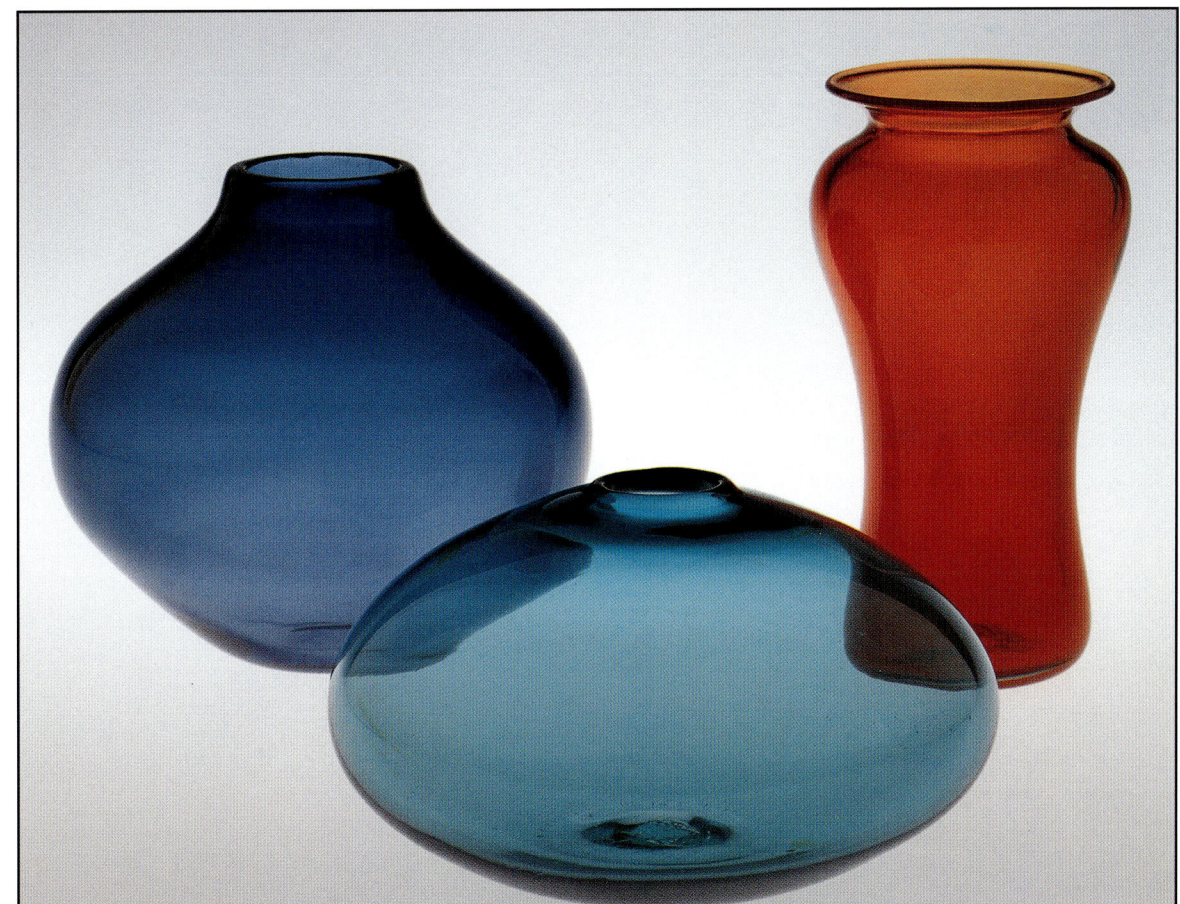

Vases, 2002, various sizes, approximately 5" h x 10" d for low vases and 10" h x 4" d for the tall ones, blown glass. *Photograph courtesy of the artist.*

Vases, 2002, various sizes, approximately 5" h x 10" d for low vases and 10" h x 4" d for the tall ones, blown glass. *Photograph courtesy of the artist.*

Celeste Starita

I became involved with glass by accident, while attending summer studies in Italy in 1992. As a material, it spoke to me and I immediately trusted it to speak *for* me. For me glass represents life, silently.

I attempt with my work to represent a journey, a sense of being, a quiet motion, and a very personal experience of space and time. Dualities are always present, and I choose single elements that translate multiple meanings. With solid glass and its processes there is positive and negative, interior and exterior, all of which play into my ideas and reveal new clues with every piece I make.

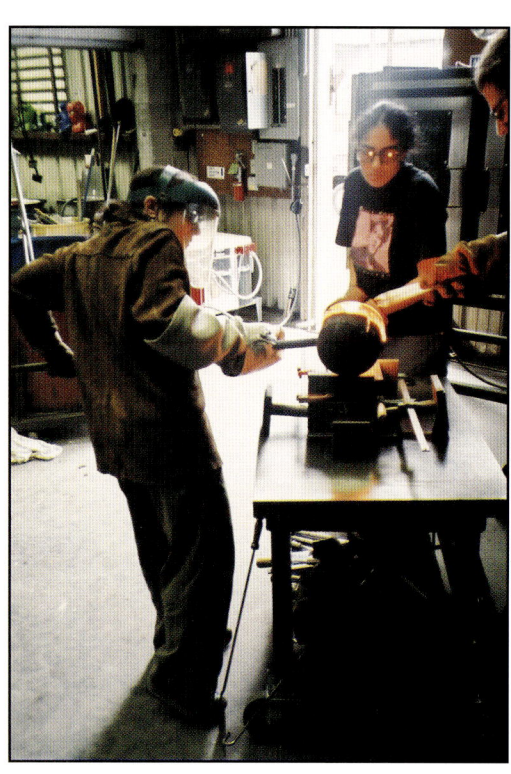

Celeste Starita. *Photograph courtesy of the artist.*

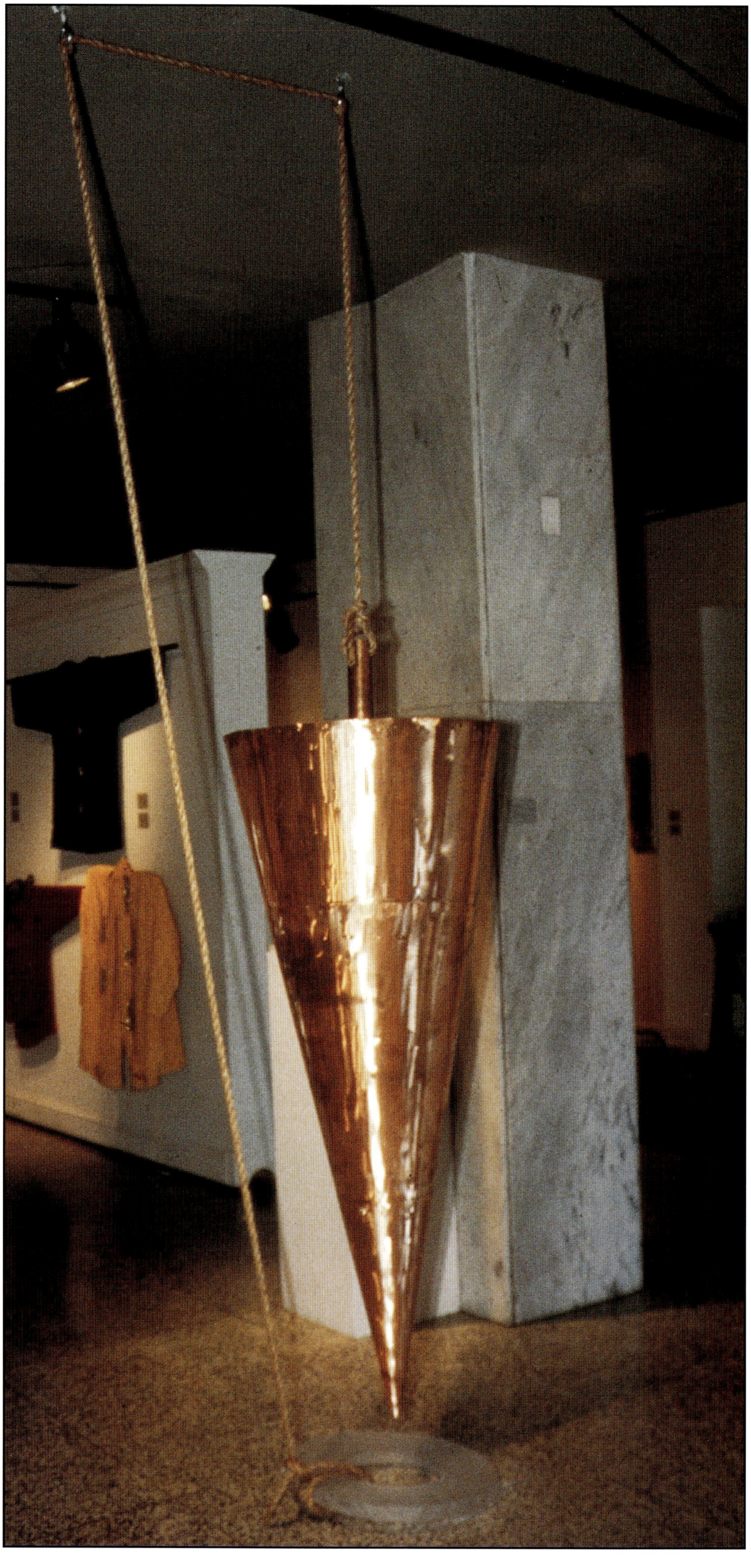

Umbillical, 1994, 8' x 2' x 2', copper, glass, rope. *Photograph courtesy of the artist.*

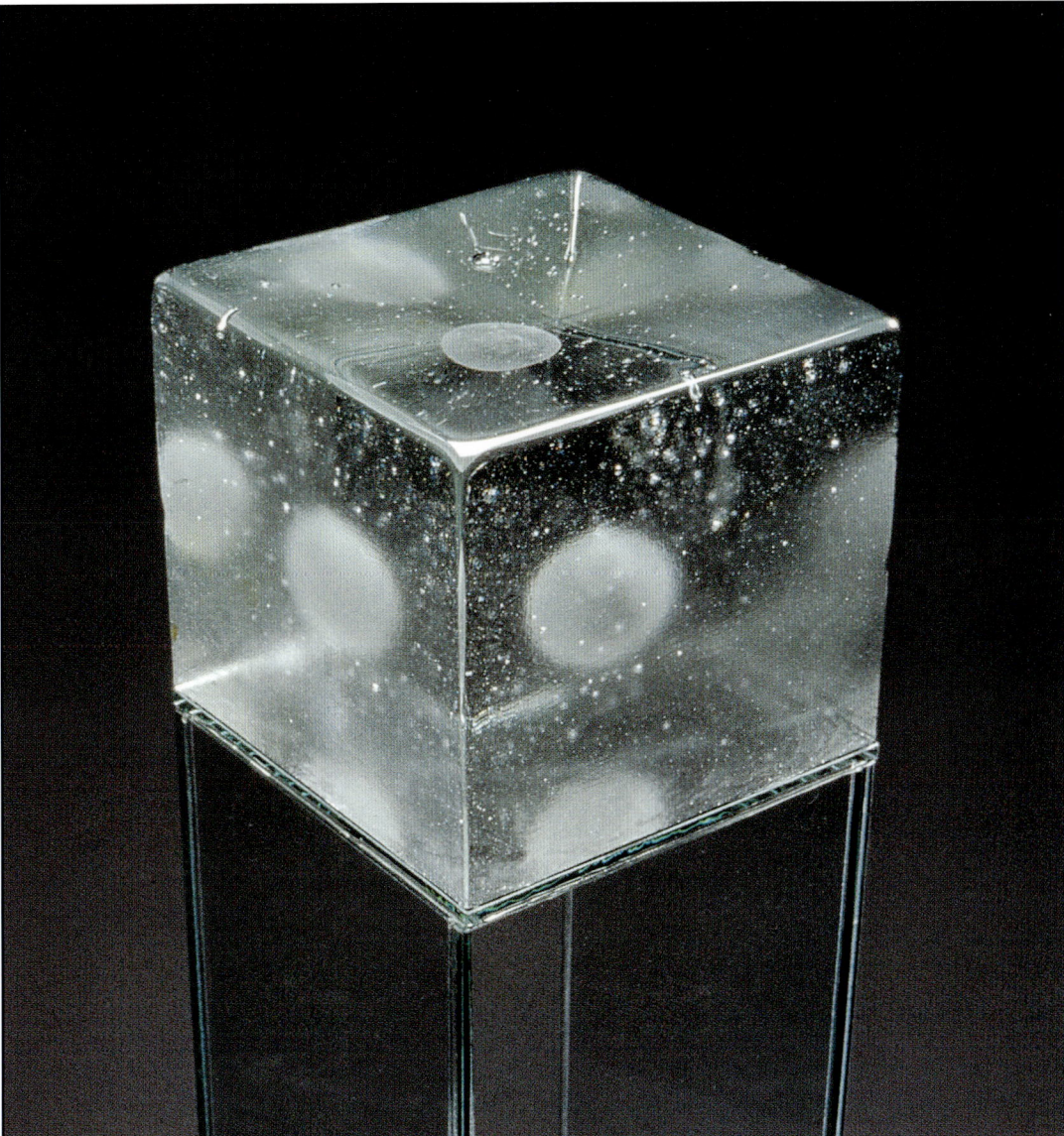

Untitled, 1999, 6" x 6" x 6", glass. Photo: Bill Wynes. *Photograph courtesy of the artist.*

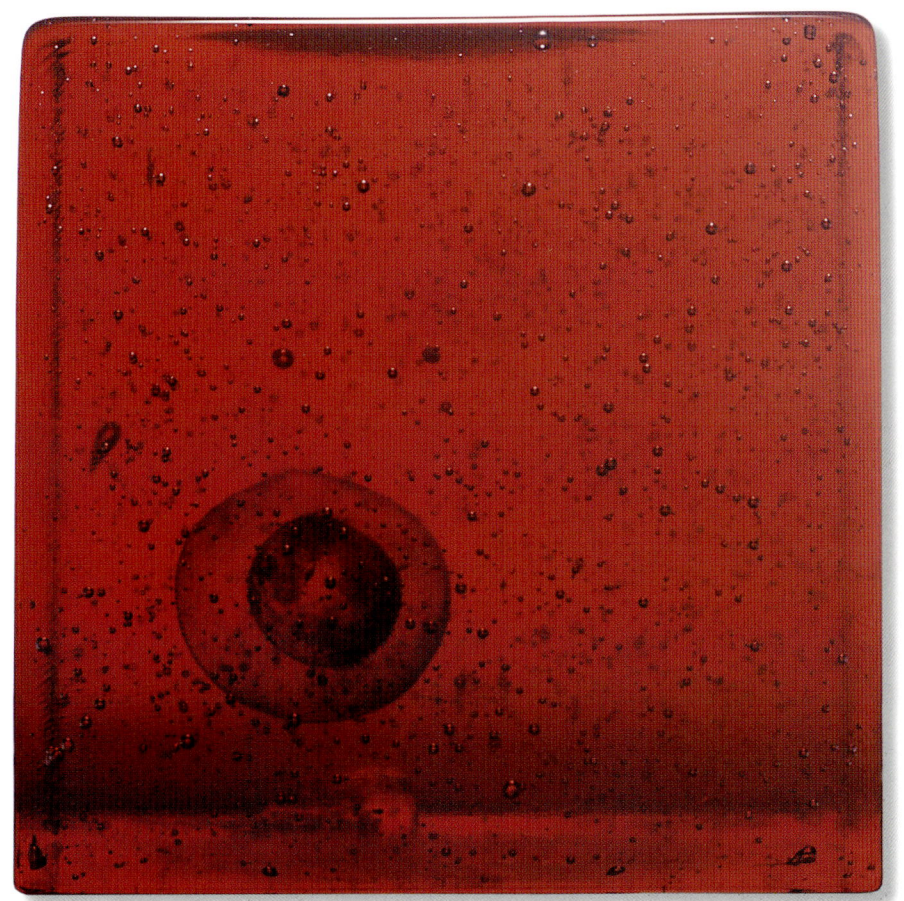

Blood/Cells, 2002, 8" x 8" x 8", cast glass. Photo: Matthew G. Hollerbush. *Photograph courtesy of the artist.*

Glossary of Glass Terms

Anneal: The slow and gradual cooling of glass from higher working temperatures to room temperature to reduce the amount of stress inherent in all types of glass.

Annealing Oven: a refractory chamber used for annealing blown and lampworked glass and for firing slumped, fused, and cast glass objects as well as vitreous enamels and lusters.

Batch: sand, soda and lime mixed with coloring oxides to be melted in a glass furnace.

Bead: a round ball usually with a hole in the center formed by winding molten glass around a wire. The tendency of glass to form a round ball when heated.

Casting: the process of making a positive form using a mold

Cire perdue: French term for lost wax casting process

Cullet: glass left over from previous melts

Enamels: low melting glass powders mixed with a resin or oil binder used to decorate glass. Can be painted, air brushed or silk-screened.

Frit: a glass that has been melted then broken into small pieces by dropping in water. Often used for pate de verre or kiln casting.

Fuse: bonding or melting together different pieces of glass with the same coefficient of expansion by means of heat.

Glass: a rigid liquid made from a mixture of oxides. Some oxides act as a flux and lower the melting temperature of the glass. Soft glasses such as lead glass and soda/lime melt at a low temperature. "Pyrex" or borosilicate glass and quartz glasses melt at a higher temperature and are called hard glasses.

Gather: glass collected on the end of a blowpipe or punty from a glass furnace.

Glory Hole: a secondary furnace used to reheat glass in the glassblowing procedure.

Investment: refractory material used in making molds for casting glass or metals.

Iridescence: a luster effect caused by spraying hot glass with chlorides or nitrates of metals such as tin and silver

Kiln: a chamber made from refractory material for the purpose of firing ceramics and glass.

Lampworking: glass that is today formed by the use of a gas fired torch. Some time called flameworking. In earlier times an oil-burning lamp was used to shape the glass.

Lost wax Casting: a casting process using by making a refractory mold over a wax positive. The wax is steamed or burned out leaving a cavity for ladling molten glass into or filling with frit for kiln casting.

Lusters: metallic oxides in a binder deposit a thin coating of metal on a glass surface when fired.

Millefiori: (a thousand flower) glass rods made by bundling many smaller rods into a pattern.

Pate de Verre: (paste of glass) a kiln casting process where a paste of finely crushed glass is pressed into a mold and fired.

Sand Casting: a process of hot casting glass by ladling molten glass from a furnace into a negative impression made in damp sand or chemically bonded sand.

Slumping: glass that has been shaped with heat and gravity by bending over or into a mold; occasionally called bent or sagged glass.

Endnotes

Introduction

1. Women and Creativity, Joelynn Sneider-Ott, Millbrae, California: Les Femmes Publishing, p. 2.
2. Ibid, p. 33.

In the Beginning: Herstory

1. Women in Prehistory, Margaret Ehrenberg, British Museum publications, London, 1989, p. 164.
2. Ibid, p. 164.
3. "A Share of Honor" Virginia Women 1600-1945, Virginia Woman's History Project, Virginia Museum of Fine Arts, W.M. Brown and Son, Richmond, VA, 1984.
4. Neikais – A Woman Glassblower of the First Century A.D.?, E Marianne Stern, Komos, Festschrift fur Thuri Lorenz zum 65. Geburtstag, Phoibos Verlag, Wein, 1997.
5. Beads and Beadmakers, Gender, Material Culture and Meaning, Lidia D. Sciama and Joanne B. Eiche, Out of Women's Hands: Notes on Venetian Glass Beads, Female Labour and International Trades, p. 47.
6. "Women Glass Painters," Peters, B.G. Binnall, The Magazine of the British Society of Master Glass Painters 16 (3), 1979-1980, pp. 26-29.
7. The Glass Industry in Sandwich, Raymond E. Barlow and Joan Kaiser, Barlow-Kaiser Publishing Co. Inc., Windham, NH, 1983, p. 287.
8. "The Hidden Women of Tiffany Studios," Maureen G. Clarke, edited by Art Femenella, Glass Art 7 (3), March/April 1992.
9. United States, Bureau of Labor. Report on condition of women and child wage-earners In the United States, prepared under the direction of Chas. P. Neill, Washington G.P.O., 1910-1913. Glass Industry #3, 1911, p. 970 (CMGL: TP853.A2.U58. 1911), pp. 282-293.
10. "Women and Glassmaking," a tardy book notice, by Paul Holister, Glass Club Bulletin #13, August 1975.
11. Glasgow Girls: Women in Art and Design, 1880-1920, editor, Jude Burkhauser, Edinburgh: Cannongate, 1990, p. 19.
12. [Walter Smith, Art Education, Boston, 1873, pp. 163-5.] Women Artists of the arts and crafts movement, 1870-1914, Anthea Callen, Angel in the Studio, New York: Pantheon Books, c. 1979, pp. 42-44 (originally published as Angel in the Studio, by the Architectural Press, London).
13. American Women Artists: From Early Indian Times to the Present, Charlotte Streifer Rubenstein, G.K. Hall & CO., Boston, 1982, p. 214.
14. Glass Focus, Beverly N. Copeland, Oct/Nov 1989, pp. 7-10.
15. "Finding a Future in the Past," Edris Eckhardt, unpublished paper, 10/25/61, Museum of American Glass archives, Wheaton Village, NJ.
16. Stanislav Libensky; Jaroslava Brychtova: A 40 year Collaboration in Glass. Edited by Suzanne K. Frantz, The Corning Museum of Glass, Prestel-Verlag.

The Sixties

1. American Women Artists: from Early Indian Times to the Present, Charlotte Streifer Rubenstein, G.K. Hall & CO., Boston, 1982, p. 324.
2. American Women Sculptors, Charlotte Streiber Rubenstein, G.K. Hall & CO., Boston, 1990, p. 444.
3. Ibid, p. 444.
4. "Thinking through Glass, Infinitely Just: Giving Peace a Chance," Erica Adams, This Side Up, January 2002, pp. 26-27.
5. YES YOKO ONO, Alexandra Munroe and Jon Hendricks, Japan Society, NY and Harry N. Abrams, Inc, NY, 2000, p. 132.
6. Visual Art in Glass. Dominick Labino, Wm. C. Brown Company Publishers, Dubuque, Iowa, 1968, p. 114.
7. The Crafts in Britain in the 20th Century, Tanya Harrod, Published for the Bard Graduate Center for Studies in the Decorative Arts by Yale University Press, 1999, pp. 327, 418.
8. "Hot Glass Feminine," Rosemarie Lierke, Neus Glass, Vol. #1, 1983, pp. 18-23.

The Seventies

1. American Women Artists: from Early Indian Times to the Present, Charlotte Streifer Rubenstein, G. K. Hall & CO., Boston, 1982, p. 324.
2. "Why Have There Been No Great Woman Artists," Linda Nochlin, Art News, January 1971, p. 3.
3. Ibid, p. 70.
4. Clearly Pilchuck, Lloyd Herman, whatcum Museum of Art.
5. Pilchuck: A Glass School, Tina Oldknow.
6. "Suzanne Harris: the Energy of Time," Artforum, summer 1980, pp. 52-57.
7. From a statement by the author, Jutta Cuny, dated 5th of April 1982.

The Eighties

1. Glass: A Contemporary Art, Dan Klein, Rizolli, 1989, p. 16.
2. Glass Art Society Journal 1984-1985, "Art, Craft and Postmodernism," Kim Levin, p. 17.
3. The Pilchuck Glass School, Tina Oldknow, The Pilchuck School and The University of Washington Press, Seattle, WA, 1996, p. 217.

The Nineties

1. "Pacific Cross Currents and Currents in Women's Glass," Dr. Susann Moeller, Neues Glas #2, 1994, pp. 54-55.
2. Betty Woodman: glass, 9/93-6/96, CIRVA, Francoise Guichon, Centre international de recherche sur le verre et les arts plastique Marseille, France.
3. "Metamorphosis: Glass Sculptures," Lynda Benglis, Matthew Kangas, Glass #82, Spring 2001, pp. 22-27.

# Selected Bibliography

American Women Sculptors. Charlotte Streiber Rubenstein, G.K. Hall & CO., Boston, 1990.

American Women Artists: From Early Indian Times to the Present. Charlotte Streifer Rubenstein, Boston: G.K. Hall & CO, 1982.

The Art Of Painting On Glass. Albinas Elskus, New York: Charles Scribner's Sons, 1980.

Artist Beware, 2nd ed. Michal McCann, PhD., Watson Guptil, 1992.

The Artist's Complete Health and Safety Guide. Monona Rossol, New York: Allworth Press, nd.

Beads and Beadmakers, Gender, Material Culture and Meaning. Lidia D. Sciama and Joanne B. Eiche.

Clearly Pilchuck. Lloyd Herman, Whatcum Museum of Art.

Contemporary Glass: A World Survey from The Corning Museum of Glass. Susanne K. Frantz, New York: Harry N. Abrams, 1989.

Contemporary Lampworking. Bandhu Scott Dunham, Salusa Glassworks, Arizona, 1994.

Contemporary Art Glass. Ray and Lee Grover, Crown Publ., 1975.

Five Thousand Years of Glass. Hugh Tait, New York: Harry N Abrams, 1991.

Glasgow Girls: Women in Art and Design, 1880-1920. Jude Burkhauser, editor, Edinburgh: Cannongate, 1990.

Glass: A Contemporary Art. Dan Klein, New York: Rizzoli International, 1989.

Glass: Art Nouveau to Art Deco. Victor Arwas, New York: Rizzoli International, 1977.

Glass: A Pocket Dictionary of Terms Commonly Used to Describe Glass and Glassmaking. David Whitehouse, Corning, NY: The Corning Museum of Glass, nd.

The Glass Industry in Sandwich. Raymond E. Barlow and Joan Kaiser, Windham, NH: Barlow-Kaiser Publishing Co. Inc, 1983.

The History of Glass. Dan Klein and Lloyd Ward, ed., London: Orbis, nd.

An Illustrated Dictionary of Glass. Harold Newman, Thames and Hudson, 1977.

Masterpieces of American Glass. The Corning Museum, Jane Shaddel Spillman and Susanne K Frantz, Toledo Museum, Lillian Nassau, Crown, NY, 1990.

More than You Ever Wanted to Know About Glass Beadmaking, Livermore, CA: GlassWear Studios, 1995.

Pate de Verre and Kiln Casting of Glass. Jim Kervin& Dan Fenton, Livermore, CA: GlassWear Studios, 1997.

Techniques of Kiln Formed Glass. Keith Cummings, A & C Black, London, Philadelphia, PA: University of Pennsylvania Press, 1997.

Neikais-A Woman Glassblower of the First Century A.D.?. E Marianne Stern, Komos, Festschrift fur Thuri Lorenz zum 65. Geburtstag, Phoibos Verlag, Wein, 1997.

The Pilchuck Glass School. Tina Oldknow, Seattle, WA: The Pilchuck School and The University of Washington Press, 1996.

"A Share of Honor" Virginia Women 1600-1945. Virginia Woman's History Project, Virginia Museum of Fine Arts, Richmond, VA: W.M. Brown and Son, 1984.

A Short History of Glass. Chloe Zerwick, Harry N. Abrams, 1990.

Stanislav Libensky; Jaroslava Brychtova: A 40 year Collaboration in Glass. Edited by Suzanne K. Frantz, The Corning Museum of Glass, Prestel-Verlag.

Visual Art in Glass. Dominick Labino, Dubuque, Iowa: Wm. C. Brown Company Publishers, 1968.

Women in Prehistory. Margaret Ehrenberg, London, British Museum Publications, 1989.

Women Artists of the arts and crafts movement, 1870-1914. Anthea Callen, New York: Pantheon Books, c.1979 (originally published as *Angel in the Studio*, by the Architectural Press, London).

YES YOKO ONO. Alexandra Munroe and Jon Hendricks, New York: Japan Society and Harry N. Abrams, Inc., 2000.

ISBN: 0-7643-1807-1
US $59.95

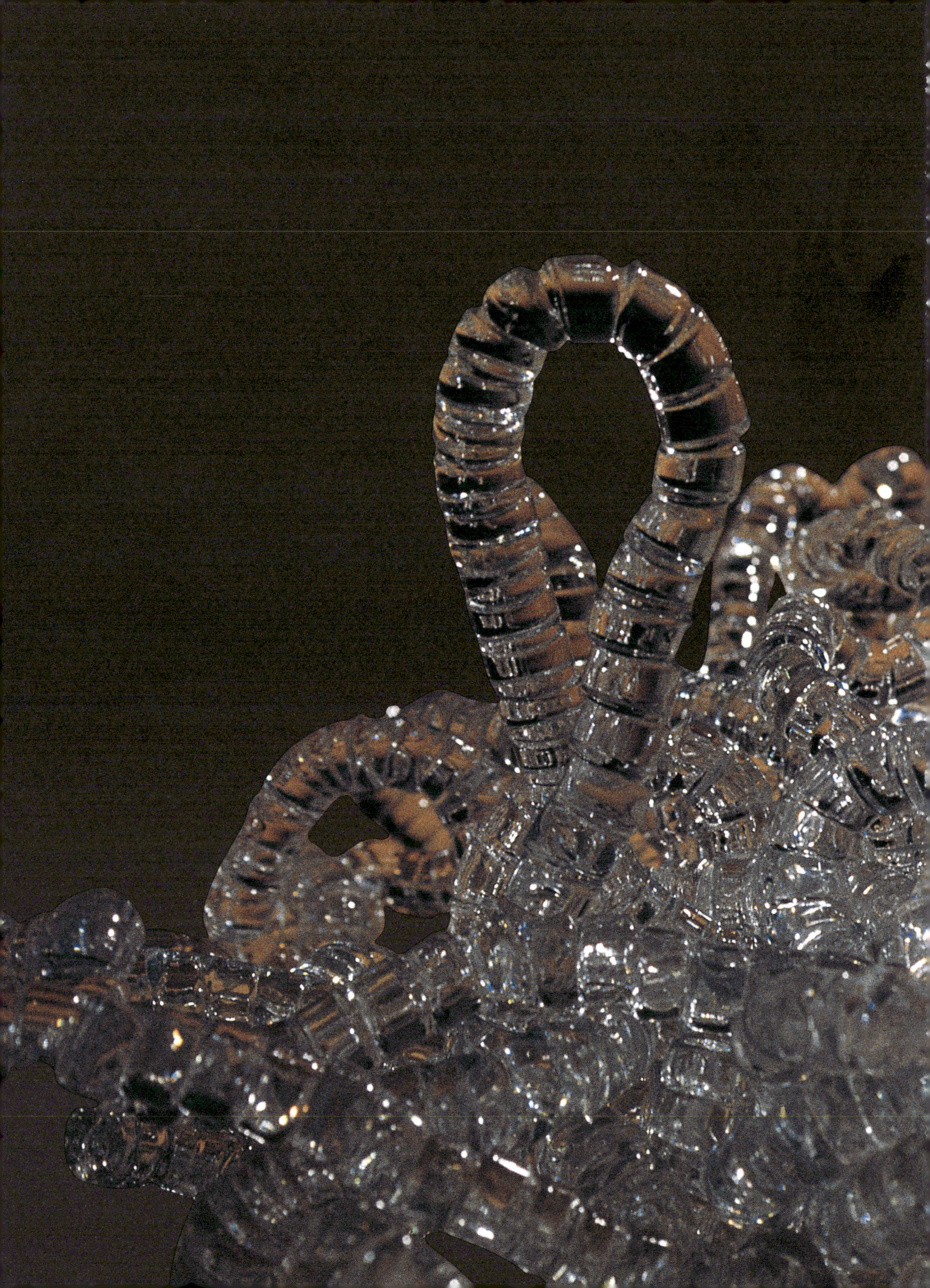